The Men Who Lost America

THE LEWIS WALPOLE SERIES IN
EIGHTEENTH-CENTURY CULTURE AND HISTORY

The Lewis Walpole Series, published by Yale University Press with the aid of the Annie Burr Lewis Fund, is dedicated to the culture and history of the long eighteenth century (from the Glorious Revolution to the accession of Queen Victoria). It welcomes work in a variety of fields, including literature and history, the visual arts, political philosophy, music, legal history, and the history of science. In addition to original scholarly work, the series publishes new editions and translations of writing from the period, as well as reprints of major books that are currently unavailable. Though the majority of books in the series will probably concentrate on Great Britain and the Continent, the range of our geographical interests is as wide as Horace Walpole's.

The Men Who Lost America

British Leadership, the American Revolution,

and the

Fate of the Empire

ANDREW JACKSON O'SHAUGHNESSY

Yale UNIVERSITY PRESS

New Haven & London

Published with assistance from the Annie Burr Lewis Fund.

Yale University Press books may be purchased in quantity for educational, business, or promotional use. For information, please e-mail sales.press@yale.edu (U.S. office) or sales@yaleup.co.uk (U.K. office).

Designed by James J. Johnson.
Set in Garamond types by Keystone Typesetting, Inc.
Printed in the United States of America.

The Library of Congress has cataloged the hardcover edition as follows:

O'Shaughnessy, Andrew Jackson.
The men who lost America : British leadership, the American Revolution, and the fate of the empire / Andrew Jackson O'Shaughnessy.
pages cm—(The Lewis Walpole series in eighteenth-century culture and history)
Includes bibliographical references and index.

ISBN 978-0-300-19107-3 (hardback : alk. paper)
1. United States—History—Revolution, 1775–1783—British forces. 2. United States—History—Revolution, 1775–1783—Campaigns. 3. Great Britain—Army—History—Revolution, 1775–1783. 4. Great Britain—Politics and government—1760-1820. 5. Napoleonic Wars, 1800–1815—Participation, British. I. Title.
E267.O75 2013   973.3'2—dc23
2012047724

ISBN 978-0-300-20940-2 (pbk.)

10 9 8 7 6 5 4 3

To my parents, John and Marjorie, and my brother Nicholas

Your failure is, I am persuaded, as certain as fate.

America is above your reach . . . her independence neither rests upon

your consent, nor can it be prevented by your arms. In short, you

spend your substance in vain, and impoverish yourself without hope.

Thomas Paine, "To the People of England," 1774

Contents

Color plates follow page 178

Acknowledgments

Since the time that we were fellow students at Oxford, Charles Stopford Sackville has been a good and generous friend who inadvertently suggested a title for this book when he mentioned that he was descended from "the man who lost America," Lord George Germain. It is hoped that he will not be disappointed that this book grants Germain a lesser role in explaining the British loss of America. Another friend of my undergraduate years, Caroline Neville, is also descended from one of the biographical subjects of this book, Lord Charles Cornwallis. Her father, Robin Neville, Lord Braybrooke, introduced me to artifacts and materials relating to Cornwallis at Audley End. She and her husband, Edward Stanley, the present earl of Derby, have subsequently made me aware of additional papers of General John Burgoyne, who married the daughter of the eleventh earl of Derby.

These personal connections influenced my decision to adopt a biographical approach, although the argument of this book is a product of my earlier study of the British Caribbean during the Revolutionary War: *An Empire Divided: The American Revolution and the British Caribbean* (Philadelphia: University of Pennsylvania Press, 2000). The writing of the book made me acutely aware of the global dimensions of British military commitments during the American Revolution. Although Piers Mackesy had previously explored this dimension in *The War for America, 1775–1783* (Cambridge, Mass.: Harvard University Press, 1964), he nevertheless concluded that defeat was due to poor leadership, while shifting the onus of responsibility from the politicians to the generals. Unlike many other historians, he was careful to show the underlying rationale for the behavior of the commanders, but he believed that the war was winnable and he implied that the outcome might have been different if Britain had appointed Sir Guy Carleton earlier to be commander in chief in America. His interpretation was contested by John Shy, who was influenced by the American experience in Vietnam. Nevertheless, the old shibboleths of blaming the leadership continue to hold sway. The case against this claim deserves further elaboration, and can be more effectively argued by viewing the war through the lens of the British.

I began work for this book in September 2001, thanks to a full year sabbatical leave from the University of Wisconsin Oshkosh and a Barra Senior Research Fellowship at The

McNeil Center for Early American Studies at the University of Pennsylvania. I am grateful to the University of Wisconsin Oshkosh Faculty Development Board, which funded my sabbatical and which was a model of professional development support throughout the University of Wisconsin system. Franca Barricelli generously chaired the department in my absence and was in every way a wonderful colleague, together with her husband Lane Earns. The McNeil Center for Early American Studies provided a vibrant intellectual home that was due in large part to the vision of its founder, Richard Dunn, and to the vitality of the present director, Dan Richter. The weekly seminars were conducted in a challenging but supportive and constructive atmosphere. My tenure as a fellow of the McNeil Center also taught me why the British so appreciated Philadelphia.

    I am grateful to those who sent me unpublished papers and references, including Charles Baxley, Richard Bernstein, Douglas Bradburn, Amy Turner Bushnell, Theodore Crackel, Douglas R. Cubbison, Harry Dickinson, James Donald, Christian DuComb, William M. Ferraro, Julie Flavell, Edith Gelles, Jack Greene, Benjamin Lee Huggins, J. Jefferson Looney, James Kirby Martin, John Minniear, Cassandra Pybus, John Roche, Robert Selig, Taylor Stoermer, Gregory J. W. Urwin, Bruce M. Venter, Mathew C. Ward, Bill Welsch, Henry Wiencek Jr., Gaye Wilson, and Neil L. York. Nicholas Cole kindly translated and identified the Latin quotes in the description of the Mischianza. It is similarly a pleasure to acknowledge those who read specific chapters or portions of the manuscript, including Bruce Bailey, Jeremy Black, Jim David, Grant Gilmore, Paul Langford, Peter J. Marshall, Pauline Maier, Holly A. Mayer, John Roche, and Leonard Sadosky. My special thanks are due to those who read and commented upon the entire manuscript: Stephen Conway, Frank Cogliano, Harry Dickinson, Julie Flavell, Ira Gruber, Michael Kranish, Maya Jasanoff, Peter Onuf, Gary Sandling, Keith Thomson, and Mark Urban. Steven Strumlauf and his wife Sonia Fox held a session of their book club to review the manuscript and gave a delightful dinner party afterwards at their home in Charlottesville. My friend Jeanie Grant Moore edited a late draft of the book that brought back happy memories of our teaching a full semester study abroad program, for two successive years, at Hughes Hall College, Cambridge University.

    I am obliged to the scholarly audiences who provided me with useful feedback. These included my graduate seminar on the topic of this book at the University of Virginia; the annual conference of the Society for Military History; the Early American Studies Seminar at the University of Virginia; the first Richard Dunn Symposium at the Autumn General Meeting of the American Philosophical Society; and The McNeil Center for Early American Studies. Michael Zuckerman invited me to speak at one of his informal "salons," which was graciously hosted at the home of George Boudreau. I was similarly the beneficiary of comments from conveners and general audiences, who included David Armitage and the Gilder Lehrman Institute Teacher Seminar; Phil Williams and the Thomas Jefferson Chapter of the Sons of the American Revolution, Charlottesville, Virginia; James Sofka and the Federal Executive Institute in Charlottesville; Bruce M. Venter and America's History,

LLC at Colonial Williamsburg; Keith Thomson and the Oxford Discovery Programme on the *Queen Mary II*; Nancy Hayward and the George Washington Symposium at Mount Vernon; Tom Reedy and the English-Speaking Union of the Sandhills in Pinehurst, North Carolina; Jack Rakove and Continuing Studies at Stanford University; and Aaron J. Palmer and the Wisconsin Lutheran College. The Order of Cincinnati sponsored my delivering their annual lectures at Hampden-Sydney College and Virginia Commonwealth University, which were respectively hosted by John C. Coombs and Sarah Hand Meacham. It was additionally stimulating to teach with Jeremy Black and Peter Onuf on the topic of British perspectives of the American Revolution for the School of Continuing and Professional Studies of the University of Virginia at Colonial Williamsburg.

Bruce Bailey was a kind host and informative archivist who guided me through papers and artifacts relating to Lord George Germain at Drayton House, which gave me the opportunity to see the war unfold through the eyes of Germain. I am grateful to the staff of the National Archives at Kew; the William L. Clements Library at the University of Michigan; the Harrison Institute and the Alderman Library at the University of Virginia. The first chapter of this book contains passages from my earlier article on George III, "'If Others Will Not Be Active, I Must Drive': George III and the American Revolution," which is reprinted by permission of the editor of *Early American Studies: An Interdisciplinary Journal* 2, no.1 (Spring 2004): 1–47. Howard Morhaim gave thoughtful advice as my literary agent, while it has been a delight to work with Christopher Rogers, the editorial director of Yale University Press, as well as with Christina Tucker, Gavin Lewis, and Margaret Otzel. Rick Britton kindly agreed to draw the maps for this book.

I owe a particular debt of gratitude to Richard Dunn, John McCusker, and Peter Onuf, who were variously responsible for my pursuing a teaching career in the United States. I shall always regard them as exemplary in their rigorous standards of scholarship and their encouragement of junior members of the profession. Since my appointment at Monticello, I have had the good fortune of being the colleague of Peter Onuf, the Thomas Jefferson Foundation Professor at the University of Virginia, whom I first met while I was a graduate student on a fellowship at the American Antiquarian Society. He has a particular gift for helping students and colleagues develop their ideas, without trying to prescribe a particular approach to history or a specific agenda. He has annually held a book workshop for the Gilder Lehrman postdoctoral fellows at Monticello. At the inaugural event of the Smith Education Center at Montalto on May 13–14, 2011, Peter similarly chaired a forum to discuss a first draft of the manuscript of this book in association with leading specialists of the British perspective of the American Revolution: Stephen Conway, Harry Dickinson, Julie Flavell, Ira Gruber, Maya Jasanoff, Michael Kranish, and Mark Urban. I remain deeply appreciative of his role and that of the other participants.

It was indeed a bonus to be able to write this book at Monticello in an office at Kenwood used by President Franklin Roosevelt in the four days leading up to D-Day. There was the constant stimulation of visiting fellows and speakers, together with the regular meetings of the University of Virginia Early American Studies Seminar at the Jefferson Library. My office is adjacent to the Jefferson Library with its impressive digital collections and the able assistance of Jack Robertson, the Foundation Librarian, and his colleagues Anna Berkes and Endrina Tay. It was also helpful to have access to Jeff Looney and the staff of *The Thomas Jefferson Papers* (Retirement Series) at the Jefferson Library, as well as Ed Lengel and the staff of *The Papers of George Washington* at the Alderman Library. As president of the Thomas Jefferson Foundation, Leslie Greene Bowman enthusiastically supported this project and granted me invaluable release time from my administrative duties to enable me to write. It is as well a pleasure to acknowledge the vision and encouragement of her predecessor, Dan Jordan, together with the senior curator of Monticello, Susan Stein. Gaye Wilson kindly assumed the role of director in my absence, despite working on her own book, with additional assistance from Mary Scott-Fleming and Christa Dierksheide. Liz Blaine and Lindsay Mericli arranged a manuscript forum chaired by Peter Onuf as the opening event of the Smith Education Center on Montalto, with its magnificent panoramic views of the Blue Ridge Mountains and Monticello. Leah Stearns and Margaret Huckaby kindly helped with illustrations. The Board of Trustees of the Thomas Jefferson Foundation has shown a remarkable dedication to research as an essential part of its mission of preservation and education. I am grateful for the support of Donald A. King, the chairman of the board, and his wife Janemarie, together with his predecessor H. Eugene Lockhart, and the respective chairs of the Scholarly Activities Committee, Charles Cullen and Jeffrey C. Walker. It is similarly a pleasure to record my thanks to former trustee A. D. Hart and his wife Margaret, who held a lunch party for me to speak about the book at their Jefferson-era home, and who represent much that is finest about Virginia.

Finally this book is dedicated to my parents and my brother. My parents read and edited the first draft of each chapter of this book. Their emigration to America, when my father John began teaching at Columbia University's Graduate School of Business, was the source of my youthful interest in the interplay of the histories of the United States and Britain. It was all the more enticing because American history was not generally part of the school history syllabus in England. My mother Marjorie took us to museums and historical sites in New York, which made me yet more curious about the historical relationship with Britain. My brother Nicholas discussed the concept of this book with me over twenty-five years ago in Oxford. My parents and brother championed my pursuing this topic and have been a constant source of support. It is with love, esteem, and gratitude that I dedicate this book to them.

Introduction

At about ten o'clock in the morning of October 17, 1781, outside the small tobacco port of Yorktown in Virginia, a lone drummer mounted the parapet of the besieged British lines, beating the call for a parley. The sound of his drum was inaudible against the background of constant firing. If it had not been for the visibility of his redcoat, "he might have beat away until doomsday." He was followed by an officer holding up a white handkerchief and carrying a message proposing negotiations for surrender. The roar of American and French cannon suddenly ceased. Ebenezer Denny, a junior officer in the Pennsylvania Line of the Continental Army, described how "when the firing ceased, I . . . had never heard a drum equal to it—the most delightful music to us all." The troops on either side stared in silence at one another from a distance of less than two hundred yards. While the drummer was sent back, the British officer was blindfolded and taken to the headquarters of General George Washington, where he delivered a message from General Charles, Earl Cornwallis proposing a cessation of hostilities for twenty-four hours to allow two officers to meet "at Mr. Moore's house to settle terms for the Surrender of the Posts of York & Gloucester." The request was refused pending the submission of more detailed terms of surrender in writing. The opposing artillery resumed firing throughout the afternoon, but the battle was really over. The guns once again fell silent throughout the night and the negotiations continued throughout the next day.[1]

At noon on October 19, the British army lowered the Union Jack. The victors were forced to wait for the pleasure of seeing their humiliated foe parade before them. Although Washington had specified that the surrender ceremony would take place at two o'clock precisely, the British and German troops did not appear for another hour. Dressed in smart new uniforms, they formed two columns more than a mile long. Their path was bordered on one side by American troops and on the other by French. There were numerous spectators from the surrounding countryside, beaming with satisfaction and joy. The onlookers eagerly awaited the appearance of Cornwallis. He was "the object of peculiar interest." A surgeon in the Continental Army, James Thacher, described how every eye was ready to gaze on the humiliated commander, but Cornwallis disappointed their eager expectations by pleading illness or "pretending indisposition." He instead sent his second in command, a ruddy-faced Irishman and "plausible talker," Brigadier General Charles O'Hara of the Brigade of Guards, who had been bayoneted at the battle of Guilford Court House and who had long believed that Britain was engaged in an unwinnable war in America.[2]

After some two hours of hushed anticipation, the vanquished British army began to advance along the Hampton Road, marching at a slow and solemn step, with shouldered arms, colors cased, drums beating, and fifes playing patriotic marches of Britain and the German states. As the captive army approached the opposing trenches, the "elegantly mounted" General O'Hara asked to be directed to the French commander, General Jean Baptiste Donatien de Vimeur, comte de Rochambeau. O'Hara removed his hat and apologized for the absence of his commanding officer. According to French accounts, he then attempted to surrender Cornwallis's sword to Rochambeau, who refused and deferred to General George Washington. An American officer added that O'Hara was mistaken: "the Commander-in-Chief of our army is to the right." It was not an error. The British preferred to surrender to the French rather than acknowledge the ignominy of defeat by the Americans. O'Hara reluctantly tried to present the sword to Washington, but was referred by Washington to General Benjamin Lincoln, who had earlier been snubbed by the British when they refused him the usual courtesies of surrender at Charleston in South Carolina in 1780. Lincoln merely returned the sword to O'Hara and gave him directions to take his troops to a spacious field to lay down their arms.[3]

As they neared the field of surrender, the royal troops became disorderly and exhibited "unsoldierly conduct," their step irregular and their ranks frequently broken. Some of them seemed to be "in liquor." When they entered the surrender field, with their spirit and pride put to the severest test, the last act of the drama was played out. They were unable to conceal their mortification. Their platoon officers appeared to be exceedingly chagrined when giving the order to ground arms. According to a New Jersey officer, the British officers in general "behaved like boys who had been whipped at school," with some biting their lips and pouting while others cried. They beat their drums "as if they did not care how." Many of the soldiers showed a sullen temper, violently throwing down their arms into a single pile, as if determined to render them useless. After an intense siege following a march of fifteen hundred miles through the south, a corporal of the 76th Foot threw down his weapon with such violence that it broke, as he shouted "May you never get so good a Master!" The round, broad-brimmed hats of the soldiers enabled them to hide their faces out of shame. It was indeed a humiliation for an army that had begun the war with an assumption of its own superior military prowess. When he beheld the soldiers so reduced from their former glory to such a miserable plight, Aedenus Burke of South Carolina reflected that he forgot for a moment their "insolence, their depredations and cruelty."[4]

Throughout much of November 1781, there was still no certain news in London of the outcome of the battle of Yorktown. As accounts of the strength of the enemy positions arrived, the mood of the government grew more anxious each day. George III and Lord

George Germain, the Cabinet minister most responsible for the conduct of the war, had been so confident of victory that the draft of the king's speech for the state opening of Parliament predicted British success in America. Germain, in particular, was aware that the outcome of the battle would determine the fate of the war and probably the future of the government of Lord North. He began to confide uneasiness on the subject to his friends. At noon on Sunday, November 25, 1781, Germain was at his London residence next to Carlton House in Pall Mall, when he received official confirmation of the news that he had been dreading. Saying nothing to a guest, he immediately ordered his coach to drive to the residence of one of the other secretaries of state, Lord Stormont, in Portland Place. After Germain imparted the "disastrous information" of the surrender of Lord Cornwallis, he and Stormont instantly drove to see the lord chancellor, Lord Thurlow, in Great Ormond Street. Following a short conference, they collectively decided to summon their nerve and go in person to the prime minister, Lord North.[5]

Between one and two o'clock in the afternoon, the three Cabinet ministers arrived at the official residence of the prime minister in Downing Street. Although he had long despaired of the war and had many times attempted to resign, Lord North reacted to the news with shock. Germain described how the prime minister responded "As he would have taken a ball in his breast." Pacing up and down his rooms for several minutes, North suddenly opened his arms, exclaiming wildly, "O God! It is all over!" North repeated the words many times in a state of consternation and distress. After North had calmed down, the ministers discussed whether to postpone the state opening of Parliament, which was due to occur in less than forty-eight hours. With many members having already arrived in the capital and others on their way, they decided against a change. They then spent several hours rewriting the king's speech, which was to be delivered from the throne in the House of Lords. The speech had originally predicted victory but was altered to make a token reference to the events at Yorktown. Germain then sent word of the "melancholy termination of Lord Cornwallis's expedition" to King George III, who was at Kew Palace on the outskirts of London. Germain then returned to his office in Whitehall, where he found additional confirmation of Cornwallis's defeat at Yorktown in a French account.[6]

As a supporter of the government and a member of Parliament, the memoirist Nathaniel Wraxall attended a dinner party with nine other guests that evening at Lord George Germain's home in Pall Mall. Apart from Thomas de Grey, Lord Walsingham, who had formerly served as an under secretary to Germain, the guests were unaware of the fateful news that Germain had received from America. Before the dinner was finished, one of the servants delivered an urgent message from the king. Looking and directing his remarks exclusively at Lord Walsingham, Germain said: "The King writes just as he always does, except that I observe he has omitted to mark the hour and the minute of his writing." George III always wrote the precise time to the last minute in his letters. Although Germain's remark was calculated to awaken interest around the table, the guests made no comment and repressed their curiosity, owing to the presence of his three daughters.[7]

The moment that his daughters left the room, Germain told the dinner party guests of his just having heard that the comte de Maurepas, the first minister of France, was "lying at the point of death." Wraxall replied that if he were the first minister of France, it would grieve him to die without knowing the outcome of the great contest between England and America. Germain responded that the French minister had survived long enough to witness the result. Wraxall thought Germain was alluding to an indecisive naval action off the Chesapeake Capes, between the fleets of Britain and France. Wraxall then explained he had meant to say that it was a shame that the dying French minister would never know the final result of the war in Virginia. Germain repeated that the French minister had survived to witness it completely: "The army has surrendered, and you may peruse the particulars of the capitulation in that paper." Without any visible emotion, Germain removed the paper from his pocket and gave it to Wraxall, who read it aloud while the other guests sat in stunned silence. The news cast a gloom over the rest of the evening as the party pondered the political fallout.[8]

The guests really wanted to know how George III had reacted to the news. They were well aware that the king would find it especially painful, as it was the most humiliating event of his reign. George III had become the driving force behind the war and had threatened to abdicate rather than accept defeat. Germain gratified the wishes of his guests by reading aloud the letter from the king, while remarking that the letter was a testimony to the king's fortitude, firmness, and consistency of character. Wraxall recalled thirty years later that the lapse of time had not erased the deep impression that the reading of the letter had made on him that evening. It contained not a word of despondency or despair, while the handwriting indicated complete composure of mind. The king wrote defiantly that the news did not make the smallest change in his views and that he was ready to continue the war. He would not admit defeat.[9]

I

The British loss of America is a subject of perennial interest, not least because it gave birth to two powerful modern nations: the United States and Canada. It was a war Britain seemingly should have won. It had spent eight years waging what the staunchest supporters regarded as a "holy war" against "dangerous" revolutionary principles, "which threaten[ed] a general subversion of every system, religious or civil, hitherto respected by mankind." Even moderates believed the retention of America was essential to the survival of Britain as a great power within Europe. According to Adam Smith, the author of *The Wealth of Nations* (1776), the "expectation of a rupture with the colonies . . . has struck the people of Great Britain with more terror than they have ever felt for a Spanish armada, or a French invasion." Britain had the advantage of a professional army, the largest navy in the world, officers who were veterans of many campaigns, the availability of military supplies, and ready access to credit. Britain had a vibrant economy, which was leading the way in agricultural innovation, commerce, banking, credit, and canal building, and was fast becoming the first industrial nation in history. It is little wonder that many contemporaries imagined that the war would be an easy triumph for Britain. When events turned out otherwise, it is equally understandable that the failure was attributed to poor leadership.[10]

The ten biographical subjects of this book were the key British decisionmakers who oversaw the conduct of the war for America. They include George III, who was portrayed in the Declaration of Independence as the tyrant responsible for the American Revolution; Lord North, the prime minister regarded as having triggered the war with his fateful decision to punish the people of Massachusetts for the Boston Tea Party through the Coercive Acts of 1774; General Sir William Howe and Admiral Lord Richard Howe, the brothers commanding the British army and navy in America during the first half of the war who are regarded as having missed the best opportunity to defeat the Continental Army in 1776; John Burgoyne, the general who surrendered at Saratoga (1777); Lord George Germain, the secretary of state for America and the chief architect of the American War in Britain; Sir Henry Clinton, commander of the British army in America during the second half of the war when he was accused by critics of inactivity; Lord Cornwallis, whose surrender at Yorktown effectively ended the British war for America; Admiral Sir George Rodney, one of the few commanders to emerge with his reputation enhanced from the war but who failed to prevent the French fleet of Admiral François-Joseph Paul, comte de Grasse, from entrapping Lord Cornwallis's army at Yorktown; and John Montague, earl of Sandwich, the first lord of the Admiralty, whom critics held responsible for the inadequacy of the Royal Navy.

These political and military leaders became the object of satire, emanating from critics who ranged from writers like Philip Freneau, Thomas Paine, Mercy Otis Warren, and Francis Hopkinson in America, to the poet Robert Burns in Scotland and the caricaturist James Gillray in England. They continue to be ridiculed in fiction, popular history, and movies. Although less crudely presented, such caricatures permeate even scholarly literature. It is glibly assumed that failure must have been a consequence of incompetent and mediocre leadership. The men who lost America were on the wrong side of history. They were associated with opposition to progress and with attempting to introduce an authoritarian style of government. They were the enemy in an event that has become part of an American national mythology wherein Britain represented antiquated aristocratic attitudes that must inevitably fail against the meritocratic and republican virtues of America. It is like a story. The end of the war is a foregone conclusion, as history progresses toward modernity.[11]

The men who lost America were able and substantial individuals who nevertheless failed. This book takes a "warts and all" approach that will consider their defects and their roles in contributing to the defeat, but it will also take issue with the popular misconception that they were simply incompetent and hidebound. The difference between success and failure is often a fine line. Horatio Gates, the American general who won the battle of Saratoga (1777), was himself defeated by Lord Cornwallis at the battle of Camden (1780), who in turn surrendered at Yorktown. Admiral de Grasse played a major role in the victory at Yorktown after winning a naval victory against Rear Admiral Thomas Graves at the battle of the Chesapeake Capes (1781) but de Grasse was defeated and captured at the battle of the Saintes by Admiral Rodney (1782). This book is an account of capable men who fought a closely contested war, but whose critics and victorious opponents are treated as giants in their respective national histories, such as Edmund Burke, Charles James Fox, and William Pitt in Britain, and Thomas Jefferson, George Washington, John Adams, and Benjamin Franklin in America.

The British generals in America were not the stuff of parody, but had much in common with modern-day military career professionals in their dedication and commitment. A career in the military was a life service. Many of the commanders were born into families with strong military traditions and associations. They joined their regiments and ships when they were little more than children. George III and his Cabinet ignored seniority to select the ablest generals in the army for command in America. The men they chose went to great lengths to improve their military skills and knowledge of warfare. They studied strategy and tactics by visiting the locations of battles, by reading the latest theories, and by training abroad. In a profession where experience counted, they were seasoned veterans who had served in junior commands in Europe and America. They had served under some of the most distinguished commanders of the age and improved their skills by leading military maneuvers during the large-scale summer exercises conducted annually by the army. They demonstrated great personal courage in action. With long absences from their families and the possibility of losing their lives for their country, their military careers required great sacrifices.[12]

The military leaders were members of an oligarchy, but they competed within that oligarchy and were fiercely ambitious. Owing to the practice of primogeniture, in which the eldest son inherited most of a family's wealth, younger sons had to seek successful careers. It was possible to buy army commissions, but the practice was not permitted for senior appointments, and at least a third of the junior appointments were not purchased. After 1760, the purchase and promotion system was subject to greater regulation. The army was even quite cosmopolitan, with many continental European officers, such as the Swiss-born generals Frederick Haldimand and Augustine Prevost, who both served in the British army in America during the Revolutionary War. The Royal Navy was more open than the army to talent and social mobility and was regarded as the best in Europe. This was a period in which success in public service could earn a fortune equal to that of a successful merchant or businessman. The officers in both services had the added incentive that success would be rewarded by governorships and sinecures. There was also the luster of national acclaim and the almost obsessive cult of heroism. The high social status of the officers of the armed services made military service a desirable occupation. Moreover, the social structure of the British military was unchanged when it defeated Napoleon. The purchase of army commissions was not abolished until 1871 at the height of the British Empire.[13]

The perception of the British leadership as incompetent has disguised the extent to which the outcome of the war was in doubt until the very end. It diminishes the achievements of American generals like George Washington and Nathanael Greene, who won against enormous odds and able opponents in a bitterly contested war; their letters were full of despair for reasons that modern readers find difficult to understand because we are conditioned to thinking that the successful outcome of the Revolution was inevitable. The British were in reality sufficiently formidable to force George Washington to spend much of the war evading battle. They inflicted major defeats on Washington at the battles of Long Island (1776), Manhattan (1776), Brandywine (1777), and Germantown (1777). The British commanders were not totally beholden to conventional European tactics of "a war of posts," in which the main aim was to preserve an army, to avoid the casualties of battle, and succeed by an emphasis on maneuver. Indeed, European warfare was not exclusively confined to such limited tactics, while many British officers had previously served in America during the French and Indian War (1756–63). The British army had more experience of frontier warfare and suppressing rebellions than any contemporary army in Europe.

British commanders adjusted their tactics to be more flexible in unconventional warfare by adapting uniforms to better suit the environment, by using light infantry, and by breaking with strict linear formations. Departing from the tradition of the infantry acting in three parallel lines, the commanders adopted loose formations of two extended lines which were not required to fire in regular volleys. Far from being hidebound, they broke with European practice by placing greater reliance on mobility and the terror of bayonet charges. During the Revolutionary War, the British infantry often fired only a single general volley before rushing the enemy with their three-sided, fifteen-inch bayonets fixed to the muzzles of their guns. The British generals additionally appreciated the psychological dimensions of the war and the importance of winning popular support. If we take seriously the capabilities of the British leadership, the achievements of the American commanders appear much greater.[14]

The political leaders in Britain were also more talented than is often appreciated. A British prime minister is admired in the United States today for facing an avalanche of hostile questions for an hour a week during Prime Minister's Question Time in Parliament. Lord North had to face such a challenge for an average of three days a week during the parliamentary sessions. The political system was never so corrupt that governments were able to assume support through patronage, and there was no equivalent of a disciplined political party to sustain them. The prime ministers of this period had to win the confidence of the House of Commons by being persuasive. Lord North was a particularly skilled public speaker who successfully defended the government and sustained majorities in the House of Commons. He was equally gifted in supervising the public accounts as first lord of the Treasury and chancellor of the Exchequer. The earl of Sandwich, as first lord of the Admiralty, and Lord George Germain, as secretary of state for America, were both able bureaucrats. They were surprisingly effective in tackling the logistical problem of amassing the largest number of troops ever sent such a distance. The majority of Cabinet members had long experience of military affairs. They were not novices.

II

The mutual recriminations within the British leadership contributed to the image of a war lost by incompetence. Lord George Germain had acrimonious relations with the successive commanders in chief in America, Sir William Howe, Sir Henry Clinton, and Sir Guy Carleton. General Clinton quarreled with Admiral Sir Peter Parker and Admiral Marriot Arbuthnot. The commanders fell out with their subordinates: Howe with Clinton; Clinton with Cornwallis, and Rodney with Rear Admiral Sir Samuel Hood. Before the advent of a more fully developed sense of nationalism in the nineteenth century, these quarrels were endemic in an era when the defense of private honor often triumphed over public service. However, such disputes were too pervasive to explain solely in terms of personalities. They were also present in other theaters of the war including Jamaica, where differences between Governor John Dalling and Admiral Parker had much the same sclerotic effect that they had between Clinton and Arbuthnot in New York. Similarly in Britain, differences between Admirals Viscount Augustus Keppel and Sir Hugh Palliser divided the Channel Fleet. The sheer multiplicity of these debilitating arguments suggests broader causes, beyond merely the indulgence of personal piques. They rather reflected competition for limited resources and a weak command structure. Furthermore, they were mirrored by similar divisions among the American revolutionaries.

The British commanders and politicians were discredited not least because their enemies triumphed and their opponents wrote the histories. This was equally true in Britain, where the view that America was lost by incompetent leadership began during the war and became the popular orthodoxy in the immediate aftermath. When in 1792 one of the earliest British consuls to the United States met President George Washington, he reported home that Washington was "a great man . . . but I cannot help thinking, that the misconduct of our commanders has given him the principle part of that greatness." Until well into the twentieth century, British historians portrayed George III and Lord North as enemies of progress who secretly conspired to introduce an unconstitutional despotic form of government in both Britain and America. This version of events was central to Whig history, which was the orthodoxy on both sides of the Atlantic. It was a view espoused by the British politician and historian, Sir George Otto Trevelyan, in his influential six-volume *History of the American Revolution* (1899–1905). In his *History of the English-Speaking Peoples* (1956–58), Sir Winston Churchill condemned the British conduct of the Revolutionary War as unequaled in the history of the country for "the multitude of errors. . . . Every maxim and principle of war was either violated or disregarded." Churchill described Lord North's government as composed of ministers "of poor quality."[15]

Surprisingly, American rather than British authors have written the most sympathetic accounts of the British side of the Revolutionary War. This was particularly true of the imperial school of history which flourished in the United States in the early twentieth century and culminated in the work of Lawrence Henry Gipson. In the anglophile wartime atmosphere of America in 1917, a film producer was even imprisoned for three years for his negative portrayal of the British in a movie about the American Revolution, called the *Spirit of '76,* following a court case entitled *United States v. The Spirit of '76.* Because the Revolutionary War was a national disgrace, British historians tended to ignore the subject. The first full-length biography of Lord North did not appear until 1913; the only scholarly biography of Sir Henry Clinton was published in 1962; and the only full-length biography of Lord Cornwallis in 1971. The American Revolution has never loomed large in British history syllabi. The major scholarly biographies of the British commanders are written primarily by Americans.[16]

The British dimension of the war remains undeveloped in most histories of the American Revolution. In contrast to the rich historiography about the Confederacy during the American Civil War, there is no equivalent literature on the British during the Revolutionary War. This is a loss for our understanding of the American Revolution. The paucity of studies is particularly remarkable when we reflect that the revolutionaries were largely reacting to British policy initiatives in the preliminaries to the war and acting defensively against British offensives during it. The British perspective is essential for making the war intelligible.[17]

III

The men who lost America were not opponents of liberty and representative government. Far from conspiring to establish tyranny in America, they regarded themselves as defending liberty and the rule of law which they believed could be safeguarded only by upholding the supreme authority of Parliament. They described themselves as Whigs and subscribed to the principles of parliamentary government established by the constitutional arrangements of the Glorious Revolution of 1688. On the eve of the American Revolution, there were popular conspiracy theories on both sides of the Atlantic. Just as colonial radicals believed that the king and a government cabal were scheming to destroy liberty in America, the British government attributed the revolution to the machinations of a small minority of rebels who wanted to seize power and declare independence. The government regarded the revolutionaries as establishing tyranny with their suppression of all dissent and their use of coercion to enforce compliance. During the first year of the war, there was the anomaly that both sides claimed to be fighting to defend the British Constitution. Both the Howes as well as Cornwallis had actually opposed the policies that led to the American Revolution.[18]

The British politicians and commanders were not ignorant bigots. They were conversant with the Enlightenment emphasis on rational thought in an era that prided itself on being an "Age of Enlightenment." George III created an outstanding library, which became the foundation of the British Museum. He made the most significant additions to the royal art collection since Charles I and founded the Royal Academy of Arts. He had a deep interest in music, architecture, astronomy, science, and agriculture. Educated at Eton and Cambridge, the earl of Sandwich was the first nobleman to participate in the public declamation of classical authors at Trinity College. He was an able linguist, classicist, and scholar of the Orient. A poet and musician, he was a patron of the theater and the opera. He had a keen interest in history, astronomy, and numismatics. In the period of the American Revolution, he supported voyages of exploration, including Captain James Cook's voyage to Australia. His name is commemorated in the Sandwich Islands in the Pacific.

John Burgoyne was a successful playwright, who was a friend of the actor David Garrick and the artist Sir Joshua Reynolds. Lord North was chancellor of Oxford University. He was described as having a lively mind, broad knowledge, and a versatile intellect by both the historian Edward Gibbon and the philosopher-politician Edmund Burke. He supported one of the earliest petitions against the slave trade and was the principal benefactor of Eleazar Wheelock's school for Indians, which became Dartmouth College. A graduate of Trinity College Dublin, Lord George Germain was a friend and chief patron of the American-born scientist Benjamin Thompson and the playwright Richard Cumberland. Sir Henry Clinton was an accomplished violin player and a serious classicist. Like Lord North, he was a friend of Edward Gibbon. Admiral Rodney was a patron of Sir Gilbert Blane, who was to become a major influence on naval medicine and the modern science of epidemiology. The program of imperial reforms that ignited the American Revolution was itself the product of an emphasis on rational thinking that we associate with the eighteenth-century Enlightenment.

The careers of some of the men portrayed in this book were revived after the war. Cornwallis achieved the most spectacular recovery when he was appointed to the highest military and civil commands in Ireland and in India. Sir William Howe, John Burgoyne, Sir Henry Clinton, and Lord Cornwallis were all promoted to the rank of full general. Burgoyne became a successful playwright. Rodney was given a peerage and emerged from the war with a reputation that was actually enhanced. Admiral Howe became a national hero with his defense of the Channel during the French Revolutionary Wars. Sir Henry Clinton was appointed governor of Gibraltar. Lord North briefly returned to power in coalition with his former opponent, the most outspoken critic of the British war for America, Charles James Fox. In the wake of the Napoleonic Wars, George III's image was transformed from that of a despot to that of a symbol of stability and a bulwark of patriotism, as Farmer George and John Bull. His popularity grew as his mental faculties and his powers diminished. Burgoyne was buried among the national heroes at Westminster Abbey. Admiral Howe, Admiral Rodney, and Lord Cornwallis were all commemorated with monuments at St. Paul's Cathedral.

IV

The biographical subjects of this book confronted obstacles of such magnitude as almost to preclude the chances of victory in America. Their greatest challenge was the popularity of the revolutionary movement and the difficulty of waging a war of counterinsurgency.

Between 1774 and 1776, the revolutionaries successfully took over control of the apparatus of government, including the assemblies, councils, court system, and local authorities, as well as the press. They ousted imperial officials. They gained ascendancy in the militias, which proved crucial in enforcing compliance, punishing loyalists, attacking supply lines, and conducting unconventional warfare against the British. The transition was relatively smooth because they already had a large measure of experience in self-government and they were able to adapt existing representative institutions. Although the Revolution was a civil war as well as a rebellion, in which families and communities were divided, the loyalists were slow to emerge as a party and failed to gain the initiative. Following the withdrawal from Boston in March 1776, Britain was not only evicted from the colonies in rebellion but threatened with an American invasion of Canada. The British leadership was thereafter confronted with the task of conquering and occupying America. When the British army was most victorious in 1776 and again in 1780, their success only served to reinvigorate and rally the militias and the Continental Army.[19]

The British commanders understood that they needed to win popular support, but this objective was often in conflict with the use of force and the imperative to win battles. Sir Henry Clinton, the British commander in chief in America between 1778 and 1782, wrote of the need "to gain the hearts and subdue the minds of America." However, the very presence of the British army helped alienate opinion in America. The British necessarily resorted to the recruitment of German mercenaries to bolster the small size of their army. Often known as Hessians, the mercenaries were recruited from a variety of different German principalities, including Hesse-Hanau, Brunswick, Anspach-Bayreuth, and Anhalt-Zerbst, and about two-thirds came from Hesse-Kassel (hence the name Hessians). Some eighteen thousand German mercenaries served in the war, during which they made up an average of a third of the total British troops in North America and 37 percent by 1781. The British similarly attempted to compensate for the size of their army by appealing to those on the margins of American society, including the slaves of rebel masters and Native Americans, but the policy helped alienate white Americans whose support Britain needed to win the war. The stories of plunder and rapes committed by the army similarly caused a backlash against the British.[20]

The men who lost America had to contend with a political system in Britain that frustrated the formulation of clear strategic priorities. The king was the nominal head of government and the army, but the powers of the monarchy were circumscribed by the political settlement between the monarch and Parliament that followed the deposition of James II in 1688. The king could not dictate strategy and policy, but rather had to obtain the agreement of government ministers and majorities of both houses of Parliament. Although he appointed the prime minister, the king had to choose a candidate who had the support of the majority of the elected members of the House of Commons. The party system was still very weak, which meant that governments were often coalitions of various factions, diluting unity of purpose. The concept of collective Cabinet responsibility, in which ministers united behind an agreed policy, had yet to evolve fully.

The British leadership was additionally impeded by the absence of a central command system to provide essential coordination between the various departments of government responsible for the war effort. The army lacked an equivalent of a general staff and had no direct control over the transportation of troops. At the outset of the war, there were a dozen different departments that administered the army. The War Office was the only department specifically responsible for the army, but its role was confined to the administrative affairs of the regiments and it was led by a civilian, the secretary at war, who did not have Cabinet rank. Until 1779, three different departments were responsible for transporting soldiers, ordnance, provisions, camp equipment, hospital stores, horses, and clothing. The different departments competed for the hiring of ships and paid different rates for freight. After 1779, the Navy Board undertook the business of transportation, which was an improvement but still involved an elaborate system by which orders for the board had to be relayed through the Admiralty. When Lord George Germain became secretary of state for the American Department in 1775, he was essentially the chief director in Britain of the war, but he had no direct control of the navy, the army transports, or the provisions. It was a fractured system of command. George Washington and the Continental Army faced similar administrative problems, but with the crucial difference that their government and army were not separated by a distance of three thousand miles.[21]

The shortcomings of the administrative system were compounded by the logistical problems of fighting a war across the Atlantic Ocean. The voyage took at least two months and sometimes three to four months round trip. The government initially assumed that the army would become relatively self-sufficient in feeding itself from territory repossessed in America. In reality, the army and navy continued to rely on provisions and supplies from Britain. The army was larger than most cities in America, with an average of 34,000 men and 4,000 horses who daily consumed 37 tons of food and 38 tons of hay and oats. According to one estimate in April 1778, the army required 127,400 pounds of candles to light 4,900 rooms. Accompanying the troops were women and children who were fed respectively on half-rations and quarter-rations. The proportion of women to soldiers doubled during the war. The government also had to feed and clothe a growing number of loyalist refugees, runaway slaves, prisoners of war, and Native Americans. There were insufficient warehouses and docking facilities in America. The supply ships were often detained and used as floating warehouses, making them unavailable for the return trip. The geographical expanse and the difficult terrain complicated logistics and diffused British forces in America.[22]

There were so many uncertainties and difficulties in providing transportation and supplies that precise timing and smooth implementation of military operations were virtually impossible. Owing to adverse winds and storms, supplies and troops frequently arrived late. The time spent assembling, loading, and unloading cargoes added further delays. The provision ships and army transports required naval convoys, which restricted the frequency and flexibility of their sailing dates. Although the amount of baggage carried by the army is often cited as an example of a hidebound European approach to warfare, the British army had little choice but to carry its provisions and camp equipment on long campaigns while moving among a generally hostile population. It did not have much opportunity to improvise for supplying its needs without alienating the local population.[23]

The need for economy was a major restraint upon military operations. The government always had to consider the necessity of keeping down the cost of the war in order to maintain the support of domestic taxpayers. For much of the eighteenth century, there was a popular fear that the country might be unable to support the burden of the national debt. This was a major issue in British politics and was largely responsible for the fatal decision to tax America. Britain was among the most highly taxed nations in Europe. Between 1700 and 1783, the per capita rate of taxation doubled and the national debt rose fifteen-fold. Furthermore, the growth in the rate of taxation far outpaced the growth in the gross national product. The interest payments on the national debt accounted for about 43 percent of tax revenues in the decade before the American Revolution, and rose from £2,735,925 to £9,406,406 between 1757 and 1783. The payments on interest and on the military accounted for between 75 and 85 percent of government expenditure.[24]

From 1778, the obstacles to British success in America escalated with the transformation of the American Revolutionary War into a global war against France, which expanded to include Spain in 1779 and the Dutch Republic in 1781. Britain was more isolated than at any other time in its history, even more than in 1940. Far from being what television documentaries invariably call the most powerful force in the world, the army was relatively small owing to the long-standing British distrust of it as a potential instrument of tyranny. British military successes consequently depended on alliances with other powers in Europe. During the successful Seven Years' War (1756–63), the worldwide conflict in which the French and Indian War was the North American theater, Britain had been allied with Frederick the Great of Prussia. William Pitt the Elder later boasted that "America had been conquered in Germany" because Prussian troops had played a crucial role in tying down French troops, enabling Britain to concentrate upon the conquest of Canada. After 1763, however, the old system of alliances broke down. Britain alienated Frederick the Great and broke the Prussian alliance by negotiating a separate peace with France, as well as being a victim of its own success because of the sheer scale of its victories which became a source of hostility and distrust elsewhere in Europe. It stood aloof from the first partition of Poland in 1772, and the War of the Bavarian Succession between Austria and Prussia in 1778–79. In June 1773, negotiations collapsed for an alliance with Catherine the Great of Russia. By the time of the American Revolution, Frederick the Great was anxious to remain on peaceful terms with France, and the French foreign minister, the comte de Vergennes, was equally determined to avoid war in Europe in order to focus resources upon Britain. It was in vain that Britain belatedly tried to negotiate a triple alliance with Russia and Austria in 1780.[25]

Even before France declared war in 1778, Britain's relations with Europe affected the war effort in America. To allay French concerns that the war in America was merely a prelude to a British attack on the French West Indies, and to appease domestic taxpayers, Britain only partially mobilized its military forces in 1775. The budget for the navy was actually cut so that the navy was too small to support the army, to suppress privateers, to provide convoys, and to blockade America. Furthermore, the navy was instructed not to intercept French ships carrying munitions and supplies to America in European waters, which precluded enforcing a meaningful blockade of America. From the beginning, France, Spain, and Holland supplied gunpowder, loans, and military equipment to America. The marquis de Lafayette was only the most famous of Europeans who voluntarily risked their lives in the early days of the struggle for American independence. They included men who played a critical role in the victory against Britain like Baron Friedrich Wilhelm Augustus von Steuben, Count Casimir Pulaski, and Thaddeus Kosciusko.[26]

After 1778, the British army and navy were engaged not only in the war for America but in the protection of the British possessions in the West Indies, the Mediterranean, Africa, and India. The army was spread throughout the globe with garrisons in outposts of empire from Antigua, Jamaica, the Bahama Islands, Minorca, Gibraltar, and Gorée in West Africa, to Bombay in India. After 1779, the army's North American garrisons included Pensacola and St. Augustine, Augusta, Charleston, New York, Newport, and Quebec. There were inland strongholds at Forts Niagara, Detroit, and Mackinaw City in the upper midwest, and at Kaskaskia in Illinois, Manchac on the lower Mississippi, and Mobile. Exclusive of Canada, they amounted to some twenty-seven different garrisons to be supplied and supervised in America. The last battle of the American Revolutionary War was fought in India. Moreover, the defense of Britain became a primary objective with the threat of attack during the summers of 1778 through 1780. In 1779, the danger of invasion was greater than at any time since the Spanish Armada in 1588. There was simultaneous concern about the possibility of a revolution in Ireland. The American War of Independence was the only war in the eighteenth century in which Britain did not have naval supremacy and did not have a "two-power" navy that was able to match the combined fleets of France and Spain. After 1778, Britain was trying to win the war in America with fewer troops and a smaller navy than it had deployed in America in 1776.[27]

The biographical chapters of this book will evaluate their subjects in terms of the constraints and the obstacles that contributed to their failure. This multi-biographical approach will enable the reader to see the war from the perspective of several individuals rather than the partial views of one participant. The sections are arranged to emphasize both victory and defeat. It was partly because the war was never a linear series of defeats that the British government persevered in the belief that victory was possible in America.

PART I

The View from London

For if America should grow into a separate empire it must of course
cause . . . a revolution in the political system of the world.

SPEECH OF LORD NORTH, November 20, 1778

CHAPTER 1

"The Tyrant"

GEORGE III

The Declaration of Independence casts George III as the leading villain of the American Revolution. It asserts that he is a prince whose character is "marked by every act which may define a Tyrant" and pronounces him "unfit to be the ruler of a free people."

John Adams, who had been a member of the committee that drafted the declaration, later admitted that it contains "expressions which I would not have inserted, if I had drawn it up, particularly that which called the King tyrant." Reminiscing at the age of eighty-eight, Adams thought it "too personal . . . too passionate, and too much like scolding, for so grave and solemn a document." He confessed that he "never believed George to be a tyrant" or to be guilty of the "cruel" acts committed in his name. In his autobiography, Adams was also critical of Benjamin Franklin for his "severe resentment" and personal animosity toward George III. According to Adams, regardless of the appropriateness of the occasion, Franklin never missed an opportunity to cast aspersions upon George III.[1]

In one of the most incongruous and remarkable encounters between former adversaries, after the Revolution John Adams and Thomas Jefferson actually met George III: the revolutionary leaders and the monarch whom they had vilified came face to face. As the first ambassador of the United States of America, Adams was presented to George III at St. James's Palace in June 1785. It was an emotional encounter between an outspoken advocate of independence and a king who had considered abdicating rather than accepting the loss of America. Dressed in a black formal coat with silk breeches and a sash, Adams told the king that the meeting would form an epoch in the history of England and America. He said that he thought himself more fortunate than his fellow citizens in having the honor to be the first to stand in the royal presence in a diplomatic role. He hoped to be instrumental in restoring the old good nature and humor between people, who, though separated by an ocean and under different governments, had the same language and a similar religion. He stressed the cultural ties that bound them, not the recent politics that had separated them. According to Adams, George III seemed much affected and answered with a tremor in his voice.[2]

Assuming an air of familiarity, George III jested with John Adams that some people believed Adams was less attached than his fellow countrymen to France. Despite his surprise and embarrassment at what he thought an indiscreet comment, Adams attempted to match the royal humor, replying that he had no attachment but to his country. "As quick as lightning," George III responded that an honest man will never have any other loyalty. After receiving a signal from the king to leave, Adams observed royal protocol by stepping backward and made his last bow at the door of the royal chamber. Accompanied back to his carriage by a royal official, Adams passed through the royal apartments where, at every stage, the serried ranks of servants, gentlemen-porters, and under-porters roared out like thunder, "Mr. Adams' servants, Mr. Adams' carriage." Adams was delighted that his person, his status, and his country had been accorded respect and kindness beyond his expectations from the king. Adams and his wife Abigail subsequently became quite fond of George III.[3]

In the summer of 1786, John Adams arranged to introduce Thomas Jefferson, who was to receive a less civil reception from George III. At the time Jefferson was not known as the primary author of the Declaration of Independence, an association that he did not promote until the rage of party politics in the 1790s. Unlike Adams, he was known to favor France over Britain in his capacity as the U.S. ambassador in Paris. On the day of his presentation, there was an unusually thin attendance at court, consisting of a few members of the royal family, government ministers, and foreign ambassadors. Other than an entry in his account book of the tips that he paid the porters at St. James's Palace, Thomas Jefferson wrote nothing of the encounter at the time. Writing thirty-five years later in his autobiography, Jefferson was more forthcoming, relating how "it was impossible for anything to be more ungracious" than the notice that George III gave "Mr. Adams and myself." He "saw, at once, that the ulcerations of mind in that quarter, left nothing to be expected on the subject of my attendance." According to Adams's grandson, the king publicly insulted them both by turning his back upon Jefferson and Adams which "was not lost upon the circle of his subjects in attendance."[4]

Jefferson certainly never ceased to blame George III personally for the breakdown in relations leading to the Revolution. Jefferson believed that from the beginning of his reign, George III had schemed to impose a tyranny on America, and wrote that "future ages will scarce believe that the hardiness of one man adventured within the short compass of twelve years only, to build a blatant and undisguised tyranny." After his return from London to Paris in August 1786, he wrote sardonically of George III as the American Messiah who had labored for twenty years to drive the nation to discover its own good, and "who had not a friend on earth who would lament his loss so much and so long as I should." In Jefferson's mind, George III always would be the villain, the antagonist in

America's primordial narrative, its myth of origin. For Jefferson, this was not propaganda but objective truth.[5]

In reality, George III had less power than virtually any other monarch in Europe. During the seventeenth century, Britain had had two revolutions of its own in which the supporters of Parliament successfully deposed Charles I and James II. After the execution of Charles I in 1649, Britain was a republic for eleven years, and following the fall of James II in 1688, Parliament negotiated a revolutionary settlement in what became known as the Glorious Revolution. It included a Bill of Rights (1689) and a Toleration Act (1689), which became the foundation of the British Constitution and ensured that the crown would henceforth govern through Parliament. The monarchy retained the power to appoint the government, but its choice was limited in practice to prime ministers who had support in Parliament. Although the system of elections was corrupt and the crown had considerable influence through patronage, the survival of the government was always dependent upon the support of independent members of the elected House of Commons. The British consequently regarded their political system as a bastion of freedom and liberty, in contrast to the absolute monarchies of Europe.

I

George III's accession seemed like the dawn of a new age with unbounded promise. It coincided with a dramatic expansion of the British Empire in America, the Caribbean, and India. In a worldwide conflict (1756–63) known as the Seven Years' War in Europe and the French and Indian War in America, Britain won a series of spectacular victories against France. There was much self-congratulation about "victories won in every quarter of the globe." William Pitt boasted that the British had overrun more of the world than the Roman Empire.[6]

In 1760, amidst great anticipation and euphoria, George III was crowned king. He was the first native English speaker to sit on the throne since Queen Anne (1702–14). At the beginning of his reign he proclaimed that he was born and educated in the country and that he gloried "in the name of Briton." He was a youth of twenty-two, who was variously described as tall, robust, graceful, affable, cheerful, fair, and fresh, with blue eyes, auburn hair, and a strong melodious voice. He was very conscious of having a tendency to corpulence which he kept in check by plenty of exercise and horse riding. Horace Walpole, whose memoirs did so much to denigrate the reputation of the king among later historians, was initially favorably impressed. He described how the king did not stand in one spot with his eyes fixed on the ground, in contrast to his seventy-seven-year-old grandfather and predecessor, George II. He walked about and spoke to everyone. In September 1761, the popular frenzy mounted when the new king chose to marry a seventeen-year-old German princess, Charlotte of Mecklenburg-Strelitz.[7]

George III seemed to embody the culture, breadth, and inquisitiveness that we associate with the age of Enlightenment. He was fluent in French and German and familiar with Italian. His interest in science surpassed that of any of his predecessors. He assembled the finest contemporary collection of scientific instruments within the first decade of his reign. He was particularly fond of astronomy and built the Royal Observatory at Richmond to view the transit of Venus in 1769. He was the patron of William Herschel, who transformed the understanding of the solar system and the universe by his discovery of the planet Uranus in the year of the battle of Yorktown, 1781. George III was fascinated by mechanical devices, especially clocks and watches, which he was able to dismantle and reassemble. He commissioned a table to chart the principles of mechanics and an air pump to demonstrate the properties of the atmosphere. He was keenly interested in gardening and horticulture, expanding the royal gardens at Kew and appointing Sir Joseph Banks as his botanist in 1771. He was similarly interested in agriculture and farming, which later earned him the nickname of "Farmer George." He was an accomplished horseman who liked to go out riding every day, and he enjoyed regular visits to the theater.[8]

George III also became the most significant royal patron and collector of art since Charles I. In 1768, he was influential in the founding of the Royal Academy of Arts, and remained closely involved in its administration, helping it relocate to Somerset House in 1780. George III was especially enthusiastic about the work of the Pennsylvania-born artist Benjamin West who was a founding member and second president of the Royal Academy. Trained by Sir William Chambers, George III was himself a competent architectural draftsman who did many of his own plans and drawings. He was a patron of many of the leading architects of his era, including James "Athenian" Stuart, Robert Adam, James Wyatt, and Thomas Sanby, and commissioned the landscape architect "Capability" Brown. He loved music. He played the flute, pianoforte, and harpsichord, collected compositions including the works of Lully, Palestrina and Scarlatti, and during his courtship of Queen Charlotte, he composed a song for her called "The Royal Bride." He several times invited the eight-year-old Wolfgang Amadeus Mozart to perform for the royal family during his visit to England in 1764. Before his departure in 1765, Mozart dedicated a set of sonatas for harpsichord and violin to Queen Charlotte. George III later tried to persuade Joseph Haydn to stay permanently in London and was instrumental in the revival of his favorite composer, George Frederick Handel. He was an enthusiastic bibliophile whose collection became the foundation of the British Library and numbered sixty-five thousand books by the time of his death in 1820.[9]

George III was conversant with the works of contemporary literary writers, philosophers, and historians like Edmund Burke, Edward Gibbon, Samuel Johnson, and James Boswell. He permitted scholars to use his library at the Queen's House, which later became Buckingham Palace. Samuel Johnson described him as "the finest gentleman I have seen," and thought him the first monarch in a hundred years to identify seriously with the interests of his people and to try to make friends with his fellow countrymen. In 1767, when the king heard that Johnson regularly visited the library at the Queen's House, he asked the librarian to introduce them and then proceeded to quiz Johnson about his views on current theological debates, his thoughts on the best literary journals, and whether there was any important work being done at Oxford University. When the king asked him about the progress of his own writing and Johnson replied that he "thought he had already done his part as a writer," the king replied "I should have thought so, if you had not written so well," which delighted Johnson as a compliment "fit for a King to pay. It was decisive." After the meeting, Johnson famously told a friend that he did not reply, since "It was not for me to bandy civilities with my sovereign." George III is wrongly alleged to have said to Edward Gibbon, "Another d——d thick square book! Always scribble, scribble, scribble! Eh! Mr. Gibbon?" It was actually said by his brother the Duke of Gloucester.[10]

<h1 style="text-align:center">II</h1>

George III did not instigate the colonial policies that triggered the American Revolution. The government ministers, not the king, were the architects of those policies, whose origins predated his reign. When he ascended the throne, George III was politically inexperienced. Throughout the 1760s he was preoccupied with the problem of forming a stable government. The king appointed the ministers of the government—the most significant of the political powers remaining to the monarchy—but his choices were confined to men who were able to command majority support in Parliament, and were governed by domestic rather than imperial considerations.

　　George III not only did not initiate the policies that led to the breakdown in imperial relations, but he was even a restraining influence on some of the more extreme measures proposed by his ministers. His first statement about affairs in America recommended that the colonies receive proper compensation for their expenses in the French and Indian War. He discouraged George Grenville's government from including a clause in the Quartering Act (1765) that permitted the billeting of soldiers in private houses in America. He later remarked that the Stamp Act was "abundant in absurdities," having "first deprived the Americans, by restraining their trade, from the means of acquiring wealth, and (then) taxed them." He supported the conciliatory colonial policies advocated by the Duke of Grafton's ministry in 1769.[11]

　　George III advised against the more draconian proposals of Lord Hillsborough, the secretary of state for America. He agreed that the abolition of elections for the Council of Massachusetts Bay might indeed "from a continuance of their conduct become necessary; but till then ought to be avoided as altering Charters is at all times an odious measure." He similarly advised against the proposal to abolish assemblies that denied the absolute sovereignty of Parliament. He argued that such action was "of so strong a nature that it rather seems calculated to increase the unhappy feuds that subsist than to assuage them." He cautioned that colonial governors "ought to be instructed to avoid as much as possible giving occasion to the Assemblies again coming on the apple of discord." He suggested that a hint be given that colonies that submitted to the Townshend Duties (1767) might be exempted from the tax on tea. He had been willing to grant such a favor to Virginia and the British West Indies in 1769, but desisted because "the Virginians were so offensive the last Spring."[12]

It was not until the Boston Tea Party (1773) that George III suddenly became actively involved in the growing imperial crisis in America. He became more vehement from the conviction that the crisis had been caused by too much lenience towards the colonies. He regretted that Britain had previously indulged them by repealing the Stamp Act in 1766. Believing that any concessions were likely to be interpreted as a sign of weakness and that they would only encourage further demands, he was against appeasement of the colonies. He was much impressed by the advice of the commander of the British army in America, General Thomas Gage, that "they will be lyons, whilst we are lambs; but, if we take the resolute part, they will undoubtedly prove very meek." He denied wishing to use force, but argued that it was the only means of success.[13]

George III saw the struggle as fundamental to the defense of order and the Constitution. A devoutly religious man, he treated political issues in moralistic terms. Later in his reign, he opposed legislation to give Catholics the vote in Ireland because he believed it his duty under his coronation oath to uphold the Anglican Church. In America, he argued that he was "fighting the battle of the legislature" in defense of the authority of Parliament to govern America. It was essential to the maintenance of order and hierarchy that the colonies acknowledge the supreme authority of Parliament. As the revolutionary movement became more republican, he became ever more passionate about crushing the rebellion and defending the dignity of kingship. He regarded monarchy as essential to liberty as part of a system of checks and balances in which the crown acted as a constitutional safeguard against the excesses of both the aristocratic and the democratic elements of government in the House of Lords and the House of Commons.[14]

George III strongly endorsed the Coercive Acts, which became the catalyst for the American Revolution. Based on the concept of collective responsibility and passed by Parliament at staggered intervals in the spring of 1774, the Coercive Acts were a series of laws that aimed to punish Massachusetts for the Boston Tea Party. George III wrote that he was unable to refrain from expressing his pleasure when he heard that the first of the acts, the Boston Port Bill, had been passed a second time without either a debate or a division in the House of Commons. When Thomas Hutchinson, the American-born governor of Massachusetts, arrived in England, George III immediately had a two-hour meeting with him and favorably impressed Hutchinson with his knowledge of America. Hutchinson wrote a word-for-word account of his conversation with the king that included descriptions of his facial expressions and body movements. George III asked Hutchinson detailed questions including whether John Adams was related to Sam Adams; he was already familiar with Sam, but wanted to know more about John. However, his questions had a random quality and lacked focus. As has been said of his architectural interests, he concentrated on detail at the expense of understanding broader themes. The king afterwards claimed that Hutchinson had assured him that he thought the Boston Port Bill was a wise measure and that he was consequently persuaded that the measure would successfully subjugate Boston. This was not the recollection of Hutchinson, who was much opposed to the bill and who wrote after the meeting that he had told the king that it was "extremely alarming" to the people of Boston.[15]

George III was pleasantly surprised by the absence of opposition in Parliament to the Coercive Acts. It confirmed in his mind the rectitude of the policy. He was glad to find that the debate had ended earlier than was expected and that the government majority was so considerable for the Regulation of the Government of Massachusetts Act, which was arguably the most unpopular of the acts. He was delighted with the results of the 1774 general election, which increased the government majority in the House of Commons, causing him to comment that the election had returned more landed gentlemen as opposed to East India nabobs and West India planters whom he thought "not ready for the battle" with America. In September 1774, months before the outbreak of actual fighting, he had concluded that the die was cast and the colonies had to either submit or triumph. In November, he was convinced that the New England governments were in a state of rebellion in which "blows must decide whether they are to be subject to this Country or independent."[16]

In November 1774, when General Thomas Gage began to have reservations about the use of force in America and urged caution and the suspension of the Coercive Acts, George III thought this the most absurd suggestion possible. He again repeated that there was no choice except to master the colonies or leave them to themselves and treat them as aliens. Prime Minister Lord North also began to shrink from the prospect of war and proposed sending out peace commissioners to the colonies to investigate the dispute. The king was opposed on the grounds that such overtures would be unlikely to make the colonies reasonable and would give the impression that the mother country was afraid. He permitted but disliked the less ambitious plan put forward by North known as the Conciliatory Proposal (1775).[17]

In 1775, George III's views over America began to differ sharply from those of the opposition speakers in Parliament. Edmund Burke and William Pitt the Elder made some of their best orations in favor of conciliation, and the Rockingham opposition group recoiled from a military solution when push came to shove. Although conspicuously passive in 1774, the merchant lobbies began to equivocate. There was a sudden profusion of petitions in favor of conciliation and peace, the first modern example of a popular antiwar protest movement, which were signed by the equivalent of one-tenth of the electorate. At the instigation of Lord Mayor John Wilkes in April 1775, the Livery of London, representing the trade associations, and the popularly elected Common Hall of the City of London petitioned the king in favor of America.[18]

The king became adamant that only the use of force was likely to succeed. In February 1775, he vowed never to look right or left, but to pursue steadily the track that his conscience dictated. He was convinced that the colonies would submit if confronted with greater vigor. In March, he reflected that the more he considered the best approach to the crisis the more he became convinced that a combination of rectitude, candor, and firmness must with time be crowned with success. After the outbreak of the war in April, he had no doubt that the British nation had lost patience with the conduct of America. He thought any action short of compelling obedience would be ruinous and culpable, and vowed that no consideration would make him swerve from the present path. He was confident that he was doing his duty and must never retreat. He became impatient with debates on America and thought the House of Commons could not possibly tolerate hearing the same speeches so frequently repeated. He insisted that "we must with Vigour pursue the means of bringing the Deluded Americans to a Sense of their Duty."[19]

George III therefore ignored colonial requests for him to serve as a mediator and readily embraced a policy of coercion. In April 1775, he broke with tradition by refusing to receive the address from the Livery of London sympathetic to America, which had obliquely compared him to the deposed Stuart King James II. He henceforth made it a policy not to receive addresses from the radical Livery and Common Hall. He particularly despised the Common Hall for its association with his nemesis, the populist politician and lord mayor, John Wilkes, who had presented the address supporting America. He regarded the petition "as fresh insolence from the Shop that has fabricated so many." Admitting that there were a thousand reasons to wish not to receive insolent addresses, Lord North tried to persuade the king against slighting the Common Hall. He warned that a change of protocol might be productive of more evils, while nothing was lost by following the traditional procedure of receiving and rejecting such addresses. Since it would only revive Wilkes's popularity if he were seen to be too studiously avoided by George III, North advised the king to alter his method of dealing with him. The king remained obdurate and unwilling "to hear myself insulted" by receiving an address instigated by Wilkes while sitting on the throne.[20]

In August 1775, George III was impatient with the progress of the ministry in issuing a proclamation of rebellion in America. He thought it necessary for the government to show determination in "prosecuting with vigour every measure that may tend to force those deluded People to Submission." Lord North then issued a proclamation in the king's name for suppressing rebellion and sedition, which accused the colonies of having proceeded "to open and avowed rebellion" and declared anyone abetting their cause to be traitors. It was necessitated by the outbreak of war and the need to cut off military supplies to the revolutionaries in Boston. However, it dashed the hopes of loyalists and moderates in the Continental Congress like John Dickinson, who still sought to compromise with Britain.[21]

By refusing to receive John Dickinson's Olive Branch Petition, which promised to support royal authority in the colonies, George III disappointed those colonists who sought his mediation. Richard Penn, a staunch loyalist and former governor of Pennsylvania, carried the petition to London, but the king avoided receiving it until after the government had issued the proclamation of rebellion and sedition. When he finally did acknowledge the petition, he refused to hear it while seated on the throne and made it clear that no answer would be given. He had good constitutional reasons for his action since the petition essentially invited him to act against Parliament. Nevertheless, George III's "contempt" rankled even the loyalist members in the Assembly of Pennsylvania. In a speech before Parliament in October 1775, the king dismissed such conciliatory gestures as "meant only to amuse, by vague expressions of attachment to the parent state, and the strongest protestations of loyalty to me, whilst they are preparing for a general revolt." His speech, which called for a speedy end to the military preparations in the colonies and for foreign assistance in suppressing the rebellion, had a great impact on colonial opinion. It was no longer tenable for colonial revolutionaries to continue to declare loyalty to the king.[22]

Throughout the summer of 1775, in his capacity as captain general of the army and prince elector of Hanover, George III began to negotiate for foreign mercenaries from Germany. Writing personally to Catherine the Great, he additionally tried to obtain Russian troops. Although he was merely carrying out a decision of his Cabinet, he had committed a double offense in the eyes of the colonists in abdicating the basic responsibility of government to provide protection and in using foreign troops against his own subjects in America. In November 1775, he opened Parliament with a speech against the daring spirit of resistance and disobedience to the law in Massachusetts. The event was witnessed by Thomas Hutchinson, who told a correspondent that it was much stronger in the manner of its delivery than when read in print. In Massachusetts, Abigail Adams predicted that the speech would stain with everlasting infamy the reign of George III.[23]

III

The part played by the king gave the colonies the impression that it was he who had rejected them rather than the other way round. Until it became apparent that he was actively committed to a policy of coercion in 1774, George III was not a target of personal attack in America. Indeed, he was treated with more deference in America than in Britain, where periodicals like the *North Briton* and the *Public Advertiser,* which published the anonymous "Letters of Junius," were comparable to the worst examples of modern tabloid journalism, replete with libelous innuendos such as the suggestion that the king's mother was having an affair with the earl of Bute. The most devastating charge in the British press was that parliamentary government had become a mockery and a mere screen for a cabal of unelected advisers, the so-called King's Friends, who used corruption and bribery to manipulate Parliament. On the other hand, until 1774 Americans concentrated their criticism upon government ministers and Parliament. John Witherspoon, the president of the College of New Jersey, observed that the king was the object of far greater insults in his own metropolis "than ever were thought of, or would have been permitted, by the mob in any part of America."[24]

Indeed, Americans continued to recognize the authority of the king, for the crux of the imperial crisis was the colonial denial of the supreme authority of the British Parliament. By 1774, colonists like James Wilson and Alexander Hamilton were writing pamphlets that denied this authority in America. At the same time, Americans continued to acknowledge the king as the sole source of imperial authority and sought his intervention against Parliament. In late 1774, they were still making declarations of loyalty to George III, even while they prepared to send representatives to the first Continental Congress. In New London, Connecticut, a royal salute was fired as the names of the local representatives were announced; in New York, a band played "God Save the King" for the departure of representative Isaac Low; the Continental Congress petitioned the king "as the loving father of your whole people" and toasted his health. Even after the outbreak of war in April 1775, the colonists indulged in the fiction that they were fighting in the name of the king against a wicked ministry and defending British liberties against Parliament. Until well into 1775, they even referred to the royal troops as the "Ministerial Army" or "the Parliament Troops." The royal arms remained on public buildings; criminal cases were tried in court in the name of the king; the Anglican clergy prayed for the king to overcome his enemies; and most provincial assemblies continued to date their laws by the year of the king's reign, while formal documents ended with "God Save the King."[25]

In *A Summary View of the Rights of British America,* the thirty-one-year-old Thomas Jefferson penned the hitherto most audacious colonial pamphlet to admonish George III. Published anonymously in Williamsburg, Virginia, in 1774, Jefferson asserted that kings were the servants, not the proprietors of the people. Despite the insubordinate tone, Jefferson called upon the king to be a mediator and even to resume the exercise of the royal veto which had fallen into desuetude since 1707 when Queen Anne became the last British monarch to veto an act of Parliament. Jefferson wrote that it behooved the king to think and to act for himself and his people, thereby inviting the king to exceed his traditional authority and act independently of Parliament. It was an opportunistic argument that reflected the desperation of the colonists to find a constitutional formula to enable them to circumvent the claims of the absolute authority of Parliament while remaining subjects of George III. They were reluctant revolutionaries. Jefferson's anonymous pamphlet was reprinted in the *London Chronicle* where he was described as "a respectable Merchant of Cumberland County in Maryland."[26]

With the escalation of the war, the fiction of opposing Parliament and not the king could not last. During the summer of 1775, John Cleaveland, a pastor in Ipswich, Massachusetts, writing under the pseudonym of "Johannes in Eremo," argued that the adage that the king could do no wrong was nonsense. He reminded his readers of the compact in which the people swore an oath of obedience to the king in return for his protecting their rights and privileges. Following the skirmishes at Lexington and Concord (April 19, 1775), Cleaveland bid "King *George* the Third, adieu! No more shall we cry to you for protection; no more shall we bleed in defence of your person." In London on October 23, 1775, an American by the name of Stephen Sayre, a former lord mayor who had returned as a merchant to his native city, was accused of a plot to kidnap George III en route to the state opening of Parliament. Allegedly, he planned to imprison the king in the Tower of London, and force him into exile in his German dominions in Hanover. The allegation was made by Frank Richardson from Pennsylvania, a lieutenant in the First Regiment of Foot Guards, who claimed that he had heard the details from Sayre.[27]

Published anonymously in January 1776, Thomas Paine's *Common Sense* ended all discretion about implicating George III. Paine did not list personal grievances against the king, but instead sought to undermine the mystique of the crown and to challenge the institution of monarchy. He mocked the contradictions in the system of monarchy, in which kings were shut away from the world yet their business required them to be all-knowing. It was not a divine institution but an artificial contrivance. It had a dubious ancestry, with forebears like William the Conqueror who was nothing more than "a French bastard landing with an armed banditti, and establishing himself as king of England." Although Paine did not mention the name of George III, he still fired some well-aimed barbs at "the Royal Brute of Britain" and "the hardened sullen tempered Pharaoh . . . the wretch, that with the pretended title of FATHER OF HIS PEOPLE can unfeelingly hear their slaughter, and composedly sleep with their blood upon his soul." Paine famously declared that one honest man was worth more to society "than all the crowned ruffians that ever lived."[28]

In the summer of 1776, the destruction of royal images, the removal of the royal arms, and the removal of the royal name represented America's symbolic break with George III. In Massachusetts, juries refused to serve "because the Writs are in the King's Name," and the Assembly passed a bill "for disusing the Kings Name in all Acts, Commissions, and Law Processes." Following the Declaration of Independence in July, the royal arms on public buildings, coffeehouses, and tavern signs were ripped, trampled, and burned, often in front of crowds shouting repeated huzzas. John Adams described how it was the fashion in Philadelphia to reverse portraits of the king and hang them upside down. There were mock trials, executions, and funerals of George III. At Bowling Green, at the southern end of modern Broadway in Manhattan, a crowd pulled down the gilded lead equestrian statue of George III, sculpted by Joseph Wilton, that depicted him in Roman garb in the style of the statue of Marcus Aurelius on the Roman Capitol. The head was severed from the body, which together with the horse was taken to Litchfield, Connecticut, where local women melted the lead into bullets. The tail, a few fragments, and the marble base of the pedestal survive in the collection of the New-York Historical Society.[29]

The colonial opposition embraced conspiracy theories claiming that the king had destroyed the traditional balance of government by gaining total control over Parliament to establish a tyranny in Britain and America. In July 1776, the Declaration of Independence exaggerated the role of George III, with its long litany of grievances against him personally. It aimed to show that he had imposed "unremitting injuries and usurpations" that had as a "direct object the establishment of an absolute tyranny." It blamed him for decisions of royal governors in which he had had no role and episodes that predated his reign. Jefferson's original draft of the declaration even listed the slave trade among the litany of grievances against George III. However, he also included a condemnation of the British people that was removed by the Continental Congress for fear that it might alienate potential support in Britain. The declaration's personal charges against the king were critical for justifying rebellion by showing that it was directed against a state of tyranny. Having for years believed in the blessings of the British Constitution, the colonists found it easier to conceive of the tyranny of an individual than the collective tyranny of Parliament. Especially in the emotionally charged atmosphere of 1776, the Declaration of Independence made for good propaganda to stir up hatred against an individual rather than a collective abstraction. As the last acknowledged source of imperial authority in America, George III was inevitably the final scapegoat.

IV

If contemporaries exaggerated his role in the origins of the dispute, George III was nevertheless crucially influential in prolonging the war, which became a personal crusade. He saw the conflict in apocalyptic terms as the most serious contest in which any country had ever engaged.[30]

George III articulated more cogently than any of his ministers the justification for the war and the vital stakes for Britain, but his emphasis shifted over time. He initially defended the war in terms of supporting parliamentary authority and the Constitution, but he increasingly argued that the war was essential to the survival of Britain as a great power in Europe. He regarded the empire as a crucial source of national wealth and power that would inevitably collapse if Britain lost America since the other colonies would soon follow and seek independence. The British Caribbean islands would be the first to cast off obedience, not in a spirit of rebellion, but rather because they were dependent on the mainland colonies for food and supplies, and Ireland would be the next domino to fall. As Britain faced a combined armada of the forces of France and Spain in the summer of 1779, George III preferred to risk an invasion rather than lose the sugar islands in the Caribbean without which it would be "impossible to raise Money to continue the War."[31]

There was no choice, the king thought, but to persist with the war or to face ruin. The loss of imperial trade and the consequent decline of manufacturing would reduce Britain to the status of a poverty-stricken island. He hoped never to live to see that day that Britain would so far lose its sense of self-esteem as to be willing to grant independence to America and consequently to fall low among the states of Europe. Four months before the British surrender at Yorktown (October 19, 1781), he remained convinced that there was but one line to follow, "for we are contending for our whole consequence whether we are to rank among the Great Powers of Europe, or to be reduced to one of the least considerable." Indeed anyone who thought otherwise did not deserve to be a member of the community. As late as November 1781, he again wrote that "the die was cast," and that Britain would be either a great empire or the least dignified state in Europe.[32]

In his capacity as captain general of the British army, George III was necessarily engaged in the planning and execution of military strategy. He collected books about warfare and regularly attended the summer encampments of the army around London. He reviewed the Guards regiments two or three times every week, copied naval charts, and collected models of major fortifications. The topographical collection in his library included records of military campaigns, fortifications, barracks and canals. He knew the strengths of the fortified towns on the continent and the soundings of the chief harbors in Europe. Under the guidance of the earl of Sandwich, first lord of the Admiralty in North's government, he became better informed on naval matters than any of his predecessors since James II.[33]

George III avidly followed every detail and initialed every page of every official document concerning the war for America placed on his desk. He read rebel newspapers, complaining on one occasion that they smelled of the pies in which they had been smuggled into New York. He did not have the final say in strategic matters and was several times overruled by the Cabinet, but he was nonetheless influential in the direction and conduct of the war. In a memorandum of 1777, he modified General John Burgoyne's plan of "The Conduct of War from Canada," criticizing him for underrating the German mercenaries and eliminating Burgoyne's option of sailing by sea from Canada to join Sir

William Howe. Although he made fewer appointments than his grandfather George II, Lord North complained that the king exerted too much influence over military promotions and assignments.[34]

George III especially favored Lord Jeffrey Amherst, a hero of the French and Indian War, whom he twice tried to persuade to become commander in chief in America, in 1775 and 1778 (Figure 13). Despite constant solicitations from the king for advice, Amherst was unwilling to commit himself in Cabinet meetings, where he was known as a man of few words. George III selected and personally appointed Generals William Howe, Henry Clinton, and John Burgoyne. He was instrumental in persuading the earl of Sandwich to appoint Admiral Richard, Earl Howe to the command of the navy in America. However, he made such appointments in consultation with the Cabinet and military advisers. Together with Lord George Germain, the secretary of state for America, he favored the high-risk strategies of generals like Burgoyne and Charles, Earl Cornwallis, rather than the caution of Sir William Howe and Sir Henry Clinton. He argued that some risk was necessary or "otherwise we shall only vegetate in this war." He preferred "to get through it with spirit, or with a crash be ruined."[35]

Owing to the void in leadership created by the doubts and hesitations of his prime minister, Lord North, George III was more than simply committed to the cause, but became the chief driving force in the war for America. Lord North was a man of considerable ability, but was unsuited to the task of a war leader. He was the first to acknowledge his shortcomings in his self-deprecating correspondence. He tellingly preferred not to think of himself as prime minister, but rather as just another member of the Cabinet who represented the Treasury. Furthermore, North lacked conviction in the cause and was increasingly despondent. He continued to hold out for a negotiated peace. At the beginning of 1778, without consulting the Cabinet, North prepared a peace plan whose terms included a complete renunciation of colonial taxation and the sending of a peace commission to America. The king was opposed and advised him not to sue for peace, since whatever he proposed was likely to be unacceptable to the Americans and to dissatisfy Parliament. Following news of the failure of North's peace commission led by the earl of Carlisle in August 1778, the king wrote that any further concessions would be a joke. In understanding that nothing short of the recognition of independence would satisfy the American Congress, George III was in many ways more realistic than Lord North.[36]

George III flattered and cajoled his prime minister to rouse him to action and keep him at the helm. He praised his financial management and his leadership of the Treasury. At the beginning of the war, his letters showed affection and respect, describing North as his sheet anchor whose ease and comfort he wanted to secure in every transaction. The king was grateful to North for replacing the duke of Grafton who had suddenly resigned as prime minister in 1770. He appreciated North's skills as a parliamentary manager who was also able and honest in the conduct of public affairs. When North defended the record of the government following the British defeat at Saratoga in 1777, the king was delighted by North's firm and dignified role in persuading the Commons "to see the present misfortune in true light, as very serious but not without remedy." He promised that he would never forget the friendship and zeal shown by Lord North, and reminded him of the support he had from the Cabinet, how sincerely he was loved and admired by the House of Commons, and how he was universally esteemed by the public, which "reflections must rouze your mind and enable you to withstand situations still more embarrassing then the present." He told him that he was too diffident of his own abilities, and was delighted when North spoke to him in a very frank manner as if "unbosoming to a friend."[37]

When flattery did not succeed, George III exhorted, goaded, and bullied Lord North. He was worried by the absence of planning and the disunity of the Cabinet. In January 1778, he urged North to deliberate without further loss of time upon the future mode of conducting the war for America. He added that it was even more important that the government have a plan to repel the attacks of opposition parties with their tactic of calling for papers and demanding inquiries; this, he wrote, "must be digested by you." He encouraged his prime minister to discuss such matters in the next Cabinet meeting and to have minutes taken in order to achieve some consensus and to unite the Cabinet when facing the questions of the opposition. He told him that he needed to explain government policy in advance to the most influential members and the independent country gentry in the House of Commons who might otherwise oppose the government because they were either not informed or did not understand the subject. These were valid implied criticisms of North's modus operandi.[38]

With the imminence of a French declaration of war at the beginning of 1778, North attempted to resign and requested that the king open negotiations with members of the opposition. He had long felt inadequate to his task and overwhelmed by the responsibilities of his position. He became particularly anxious over his inability to negotiate a peace that was satisfactory both to the Patriots and "to the present zealous friends of government." He believed his continuance in office to be an obstacle to any chance of a negotiated peace with America, and feared that whatever he did must inevitably cause him misery and disgrace. Pleading that his health and understanding were greatly impaired by struggling so long in an office to which he was unequal, North asked the king to choose a successor less tainted by past policies. In March 1778, he asked to be relieved immediately since the longer he remained in office the worse the consequences. He asked that his continuance in the government should not be made a necessary condition of negotiations to appoint a successor. The present situation required "*new* men and *able* men." North wrote that he regarded capital punishment as preferable to the constant anguish of mind that he felt while he continued to be prime minister.[39]

North complained that the king had constantly refused to grant him permission to resign, with the result that the issues had become more difficult, leaving him even more unequal to his role as prime minister. He wrote that he could not conceive what induced the king to be so determined to keep him, despite so much evidence of his unfitness for his position. He believed that the king saw the state of the country in a better light than it deserved, when public and private credit was so low: he doubted whether the country could continue to obtain loans to finance the war for two more years, reminding the king that "the power of borrowing had been hitherto the principal source of greatness and weight of Great Britain." He thought the king should be glad if an accommodation with America prevented a war with France. North feared that Britain would suffer more than her enemies from the continuance of the war, not "by defeats, but by an enormous expense, which will ruin her, and will not in any degree be repaid by the most brilliant victories." He warned that the consequent economic hardships would "be attributed to the obstinate perseverance in the American War."[40]

George III was impatient with North's "always recurring" to the need for a total change of government. The king made it clear that he would never voluntarily consent to his resignation, which he would treat as a personal act of betrayal. In March 1778, he sent a remarkable letter to North in which he demanded to know whether he did indeed intend to desert him at the hour of danger. He wrote that he was becoming more exasperated with North constantly suggesting measures that he had repeatedly told him he would never submit to "as I look upon it as disgraceful to me and destruction to my kingdom, and Family." He complained that he was tired of North never ceasing to talk about his resignation and peace negotiations with America. He regarded North's avowed despondency as highly detrimental to the service of government, and felt obliged to ask him whether he intended to remain in power, a query to which he expected "explicit answers in writing." He implored North to cooperate with him and exert himself in putting vigor and activity into every department of government. North replied by repeating his request to quit, but he fatally agreed to serve the rest of the parliamentary session in expectation that the king would soon appoint a successor as prime minister. North begged, "let me not go to the grave with the guilt of having been the ruin of his [sic] King and country."[41]

George III alternated between appealing to North's loyalty and chiding him. He implored him to remember that his resignation would be detrimental to the crown and the public, whose interests were inseparable. He gave North several pep talks in which he warned him that the greatest part of his difficulties arose from his proceeding too far with plans, especially appointments to offices, without consulting him. George III asked where else might North find a greater confidant "to repose his undigested thoughts more safely than in the breast of one who had ever treated him more as his friend than minister." In November 1778, the king became positively hostile. He demanded that

North complete a plan "forthwith" for dealing with the opposition in the next Parliament. A week later, he berated him for his dilatoriness and failure to do what he had asked. When North responded that he was conscious and certain that he had neither the authority nor abilities requisite for his position, it occasioned an outburst from the king, who demanded an explanation in writing of what he meant by not having the authority.[42]

George III had become so distrustful of his wobbling prime minister that he began to monitor him through two members of North's inner circle—Charles Jenkinson, the secretary at war, and John Robinson, the secretary to the Treasury. North was incensed when he discovered a letter from the king to Robinson criticizing him. In a series of sycophantic and ingratiating letters, Jenkinson commiserated with the king on his disagreeable situation in having to deal with North; aware that North knew nothing of this, Jenkinson was nervous about being seen too often at court in case it alerted North's suspicions. He reassured the king that the prime minister would not resign if his resolve was stiffened; his weak mind needed only the king's support and firmness to help him recover his spirit. He encouraged the king to discount North's protestations and threats of resignation because he really intended to remain in government as long as possible. On another occasion, he suggested that North's declarations were merely pretexts to shift the blame and responsibility for the war to the king, concluding that "The Meaning of all this, is, that He may have it to say to the World that He is ready to retire, but that your Majesty insists on His continuing in His present Situation." According to Jenkinson, Robinson thought him a prophet for predicting that North would never voluntarily give up power.[43]

Far from vacillating, North was undeviating in his requests to resign. In June 1779, Jenkinson wrote to the king saying that North was in good spirits and determined to go on, but North wrote to the king that he hoped that he would not think it unbecoming of him to renew his request to resign at the end of the session. North reminded the king that he had tried to resign every year since he had taken office, for which he blamed himself, but he was now convinced that his presence was among the principal causes of the perilous state of the country. His attitude was unchanged later in the year when he wrote that he was contented to retire without an honor or sinecure since he was "really so broken" and did not feel able to trust his own judgment. North claimed that he had been miserable for ten years in obedience to the king, and was unable to endure the combination of misery and guilt, especially when nobody approved his conduct. North's desire to resign remained unchanged throughout the last two years of his premiership. In November 1779, he wrote to the king that it was absolutely necessary that he should be permitted to retire and be replaced following the end of the parliamentary session. Much to the chagrin of George III and Jenkinson, in April 1780 North was so distraught that he spoke of his desire to retire in favor of his leading parliamentary opponent, Charles James Fox.[44]

George III had no alternative but to retain Lord North if he wanted a prime minister who was both willing to continue the war and able to command the support of the House of Commons. Horace Walpole understood the king's situation, namely that he "had nobody to put in his place." The king admitted as much, telling Lord George Germain, "altho' he is not intirely to my mind, and there are many things about him I wish were changed, I don't know any who wou'd do so well."[45]

George III equated opposition to the war with treason and was therefore not inclined to negotiate with the opposition parties. He ridiculed those who supposed the Americans to be "poor mild persons who after unheard of and repeated grievances had no choice but Slavery or the Sword." He talked of "that perfidious man" and "trumpet of sedition" who was the leading opponent of the government, William Pitt the Elder, earl of Chatham. North had wanted to be replaced by Chatham who, although fiercely opposed to the war, was adamant that Britain should not grant independence to America. North wrote bluntly that the king's only objection was his fear of the domineering Chatham assuming too much authority. In April 1778, during a speech on America in the House of Lords, Chatham dramatically collapsed and soon afterward died, removing the most viable alternative candidate to replace North as prime minister. George III was appalled when the House of Commons voted Chatham a state funeral and a monument in Westminster Abbey, finding the compliment "rather an offensive measure to me personally."[46]

Rather than allow the opposition leaders into government, George III was willing to risk a constitutional crisis. This was clear from a series of letters he wrote to North during March of 1778. The king solemnly declared that nothing would bring him to deal personally with Lord Chatham. He wrote that it was "not private pique, but an opinion formed on an experience of a Reign of now seventeen years, that makes me resolve to run any personal risque rather than submit to Opposition." The king was insistent that he would not be made a slave by the opposition for the remainder of his days. He preferred to risk his crown than do what he regarded as "personally disgraceful" by withdrawing from America. He thought it impossible "that the nation shall not stand by me, if they will not, they shall have another King, for I will never put my hand to what would make me miserable to the last hour of my life." In reference to the two opposition leaders, the marquess of Rockingham and the earl of Chatham, the king wrote that "rather than be shackled by those desperate Men," he would "rather see any form of Government introduced into this Island and lose my Crown than wear it as a disgrace."[47]

Upon Chatham's death, the only alternative to North was opposition leaders who were committed to ending the war and therefore unacceptable to George III. After the French entered the war in 1778, the Rockingham party wanted an immediate end to the war and became reconciled to granting American independence. The earl of Shelburne, who replaced Chatham as an opposition leader, was more ambivalent about this than Rockingham. He wanted an immediate end to the war, but hoped that it might be possible to continue an informal imperial relationship with America. His policy was to leave the revolutionaries to themselves, hoping that they would soon send commissioners to offer terms. Since the king found none of these aims acceptable, he had to keep North in power. Toward the end of his life, North defended himself by saying, "year after year, I entreated to be allowed to resign, but I was not allowed, and was earnestly entreated to remain." He remained on board until the bitter end, but who was driving the war?[48]

George III declaimed, "If others will not be active, I must drive." By dint of his forceful personality and his pertinacity in the closing months of 1779, the king kept the discordant elements of the government together. He bolstered his ministers against an opposition containing the talents of some of the most brilliant parliamentary orators, including Edmund Burke, Charles James Fox, and the earl of Shelburne. He rallied his ministers to face a growing international threat. In June 1779, Britain faced the most serious danger of an invasion since the Spanish Armada from the combined fleets of France and Spain. In the Caribbean, Grenada and St. Vincent fell to the French. Ireland seemed to be going the way of America with tens of thousands of people arming themselves in the Volunteer Movement, which was purportedly for self-defense, but soon began to lobby for greater autonomy. There was a virtual stalemate in the war in America. The government majorities were dwindling in the House of Commons where Sir William Meredith made a motion for peace, declaring that no nation had "ever sent fleets and armies of such strength and magnitude on so remote a service as those which Great Britain has poured into America." Lord North asked again to be allowed to resign at the end of the parliamentary session.[49]

George III was undaunted. He was ready both to ride the occasional defeat in Parliament and to call the bluff of ministers who threatened to resign. He wrote to North that he had frequently heard him say that the advantages to be gained by this contest could never repay the expense, which he likened to the attitude of a tradesman with his weighing scale behind his counter. George III conceded that no sane individual would now argue "the laying of a tax was deserving of all the evils that have arisen from it," but step by step the demands of America had risen—independence was their object, to which "this Country can never submit." There was no price too high to pay. On June 21, 1779, George III summoned the Cabinet to his personal library at the Queen's House—the first time a monarch had done so since the reign of Queen Anne. At the meeting, he refused to give any intimation of the reason for the meeting. He broke normal protocol by inviting the Cabinet to sit down around the library table with himself at the head. Lord George Germain told one of his under secretaries that he "began to think that they were going to be dismissed, and very probably they all thought the same thing."[50]

At this remarkable occasion, George III rehearsed the history of the colonial struggle, expressing regret only for changing his ministry in 1765 and consenting to the repeal of the Stamp Act in 1766. He praised the earl of Sandwich for building up the navy, and the Treasury "for the very abundant manner in which the war in America had been supplied." He defended the generals in America—Howe, Burgoyne, and Clinton—of whom originally "everybody approved." He said that it was "his principle, and it was [his] resolution to part with his life rather than suffer his dominions to be dismembered, for he held it to be his duty to God and his people to preserve them intire at whatever hazard or inconvenience to himself." He "therefore expected firmness and support from his ministers." He was willing to make new appointments to the Cabinet if they desired, "but in all events he expected they would support him." He spoke for nearly an hour, not "by way of speech or formal harangue, but as a plain narrative, delivered in conversation." He subsequently wrote to Lord North that "I hope after having so fully stated my sentiments this day . . . every one felt how I am interested in the present moment, and consequently will feel that they can alone hope for my Support by shewing zeal, assiduity, and activity." As he later told North, he wanted to infuse the ministers with his spirit but waited, in the hope of finding them more resolved, until the declaration of war with Spain. North continued on the brink of resignation, but the king had kept the show on the road.[51]

Writing in the 1940s, the historian Sir Herbert Butterfield found George III's robust and unflagging determination to fight to the last to be almost Churchillian. The king's letters resounded with rallying refrains calling for firmness, resolution, boldness, zeal, alacrity, and vigor. He regarded firmness as the characteristic of a true Englishman. He vowed to march on "whilst any ten men in the kingdom will stand by me." He admitted that "the times are certainly hazardous, but that ought to rouze the Spirit of Every Englishman to support me." He would never surrender: "every man not willing to sacrifice every object to a *momentary* and inglorious Peace must concur with me in thinking that this Country can never submit." He called for sacrifice: "We must stretch every nerve to defend ourselves, and must run some risks, for if we are to play only a cautious game ruin will inevitably ensue."[52]

In order to hasten the fitting out and sailing of the fleets of the Royal Navy, George III made personal visits of inspection to the naval yards at Chatham, Sheerness, and Portsmouth. In 1779, he enlisted his fourteen-year-old son Prince William in the navy as a midshipman, and in December 1780, he sent another son, Prince Frederick, to pursue military studies in Hanover. His martial spirit was evident in the portrait that he commissioned from Benjamin West. It depicted George III as captain general of the army, standing in a scarlet uniform and holding plans of military encampments, against a background of the *Royal George* firing a salute and a detachment of the 15th Light Dragoons, led by Lord Jeffrey Amherst and the marquess of Lothian (Figure 3). In about 1776, George III changed his principal royal retreat from Kew to a more warlike residence, Windsor Castle. The castle was decrepit, but the otherwise frugal king began extensive renovations, and from 1778, he began to spend more and more time there, which was also conveniently located for hunting. When he was in residence at the castle, a military band played every night. Between 1777 and 1779, he introduced a military-style dress known as the Windsor Uniform to be worn in court, following the practice among the princes of the Holy Roman Empire.[53]

V

The opposition parties were in no doubt about who was the driving force behind the continuance of the war, and they changed their tactics accordingly, to demonstrate against the king personally. The Rockingham Whigs launched what Edmund Burke dubbed an "economical reform" program that aimed not so much to improve the efficiency of government and prevent waste as to reduce the influence of the king's ministers in the House of Commons. The plan took the form of several bills to limit the number of "placemen"—members of the House of Commons who held appointments and sinecures from the king. In December 1779, the early stages of the "economical reform" movement gained additional momentum from outside Parliament with the launch of the Yorkshire Association by Christopher Wyvill, an Anglican clergyman and local landowner who led what became a nationwide petitioning movement for the reform of Parliament.

In a series of celebrated parliamentary speeches, Charles James Fox emerged as the nemesis of George III and the war. He held the king responsible for war's misfortunes and the dismantling of the empire, made ominous references to revolution, and invoked the memory of the overthrow of the Stuarts. There were many such allusions. William Cowper, the poet and satirist, wrote that he was not alone "in thinking that you see a striking resemblance between the reign of his present Majesty and that of Charles I." Cowper cited the undue extension of crown influence, the discountenancing and displacing of men obnoxious to the court, and the waste of public money, as "features common to both faces." The caricaturists followed suit, depicting George III as a despot. As in America, it became more difficult for the opposition to maintain the fiction that the "king can do no wrong" and that the war was due to the bad advice of evil ministers, because the king was visibly and actively pursuing a war that had become anathema to them. There was talk in opposition circles that victory in America might mean the beginning of a much more powerful monarchy in Britain.[54]

In April 1780, the personal opposition to the king reached a crescendo with the passing of a series of resolutions by John Dunning, which culminated in the motion "that the influence of the Crown has increased, is increasing, and ought to be diminished." The motion carried by 233 votes to 215 in the House of Commons, indicating that even some traditional supporters of the government felt that the king had become too obtrusive. It was a major defeat for the king, who wished that he "did not feel at whom they are *personally levelled*," but reassured himself that the rank and file members had gone "farther than they intended . . . for it cannot be the wish of the Majority to overturn the Constitution." He blamed instead "Factious Leaders and ruined Men."[55]

Some modern commentators have dismissed the motion as an opposition sham and a bald attempt to seize power, showing nothing more than "a sublime and beautiful disregard of easily ascertainable facts and trends." They contend that the reformers "stirred up a great deal of fuss about nothing," because the number of placemen had already reached its zenith in 1761 and had declined by over a fifth by 1780. The rotten boroughs controlled by the government similarly decreased. Furthermore, there were precedents in the reign of George II for some of the actions of George III.[56]

This is an argument that attempts to reduce the influence of the king to a mathematical formula. The growing influence of the king in driving the war was not to be measured in the number of royal officeholders in Parliament but in the force of George III's character and especially his dominance of Lord North. By introducing legislation to reduce the number of officeholders, the opposition merely chose a symbolic weapon with which to strike at the personal authority of the king. The rise in royal influence was evident in George III's role in persisting with the war for America. He refused to negotiate with opposition leaders unless they signed an agreement "to keep the empire entire." He would permit neither independence nor the withdrawal of troops in America. As a condition to any negotiations with opposition leaders, he made it a minimum requirement that they provide assurances that they intended to strain every nerve to keep the empire intact, that they would prosecute the war with vigor in every area, and that they would treat past policies with respect. He warned that these were the "farthest lengths" to which he was prepared to go, and that anyone who thought the difficulties of the times might force him to make further concessions was much mistaken. He was "willing to sacrifice any member of the cabinet" in a coalition with the opposition, but he was emphatic that policies should not be changed. He would rather "be beat in Parliament, than see everything ruined by an ignominious treaty with Opposition." During negotiations with the opposition in the summer of 1780, a major obstacle was their "evasive answer" regarding their future policies toward America. George III was only prepared to admit members of the opposition to government "if it can be attained without a violation of my Principles." According to his modern apologists, he confined himself to advising and selecting ministers, but this was tantamount to dictating policy.[57]

The contest with the opposition became personal. George III became all the more implacable about keeping the opposition leaders out of government when they began to support measures to limit the influence of the crown with the "economical reform" bills. The continuation of the war was entwined with the defense of his powers at home. He was determined to keep out what he regarded as a dangerous faction that he associated with the same principles and doctrines as those of the revolutionaries in

America. He especially regarded Charles James Fox as "inseparably implicated with rebellion" for his highly charged speeches in which he mischievously compared George III and Catherine the Great, observing that the only major difference was that Russia's empire had expanded under Catherine and that the British Empire had sunk into contempt under George III. The king suspected the opposition of planning to change the Constitution. He was less bothered than North about parliamentary defeats, dismissing them as "the momentary whims that strike Popular Assemblies." The interests of his country and his own interest were conveniently allied in his mind. The opposition correspondingly began to equate a victory in America with a victory for the personal power of George III.[58]

By refusing to allow the resignation of the Lord North and in favor of opposition leaders committed to granting independence to America, George III effectively prolonged the war. In June and July 1780, his views on America stymied negotiations for a coalition with the marquess of Rockingham. It was a bitter blow to Lord North. The king understood the need to strengthen the government from the ranks of the opposition, and he was willing to change some of his ministers, but not his measures. Until June 1780, the position of the king and the Cabinet was becoming desperate as they faced a united opposition and dwindling majorities in Parliament, but the hand of fate rescued the king. The fortunes of the war began to improve, supporting his contention that victory was possible. His optimism was never entirely misplaced because it was never a war of constant reversals and defeats. In April 1780, Admiral Sir George Rodney narrowly missed defeating the French fleet of Admiral Luc Urbain de Guichen off Martinique, which would have given Britain naval superiority over France. In May, Sir Henry Clinton accepted the surrender of Charleston in South Carolina, capturing an army of five thousand men. In August, Lord Cornwallis defeated Horatio Gates, the hero of Saratoga, at the battle of Camden and took prisoner much of the remaining southern detachment of the Continental Army. In September, General Benedict Arnold of the Continental Army defected from his command of West Point to join the British. The propaganda value of the defection of one of the highest-ranking and most illustrious of the rebel American generals was heightened by public outcry in Britain at the hanging and brave death of his British accomplice, the popular Major John André.[59]

The king was vindicated, and his fortunes abroad were matched by the troubles of the opposition at home. The brief union of the opposition parties was again split between the former followers of the earl of Chatham, led by the earl of Shelburne, and those of the marquess of Rockingham. They divided on the issue of parliamentary reform that was supported by Shelburne, but not by Rockingham. Between June 2 and 11, 1780, the growing support for reform and a change of government was checked by the ferocity of the Gordon Riots in London, purportedly anti-Catholic demonstrations against the enlightened Catholic Relief Act of 1778. In scenes that Charles Dickens was to evoke in his novel *Barnaby Rudge* (1841), London was turned over to six days of rioting and hundreds of people died. Nine years before French revolutionaries would storm the Bastille, crowds numbering as many as fifty thousand released prison inmates, and burned Newgate Prison and the Clink. The mob attacked the homes of government ministers, and some fourteen thousand demonstrators attempted to burst into the House of Commons. St. James's Park and Hyde Park became encampments for eleven thousand troops. The army tents looked almost picturesque covering St. James's Park all the way from the Queen's House to the Horse Guards. To the mystification of the opposition leaders, the riots helped discredit the extraparliamentary reform movements and the demand for a change in government. In November, the king sensed a change of mood in which his adversaries in the corporation of the City of London, the former stronghold of John Wilkes, "thought much worse of the Opposition" and had come to believe that a change of government "must be disadvantageous to the Public." North abandoned attempts to negotiate with the opposition and called a quick election to gather support from the nation.[60]

The opposition parties made the classic error of indulging in shrill rhetoric and appearing too sympathetic to the enemy. This was particularly true of Charles James Fox, who "from the union of birth, connections, talents, and eloquence" became the star of the opposition, but who was distrusted as a demagogue and a radical by the independent members of the House of Commons. Fox was openly scathing of the very members whose support was essential, those that "choose to call themselves country gentlemen," whom he derided for their "unlimited attachment to every court measure" and for persisting in support of policies that "do not promise the attainment of a single object." With his dark undertone of revolutionary change, Fox backfired by making personal attacks on the king.[61]

Fox reinforced the impression that he was unpatriotic by seeming to glory in the military reversals of his country. Fox and his supporters sat on the opposition benches dressed in the blue frock coats and buff waistcoats that were the old colors of the Whigs but were also associated with the uniforms of the Continental Army.[62] In a speech of November 9, 1780, he vowed as long as he lived, "he never would agree to join in a vote of thanks to any officer, whose laurels were gathered in the American war," not even his own brother who was serving in America. Fox compounded distrust of his political character by his dissolute lifestyle. It was said that he loved only three things—women, play, and politics—yet he failed to ever make a creditable connection with a woman, lost his fortune gambling, and remained for most of his life in opposition. The country gentry and the rising middle class were more attracted to the virtuous domestic lifestyle and religious devotion that were characteristic of both George III and Lord North.[63]

While Charles James Fox was still able to charm and impress his detractors, Lord Shelburne, the most intellectual and most visionary of the opposition leaders, was widely disliked. Shelburne was regarded as untrustworthy, causing him to be dubbed "the Jesuit of Berkeley Square" or Malagrida (the name of a Spanish Jesuit). The dramatist Oliver Goldsmith thought the comparison with Shelburne most unfair, "for Malagrida was a very good sort of man." Shelburne was perceived as alternating between a cold imperiousness and utter obsequiousness. His interest in parliamentary reform was regarded as too radical even by the Rockinghams. George III and Lord North's political and social conservatism was simply more appealing to the prejudices of the majority of the members of Parliament than the reforming views of the leading opponents of the war in America.[64]

VI

Even after the British defeat at Yorktown in 1781, George III's fixation on winning the war at all costs was unabated. He was unbowed. He regarded the defeat as a temporary setback and was ready to continue. He was confident of parliamentary support once the members had recovered a little from the shock of the bad news and had contemplated the necessity of carrying on the war to spare the country from being totally diminished in stature. He could accept neither the verdict of military defeat nor the collapse of parliamentary support. He was adamant that he would never allow himself to be an instrument in the separation of the two countries, and that he was ready to be driven "to the wall [to] do what I can to save the empire." With the news of Yorktown arriving on the eve of the annual opening of Parliament, the king's speech had to be hastily rewritten because the original draft had confidently predicted a speedy and victorious termination of the war. At midnight before the opening day, George III refused to accept the revised version of his speech but insisted that it be changed to indicate that the government had no intention of withdrawing from America. He declared that he would be undeserving of the trust and loyalty of a free people "if he consented to the sacrifice, either to his own desire for peace, or to their temporary ease and relief, those essential rights and permanent interests, upon the maintenance and preservation of which the future strength and security of Great Britain must depend."[65]

Delivered from the throne in the House of Lords on November 27, 1781, the final version of the king's speech caused much astonishment by making only a passing reference to the "late capture of Lord Cornwallis and his army" which "had been very unfortunate" to the king's "arms in Virginia, having ended in the loss of his forces in that province." The royal speech continued that "the late misfortune in that quarter called loudly for the firm concurrence and assistance of parliament, in order to frustrate the designs of their enemies, which were equally prejudicial to the real interests of America, and to those of Great Britain." It "still declared his perfect conviction of the justice of his cause" and his intention to continue to prosecute the war.[66]

In the aftermath of Yorktown, George III's desire to pursue the war was no longer shared by the majority of the Cabinet. When Lord George Germain, the only Cabinet member to advocate continuing the war, was removed from the government in January 1782, Lord North told him that "your being out of the way wont mend matters, for the king is of the same opinion." Indeed, George III told North that if Germain's departure indicated government acceptance of American independence, "you must go further; you must remove ME." The king demonstrated his continued support for Germain by creating him Viscount Sackville. North commented to his secretary that the king was willing to change his ministers, but not his policies, expecting "me *alone* to carry on that plan which appears to me in our present circumstances ruinous and impracticable."[67]

In March 1782, George III was "mortified" when Lord North made clear his intention to resign. North finally confronted the king, explaining that he could longer remain in office because he had lost the support of the majority of the House of Commons. In a remarkably defiant and bold rebuke, North wrote that "in this country, the Prince on the Throne cannot, with prudence, oppose the deliberate resolution of the House of Commons." He reminded the king that his forebears had consented to changes in government in order to prevent the terrible consequence of a clash between the two branches of government. Parliament had altered its "sentiments, and their sentiments whether just or erroneous, must ultimately prevail." In a very revealing statement, he credited the king with "having persevered, as long as possible, *in what You thought right*" (my italics). North wrote that the king could consequently lose no honor if he yielded, "as some of the most renowned and most glorious of your Predecessors have done, to the opinion and wishes of the House of Commons." George III threatened that North would forever forfeit his regard if he did not give him more time to decide what to do. According to the hostile gossip of Horace Walpole, when Lord North came to take his formal leave, the king said, "Remember, my Lord, that it is you who desert me, not I you."[68]

George III did not forgive the resignation of Lord North. He afterwards quarreled with him over the debt from the election of 1780, and initially tried to insist that North be personally liable for the cost. The breach became permanent when North later allied himself with the nemesis of the king, Charles James Fox. The two former antagonists formed a brief and remarkable coalition in government known as the Fox-North ministry (April–December 1783). Determined to oust them from office, George III instructed his friends in the House of Lords to vote against a government bill for the management of the East India Company, and thereby succeeded in bringing the ministry down.

When he was finally forced to yield to American independence, George III drafted a letter of abdication to Parliament. Claiming that all his difficulties in America had arisen from "his scrupulous attachment to the Rights of Parliament," he spoke of his devotion to the British Constitution. He complained of the "sudden change in Sentiments" in what he pointedly referred to as "one Branch of the Legislature," which had "totally incapacitated Him from either conducting the War with effect, or from obtaining any Peace but on conditions which would prove destructive to the Commerce as well as essential Rights of the British Nation." With much sorrow, he announced that he found that he could be of no further utility to his country, which had driven him "to the painful step of quitting it for ever." He therefore resigned "the Crown of Great Britain and the Dominions appertaining thereto to His Dearly Beloved Son and lawful Successor, George Prince of Wales," who he hoped might be more successful in his endeavors for the prosperity of the British Empire. His letter of abdication was never submitted.[69]

On December 5, 1782, George III had to give a speech to Parliament acknowledging the independence of the United States of America. As he read the word "independent," his voice was "constrained." According to Elkanah Watson, a young American merchant, George III "hesitated" and "choked" over the words "free and independent states" but otherwise delivered the speech with "ill grace." George III spoke candidly of having sacrificed his own wishes to the opinion of his people. Although sympathetic to him, Nathaniel Wraxall described the speech as "among the most singular compositions ever put in the mouth of a British sovereign." It included passages more suitable to the spirit and language of a moralist or a sage than of a monarch. It had a kind of invocation or prayer in the middle in which George III implored divine intervention to avert the calamities that might befall the former colonies in consequence of their becoming independent states and repudiating monarchical power. Wraxall wrote that the speech was the subject of mirth and satire, while Edmund Burke called it "insufferable." The personal blow of conceding independence was made more tragic by the death of George III's favorite son, the four-year-old Octavius.[70]

When he was asked whether he would be willing to receive an ambassador from the United States in 1783, George III replied emphatically that it could never be agreeable to him and he would have a very bad opinion of any Englishman who accepted "a minister for a Revolted State," which he predicted for many years "cannot have any stable Government." He also balked at the idea of sending a permanent diplomatic representative to the United States. He declined to observe the usual courtesy of giving jewelry and portraits to the American peace negotiators in Paris, and was glad to be out of town on the day of the proclamation of the final peace, which he thought was the beginning of the end of the British Empire. He regarded the willingness of the nation to make terms as a tragic consequence of religion and public spirit having become "absorbed by Vice and Dissipation," and wrote that he was deeply wounded that the separation of the former colonies happened in his reign. He never relented from the view that it was the most justifiable war that any country had ever waged.[71]

VII

George III enjoyed an apotheosis in the later stages of his reign. This was particularly evident in the contemporary caricatures of him in which his image was transformed from the oriental despot of the later years of the war for America, to that of John Bull, the national icon who popularly symbolized the rugged and masculine qualities of the British. His frugal lifestyle and his interest in agriculture became assets, causing him to be depicted as plain Farmer George. "God Save the King" began to outstrip "Rule Britannia" in popularity, and the custom began of playing it regularly before theater performances. Earlier in his reign, the king's need for a magnifying glass had been a boon to caricaturists as a symbol of his political myopia, but it later became a satirical prop in portrayals of him trying to see such diminutive opponents as Napoleon. The pageantry of royal occasions became grander and more popular. Formerly a thorn in the side of the king, John Wilkes presented him with the freedom of the City of London for his support for the "legal prerogative of the Crown, *and* constitutional rights of the people." Thirty thousand people flocked to his funeral despite the intention to keep it private.[72]

It helped that he had been the longest-serving monarch since Elizabeth I, having ascended the throne before many of his subjects were born. In addition, his reign had coincided with a major period of economic and industrial growth, as well as being a golden age of literature, with such figures as Samuel Johnson, Edward Gibbon, Oliver Goldsmith, Jane Austen, Sir Walter Scott, and William Wordsworth. After 1792, the French Revolution enhanced his stature. It enabled him to become the personification of national identity, a symbol of continuity and stability, in which monarchy remained distinctive and seemingly more legitimate than the self-appointed emperorship of Napoleon. It galvanized the landed and clerical elites, who were anxious to show solidarity and to contrive popular support for the crown from fear of the egalitarian revolutionary zeal of France. The press joined in the acclaim, helping to cultivate public support, and urban leaders, keen to develop civic pride, sponsored royal celebrations aided by the growth of independent voluntary organizations that were anxious to distinguish themselves from radical sects.[73]

George III's personal character traits played to his advantage. Outside radical circles, his stubborn resistance to change was regarded as a merit in a revolutionary period. His undoubted courage won him applause when he did not flinch in response to assassination attempts: one by Margaret Nicholson in 1786 and another by James Hadfield in 1800. Freely intermingling with his subjects, he was informal and personable. Despite her dislike of his white eyebrows and red face, he won the enthusiastic approval of Abigail Adams.

George III's private virtues had always gained him respect. In a period known for its aristocratic decadence, he was faithful to his wife, Queen Charlotte, by whom he had fifteen children. After nineteen years of marriage together, he thanked "heaven for having directed my choice. . . . I could not bear up did I not find in her a feeling friend to whom I can unbosom my grief." Her "excellent qualities appear stronger to me every hour." Even at the height of his illness, she wore ever larger miniature portraits of him on a long chain.

He loathed the vice and promiscuity of his age. Ever concerned about the dignity of the monarchy, he quarreled with his brothers when they married women without his permission whom he regarded as unsuitable, and even when he reconciled with them, he refused to receive their wives. He similarly clashed with his sons over their keeping mistresses and he was resistant to his daughters getting married for lack of eligible European princes. He was frugal, living modestly for a prince and with a regular routine. He did not even keep a wine cellar but bought directly from merchants when the occasion required. His habits were to appear exemplary in comparison to those of his eldest son, George, prince of Wales, whose dissolute lifestyle became notorious after the war.[74]

George III's popularity reached its peak when it was widely believed that he was going mad. Throughout the American war, he was in perfect health and did not exhibit any of the symptoms of his later illness, although after falling off a horse at the time of the passage of the Stamp Act in 1765, he had had an attack of symptoms that were to reappear and eventually to afflict him permanently. In the summer of 1788, he had such a prolonged and serious malady that it provoked a political crisis over whether he should be replaced by his son as regent. His symptoms included delirium, insomnia, paranoia, incoherent rambling speech, a rapid pulse, and deteriorating eyesight. It was likely porphyria, a blood disease that causes neurologic attacks and the distinctive symptom of purple-colored urine, which was present in George III. He underwent various humiliating forms of medical treatment in which he was tied to a chair and confined. During his illness in 1788, he told his daughters that he was luckier than Shakespeare's King Lear in his madness, for he had no Regan or Goneril to bully him, but three Cordelias to look after him.[75]

In October 1810, George III made his last public appearance as king. Looking like Lear in his long white beard, he spent much of his final decade a virtual prisoner at Windsor Castle while his son reigned in his place as Prince Regent. He inspected imaginary military parades and had fond conversations with the long-dead Lord North. He continued to play his harpsichord in an effort to hear. According to one of his doctors, he appeared "to be living in another world' and had "lost almost all interest in the concerns of this." Queen Charlotte ceased to visit him, because his symptoms were so violent and he suffered so much from dementia that he did not recognize his own family, and eventually she predeceased him. George III outlived the other British commanders and politicians who had participated in the loss of America. On January 29, 1820, George III died at the age of eighty-one and was buried at St. George's Chapel, Windsor. His popularity had continued to rise partly because of the waning of his political influence. He presented no threat, and he could be safely regarded as a symbol of national pride.[76]

In terms of wielding real executive power, George III's reign was the last hurrah of the British monarchy. His lengthy illness and the unpopularity of his son helped hasten the decline of the crown's influence, which thereafter gradually waned to a token role in what was to be described as a republic disguised as a monarchy. In 1761, George III had unwittingly contributed to the financial decline of the monarchy by accepting a fixed income instead of receiving revenues from crown lands and an annual vote of funds by Parliament. The 1780s "economical reform" movement, which aimed to curb the number of placemen and royal office holders in the House of Commons, made only minor strides, but it gave symbolic momentum to the reduction of crown influence over Parliament. There were other, deeper trends at work, including the rise of the concept of Cabinet responsibility that enabled ministers to impose their collective will on the monarch. The role of the crown was also reduced by the rise of popular participation in politics through lobbying and extraparliamentary agitation. In the early nineteenth century, the gradual disappearance of the aristocratic parliamentary factions and their replacement by a disciplined two-party system greatly reduced royal power.

George III had tried to console himself over the loss of America with the thought that "I should be miserable indeed if I did not feel that no blame on that Account can be laid at my door, and did I not also know that knavery seems to be so much the striking feature of its Inhabitants that it may not in the end be an evil that they become Aliens to this Kingdom." During his emotional meeting with John Adams in 1785, George III gave a fitting epitaph to his own role in the American Revolution:

> I wish you, sir, to believe, and that it may be understood in America, that I have done nothing in the late contest but what I thought myself indispensably bound to do, by the duty which I owed to my people. I will be frank with you. I was the last to consent to the separation; but the separation having been made, and having become inevitable, I have always said, as I say now, that I would be the first to meet the friendship of the United States as an independent power.

Better than many of his aristocratic opponents, George III appreciated the portent of the American Revolution for the end of the Ancien Régime in Europe. He had defended what he considered his rights, which he regarded as essential to the preservation of the liberties of the people, against politicians who he believed were trying to change the balance of power by removing the check of royal authority over Parliament. He had used every means to defend the empire against revolutionaries whose victory he believed would annihilate the national greatness of Britain. He had unapologetically defended an order of monarchy, hierarchy, religious orthodoxy, and empire that he regarded as the world turned the right way up.[77]

CHAPTER 2

The Prime Minister

LORD NORTH

O n the evening of June 22, 1779, Prime Minister Lord North wept before the House of Commons. In a scarcely veiled reference to the resistance of George III, he told the members that he had long wished to resign but that he had been prevented. He had indeed made many such requests to the king. Earlier in June, North had yet again asked to be replaced as prime minister, offering to leave the government, if his presence was an obstacle to a choice of successor and explaining that he was unequal to the task and that abler hands were needed to save the country.[1]

The spectacle of the Lord North breaking down in Parliament in the midst of the war was nothing new. Since the French entry into the war in 1778, North had been in a state of virtual paralysis, during which his postponement of decisions became chronic. In March 1778, he told the House that he had wanted to resign for ten years. After being lambasted in a speech by Charles James Fox in December, he wept in the House "in the most pitiable lamentation." His state of mind was unchanged a year later when a verbal assault by the opposition regarding his absences caused him to excuse himself with tears and mention the death of his son earlier in the year. Even before the outbreak of the war, North had broken down on at least two occasions. This won him little sympathy, for he was assumed to be bluffing. Such cynicism seemed justified, since these episodes were soon followed by defiant speeches asserting his intention to remain in office. On being challenged to make good his desire to resign by Charles James Fox in June 1779, North replied that he could not do so until a suitable replacement had been appointed. He insisted that it was his duty to stay in office when events were so critical.[2]

North wanted to resign because he had lost faith in the British effort to recover America. He was acutely aware that he was personally blamed for the failure of the war effort. As early as 1776, Madame de Castries, the wife of the French ambassador, noticed Lord North among the Knights of the Garter and asked if he had been appointed a member of the order "for having lost America." In the *Public Advertiser* in 1778, "Philopoemen" told North that he was mistaken if he thought that he could escape by blaming the generals, since the cause of his disappointment originated in the imbecility of his own counsels. In the House of Commons in 1780, a member accused North "of being author of the loss of America." North's reservations about the war were not shared by George III, nor by the majority of the members of the Cabinet or his own parliamentary supporters, who opposed North's attempts to open negotiations with the Continental Congress. This tension was the primary reason that North wanted to resign. He believed that the revolutionaries were unlikely to make terms with the man that they regarded as responsible for instigating the war. He saw himself as an obstacle to peace.[3]

North's motives for remaining in power were complex. His critics believed that he was insincere about his wish to resign, which they regarded as a tactical maneuver to shield himself from responsibility if Britain lost America. He himself blamed the king for making him stay through moral pressure. The two had known one another since childhood. North's father was a tutor of George III and a friend of the King's father, Prince Frederick. North was the godson of George III's father after whom he was named Frederick, Lord North. There was even an obelisk presented by Prince Frederick in the grounds of the North family home at Wroxton Abbey in Oxfordshire.[4]

North was also literally in the King's debt. In 1772, the King made North a Knight of the Garter, the first sitting prime minister to receive the honor since Sir Robert Walpole. George III gave North's wife the valuable sinecure of ranger of Bushy Park outside central London, including a salary and a house that North was to use as his favorite retreat from his official residence in Downing Street. The king appointed North's father, the earl of Guilford, as treasurer to the queen, and his brother, Brownlow North, as bishop of Worcester. In September 1777, the king paid off North's debts to the amount of £16,000, writing that he wished no other return "but your being convinced that I love You as well as a Man of Worth as I esteem You as a Minister." In 1778, "as a fresh mark of my regard," the king gave him the lucrative sinecure of the Wardenship of the Cinque Ports. He also promised him the richest office in the gift of the crown—the first tellership of the Exchequer. The King urged North to remain "at the head of the Treasury where many Opportunities will of course arise by which I may benefit your family."[5]

North regarded himself "under such obligations to the King that I can never leave his service while he desires me to remain in it and thinks I can be of use to him." North felt "tied to the stake." In March 1778, his quandary was made even more difficult when the king threatened to abdicate rather than make terms with the opposition and concede independence to America. North feared that his own resignation might precipitate a crisis, and "talked much of the confusion his immediate resignation would occasion." When most of the members of the Cabinet were members of the House of Lords, North had always wrestled with the problem of the absence of a potential successor who could provide the crucial lead necessary in the House of Commons. North was also under pressure from his domineering father, who wanted him to use his influence to obtain benefits for the family and who corresponded with George III while North was prime minister.[6]

I

When he became prime minister in 1770, Frederick, Lord North, was thirty-eight years old. He was an easy object of satire, with an awkward and ungainly appearance. He was described as corpulent with thick lips, bushy eyebrows, a tongue too big for the mouth, a bulbous head, and a disproportionate body. Horace Walpole famously referred to his large eyes that rolled about to no purpose and gave him the air of a blind trumpeter. His eyelids were so heavy that they sometimes gave the impression that he was asleep, which, together with his tendency to nap during debates, contributed to his reputation for lethargy.[7]

North's appearance notwithstanding, even his opponents were fond of him, with his self-deprecating humor and urbane manner. He appeared constantly jovial to the extent that anger and resentment seemed foreign to his nature. He was celebrated for his wit and conversation, laced with literary anecdotes and historical references that revealed a profound knowledge of Europe. Upon completing his education at Eton and Oxford, he had traveled for three years on the continent, where he became fluent in French and conversant in German and Italian. A gifted classicist, he continued to study Greek and Latin until the end of his life. Edward Gibbon dedicated the fourth and final volume of *The Decline and Fall of the Roman Empire* (1787) to Lord North, writing of "the lively vigour of his mind, and the felicity of his incomparable temper." The memoirist Nathaniel Wraxall endearingly described North, saying that it was impossible to experience dullness in his society. He remembered him as the least affected and pompous of any prime minister. North was always happy to throw aside his public character.[8]

North inherited a revolutionary situation in America. Since at least the 1750s, there had been proposals to restructure the colonial government there. With the elected colonial assemblies claiming the same privileges as Parliament, there was a sense that British authority had been eroded and needed to be reasserted. The British state was in the process of expanding, becoming more powerful militarily, and increasing central authority, which gave greater impetus to policies aimed at reforming and strengthening imperial government. In a period of heightened nationalism and imperial pride, there was an awareness of a need for a more rational and integrated empire. There was a belief that trade with the colonies was the foundation of national prosperity and therefore needed to be more closely regulated. Following the end of the Seven Years' War in 1763, the problem of governing America became more urgent with major acquisitions of territory in the upper midwest, Canada, India, and the Caribbean. As a result of the war,

Britain's national debt had doubled to £133 million. The annual interest on the debt alone was £5 million when annual revenues amounted to only £8 million. The government believed that the burden should be shared with the colonies, on the grounds that they had benefited from the war.[9]

In the decade before Lord North became prime minister in 1770, six successive governments had introduced a series of colonial policies that precipitated a revolutionary crisis in America. Often made at the behest of different departments and interest groups, these reforms were piecemeal measures that lacked the coordination necessary to create a coherent system. After the Seven Years' War, the home government had attempted to regulate imperial trade more rigorously, to prohibit the colonies from issuing paper money, and to limit westward expansion in America. The administration of Lord Bute in 1762–63 had made the momentous decision to keep a peacetime army of ten thousand British troops in America. With the object of defraying the cost of imperial government and offsetting the national debt, the various administrations had attempted to levy direct taxes upon America. In 1765, Prime Minister George Grenville had tried to impose a stamp tax in America and the Caribbean, and in 1767, Charles Townshend had imposed duties on specified imports, which included a tax on tea, in America. These policies were vigorously and often successfully resisted in the colonies. They gave rise to radical leaders, organized popular resistance, a heightened political consciousness, intercolonial unions, and a profound distrust of Britain. By generating a constitutional debate about the limits of imperial power, the colonists articulated and defined a coherent set of political ideas to justify their opposition to Britain. There was a breakdown in the relations of colonial governors and the elected assemblies which had already reached a total impasse in South Carolina. On March 5, 1770, the day that North made his first speech as prime minister, British troops in Boston fired on a crowd in what became known as the Boston Massacre. The situation was ripe for rebellion.[10]

Before he became prime minister, North had advocated and supported the policies that led to the crisis, including the right of Parliament to tax America. In 1768, he had assured friends that the presence of troops in the colonies would facilitate the collection of the Townshend Duties (1767). He had been described by one official as "wholly and absolutely" in favor of coercive measures in the colonies. North had spoken against Parliament hearing a petition from the Assembly of New York that questioned the right of Parliament to tax America. In a phrase that later returned to haunt him, he had said he would oppose the repeal of the Townshend Duties "until he saw America prostrate at his feet." He added "America must fear you before they will love you." William Bollan, the colonial agent for Massachusetts, had described North as showing himself in the House of Commons determined not to permit any future concessions to America. During the government of the duke of Grafton, North had cast a deciding vote against the repeal of the tea duty.[11]

Upon becoming prime minister in 1770, North was more conciliatory in his colonial policy. He did not have the unyielding attitude of the former prime minister, George Grenville, or the secretary of state for America, the earl of Hillsborough. He removed all the Townshend Duties except the tax on tea—a significant concession, especially given that he had previously insisted that he would not repeal any of the duties until colonial opposition had subsided. He justified the retreat on the grounds that the duties did not make commercial sense, because they were effectively an export tax on Britain. His government further eased tensions by removing troops from inside Boston and by overriding the Currency Act of 1764 to permit the issue of paper money among colonies south of New England. North continued to appease colonial opinion by relaxing the regulation of western expansion, which had been limited by the Proclamation Line of 1763. When his leniency on the issue of western expansion caused the resignation of the earl of Hillsborough as secretary for America, North replaced Hillsborough with his own stepbrother, the earl of Dartmouth, who was much more sympathetic to the Americans.

North's views and actions were certainly not those of a prime minister intent on tyranny in America. He wanted to defuse the situation in the colonies in part to secure the stability of his government in Britain. He was politically vulnerable, for he did not have his own party following but relied upon the support of a coalition of different factions. Furthermore, he was temperamentally averse to confrontation. He had a habit of postponing difficult decisions, hesitating and changing his mind, to the extent that he was accused by critics of lacking principles or coherent ideas. It is still debated whether he really had a consistent policy on America. He was ambivalent as to whether to be lenient or firm, wavering between compromise and coercion. He did not wish to appear to be weak or to be retreating in response to the threats of colonial radicals. His uncertainty reflected the quandary of political leaders in both government and opposition in Britain who wanted to avoid conflict with the colonies while affirming the supreme authority of Parliament to govern America.[12]

North was willing to make concessions as long as they did not compromise the rights of Parliament, and consequently he retained the tea tax, arguing that it was a luxury tax, a light duty that the colonies could easily afford, and not a tax on a product of the mother country. He reminded the House of Commons that earlier acts of leniency had not inspired obedience or moderation, but had rather "encouraged them to insult our authority, to dispute our rights and to aim at independent government." The time to exert the right of taxation was when that right was denied. He warned that "to temporize is to yield, and the authority of the mother country, if it is now unsupported, will, in reality, be relinquished for ever."[13]

Despite his more conciliatory approach, Lord North was ultimately responsible for the policies that precipitated the American Revolution with the East India Tea Act (1773) which aimed to remedy the financial problems of the East India Company by withdrawing the duties on tea exports from Britain to America. It would thereby make tea cheaper in America and improve sales for the East India Company. However, it would also increase the revenues from the tea tax, the most profitable of the Townshend Duties, and uphold the right of Parliament to tax America. It also granted monopolies for selling tea to favored colonial merchants. North was well aware of the adverse implications of the East India Tea Act for America. The East India Company had tried to persuade North to repeal the tea tax there, and lest it appear that the government was appeasing America, the chairman of the East India Company even offered to petition Parliament. An opposition party speaker warned that if the duty remained, the colonists would not take the tea. Opponents proposed an alternative solution of simply continuing the export duty on tea in Britain and removing the tea tax in America.[14]

The issue of taxation had immense symbolic importance on both sides of the Atlantic. Like most of his fellow members of Parliament, North regarded the right of Britain to tax America as integral to the absolute and indivisible supremacy of Parliament over America. The concept of parliamentary sovereignty was more than an abstract doctrine. It had an emotional resonance as a constitutional victory won against the monarchy in the Glorious Revolution, following the deposition of James II in 1688. It was regarded as essential for the protection of liberty in general. For Britain, the right to tax the colonies was fundamental to its authority to govern America. At the same time, taxation united colonial opposition more than any other grievance. The colonists regarded direct imperial taxes as a potential instrument of tyranny. They insisted upon their right to be taxed exclusively by their own representatives, which they believed was essential to the influence and survival of their elected assemblies. The issue of taxation and representation raised a fundamental contest over sovereignty and the limits of British authority in America.[15]

North was willing to promise no new imperial taxes, but was adamant about retaining the tea duty as a symbolic assertion of British sovereignty over America. He did not anticipate any difficulties because the tea duty was already being paid in the colonies, and the new act made tea cheaper. He calculated that individuals in America paid one-fiftieth of the taxes paid by Englishmen, and later defended himself by saying that it would have been "impossible for him to foretell that the Americans would resist at being able to drink their tea at nine-pence in the pound cheaper." North was so far from suspecting any adverse reaction in the colonies that the Treasury did not even inform the secretary of state for America of the anticipated arrival date of the tea ships in America. The colonial governors were consequently not forewarned. Lord North's East India Tea Act was a major miscalculation that resulted in the Boston Tea Party, in which Boston revolutionaries, dressed as Mohawks, dumped cargoes of East India Company tea into Boston Harbor (1773).[16]

Outraged by the Boston Tea Party, North introduced the Coercive Acts (known in America as the Intolerable Acts), which were passed in stages over the spring of 1774 and which triggered the Revolutionary War in America. He intended these acts to make an example of Massachusetts, because it was the colony "where opposition to the authority of Parliament had always originated," as well as being the home of "the irregular and seditious proceedings of Boston." North acted in the belief that previous concessions had only encouraged greater demands and that anything short of forceful measures would give the impression of a lack of resolution. It was essential to show America "that we are in earnest, and that we will proceed with firmness and vigour. This conviction would be lost, if they found us hesitating and doubting." Like many of his colleagues, North believed that the opposition in the colonies was not a popular movement, but rather a conspiracy of a minority who were intent on independence. The quarrel was not with all the colonies, but those that denied the authority of Parliament. North thought colonial grievances not only empty of substance, but an excuse to plunder ships, avoid the trade and navigation acts, and escape paying debts. He defended his measures as necessary for protecting colonial officials and those who had remained loyal. The issue was "whether we have or have not any authority in that country."[17]

North claimed that he had the support of the nation for the Coercive Acts, which did indeed pass with overwhelming majorities in Parliament. In London, Benjamin Franklin expressed dismay that "we never had since we were a people so few friends in Britain. The violent destruction of the tea seems to have united all parties here against our province." Even the opposition parties in Parliament condemned the Boston Tea Party. The traditional supporters of colonial grievances, like the merchant community in London, critically failed to intervene in support of America.[18]

Following the Boston Tea Party, there was a national mood of retribution in Britain. The *Middlesex Journal* called for the hanging of "about one hundred of these puritanical rebels in Boston." Charles Van told the House of Commons that "the town of Boston ought to be knocked about their ears and destroyed. Delenda est Carthago. . . . I am of opinion you will never meet with that proper obedience to the laws of this country, until you have destroyed that nest of locusts." He later argued that if the inhabitants of Massachusetts Bay opposed some of the measures before Parliament, "I would do as was done of old in the time of the ancient Britons, I would burn and set fire to all their woods, and leave their country open, to prevent the protection they now have: and if we are likely to lose that country, I think it is better lost by our own soldiers than wrested from us by our rebellious children." In an early draft of his pamphlet *Taxation no Tyranny*, Samuel Johnson declared that if he were in power "the first thing he would do, would be to quarter the army on the citys, and if any refused free quarters, he would pull down that person's house, if it was joyned to other houses, but would burn it if it stood alone." Johnson complained when his incendiary passage was expunged by the government, which had commissioned him to write the pamphlet.[19]

Following the passing of the Coercive Acts, Lord North was despised in America. His effigy was burned in Virginia. In Massachusetts, his name was invoked as an expletive at the inconvenience of moving goods by road owing to the closure of the port of Boston, which was called Lord North's Act: a hard jolt caused by a stone was accompanied by "Damn Lord North!" The wagons became known as Lord North's Coasters. If the wheels of a carriage ran into a rut, it was blamed on Lord North's Road. Even the clergy had "something to say in their Prayers about *Lord North*," with one declaiming from the pulpit, "*O! Thou Lord of the East & of the West, & of ye South! Defend us against Lord North!*"[20]

II

North suddenly began to have misgivings about the use of coercive authority when he realized that the sanctions were failing to isolate Massachusetts from the rest of America. He began to appreciate the full scale of colonial opposition when news arrived of the outcome of the secret deliberations of the Continental Congress, which had unanimously passed the Suffolk Resolves (September 17, 1774), urging civil disobedience and defensive preparations against the Coercive Acts. On December 15, 1774, the *London Evening Post* printed the articles of the Continental Association, by which the Continental Congress had voted to impose an economic boycott against Britain. North and his Cabinet had not anticipated the extent and intensity of colonial resistance. They had been misled by intelligence reports about divisions within the Continental Congress, and had assumed that the mere threat of force would be sufficient to quell resistance and that the other colonies would dissociate themselves from Massachusetts. It was a belief encouraged by secret government interception of correspondence from America that gave the impression that only a minority supported the actions of Massachusetts. The government's view was reinforced by those most familiar with conditions in America, like William Bull, the American-born former governor of South Carolina, and Josiah Martin, the Antiguan-born governor of North Carolina.[21]

As George III and the rest of the Cabinet became more resolute in their commitment to coercion, North sought to find a peace formula, together with the earl of Dartmouth. Lord Beauchamp told Horace Walpole that "he saw the disposition [of the government] was to give way." Thomas Hutchinson, the American-born former governor of Massachusetts, "plainly perceive[d] that it would have been agreeable" to the prime minister "to have found something in the Petition [from the Continental Congress] that would lead to an accommodation." Horace Walpole believed that North had hurried to introduce the budget before Christmas "to prevent reinforcements being sent to America." North was accused by a fellow member of the government of frequently changing his language, declaring at times that he did not mean to tax America, and seeming besides "to speak but slightly of the right of taxation, and giving some intimation even of consenting to the repeal of the tea duty." Edward Gibbon was "more and more convinced that with firmness all may go well; yet I sometimes doubt Lord N."[22]

North favored a royal commission with the authority to negotiate a settlement with the Americans, but he was discouraged by George III, and instead pursued secret negotiations with Benjamin Franklin through third parties. His intermediaries were Dr. John Fothergill, the physician to Lord Dartmouth, and David Barclay, a Quaker banker who was a friend of Lord Hyde, the chancellor of the Duchy of Lancaster. North received daily reports of their conversations. Barclay told Franklin that North's government wanted to avoid a civil war, and that it desired to get out of its present embarrassment on any terms, while preserving its honor and dignity. At a meeting in early December 1774, Forthergill assured Franklin that although some members of the Cabinet were violent, others, "he had *good reason* to believe . . . were differently dispos'd." Barclay and Forthergill sought to know what terms might be acceptable to the colonies for a reunion, to which Franklin replied by drafting a paper entitled "Hints for Conversation upon the Subject of Terms that may probably produce a Durable union between Great Britain and her Colonies."[23]

Admiral Howe simultaneously made peace overtures through his sister, Caroline Howe, who invited Franklin to their home for a game of chess. According to Franklin, she was "fancying she could beat me." She broached the subject of peace negotiations by saying, "And What is to be done with this dispute between Britain and the Colonies? I hope we are not to have a Civil War?" On Christmas Day, 1775, they met for another game of chess when she introduced Franklin to her brother. Like Barclay and Fothergill, Howe "gave it . . . as his sincere Opinion that some of the Ministry were extreamly well dispos'd to any reasonable Accommodation, preserving only the Dignity of Government," and he invited Franklin to "draw up in writing some Propositions containing the Terms on which . . . a good Understanding might be obtained." At another meeting, Howe told Franklin that he "could now assure him of a Certainty that there was a sincere Disposition in Lord North and Lord Dartmouth to accommodate the Differences with America, and to listen favourably to any Proposition that might have a probable tendency to answer that salutary Purpose." He asked Franklin what he thought of the idea of sending commissioners to America to make inquiries and negotiate. Thomas Pownall, a former governor of Massachusetts, similarly told Franklin that North did not approve of the coercive policies and that "he was well dispos'd to promote a Reconciliation upon any Terms honourable to the Government."[24]

On February 20, 1775, to the dismay of the king and the bewilderment of his own political supporters, North introduced his Conciliatory Proposal into the House of Commons. He was seeking a way out from the escalation of the conflict that did not appear to be a total capitulation. He offered to allow the colonies to tax themselves if they made an adequate contribution toward the cost of their administration. Although he admitted that Parliament could not give up the right to tax America, North would not "hesitate a moment to suspend the exercise of that right," if the colonies agreed to raise their share of the revenue. He acknowledged that some members might accuse him of negotiating with rebels, but he retorted that "it has never been said that all Americans are rebels" and that he would be happy if he could "open the door even to rebels to return to their duty." In a journal of his negotiations in London, Benjamin Franklin wrote that the Conciliatory Proposal included his advice to give up the tea and sugar duties and that North originally planned to incorporate the more radical plan of David Barclay who had conferred with Franklin.[25]

It was subsequently claimed that the Conciliatory Proposal was not a sincere gesture, but a maneuver rather than a concession, designed to divide opinion in America and to consolidate support in Britain. Opponents contended that the proposal did not allow direct negotiations with the Continental Congress. They also objected that North continued preparations for war and further retaliatory measures. Thomas Jefferson argued that the Conciliatory Proposal did not address the main issue, which was not merely the mode of raising taxes, but the freedom of allocating and controlling tax revenue. Franklin likened North's offer to "a Highway-man who presents his pistol and hat at a Coach-Window, demanding no specific Sum, but if you will give all your Money or what he pleas'd to think sufficient, he will civilly omit putting his own Hand in your Pockets. If not, there is his Pistol." The Conciliatory Proposal also did not resolve numerous other colonial grievances, like the presence of the British army in America and the enforcement of the Coercive Acts. Furthermore, the news of the terms did not arrive until after the first skirmish of the Revolutionary War at Lexington and Concord (April 19, 1775).[26]

North's gesture was not, however, a cynical maneuver. He had in fact introduced the measure in defiance of the views of the king, his Cabinet colleagues, and his parliamentary supporters. It threatened a revolt within the government among the followers of the Duke of Bedford, aggressive advocates of a coercive policy in America whose support was essential for maintaining North's majority in the House of Commons. The Conciliatory Proposal was a remarkable act of political courage, especially for a man who detested confrontation and who was regarded by opponents as a pliant tool of George III. North was so uncertain of a majority in the House of Commons that he solicited the support of the opposition parties, to whom he gave advance notice of his motion, which was extraordinary, "it not being usual to notify any but the friends of Government on such occasions."[27] His hesitancy was evident from his long speech justifying the Conciliatory Proposal, which was regarded as one of his worst and most clumsy orations, owing to "the perplexity of some of its construction" and "the obscurity in the words," which left some members unsure of what he was intending. Walpole recollected that the Conciliatory Proposal was "received with astonishment and indignation," for the government "had worked up both the Parliament and the people to such a frenzy for the supremacy over

America, that a proposal of terms to them seemed a debasement of this country's dignity."
The *Annual Register* described how the government supporters looked at each other with
amazement and seemed at a loss to understand North.[28]

The government benches were in disarray, with North's own supporters the first
to speak against his Conciliatory Proposal and he was forced to intervene in the debate six
times. Benjamin Franklin described the caballing and whispering in a full and expectant
House of Commons, and the alarm of the Bedfords who "began to exclaim against the
Minister for his Timidity, and the Fluctuation of his *Politicks;* they even began to count
Voices, to see if they could not by negativing his Motion, at once unhorse him, and throw
him out of Administration." According to Edward Gibbon, the government members
went into "the House in Confusion every moment expecting that the Bedfords would fly
into Rebellion." Far from seeming a cynical maneuver to divide the Americans, the
Conciliatory Proposal appeared to government supporters to "give up every ground they
had gone upon in the whole course of American measures," contradicting "all acts and
declarations of parliament," while seemingly acknowledging that there was "something
really grievous in the idea of taxing America by parliament." The treasurer of the navy, Sir
Gilbert Elliot, helped spare North the humiliation of defeat at the hands of his own
supporters by arguing that the proposal did not represent a retreat and that no relaxation
of severity was intended. North assuaged supporters by assuring them that the proposal
was consistent with the policy of coercion. The tactic worked, but at the cost of the
credibility of his conciliatory gesture.[29]

North had tried to please both sides by the threat of force and the incentive of
limited concessions in an effort to prevent a war. He was in a dilemma since he could not
make further concessions without alienating the king and government supporters in the
House of Commons. It was essential for any eighteenth-century prime minister to be able
to balance the support of both, since neither could be taken for granted. He had to be able
to retain the support of the independent country gentlemen who were unaffiliated with
any faction and who were generally reliable supporters of the government, but who were
capable of voting independently and forcing his resignation. As Charles Jenkinson told
Thomas Hutchinson, there were about "150 members, a sort of Flying Squadron, that
you don't know where they will be in a new question." North was always aware of his
political vulnerability.[30]

North had courted danger when he introduced his Conciliatory Proposal, yet he
persisted with another perilous attempt at negotiation with Continental Congress, even
though its existence was not formally acknowledged by the government and its very name
was so taboo in government circles that it was referred to obliquely as "a meeting held at
Philadelphia." North met with Gilbert Barklay, an English resident of Philadelphia, and
gave him a letter, which Barklay arranged to have submitted to the Continental Congress.
The letter urged "all the colonies" to accept the Conciliatory Proposal, which "will

remove every grievance relative to taxation, and be the basis of a compact between the colonies and the Mother Country." It warned that "the temper and spirit of the nation" was opposed to any more concessions, that there was not the least possibility of a change of government, and that the British people were united in their willingness to take any effectual action against the rebellious colonies. North made himself readily available to Americans in London like Ralph Izard, Hugh Williamson, John Ewing, and Henry Cruger, who were acting as intermediaries with the Continental Congress. North was more loath to go to war than his Cabinet colleagues, and he became increasingly doubtful of the prospect of victory in the summer of 1775. After hearing news of the heavy British casualties at the battle of Bunker Hill (June 17, 1775), North confided to William Eden that he did not think a military conquest of the colonies possible.[31]

North had much in common with opposition leaders, who similarly believed in the principle of the supremacy of Parliament, but who questioned the expediency of war with America. Like Lord North, they were accused of posturing. During the 1760s, they had variously held power when they had initiated and supported the very policies that had led to the crisis. In 1774, many opposition members had voted for the Coercive Acts. They later defended themselves, claiming that the government had given them "defective and partial information." As General John Burgoyne was to observe, whichever party fathered the rebellion, "all parties in England nursed it into manhood." Among the major parties in Parliament, there was very little diversity of opinion on the question of America. The opposition parties put forward their own plans for conciliation, but they had little more chance of success than the government, since they also believed in the absolute supremacy of Parliament over America. Apart from radicals and religious nonconformists outside of Parliament, the earl of Chatham and his small party were alone in opposing the right of Parliament to tax America. However, Chatham's plan of conciliation required the colonies to provide permanent revenue for their administration and to permit the billeting of troops. The opposition parties were divided and therefore did not coordinate their efforts against the government.[32]

In 1775, Britain became increasingly divided over the subject of America. John Wesley, celebrated as the founder of Methodism, wrote a pamphlet in support of the government, which admitted that all his prejudices were against the claims of the colonies, but, "waiving all considerations of right and wrong," Wesley asked himself whether it was "common sense to use force toward the Americans." James Boswell exclaimed that the ministry was mad "in undertaking a desperate war." As Johnson told Mrs. Thrale in August 1775, America was so much the popular subject of discussion that it "now fills every mouth, and some heads." It was a very different situation from eighteen months earlier when, according to Edmund Burke, "any Remarkable Highway Robbery at Hounslow Heath would make more conversation than all the disturbances of America." The debate raged in the newspapers. There was much sympathy for the Americans in the *Political*

Register, the *London Chronicle,* and the *London Evening Post,* together with some of the provincial papers, like the *Leeds Mercury,* the *Bath Journal,* and the *Birmingham and Stafford Chronicle.* When Major General Richard Montgomery was killed fighting the British in Quebec, he was treated as a hero in the opposition paper the *Scot's Magazine* which likened him to General James Wolfe. The *Evening Post* reported the story of Montgomery's death with a black border and *The Morning Post* speculated that Montgomery would not have wanted anyone to shed tears except "for my country's sake!"[33]

In 1775, in the largest public petitioning campaign of the era, rival petitions supported and opposed the war, representing twelve English counties and forty-seven boroughs, with some 45,000 signatures. More people signed the opposition petitions than the progovernment petitions. Throughout 1775, a substantial proportion of letters to the press condemned the government for folly, ignorance, deception, and wickedness. Subscription societies were formed to support or oppose the war, including the Constitutional Society, which placed an advertisement from the radical John Horne Tooke to raise funds for the widows, orphans, and elderly parents of those Americans who had been "inhumanly murdered by the King's troops" at Lexington and Concord. The chief center of opposition to the war was London, which made up a tenth of the population of England and Wales. Religious dissenters in Britain, like Dr. Richard Price and Joseph Priestley, were particularly sympathetic to the revolutionaries. The cause of the colonial rebellion was also popular among English radicals like Major John Cartwright and John Sawbridge. The division of popular opinion had an economic and social dimension, with artisans and tradesmen more likely to oppose the war than the landed gentry and professional classes.[34]

North was concerned by the rise of domestic opposition to the war. He remained at odds with other Cabinet members over the issue of a negotiated settlement with America. It was a subject of public comment that North was thwarted and overruled and that he "did not approve of the violent measures" of his colleagues. Following the resignation from the Cabinet of members who opposed the war, North became more isolated within the government. The duke of Grafton resigned as lord privy seal in opposition to the war. After playing a leading role in encouraging North to find a peace formula, the earl of Dartmouth resigned as secretary of state for America to be replaced by the much more belligerent Lord George Germain. Following the defections of General Henry Seymour Conway and Lord Thomas Lyttelton, North also lost two of his ablest government speakers in the House of Commons. North was determined to keep Dartmouth in the cabinet, to the extent of precipitating a crisis by threatening to resign if Dartmouth was not appointed lord privy seal.[35]

North still believed that some of the rebel colonies might be persuaded to reconsider, because they were still fighting what they called a war for the redress of grievances and continued to deny that they sought independence. North wished to offer pardons to colonists who swore allegiance to Britain, as well as to create a peace commission with wide discretionary powers, but he delayed submitting a proposal, owing to the opposition of the earl of Suffolk and the earl of Sandwich. Despite the impatience of George III, North was reluctant to issue a proclamation declaring sedition and rebellion in America. It was only produced under duress from the king, and was written by Suffolk and William Eden, not by North. In a clause of a bill prohibiting trade with America in November 1775, North finally succeeded in obtaining a peace commission with authority to pardon those "disposed to return to their duty." The policy brought him into conflict with Lord George Germain, who was against the peace commissioners receiving the discretionary authority to grant pardons as North desired. Germain believed it was necessary to win the war to negotiate from a position of strength and wanted to make an acknowledgment of parliamentary authority a prerequisite for any pardon.[36]

The internal government disagreement over the terms of the peace commission caused a critical five-month delay in the appointment of the commissioners. North, Dartmouth, and Germain each threatened to resign, but were dissuaded by George III. When the crisis was resolved in May 1776, Germain was the victor to the extent that the commissioners were given little discretionary power to make concessions. However, his success was partly undermined by the appointment of the Howe brothers, who had earlier opposed the policies that had helped to precipitate the war, to be both peace commissioners and military commanders in America. In consequence, government strategy was unclear and inconsistent. Walpole described how the "contradictory language of Lord North and Lord George Germain, left Parliament wholly in doubt whether they meant peace or war, and, if peace, whether they would grant America a moderate peace, or whether they would expect implicit submission." Lord John Cavendish complained that the Cabinet did not have a policy: "it was one day peace, another day war." The opposition held that "the mixt system of war and conciliation" was "highly improper," arguing that government policy "whether of peace or war, should be clear, simple, and decided," rather than mired in "doubt, perplexity and darkness."[37]

North was much more skeptical than both the king and the majority of his Cabinet colleagues about the prospects of a military victory. In September 1776, the king privately confided that he differed greatly from North as to the likelihood of bad news from the campaign in New York. In August 1777, North wrote to William Eden, a confidant and an under secretary of state, that "it has for many months been clear to me that if we cannot reduce the Colonies by force now employed under Howe and Clinton and Burgoyne, we cannot send and support a force capable to reduce them." While North was drafting the king's speech for Parliament in November 1777, his resigned mood was all too apparent when he asked Eden, "How shall we mention America? Shall we be very stout? Or shall we take advantage of the flourishing state of our affairs to get out of this d—d war, and hold a moderate language?" He added that even the most spectacular success would serve only to help get out of the dispute as soon as possible. North was accused in letters to the press of mistaken moderation and a cringing approach.[38]

III

After the British defeat at Saratoga in 1777, North was willing to make almost any concession short of independence. He was becoming even more despondent and doubtful of success owing to the military setbacks. He thought it inevitable that France would make a treaty with the Continental Congress, and that consequently America would forever be "torn from us and the West Indies must follow. With these apprehensions I own myself to be for peace on any terms." He did not believe that Britain could wage war on all fronts and feared the ebbing of support for the government in the House of Commons. North renewed his attempts for a negotiated peace with the unintended consequence of hastening the war with France; the French foreign minister, Charles Cravier, comte de Vergennes, was fearful of a settlement between Britain and the United States, which they were encouraged to think possible by Benjamin Franklin.[39]

Influenced by William Eden, who had family interests in America, North attempted secret negotiations with the Continental Congress through the agencies of Paul Wentworth, William Pulteney, and David Hartley. Only two days after the news of Saratoga arrived in London in December 1777, Wentworth was sent to Paris to negotiate with the American commissioners, Benjamin Franklin, Silas Deane, and Arthur Lee. Born in New Hampshire, he was a former agent of the colony in London and a successful businessman, who had worked in Paris. He was instructed to find out what terms of settlement were acceptable, and was authorized to inform the American commissioners that Britain had moderated its language, sentiments and expectations. In March 1778, William Pulteney arrived in Paris in a similar attempt to open negotiations. An independent member of Parliament, he had published a pamphlet sympathetic to American objections to taxation without representation, entitled *The Present State of Affairs with America.* In April, David Hartley,. a friend of North and Franklin, and one of the most vociferous opponents of the war for America in the House of Commons, met with Franklin. Hartley had instigated the mission, but North encouraged him with the assurance that he could not serve the country more essentially than by cultivating every opportunity to further peace. As late as April 1779, Hartley told Franklin that North might agree to a tacit acknowledgment of independence during a ten-year truce, followed by a final settlement.[40]

While conducting secret diplomacy in France, in 1778 North arranged to send negotiators to America who became known as the Carlisle Peace Commission. North significantly did not consult his Cabinet colleagues, but rather developed his plan in association with a small circle of his junior ministers and officials, William Eden, Charles

Jenkinson, and John Robinson. Having originally proposed the initiative to North, Eden later recollected that this latest peace initiative was very much disliked by the paymaster general, Richard Rigby. He also described how Attorney General Lord Thurlow read over the terms of the peace commission "with one of his sourest countenances, and then said 'Mr. Eden, tell Lord North from me that I think this the most wretched and disgraceful of all measures, and that it will lose America and ruin England.'" Eden replied to Thurlow by asking whether he really wanted him to report back "such a harsh judgement in such unqualified terms" to which Thurlow was emphatic that he wanted his exact words repeated to North. Nevertheless, in his anxiety to make the terms of his offer known in America, North sent out a draft version of the bill establishing the commission before it had even been approved by Parliament.[41]

North "expected to be roasted" when he presented his objectives to the House of Commons. His plan offered to yield entirely on the question of taxation and once again to appoint a peace commission with the authority to negotiate directly with the Continental Congress "as if it were a legal body." He wanted the commissioners to be given broad discretionary powers to negotiate. He was willing to offer legal recognition of elected officials and to consider admitting American representatives into the House of Commons. The commissioners were empowered to promise the future preservation of colonial charters against imperial interference, the withdrawal of the army in peacetime, the appointment of judges with life tenure, election to public offices, the exclusive appointment of Americans to customs offices, and the continuation of the Continental Congress. North secretly instructed the commission not to make American independence a stumbling block to negotiations, but instead to arrange an armistice and request further instructions from London. Before the drafts of the bills to authorize the commission were completed, North sent a copy of the terms to General Sir William Howe to be forwarded to Congress.[42]

In his speech announcing his new peace initiative, North gave what the *Annual Register* described as "a recital of his creed in all American matters," in that he asserted peace had at all times been his governing principle. The Coercive Acts had appeared necessary at the time, but "in the event had produced effects which he never intended, nor could possibly have been expected." North recalled how he had made his Conciliatory Proposal "before the sword was drawn," but it had been represented as a scheme "for sowing divisions," and was consequently rejected by the Continental Congress. He acknowledged that the war had turned out differently from what he had expected and that he was disappointed with the results. In the House of Commons, his proposal to yield almost everything but token authority over America was heard with profound attention, followed by "a dull melancholy silence," which transformed into "astonishment, dejection, and fear." His claim that the sentiments in his speech were "those which he had always entertained" was contrary to the understanding of the members who had thought him to be the person "the most tenacious of those parliamentary rights which he now proposed to resign." There was even suspicion that the government was hiding something "alarming and extraordinary," which alone could explain "such an apparent change in measures, principles and arguments." Hutchinson suspected that the majority of government supporters disliked the measure but felt obliged to vote for it.[43]

North's own friends and supporters "strongly condemned" his proceeding with the peace commission. The opposition parties broadly supported North's plans, but they were merciless in taunting North for his conversion to their views, wondering "whether the lance of Achilles could cure the wound which it had inflicted." Charles James Fox "congratulated his own party on the acquisition of so potent an auxiliary" as Lord North. He was glad to find the terms to be offered by the peace commission similar to those rejected by North when proposed by Edmund Burke in 1775, and "observed that the Noble Lord was so perfect a proselyte, that the very same arguments which had at the time been so ineffectually used by the minority, was now adopted by his Lordship." Walpole described the scene in the House of Commons when Fox rose "and after pluming himself on having sat there till he had brought the noble Lord to concur in sentiments with him and his friends," asked the prime minister whether it was true that a commercial treaty had been signed in the last ten days between France and America. Lord North was "thunderstruck and would not rise." It was the first official news of the French alliance with the United States.[44]

Led by the thirty-year-old earl of Carlisle, North's peace commission was stillborn. It was overshadowed by the outbreak of war with France; it did not have the support of the majority of the cabinet, especially Lord George Germain; the commissioners were inexperienced and lacked stature, and they were divided among themselves and became a subject of scandal in America. Their discretionary authority to offer pardons was considerably reduced in the final version of their instructions. They were not forewarned by the government of secret orders permitting General Howe to withdraw from Philadelphia to free troops to conquer St. Lucia in the Caribbean, weakening their negotiating position. The earl of Carlisle was incredulous that such a critical mission should be sacrificed for "an insignificant West India island in the most unfit season of the year." The commission's hand was further undermined by the arrival of a superior French fleet under Admiral d'Estaing, and by the popular belief that America would soon be able to "extort the Concession of Independence from Great Britain." The commissioners spent almost six fruitless months in America, where their terms were rejected by the Continental Congress.[45]

North had behaved strangely throughout the affair. He allowed the instructions to the commissioners to be changed by Germain and the earl of Suffolk, who insisted that the revolutionaries renounce their "pretensions to independence" and that they seek the forgiveness of the king before the start of any negotiation. North had earlier said that any such condition would ensure failure. He had previously threatened resignation when Germain had wanted to impose similar conditions on the Howe brothers in 1776, but he made no resistance on this occasion. He seemingly lost interest in the selection of the peace commissioners, leaving William Eden feeling betrayed because he was a personal friend of North and a member of the Carlisle Peace Commission. Before his departure for America, Eden had been perplexed at his casual treatment by Cabinet ministers, whom he described as behaving toward him "very much in the stile of a common acquaintance who is stepping from your Room to the water Closet, and means to return in five minutes."[46]

North seemingly gave up on the commission before it left for America. After making secret contact with Franklin in Paris, he discovered that the commission's terms were unlikely to be accepted. He had no support from the king or from his Cabinet colleagues. He found it difficult to recruit experienced and qualified individuals to serve on the commission: the earl of Carlisle had not even featured in the original list of potential candidates. At the very moment that the Cabinet was preparing for a much wider war with France, North was in a state of personal turmoil. He wrote impassioned letters to the king requesting to resign in favor of the earl of Chatham, who was the only opposition leader unequivocally opposed to granting independence to the United States. North's personal crisis became all the more acute with the sudden death of Chatham, who had dramatically collapsed in the midst of a speech in the House of Lords.[47]

Although the Carlisle Peace Commission was a failure, the initiative showed that North was willing to concede the very issues for which Britain had first contended in America. In the words of Walpole, "the Administration ventured on taking the very opposite part to all they had been doing," and North had presumed to tell the British "that they must abandon all the high views with which they had been lulled, and must stoop to beg peace of America *at any rate.*" Edward Gibbon humorously compared the reversal of North's American policy to the injunction in the Anglican liturgy that "all the People shall say, after the Minister, turn us again O lord and so shall we [be] turned." A writer in the *Morning Post* accused North of offering "terms of humiliating reconciliation" to a "race of unnatural and ungrateful bastards" and "confessing by your own tacit acknowledgement, that they are invincible." North had been willing to concede independence in all but name. Thereafter, the war was more a matter of saving face to maintain nominal control of America. In the withering words of Isaac Barré, the government was ruining the nation "merely upon a punctilio of honour."[48]

The abolitionist Granville Sharp later recalled that North had been prepared to accept American independence in January 1778 "but was unhappily deterred from openly declaring it, by the violent opposition that was made." In June 1778, North had written to Eden that nothing but independence was the "avowed purpose of the Americans: they think they can bring it about and nothing less will satisfy them." He regretted that it was not politically expedient to propose to grant them independence while "we cannot, I am afraid, be sure of preventing it by any exertion of force." North's youngest daughter was to relate how she believed that her father never "entertained any doubt as to the justice of the American war, yet I am sure that he wished to have peace made three years before its termination," but that he had allowed himself to be persuaded to remain in office by George III.[49]

I V

North's reservations about the use of force were hardly conducive to making him an effective war leader. He was no earl of Chatham who had led Britain during the Seven Years' War. Although devoted to North, Nathaniel Wraxall thought him especially deficient in one important aspect: "he knew not how to inspire terror, like the first Mr. Pitt." North was too amiable and too averse to confrontation. The lord advocate of Scotland, Henry Dundas, similarly said of North that "He wants only one quality to render him a great and distinguished statesman—I mean a more despotic and commandeering temper." According to the duke of Newcastle, Chatham "with all his faults" was unequaled in his ability to "plan, or push the execution of any plan agreed upon." Although a supporter of the government, Samuel Johnson hoped that Chatham might replace North because he "was a Dictator: he possessed the power of putting the State into motion; now there is no power; all order is relaxed."[50]

North was the first to admit his shortcomings, but he specifically rejected the title of prime minister. He prohibited his family from using the term, "saying there was no such thing in the British Constitution." In 1778, he told the House of Commons that he "did not think the constitution authorized such a character. He stood responsible as one of his Majesty's Cabinet Council, but not as that animal called a Prime Minister." The following year, he reminded the members that "he never had pretended to be the Prime Minister, and had only acted as one member of the cabinet. . . . He meant to evade nothing but the presumption of his being Prime Minister, a presumption which he never assumed and which therefore he ought not to be charged with." When Charles James Fox nevertheless called him the first minister, North assured him that he was mistaken and said that he knew of no such minister. He wished merely to be considered as the head of a very important department, who worked in concert with Cabinet colleagues.[51]

It was indeed the case that the leading minister in the Cabinet was not consistently called the prime minister, and that the office was still in the process of evolution at the time of the American Revolution. Although the office had earlier antecedents with the first ministers of the later Stuarts, the title is traditionally associated with Sir Robert Walpole, who is credited with being the first prime minister of Britain. Usually associated with the first lord of the Treasury, the role remained undefined. North's contemporaries compared him adversely to Sir Robert Walpole. Samuel Johnson complained of North to James Boswell that "There is no Prime Minister. There is only an agent for the government in the House of Commons." The country was governed by the Cabinet, "but there is no head there, as in Sir Robert Walpole's time." Charles Jenkinson told Thomas Hutchinson that North did not have "the influence of Sr R. Walpole." North's contemporaries evidently forgot that Walpole had fallen from office primarily because of early British reversals in the War of the Spanish Succession (1740–48).[52]

North himself believed that he needed to be replaced by someone who acted as "the director and dictator of the leading measures of government." He was the first to admit that "there should be one capable of forming wise plans, and of combining and connecting the whole force and operations of government. I am certainly not such a man." He repeatedly warned that national affairs could not be properly conducted "until there is a person in the cabinet capable of leading, of discerning between opinions, of deciding quickly and confidently, and of connecting all the operations of government, that this nation may act uniformly and with force." North added that he was "not such a man, and yet holds the situation in which such abilities and qualities are at present expected." He warned George III that "it is not possible to expect much exertion from a man under the dominion of such sentiments."[53]

It was because North felt inadequate to his task and because he doubted the wisdom of persisting with the war that he pleaded for permission from George III to resign. His youngest daughter later recollected that he often looked wistfully from the windows of the prime minister's residence in Downing Street at his former home, lamenting that he had never been happy since he moved. Even before the war for America, North was uncomfortable in his position and wrote to his father that "it must always be my wish to be released from a station which is too great for my abilities before I have entirely forfeited the little reputation I may have gained, and done more mischief to the Public by my want of knowledge, activity and talents." After France declared war on Britain, his requests to leave office became more frequent and more public.[54]

North was reputedly saying in private that he did not know "what in the world to do, if I wish ever so much to resign and give up business I can't, I am not my own master, I am tied to a stake and can't stir." John Robinson described him as "the most altered man I ever saw in my life, he has not spirits to set to anything." In November 1779, North confided to his stepbrother: "I am in a fever with my situation. I have been kept in it by force." He regarded himself as holding up a falling house whose collapse he could not prevent. As Lord Cornwallis marched into Virginia in 1781, North wrote to his father that he did not feel that he had either conducted himself to his own credit or to the benefit of the public: "I have not done well in my situation, I can truly say it is a situation which I never sought, and I have been severely punished for all the harm I may have done by the increasing anxiety and uneasiness I have undergone."[55]

North's indecision and his inability to assert himself among Cabinet colleagues were major liabilities in a wartime leader. Following the declaration of war by France, North admitted to the king that he "never could, nor can decide between different opinions." One of his junior ministers attributed "the delays which attend business of all sorts, to Lord North's consulting so many persons, who are of very different opinions: and from the difference he remains undecided himself for some time, and after he appeared decided, is apt to change." His closest advisers despaired of his ability to provide direction and momentum. In the summer of 1780, John Robinson lamented that "nothing is done, no line fixed . . . no Cabinet fixed, no previous Meeting. . . . It is impossible in this State we can ever drag on without endangering everything." A letter to *The Caledonian Mercury* from "A LOVER OF SPIRIT AND CONSISTENCY IN A PRIME MINISTER," attributed national problems to "the want of some bold and enterprising spirit, to animate and direct our public counsels, and to give consistency, vigour and finally success to our national measures. In a word it is entirely owing to the want of a Prime Minister."[56]

North's Cabinet colleagues were openly disdainful of his leadership. Lord Hillsborough thought North "a good man, but apt suddenly to resolve on a thing, which upon second thoughts he repented of." The first lord of the Admiralty, the earl of Sandwich, told the king that he intended to write to North to urge upon him the necessity of taking a firm lead in the Cabinet and of acting decisively "with the spirit that becomes the principal person" in the government. Richard Rigby, the paymaster general, attributed all the problems of the government to the indecision and weak management of North. Lord Thurlow, the lord chancellor, complained that matters destined for the Cabinet were not sufficiently prepared to enable them to judge properly. In an outburst to John Robinson, he said "DAMN HIM, nothing can goad him forward, he is the very clog that loads everything." North distrusted his colleagues and complained that they did not reciprocate his loyalty to them. He was hurt that Sandwich "has conceived such a mean opinion of my intelligence, and all my suggestions," but added pathetically in parentheses, "perhaps deservedly."[57]

The consequence of North's leadership was a divided Cabinet that postponed difficult decisions and often left military goals nebulous. In what he called government by departments, North was surrounded by strong personalities in the Cabinet who feuded with one another and pursued conflicting initiatives. John Robinson, his trusted secretary to the Treasury, decried the situation, arguing that "war can't be carried on in departments, there must be consultation, union, and a friendly and hearty concurrence in all the several parts which set the springs at work." Robinson described a Cabinet that was totally disjointed, that lacked mutual respect and affection. The rivalries between ministers were mirrored in the disputes between their subordinates, especially between the army and the navy. All this helped create a tone of rancor and recrimination.[58]

Admitting that he was "quite unacquainted with Military punctilios," North deferred to colleagues with regard to strategy, but his inability to be decisive or assertive adversely affected the conduct of the war. In the crucial months of preparation before the outbreak of the war, the American loyalist Thomas Hutchinson found it "strange to see every office in a state of inaction." Hutchinson was told by Lord Hillsborough that "all the languor about America was owing to Lord North's aversion to business." He commented in his diary that "it is certain that business is in a strange languid state, and the Prime Conductor seems to leave more to other persons than has been usual."[59]

North's inability to provide decisive leadership became a particular liability as war broke out with France. From 1778, his Cabinet was divided over strategy, between those who wanted to continue the land war in America and those who wanted to make a strategic withdrawal from there to concentrate resources on a naval war with France. The two ministers most responsible for the conduct of the war were opposed. Lord George Germain was committed to the war in America, and the earl of Sandwich was more concerned with the naval defense of Britain. They were both strong personalities who often acted independently. Germain wanted to send an immediate naval reinforcement to America to prevent the French from gaining the advantage, but Sandwich advocated a more reactive policy of shadowing the French navy to prevent the possibility of its gaining superiority in European waters. The differences between the ministers resulted in the delays, compounded by bad weather and the slowness of military operations, that gave the initiative to Admiral d'Estaing who captured Dominica. The government was lucky that the damage was not greater. The Cabinet never resolved the military priorities, with the consequence that resources were overstretched and naval protection of the army was often inadequate. The government relied instead on improvisation and luck. North had anticipated as much and had written privately at the time to the king suggesting withdrawal from America.[60]

The deficiencies in North's leadership were not due solely to his personal shortcomings. He was subject to excessive demands, combining the responsibilities of several departments: he was not only prime minister, but also leader of the House of Commons, first lord of the Treasury, and chancellor of the Exchequer. He also played a larger role in foreign policy than is generally appreciated. As he explained to the king, "To perform the duties of the Treasury, to attend the House of Commons at the rate of three long days a week, to see the numbers of people who have daily business with the first Lord of the Treasury, and to give all thought to the principal measures of government in this very alarming crisis is enough to employ the greatest man of business, and the most consummate statesman that ever existed." In a period when government was still very personal, he had to field requests that extended from a barrage of patronage seekers to a personal letter from Baroness von Riedesel, the wife of the German commander in Canada, asking permission for her carriage to be admitted duty-free into England.[61]

At the Treasury, North had a staff of twenty-three clerks who oversaw the purchases and provisioning of the army. They negotiated the contracts with merchants and suppliers, and oversaw the purchase of every necessity, including butter, oats, flour, tents, hay, blankets, coal, candles, barrack furniture, and clothing. Until 1779, his department was also responsible for the shipping of the provisions and for military transports to convey the troops to America. In 1778, the Treasury had a fleet of 115 ships with a total tonnage of 30,052 tons. Between 1775 and 1782, North missed only 23 of the 670 meetings of the Treasury board, over half his few absences being due to ill health. In 1781, his department was responsible for contracting for supplies for and provisioning 86,000 troops. It increasingly made bids for supplies more competitive and required greater accountability from contractors. After 1779, army complaints about the quality of provisions significantly declined. With the French entry into the war, North suggested to the king that he might be relieved of the chancellorship of the Exchequer in favor of Charles Jenkinson. William Eden wrote to him of the absurdity of the prime minister spending at least two-thirds of his time dealing with contracts, jobs, and private petitions involving petty amounts of money.[62]

North's greatest fault was his failure to unite the Cabinet behind an agreed policy, but this was partly due to the political system. The modern concept of Cabinet responsibility, in which ministers unite in support of government policies, was yet to evolve fully. The prime ministers of the eighteenth century did not even choose all the members of the Cabinet but had to negotiate with the king to form a mixed Cabinet in which some members gave minimal support to the prime minister. Lord Edward Thurlow was openly disdainful of North but was appointed to the Cabinet as lord chancellor by George III. North's Cabinet began to act collectively only in the later stages of the war, when it adopted formal minutes of decisions and an agreed policy.[63]

North confronted daunting problems at home and abroad. From 1778, his indecisiveness became chronic with the prospect of failure in America and with Britain fighting alone in a global war against France, joined by Spain in 1779 and by the Dutch Republic in 1781. For three summers from 1778 to 1780, Britain faced the threat of a French attack upon its coast. The government was also concerned about the revolutionary potential of the armed Volunteer movement in Ireland, which was formed on the pretext of danger from abroad and the removal of British troops for service in America. Ireland was in a severe economic recession, and North was constantly distracted by the need to address the situation there. In September 1779, he was spending eighteen hours a day on matters related to Ireland and the East India Company. The following month, he wrote to Eden that he trembled at every letter from America.[64]

In 1779, there seemed a real danger of the government falling from power, with the Cabinet at loggerheads and its parliamentary majority dwindling. North was particularly anxious about the possibility of defection by members of his Cabinet. There were differences among them over strategy, but there was also a power struggle for seniority. In March 1779, when the earl of Suffolk's death created a vacancy for one of the offices of secretary of state, North left the position unfilled for six months because there was such bitter rivalry among the contenders. The attorney general, Alexander Wedderburn, lobbied for the post to North's consternation. In October, Lord Gower resigned as lord president of the Council in protest at the handling of events in Ireland, and gave a withering critique of the weak state of the government. In November, Gower's resignation was followed by that of Secretary of State Lord Weymouth. The *Annual Register* commented that "the ministers seemed as little united as the people." In May 1780, Richard Rigby, one of the most effective government spokesmen, resigned as paymaster general in opposition to the war, after having been a leading advocate for it. The government majority fell from a comfortable 150 to around 80–90. The supporters of the government became less spirited and enthusiastic in debates. The royal officeholders, upon whose support the government could usually rely, became less reliable in their attendance at Parliament.[65]

North faced an emboldened opposition, who shifted their tactics from questioning the war's legitimacy to criticizing its conduct. In January 1779, the opposition successfully exploited the court martial of Admiral Augustus Keppel, who was accused of having failed to sufficiently engage the French fleet at the battle of the Ushant. It was a popular cause because it was believed that the trial was politically motivated: Keppel was an opponent of the war and an ally of Charles James Fox. In February, Keppel's acquittal caused an outburst of antigovernment celebrations, enabling the opposition to challenge Sandwich. In March, North was only able to avert a government defeat on a motion to censure Sandwich by arguing that it would be a vote of no confidence in the government. In June 1779, Generals John Burgoyne and Sir William Howe defended their respective commands in America before Parliament. The House of Commons was treated to the remarkable spectacle of generals and government ministers blaming one another for the fiasco that led to the British defeat at Saratoga.

The opposition parties came close to victory in what became known as the movement for "economical reform," which was aimed more at curtailing executive power than promoting financial savings. In December 1779, the Reverend Christopher Wyvill convened a meeting of the local gentry in Yorkshire to petition Parliament against the perceived waste of public money. Wyvill's campaign led to a much broader movement for reform in the guise of a county petitioning campaign. The opposition parties began to unite and adopted elements of the program of the Wyvill movement in Parliament. In March 1780, the opposition won a vote to abolish the Board of Trade. In April 1780, they passed Dunning's motion that asserted that the influence of the Crown had increased, was increasing, and ought to be diminished. The near success of the opposition, combined with the divisions in the Cabinet and the expansion of the war, explain why North revealed such despair in his letters to George III. He was genuinely hurt by unfounded claims of personal corruption.[66]

As always, North was concerned about the financial toll of the war and the growing national debt, which had been a major factor in his misgivings about going to war in the first place. By 1778, the war's cost amounted to 11 percent of national income. North increased taxes by 30 percent, but the revenue from taxation still covered only about 20 percent of the cost of the war. The taxes were so pervasive that he jested that he intended to impose a tax on hairdressers. During the course of the war, the national debt rose from £127 million to £232 million, and the total cost of the war was £52.5 million. North was rebuked by the king for his belief that the "contest could never repay the expence."[67]

North's task was made more difficult by the most merciless personal lampoons and press attacks since the days of Sir Robert Walpole. North was indeed subject to more press scrutiny than any previous prime minister because of the growing popularity of newspapers and the recently won right of journalists to report debates in Parliament. In the later stages of the war, total daily newspaper sales amounted to an estimated 40,000 in London. Newspapers were circulated in coffeehouses and private residences where each copy was read many times. Since the papers were sometimes read aloud, it was possible for almost anyone, regardless of class or gender, to follow both the war and the operations of the government in detail. Lord North became the main press scapegoat for British failure in America. He suffered a barrage of personal invective which he shrugged off in public, but he confided to the king his fear that his reputation was being destroyed. The letters to the press and the satires were savage. North felt overwhelmed, and with good reason.[68]

V

North left much to be desired as a war leader, but the war could not have continued without the exceptional qualities that he possessed in other respects. As a speaker and advocate of government policy, he excelled in the House of Commons. Since government majorities could not be taken for granted, his presence and popularity in the chamber were critical. Contrary to the charges of his opponents, North had to govern through persuasion. Although there were members who held government offices, known as "placemen," and others who owed their seats to government patronage, their loyalty was not unequivocal and they accounted for only about a fifth of the membership of the House of Commons. The majority of independents generally voted with the government, but could not be taken for granted. They could at any time bring down a government by voting with the opposition.

Nathaniel Wraxall watched Lord North often in the House of Commons and described glowingly how "That assembly presented, in fact, a theatre on which he acted the first personage, where he attracted almost all the attention." North was "powerful, able, and fluent in debate," regularly speaking without notes for two hours. North spent at least three days a week in the House of Commons. Often having just met with the king, North would be in court dress, with the Garter star and a broad ribbon of royal blue, causing him to be referred to in debate as "the noble lord in the blue ribbon." His absence was so rare that newspapers commented when he did not appear in the chamber. Before beginning their public business at about three o'clock in the afternoon, the members awaited his arrival expectantly, and the debates typically lasted another six to eight hours. The House sometimes sat until after midnight without a recess the next day. North regularly proposed the motion on major issues and was generally the leading spokesman for government policy, and often waited until the end of a debate to have the last word. In 1774, he gave 104 speeches on the subject of the Coercive Acts and the Quebec Act alone.[69]

According to Wraxall, "In brilliancy of wit, Lord North alone could compete with [Edmund] Burke." Although North had "a deep untuneable voice" which was monotone and unnecessarily pompous, his speeches were celebrated for their clarity, their elegance, and their grasp of the issues. He deflected the opposition by his wit. Horace Walpole described how "whatever the subject, except on the danger to his own person, he treated the whole with mirth and ridicule." Thomas Townsend similarly wrote that "happen what will, the noble Lord is ready with his joke" and that North treated even the most distressing events "as subjects of merriment, of gaiety, and of repartee." Wraxall admitted that North was sometimes too flippant, but found it "impossible to resist the effect of Lord North's talents for ridicule."[70]

His was not a malicious wit, but amusing and frequently self-deprecating. When he fell asleep during a debate on the state of public finances, he was prodded awake by a colleague just as a speaker was referring to national revenues and expenditures in 1689, to which North said, "Zounds, you have wakened me near one hundred years too soon." In another debate, when a member claimed that he was asleep, North responded, "Would to God I were." In January 1778, when North was questioned in Parliament about the condition of the quarters of British troops in Philadelphia, he replied that they were so good he wished he could pass the next three months there. When Charles James Fox accused him of idleness and listening to flatterers, North replied "that he passed a great deal of time in that House, where he could not be idle and it was plain not *flattered.*" When "during one of his violent philippics at the profusions" of the government, Edmund Burke mispronounced a Latin word, North called out the correct pronunciation and "Burke by some nod or expression signified his acknowledgement" of his error. When an opposition member questioned his still speaking of "our rebellious subjects," North rejoined "very well, then, I will call them the gentlemen in Opposition on the other side of the water."[71]

North delighted in the theater of parliamentary debate and appreciated the talents of his opponents, especially the oratory of Edmund Burke. After a speech by Burke, North once responded "And now Mr. Speaker I believe I have replied to everything which has fallen from the honorable gentleman, except his wit. That, I readily acknowledge, is unanswerable, he being greatly my superior in that respect." In spite of the acrimony with which Burke frequently treated Lord North, Wraxall said that no man in the House of Commons appeared to enjoy Burke's "sallies of wit more than the First Minister." North even laughed at jokes at his own expense, like the occasion when Burke "convulsed the House and shook Lord North's sides with laughter by comparing the thin, lean member of Parliament," when North first became a member of Parliament, "to the *Vulpecula,* or weasel of Aesop, who afterwards become so large and sleek as to be unable to effect his retreat."[72]

Since 1547, the House of Commons had met in St. Stephen's Chapel in Westminster Palace. The former choir stalls of the chapel became the benches of the members and the altar was replaced by the speaker's chair. Sir Christopher Wren readapted the chapel into a debating hall with a flat ceiling, galleries, and Romanesque windows facing the River Thames. Partly because the building was too small to seat comfortably more than two-thirds of the total membership of 558, the debating chamber had an intimate, clubbable atmosphere. Even on important issues, the attendance rarely exceeded 300 and was more usually about 150. The lobby and the debating chamber were divided by a screen, which had formerly separated the original chapel and antechapel. The government ministers and leading members of the opposition generally sat on opposing sides on the front benches, but there was otherwise no formal seating arrangement, so that opposition and government members intermixed. The voting was frequently done by shouts of yea or nay, rather than by formal counting. After the annual opening of Parliament by the king, usually in late November, the sessions lasted over six months. The major business was conducted between Christmas and Easter.[73]

During one of the finest eras of parliamentary debate, North excelled as a speaker. The standard of the exchanges was so high and the membership was so intolerant of poor performances that Edward Gibbon admitted in his autobiography that he never had the courage to speak in a debate. Gibbon had particularly wanted to speak on American affairs, but "dreaded exposing myself" and remained in his seat "safe but inglorious." Although the House of Commons had the atmosphere of a club, with a membership belonging mostly to distantly related members of the landed classes, only half the members ever made a speech during the entire course of their parliamentary careers. Sitting in the House of Commons throughout the American Revolution, Gibbon recalled with gratitude the sessions that he believed had helped train him as a historian, by educating him in the arts of government. He had the "near prospect of the characters, views, and passions, of the first men of the age." He heard "agitated the most important questions, of

peace and war, of Justice and Policy" which were debated with "eloquence and reason."
He regarded North as "a consummate master of debate, who could wield with equal
dexterity the arms of reason and ridicule."[74]

North faced an opposition composed of many of the most talented and most
esteemed speakers of the day, whom he frequently outmaneuvered in debate. He became
skilled at deflecting opponents by exuding an "unalterable suavity" and an urbane demeanor so that the "bitter sarcasms and severe accusations leveled at him always seemed
to sink into him like a cannon-ball into a wool sack." It was North who coined the still
popular phrase of "roasting a minister" to describe opposition attacks. He was particularly deft at changing the topic of a debate and at diversionary tactics. He was also
practiced in the art of eluding and evading precise questions, giving nothing away. True,
Edward Gibbon did not think the opposition of "such superiority either of measures or
abilities," and other commentators agreed with him. In the opinion of Horace Walpole,
Edmund Burke often "lost himself in a torrent of images and copiousness." Wraxall
similarly thought that Burke's "ideas outran the powers of *utterance*," and that although
Burke "instructed, delighted and astonished, he frequently fatigued." David Hartley was
the most zealous opponent of the American war in the House of Commons. He rarely
spoke on any other issue, but according to Wraxall, "his rising always operated like a
Dinner Bell," and he was accused by an opponent of giving a tedious speech more
appropriate for an American Congress than a British Parliament. During the course of
one of his speeches, in which two-thirds of the members walked out, Hartley had occasion to read out the proclamation of riotous assembly from the Riot Act, causing Burke to
grab him by the coat saying, "the Riot Act! To what purpose! Don't you see the mob is
already completely dispersed?"[75]

The opposition parties were too divided among themselves to overthrow the
government. They had initially disagreed among themselves on the right of Parliament to
tax America, and they remained divided over the terms of a settlement of the conflict. In
1779–80, they found common cause in their opposition to the war and began to coalesce,
but in June 1780, the brief collaboration among the opposition parties ended with the
anti-Catholic Gordon Riots. The fanaticism of the riots redounded to the benefit of Lord
North. One of the evenings during the riots, a mob massed outside his official residence
in Downing Street. North had soldiers in the house to protect him, and one of his dinner
party guests called Jack St. John was armed, causing North to exclaim, "I am not half so
much afraid of the mob as of Jack St. John's pistol." As night was coming in and the guests
finished their wine, North led them onto his roof at Downing Street where they "beheld
London blazing in seven places, and could hear the platoons regularly firing in various
directions." The revolutionary potential of the riots caused a reaction against the opposition parties, who themselves became divided in their own response to these events. A
member of the Cabinet admitted that "the opposition is so universally detested and

feared" that the government continued to be supported by the nation, a support to which it was "not entitled but from *comparison*."[76]

Outside Parliament, North appreciated the importance of propaganda and attempted to influence domestic opinion in support of the war. At the beginning of the war in 1775, he and Robinson successfully solicited mass petitions in support of the government to counteract the petitions of the opposition. North recruited some of the leading writers of the period to compose propaganda pamphlets in support of the war, most famously Samuel Johnson, whose *Taxation No Tyranny* was published in March 1775. There were four editions within the first month. Three weeks after the publication, Johnson was awarded an honorary D.C.L. by Oxford University whose chancellor was none other than Lord North. The portrait artist Allan Ramsay "left off painting, and was a constant scribbler for the Court in the newspapers." Another government writer, John Mein, wrote newspaper articles under the pseudonym of "Sagittarius," in which he entertained readers with jibes, like his description of Franklin before the war as an "old factious agent, who vomits out his venom in the newspapers." North made use of the writing talents of John Wesley; of James Macpherson, the author of the literary fraud, *The Poems of Ossian;* together with the loyalist Joseph Galloway, the pamphleteer John Shebbeare, and the MP Sir John Dalrymple. In the later years of the war, the pamphlets of Galloway and Macpherson "threw responsibility onto the generals and admirals" for the problems of the American War.[77]

Lord North was not only an effective speaker, but also a parliamentary manager who maintained government majorities until several months after the final British defeat at Yorktown. He defied the expectations of contemporaries by remaining continuously in power for longer than any prime minister since Walpole. As Wraxall observed, North had "attained in the course of years that intimate knowledge of the Lower House, its formation, composition, and the modes of conducting or influencing it as a body which nothing can confer except long habits of debate and the necessity of daily attendance." In 1775, North deflected the petitions critical of the war to a committee for the framing of commercial regulations that Edmund Burke called the "Committee of Oblivion." In 1774 and 1780, North twice caught the opposition off guard by calling early elections. After news arrived of the British defeat at Saratoga, North evaded the opposition's onslaught with a six-week adjournment of Parliament. He appointed some particularly gifted junior politicians to assist him in the task of managing the government majorities, including John Robinson and Charles Jenkinson. Robinson performed some of the functions of a modern government whip by helping to turn out the vote of the government supporters, and kept detailed records of the political persuasions of every member and the likely outcomes of elections in every district.[78]

North played a critical role in sustaining the American war through his financial expertise. Eighteenth-century prime ministers were generally well versed in finance because of concerns about the national debt. It was partly to reduce the debt that Britain had attempted to levy taxes in America. At the beginning of the American Revolution, the national debt was £245 million, while revenue from annual tax income was about £12 million. The servicing of the debt later rose to 66 percent of total tax revenues. During the war, the British government borrowed £91.8 million and paid a total of £115.3 million on the debt. North negotiated the loans himself and masterminded the difficult task of seeking additional funding from Parliament. The task became more difficult as creditors demanded greater incentives and better rates of return. In speeches lasting about two hours, North introduced the budget, for which "he was esteemed particularly lucid, clear, and able." According to Nathaniel Wraxall, the day that he announced the annual budget was "a day of triumph to his friends and supporters who exulted in the talent which he displayed whenever he exhibited the state of the national finances or imposed new pecuniary burdens." His skill seemed to Wraxall "deserving of the encomiums lavished on it."[79]

North was an innovator who made important financial reforms, which were continued by William Pitt the Younger. He believed that merit and ability should be the chief criteria for promotion in the Treasury. In 1780, he began a comprehensive review of the accounting system by creating the Commissioners of Public Accounts. In his last months as prime minister, he invited competitive loan offers, rather than use the traditional method of bargaining with individual lenders. The British financial system and the ability of governments to obtain credit was a major source of the strength of the British state in relation to the rest of Europe. It was a testimony to North's abilities that Britain remained solvent while France was bankrupted by its participation in the American War of Independence.[80]

VI

With the words "O God, it is all over!" North showed that he understood the significance of the British defeat at Yorktown. As Nathaniel Wraxall discovered at Germain's dinner party that evening, George III wanted to persevere, and so did Germain. North initially gave no public indication that the government had any intention of withdrawing from America.[81]

It was a testament to his popularity and his political skills that he managed to sustain his government for over three more months. A vivid impression of the final gasps of the government of Lord North is conveyed by Wraxall, who believed that he had witnessed the greatest "assemblage of first rate talents on the Opposition benches" in the history of Parliament. North faced an opposition that "beheld a constellation of men of genius." Their formidable talents had been strengthened by the accession of Chatham's son William Pitt the Younger, and of the playwright Richard Sheridan, "two of the most resplendent luminaries produced during the course of the eighteenth century," who began their parliamentary careers within days of one another and who "were preparing to unfold their powers." The twenty-one-year-old William Pitt had aroused such expectations among those who remembered his father that every ear was attentive to the son, "thus removing all the impediments that present themselves in the way of ordinary men when attempting to address Parliament." On hearing Pitt speak, Edmund Burke declared that he was "not merely a chip off the old block, but the old block itself."[82]

North was ultimately driven from power by his refusal to make a clear commitment to military withdrawal from America. The defection of the independent members was instrumental in his downfall. North confided in friends that it was futile to continue the war, and visibly indicated his real opinion when he suddenly moved away from the government front benches in the midst of Lord George Germain's speech urging the continuation of the war for America. North told Parliament he was unwilling to declare any intention of ending the war, because it would weaken the negotiating position of Britain with the United States. He privately did not want to defy George III openly, but rather to persuade him to accept the inevitability of the loss of America.[83]

As members became doubtful of the intention of the North ministry to end the war, the government majority dwindled. In late February 1782, the government won by only one vote against a motion of General Henry Seymour Conway urging that the war "no longer be pursued for the impracticable purpose of reducing the inhabitants of that country to obedience by force." A few days later, Conway defeated the government over another motion to the effect that the continued prosecution of an offensive war in America threatened British security by weakening the chances of victory in Europe. On March 15, the final blow was a government majority of only nine votes against an opposition motion of censure proposed by an independent member who accused the government of having "reduced the country from a state of glory and prosperity to calamity and disgrace." Although army officers were usually reliable government supporters, sixteen voted with the opposition and only fifteen against the motion. Wraxall suspected that North "did not really regret" the moral defeat of the government. North wanted to be released from the burdens of office.[84]

On March 27, North went out with aplomb and characteristic humor. On the eve of what amounted to a vote of no confidence, he composed his resignation letter to the king. Writing with an uncharacteristic vehemence, he reminded the king of his constitutional duty to bow to the expressed wishes of the elected majority of the House of Commons. North gave no warning of his decision to his supporters. Following a meeting of an hour and a half with George III, North set off late to the House of Commons. With some four hundred members in attendance in the early afternoon, the chamber was unusually full, and "all eyes were directed towards the door each time that it opened." Entering in full court dress and his ribbon over his coat, North was greeted with howls of "Order" and "Places." As soon as he reached the government front bench, he rose and attempted to address the speaker, but his voice was drowned by a clamor "from all quarters of the most violent description," demanding that precedence be given to a prior motion of the earl of Surrey.[85]

Disregarding a motion by Charles James Fox that "the Earl of Surrey do now speak," North silenced the House by announcing his resignation. Wraxall recalled that "it is not easy to conceive the effect which this declaration produced in a popular assembly," where there was scarcely an individual who did not hear him without exuding joy or concern, "which emotions were heightened by surprise." North vowed that he would not run away, but would remain "to be found as much as ever, and would not on any account avoid an enquiry" into his public conduct. As he departed, he told a friend to come home and dine "and get the credit of having dined with a fallen minister on the day of his dismissal." He had arranged for his carriage to make a quick escape before the members "dispersed in all directions to spread the intelligence through the capital." Having made his way ahead of most of them, he turned to those persons who were near him as he entered his carriage and, "with that placid temper that never forsook him," North said "Good night, gentlemen; you see what it is to be in the secret." It was a humorous jibe at conspiratorial theories about the inner workings and secrecy of the government.[86]

VII

The younger members of Parliament had never known any ministers other than Lord North at the head of the Treasury and the earl of Sandwich as first lord of the Admiralty. Wraxall described how it was "difficult to recognize them again in their new seats dispersed over the Opposition benches, wrapped in great coats or habited in frocks and boots." It excited more astonishment still to see the former members of the opposition no longer in their blue and buff coats associated with the Continental Army, but "ornamented with the appendages of full dress or returning from court decorated with swords, lace, and hair powder."[87]

North's relegation to the opposition benches was brief. In an unlikely coalition with Charles James Fox, he returned to power a year later in 1783, though he significantly showed no desire to be prime minister and deferred to Fox. During its short-lived tenure of nine months, the Fox-North coalition was widely regarded as an unscrupulous and cynical alliance. It diminished the reputation of North among some of his most loyal supporters, who defected to join the rising star William Pitt. He later told his wife that he regretted it more than any action in his life. Nevertheless, North continued to remain loyal to Fox, and even wore the blue and buff livery to a party of the prince of Wales at Carlton House. His home became a popular resort among former political opponents including Fox, Burke, and Sheridan. It was located on the opposite side of Grosvenor

Square from the home of the ambassador of the United States, John Adams, who was close enough to see through Lord North's windows. Adams's wife Abigail remarked that "we have not taken a side with Lord North, but we are still opposite him."[88]

Lady Charlotte Lindsay, North's youngest daughter, thought it "probable that the anxiety of mind which he suffered during the unsuccessful contest with America" was the cause of the breakdown of North's health. Over of the next five years, he became totally blind, an affliction that he bore with patience and resignation. The playwright Richard Cumberland visited him in this period, when all "but his illuminated mind was dark around him." Cumberland praised the way North "when divested of that incidental greatness, which high office for a time can give, self-dignified and independent, rose to a real greatness of his own creating." He still "possessed a boundless fund of information for the instruction and delight of others." During sleepless nights, North suffered fits of depression, and his wife would read to him until he fell asleep. He continued to make occasional speeches in the House of Commons. On his final appearance in the chamber, his blindness necessitated that he be led to his seat by his son.[89]

His humor never deserted him, as on the occasion in Tunbridge Wells when he encountered the equally blind Colonel Isaac Barré, who had coined the phrase "Sons of Liberty," and who had consistently sparred with North in opposition to the war in America. North said to Barré "Though you and I have had our quarrels in the past, I wager there are not two men in England who would be happier to see one another today!" Although he enjoyed the company of others, North was at his best with "only his family, or one or two intimate friends" during weekends in the country. His wife was only sixteen when they married and was seven years his junior. His daughter wrote of the marriage that "there never was a more happy union than theirs during the thirty-six years that it lasted," and that we "never saw an unkind look, or heard an unkind word pass between them; his affectionate attachment to her was as unabated, as her love and admiration of him."[90]

His daughters read to him by turns, wrote his letters, led him on walks, and were his constant companions. North liked to have his oldest daughter read from Shakespeare. In the last ten days of his life, she read to him for "a great part of every day with her usual spirit, though her heart was dying within her." She also read from the French newspapers containing accounts of the outbreak of the Revolution, to which he responded "I am going, and thankful I am that I shall not witness the anarchy and bloodshed which will soon overwhelm that unhappy country."[91]

On the day of his death on August 2, 1792, North talked of his "considerable anxiety on the subject of his character and fame—that he should have wished to know how he stood and would stand with the world." He summoned his family to his bedside when he knew that he had but a few hours to live. After they had gathered round him, he reflected on his political career, claiming that it gave him satisfaction that he could look back without regret. According to his nephew, he "then took leave of his family," and, after thanking them separately for their great kindness and attention to him, he passed away without a struggle or a groan. He was sixty years old.[92]

North defended his role in the war for America to his death. He insisted that it "did not originate in a despotic wish to tyrannise America, but from the desire of maintaining the constitutional authority of Parliament over the colonies." He admitted that the war with America had "been unfortunate but not unjust," adding that if he had been forced to "mount the scaffold in consequence of the part that I have performed in its prosecution, I shall continue to maintain that it was founded in right and dictated by necessity." He denied that it was ever a war waged by the crown against the wishes of the people, but rather "a war of Parliament, sanctioned through its whole progress by both Houses. It was more. It was a war of the people, undertaken for the purpose of maintaining their rights over the dependencies of the Empire." In later years, he had reminded the House of Commons that it had been a popular war at its commencement and that it was absurd to pretend that the crown had the influence to procure almost unanimous majorities in Parliament. It was only the failure of the military campaigns that eventually made it unpopular when "the people began to cry out for peace," but still it was a war approved by the people at large. He argued that even if Parliament had been reformed to reflect the views of the people more accurately, it would still have supported the war for America.[93]

PART II

Victory and Defeat in the North (1776–1778)

It was a little hard, that after a man had devoted his whole time and talents (however poor the latter might be) to the service of his country, that the *event,* and not his conduct, should determine his character; that to be *unsuccessful* and guilty should be the same thing, and that he should be held up as a public criminal, for not doing what could not be done!

ADMIRAL HOWE

I believe, where war is concerned, few men in command would stand acquitted, if any after-knowledge of facts and circumstances were brought in argument against decisions of the moment.

JOHN BURGOYNE

CHAPTER 3

The Peace Commissioners?

THE HOWE BROTHERS

On May 25, 1775, HMS *Cerberus*—a sixth-rate warship of twenty-eight guns—sailed into Boston harbor with troop reinforcements from Britain. Named after the three-headed dog of classical mythology that guarded the gates of hell, the ship carried three major generals—William Howe, John Burgoyne, and Henry Clinton, all of whom had received their promotions on the same day. Howe was the most senior because of his years of continuous service in the army, whereas the fifty-eight-year-old Burgoyne was second in seniority to Howe in spite of being the oldest among them. Clinton was the youngest and most junior of the three generals. He was painfully shy and spent much of his time on deck, escaping a confined cabin with six roommates and suffering acute seasickness. During the "very disagreeable passage" of seven weeks, there was nevertheless an atmosphere of camaraderie among the three aspiring commanders, who held one another in high esteem. They were each about to embark on a service in which they would compete for command, glory, and victory in America.[1]

Howe, Burgoyne, and Clinton represented the best of the general officers in the British army. They had been selected to command in America from 119 possible candidates who ranged in rank from major generals to full generals. They had not been appointed on the basis of seniority or patronage. Although senior to both Burgoyne and Clinton, Howe ranked only 111th in rank of the 119 generals in the British Army. Since generals never retired, the choice was limited only by age and health. Others were disqualified by their lack of suitable training, their political opposition to the war, or their refusal to serve in America. This left about a third of the total number to be considered as possible candidates, of whom twelve were thought outstanding. The government congratulated itself upon the final selection. As George III later reminded his Cabinet, the three major generals were "thought the best in his service to command the troops" in America, and in the House of Commons, Lord George Germain described them as "the fittest men for the service in the army." Although John Burgoyne claimed that they were the personal choice of the monarch and although such appointments were ultimately the prerogative of the crown, George III said that their selection had been unanimously approved by the Cabinet.[2]

In 1775, members of Parliament ridiculed the idea that the army would encounter significant resistance in America. In the House of Commons, speaker after speaker told "ludicrous stories" of the military incapacity of Americans to the great "entertainment of the House." It was claimed that the Americans "were neither soldiers, nor could be made so; being naturally of a pusillanimous disposition, and utterly incapable of any sort of order or discipline." It was said that owing to their laziness, lack of cleanliness, and defects of character, "they were incapable of going through the service of a campaign," and that they "would melt away with sickness before they could face an enemy." On February 2, Colonel James Grant told the House that the Americans "would never dare to face an *English* army." A veteran of the French and Indian War and former governor of East Florida, Grant claimed that five thousand regular troops could march from one end of America to another without serious opposition. In April, Richard Rigby said that "it was romantic to think they [the Americans] would fight." There was a debate as to whether the militiamen and minutemen should be considered enemy belligerents, with the rights and status of a nation, or merely traitors and rebels who should not be dignified with the conventions of war and prisoner exchanges.[3]

The home government had sent Howe, Burgoyne, and Clinton to quash the rebellion and to bolster Lieutenant General Thomas Gage, who combined the role of governor of Massachusetts and commander in chief of the British army in America. Gage had lived twenty years in America and was married to an American. During the French and Indian War he had raised a light infantry regiment that was trained to fight under the irregular conditions of warfare in America. With a tall slender physique, he was a popular and mild-mannered officer who was admired as a man of great integrity even by his critics. Before Lord North became prime minister in 1770, Gage had urged the home government to use force to put a speedy end to sedition in the colonies. He had warned that moderation and forbearance would only stiffen resistance.

In the final months of 1774, Gage suddenly began to equivocate. He proposed suspending the Coercive Acts on discovering that all of the thirteen colonies were embracing the cause of Boston. The following year, he became despondent of a military solution without doubling the number of troops to a minimum of twenty thousand. He observed that the rebels knew what they were about and that "in all the wars against France they never shewed so much conduct attention and perseverance as they do now." The home government turned against him, thinking him too timid and supine, and he became known in the army as the "Old Woman." In the opening salvo of the war on April 19, 1775, Gage had suffered a serious reversal and heavy casualties when he sent an expeditionary force twenty miles into the countryside to seize weapons and revolutionary leaders believed to be located at Lexington and Concord.[4]

Before the land reclamation projects of later years, Boston was located on a virtual island with just a narrow strip of road connecting the peninsula to the rest of the continent. Howe, Burgoyne, and Clinton arrived to find the British army and its loyalist supporters besieged by thousands of revolutionary militiamen who had begun to encircle the city in the days following the skirmish at Lexington and Concord. Surrounded and outnumbered, the army was invested by what Burgoyne described as "a rabble in arms, who flushed with success and insolence, had advanced their sentries to pistol shot of our out-guards." The naval ships in the harbor were exposed to rebel cannon fire. The troops, officers, and inhabitants were still "lost in a sort of stupefaction which the events of the 19 of April had occasioned." They vented emotions ranging from censure and anger to despondency. Howe, Burgoyne, and Clinton found the walls of their residences daubed night after night with mock royal proclamations threatening vengeance on the rebels. They were similarly ridiculed in messages of congratulation.[5]

On June 17, 1775, less than three weeks after their arrival, the three major generals had their first taste of battle in America at Bunker Hill. Henry Clinton described the astonishing perseverance with which the revolutionary militia overnight fortified the high ground at Breed's Hill and Bunker Hill, located to the north of Boston across the Charles River on another peninsula called Charlestown. In preference to a strategy suggested by Clinton, Gage opted for a plan proposed by Howe. Far from contemplating a crude frontal attack, Howe envisaged a turning movement, with a feint attack to distract from the main thrust of the army against one of the enemy flanks. It was to be preceded by naval cannonade from the harbor and the blast of field artillery. Howe showed great courage by personally leading the assault, and at one stage of the battle, he was the only officer in the front rank left standing. In an eyewitness account, Sergeant Roger Lamb described Howe as acting with "coolness, firmness, and presence of mind." Like other British eyewitnesses, Lamb was impressed by the marksmanship of their opponents who "behaved with great resolution and bravery, and by no means merited the appellation of *cowards,* with which they were so often branded in England." Howe was appalled to witness wave after wave of his infantry felled by repeated volleys of accurate enemy fire. As he watched in disbelief while his elite light infantrymen were repulsed, he wrote that he had never experienced such a moment before.[6]

Howe's plan was poorly implemented because of the inexperience and indiscipline of his mostly raw troops. The effectiveness of the assault was blunted by a six-hour delay waiting for high tide, and by fences that were completed by the rebels just before the attack. However, it was the failure of his troops to keep advancing with their bayonets in the face of enemy fire that made the price of victory so high. Contrary to his orders, they stood, retreated, and tried again. The British won the battle of Bunker Hill, but at such a cost in the lives of men that Henry Clinton wrote in his memoirs "a few more such victories would have shortly put an end to British dominion in America." Some of the oldest officers and soldiers "declared it was the hottest service they had ever seen." Of an estimated 2,200 troops engaged, there were 1,054 casualties. The overall fatality rate was relatively standard for battles in Europe. It was the proportion of officers killed that was startling—amounting to over one-eighth of all British officers killed during the American Revolutionary War. Howe wrote that when contemplating "the loss of so many brave officers, I do it with horror." On July 25, 1775, the return journey of the *Cerberus* brought official confirmation of the news of the British losses at the battle of Bunker Hill to England.[7]

Gage was the first in a succession of military commanders to be blamed for the British defeat in America. On October 10, he handed over his command to William Howe and left Boston on the official pretext that he was to consult with government ministers in London. The historian Edward Gibbon wrote that good men rejoiced when they heard of his recall. According to John Burgoyne, "the secret and real reason" that Howe had not wanted to serve in America was because he had a "low opinion" of Gage and "dreaded acting immediately under the orders of an officer whose talents were far inferior to his command." Indeed, Gage initially misled the home government by giving the impression that resistance might easily be overcome and that opposition was largely confined to Boston. When he reversed his opinion to predict widespread support for the revolutionary movement and the need for a much larger military force, the government became intent on replacing him.[8]

Gage disappeared into relative obscurity, supporting his large family on a small income in England, but he lived to see his successors suffer similar humiliation. In 1778, he sat on the commission of inquiry into General John Burgoyne's conduct at Saratoga. Promoted to a full general after the fall of Lord North's government in 1782, Gage died five years later at Portland Place in London. Burgoyne wrote at the time of Bunker Hill that it was no reflection on Gage to say that he was unequal to the command in America, because "few characters in the world would be fit"; the position required "a genius of the first class, together with uncommon resolution, and a firm reliance upon support at home." It was a situation "in which Caesar might have failed."[9]

In almost four months before the signing of the Declaration of Independence, the British lost America. On March 17, 1776, after almost eleven months under siege, General Howe withdrew all his 6,000 troops and 900 sick from Boston. They were accompanied by some 1,100 American loyalists who were mostly ordinary people such as farmers, artisans, and tradesmen. Although the home government had ordered the withdrawal as a tactical retreat, it was humiliating because it was precipitated by enemy troops and militia commanded by George Washington, the forty-three-year-old Virginian appointed by Congress to turn the rabble gathered around Boston into professional soldiers of the

Continental Army. Washington had been able to make up the deficiency in his artillery thanks to Benedict Arnold's and Ethan Allen's capture of the British fortresses of Ticonderoga (May 10, 1775) and Crown Point (May 12, 1775) near Lake Champlain. In a remarkable feat of endurance, Henry Knox arranged for fifty-eight mortars and cannon from the fortresses to be dragged by boats, sledges, and oxen three hundred miles south to Boston. Knox was a twenty-five-year-old former Boston bookseller whose military knowledge was mainly derived from reading. In another daring and enterprising effort, the besiegers had dug trenches and mounted the guns overnight on Dorchester Heights and had begun to bombard the British garrison in Boston.[10]

While William Howe's army awaited reinforcements in Halifax, Nova Scotia, British authority collapsed from Georgia to New Hampshire as the rebels won control of the militias, the law courts, the presses, and the assemblies. The royal governors either fled into exile or sought refuge on board warships. The vaunted military superiority of the British was shown to lack substance. In Canada, the British were forced on the defensive by Generals Benedict Arnold and Richard Montgomery who led a detachment of the Continental Army in taking Montreal and besieging Quebec. The fifty-one-year-old British governor and commander in chief in Canada, Guy Carleton, only escaped capture by disguising himself as a farmer to escape from Montreal to Quebec. The British lost the initiative and were crucially unable to protect and defend those who remained their supporters and friends in America, where they were known derogatorily as Tories. The first year of the war ended in retreat for the British and a propaganda coup for the forces of rebellion in America.

The arrival of Howe, Burgoyne, and Clinton had not deterred the revolutionary movement. Grandiosely styled a "triumvirate of reputation" by Burgoyne, they were lampooned in doggerel by a London wit:

> Behold the *Cerberus* the Atlantic plough,
> Her precious cargo, Burgoyne, Clinton, Howe.
> Bow, wow, wow!

The *Cerberus* and its three illustrious passengers were to suffer grim fates in America. While stationed off New London in 1777, the *Cerberus* narrowly evaded becoming the victim of one of the first underwater mines, developed by David Bushnell, the Connecticut-born inventor of a man-propelled submarine known as the *American Turtle*. The *Cerberus* was less fortunate the following year. After unsuccessfully attempting to escape two French frigates on August 5, 1778, the *Cerberus* was scuttled and blown up by her own crew off shore at Newport, Rhode Island. As for the three major generals, they would each hold senior command, each preside over major reversals, each suffer humiliating recalls, and become each other's critics and bitter rivals. Their names would be indelibly associated with the British loss of America.[11]

I

If British defeat seemed inevitable after the withdrawal from Boston, the Howe brothers were to reverse the situation with a spectacular series of victories beginning in the summer of 1776. In July, Major General William Howe was joined by his older brother Admiral Richard, Lord Howe, who commanded the British fleet in North America. The Howe brothers were distinctive and impressive. They were physically imposing, with tall athletic builds and swarthy complexions which caused Admiral Howe to be nicknamed in the navy "Black Dick," and General Howe to be called "the savage" by his sister and mother. Like Lord North, the brothers resembled George III, and indeed their mother was believed to be an out-of-wedlock daughter of George I. Their father had been governor of Barbados who had died before either of his sons had reached their teens.

The Howe brothers were close and supportive of one another. Their joint commands created the potential for successful combined operations between the army and navy, which was a crucial advantage for launching amphibious attacks against the major cities along the East Coast of America. The brothers were each known for their almost reckless courage. They kept their own counsel and were famously taciturn. In his description of "those brave and silent brothers," Horace Walpole remarked that General William Howe "was reckoned sensible, though so silent that nobody knew whether he was or not" and that the admiral was as "undaunted as a rock and as silent." According to Nathaniel Wraxall, Admiral Howe expressed himself in such a convoluted style that "it was by no means easy to comprehend his precise meaning." Charles Stedman, an American-born officer in the British army, wrote of "the hauteur and frigid reserve" in the deportment of the admiral which "ill qualified him as a soother and a mediator between two contending parties."[12]

Their oldest brother, George Augustus, third Viscount Howe, had been a hero in America, having been killed in action at Ticonderoga in the French and Indian War. He was famous for wearing hunting shirts and trousers, and living in a frontier manner. He was honored by the General Court of Massachusetts Bay, which voted £250 to erect a monument in his memory in Westminster Abbey. In the second pamphlet in his essays on *The American Crisis,* Tom Paine accused William Howe of being forgetful in brandishing "his sword against those who, at their own charge, raised a monument to his brother."[13]

The Howe brothers had exemplary military records and were veterans of many campaigns. After attending Eton in 1746, William Howe began his lifelong career in the army at the age of seventeen as a cornet in the Duke of Cumberland's Light Dragoons. Under the cover of darkness during the French and Indian War in 1759, he led the advance guard of Major General James Wolfe's force that scaled the Heights of Abraham and captured Quebec. William Howe was similarly prominent in the capture of Montreal in 1760 and Belle Île on the coast of Brittany in 1761, and in the conquest of Havana in 1762. On his arrival in Boston in 1775, he was described as being held in great repute, and much esteemed both for his "military genius, and care for his army."[14]

After short stints at two schools favored by the upper classes for the education of their teenage sons, Westminster and Eton, Admiral Lord Howe had joined the navy at the age of thirteen in 1739. Aged twenty-two, he became the captain of the flagship of Rear Admiral Charles Knowles. He accompanied George Anson on his voyage around the world. He was rapidly promoted to first lieutenant in the spring of 1745 and captain in the spring of 1746. As captain of HMS *Dunkirk* in 1755, Howe fired the first shot of the Seven Years' War, and he led a British squadron in the great naval victory at Quiberon Bay off the coast of France near St. Nazaire in 1759. Commanding the *Magnanime* in 1760, he anchored within sixty yards of the French fortress of Île d'Aix. As he and a pilot stood heroically alone, he made the rest of his deck crew lie down in order to bombard the fort at such close quarters that it capitulated within thirty-five minutes. Admiral Howe ultimately spent fifty-nine years in active service and became one of the most celebrated naval commanders of the age.

The military experience of both brothers gave them familiarity with both the Caribbean and North America, and they were also practitioners and innovators in tactics best suited to the conditions of warfare in North America. Together with George, General William Howe had helped to develop the use of light infantry during the French and Indian War. These faster and more agile troops were better adapted than heavy infantry for conditions in America, and although the army had dabbled in their use for over thirty years in Europe, they were not formally introduced into each foot regiment until after they had proven their worth in America. Together with the grenadiers, the light infantry companies were the elite of each regiment and were often placed as flank companies. They were occasionally formed into special battalions. Howe's knowledge of light infantry and unconventional warfare was important in his selection as commander in chief.[15]

In England in the summer of 1774, William Howe had intensively trained seven companies of light infantry on Salisbury Plain and demonstrated their capacity in front of George III at Richmond. He was known for his careful and regular inspections that made his troops some of the fittest and most active in the British army. Lord George Germain wrote that nobody understood better than Howe the past lessons of warfare in America and the need for light troops who had been "taught to separate and secure themselves by trees, walls, or hedges." Germain was persuaded that Howe would "teach the present army to be as formidable" as the troops Howe had led in Canada during the French and Indian War. In December 1775, he was described by George Washington as the "most formidable enemy America has."[16]

Admiral Howe was one of the most influential admirals in the development of the eighteenth-century Royal Navy. Beginning with his time commanding squadrons and flotillas in the Seven Years' War, he was interested in revising the system of signals and fighting instructions that so frequently plagued commanders during fleet maneuvers and battles. He took a keen interest in administrative detail. During his command of the *Magnanime* in 1759, he kept a "captain's order book" in a novel attempt to improve the management of officers and crew. He made radical proposals for altering the ship's guns, including the use of priming tubes, flannel cartridges, and locks on the cannon to improve safety and the rate of fire. His ideas were fully adopted in the navy twenty years later.[17]

Admiral Howe pioneered the naval code of practice for amphibious warfare, in which the navy transported and gave logistical support to the army in beachhead landings. As with the signal system and fighting instructions, there was no standard procedure for amphibious warfare before May 1758. Howe issued what became the standard directives and signals for embarking and landing troops in hostile surroundings, together with regulations for maintaining the chain of command for army transport ships. He also introduced flat-bottom boats, able to carry half a company of infantry or twenty-five men, with hinged bows that acted like gangplanks to enable the troops to disembark quickly. He likely had a role in their design.[18]

The Howe brothers were both members of Parliament and both ambivalent about the war in America. In 1766, Admiral Howe had been one of the few members of Parliament who wanted to receive the petition of the Stamp Act Congress in New York. Like Edmund Burke, he believed in the absolute authority of Parliament over America, but he thought it inexpedient to require a formal acknowledgment of supremacy from the colonies. In 1774, William Howe opposed the Coercive Acts aimed at punishing Massachusetts. In a general election of the same year in Britain, he assured his Nottingham constituents that he would refuse an invitation to command British forces in America. Beginning with a meeting on Christmas Day in December 1774, Admiral Howe tried to open negotiations by meeting with Benjamin Franklin in London. His sister, Caroline Howe, told Franklin that she wished that Admiral Howe was going as a peace commissioner to America which she "should like much better than General Howe's going to command the Army." In March 1775, the admiral lamented the strictness of a bill to restrain the trade of New England, but nevertheless voted for it, claiming that it was necessary "as the only moderate means of bringing the disobedient provinces to a sense of their duty, without involving the empire in all the horrors of civil war."[19]

In Britain, the political opponents of the war had some support within the army and navy, where a few officers declined for reasons of conscience to serve in America. They included generals such as Lord Frederick Cavendish, Henry Seymour Conway, Sir George Howard, and Sir John Griffin. According to Horace Walpole, General Conway caused much offense by saying in Parliament that an officer who disapproved of the war ought not to go to America, but some officers followed his advice. Major John Cartwright refused the invitation of Admiral Howe to be one of his naval lieutenants in America, writing that it would be a desertion of his principles. The earl of Effingham resigned his commission when his regiment was ordered to America, thinking it inconsistent with his character and unbecoming of his dignity to enforce policies that he had opposed in Parliament. He wrote to the secretary for war that he was unwilling to deprive fellow subjects of those liberties "which form the best security for their fidelity and obedience to government." He expressed dismay at being obliged to quit the profession of his ancestors, to which he had applied himself since childhood and had intended to dedicate his future. In a speech in the House of Lords in May 1775, Effingham said that the moment had arrived that he most dreaded, when his military profession had become incompatible with his duty as a citizen.[20]

The Howe brothers were typical of the majority of army and navy officers in believing that "it was no part of their military duty to enquire into the justice or policy of the quarrel," once the decision to go to war had been determined by the king and Parliament.[21] When an irate constituent challenged him over breaking his election promise and accepting a command in America, William Howe replied that the private sentiments of every man should give way to public service at a time of crisis. He had actually sought the command from the government, which he justified as a duty but which also reflected his military ambition. In November, Admiral Howe told the House of Commons of his painful struggle between "his duty as an officer, and his duty as a man" in which "if commanded his duty was to serve," but otherwise he would decline. By January 1776, the admiral had become more defensive of the war, arguing that since the designs of the colonial opposition had become fully known, "we had no alternative left but to push our operations by sea and land with vigour, or for ever relinquish our claims, and submit to whatever terms America thought fit to prescribe."[22]

The brothers not only held the military command, but they were also jointly appointed to be peace commissioners. Admiral Howe had insisted upon being named a peace commissioner as a condition of his accepting the naval command in America. He had wanted the peace commission to have wide-ranging powers to grant pardons and to offer concessions as well as to consist solely of himself and his brother. He was opposed by the secretary of state for the American Department, Lord George Germain, who threatened resignation rather than allow such discretionary authority to the Howe brothers and wanted pardons restricted to those who swore oaths of allegiance, with no additional concessions.[23]

Germain blocked Howe's appointment until he had succeeded in limiting the terms of the peace commission to prevent the admiral from granting any significant concessions or acting on his own initiative. However, he did reluctantly agree to allow the two brothers to serve as the sole peace commissioners. In the view of one Cabinet insider, the government was in an invidious position and could not afford to risk alienating the brothers by denying their terms. The Howe brothers therefore had dual roles as military commanders and peace commissioners in America.[24]

II

According to a rifleman on Staten Island, the approach of the British army and navy looked like London afloat. Another eyewitness said he could not believe his eyes: the invasion fleet was like a forest of trimmed pine trees. On a Saturday afternoon on June 29, 1776, New Yorkers watched the approach of an armada of about 9,000 troops, accompanied by 110 ships, with General Howe aboard the frigate *Greyhound,* arriving from Halifax. General Henry Knox of the Continental Army and his wife, Lucy, watched in horror from their breakfast table on the second floor of one of the grandest mansions in Manhattan at No.1 Broadway. The city was instantly in uproar, "the alarm guns firing, troops repairing to their posts, and everything in the height of bustle." Knox wrote to his brother "My God, may I never experience the like feeling again!"[25]

As the invading armada continued to gather, Howe waited in daily anticipation of being joined by his brother and the grand fleet from England. On Monday, July 12, 1776, at about seven o'clock in the evening, there were cries of joy "almost like that of a Victory" upon the arrival of the fleet led by Admiral Howe aboard his flagship, the sixty-four-gun HMS *Eagle*. The fleet made a fine appearance with colors flying, guns saluting, and men. There were nearly 150 ships of varying sizes including 10 large warships, 20 frigates, numerous transport ships, 10,000 seamen, and 11,000 troops. On August 1, another contingent of 2,000 troops and 45 ships, together with Major Generals Henry Clinton and Lord Charles Cornwallis, joined Howe. They were returning from an unsuccessful expedition led by Clinton against Sullivan's Island in Charleston, South Carolina.[26]

The force continued to grow with the arrival of an additional 3,000 British troops and another 8,000 mercenaries from Germany. Packed like herrings on board their ships, the tall men were neither able to stand up between decks, nor sit up straight in their berths. There were six men to each berth—which was intended for only four—with the consequence that the men slept in what was called "spoon fashion": in order to turn in bed, one would call "about face," and they would all turn together. It had required the service of almost the entire British merchant fleet to carry troops to America from different embarkation ports in Canada, Germany, Ireland, and England.[27]

It was the largest British expedition ever sent across the Atlantic. Two-thirds of the total British army and 45 percent of the Royal Navy were serving in America and the Caribbean. There were some four hundred ships of varying sizes in New York. The combined invading force was greater than the estimated 30,000 population of Philadelphia, the largest city in America. A seventy-four-gun ship alone had at least 600 crew members and larger vessels had even more. Howe's army of over 32,000 troops greatly outnumbered the 19,000 troops of Washington. General James Grant wrote on the eve of the campaign: "if a good bleeding can bring those Bible-faced Yankees to their senses— the fever of Independence should soon abate."[28]

Following his withdrawal from Boston, Howe had transformed the army while stationed in Halifax. Together with Burgoyne and Clinton, he believed that inexperience and poor training had undermined its performance at Bunker Hill, and he repeatedly disembarked them for training from the transport ships where they lived in cramped and freezing conditions. Exhibiting the characteristics that had made him such an effective brigade commander, Howe drilled each regiment in light infantry tactics. In order to adapt to the conditions of warfare in America, he introduced looser infantry formations with wider gaps between each man and only two lines deep rather than the conventional three used in Europe, allowing for greater mobility across broken ground. His two-line loose formations later became the standard practice of the British army. Howe permitted changes in uniforms to make them better adapted to local conditions, with shorter jackets, fewer frills, and smaller caps. He favored and promoted officers familiar with light infantry training throughout the army.[29]

General Howe's object was the conquest of New York, which had major strategic advantages. John Adams described it as "a kind of key to the whole continent," and in the opinion of Lord George Germain, "as long as you maintained New York the continent was divided." New York was a major port and potential naval base, and its possession depended upon sea power which played to the strength of the British. Owing to its situation at the mouth of the Hudson River, its conquest opened up possibilities for penetrating the interior along the Hudson north to Lake Champlain and Canada, creating the potential to cut off New England. Furthermore, the city and the region of the lower Hudson were thought to be centers of loyalist support for the British. Manhattan Island was still largely farmland and forests, with a rough and craggy terrain that survives in areas like Central Park. The center of population was on the southern tip of the island in the region of Wall Street and lower Broadway.[30]

On Thursday, August 22, 1776, after a night of terrible thunder and lightning, the Howe brothers launched an amphibious attack on Long Island. At 8:00 A.M., Generals Clinton and Cornwallis led the advanced guard of 4,000 elite light infantry troops to occupy the southwest of Long Island. In two and a half hours, Howe landed 15,000 men and 40 pieces of cannon near the town of Utrecht. He subsequently increased their number to 20,000. Believing that Howe would first attack Manhattan, Washington had stationed only 9,000 troops on Long Island, where they were positioned along the Guana (Gowanus) Heights and the Brooklyn Heights.[31]

Five days after the landing, Howe outwitted and defeated Washington at the battle of Long Island (also known as the battle of Brooklyn or the battle of Brooklyn Heights). In a seeming repetition of his tactics at Bunker Hill, Howe played to the expectations of his opponents by opening with a frontal assault by his Hessians. It was a feint suggested to him by Henry Clinton. Leaving his tents standing and camp fires burning at about 9:00 P.M., Clinton led the main army nine miles around the rear of the

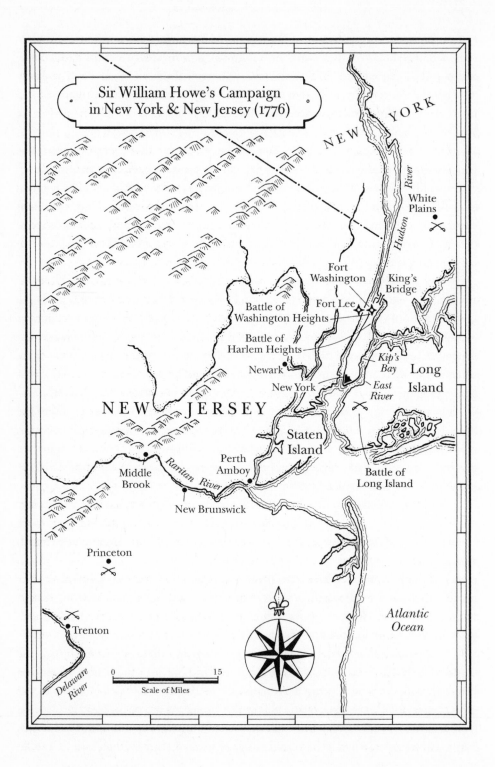

Sir William Howe's Campaign
in New York & New Jersey (1776)

NEW YORK

Hudson River

White Plains

Fort Washington

King's Bridge

Battle of Washington Heights

Fort Lee

Battle of Harlem Heights

Newark

Kip's Bay

Long Island

New York

East River

NEW JERSEY

Staten Island

Middle Brook

Raritan River

Perth Amboy

New Brunswick

Battle of Long Island

Princeton

Atlantic Ocean

Trenton

Delaware River

0   15

Scale of Miles

enemy, via a virtually unknown and unprotected route, suggested to him by a local loyalist, known as the Jamaica Pass. The result was a rout in which the British took three generals, and inflicted losses of between 700 and 1,000 enemy troops. As Howe prepared to begin an elaborate siege of the remaining enemy position on Brooklyn Heights, Washington and his men made a remarkable nighttime escape across the East River to Manhattan, availing themselves of the cover of darkness and morning fog.

Following the great victory at Long Island, the British were delirious with expectations of imminent success and the end of the war. Cornwallis predicted that "in a short time their army will disperse and the war will be over." General Hugh, Lord Percy, wrote to his father that the campaign would put a total end to the war, and wrote to Lord George Germain that "this business is pretty near over." The success similarly aroused high expectations among government circles in Britain. George III conferred the coveted Order of the Bath on William Howe, who was thereafter known as Sir William Howe.[32]

With the battle for the control of Long Island over, Howe began the battle for control of Manhattan. On September 15, 1776, he began with an attack upon Kip's Bay, a small cove which is now landfilled at the end of East 34th Street. It was undefended by enemy artillery, there was open meadow that precluded the enemy from concealing themselves, and it was close to the Post Road which was one of the major arteries from lower Broadway to what is today the upper East Side. The attack began with a suitably dramatic opening salvo when five naval ships bombarded the shores from a distance of less than two hundred yards. With 4,000 British and Hessian troops, Clinton led the first invasion party in an uncontested landing, which precipitated a general panic and retreat among the defending militia, to the visible ire of George Washington. Entire rebel companies disbanded and returned home. The original contingent of 13,000 Connecticut militia dwindled to 2,000. Between 1775 and August 1776, some 18,000 civilians had evacuated New York City in anticipation of the arrival of the British, and the population fell to 5,000. By the late afternoon of September 15, the invaders had occupied lower Manhattan. At Old Fort George, a woman hauled down and trampled the Union Flag of the Continental Army and raised the Union Jack.[33]

By late September, however, Howe was already having misgivings about the possibility of ending the war in a single campaign. Washington had occupied strong defenses at Harlem Heights, the high ground in Manhattan between the Harlem and Hudson rivers around modern 125th Street. Believing that the enemy was "too strongly posted to be attacked in front," Howe chose to try to encircle Harlem Heights by landing troops above the northern tip of Manhattan Island in Westchester County. His move forced Washington to abandon his defenses and retreat eighteen miles north across the Harlem River to White Plains. On October 26, 1776, the two armies faced off against one another at the battle of White Plains. Howe's main offensive had to be postponed owing to a violent rainfall that made the ground so slippery that he deemed it too risky to march uphill. Nevertheless, his earlier flanking movement forced Washington to retreat, leaving behind two exposed rebel fortresses—Fort Washington and Fort Lee on either side of the present day George Washington Bridge—which secured communications between Manhattan and New Jersey. On November 16, Howe's German mercenaries stormed Fort Washington and took some 2,837 prisoners, including 230 officers. On November 29, in an effort to cut off Washington's retreat to Hackensack, Cornwallis captured Fort Lee along the Jersey shore of the Hudson River. The British had gained possession of Manhattan, which became their headquarters and main base in America for the duration of the Revolutionary War.[34]

With the capture of Manhattan, Howe sent Cornwallis in pursuit of Washington into New Jersey as far as New Brunswick, only sixty miles north of Philadelphia. Washington's army numbered only about thirty-five hundred, from a peak of twenty thousand in August. On December 1, 1776, Cornwallis just missed intercepting Washington crossing the Raritan River at Brunswick. Howe proceeded to set up an eighty-mile-long chain of garrisons in East Jersey for the purpose of provisioning his army in New York during the winter. With a view to ending the war by a final blow against New England, he sent Clinton to capture Newport, Rhode Island, which surrendered without resistance on December 8. It was the best bay on the east coast for anchoring the fleet, and ideally located for attacks upon New England. In another major coup, the British caught General Charles Lee, a former British army officer and one of the most senior generals in the Continental Army. His captors made his horse drunk in their undisguised pleasure. They included men whom Lee had once commanded as a British officer in Portugal under John Burgoyne.

It was the lowest ebb of the revolutionary cause. Serving in Washington's army, Thomas Paine began the first of his series of rebel propaganda tracts entitled *The American Crisis,* with the words, "These are the times that try men's souls." Since July, Howe's army had taken 4,500 prisoners including four generals, 235 iron cannon, 24,000 shells, 17,000 cannonballs, and some 2,800 muskets. He had won four major battles, at Long Island, Kip's Bay, White Plains, and Fort Washington. The Continental Congress fled from Philadelphia to Baltimore. Washington wrote that "our affairs are in a very bad way . . . the game is pretty near up—owing in a great measure to the insidious arts of the enemy."[35]

III

Despite their spectacular successes, the Howe brothers are generally regarded as having missed the best opportunity of winning the American Revolutionary War. General Sir William Howe seemingly failed to follow up victories to trap Washington and the Continental Army. After the battle of Long Island, he had not pursued the remnants of

Washington's army or prevented its escape to Manhattan. After the skirmish at Harlem Heights, Howe's army had waited more than a month before his next move, while making no effort to trap Washington in Manhattan by cutting off his escape route across the Hudson. At White Plains, Howe waited three days, enabling Washington to move his supplies to the safety of New Jersey, and then failed to pursue Washington. By instructing Cornwallis not to go beyond New Brunswick Howe may have missed one of his best opportunities to ensnare Washington. In 1777, known ominously as the Year of the Hangman, because the three sevens looked like three gallows, he lost time by not opening the campaign until June.

Howe's lethargy was attributed by critics to his hedonistic lifestyle. Howe's wife, Frances, the daughter of the Right Hon. William Conolly, of Castletown in County Kildare, had remained in England. During the siege of Boston, Howe began an affair with Elizabeth Lloyd Loring, whom he publicly accompanied on social occasions and who became known among his officers as "the Sultana." She was the wife of an American loyalist, Joshua Loring, whom Howe promoted to be commissary for prisoners, in which role he was detested for his alleged mistreatment of the men in his charge. Following the delay in opening the campaign, the relationship was mocked in popular verse:

> Sir William, he, snug as a flea,
> Lay all this time a-snoring;
> Nor dreamed of harm, as he lay warm
> In bed with Mrs. Loring.

Another ditty was written by a loyalist:

> Awake, arouse, Sir Billy,
> There's forage in the plain,
> Leave your little filly,
> And open the campaign.

The *London Evening Post* suggested that Elizabeth Loring had been purchased from her husband in return for a contract, and that the country had to "Pay the Piper for the Pimping." Howe shared with her a taste for drinking and gambling. He was very different from his abstemious brother, but such indulgence was probably more a consequence than a cause of delays in the movement of the army.[36]

General Howe's extreme caution was more explicable in terms of the strategic ideas that he shared with his brother. In their joint capacity as commanders and peace commissioners, the brothers aimed to win by a combination of military pressure and offers of conciliation. They had a sophisticated approach that indicated an appreciation of the political and psychological elements of warfare. Since they were attempting to suppress a rebellion among fellow subjects rather than fight a foreign war, they were wary of using destructive methods that might alienate the majority of the population. They favored a more humane approach in order to both win the support of the people and create the conditions necessary for a harmonious postwar reconstruction of civil government. They anticipated that the combination of overwhelming force and conciliatory gestures would be sufficient to persuade the rebels of the futility of resistance. Although he had originally intended to win by a decisive battle, General Howe shifted his tactics with an emphasis upon maneuver rather than trying to trap Washington in Manhattan, a change that fatally lost him the best chance to win the war. Similarly, Admiral Howe never seriously attempted to attack and burn ports along the coast because he believed it would make reconciliation more difficult and force people to fight by starving them. Captain Johann von Ewald, a *Jaeger* (light infantryman) in the Hessian army, was mystified by the restraint of General Howe until he "perceived what was afoot. We wanted to spare the King's subjects and hoped to terminate the war amicably, in which assumption I was strengthened the next day by several English officers."[37]

Before leaving Britain, General Howe had explained his view of the situation in America. He contended that the insurgents were in a minority, and believed that the opponents of imperial revenue duties would return to obedience in return for a redress of their complaints. He further claimed that the few who sought independence would relent once they discovered that "they were not well supported in their frantic ideas by the more moderate." After his landing at Staten Island in July 1776, General Howe wrote that he had great reason to expect a large body of inhabitants to join the army from New York, New Jersey, and Connecticut. He believed that they were only waiting for the right opportunity "to give Proof of their Loyalty and Zeal for Government." Serving in the commissariat department, Charles Stedman later suggested that Howe had been hoping that his victory at Long Island "would produce a revolution in sentiment capable of terminating the war without the extremity which it appeared to be, beyond all possibility of doubt, in his power to enforce."[38]

It was indeed an axiom of British policy that the majority of Americans were loyal, and that the revolution was nothing more than a coup achieved by "the intrigues of a few bold and criminal leaders." It was not a spontaneous popular movement, but rather a "contagion," in which the "flames of sedition" were started and spread by an "armed faction," a few firebrands, "a rascally banditti," or "a set of puritannick ingrates," who had usurped legal authority in an experiment that was likely to end in anarchy and oppression. In Britain, the advocates of war saw themselves as liberators of a "deluded and unhappy multitude" against "the arbitrary tyranny of their leaders" and their "tyrannical Congress, Committees, Conventions." They were rescuing "a vast number of our fellow subjects in America from the despotism not to be exceeded in the history of mankind." It was a view that seemed reasonable given the tactics of intimidation used by local committees of safety to purge the loyalists by various means ranging from tarring and feathering and confiscating property to arrest and execution. It was a view promoted and reinforced by former colonial officials and by American loyalist exiles in Britain.[39]

Admiral Howe was especially idealistic about the possibilities of a negotiated settlement. On arrival in New York, he issued a proclamation announcing his powers as peace commissioner to grant pardons and to declare peace. The troop transports that accompanied him tellingly had names like *Good Intent, Friendship, Amity's Admonition,* and *Father's Good Will.* General Howe warned his older brother that the declaration of the peace commission was likely to be ineffectual, but the admiral was adamant about showing "the people of America that the Door was yet open for Reconciliation." Upon arrival in America, Admiral Howe immediately attempted to open negotiations by sending an officer with a flag of truce across the bay to Manhattan with a letter for "Mr. Washington." The officer returned with a reply that there was no such person other than General Washington. Admiral Howe tried again with a letter addressed to "George Washington, Esq., etc. etc." It was again declined. Finally, the admiral succeeded in setting up a meeting between his adjutant general and Washington at No. 1 Broadway. It accomplished nothing because it failed to recognize the changed situation in America following the Declaration of Independence on July 4, 1776. The contest was no longer about redressing grievances. It was a struggle for independence.[40]

On September 11, 1776, Admiral Howe convened a peace conference at Staten Island while his brother prepared the invasion of Manhattan. The admiral met with a delegation from the Continental Congress consisting of John Adams of Massachusetts, Benjamin Franklin of Pennsylvania, and Edward Rutledge of South Carolina. He omitted mention of some of the more awkward preconditions of peace that had been stipulated by the home government. The terms were still so unattractive that they were actually published by the Continental Congress. When Howe explained that he could only negotiate with them as "private gentlemen of influence," John Adams replied that he might "consider me in what light you please . . . except a British subject," causing Howe to observe to Franklin and Rutledge that "Mr. Adams is a decided character." In the words of Howe's private secretary, Ambrose Serle, "they met, they talked, they parted." It was the only official meeting between representatives of the two governments until the end of the war.[41]

After their successful landing on Manhattan, the Howe brothers tried again with a direct appeal to the people. On September 19, 1776, they issued a joint declaration that announced that the king was willing to revise royal instructions and parliamentary legislation relating to America. In London, the government was caught unaware when confronted by the opposition parties with news of the declaration. Lord North referred questions about its authenticity to Lord George Germain. It was greeted with ridicule on all sides. The brothers still persisted. On November 30, 1776, as the Continental Army was withdrawing through New Jersey, they issued another proclamation that offered to pardon anyone who swore an oath of allegiance within sixty days. It embarrassed the government. In the House of Commons, General Henry Seymour Conway was critical of what he called a mixed system of war and conciliation. He argued that the objectives of the campaign "should be clear, simple and decided, not involved in doubt, perplexity, and darkness." The contradictions in the objectives of the two brothers mirrored the divisions within the government about the conduct of the war.[42]

The peace overtures were not sufficient in themselves to explain the failure of Howe to act with greater vigor against Washington. Even before his arrival in New York, General Howe was more skeptical than his brother about the possibilities of negotiation, writing that there was not the least prospect of conciliating the continent until the rebel armies had been "roughly dealt with." With remarkable prescience and shrewdness, he confessed that he was doubtful of an outright victory when the enemy was unlikely to engage on equal terms in open battle and when his opponents had the advantage of "having the whole country." The enemy army would instead retreat a few miles beyond the navigable rivers "where ours cannot follow them." Although he appreciated that there were many inhabitants who were "well affected" to Britain, he doubted that they would assist "until his Majesty's arms have a clear superiority by a decisive victory." He attempted numerous times to win decisively. If his objective seemed to vacillate between seeking out the enemy army and occupying territory, it was because he was unable to draw out Washington.[43]

Howe was cautious because he could not afford to sustain heavy casualties in America. As he told a parliamentary committee of inquiry in 1779, he thought it his duty "not wantonly to commit his majesty's troops, where the object was inadequate." "Light Horse" Henry Lee retrospectively claimed that Howe lost his nerve after witnessing the battle of Bunker Hill. It was common to have the casualty rates in eighteenth-century battles of about a third of the troops. In response to criticism of his failure to pursue the enemy aggressively after the battle of Long Island, Howe insisted that if he had continued to fight, "the only advantage we should have gained would have been the destruction of a few more men," at a cost of perhaps a thousand or fifteen hundred of his own men, which "would have been but ill repaid by double that number of the enemy." He could not have destroyed Washington's army, which was mostly in Manhattan. At White Plains, Howe was more eager to engage than his generals, but he denied that he could have cut off Washington's retreat into New Jersey. Howe had given Cornwallis orders not to pursue Washington further than New Brunswick because his detachment might have become dangerously exposed owing to the proximity of another rebel army commanded by General Charles Lee. The troops were in any case exhausted by the pursuit.[44]

IV

It was when Howe was bold that he suffered his greatest setbacks. While still giddy with the success of the landing at Kip's Bay in Manhattan, elite British light infantry troops pursued and taunted retreating enemy rangers by sounding the "View halloo!" (which signified that the fox is in sight and on the run). The provocation incensed Washington's adjutant general, for whom "it seemed to crown our disgrace." The encounter occurred in the area of the current location of Columbia University on the upper West Side. The British troops included the kilted Scottish Royal Highland Regiment, otherwise known as the Black Watch, which had fought in America during the French and Indian War. The most intense fighting occurred at about noon in a buckwheat field around present West 120th Street between Broadway and Riverside Drive. Instead of a repetition of the rebel flight at Kip's Bay, the British not only met determined resistance, but suffered the humiliation of having to turn their backs in retreat when they were nearly cut off, although they eventually recovered and put the enemy to flight. After what he called a "pretty sharp skirmish" that became known as the battle of Harlem Heights (September 16, 1776), Washington appreciated that "this little advantage has inspired our troops prodigiously . . . they finding that it only requires resolution and good officers to make an enemy (that they stood in too much dread of) give way." Howe waited a month before making another advance, using the intervening time to gather intelligence and to consolidate his position in Manhattan.[45]

Howe discovered the perils of an ambitious strategy even more dramatically when he entered New Jersey. Buoyed by the capture of Manhattan and Long Island, he saw an opportunity to occupy a large area of territory and to provision the army. With the encouragement of Lord Cornwallis, Howe spread his army in a chain of garrison posts, known as cantonments, across the breadth of New Jersey, between Perth Amboy and the Delaware River. Clinton advised against the strategy on the grounds that the enemy had already shown skill in attacking isolated posts. In a letter to Germain on December 20, 1776, Howe admitted that his posts had been "rather too extensive" when his army entered winter quarters in New Jersey. He had every reason to be relatively confident, however. He had advanced 170 miles in two months, and the enemy army was shrinking since it was largely composed of citizen militiamen whose enlistments were due to expire before the end of the month.[46]

In what became one of the iconic moments of the Revolutionary War, George Washington returned with his army across the Delaware River. Howe was a victim of his own success. He had driven his opponent into making a desperate bid. With some troops marching shoeless through the snow, Washington and his ill-equipped and ill-fed men defied a major storm, floating ice, and swift currents in the river. In a stunning counteroffensive that lasted less than two weeks, Washington surprised and captured the garrison of German Hessian troops at Trenton on December 26, 1776, and forced Howe to retreat from all his posts in New Jersey, except a small area around the River Raritan.

It is likely a myth that the fourteen hundred Hessians at Trenton were asleep or drunk after celebrating Christmas. Following constant alarms occasioned by enemy militia, the garrison had been on duty throughout Christmas Day. They were commanded by fifty-six-year-old Colonel Johann Rall, who had led the successful assault on Fort Washington and won the esteem of Howe. Rall was so nervous about an attack that he set up outposts beyond the town and insisted that one company of troops sleep with their muskets ready. Complaining that his garrison had not slept owing to constant raids, he sent dispatch riders with an escort of a hundred men and two guns to impress his difficulties upon the senior commanding officer, General James Grant, and appealed for British troops to be stationed nearer him at Maidenhead. However, contemptuous of the rebels, he neglected to build redoubts or fortifications for his artillery. "Incessantly intoxicated with strong liquors," Colonel Rall may have been drunk the previous evening. In any case, he failed to open a letter warning him of an imminent attack. He was to be killed in a short battle of less than an hour in which Washington's force killed or captured nine hundred men with the loss of only one officer and a private. Although Howe blamed Rall for the disaster at Trenton, Lord George Germain later commented that Howe should never have posted such a small force so close to the main enemy army.[47]

Determined to regain support and restore the morale of the Revolution, Washington crossed the Delaware again in late December and circumvented a force of 7,000 men led by Lord Cornwallis to inflict another blow against a rear garrison of the British army at Princeton (January 3, 1777). During this raid of great daring and stealth, Washington shouted "It's a fine fox chase, boys!"—a clear allusion to the hunting metaphor earlier used by the British. He estimated that he captured or killed 500 to 600 men against the losses listed by Howe at 276. Suffering casualties of thirty soldiers and fourteen officers, he destroyed the British 4th Brigade guard at Princeton.[48]

It was because of his expectation of widespread loyalist support that General Howe had dispersed his garrisons so widely in New Jersey. He originally intended not to post his forces beyond New Brunswick and Newark, but was encouraged to expand further when almost five thousand Americans swore oaths of allegiance, including one of the fifty-six signers of the Declaration of Independence, Richard Stockton. In occupying Trenton, General Howe had hoped to incorporate what he believed to be strongly loyalist country to the east of Princeton in the county of Monmouth. The belief was increasingly contradicted by experience. In December 1776, Admiral Howe told his secretary that "all the People of Parts & Spirit were in the Rebellion." In the spring of 1777, Colonel William Harcourt, the commander of the 16th Light Dragoons, wrote home from New Brunswick, "You may be assured that we are almost without a friend (I mean from principle) on this side of the Atlantic . . ." In July, Major General James Grant, who had once boasted that he could subdue the entire country with five thousand troops, admitted that "we have no friends." During the parliamentary inquiry into his conduct in 1779, Howe defended himself by saying that he "found the Americans not so well disposed to join us, and to serve us" as he had been "taught to expect." Howe had equally underestimated his enemy and the chances of a counterattack.[49]

Far from finding latent support in New Jersey, the British occupation was subject to continued resistance in small-scale partisan warfare known as *petite guerre*. As Cornwallis was to discover in his later conquest of South Carolina, the British army was plagued by constant raids and ambushes by local militia and citizen bands. Howe's communications were frequently cut off between Amboy and New Brunswick. Throughout the campaign, Howe had difficulty obtaining intelligence from the inhabitants about the local terrain. Since it was mostly "wood, creeks and swamps," he had to move cautiously and was unable to rely on accounts from "inhabitants entirely ignorant of military description." His army suffered some of its worst setbacks when mounting foraging parties, in which they were opposed by rebel groups as large as seven hundred to a thousand men. Sir James Murray, a young Scottish officer, described one such encounter in which an officer and sixty men were killed. By the end of the winter of 1776–77, Howe had lost half his army. More troops were killed in minor forays than in battles.[50]

Howe was also impeded from pursuing a bolder strategy against Washington by the difficulties of obtaining supplies, transport, and food, a logistical problem that vexed him at every turn and continued to plague the army throughout the war. It was because of the shortage of shipping and supplies that Howe had delayed his withdrawal from Boston in 1775 and his departure from Halifax to begin the campaign in New York in 1776. The shortage of food restricted his strategic choices when he had to capture territory in order to sustain and feed his army, since he otherwise had to import his supplies and food from Britain. It was a factor in his decision to secure New York before attempting to defeat Washington's army, and in his "much criticized" decision to take Rhode Island in 1776. The need for forage and food was also a motive for invading New Jersey. The demand for food increased with the arrival of loyalist refugees in New York and the destruction caused by a mysterious fire there in September 1776. The need for food was the primary reason for mounting foraging parties that resulted in such heavy casualties during the harsh winter in New Jersey. Similarly, the shortage of boats was a problem that Cornwallis claimed prevented him from crossing the Delaware River in pursuit of Washington.[51]

Even before the war escalated into a global conflict with France and Spain, British resources were overstretched in America. Admiral Howe had insufficient ships to both support the army and mount a naval blockade. In 1776, even if he had wished to enforce a blockade, he had only fifteen spare ships to cruise the Atlantic coast. Furthermore, it was often impractical for warships to negotiate the coastal creeks and tide harbors. Although Howe attempted to improve the dockyard facilities in New York, he had to send ships to be refitted at English Harbour in Antigua, or Port Royal in Jamaica, or one of the dockyards in England. Without an effective blockade the enemy was able to import vital military supplies for the Continental Army and launch privateers with a devastating impact on British trade. Although his squadron retook 26 British ships and captured 140 enemy ships, Admiral Howe was never able to keep more than about 30 warships blockading the East Coast.[52]

Britain had jeopardized its own security and that of its empire in order to mount the offensive in America in 1776. It reduced garrisons in England, Scotland, Ireland, and the West Indies. Hanoverian and German mercenaries replaced British troops to garrison Minorca and Gibraltar. At the beginning of the war, approximately 12,500 British troops garrisoned Ireland (the equivalent of almost a third of the British army), Dublin contained one of the largest systems of barracks in Europe, and the Irish Parliament was required to fund the cost of 15,000 troops. Unlike England, Ireland was predominantly Gaelic speaking and Catholic (with a ratio of at least three Catholics to every Protestant). Although German mercenaries replaced some of the British troops sent to America, the garrison fell to a quarter of its prewar level, raising fears of potential insurrection. In March 1776, nine ships of the Continental Navy and 100 Continental marines successfully attacked Nassau in the Bahamas island of New Providence, and occupied the town and fortress for two weeks. The marines removed military stores including gunpowder, and took the governor prisoner to New England. It was the first amphibious landing of the rebel navy and the first engagement of what later became the United States Marine Corps.[53]

The redeployment of troops to America was a cause of a Jamaican slave rebellion in the summer of 1776. The island had a slave population that outnumbered whites by twelve to one, and the revolt began when one of the two regiments garrisoning the island was about to embark for New York to reinforce General Howe. The slave leaders were aware that there were fewer troops on the island "than at any other time in their memory," and that the local naval force was about to convoy a homeward-bound merchant fleet. They knew that "the English were engaged in a desperate war, which would require all their forces elsewhere [so that] . . . they could not have a better opportunity of seizing the country to themselves." An inquiry by the island assembly concluded unanimously that the slaves had "placed their strongest hopes" on the withdrawal of the troops, which was the primary cause of the conspiracy. In the meantime, the valuable merchant convoy was delayed, enabling rebel privateers to equip and prepare. It was eventually separated from its naval escort by bad weather, leading to losses to enemy privateers valued at over a million pounds sterling.[54]

In his election bid of 1774, General Howe had told his constituents that it was beyond the power of the entire British army to conquer America. In Boston in July 1775,

General Hugh, Earl Percy, complained that the army was "so small that we cannot even afford a victory, if it is attended with any loss of men." In a speech in the House of Commons in November 1776, General Henry Seymour Conway said that the military force "was totally inadequate to the purposes of absolute coercion" in America. Edmund Burke observed that none of the members with military experience were willing to vouch for the sufficiency of the military force. Secretary at War Lord William Barrington warned that the Americans "may be reduced by the fleet, but never can be by the army." The army was not adequate to simultaneously fighting a war while garrisoning Britain, Ireland, Jersey, the Caribbean, Minorca, Gibraltar, and India.[55]

V

The lack of supplies and troops caused General Howe to revise his original campaign plan for 1777 and thereby contributed to the disastrous sequence of events that led to the defeat of General Burgoyne at Saratoga. In a letter to Lord George Germain of November 30, 1776, Howe outlined an ambitious strategy for the conquest of New England. It included an army of 10,000 marching to Albany to meet another British army from Canada that was to be commanded by General John Burgoyne. However, it required 15,000 additional troops to provide a total of 35,000 troops in opposition to the anticipated 50,000 troops voted by the Continental Congress. After suffering the setbacks at Trenton and Princeton, Howe submitted another more modest proposal that made no mention of sending his army north to meet Burgoyne's army at Albany.[56]

On January 20, 1777, Howe radically revised his plan with a new objective of capturing Philadelphia, which he thought an easier target than New England. He expected less opposition because he still believed that the loyalists were predominant in Pennsylvania. Although he was ultimately proved wrong, it was a justifiable view. There were significant pockets of loyalist support in Philadelphia and in the neighboring counties of Bucks and Chester. Thomas Paine complained of the numbers of people in Pennsylvania "who are changing to whig and tory with the circumstances of every day." It was easy to exaggerate the extent of loyalist support because of the pacifist stance of the Quakers and the neutrality of many German sects like the Mennonites, Amish, and Dunkers. Moreover, Howe regarded Philadelphia as the capital of the American Revolution. It was the location of the Continental Congress and the largest city in British North America. Having never given up his desire to crush the Continental Army, Howe anticipated that Washington would "risk a battle to protect that Capital." In a later testimony, Howe said that it had always been his opinion that "the defeat of the rebel regular army" was the surest road to victory.[57]

Howe was deterred before the campaign even started because his plan for victory required a larger army. He was expected to win with fewer troops than he had commanded during the conquest of New York and an army that was small by the standards of warfare in Europe. He ultimately received 2,900 reinforcements, a fifth of the number that he originally requested and half what he thought necessary just to attack Philadelphia. His relations with Lord George Germain began to sour. He was angered that Germain included the sick and wounded when calculating the number of troops available for offensive operations in America. He resented Germain's assurances that the shortage of troops would be compensated by "the weakness of the enemy, and the good inclination of the inhabitants." Howe interpreted the failure of the home government to send more troops as evidence that his own opinion no longer carried weight and that he did not have the confidence of the ministers. Indeed, Germain became sarcastic in his letters to Howe, and his dissatisfaction was reflected in progovernment newspapers in Britain. In June and July, the *Morning Post* published articles critical of the tardiness of the brothers in sending reports, and sought their recall.[58]

In his defense of the campaign before the House of Commons in 1779, Howe ridiculed the expectation that he could have made major new conquests with a force that was sufficient only for the seizure and occupation of New York. In an argument encapsulating the British problem in America, he asserted that it was self-evident that "the power of an army must diminish in proportion to the decrease of their numbers" and that their numbers in the field must necessarily decrease "in proportion to the towns, posts, or forts, which we take, and are obliged to preserve." The shortage of troops was mirrored by the inadequate size of the fleet, for in order to support the operations of the army, Admiral Howe virtually suspended the blockade of the coast of America. Sir William Howe had begun the campaign with an army "14,000 short of the number I had expected." He had an army of conquest, but insufficient troops for the large-scale occupation necessary for the recovery of America.[59]

Because of the shortage of troops and the threat posed by the enemy to his communications, Howe again changed his campaign plan with the decision to go by sea to Philadelphia rather than take the shorter route by land from New York. This further delayed the start of his campaign. In a letter to Germain on April 2, containing his proposal to "invade Pensilvania by Sea," Howe wrote that "restricted as I am from entering upon more extensive Operations by want of force, my Hopes of terminating the War this year are vanished." He thought it possible that by the end of the year, he might be in possession of New York, the Jerseys, and Pennsylvania, "tho' this in some Measure must depend upon the successes of the Northern Army" commanded by General John Burgoyne. Before getting under sail on July 7, he warned Germain that "I do not suppose" the planned junction of the two armies at Albany "can happen this Campaign." He added that "a Corps of 10,000 effective fighting Men I think would ensure the Success of the War to Great Britain in another Campaign."[60]

Owing to the late arrival of the convoys of stores and camp equipment from

Britain, Howe felt unable to open the campaign until June 7. Never wavering in his belief that the surest means of winning the war was the destruction of Washington's army, Howe lost another six weeks in attempting to lure Washington from his encampment at Middle Brook, on the hills above the Raritan in New Jersey. Even after he had begun to embark his troops for Philadelphia, he pulled them back and crossed the river when he thought he had another chance to trap Washington. The futility of such cat-and-mouse games left him little alternative but to conquer territory and to build up loyalist support.[61]

On July 23, the Howe brothers finally launched the expedition to Philadelphia with a combined armada of 13,000 troops and 225 ships. Owing to General Howe's disdain for the German mercenaries, only 4,441 of his troops were Hessians. He left the remainder with Clinton in New York who had a total of 9,000 troops. According to an official report of rations, Howe's army was accompanied by 652 women and children. The women were wives, common-law partners, and camp followers who acted as nurses, seamstresses, launderers, cooks, and vendors.

In the meantime, General John Burgoyne was marching south from Canada with the object of meeting Howe's army at Albany. Howe had delayed his departure from New York until he was confident that Burgoyne's expedition was well under way.[62]

Upon arrival at the mouth of the Delaware River on July 30, Howe lost more valuable time by his decision not to land his army there, but to proceed via Chesapeake Bay to the Head of Elk (near modern Elkton in Maryland), fifty-five miles south of Philadelphia. The change added another month to his journey during which the troops suffered cramped conditions aboard ship at the height of summer. In England, the *St. James's Chronicle* published a satirical article alleging that the government had made unsuccessful inquiries in search of Howe's whereabouts in Knightsbridge, on the Serpentine River, and at the Lost and Found Office in Holborn. Howe's decision not to land at the Delaware was due to naval intelligence about the proximity of Washington's army and the hazards of landing in marshy terrain along that river. It was also motivated by his intention to cut Washington off from the military depots in York and Carlisle, Pennsylvania. He anticipated no opposition in Maryland and southern Pennsylvania. However, the delays to the expedition precluded any chance of Howe marching north to Albany to join Burgoyne's army from Canada. After arriving at the Head of Elk on August 30, Howe again warned Germain that he would be unable to fulfill his orders to complete the recovery of Pennsylvania "in time for me to co-operate with the Northern Army."[63]

Howe enjoyed considerable success in meeting his objectives for the campaign of 1777. As he had anticipated, his march north was opposed by Washington who attempted to prevent the British army from crossing the sharp banks of the Brandywine Creek. It was an excellent defensive position for the enemy army with hills and forests along a deep valley. Varying in width between 50 and 150 yards, the creek could only be forded in seven places, of which the most accessible was Chadd's Ford on the main route from Kennett

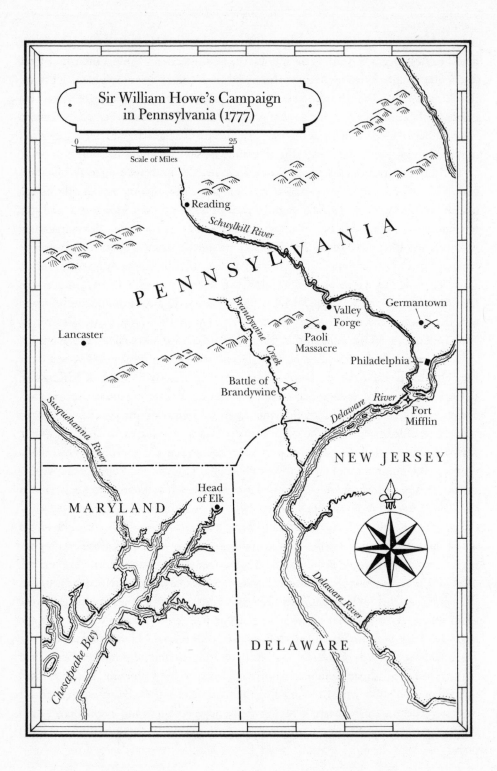

Sir William Howe's Campaign
in Pennsylvania (1777)

0   25
Scale of Miles

Reading

Schuylkill River

PENNSYLVANIA

Brandywine Creek

Valley
Forge

Germantown

Lancaster

Paoli
Massacre

Philadelphia

Battle of
Brandywine

Delaware River

Fort
Mifflin

Susquehanna River

NEW JERSEY

Head
of Elk

MARYLAND

Delaware River

Chesapeake Bay

DELAWARE

square to Philadelphia. At the battle of Brandywine on September 11, Howe repeated the strategy that had served him so well at Long Island, by deceiving the enemy into expecting a frontal assault by troops commanded by General Wilhelm von Knyphausen. Beginning in darkness at about two o'clock in the morning, Cornwallis with 7,500 men marched twelve miles across the forks of the Brandywine in order to turn the enemy's right at Chadd's Ford. As Cornwallis engaged the enemy rear at about 4.30 P.M., Knyphausen simultaneously launched a frontal attack. After two and a half hours of what General Henry Knox called "the most severe action that has been fought in this war," Washington was forced into retreat across the Schuylkill River with 300 of his men killed, around 600 wounded, and another 400 taken prisoner, against 90 British dead and 488 wounded. In the early hours of September 19, a messenger arrived in Philadelphia to warn of the rapid approach of Howe's army. The Continental Congress adjourned the next day and moved to Lancaster, Pennsylvania, and about a quarter of the population left the city in advance of the arrival of the British. Writing in his journal after the battle, Captain von Ewald reflected that "one will perceive that General Howe is not a middling man but indeed a good general."[64]

Howe yet again displayed the talents of an able tactician. Washington still attempted to obstruct his advance on Philadelphia, by leaving a division commanded by "Mad" Anthony Wayne on the south side of the Schuylkill River. General Charles Grey earned the sobriquet "No Flint" Grey when he ordered his troops to remove the flint from their rifles and to use only their bayonets in a surprise nighttime attack on September 21, in which they surrounded Wayne's camp two miles south of the Paoli Tavern. In what became known as the "Paoli Massacre," some three hundred Americans were killed compared to eighteen British losses. Howe then successfully deceived Washington by moving his army upriver away from Philadelphia in a feint to give the impression that he was about to attack the rebel arsenal at Reading and outflank the Continental Army.

At about ten o'clock on the morning of September 26, Lord Cornwallis at the head of both English grenadier battalions as well as Hessian grenadiers, along with a part of the artillery, marched in triumph into Philadelphia, with the bands playing martial music. As the army entered from Germantown along Second Street, the inhabitants thronged along the streets to see them and seemed "to rejoice on the occasion, tho' by all accounts many of them were publickly on the other side before our arrival." According to Captain John Montresor, the troops received the "acclamations of some thousands of inhabitants, mostly women and children." As the rear of the army with the light dragoons passed, the band played "God Save the King." Although frightened by the somber demeanor and moustaches of the Hessians, a boy of ten marveled at their fine martial appearance, their friendly attitude, and their hearty handclasps. Another observer was appalled by the motley camp followers of animals, goats, asses, wagons, horses, and women.

In her house on the south side of Chestnut, Deborah Logan observed "what we thought the haughty looks of Lord Rawdon and the other aide-de-camp" of Lord Cornwallis.[65]

Washington narrowly failed to inflict a counterblow against the British in Pennsylvania similar to his victories at Trenton and Princeton. At 3:00 A.M. on October 4, his army of 8,000 regulars and 4,000 militia made contact with patrols of the 9,000-strong British outpost at Germantown. Howe had not fortified the town, trusting that the enemy would not have "dared to approach after so recent a defeat as that of Brandywine." In any case he was distracted with clearing the Delaware River in order to supply Philadelphia. When he received news of the attack, he said "That cannot be!" During the two-and-a-half-hour battle at Germantown, he witnessed the line of his troops being driven back, causing him to furiously exclaim, "For shame, Light Infantry, I never saw you retreat before, form! form!" There was thick early morning fog which reduced visibility to thirty yards or less. When Howe suddenly came under fire, an officer of the 52nd Regiment recalled that "we all felt pleased to hear the grape rattle about the Commander-in Chief's ears after he had accused the battalion of having run away from a scouting party." During the battle, Washington returned Howe's dog with a note sending his compliments, writing that the dog "accidentally fell into his hands, and by the inscription on the collar, appears to belong to General Howe." Washington had nearly triumphed but for confusion caused by the fog, and the stubborn resistance of the British 40th Regiment which had occupied Chew House in the north of Germantown. The building was "riddled by cannonballs and looked like a slaughter house with blood splattered around" from the incessant fire of the enemy artillery commanded by General Henry Knox. The day was saved for Howe by the arrival of reinforcements under Cornwallis from Philadelphia.[66]

During their nine-month occupation of Philadelphia, the British revived the entertainments suppressed by the Continental Congress. There were cockfights, horse races, and cricket matches. The Southwark Theatre reopened with British officers joining a troop of actors known as "Howe's strolling players," who largely performed farces and at least one Shakespeare play, *Henry IV, Part I.* There were performances once or twice a week with the proceeds donated for the care of widows and orphans of the army. The audiences could enjoy spectacles like Lord Cathcart playing the role of a servant and being kicked on stage in George Farquhar's *The Inconstant.* The British also opened clubs and assembly rooms in Philadelphia, and the senior officers gave private balls, concerts, and dinners. The City Tavern hosted a ball every Thursday, as well as acting as the largest gambling club, with a faro bank kept by the Hessians, where "everyone from the Commanding General to the youngest ensign assembled." The bids were as high as a thousand guineas and fifty thousand dollars, which ruined many good officers, some of whom "shot themselves out of desperation," while many were forced to sell their commissions and leave the army. The editor of the *Pennsylvania Evening Post,* the first newspaper to print the Declaration of Independence, switched allegiance to publish articles in support of Britain. The State House (Independence Hall)—where the Continental Congress had voted for the declaration—became a prisoner of war camp. In the grounds, the army drilled and paraded daily, and the bandsmen gave regular public concerts. Their barracks extended from Second to Third Street and from Tammany to Green Street, and Howe moved his headquarters to the Morris mansion at Market Square. Philadelphia became a garrison city.[67]

Despite deceptive appearances, the British were far from luxuriating in Philadelphia while Washington and his army suffered at Valley Forge. Every public building was used to house two thousand sick and wounded British and Hessian soldiers. The army was placed on half-rations, and there was a shortage of medical and hospital supplies that caused tension between the British and the Hessians. Unable to obtain supplies, the city became a prison for as many as fifty thousand inhabitants and troops. The journals and letters of officers complained of the extortionate prices of every necessity. Howe had difficulty in trying to arrange a quasi-civilian government, causing conflict with the leading Philadelphian loyalist, Joseph Galloway, who was to become Howe's greatest critic in England.[68]

As early as October 16, the success of the Philadelphia campaign was suddenly overshadowed by rumors that Burgoyne had surrendered his entire army at Saratoga in upstate New York. It was the turning point of the war. While rumors were still pending on October 22, General Howe wrote a letter of resignation to Lord George Germain in which he complained of the "little Attention . . . given to my Recommendations since the Commencement of my Command." His Philadelphia campaign seemed nothing more than a frivolous excursion, and worse still a distraction that contributed directly to the British defeat at Saratoga. News of his victory at Philadelphia and Burgoyne's defeat at Saratoga appeared almost simultaneously in newspapers in Britain. In the words of a correspondent in the *Morning Post*, "the joy of General Howe's success has been so soon followed by the mortifying news of the brave General Burgoyne." Like an actor who had missed his cue, Howe was accused of having ignored orders to form a junction with Burgoyne at Albany.[69]

VI

Howe had been well aware that he was expected to make contact with Burgoyne's army and assume overall command when it reached Albany from Canada. The home government had planned to cut off radical New England along the Hudson River from the rest of America. This was to be achieved by Burgoyne's army marching south from Canada and Howe's army marching north from New York to converge at Albany. Howe and his brother were also expected to strike against the coast of New England. This had already been the plan for 1776 when Germain hoped that Howe would meet the army of General

Sir Guy Carleton advancing south from Canada. It was then aborted only because Carleton failed to take Fort Ticonderoga and his army returned to Quebec. In the first iteration of his plans for the campaign in 1777, Howe had included the concept of a junction with Burgoyne's army at Albany.

Lord George Germain had reminded Howe that he was expected to link with Burgoyne and undertake raids on the coast of New England. On July 5, Howe acknowledged the receipt of a copy of Germain's instructions to the governor of Canada stipulating that Burgoyne "must never lose view of their intended junctions with Sir William Howe as their principal objects." On August 16, Howe received a letter from Germain sent on May 18 "trusting . . . that whatever you may meditate, it will be executed in time for you to co-operate with the Army ordered to proceed from Canada." According to an account assiduously circulated by the earl of Shelburne, Germain delegated the task of writing and sending the plan of the campaign to one of his under secretaries, Christopher D'Oyly, because he was impatient to leave for his country home at Stoneland and consequently did not wait to see his instructions carried out by D'Oyly. William Knox, an under secretary in the American Department, later confirmed the substance of the story, with the exception that he claimed that Howe acknowledged the receipt of the letter containing the plan but suppressed the contents, while no copy was kept in London. Knox may indeed have intended to imply a conspiracy and cover-up involving D'Oyly as a friend of Howe. In any case on September 3, Germain wrote again to Howe of "the Joy you must have derived from the Accounts of General Burgoyne's rapid Progress, and the fair Prospect which you may now have of an earlier Junction."[70]

From conversations with army officers who had returned from London, Howe was also aware of the expectation that he would join Burgoyne. On May 8, he met with a Major Nisbet Balfour who had been sent by Germain to urge the Howes to carry out raids on the coastlines of Massachusetts Bay and New Hampshire in support of Burgoyne. On July 5, Sir Henry Clinton returned to America from England where he had spent time with Germain. He was very familiar with the plan to unite the armies along the Hudson and finish the campaign in 1777. While Howe was still in New York, Clinton implored him to abandon the proposed Philadelphia campaign in order to join with Burgoyne at Albany. His case was weakened by their mutual dislike of one another. As Clinton wrote in his unpublished memoirs, "by some cursed fatality we could never draw together." Apart from the strategy at the battle of Long Island, Howe had consistently rejected alternative plans proposed by Clinton.[71]

By mid-July 1777, the majority of Howe's senior officers had advised against the Philadelphia campaign, including "No Flint" Charles Grey and Sir William Erskine. Cornwallis supported Howe, dismissing the opposition of another staff officer, Sir William "Woolly" Erskine, saying "Faugh! Faugh! Wooly only wants a junction with Burgoyne so that he may crack a bottle with his friend Phillips." Even George Washington believed that Howe "certainly ought now, in good policy, to endeavor to cooperate with General Burgoyne." When it became apparent at the end of July that Howe was abandoning Burgoyne, Washington still thought it so improbable that he wrote that he could not "help casting my eyes continually behind me."[72]

Howe justified his own conduct on the grounds that Germain had endorsed his various plans for the conquest of Philadelphia. He further argued that he did not have the troops or ships to both conquer Philadelphia and mount raids on New England. He doubted that he had the capacity to hold territory over the winter in a region that was so hostile. In regard to the planned junction along the Hudson, Howe claimed that he would have been accused of wasting the campaign "merely to ensure the progress of the northern army." He added revealingly that it might have been said that he "had enviously grasped a share of that merit" from Burgoyne. Howe had given advance warning both to Germain and to Burgoyne that he would be unable to march north to Albany.[73]

There was little danger of Howe stealing the thunder of Burgoyne, but there was a real chance that he might be eclipsed by Burgoyne blazing a trail from Canada. Howe was the commander in chief, but he was given a subordinate role in the plan for the junction at Albany, whereas his modified plan to take Philadelphia offered him the opportunity to shine as much as Burgoyne. In choosing to attack by sea, furthermore, the Howe brothers were able to play to their greatest strength in combining the army and navy. They would be able to display the talents that had given them prominence in their respective services—the use of light infantry and amphibious warfare. Burgoyne, for his part, had been disappointed that he had not originally been appointed commander in chief rather than Howe. Clinton was upset at being given a cameo role of commanding the forces in New York with an inadequate force to fend off Washington's army and create a diversion in favor of Burgoyne. The general strategy of 1777 had thrown the apple of discord among the three generals who had traveled so amicably together aboard the *Cerberus* to Boston.

Howe was too professional a soldier to have deliberately allowed Burgoyne to fail at Saratoga. He had indeed expected him to succeed. Howe did not sail from New York until after he had received news of Burgoyne's capture of Fort Ticonderoga, and he did not thereafter expect the northern army to face serious opposition. This was the real source of the seemingly lax instructions and lack of coordination among the campaigns of 1777: the whole plan was predicated on the anticipation of support from the majority of the population and of a weak enemy. After hearing of Burgoyne's victory at Ticonderoga, Howe wrote: "I apprehend Genl Burgoyne will meet with little interruption [other] than the Difficulties he must encounter in transporting stores and provisions for the supply of his Army." He instead hoped that the success of Burgoyne in the north might deflect Washington's forces in Pennsylvania. He was not in the least concerned that Washington might march north, since "the strength of Genl. Burgoyne's army is such as to leave me no

Room to dread the Event." For his part, Burgoyne was equally confident that he would not need help from Howe. He was still with Governor Sir Guy Carleton when a message arrived from Howe warning him not to expect much assistance during the march south of Ticonderoga. As for Germain, he assumed that Howe would be able to complete the Pennsylvania campaign in time to support Burgoyne. He was unperturbed when he discovered that the junction was unlikely to happen, writing that it would be "more honour for Burgoyne if he does the business without any assistance from New York." Germain was more worried about Howe than about Burgoyne, and thought it was the former who might need assistance from the latter. Indeed, he only regarded a junction as desirable rather than essential.[74]

The root cause of the defeat was not that there were too many cooks spoiling the broth in the planning of the campaign, but that the politicians and the generals had all assumed little opposition from the enemy and widespread loyalist support. The various plans underestimated the popularity of the independence movement and of what John Adams called the real American Revolution—the radical change in the principles, opinions, sentiments, and affections of the people with the spread of republican ideas enshrined in the Declaration of Independence. Thomas Jefferson went beyond the usual formula of listing grievances used in the many regional declarations of independence by towns, counties, and states. His genius was to begin by establishing a broad set of popular principles—his "self-evident truths." Influenced by his love of poetry and music, the declaration was written in a rhetorical and persuasive style that rivaled Jean-Jacques Rousseau and Thomas Paine. As Jefferson readily admitted, it was not intended to be original but to capture the popular thought of the time—what he called the American mind.[75]

The Declaration of Independence articulated the radical republican creed of the American Revolution. Its promise of a better future gave purpose to the struggle, beyond simply changing one ruling elite for another. Republicanism invoked a language of liberty, natural rights, representation, and equality, the meaning of which was sufficiently ambiguous and elastic to allow for more utopian and radical interpretations than originally intended. It appealed to the aspirations of ordinary people, and was well suited to the relatively egalitarian social conditions among the free white population in America. The republican ideology of the revolution led to actual changes in state constitutions that permitted greater participation in government and new emphasis upon actual representation. When combined with messianic religious overtones and a sense of righteous indignation, it was a compelling formula for what the revolutionaries dubbed "the Glorious Cause." There was a thrill and excitement that they were beginning the world anew. British and loyalist claims that the majority of people were being duped by a few unscrupulous revolutionaries were less persuasive than the popular conspiracy theory of a deliberate pattern of British policy to create a tyrannical system of government in America.[76]

The popularity of revolutionary ideology was reinforced by the threat of coercion against anyone who resisted. In the Association of 1774, the Continental Congress had set up committees of safety (also known by other names such as committees of observation) in every town and county to enforce the boycott against British trade. The role of the committees expanded in the initial absence of local government. They administered test oaths and laws together with the justices of the peace, and they acted in concert with the militia to police the population and purge loyalists. Their presence forced ordinary people to make choices. In areas of apathy or opposition, the militia of other regions intervened. The requirement that citizens serve in the militia forced those who were neutral to identify themselves actively with the revolutionary cause or go into exile. The British interpreted such coercive methods of recruitment as evidence of the tyranny and desperation of the revolutionaries. Still, although opinion continued to shift among what is called today "the silent majority," the population increasingly embraced the revolution.[77]

The opposing sides began to regard one another as foreigners and not as brothers engaged in a civil war. A British marine captain described the American people as a "levelling, underbred, artfull, race of people," devoid of principles, "a sad set of Presbyterian rascals." He was so perturbed by their formality of dress and their deliberately slow speech that he longed "to shove a soup ladle down their throat[s]." The officers and soldiers frequently alluded to their opponents as cowardly because of the unconventional tactics of the militiamen and their avoidance of open battle. During the retreat from Lexington and Concord in April 1775, soldiers had vented their anger at being shot from behind bushes by ransacking houses. Major John Bowater of the Marines wrote about being hurt beyond conception when he contemplated fine men aged as young as fifteen who had lost limbs. He every day cursed "Columbus and all the discoverers of this Diabolical Country." There was also an ideological component. The British regarded their opponents as criminals who were committing acts of rebellion and treason that did not entitle them to the usual conventions of war.[78]

The presence of British soldiers, known as "Bloodybacks" and "Lobsters," helped alienate popular opinion in America. Although there were many instances of soldiers making friends among the Americans, a British officer admitted that the troops more typically "planted an irrecoverable hatred wherever we went." Between a quarter and a third of Howe's army were German mercenaries. It was one of the most consistent complaints of the various declarations of independence at the local and state level that the British had used foreign mercenaries against their fellow subjects. The British relied on the terror inspired by the bayonets of the infantry and the charge of the cavalry. It was often successful in causing opponents to flee but it resulted in terrible carnage and bloody mutilated carcasses. The British had difficulty in distinguishing between enemy combatants and civilians because militiamen did not wear uniforms or carry standard weaponry, often conducting raids in small bands without officers. In December 1776, Howe ordered that armed men who were neither officers nor in uniform but who fired at troops should be hanged without trial as assassins. The subject was debated in Parliament.[79]

Although there were atrocities committed by both sides, those attributed to the British were recounted in the revolutionary press and helped perpetuate the image of a hostile foreign presence. After the battle of Long Island, there were accounts of the bayoneting of prisoners of war and even the massacre of provincial troops in newspapers on both sides of the Atlantic. During an engagement fifty miles north of Philadelphia at Crooked Billet (May 1, 1778), a report to the revolutionary Pennsylvania Council claimed that British troops had burned alive fully clothed men in buckwheat straw and committed acts of butchery worse than those of the most brutal savages. The more poignant tales of revolutionary courage and sacrifice created national martyrs and heroes. Howe ordered the execution without trial of Nathan Hale, a graduate of Yale and an officer in the Continental Army, who was hanged for spying in New York on September 22, 1776. Captain John Montresor, the chief engineer of the British army, wrote to Enoch Hale describing how his brother had mounted the gallows with the words, "I only regret that I have but one life to lose for my country."[80]

Even though these were crimes punishable by death, British troops committed acts of rape and plunder. The twenty-two-year-old Lord Francis Rawdon described how the "fair nymphs" made the men as riotous as satyrs for "fresh meat." He quipped that a girl could not step into the bushes to pluck a rose without running the imminent risk of being ravished, adding that they "are so little accustomed to these vigorous methods that they don't bear them with proper resignation." He recounted with equal levity instances of gang rape by seven men and another by a group of grenadiers.[81]

The practice of plunder was a notorious problem. General Howe attempted to suppress it with a series of proclamations and occasional executions, but then, to the consternation of Lord Cornwallis, he increasingly turned a blind eye. It was difficult to regulate plunder because the army was unable either to purchase sufficient food locally or import enough from Britain, so that the troops often suffered from hunger. Furthermore, plunder was regarded as part of the legitimate spoils of war.

Plunder was all too often indiscriminate against friends and foes alike. There was even a special vocabulary for it within the army where it was called "grabs" and "lobs." In New Jersey, Major Charles Stuart condemned the way the soldiers judged everyone rebels, "neither their clothes nor property spared, but in the most inhuman and barbarous manner torn from them." Although repeated orders were "given against this barbarity," they were disregarded because the crime was not punished and "Thus we went on persuading to enmity those minds already undecided, and inducing our very Friends to fly to the opposite party for protection." Major Stephen Kemble, from a loyalist family in New York, decried the unmerciful pillaging—"no wonder if the Country People refuse to join us." He described marauding that was so outrageous and cruel that the troops threatened death to anyone who opposed them and even violence against their own officers. In British-occupied Philadelphia, the plundering by the troops antagonized the civilian population and not least the American loyalists. The soldiers stripped houses, furniture, fences, gates, and sheds for firewood. The British officers and the loyalists often blamed the Hessians and female camp followers, but in fact the practice was universal. The possessions of avowed rebels were regarded as fair game. After occupying the home of Benjamin Franklin in Philadelphia, Major John André looted his books, musical instruments, and scientific equipment despite the protests of his friend, the young Swiss-born officer Pierre Eugène du Simitière. Possibly acting under orders, André took the Benjamin Wilson portrait of Franklin which he gave to General Charles "No Flint" Grey. The portrait hung in the ancestral home of the Greys until 1906 when it was returned to the United States and now hangs in the White House.[82]

The process by which the presence of the British army alienated popular opinion was evident in Queens County in Long Island, one of the first areas to be recaptured by Howe in 1776. It comprised the towns of Newton, Flushing, Jamaica, Hempstead, and Oyster Bay. At the beginning of the war, the population was largely neutral or loyalist. Only 12 percent of the inhabitants had renounced allegiance to the crown, compared to 27 percent who identified themselves as loyalists. Their attitudes changed during the course of the war when they were under military rather than civil government. They were also the victims of plunder not only by soldiers but also by corrupt commissary officers who purchased supplies and provisions from them. They suffered billeting of soldiers in their private homes during the winter. The inhabitants were unsuccessful in their recourse to law. It did not help that the British turned the churches and meeting houses of what they regarded as nonconformists and "rascally sects" into prisons and barracks. Unlike seventeenth-century Tories, the American loyalists were not believers in passive obedience and divine right, but shared the belief of their fellow countrymen in the rule of law, liberty, and government by consent. They believed that the rebellion was unjustified because there was not an absolute state of tyranny and because the unpopular measures of the imperial government were reversible by other means. In the later stages of the war, the residents of Queens County increasingly voted for candidates for town meetings who were neutral, rather than avowed loyalists.[83]

In consequence of all these abuses, there was decreasing loyalist support for the British in America. Contrary to General Howe's expectations regarding the strength of the loyalists in Pennsylvania, before his landing in the Chesapeake, the inhabitants deserted their homes, drove away their livestock and removed their arms. Instead of finding support on his arrival, he complained that "the prevailing disposition of the inhabitants . . . seem to be, excepting a few individuals, strongly in enmity against us." In Philadelphia, Howe was surrounded by a hostile countryside. He spent two months opening the Delaware River against determined resistance by Washington's army and revolutionary militia who tried to cut off supplies to the city. His campaign culminated in the bombardment and capture of Fort Mifflin.[84]

The chimera of loyalist support had lured Howe into extensive operations in New Jersey and Pennsylvania, and it had been the pretext for an ill-fated campaign of Henry Clinton in North and South Carolina in 1776. Nevertheless, the British continued to be beguiled by the promise of countless legions of loyalists elsewhere in America. The belief was sustained by the seeming decline in enthusiasm for the revolutionary cause and the difficulty of obtaining volunteers for the Continental Army after 1776. Thomas Paine wrote of the "summer patriots and the sunshine soldier," and Washington complained initially of the apathy of the population in New Jersey and Pennsylvania. The British obtained useful intelligence from the population in southeastern Pennsylvania, and Howe believed that loyalist sympathies began to revive during his occupation of Philadelphia.[85]

The latent potential of the loyalists was never disproven because the British never held swathes of territory for long enough to test the possibilities of the restoration and the reconstruction of imperial government. The loyalists were disappointed when they did rally, only to be forsaken by the British as happened in Boston, North Carolina, and New Jersey in 1776. It did not help that the British did not restore civil government in New York or Philadelphia. The commanders did not trust the allegiance of the population and it was militarily inconvenient to negotiate with an elected assembly. It was a chicken-and-egg situation. The British needed to demonstrate that they were able to hold territory to attract support and allegiance, but such a strategy overextended the army. Following the conquest of New Jersey in the winter of 1776–77 and of Philadelphia in 1777–78, British power imploded in the wake of popular insurgencies.

VII

The debacle at Saratoga has inevitably overshadowed the success of Howe's Pennsylvania campaign against Washington. It was after the conquest of Philadelphia that Washington and his army endured the infamous winter encampment at Valley Forge. Their sacrifice and endurance became one of the abiding national images of the war. It was after the conquest of Philadelphia, too, that Washington's leadership was challenged by the Conway Cabal. Although it is doubtful that there was a real conspiracy to replace Washington with Horatio Gates, Washington himself believed that there was a movement to supplant him and confronted his critics through the medium of the Continental Congress. Washington and his army were to emerge stronger from the trials of the Conway Cabal and Valley Forge, but this is apparent only with hindsight. The number of his troops fit for duty dropped from 14,122 in December 1777 to 7,316 in March 1778. Despite the victory at Saratoga, the winter of 1777–78 represented a period of great vulnerability in the cause of independence, thanks to the success of Howe's campaign in Pennsylvania.[86]

On May 25, 1778, three years to the day since he had first arrived in America aboard the *Cerberus,* Sir William Howe sailed from Philadelphia to England on the *Andromeda,* named after the princess of Greek legend who, after being chained to a rock, escaped the sea monster Cetus. The name was appropriate, for following the outbreak of war with France and new orders from London to return his army to New York, his last duties involved preparing the evacuation of Philadelphia which he had so dearly won. Howe had been popular among his officers who arranged a remarkable farewell event. Known as the Mischianza, it began with a regatta, followed by various entertainments that included fireworks, gun salutes, and a grand dinner. Sir William Howe blamed his resignation on the "little attention" that the government had paid to his advice and the lack of confidence that he had received from his superiors. He became even more indignant when Germain made no effort to dissuade him from resignation and did not observe the usual courtesies of thanking him for his service. Howe returned determined to vindicate himself in England.[87]

Always close to his younger brother, Admiral Howe also requested permission to resign. Both brothers had received increasingly sarcastic letters from Lord George Germain. Admiral Howe was congratulated by Germain for his indulgence in not suppressing subsistence fishermen and allowing swarms of rebel privateers off the coast of France. Indeed, Howe had always given priority to supporting the army, rather than blockading the coast and launching raids. There was a long history of differences between himself and Germain that dated from their service together in the Seven Years' War and their disagreement about the terms of the peace commission in 1776. Admiral Howe also had a poor relationship with the earl of Sandwich. The admiral told his secretary that he had never enjoyed the confidence and civility of any government minister since the resignation of the earl of Dartmouth in 1775. He was especially upset at the treatment of his brother.[88]

While Admiral Howe was awaiting his successor in 1778, he was to demonstrate some of those qualities that later made him a hero in the naval war between Britain and France. He assisted in the final evacuation of Philadelphia, with his fleet accompanying the transports with military supplies and loyalists. As he cleared Delaware Bay on June 29, Howe received his first intimation of the sailing of a French fleet commanded by Admiral Charles Hector Théodat, comte d'Estaing, who was sent specifically to entrap Howe's fleet along the east coast. Within nine days of sailing out of the Delaware, Howe heard that the French fleet was already off the coast of America. His fleet was outnumbered with the possibility that the British army might be encircled and trapped in New York or Rhode Island. A young lieutenant in the 4th Regiment described the way that Admiral

Howe met the crisis with the "same cool tranquility and clearness [that] attend[ed] all his orders," seemingly unperturbed by the multiplicity of demands upon him. For eleven days, the two fleets faced one another, and Howe made a strong enough showing to dissuade d'Estaing from attacking New York. In addition, he successfully defended the British garrison at Newport in Rhode Island against d'Estaing. Britain might otherwise have lost the war much earlier in New York or Newport. Finally, on September 26, 1778, Admiral Howe sailed for England.[89]

In the meantime, General Sir William Howe had demanded a parliamentary committee of inquiry to clear his name of any responsibility for the events leading to Burgoyne's surrender at Saratoga. This became a personal parliamentary battle between the Howe brothers and Lord George Germain. There was a chance that the brothers would prevail; they were close to George III who was willing to dispense with Germain, the other government ministers were prepared to retain the Howes in command in America, and their friends rallied in their support. The dowager viscountess, Charlotte Howe, likened by the newspapers to a "Roman matron," accused Germain of abusing her sons by employing hacks to plant derogatory articles about them in the newspapers. Their friend Christopher D'Oyly resigned in protest as under secretary to Lord George Germain in the American Department. Although Germain triumphed, General Howe was courteously received at court and Lord North approached Admiral Howe about replacing the earl of Sandwich as first lord of the Admiralty. They lost the support of the king, however, because they argued that the war in America was unwinnable, causing him to write to Lord North "L[ord] Howe should mind his own business and take the Plans as he found them."[90]

The Howe brothers became an embarrassment to the government and a boon to the opposition parties. Between April 22 and June 30, 1779, a committee of the whole House examined the war in America in what became an inquiry into the conduct of the Howes. Sir William began with his defense before the House of Commons which he subsequently published as a pamphlet. On April 29, Admiral Howe made a speech accusing the government of character assassination against himself and his brother through the use of pamphleteers, newspapers, and coffeehouse runners. In May, the brothers succeeded in having witnesses called, including Lord Cornwallis whose examination was much anticipated. His evidence proved disappointing, however, because he insisted upon keeping to the facts and refused to pass judgment on the decisions of his commander. He was due to return to command in America.

The attempt of the brothers to vindicate themselves was tantamount to a vote on the competence of the ministry of Lord North. They failed because the government still held a large majority in the House of Commons, and the inquiry was eclipsed by news of the declaration of war with Spain. On June 29, the committee of inquiry was adjourned. The issue was kept in the public eye by a campaign of twenty-five pamphlets whose primary authors were two American loyalists living in London, Joseph Galloway and Israel Mauduit. Galloway had been the prime witness against the Howe brothers during the hearings in Parliament. Mauduit's pamphlets, which called for both brothers to be impeached, were written with the connivance of Germain. The pamphlet campaign provoked Sir William Howe to publish an edited version of a speech in his own defense that he made in the House of Commons in 1780.[91]

VIII

The careers of the brothers did not end in ignominy. Following the fall of the government of Lord North, General Howe became a member of the Privy Council, lieutenant general of the Ordnance, and colonel of the 19th Regiment of Dragoons. During the French Revolutionary War, he was promoted to full general and had an important role in supervising the defenses of Britain against Napoleon. He subsequently became governor of Berwick-upon-Tweed (1795–1808) and Plymouth (1808–24), and succeeded Admiral Howe as fifth Viscount Howe in the peerage of Ireland. He outlived both Burgoyne and Clinton, and died childless at the age of eighty-five in Plymouth on July 12, 1814, a year before the battle of Waterloo. He was buried at Twickenham outside London.

Admiral Howe became one of Britain's most celebrated naval commanders. After the fall of the government of Lord North in April 1782, he was promoted to full admiral and became commander of the Channel Fleet. In October, he led the famous relief expedition of the British garrison in Gibraltar. Between 1783 and 1788, he was head of the navy as first lord of the Admiralty during the premiership of William Pitt the Younger. He was raised in the peerage to an earldom with the title of Earl Howe and Baron Howe of Langar in 1788. On the death of Admiral George Rodney in May 1792, he was appointed vice admiral of England. It was during the French Revolutionary Wars that his reputation reached its peak when he defeated the French fleet of Admiral Villaret-Joyeuse off Ushant in 1794. He inflicted some seven thousand casualties, capturing six ships of the line and sinking another, in what became known as the Glorious First of June. Howe was said to have been almost constantly on deck for five days and four nights while the fleets were in regular contact.

The Glorious First of June was the first major British naval victory of the French Revolutionary and Napoleonic Wars. It was to be commemorated in prints, souvenirs, ceramics, mugs, coins, and tokens. It was painted by the artist Mather Brown, who did portraits of John Adams and Thomas Jefferson while they were in London in 1786. On board his flagship *Queen Charlotte,* Howe was presented with a diamond-hilted sword by George III. His senior officers were given Irish peerages, including Admiral Thomas Graves and Sir Samuel Hood who had both commanded at the battle of the Chesapeake Capes in which they had been outmaneuvered by the French fleet off Virginia during the

Revolutionary War. In 1796, Howe was appointed admiral of the fleet and general of the Marines. Among his last official duties in Portsmouth, Howe presided over the court martial of Admiral Sir William Cornwallis, the brother of General Lord Charles Cornwallis, who was accused of disobeying an order from the Admiralty. He found in favor of Admiral Cornwallis. In 1797, he became a member of the Order of the Garter.

After fifty-nine years of service in the navy, Howe had the opportunity to practice the conciliatory approach that he had advocated in America when he was personally asked by George III to negotiate with naval mutineers at Spithead in May 1797. The entire Channel fleet was in mutiny, and there had been actual bloodshed in which unpopular officers had been forced to leave their ships. Despite severe inflation and raises given to the army in the 1790s, the wages of the ordinary sailor had not increased since 1652. Howe was known to be popular with the ordinary seamen, earning him the sobriquet "the sailor's friend." He had shown concern for their welfare and conditions throughout his career. He was rowed out to each ship where he received petitions and listened to grievances. By offering concessions and a royal pardon, he successfully ended the mutiny with the fleet sailing again a month later. It was his last official duty—and the outcome he had wanted for America.[92]

During the final years of his life, Admiral Howe suffered from considerable pain caused by gout which had afflicted him for over thirty years. He needed crutches to walk between the rooms of his London home, and had frequently sought relief from the spa waters at Bath as well as trying the fashionable "electricity" treatment used to cure gout. He died at his home in Grafton Street in London, on August 5, 1799, aged seventy-three, and was buried "without pomp or parade" in the family vault at the parish church at Langar in Nottinghamshire. His grief-stricken wife Mary was five years his junior and survived him by almost exactly a year. She was from a landed family by the name of Hartopp, and they had been married for forty-one years and had three daughters. A portrait of her early in their marriage by Thomas Gainsborough has been described by one art critic as the most forceful portrait ever painted of a woman by that artist (Figure 15). After the war in America, they spent much of their time together between their home in London and Porter's Lodge, their country estate in Hertfordshire, but Mary also accompanied him from London when he went to negotiate with the mutineers at Spithead. The couple left considerable properties in England and Ireland. A monument to Admiral Howe by John Flaxman, commissioned by the government in 1803, was emplaced in St. Paul's Cathedral in 1811.[93]

CHAPTER 4

"The Old Gamester"

JOHN BURGOYNE

London greeted the news of the British surrender at Saratoga with disbelief. From early November 1777, rumors of an impending disaster had begun to circulate. At the beginning of December, there was still such incredulity and doubt that a correspondent of the *Morning Chronicle* called upon readers to resist "mischievous impressions" put about by the agents of darkness and "channels of infamy and falsehood." The newspapers were simultaneously printing descriptions of the victorious exploits of Sir William Howe and his occupation of Philadelphia. On December 4, the first reliable confirmation of the defeat arrived in a letter from the governor of Canada, Sir Guy Carleton. George III "fell into agonies on hearing the account." According to Horace Walpole, the king tried to disguise his concern by affecting to laugh and pretending "to be so indecently merry, that Lord North endeavoured to stop him." When challenged by opposition speaker Isaac Barré in the House of Commons, Lord George Germain was forced to acknowledge news of the defeat in a speech which "struck the house with astonishment; and such a gloom appeared on the countenance of every member, as might be supposed to have settled on the face of every Roman senator, when the defeat at Cannae was announced in the senate." On December 15, any lingering doubt was dispelled when the official account of the surrender reached London.[1]

Anthony Morris Storer, the member of Parliament for Carlisle, wrote to a friend that he could have no idea what an effect the news of the defeat had on the minds of people in London. He said that those unconcerned about the war were suddenly awakened from their lethargy to see to "what a dreadful situation we are reduced." He thought everyone at fault "at this dreadful check." As to whom to blame, no one could say, but "all seem, however, to be willing to excuse Burgoyne." The *General Evening Post* described the way that the patrons of coffeehouses had become armchair generals: "having only fought battles in books, or formed attacks upon paper, by a comfortable fire-side," they variously judged the conduct of General Burgoyne.[2]

John Burgoyne, the general who commanded the British army at Saratoga, seemingly embodied the image of the aristocratic dilettante and buffoon who was inevitably defeated by the simple, practical merits of the opposing commanders. Both a soldier and a playwright, he was a showman with staged mannerisms and speech. There was a rash quality in his propensity for gambling and cavorting. Burgoyne was said by one contemporary to have "more sail than ballast." His theatrical personality made him a popular subject of parody in contemporary satires and lampoons. Horace Walpole variously called him "General Swagger" and "Julius Caesar Burgonius," and described him as "a vain, very ambitious man, with a half understanding that was worse than none." According to Nathaniel Wraxall, Burgoyne's appearance seemed more fitted to a drawing room than a military camp.[3]

In a portrait by his friend Sir Joshua Reynolds of 1766, Burgoyne appears a glamorous figure with long, dark brown hair (Figure 16). His head is turned, so that he gazes to one side with a look of determination. His face is pale with dark rims around the eyes. The dramatic effect of the portrait is emphasized by a battle scene in the background and darkened clouds from the smoke of war. He is wearing the full brocaded scarlet uniform of a general, a fashionable grey waistcoat with black lining, together with the silver buttons and epaulettes of his cavalry regiment, the 16th Light Dragoons. His right hand clasps a saber while his left hand rests on his waist. He was the subject of more satires and biographies than any of the British commanders during the Revolutionary War. He was portrayed in George Bernard Shaw's play, *The Devil's Disciple* (1897). Indeed, Burgoyne has become the popular stereotype of the men who lost America.[4]

Burgoyne was in fact the least aristocratic of the British commanders in America. The Howe brothers were the sons of an Irish viscount, Clinton was the cousin of the second duke of Newcastle, Cornwallis was an earl, and Thomas Gage was the second son of an Irish viscount. Burgoyne was plain "Gentleman Johnny." He was descended from landholding gentry who had lived in Sutton in Bedfordshire at least since 1500. Like many gentry families, they had profited from the opportunity to obtain land following the dissolution of the monasteries. They had sat in Parliament since the 1560s and had supported Parliament in the English Civil War against Charles I. It was a respectable pedigree, but there was speculation about Burgoyne's legitimacy. Horace Walpole repeated the rumor that he was the out-of-wedlock son of Lord Bingley, chancellor of the Exchequer under Queen Anne, an allegation supposedly made by Lady Bingley. The story gained some currency when John Burgoyne's mother was left a substantial bequest by Lord Bingley. In the event of having no legitimate offspring, Bingley had intended the rest of the estate to go to "my godson, John Burgoyne" in return for taking his surname Benson.[5]

Burgoyne instead cultivated his own influential connections with the earls of Derby who owned extensive lands in Lancashire in the northwest of England. The first earl of Derby had played a decisive role in putting the Tudors on the throne of England at the battle of Bosworth in 1485; the fifth earl had been a patron of William Shakespeare who performed as an actor at Knowsley, the Derby family home near Liverpool; and the twelfth earl established the still popular annual horseraces, the Oaks and the Derby. The family was a major political presence in the northwest of England, especially in Lancashire including Liverpool. Burgoyne met James Smith Stanley, who later became Lord Strange and heir to the earldom of Derby, while they were both at Westminster School in London. Although five years younger than Stanley, Burgoyne remained a close friend of a man of "whose integrity and political judgment I had the highest veneration, and who was besides my benefactor, my patron and my friend." At the age of twenty-eight, Burgoyne became his brother-in-law when he eloped with the fifteen-year-old Lady Charlotte Stanley, the youngest of six daughters of the eleventh earl of Derby. Her father disapproved but was eventually reconciled to the marriage. It was a testimony to the charisma and charm of Burgoyne that his relationship with the Derby family survived the death of Lord Strange in 1771 and the death of Lady Charlotte in 1776.[6]

The patronage of the Derby family assisted Burgoyne in his driving ambition to rise to high rank and fame as a cavalry officer. Burgoyne was descended from a family with a military tradition that had been granted the right to bear arms in the reign of Henry VII. His father had been a captain in the army, but gambled away the family fortune and died a debtor. After leaving school at the age of fifteen, John Burgoyne entered the army as a subbrigadier in the Horse Guards. His military career was twice interrupted at the cost of his seniority in the army, which he was to regret. On the first occasion, for reasons that remain obscure, he sold his commission in the Horse Guards in November 1741, and then returned as a cornet with the 1st Royal Dragoons, known as "the Royals," with whom he rose to the rank of captain and saw active service against the French during the War of the Austrian Succession (1740–48). His regiment made repeated charges at the battle of Fontenoy (1745) in the Austrian Netherlands (Belgium). After marrying Lady Charlotte Stanley in 1751, he again sold his commission and escaped his creditors by moving to France. The couple visited Rome, where Burgoyne was painted against the background of the ruins of the Colosseum by the artist Allan Ramsay, who later did the coronation portrait of George III. Burgoyne's commitment to a military career was suggested by his daily reading of the leading military manuals of the period and his conversing on military issues with authorities such as the future French minister, the duc de Choiseul. After the birth of a daughter in 1755, Burgoyne was accepted into the Derby family by his father-in-law and resumed his military career in England.[7]

Burgoyne made his reputation as a soldier in Europe during the Seven Years' War. Returning to the army as a captain in the 11th Dragoons, he distinguished himself in a landing near Saint-Malo on the coast of Brittany in 1758, one of several unsuccessful coastal raids aimed at gaining the offensive against France. The expedition involved the same men who were later to blame one another for British strategy in America before Saratoga, including Lord George Sackville (Germain), William Howe, and Lord Richard Howe. Burgoyne was afterwards appointed lieutenant colonel of the 2d Regiment of Foot Guards. A still greater honor and profit for an officer of his relatively junior status, he was chosen to raise a new light cavalry regiment, the 16th Light Dragoons, who were commonly known as Burgoyne's Light Horse. The cavalry regiments had greater social éclat, so that the purchase of commissions was more expensive than for infantry regiments.

In recruiting and commanding his new regiment, Burgoyne demonstrated flair and originality. He did not resort to the time-honored technique of delegating the raising of men to recruiting sergeants but personally undertook the responsibility doing so in Northamptonshire. He wined and dined the local gentry, encouraging them to join as officers or to use their influence to entice men to enlist. Burgoyne distributed posters that highlighted the glamour and excitement of service in a light cavalry regiment with promises of the finest horses in the world, "superb clothing," and the "richest accoutrements." He offered a life of universal respect in which members of the regiment would be courted by the rest of society and admired by women. Burgoyne appealed in his advertisements specifically to the unemployed and poor, quoting from Shakespeare that "There is a tide in the affairs of men, which, taken at the flood, leads to a fortune." He signed off, "Nick in instantly and enlist."[8]

Burgoyne wrote a code of conduct for the officers of his new cavalry regiment that was unparalleled in the British army until the early nineteenth-century reforms of Sir John Moore. Reflecting the humanitarian ideals of the Enlightenment, the code was introduced not "as the orders of a commanding officer, but as the sentiments of a friend, partly borrowed and partly formed upon observation and practice." He prohibited officers from swearing at soldiers and exhorted them to treat their troops as "thinking beings." Insisting on "complete social equality" between officers in private conversation, he encouraged informality, and even the occasional joke, with the men on suitable occasions. He suggested that officers devote some time each day to studying. He recommended that they learn to read French since "the best modern books upon our profession are written in that language." He stressed the importance of writing skills and the ability to draw. He thought it imperative that an officer should be capable of doing the tasks he required of his men, stressing that officers should be able to dress, bridle, and equip horses. They should know every strap and buckle. Such familiarity would enable them to review their troops more critically and to hold them to higher standards.[9]

Burgoyne won his greatest military laurels in Portugal, the oldest ally of Britain. Following the declaration of war by Spain in 1762, Burgoyne was sent to defend Portugal under the command of Wilhelm, count of Schaumburg-Lippe (Count La Lippe), a German military adventurer who was one of the foremost artillery officers of the age, reputed to be an out-of-wedlock son of George I. In order to prevent the Spanish forces from coming across the border to attack Lisbon, Burgoyne led a mixed force of different foreign nationals in the bold capture of the walled frontier town of Valencia de Alcántara. After a forced march of fifty miles, he led a cavalry charge that took the colors of three Spanish regiments. When the Spanish later recovered and began to invade Portugal, Burgoyne sent Charles Lee to take a Spanish post and depot at Villa Velha, a village flanked by two decaying Moorish castles. Lee later became a general in the Continental Army in America. Burgoyne was promoted to the rank of full colonel, and received a diamond ring from the king of Portugal that was personally presented by the first minister, the Marquis de Pombal. La Lippe wrote an encomium about Burgoyne's service which was published in *The Gentleman's Magazine,* and paid for the 1766 portrait of Burgoyne by Sir Joshua Reynolds which is now exhibited in the Frick Collection in New York.[10]

I

Burgoyne was a remarkably progressive and successful commander. In 1765, he traveled through Europe with the object of studying the different national armies, as well as of conversing with veterans and commanders like Prince Ferdinand of Brunswick. With introductions he secured abroad from the earl of Chatham, he visited the battlefields of central Europe and talked to the "principal actors on both sides." He attended lectures in mathematics and languages at the Brunswick Military Academy. In Prague, he dressed in disguise to observe a military base of the Holy Roman Empire and witnessed drill parades of Bohemian and Moravian troops of the Austrian army.

On his return to England, Burgoyne wrote a pamphlet, *Observations and Reflections Upon the Present Military State of Prussia, Austria, and France,* that compared the national armies of Europe. After completing a draft in 1766, he sent it to the earl of Chatham who had presided in government over the great British victories of the Seven Years' War. Burgoyne's pamphlet showed his ability to think conceptually about warfare. He made a shrewd sociological argument that training and tactics reflected national character. While admiring the assiduity and meticulousness of Frederick the Great of Prussia, Burgoyne was critical of his methods of training that degraded "all intellectual faculties" and reduced men "as nearly as possible to mere machinery." He did not think such techniques transferable to British soldiers who he insisted should always be treated as "thinking beings." Their officers should instead appeal to their reason, their patriotism, and their camaraderie. He thought that a system whose maxim was "not to reason, but to obey" was a liability among senior officers who became nothing more than "expert artificers."[11]

Burgoyne was impressed by the quality of Irish émigrés who had risen to senior ranks in the armies of Europe, especially among the Catholic powers of France, Austria, and Spain. They included the "Wild Geese," the Irish brigade of Jacobites, who turned the fortune of Marshal Saxe's army against the British at the battle of Fontenoy (1745). Burgoyne hinted that Britain should enlist Roman Catholics, including Irish Catholics, who were traditionally excluded from service in the army. Although always concerned with his own sartorial elegance, he believed that the clothing of soldiers should be designed with a view to "lightness, warmth and ease." He stressed the importance of adequate pay for the morale and quality of an army. His concern for the treatment of his troops earned him the sobriquet of "Gentleman Johnny."[12]

Although his pamphlet was impressive for its erudition, it was also shameless self-promotion in anticipation of the outbreak of another war in Europe. Burgoyne used every means to advance his career in the army. He lobbied aggressively even by eighteenth-century standards. Within a year of rejoining the army in 1757, he wrote to the commanding officer expressing resentment at "serving *under* so many men whom I had commanded." He had an overweening desire to make up for the earlier intermissions in his military career which had lost him seniority among his contemporaries. In Portugal in 1762, he was the only British lieutenant colonel to be given the temporary rank of brigadier general to enable him to command the Portuguese as well as the British. He was not satisfied and wrote to the prime minister, the earl of Bute, seeking to be made a full colonel. Bute replied that it was not possible since there were a great many more senior lieutenant colonels. The explanation did not appease Burgoyne, who applied again to the secretary at war, Charles Townshend. He became even more importunate when he heard about the promotion of other lieutenant colonels who included Henry Clinton. He protested that the other promotions were not based solely on merit but upon family weight. He warned that denial of his promotion would be a slight to his patron Lord Strange, and made his claim to be "upon the same list as Mr. Clinton." Bute relented and made him a full colonel "out of regard to Lord Strange, and your own merit."[13]

Like many aspiring army officers, Burgoyne pursued a simultaneous career in Parliament. When he was first elected as MP for Midhurst in 1761, he was one of sixty-three army officers in the House of Commons. Although he regarded himself as an independent, he rarely deviated from the politics of Lord Strange, whom Walpole regarded as one of the foremost speakers in the Commons. Burgoyne did not speak in debates for much of his first ten years in Parliament. In the election of 1768, he stood to represent the town of Preston in north Lancashire, where many of the residents were tenants of the earl of Derby. Although the national electorate consisted of less than 20 percent of adult males, the right to vote varied considerably between constituencies. In this case, the earl of Derby had recently persuaded the House of Commons to enfranchise virtually all the male householders in Preston. As the earl of Derby's nominee, Burgoyne's candidacy challenged the power of the local burgesses who had previously held the exclusive right to choose the town's MP. It became a contest over the future political control of Preston. The election was violent, with looting, fist fighting, and gangs roaming the streets, so that the candidates had to be protected by bodyguards.[14]

Burgoyne went to the poll carrying a loaded pistol in each hand, which he justified as necessary for his own protection but which his opponents claimed he used for intimidation. He wore his regimental uniform and was accompanied by a guard of soldiers. Allying himself with the large population of religious dissenters, he won the election. However, he paid a price for his success when the town burgesses sued him for intimidation and won their case in the Court of King's Bench. Burgoyne was fined the considerable sum of £1,000, and some of his supporters were fined £100 each. His three sergeants and drummers were sent to prison but not fined because they were too poor. The popular anonymous newspaper letters of Junius alleged that, in return for political support, the duke of Grafton, the prime minister, paid Burgoyne's fine and rewarded him with the lucrative sinecure of governor of Fort William in Scotland. Junius protested that such appointments were intended as pensions in reward to retired military personnel for good service and that it was hardly merited by one who "was not very conspicuous in his profession." Junius wrote of Burgoyne that "no man was more tender of his reputation," and proceeded to imply that he was a card shark who preyed on drunken young noblemen in games of piquet. A few years later, Burgoyne leapt to his feet clutching his sword when the accusation was repeated in the House of Commons.[15]

In 1772, Burgoyne was promoted to the rank of major general, together with William Howe and Henry Clinton. George III admired Burgoyne's cavalry regiment which he regularly inspected, watching exercises on Wimbledon Common. George III raised the regiment to a royal unit in 1766, and the 16th Light Dragoons thereafter became known as the Queen's Light Dragoons.[16]

Burgoyne rode the wave of success. He sought out the most fashionable venues and society in London. Always fond of theater and the world of the arts, he was a friend of the Shakespearean actor David Garrick as well as of Sir Joshua Reynolds. He was a member of the sparkling circle of Georgiana Cavendish, the duchess of Devonshire. He befriended both government and opposition politicians including Edmund Burke, Lord North, Charles James Fox, George Selwyn, the earl of March and Queensberry, and the duke of Devonshire. He was regularly in attendance at the Green Room of the Drury Lane Theatre. He dined at the Thursday Night Club and at the Star and Garter in Richmond, and he frequented the gaming tables of Brooks's Club and White's Club. He went to the horseraces at Salisbury and Newmarket. After the Preston election in 1768, he purchased stylish new homes in London and in Lancashire. He employed the Scottish architect Robert Adam to totally renovate his London house which is still standing at 10 Hertford Street in Mayfair. He built Cooper Hill at Walton-le-Dale in Lancashire, on the site of a Roman military encampment, near Patten House, the home of Lord Strange. Burgoyne designed the house, which was supposedly the first in England to have a lightning rod as invented by Benjamin Franklin.[17]

In June 1774, Burgoyne wrote his first play which was later performed in the West End as *The Maid of the Oaks.* Written as part of a newly fashionable *fête champêtre,* or rural festival, it celebrated the engagement of his twenty-one-year-old brother-in-law, Lord Edward Smith-Stanley, later twelfth earl of Derby, to Lady Betty Hamilton, the daughter of the duke of Argyll. It was held at The Oaks, a country house and hunting lodge that Burgoyne leased from the Derbys near Epsom in Surrey, about fourteen miles southwest of central London. At the extravaganza, costing more than the house at £500,000, Burgoyne was the master of ceremonies. He greeted the guests, whom he conducted to a "voluptuous scene" with a specially created orange grove, concealing a band playing minuets composed for the occasion by the violinist François Hippolyte Barthélemon, accompanied by the acclaimed soprano Polly Young and the drunken, fiddle-playing earl of Erskine. There were fireworks, archery stands, and ninepins, with shepherdesses on velvet-clad swings and kicking nymphs hanging from trees. There were young men bowling and playing skittles, surrounded by merry rustics in scenes evoking Arcadia. The female guests received a bouquet of flowers presented by two Cupids. Many of the entertainers were thespians who belonged to the troupe of celebrated actor David Garrick from the Theatre Royal in London. A temporary tented pavilion designed by the architect Robert Adam contained a ballroom adorned with Etruscan art and seats covered in crimson.[18]

After dinner, the guests watched Burgoyne's masque which was later revised by David Garrick and performed as a five-act play at the Theatre Royal. It anticipated musical comedy, which was to become so popular among the rising middle classes. The plot was a farce in which a gentleman is due to be married to a simple country girl who is an orphan. A friend of the groom tries to stop the marriage, questioning the motives of the bride and denouncing all English women as covetous, and the groom's father threatens to disinherit him, but all to no avail. The wedding proceeds when the guardian of the bride reveals that he is her father, that she is an heiress, and that he had kept her real identity secret to ensure that she would only be married by someone who genuinely loved her. The play was notable for the advocacy of women's equality by one of the characters, played by Frances Abington, the subject of a portrait by Sir Joshua Reynolds now at the Yale Center for British Art. The scenery was painted by the noted artist Philip James de Loutherbourg. The couple whose engagement the play commemorated had a less happy ending. They last appeared together in the drawing room of St. James's Palace on May 2, 1778, before the countess eloped and had a child by a former lover, John Frederick Sackville, the son of the earl of Dorset and nephew of Lord George Germain.[19]

II

Burgoyne prided himself on his political independence, but occasional opposition to the government was also an avenue to political rewards in exchange for future support. Following a dispute over the Falkland Islands off Argentina in 1770, he voted against a peace treaty with Spain. George III wrote to North that "seeing Colonel Burgoyne's name on the side of the minority appears so extraordinary that I almost imagine it was a mistake." Burgoyne voted against the Carib War in St. Vincent in 1772–73 in which the planters on the island had tried to take over the land of the native people, and which precipitated a heated debate about the rights of indigenous peoples with Burgoyne supporting the Caribs. After some equivocation, he supported the Royal Marriage Act (1772) to give George III the authority to prohibit members of the royal family from marrying without the permission of the crown. George III wrote to North that if Burgoyne had failed to support the measure, "I should have felt myself obliged to name a new Governor of Fort William."[20]

Burgoyne became more politically active and attempted to make his reputation on the subject of the East India Company that ruled British India. It was a commercial corporation with its own army, navy and administrators, and even its own flag with stars and stripes. The company seemed incapable of self-regulation and was in severe debt owing to the increased cost of defending and administering its expanded territories, but the government regarded it as too big to fail. Burgoyne proposed a series of measures to restore the credit of the company and the public faith in it, including a reduction in dividend payments to stockholders and a grace period for the payment of its debts. He argued that such temporary solutions needed to be accompanied by a series of fundamental reforms in the administration of the company and the financial ethics of its employees.[21]

In April 1772, Burgoyne made a major parliamentary speech in which he asserted that the government must "hold up the mirror of truth to the Company," the deficient regulation of which excited and gave play "to the vicious passions of men." He proposed and then chaired a select committee of investigation which turned into a sensational exposure of corruption within the company. His committee included Lord George Germain, Lord Richard Howe, Isaac Barré, and Charles James Fox. Burgoyne sought more government oversight and intervention in the company's affairs, whereas Lord North wanted the relationship between the state and the company left more ambiguous. It was a very sensitive issue touching upon the rights of private property and also raising the fear that state control might open the floodgates to political corruption by giving the government a wealth of new patronage. North was not keen to publicize the fraudulent activities of the company employees and set up his own secret committee aimed at undermining the committee established by Burgoyne. North granted the company a loan while insisting that the government was not obliged to save private enterprises that were foundering.[22]

On May 3, 1773, Burgoyne responded that reforms were meaningless without identifying and punishing former crimes. He revealed the discoveries of his own committee, exposing the most prominent, wealthiest, and most successful of the East India Company servants, Robert Clive, known as Clive of India, who had done much to consolidate British power in the subcontinent. He had been the victorious commanding general at the battle of Plassey (1757), for which he became Baron Clive of Plassey and which was significant in expanding British power in Bengal. Lord Clive was connected with the government of Lord North, and had a small following of members who owed their seats to his patronage. Following the revelations, Burgoyne was successful in passing a series of resolutions in the House of Commons asserting that the British state owned all territorial acquisitions acquired by the East India Company and that private gifts acquired by company servants were illegal. However, he was defeated in his attempt to formally censure Lord Clive who made a spirited defense, in which he famously said that "I stand astonished at my own moderation" in taking perquisites and gifts. Following the ordeal of the investigation by Burgoyne, Clive suffered sleeplessness and became addicted to opium. In November 1774, Clive of India committed suicide at his London home in Berkeley Square.[23]

Unlike the Howe brothers and Cornwallis, Burgoyne consistently supported authoritarian policies in America. In 1766, he voted against the repeal of the Stamp Act and in favor of the Declaratory Act, and in 1774, he supported the Coercive Acts which triggered the Revolutionary War. His views were conventional. He believed in the supremacy of the British Parliament over America, and regarded America as a child who had been ruined by the misplaced indulgence, "lenity and tenderness" of Britain. However, he stressed his desire to see the crisis solved by persuasion. In a debate on the tea duty on April 19, 1774, he claimed that he did not wish to see the colonies "prostrate at our feet," an invocation of an unfortunate speech years earlier by Lord North. He said that he did "not wish to see America conquered by the sword, and bowing to force, but convinced by reason." He believed in consultation in all matters and in treating the colonies as a partner in empire. He denied that removing the tea duty would remove all grievances in America, since it was "the right of taxation they contend about, not the tax; it is the independent state of that country upon the legislature of this, which is contended for." During his speech, the members became inattentive and noisy, "being tired of the debate." It was quipped that "the General belonged rather to the heavy than the light horse." Walpole described him as a pompous speaker who made studied and florid speeches. which were not striking.[24]

III

When he was invited to assume a junior command in America in February 1775, Burgoyne was reluctant to accept until he was personally persuaded by George III. He received his first intimation of the appointment in January from Charles Jenkinson who was a confidant at the Treasury of both the king and Lord North. While they walked together among a crowd outside the House of Commons, Jenkinson said that he wished Burgoyne were in America "with a look and emphasis that conveyed more than accidental conversation." Burgoyne suspected that Jenkinson was sounding him out, and replied that "every soldier must go where he was ordered" but that he "believed in the present state of things, *that* service would not be desirable to any man." On February 2, Burgoyne was summoned by the secretary at war, Lord Barrington, who began by informally talking about the previous evening's debate on America which had kept the members late and "was very tiresome." Barrington made other various "chit-chat observations of that sort" and then suddenly mentioned, "with an abruptness something like what Horace recommends to an epic poet," that he hoped "everything in America would mend" with the arrival of Burgoyne. Barrington broached the subject with a total indifference of expression and tone of voice.[25]

Burgoyne thought this manner of breaking the news "rather singular" when it was "one of the most important, of the most unexpected, and . . . *the most disagreeable events of my life.*" Although he was secretary at war, Barrington was opposed to going to war with America. If war was inevitable, he argued against using the army in favor of a naval blockade. Earlier in his career, Burgoyne had offended Barrington by writing to remind him of his important connections and ridiculously complaining that he had not received a chaplain and choir for his new cavalry regiment—which would have increased his income from the regiment. The request elicited a furious reply from Barrington that Burgoyne was comparing himself to more senior officers of "uninterrupted service to the army," and that he had already received "a series of favours of which the army does not furnish a precedent, and to which with all his amiable and valuable qualities as a man he had not the least claim as a soldier."[26]

When Burgoyne responded that he would decline the service in America if it was optional, Barrington hastened to assure him that he believed Burgoyne to be the personal choice of the king, who had not been influenced by anyone and who had selected the generals "with no view than to scrupulously appoint to each particular service the person in his judgment best adapted to it." Burgoyne professed that he felt it an honor "to be classed with such colleagues" and asked the minister to convey his ready obedience to the king.[27]

Burgoyne ascribed his own hesitation in accepting the command to private family matters. He was concerned by the growing incapacity and illness of his wife. The couple had lost their only child, a ten-year-old daughter, Charlotte Elizabeth Burgoyne, who was buried in the North Cloister of Westminster Abbey in 1764. Burgoyne wrote of the pain of separating "for a length of time, perhaps for ever, from the tenderest, the faithfullest, the most amiable companion and friend that ever man was blessed with—a wife in whom during four and twenty years I never could find a momentary act of blame!" He feared that his death might leave her financially embarrassed: "To supply the requisites of her rank, to reward the virtues of her character, I could only bequeath her a legacy of my imprudences."[28]

Burgoyne was also professionally unhappy with the appointment because it did not give him an independent command but simply made him an adjunct to two more senior major generals. He wrote that he "began to feel regret at being selected merely to make up a triumvirate of reputation." Burgoyne lobbied members of the government to become governor of New York and replace William Tryon. He tried to patch up his relations with Lord North following their differences over the East India Company. He talked to Charles Jenkinson who he believed had nominated him for the post with the intention that he alone should be commander in chief in America. He met with Lord George Germain. He told General William Howe of his desire to be "employed in some more active station than the mere inspection of a brigade." He became convinced that Lord North supported him but that William Howe had used "every engine of interest" against him. There was a rivalry for command before the generals had even departed aboard the *Cerberus* from England.[29]

Before leaving England, Burgoyne gave a speech in the House of Commons in favor of the government's American policy. His active participation in debate was in contrast to the silence of Clinton and Howe, who were fellow members but who never gave a speech until much later when they defended their commands in America. Burgoyne explained his intervention on the ground that there was much public speculation about the sentiments of the military commanders in regard to America. There was particular concern that the generals had such latitude in their orders that they might be influenced either by inflammatory speeches in favor of violence or by advocates for humiliating concessions. He said that he intended to conduct himself with both bravery and compassion. The army would inevitably be made the instrument of correction, but it should desist from "the sudden and impetuous impulse of passion and revenge."[30]

Burgoyne conceded that there was "a charm in the very wanderings and dreams of liberty that disarms an Englishman's anger." The British should remember that they are "contending against fellow subjects and brothers," but it should not be forgotten that they were fighting for the fate of the British Empire. He believed all the governments in the previous ten years had some share in the errors that had been committed, but it had become a simple issue as to whether the representatives of the nation were willing to support the conviction of "the great rational majority of people in England" of the supremacy of Parliament. Britain would otherwise revert to "primitive insignificancy in the Map of the World and the Congress of Philadelphia" would become "the Legislature to dispense the blessings of Empire." Walpole called Burgoyne's speech a "set oration" but said that it was admired, and Burgoyne had the speech published. It was one of the very few hostile British tracts to be reprinted and circulated in America in 1775.[31]

Shortly before leaving London for Portsmouth, Burgoyne had a breakfast meeting with Thomas Hutchinson, who was then regarded as the best-informed and most prominent American loyalist in Britain. Burgoyne was openly critical of the government, the absence of vigorous direction, the indecision of the Cabinet, and the aptness to procrastinate. Although he was due to sail in just over a week, he had not received any formal instructions. On the morning of April 18, 1775, upon his embarkation from

Portsmouth for America, Burgoyne entrusted a letter to a friend which, in the event of his death, was to be sent to the king seeking royal protection for Lady Charlotte Burgoyne. The letter repeated his fears about his leaving his wife in "very narrow [financial] circumstances" when her health was weak. He wrote that she had committed no fault except that of love and generosity in choosing him against the wishes of her family. Despite his many absences, they had never been estranged from one another.[32]

IV

Burgoyne was predictably frustrated and impatient in Boston, where he was nicknamed "General Elbow Room" because he was reputed to have said, "Well, let *us* get in and we'll soon find elbow-room." Within three weeks of his arrival, Burgoyne was writing to Lord North that his position left him powerless to enable him to contribute to the military situation in America. He requested to take a leave of absence to return to England before Christmas. In a letter to one of the secretaries of state, he described himself as "a useless spectator" at the battle of Bunker Hill (June 17, 1775). As the most junior of the major generals, he led the artillery which was briefly engaged in a cannonade of the enemy. He complained that his lot placed him "in a motionless, drowsy, irksome medium, or rather vacuum, too low for the honor of command, too high for that of execution." It was a situation he said that he had foreseen and predicted.[33]

Burgoyne wrote vivid accounts of Bunker Hill. He intended them for circulation and sent letters unsealed to allow his wife to make extracts before forwarding them to his correspondents. His letter to Lord Palmerston included an account of the death of Major John Pitcairn, who had commanded the advance guard on the march to Concord. At Bunker Hill, he led the final assault on the enemy lines, with the cry "now for the glory of the Marines!" He was believed by tradition to have been killed by Peter Salem, a black soldier depicted in the famous painting of the scene by John Trumbull. Burgoyne described the way that Pitcairn's son, who was also an officer in the Marines and who was near his father when he fell, "carried his father upon his back to the boats, about a quarter of a mile, kissed him, and instantly returned to his duty." Burgoyne thought about the war in artistic and melodramatic terms, concluding this account by saying that the scene "in the hands of a good painter or historian, would equal the most that can be found in antiquity." He elsewhere described himself as an insignificant actor in a great cause.[34]

Burgoyne indeed urged the government to use propaganda to persuade not only the enemy but public opinion everywhere. Historian George Athan Billias credits him with understanding psychological warfare and "grasping the implications of the revolutionary idea that the British were fighting a people in arms rather than a professional army," and that they were engaged in a war of ideology. Burgoyne wrote that it would be wise policy to promote the impression of the superiority of regular troops over enemy irregulars through writing and discourse. He proposed that the government commission the composition of a manifesto before the next campaign. He was aware of the importance of persuasion and the possibilities of altering perspectives through rhetoric. On June 12, 1775, General Thomas Gage chose Burgoyne to write a proclamation imposing martial law on Massachusetts that aimed to divide the population by offering pardons to those who lay down their arms and by threatening those who continued to resist. Although it has since been ridiculed for its rhetorical flourishes, it represented an attempt at persuasion.[35]

Burgoyne similarly hoped to influence opinion in his public correspondence with the British-born General Charles Lee who had served under him in Portugal before becoming disenchanted and emigrating to America. Lee was one of the most original and innovative strategists among the generals of the Continental Army, and had advocated fighting an exclusively guerrilla war against the British. He initiated the exchange with Burgoyne, of whom he wrote that there was "no man whose esteem and affection could, in my opinion have done me greater honour." His purpose in writing was to warn Burgoyne not to be misled by the misrepresentation of the views of Americans in Britain. Lee had traveled the entire extent of the eastern seaboard and conversed with all orders of men, among whom he found that "the same spirit animates the whole" and that they were "determined to preserve their liberties or perish." Lee predicted that any attempt to crush the rebellion "must be ineffectual. . . . You cannot possibly succeed." Burgoyne replied that there was no state of tyranny and that it was still possible to obtain a redress of grievances from Britain. He wrote that he was "no stranger to the doctrines of Mr. Locke, and others of the best advocates of the rights of mankind," and declared his "reverence almost amounting to idolatry upon those immortal Whigs who adopted and applied such doctrine" under the Stuarts. Burgoyne suggested a meeting, but it was discouraged by both the home government and the Continental Congress.[36]

Burgoyne displayed his boredom by seeking amusements in Boston. He established a riding school in the Old South Meeting House, thereby snubbing the New England Congregationalists. When he was taken prisoner after Saratoga, he was bitterly reminded of his riding school by his captors as they passed through Boston. Burgoyne also wrote plays for the private theatricals of the British army which were mostly staged at Faneuil Hall. He wrote the prologue and epilogue for an adaptation of Voltaire's *Zara*, ridiculing the prudery of the Congregationalists. Lord Rawdon read the prologue and a ten-year-old girl delivered the epilogue. Burgoyne also wrote a farce entitled *The Blockade of Boston* that portrayed George Washington "as a bumbling figure with an oversized wig and trailing sword." As the curtain rose on the first night, an orderly sergeant ran onto the stage shouting "The Yankees are attacking." The audience applauded and laughed until they heard real alarm guns, and the officers immediately dispersed to go to their units and posts "leaving the Ladies in the House in a most Terible Dilema." Mercy Otis Warren parodied Burgoyne in her own play *The Blockheads* (1776), in which he was called "Elbow Room." She was intimately connected with the rebel movement in Boston and was the sister of the Patriot leader James Otis. She later wrote a three-volume history of the war that was among the earliest accounts by an American.[37]

Burgoyne continued to send home schemes and plans for ending the war. After he witnessed Bunker Hill, his thinking evolved. He viewed the rebellion broadly in both its political and military dimensions, simultaneously advancing alternative political and military solutions. Like the Howe brothers, he favored first trying a peaceful approach and a negotiated settlement. Burgoyne suggested that he be released from service to go on a fact-finding trip to those states that had yet to experience the full impact of the war. He denied any desire to have a formal commission, but simply to act as "an individual member of Parliament, a friend to human nature, and a well-wisher to the united interests of the two countries."[38]

He also elaborated on a military solution, giving a grim portrayal of conditions in Boston. He did not disparage the rebels, noting that their defense had been well conceived and obstinately maintained at Bunker Hill. Their retreat was no flight but was covered with bravery and military skill. They were experts in the use of firearms. Their leaders might be "profligate hypocrites," whose political ideas were "founded upon false principle . . . supported only by sophistry and frenzy," but they often had "great ability." The countryside was surrounded with fortifications, so that rebels driven from one hill simply retrenched on the next, necessitating continual sieges against them. The British troops were only sufficient to secure convoys and communications between the army and the supply depots against an enemy "who are all light troops." There were insufficient cattle and forage. The sick and wounded were without provisions and even broth. The army lacked intelligence, not just of the rebel congresses but of activities among the hills just half a mile away. In fact, Burgoyne thought it desirable to evacuate Boston. There were insufficient troops and supplies to remain in the city.[39]

Burgoyne proposed that the situation in Boston might be eased in the short term by the British fleet attacking off the coast of Rhode Island. The expedition might "try the temper and strength of places, by degrees, to the southward." It might also be a diversion to cover and facilitate greater objects—namely New York—whose possession Burgoyne regarded as strategically vital to holding America. Long Island was potentially an excellent source of supplies and provisions to support operations along the Hudson River. He envisaged cutting off New England by the junction of two armies marching toward one another along the Hudson from New York and from Canada.[40]

Burgoyne wrote that Britain and Ireland did not have sufficient forces to subdue the rebellion, a view that he claimed represented "the sentiments of those who know America." He thought it necessary to raise a large army of foreign mercenaries to begin the operations up the Hudson, while the army from Canada should include British regulars and Canadians together with a "large levy of Indians." Burgoyne's wish to employ Indians was later attributed to Germain, but Burgoyne recognized "that the rebels are more alarmed at the report of engaging Indians than at any other measure" and he therefore recommended "the expediency of diligently preparing and employing that engine." He additionally suggested that the insufficient number of regular troops might also be compensated by "a supply of arms for the blacks, to awe the southern provinces, conjointly with detachments of regulars." The army operations should be supported by a large naval fleet sweeping across the whole eastern seaboard, which might "possibly do the business in one campaign." Britain could not afford half-measures, which would only produce "much fruitless expense, great loss of blood, and a series of disappointments."[41]

V

Before the end of December, Burgoyne was back in London where he was able to start jockeying for a better position in America and to become more closely acquainted with Lord George Germain, the secretary of state for America. Burgoyne continued to develop his thinking for the next campaign on the voyage home and presented the results to the Cabinet in a paper entitled "Reflections upon the War in America." He recommended a more effective blockade of the coast to cut off supplies to the rebels. In common with the campaign plan for 1776, the main objective remained a junction of two separate armies moving north from New York and south from Canada.

Burgoyne's revised version was noteworthy because it showed a respect for rebel fighting ability and appreciation of the problems posed by warfare in America. The rebels were unlikely to risk a general combat or a pitched battle. They preferred to use earthworks and palisades made from felled trees to cover and entrench themselves. Burgoyne dismissed the low opinion of the militia that was so prevalent among fellow officers. He thought it adept at using the terrain to its advantage with its woods, swamps, stonewalls, enclosures, and hiding places. "Every private man was his own general, who will turn every tree and bush into a kind of temporary fortress" from whence, after firing his shot with "deliberation, coolness, and certainty which hidden safety inspires," he skipped to another vantage point and then the next. He concluded that the enemy militia was a respectable adversary even in retreat.[42]

Burgoyne stressed the importance of mobility and flexibility to contend with conditions of warfare in America. He argued for an increase in the size of the light infantry which should become the standard in the British army. He envisaged using artillery to dislodge the rebels followed by a resolute attack of light infantry. In order to mount a more effective blockade of the coast, he suggested the use of smaller armed craft varying from schooners of ninety tons to rowboats. He imagined these smaller boats acting like satellites, oscillating around the primary planet of a large warship or frigate.

They would be the equivalent of light infantry in their ability to navigate every inlet, passage, and sound.[43]

Burgoyne was successful in his bid for advancement and was appointed second in command to Guy Carleton, the governor and commander in chief in Canada (Figure 19). The government had originally intended to appoint Henry Clinton, but he was commanding the expedition that ended in failure in Charleston. The appointment proved bittersweet. Burgoyne's wife lost both her parents within two days of each other while he was in England, and her own health was already ailing when her grief was compounded by the death of her favorite sister. Burgoyne sought to remain with her and considered resigning his commission, but in March 1776, he reluctantly sailed again for America.

As a huge armada of troops and ships assembled off New York under the command of William Howe, Burgoyne arrived with a massive reinforcement in Canada. Between early May and the middle of June 1776, the garrison of nine hundred British regulars swelled to twelve thousand troops, a third of whom were German auxiliaries primarily from Brunswick. Burgoyne's convoy included a talented group of general officers serving under him, like the forty-one-year-old Baron Friedrich von Riedesel, who commanded the three German brigades, and the forty-five-year-old artillery commander Major General William Phillips, who had previously served with Burgoyne in Portugal. Phillips was later described by Thomas Jefferson as "the proudest man of the proudest nation on earth." Brigadier General Simon Fraser led the 24th Foot. During the Seven Years' War, Fraser had commanded a light infantry unit and served as aide-de-camp to the duke of Brunswick. He gained acclaim for attacking and driving off four hundred French troops with only fifty men at the north German village of Wezen in 1761.[44]

Since December 1775, Quebec had been under siege by a small but valiant force of the Continental Army led by Generals Richard Montgomery and Benedict Arnold. The assault was launched at midnight during a blizzard on December 31. Montgomery, a former British officer and a friend of Charles James Fox, was one of the first to be killed in the initial attack, and Arnold was wounded in the leg and forced to return to Montreal. The siege gradually lost momentum owing to dwindling enlistments and a smallpox epidemic that spread throughout the continent during the years of the Revolutionary War. With the melting of the ice along the St. Lawrence River and the imminent arrival of the reinforcements commanded by Burgoyne, Arnold abandoned the siege and began to withdraw.[45]

Burgoyne reached Quebec to find Guy Carleton already in pursuit of the retreating Continental Army. Carleton had been acting governor for a decade. Six feet tall, with an impressive military posture, he was known as cold and haughty but was regarded as a very capable officer who had been a close friend of the hero James Wolfe. As described by Sergeant Roger Lamb, "his presence was itself a garrison, he was a man of ten thousand eyes, and was not to be taken unawares." In 1776, Carleton was the most senior British

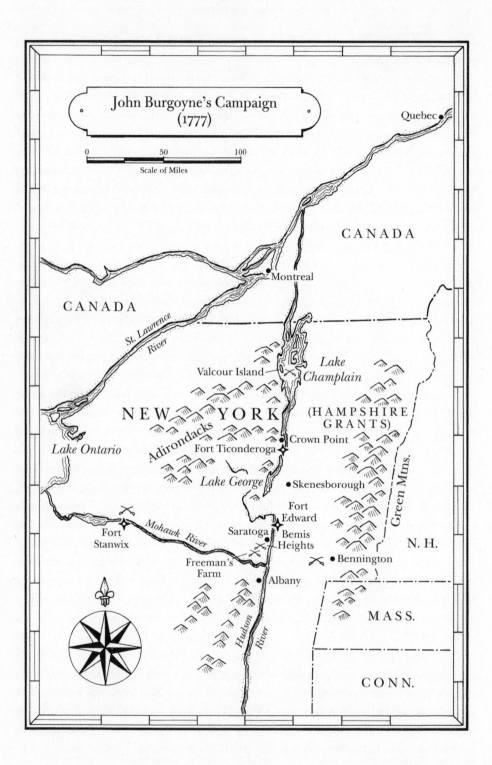

John Burgoyne's Campaign
(1777)

0   50   100
Scale of Miles

Quebec

CANADA

Montreal

CANADA

St. Lawrence River

Valcour Island

Lake Champlain

NEW YORK

Adirondacks

(HAMPSHIRE GRANTS)

Lake Ontario

Fort Ticonderoga

Crown Point

Lake George

Skenesborough

Green Mtns.

Fort Stanwix

Mohawk River

Fort Edward

Saratoga

Bemis Heights

N. H.

Freeman's Farm

Bennington

Albany

Hudson River

MASS.

CONN.

army officer in America. The European population of Canada consisted of some three thousand British subjects, who were mainly merchants and artisans, and as many as seventy-five thousand French Canadians. Carleton had shown vision in integrating the largely French population into the British Empire by persuading the home government to restore French law and to tolerate the Roman Catholic Church. He was against the establishment of an elected assembly because it would have allowed three thousand Protestant British subjects to rule over the majority French Catholics. His advice prevailed and was eventually enshrined in the Quebec Act (1774). The act alienated the British minority who were consequently sympathetic to the Revolution. However, the concessions proved enough to maintain the neutrality of the French population, though insufficient to obtain their active support in the war.[46]

At the end of May 1776, Burgoyne followed Carleton to Three Rivers (Trois Rivières), an Indian settlement on the St. Lawrence River between Montreal and Quebec. The Continental Congress had poured resources into the invasion of Canada, sending an additional fifty-three hundred troops to make a second attack on Quebec. Just as the British overestimated the extent of loyalist support in America, the Continental Congress exaggerated the potential for support for the Revolution among the inhabitants of Canada. Near Three Rivers on June 8, Fraser drove back an advanced guard of enemy reinforcements commanded by Major General John Sullivan of the Continental Army.

While Howe prepared to invade New York, Burgoyne pursued the retreating army of Sullivan, during which "some of his men nearly caught Arnold prisoner." His troops raced in transport boats to overtake their opponent, but contrary winds enabled the armies of Sullivan and Arnold to unite at St. Johns, and Burgoyne arrived there in time to see them rowing away toward Lake Champlain. He and Carleton were unable to continue the pursuit for lack of boats to cross the lake, but by the beginning of July 1776, Burgoyne had driven the enemy from Canada. Benedict Arnold was the last to leave. He supposedly shot his horse to prevent it being captured and vowed that he would return to recapture Canada. He did not return until after the war—as a British subject.[47]

Like William Howe, Carleton was cautious and persisted in the belief that conciliatory behavior might lead to a rapprochement. He released prisoners of war and showed them clemency in the hope that this might sway opinion in America. They included Daniel Morgan, "the Old Wagoner," who later became a general of the Continental Army and the victor at the battle of Cowpens (1781). Rather than lose precious time waiting for boats, Burgoyne sought permission to lead a force across Lake Ontario and cut off the enemy before they could attempt to block the British from crossing Lake Champlain into upstate New York. Burgoyne also hoped that his proposed diversion might assist William Howe in marching north from New York and joining with Carleton along the Hudson. Burgoyne's request was refused by Carleton, who lost weeks waiting for his guns to be dragged down from St. Johns, his boats to be disassembled to enable him to cross the ten-mile portage near Chambly, and his marines to arrive from the St. Lawrence. The delay allowed the enemy force to strengthen their fortifications at Crown Point and Ticonderoga, the former situated at the north end of Lake George and the latter near the southern end of Lake Champlain.[48]

Upon Carleton's resuming his advance along the Richelieu River, his progress was blocked by a flotilla prepared by General Philip Schuyler, who had appreciated the importance of maintaining naval superiority on Lake Champlain. The fleet was hastily completed by Benedict Arnold, and Carleton lost vital time building ships to engage Arnold. Although he triumphed against Arnold in a naval battle off Valcour Island (October 11–13, 1776), the delay enabled Colonel Thaddeus Kosciusko, the Polish engineer, to strengthen the massive fortifications at Fort Ticonderoga whose strategic location on Lake Champlain guarded the entry into New York. On November 3, Carleton seized the fortress of Crown Point which was a natural stepping stone to the capture of Ticonderoga. The distance between the fortresses was only fifteen miles. Owing to the onset of winter and the strong garrison of the Continental Army at Ticonderoga, Carleton decided to return to Canada and give up Crown Point. He had successfully defended Canada against an invasion that had cost the enemy five thousand men. However, his failure to continue his offensive meant that he was unable to fulfill his mission of supporting the operations of William Howe's army in New York.[49]

As he had done during the siege of Boston, Burgoyne once again took leave to return to Britain. He had assumed that Carleton would retain Crown Point for the opening of the campaign the following year, and it was only after he had departed that he discovered that Carleton had given up the fortress. Like Clinton under Howe, Burgoyne balked at not having his advice accepted by Carleton, and though he did not openly challenge Carleton, he spoke of his frustration in a letter to Clinton occasioned also by the fact that in June 1776 during his absence from England, his wife had died and been buried next to their daughter in the North Cloister of Westminster Abbey. In writing to Clinton, Burgoyne sought the consolation of a fellow widower. He told Clinton that he had nearly burned his letter knowing, "too well your mind to think you can read it without pain." He then proceeded to complain of Carleton's conduct of the campaign in Canada. While telling Germain that he was returning to England because of his health and the need to attend to the affairs of his late wife, Burgoyne wrote to Clinton that he was returning because "a secondary station in a secondary army is at no time agreeable." The day after his arrival in England on December 9, 1776, Burgoyne met with Lord George Germain. It was an opportune moment.[50]

Germain was disappointed with the progress of all his commanders—Guy Carleton in Canada, William Howe in New York, and Henry Clinton in South Carolina— who had failed to win a decisive victory with the huge forces that Germain had sent to America in 1776. More than ten weeks before Carleton vacated Crown Point, Germain and the Cabinet had decided that Burgoyne was to supersede Carleton, but the order did not reach Canada until the spring of 1777. Far from acting from spite, Germain aimed to preserve the seniority of Howe, who was junior to Carleton, before the anticipated junction of the two armies at Albany. Nevertheless, Germain's relationship with Carleton became acrimonious, with Carleton sending him indignant, rancorous letters. Although an admirer of Carleton, George III thought him "highly wrong in permitting his pen to convey such asperity to the Secretary of State." Germain dismissed Carleton's subsequent conduct of the campaign as being "without sense or vigour." He tried to prevent George III from conferring upon Carleton the Order of the Bath in reward for his successful defense of Canada.[51]

Burgoyne was to deny that he had ever endeavored to supplant Sir Guy Carleton in command of the British forces in Canada. When Burgoyne had departed for England, Carleton gave him a draft proposal to present to the government for the campaign of 1777. During the home voyage, Burgoyne edited and expanded Carleton's plan into a sixteen-page report entitled "Memorandum & Observations Relative to the Service in Canada." Burgoyne added his own clearly marked commentary, headed "Observations," in which he critiqued and expanded upon "General Carleton's Requisitions."[52]

In addition to meeting with Germain, Burgoyne obtained an audience with George III, who had already concluded that Carleton "may be too cold and not so active as might be wished" and needed to be replaced by "a more enterprizing Commander." The king recommended Burgoyne for the command to Lord North. On Christmas Day 1776, before he had even been appointed to command the army in Canada, Burgoyne placed a bet of one pony—the equivalent of fifty guineas—against the opposition leader Charles James Fox, in the wagers book at Brooks's Club in London, that he would "be home victorious from America by Christmas Day, 1777." In early January, there were newspaper reports of his riding with George III for almost an hour in Hyde Park.[53]

Burgoyne spoke the same language as Germain and George III, with promises of bold strokes in contrast to the seemingly hesitant strategies of Carleton and Howe. At the end of February, he presented Germain with a memorandum entitled "Thoughts for Conducting the War from the Side of Canada." It had the specific objective of the northern army uniting in Albany with Howe's army from New York, with the aim of cutting off New England from the rest of America by control of the Hudson River, which was navigable as far as Albany. The idea of a junction between two armies had, of course, already been an objective of the campaign in 1776 when General Howe had been expected to join forces with Carleton's Canadian army.[54]

In his memorandum, Burgoyne deviated from earlier plans only by suggesting some additions, most notably a third diversionary force to march via Lake Ontario and Oswego to the Mohawk River. The purpose of this third force was as much political as strategic. It was to support loyalists along the Mohawk Valley. It was to be commanded by

Barry St. Leger, a veteran of frontier fighting during the French and Indian War. Burgoyne additionally proposed an attack on Connecticut. His memorandum left open an option to embark the army by sea from Quebec to New York to join Howe. However, he did not think the sea route to be an equally effective strategy "to close the war" as one by land. He significantly failed to offer thoughts regarding the transportation and provision needs of the army after it had reached Fort Edward. It was as if he did not expect any obstacles once he had crossed Lake Champlain and captured Fort Ticonderoga.[55]

VI

In March 1777, Burgoyne was appointed to the command of the northern army in Canada. Germain had previously approached Henry Clinton who was also in London. He had told him that the job was his for the asking, but Clinton was too diffident. Burgoyne showed no such modesty. He was poised to take the limelight. His appointment displaced both Carleton and Clinton; it relegated Howe to the subsidiary role of supporting a junction at Albany. His subsequent behavior throughout the campaign suggested that he thought he could succeed alone, and that he never imagined that he might need assistance from the very generals whom he had trumped.

On April 2, 1777, the fifty-five-year-old Burgoyne sailed for Canada from Plymouth aboard the *Apollo*. His orders from the home government embraced the essentials of his original plan, with minor modifications which he later blamed for the failure of the campaign and which he attributed exclusively to Germain. His orders eliminated some of the suggestions that he had proposed in his memorandum. He was not given permission to make an eastward feint toward the Connecticut River nor to travel by sea to New York. These changes were in accordance with the comments of George III, written in his own handwriting, entitled "Remarks on '*The Conduct of the War from Canada.*'" They were based on at least two other memoranda and very likely on the opinion of Lord Jeffrey Amherst, the lord lieutenant of the ordnance, who was a favorite military adviser of the government and a hero of the French and Indian War. Burgoyne expressed no concern at the minor revisions but rather satisfaction that the material part of his plan had been adopted by the king and Cabinet.[56]

Before his departure from England, Burgoyne wrote to Howe with details of his orders to join him at Albany. Soon after his arrival at Quebec on May 6, 1777, Burgoyne wrote to Howe again, repeating that he was to command the army from Canada and that his orders were to force a junction with him. He soon after received a letter written by Howe to Carleton which made clear that Howe would be unable to reach him at Albany. Howe explained that his force was too small to detach a corps along the Hudson River, and that should Burgoyne think it expedient to advance beyond the frontiers of Canada, he would have "little assistances from hence [New York] to facilitate his approach." Howe warned that he would probably be in Pennsylvania when Burgoyne was ready to advance into New York, and that Burgoyne must "pursue such Measures as may from circumstances be judged most conducive to the Advancement of His Majesty's Service." Burgoyne was unperturbed by the message and subsequently defended himself saying that it "had never weighed on my mind." He thought it had been written before Howe received new instructions from Germain, "which I must have supposed to relate to co-operation" with Howe at Albany.[57]

The preparations for the expedition were not propitious. Burgoyne wrote that he was surprised and mortified "to find a paper handed about at Montreal publishing the whole design of the campaign almost as accurately as if it had been copied from the Secretary of State's letter." His force was nearly a third below the number that he had requested consisting of 7,300 men rather than the 11,000 specified in his original memorandum. He commanded 6,740 regular soldiers, of whom 3,724 were British and the rest mostly German mercenaries from Brunswick. Like Howe and Clinton, he much preferred British troops to German. It was largely just prejudice, but the mercenaries did pose operational difficulties because of the difference of language and the problem of integrating them into a single fighting force. However, Burgoyne's force included some of the oldest and best regiments in the British army. His officers included thirty future generals and four members of Parliament.[58]

The expedition recruited only four hundred Indians rather than the proposed thousand. They included warriors of the Iroquois and Algonquin nations from areas between Quebec and Lake Ontario and beyond. The Iroquois League or Six Nations had been a powerful presence in upper New York. At the Council of Oswego in 1775, Joseph Brant (also known as Thayendanegea) who was a chief of the Mohawks, and Sir Guy Johnson, the British superintendent of Indian affairs, had negotiated an alliance with the Mohawks, the Senecas, the Onondagas, and the Cayugas, though they failed to win over the Oneida and Tuscarora peoples who sided with the Continental Congress (Figure 18). During the winter of 1775–76, Brant and Johnson had gone to London where Brant's father had been one of the four native chiefs to visit Queen Anne in 1710. Brant was to join the second expedition from Canada along the Mohawk, commanded by Barry St. Leger, which aimed to encourage loyalist support and create a diversion in favor of Burgoyne's march to Albany. In Burgoyne's expedition, there were also Ottawas and Abenakis from Odanak, Bécancour, Caughnawaga, Saint Regis (Akwasasne), and the Lake of Two Mountains (Oka). According to historian Colin G. Calloway, the majority of these warriors were coerced into joining the expedition. The courting of their support by both sides certainly placed Indians in an invidious position of choosing between the lesser of two evils.[59]

Burgoyne had only eight hundred militia and French Canadians rather than the two thousand that he had anticipated in his memorandum to Germain, and within two months their numbers dwindled through desertion to thirty. Carleton was scathing about Burgoyne's expectation of assistance from the Canadians, which he said "was surely not [based] upon information proceeding from me." Although Carleton by implication blamed Germain, Burgoyne had made the original estimates, despite the low turnout of Canadians during Carleton's offensive of 1776. Unlike William Howe, Burgoyne did not seek permission to change the plan when it was apparent that he lacked the minimum troops that he had earlier deemed a necessary condition for success.[60]

Burgoyne was also accompanied by his mistress, who was the wife of a commissary officer named Rousseau. Other women traveling with the army included the pregnant Lady Harriet Acland, the daughter of the earl of Ilchester and wife of the commander of the grenadiers, Major John Dyke Acland. They were later joined by the thirty-eight-year-old Baroness Frederika von Riedesel, the wife of the German commander, and her three little daughters. She was determined to join her husband and spent over a year making the journey from Germany. She wrote a journal of her time in America, which was published in 1800. There were officially about 225 women and 500 children among the camp followers of the army, although it was alleged at a subsequent inquiry that the number of women was closer to 2,000.[61]

The expedition was debilitated from the start by the lack of carriages, wagons, carts, horses, and drivers to haul the artillery and supplies. Burgoyne was to be criticized for the amount of artillery and supplies that he took with him, which impeded his advance across forests, rivers, and areas of virtual wilderness. His train of artillery consisted of 138 field pieces and siege equipment, which required fifteen hundred horses to haul. He justified the artillery as "formidable to raw troops" and opponents who were adept at building entrenchments, and as necessary for attacking and defending Ticonderoga and Albany. However, there is no contemporary evidence for the popular story that he used thirty carts to carry his personal possessions. Burgoyne spent a month in Canada trying to obtain four hundred horses—less than a third of his requirements—and five hundred wagons. He and Carleton had likely assumed that they could make up the deficiencies with *corvées,* detachments of unarmed provincials impressed by the government to repair roads, carry provisions, and provide temporary labor.[62]

Burgoyne appreciated the power of words in warfare. From his office desk aboard ship, he had written a proclamation to the Americans that was printed and published on June 24, 1777. It denounced "the present unnatural rebellion" as establishing "the compleatest system of Tyranny that ever God in his displeasure suffered for a time to be exercised over a forward and stubborn generation." The assemblies and committees of the rebels had inflicted "Arbitrary imprisonment, confiscation of property, persecution and torture, unprecedented in the inquisitions of the Romish church." He invited the population to return to the blessings, protection, and security of legal government. He darkly threatened that he had "but to give stretch to the Indian Forces under his direction," who he claimed "amounted to thousands," and who would overcome "the hard-ened enemies of Great Britain." He wrote ominously of the vengeance of the state against willful outcasts, and conjured images of devastation, famine, and "every concomitant horror that a reluctant but indispensable prosecution of military duty must occasion."[63]

On June 21, 1777, Burgoyne addressed a congress of four hundred Indians near present-day Willsboro on the River Bouquet, which ran eastward from the Adirondacks about forty miles north of Fort Ticonderoga. He called upon the warriors to go forth "in the might of your valour and your cause" to strike at the "disturbers of public order, peace, and happiness—destroyers of commerce, parricides of the State." His speech cautioned against brutality. He prohibited bloodshed against unarmed opponents and the use of knives or hatchets against elderly men, women, children, and prisoners. He similarly only permitted the scalping of dead enemies. He offered rewards for prisoners and asked that they be well treated.[64]

In both England and America, Burgoyne's speeches and proclamations alter-nately aroused horror and derision. He and the home government were condemned for employing Indians by both the opposition in Parliament and the revolutionaries in America. The earl of Chatham claimed to discern a frown on the faces in the tapestry looking down upon the House of Lords. According to the memoirs of Horace Walpole, even government ministers "laughed at his pomp." Edmund Burke parodied Burgoyne's oration to the Indians, with Burgoyne as the keeper of lions during a riot in the zoo at the Tower of London. Burke imagined him flinging open "the dens of the wild beasts" with an address to "My gentle lions, my humane bears, my tender-hearted hyenas, go forth! but I exhort you as you are Christians, and members of a civilized society, to take care not to hurt any man, woman, or child!" Burke's speech was so humorous that Lord North became convulsed with laughter, the tears rolling down his plump cheeks.[65]

Burgoyne's use of Indians, French Canadians, and German auxiliaries alienated popular support in America by making his advance seem like a foreign invasion. The Canadians were suspected as potential agents of tyranny, because they were mostly French and Roman Catholics who were popularly identified with the absolutist regimes of continental Europe. The Declaration of Independence had referred to the Germans "as large Armies of foreign Mercenaries," who had been transported "to compleat the works of death, desolation and tyranny," and spoke of "the merciless Indian Savages, whose known rule of warfare, is an undistinguished destruction of all ages, sexes and conditions." The employment of such forces was revealing of the dilemma facing the British, whose insufficient manpower necessitated their allying with the most margin-alized elements of American society.[66]

Avoiding the delays that had beset Carleton in 1776, Burgoyne's invasion force set off in a grand procession down Lake Champlain, surrounded by vistas of the Adirondacks to the west and the Green Mountains to the east. As his convoy of boats approached the wildest part of the lake, the weather was remarkably fine and clear, with not a breeze stir-ring. His whole army appeared "in such perfect regularity as to form the most complete and splendid regatta you can possibly conceive." It was a majestic sight, with the Indians in the vanguard in their birch canoes holding between twenty and thirty men each, followed by the gunboats, together with brigs and sloops, and women camp followers in the rear. The fleet presented a formidable appearance as it became visible on the horizon from Fort Ticonderoga. It easily crushed the rebel naval resistance, which was minor compared to the opposition of the previous year by Benedict Arnold at Valcour Bay.[67]

VII

Although Horace Walpole wrote scathingly of "General Swagger" who "promises to cross America in a hop, step, and a jump," Burgoyne initially achieved dramatic effect in the swift momentum of his descent into America. It took him little over a week to advance the same distance that Carleton had covered in four months in 1776. He not only succeeded where Carleton had failed by taking Crown Point, but he also took the glitter-ing prize of Fort Ticonderoga, the largest fortress complex in North America with the capacity to hold up to twelve thousand men. Located at the south end of Lake Champlain in upstate New York, it occupied a critical strategic site for command of both that lake and Lake George. The rebels had spent over a year strengthening the fort. Between July 2 and 6, Burgoyne laid siege to Ticonderoga. His artillery officer, Major General William Phillips, favored mounting guns on an unguarded promontory called Sugar Loaf Hill (later Mount Defiance) overlooking the great fortress. He was famously said to have advised "Where a goat can go, a man can go, and where a man can go, he can drag a gun." Upon seeing the British advantage, the besieged rebel garrison of 1,567 men evacuated and escaped unharmed, leaving Burgoyne the master of Ticonderoga.[68]

Before confirmation of the victory arrived, expectations of success ran high within government circles. The lord advocate for Scotland, Henry Dundas, was so ex-cited that he could hardly wait for the post. William Eden, an under secretary of state and a confidant of Lord North, thought the campaign was close to ending the rebellion. William Knox, an under secretary of state for the American Department, predicted that there would be a special newspaper edition announcing a great victory. John Robinson, secretary to the Treasury, advised Lord North to delay the opening of Parliament until the arrival of good news from America. When news of the capture of Ticonderoga arrived in London, George III was said to have run into the boudoir of Queen Charlotte exclaim-ing, "I have beat them! Beat all the Americans!" [69]

Burgoyne was the man of the moment. He was rewarded with the brevet (tempo-rary) rank of lieutenant general, and was also invited to become a member of the Order of the Bath. Before he had even left England, Burgoyne had assumed that he would receive such an offer, and had asked that it be declined on his behalf by the earl of Derby. It was an odd decision for one so brazenly ambitious. George III had personally revived the prestige of the order, and made such awards only sparingly to maintain its exclusivity and status. However, he had already conferred knighthoods and membership of the order on Sir William Howe, Sir Henry Clinton, and Sir Guy Carleton. A gambler by nature, Burgoyne was playing for the highest stakes in anticipation of a yet higher honor. General George Washington predicted that Burgoyne's successes "may precipitate his ruin," and that he would pursue "that line of conduct which of all others is most favorable to us."[70]

Burgoyne had to leave over a tenth of his regular army to garrison the massive fortifications at Ticonderoga, a force that he had wrongly assumed he might replace with reinforcements from Canada. His request for additional troops was initially denied by Carleton on the grounds that he did not have the authority to reassign his troops outside Canada owing to very precise orders from Germain. Although there is no evidence that he acted from malice, Carleton was incensed by Germain's treatment of him and requested to resign as governor in late June 1777. While Burgoyne was in England, Carleton did little to obtain horses and wagons in preparation for Burgoyne's campaign. He was opposed to the use of Indians and obtained only four hundred for Burgoyne while managing to raise a thousand for the expedition of St. Leger along the Mohawk. He had waited two weeks before giving Burgoyne the letter to himself from Howe with the critical information that he was unlikely to be able to join Burgoyne in Albany. Carleton appreciated the importance of the letter, which he passed on to Burgoyne with the comment that Howe was "wishing you a happy and Successful Campaign." After Burgoyne had departed from Canada, Carleton wrote to Germain of "those evils which might naturally follow to the publick from the chief commands being given to an inferior officer" while he was "to act as a subaltern office[r]" in his own government under Burgoyne. Burgoyne never blamed Carleton. He later always went out of his way to acknowledge his assistance.[71]

Like Howe after the conquest of New York, Burgoyne did not expect much opposition after the conquest of Ticonderoga, but anticipated a triumphal procession through loyalist territory south to Albany. He easily outnumbered the forty-five hundred troops of the Continental Army under General Philip Schuyler, who was unpopular among New Englanders because he had championed land claims of New York against Massachusetts and New Hampshire. They preferred General Horatio Gates, which led to a leadership contest between Schuyler and Gates. According to the testimony of one British officer, "the army in general did not think" that the rebels "would make a stand any where." Burgoyne was so confident of success that he requested leave to return over winter to Britain and was disappointed that his orders did not permit him to attack Connecticut. General Howe similarly thought it would be plain sailing for Burgoyne after Ticonderoga. He waited until he heard confirmation of the victory and then embarked with the fleet from Staten Island for Philadelphia. Howe believed that he was creating a diversion in favor of Burgoyne by drawing away the troops commanded by George Washington, and Burgoyne gave no hint that he would need help.[72]

Burgoyne began a relentless pursuit of the escaped garrison from Ticonderoga, which necessitated his proceeding by land through Skenesborough, now Whitehall in New York, rather than by water across Lake George toward Albany. Although he was to justify the decision on the ground that he only had enough shipping to send his baggage and supplies across the lake, he wanted to maintain the appearance of a victorious advance, whereas the lake route would have required him to double back to Ticonderoga. While still at Crown Point, Burgoyne had issued a general order that "this army must not retreat." In his later defense of the campaign, he admitted that he was influenced by the negative general impression that "a retrograde movement is apt to make upon the minds both of enemies and friends." At Skenesborough, his army was joined by some six hundred loyalists, which seemed to confirm earlier optimism in regard to the political persuasions of the local inhabitants.[73]

Burgoyne was obliged to suspend operations to await the arrival of provisions, transportation, and tents. He later recalled that for every hour that he contemplated the strategy of the army, he had to spend another twenty wondering how to feed it. Furthermore, his progress was contested at every stage. An advance force commanded by Simon Fraser encountered unexpectedly fierce resistance from a rearguard of the retreating rebel garrison. Having marched 150 miles in a few weeks, Burgoyne's army took almost a month to go 22 miles from Skenesborough to Fort Edward on the Hudson. The troops were so short of wagons that they used a hundred boats each pulled by six or more horses. Their path was obstructed every ten or twelve yards by great trees that the rebels had felled lengthways with their branches interwoven. They had to build some forty bridges to cross deep ravines and to construct a logwood causeway over a morass two miles wide. They marched through heavily wooded forests, creeks, marshes, morasses, swamps, and hilly countryside. The conditions were made worse by heavy rainfall. The few clearings and farms were desolate, as Schuyler was conducting a scorched-earth retreat and his troops were driving away cattle. Burgoyne was accompanied by fourteen hundred horses in a region destitute of forage, and his force was slowed down by the long artillery train. There were not even enough horses to mount his German dragoons. In the meantime, the Continental Army was reinforced by troops sent by Washington under Brigadier Generals Benedict Arnold and Benjamin Lincoln.[74]

Upon approaching Fort Edward, Burgoyne suffered a major setback in attempting to win support among the local population with the killing of Jane McCrea, which became a legend of British brutality in America. Her death allegedly occurred from the blow of a tomahawk following a quarrel between two of Burgoyne's Indians over the reward for accompanying her as bodyguards to meet her fiancé in the army. She was a curious heroine for the revolutionary cause, because she was engaged to a loyalist officer called David Jones. Nevertheless, the incident was used by the revolutionaries as propaganda. In a published letter to Burgoyne, General Horatio Gates of the Continental Army expressed abhorrence "that the famous lieutenant-general Burgoyne, in whom the fine gentleman is united with the scholar and soldier, should hire the savages of America to scalp Europeans, and the descendants of Europeans." Gates embellished the incident with a sentimental account of the "young lady lovely to sight, of virtuous character and amiable disposition . . . scalped and mangled in the most shocking manner." He portrayed her "dressed to meet her promised husband," but instead meeting murderers "employed by you." The fact that Jane McCrea was engaged to a loyalist made the episode more poignant because it suggested that Burgoyne was unable to control his Indian allies and that they were capable of indiscriminate murder of Americans. The account by Gates was published in every newspaper in America between August and October 1777. The incident became one of the enduring images of the American Revolution in depictions like the celebrated painting by John Vanderlyn in 1804.[75]

Upon reaching Fort Edward, Burgoyne's supply lines extended 185 miles to Montreal. He was so short of provisions that his "army could barely be victualled from day to day." Nevertheless, he remained optimistic, writing to Clinton that he expected to reach Albany no later than August 23. Clinton wrote in his memoirs that this letter showed Burgoyne "to be in the highest spirits, and did not contain an expression that indicated either an expectation or desire of cooperation" from Howe.[76]

Burgoyne waited another week at Fort Edward. He had lost his original momentum owing to the shortage of provisions, and he ideally wanted to accumulate a three-month supply before his arrival in Albany. It was because of the lack of forage for the horses that Burgoyne sent out an expedition to Bennington, the location of a military depot together with food supplies of grain, flour, and cattle. Burgoyne had heard that it was lightly guarded by militia, and he also acted under the belief that the enemy was "broken and disconcerted" and that the sympathies of the local population were "five to one" in favor of Britain. Although Riedesel had recommended a raid into the Connecticut valley, Burgoyne ordered a much more ambitious operation, sending the German detachment further south under the command of Lieutenant Colonel Friedrich Baum. Burgoyne wanted to continue his advance and reunite with Baum's detachment on the way to Albany. He was later accused of sending an inadequate force too great a distance.[77]

What followed was a stinging defeat for the detachment (August 16), for which, like Howe after Trenton, Burgoyne blamed the German officers. He claimed that Baum had failed to observe instructions to proceed with the "utmost caution" by establishing posts for a secure retreat, and to avoid an engagement without the "certainty of success." Instead of meeting with support, Baum's detachment was infiltrated by enemy troops pretending to be loyalists. He was also simply unlucky that two thousand rebel militiamen from New Hampshire and Massachusetts had coincidentally planned to rendezvous at Bennington under the command of Colonel John Stark, a veteran of Bunker Hill. During the ensuing battle, Baum's troops were surrounded and outnumbered in a double-double envelopment by four flanking columns of enemy militia. Burgoyne sent a relief expedition of dismounted German dragoons commanded by Lieutenant Colonel Heinrich von Breymann. Impeded by their cumbersome cavalry uniforms with thigh-high jackboots and giant spurs, Breymann's men nearly suffered the same fate as those of Baum. Breymann was shot five times in his coat and once in his leg. Burgoyne's two expeditions lost more than a thousand men in the attempt to capture the arsenal and provisions at Bennington.

Although Baum had shown poor judgment in the execution of the mission, the real cause of failure was the misleading intelligence about the strength of American loyalists. Baum was outnumbered by over two to one, which was indicative of the popular support for the Revolution in New England. Within less than a week, a tenth of the adult male population had enlisted for service in the militia of New Hampshire. Similarly the expedition led by Barry St. Leger failed to stir a loyalist rising along the Mohawk and to divert the enemy from Burgoyne. After an unsuccessful siege of Fort Stanwix, St. Leger withdrew when he was one hundred and twenty-four miles from Burgoyne's army at Fort Edward. Unlike Burgoyne, he did not feel compelled to obey the letter of his instructions from Germain to proceed down the Mohawk River to Albany and put himself under the command of Sir William Howe.[78]

At the end of July, Burgoyne wrote that he was ignorant of Howe's movements. He discovered that at least two of his messengers had been hanged by the enemy and suspected the same fate had attended messengers sent by Howe. On August 3, he received a two-week-old letter from Howe that made clear that his objective was Pennsylvania, where he expected to encounter Washington. Howe promised to follow Washington if he moved northward and assured Burgoyne that Clinton would "act as occurrences may direct" in New York. Burgoyne did not communicate the contents of Howe's letter to his men or even fellow commanders like Riedesel. He was subsequently informed by Clinton that Howe had gone to the Chesapeake. On August 20, Burgoyne admitted to Germain that the prospects for his campaign had become "far less favourable," since the majority of the population supported the Revolution and the enemy conducted themselves "with a secrecy and dispatch that are not to be equaled."[79]

In the same letter to Germain of August 20, Burgoyne rehearsed what became his exculpatory argument after Saratoga. If it had not been for positive orders to the contrary, he claimed, he would have considered it his duty to remain stationary or even to withdraw to Fort Edward "where my communication with Lake George would be perfectly secure, till some event happened to assist my movement forward." However, Burgoyne insisted that his orders did not give him the discretion to stay inactive, but rather required him to "force a junction with Sir William Howe." He wrote that he never foresaw that he would be left to pursue his own way through "such a tract of country, and hosts of foes without any co-operation from New York." He ended with a flourish that whatever his fate, he was confident that his good intent would not be questioned.[80]

Burgoyne was hedging his bets by blaming his orders for his decision to advance. He had himself vowed that his army would never turn back, and he had been critical of supine tactics of Gage in 1775 and Carleton in 1776. He had made his reputation by daring and boldness, while none of the other British generals felt bound by their orders to pursue a course of folly. In contrast to Burgoyne, Howe had revised his orders from home throughout the campaign and later blamed Germain for not giving him sufficiently positive orders to go to Albany. Germain had made it his maxim that commanders should have discretion, because they were the most competent judges of conditions in America. Burgoyne had never defined what he meant by a junction or communication, and what he expected to achieve on arrival in Albany. It had always been an ultimate rather than an immediate goal of the campaign. As Germain observed of the original plan proposed by Burgoyne, "a co-operation of Howe's army was not expected . . . the expedition [was] undertaken as an independent enterprise to be executed by the force allotted for it." Burgoyne had even written that he would need heavy artillery to defend Albany in the event of his spending "winter there, without communication with New York." Burgoyne might have been more persuasive if he had argued that he felt morally compelled to advance by his promises to the government, as well as by the expectations of both his army and Lord George Germain.[81]

Later on, facing an inquiry before Parliament, Burgoyne was inconsistent in simultaneously blaming his orders and arguing that he was under pressure from his own troops to continue. He called former officers as witnesses who testified that the troops thought it their indispensible duty to risk an action before returning to Canada: given their temper and language, they would have been satisfied with nothing less than crossing the river to fight the enemy. Quartermaster General Captain Money said that if they had returned without fighting "the army would never have forgiven the general, nor the general have forgiven himself." The earl of Harrington, who was captain of the 29th Foot, said "that General Burgoyne's character would not have stood very high either with the army, this country, or the enemy, had he halted at Fort Edward." In his published defense of the campaign in 1780, Burgoyne claimed "that no proof that could have been brought from appearances, intelligence or reasoning, could have justified me to my country, have saved me from the condemnation of my profession, or produced pardon within my own breast, had I not advanced, and tried a battle with the enemy." He had only to recall the criticism of Carleton by Germain after the retreat from Crown Point in 1776.[82]

VIII

On September 14, Burgoyne crossed the Rubicon when his army used a bridge of boats to pass the Hudson River. He had been warned that all safety of communication would cease the hour that he did so and severed his two-hundred-mile supply line from Montreal. His officers and troops had earlier discarded all their baggage except essentials, and although his men spent virtually a month trying to collect provisions to last thirty days, he later claimed that he only had provisions for thirteen days. However, there was no sense of impending doom among his officers and men. The army was in good spirits and keen to engage the enemy. Baroness von Riedesel recalled in her journal "the high hopes of victory and of reaching the promised land," and the enthusiasm with which they heard Burgoyne rally them with the words "Britons never retreat." Burgoyne never told his army that it was unlikely to be met by Sir William Howe, but then he had never suggested that the success of his campaign was predicated on such a junction.[83]

Meanwhile, the revolutionary forces awaited Burgoyne's advance at Bemis Heights, under General Horatio Gates, commander of the Continental Army in New England. A former British army officer, Gates had fought in both America and the Caribbean during the French and Indian War. His mother had been the housekeeper to the duke of Leeds and he was reputed to be the duke's out-of-wedlock son, while his godfather was Horace Walpole. A ruddy-faced man who wore thick spectacles, Gates was possibly even more ambitious and political than Burgoyne. Perceiving an opportunity to cut off Burgoyne, George Washington had reinforced Gates with troops commanded by Daniel Morgan and Benedict Arnold. Known as "Old Wagoner," Daniel Morgan was a large man, six feet tall and weighing two hundred pounds, who commanded a crack regiment of riflemen carrying Kentucky and Pennsylvania weapons that were much more accurate than the smoothbore Brown Bess muskets of the British. Popularly remembered as a traitor in the United States, Benedict Arnold was previously an American hero who had helped lead the successful capture of Ticonderoga and the invasion of Canada in 1775. He had frustrated Carleton's advance at Valcour Island in 1776, thereby preventing an earlier planned junction of the British army at Albany.

Gates's force had the advantages of interior lines, better intelligence, numerical superiority, favorable terrain, plentiful provisions, and ease of resupply and reinforcement. Commanding the route to Albany, Bemis Heights was an ideal position for defense on a plateau with steep bluffs rising some two to three hundred feet overlooking a narrow defile on the west side of the Hudson River. The area was heavily wooded, with an occasional clearing for a farm, which made it difficult for Burgoyne to maneuver his army and make effective use of his artillery. The terrain favored the skirmishing tactics of the rebel militia and riflemen. Burgoyne faced an invidious choice of either running a gauntlet of enemy fire or launching a frontal attack against a well-entrenched enemy. His opportunity of retreat was gradually closed by enemy troops who began to retake some of the forts and supply posts on the way to Canada, including Fort Edward.

Over the course of a month, Burgoyne was defeated in an interconnected series of engagements in the environs of Saratoga. After crossing the Hudson, most of the accompanying Indians left his army. Although he was later dismissive of their utility, his army was blind without the Indians acting as scouts. His knowledge of enemy movements was hindered by the hilly and forested landscape. His center column approached a small clearing known as Freeman's Farm, named after the farmer whose abandoned cabin stood in the midst of a field which was mostly obscured by woods. Although only four miles apart, the opposing armies had been unaware of each other until one of Gates's patrols fired upon a British foraging party who were digging potatoes on another abandoned farm.[84]

On September 19, Burgoyne sent a detachment of Tories, Canadians, and Indians to establish outposts on an undefended height overlooking Gates' army at Bemis Heights. From this vantage point, he hoped to use his artillery before ordering his infantry to force the rebels back to the Hudson. This instigated the battle of Freeman's Farm (also known as the first battle of Saratoga), in which Burgoyne's troops were outnumbered by the forces of Gates. Burgoyne had always trusted in British bayonet charges to ensure victory, but his men's repeated attempts to charge were ineffectual owing to the thickness of the wood and the accuracy of the enemy riflemen, some of whom were hanging from trees. Burgoyne's plan to take the height was foiled by Benedict Arnold, who perceived a weakness in the British center and an opportunity to divide Burgoyne's force by attacking the German troops of Baron von Riedesel. According to the eyewitness account of Roger Lamb, an Irish-born private in the army, Burgoyne "behaved with great personal bravery, he shunned no danger; his presence and conduct animated the troops (for they greatly loved the general)." In his narrative which was turned into a novel by Robert Graves, Lamb described how Burgoyne "delivered his orders with precision and coolness; and in the heat, fury, and danger of fight maintained those true characteristics of the soldier—serenity, fortitude and undaunted intrepidity." Between a third and a half of the British soldiers were wounded, killed, or taken prisoner, during four hours of incessant fire on both sides of which Lamb wrote: "Few actions have been characterized by more obstinacy in attack or defence." The 62nd Regiment began the battle with 350 men of whom only four or five officers and sixty soldiers remained effective by early evening. In one artillery detachment, the captain and thirty-six of the forty-eight men were either killed or wounded.[85]

There was not a moment of respite from the smoke. When one marksman spotted the lace decoration of a saddle, he thought he had killed Burgoyne, but he had actually wounded a Captain Green, the aide-de-camp to Major General Phillips. The army abounded with officers in their teens. Among the casualties of the 20th Regiment, three young officers were buried together, of whom the oldest was seventeen. The sixteen-year-old Lieutenant Hervey, who was the nephew of the adjutant general of the British army, took his own life with an opium overdose to avoid an excruciating, slow death with the words, "Tell my uncle I died like a soldier." Burgoyne was close to defeat when the British army was rescued by the arrival of Riedesel and his Brunswickers. The British held the field in a last desperate bayonet charge, but with crippling losses.[86]

Burgoyne intended to resume the offensive the next day but was dissuaded by Fraser. Heartened by a message from Sir Henry Clinton that he would "make a push" northward from New York to deflect Gates, Burgoyne again called off an attack and instead began to entrench by building redoubts along the two-and-a-half-mile front of his army. The two sides were deadlocked for seventeen days, during which Gates was reinforced by over six thousand Connecticut, Massachusetts, New Hampshire, and New York militiamen, giving him a total of fifteen thousand rank and file. In the words of Sergeant Lamb, these "numerous parties of militia . . . swarmed around like birds of prey." Burgoyne's outposts were subject to raids by Oneida, Tuscarora, and Stockbridge Mohican warriors, from the only native tribes to ally with the Continental Army. The armies were in such close proximity that there was constant skirmishing, with not a day or night passing without the "roaring of cannon and whistling of bullets." The British officers and men slept in their uniforms ready for action at any time. Burgoyne put all his hope in the prospect of a relief expedition by Clinton.[87]

It was not until September 21 that Burgoyne indicated that he needed help from Clinton, and asked him to attack or menace Fort Montgomery, on the Hudson fifty miles upstream from New York. Clinton was already angry that Howe had gone to Philadelphia and left him in a "most starved defensive" in New York. He recalled in his memoirs that Burgoyne, "so far from calling for assistance, scarcely even hinted that he expected cooperation" until the arrival of his letter on September 29. Burgoyne still failed to communicate the urgency of his situation to Clinton. Except for the check at Bennington, Clinton described how every account before October 5 had "represented his progress . . . as most flourishing." Burgoyne had difficulty communicating with Clinton. They wrote to one another in cipher: each had an hour-glass shaped frame with which to isolate a message from the rest of the text and decode it. The messengers had difficulty moving through enemy territory and despite swallowing a message wrapped in a silver musket bullet, Lieutenant Daniel Taylor of the 9th Regiment of Foot was intercepted and hanged as one of the unfortunate couriers. On October 3, Burgoyne put his troops on short rations while assuring them that "there were powerful armies" ready to come to their assistance. He was banking on help from Clinton, who left the same day with three thousand men up the Hudson. It was a vain hope, however, since Clinton did not have sufficient troops to mount a rescue mission and aimed merely to open up the Hudson River as far as Albany. He might at best create a diversion to draw away some of Gates's troops.[88]

On the eve of the battle of Bemis Heights (also known as the second battle of Saratoga), Gates had the measure of Burgoyne, and predicted that despair might cause him to risk all upon one throw, saying "he is an Old Gamester." Burgoyne ignored General Riedesel's proposal to retreat to Fort Miller where he could maintain a line of communications to Canada. When the battle commenced on October 7, Burgoyne personally led fifteen hundred men against the left wing of the enemy army in an effort to occupy the hill whose capture had evaded him during the first battle. In this crisis, Sergeant Lamb wrote that he "appeared cool and intrepid." When Gates's troops simultaneously broke the right and left flanks of his army, Burgoyne ordered a general withdrawal, but the messenger was wounded before he could deliver the command. Acting without authority from Gates, Benedict Arnold assumed the direction of the field and rushed into the fray, rallying the rebel troops to prevent British artillery from firing upon their lines. A German soldier fired point-blank at Arnold in the same knee in which he had been wounded at Quebec. The shot crippled Arnold for life, leaving one leg shorter than the other, but did not prevent his turning the battle into a decisive rebel victory. Burgoyne himself had been dangerously exposed during the battle when a shot passed through his hat and another tore his waistcoat. He claimed that he might have struck a fatal blow against the enemy but for Arnold.[89]

The campaign began to wear an aura of tragedy. General Simon Fraser, who had been both friend and adviser to Burgoyne, was shot and mortally wounded. He was nursed through the night by Baroness von Riedesel, and buried the next day at sunset on the battlefield in accordance with his dying wishes. The voice of the officiating chaplain never wavered during the funeral while enemy batteries fired into the midst of the mourners who were covered in dust thrown up by cannonballs. Burgoyne described "the mute but expressive mixture of sensibility and indignation upon every countenance," believing that the memory would remain "to the last of life upon every man who was present." Burgoyne was similarly moved by the plight of Lady Harriet Acland. She had endured all the privations of the campaign to be with her husband. After he was shot through both legs and taken prisoner during the battle, she went into the enemy camp to nurse him. Burgoyne was affected by the courage and forbearance of a woman habituated to "all the soft elegancies, and refined enjoyments, that attend high birth and fortune." He had lost some 600 men in the battle against 150 enemy losses.[90]

Like Cornwallis at Yorktown, Burgoyne was surrounded and outnumbered when he surrendered at Saratoga. After the repulse of his attack on October 7, he retreated to Old Saratoga, now called Schuylerville. With his army close to starvation and subject to constant fire, Burgoyne held a council of his general officers, together with regimental commanders and even captains, who voted unanimously to surrender. Burgoyne had some 6,500 men, but less than 4,000 fit for action, against 20,365 effectives under Gates. In the midst of anguish, with surrender inevitable, Baroness von Riedesel described Burgoyne as "having a jolly time" and "spending half the night singing and drinking and amusing himself in the company of the wife of a commissary, who was his mistress and, like him, loved champaign." During these final days, the baroness recalled the moaning at night of a dying lieutenant, whose arm had been torn away at the shoulder by a cannonball, which was "doubly gruesome as the sound re-echoed through the cellar."[91]

Between October 13 and 17, Burgoyne opened negotiations for surrender. He was able to obtain liberal terms from Gates who was fearful of the advance of Sir Henry Clinton's advanced corps, led by Major General John Vaughan, that approached within forty-five miles south of Albany. Burgoyne played a game of brinksmanship to the very end, threatening to break off the negotiations and reconvening his council officers to consider reversing the surrender agreement when he thought he again had a chance. The surrender terms were more like an armistice, and Burgoyne attempted to disguise the reality of his surrender by having the agreement named the Convention of Saratoga. The terms permitted Burgoyne's army to return to Britain on condition that it never again served in America.[92]

During the subsequent surrender ceremony, a witness described how the drums seemed to have lost their formerly inspiring sound. The band played the "British Grena-diers," a favorite of the British army in America, "which not long before was so animat-ing, yet then it seemed by its last feeble effort as if almost ashamed to be heard on such an occasion." Gates spared the British further humiliation by keeping his army out of sight in the woods as the vanquished troops piled their arms while his fifes and drums played "Yankee Doodle." In a scene that was repeated at Yorktown, some of the British soldiers broke the butts of the muskets as they threw them down with impotent rage and defiance. The commanders raised their hats to one another. Burgoyne said to the former half-pay major of the British army, "The fortunes of war, General Gates, have made me your prisoner." Gates replied: "I shall always be ready to bear testimony that it has not been through any fault of your Excellency."[93]

The Convention of Saratoga was never honored by the Continental Congress, on the grounds that some of the soldiers had kept their cartouche boxes and that Bur-goyne had said that "the public faith is broke" when he was unhappy with his accom-modation in Boston. It conceded too much to the British. Burgoyne's army might have been retained in America or used as a replacement at home for troops sent for service in America. Sir William Howe did, in fact, secretly plan to send the German troops to Britain while retaining the British troops from Saratoga in America. The surrender agreement turned out to have been no more than a face-saving formula for Burgoyne.

The prisoners appeared "a sordid set of creatures in human figure—poor, dirty, emaciated men" when they marched into Cambridge. The great number of women accompanying them "seemed to be the beasts of burden, having bushel baskets on their backs, by which they were bent double." They were barefoot and clothed in rags. The continued imprisonment of Burgoyne's army became a source of grievance among the British high command and the ministry in London.[94]

For eight weeks during the winter of 1778–79, the four thousand convention prisoners marched 641 miles from Cambridge to Charlottesville. Nearly half of them were Brunswickers from Germany. They were kept in the Albemarle Barracks where their former path to imprisonment is now called Barracks Road. With a population larger than any town in Virginia, the prison barracks became a shanty town with poor conditions and little protection for the ordinary soldiers. Nevertheless, a company of British soldiers built a "comedy theater" where they performed two plays every week, with changes of scenery and a sign with the words: "Who would have expected all this here!" According to one of the German officers, the drummers were turned into "queens and belles." The officers lived in grander style, renting the plantation houses of local gentry. Major General William Phillips lived at Blenheim, the home of Edward Carter. Thomas Jefferson frequently entertained some of the German and British officers at Monticello. He wrote to Phillips that the war that divided their countries should not be the source of animosity between individuals, and Phillips reciprocated with invitations to Jefferson to be a guest in his box at the camp theater and to dine at Blenheim. Jefferson was particularly fond of Captain Baron de Geismar with whom he played the violin. Martha Jefferson accompanied them on the piano, while Baroness von Riedesel led the dances in the late evening at Monticello. After his release, Geismar gave his sheet music to Jefferson, writing "Be my friend, do not forget me and persuade yourself of my Sincerity." Many of the convention prisoners successfully contrived to escape during their captivity, and a number of them rejoined the British army in New York. In November 1780, the three thousand remaining prisoners were moved to Maryland. Escapes continued, and there were only 472 prisoners left when they were eventually released in 1782.[95]

IX

After the surrender at Saratoga, Burgoyne finally reached Albany as a prisoner rather than a victor. He wrote to his nieces that he was so exhausted that he could scarce hold his pen, and described his situation as attended with perplexity, distress, and trial that affected all his faculties and feelings. He was bitter that he had been "surrounded with enemies, ill-treated by pretended friends, abandoned by a considerable part of my own army, totally unassisted by Sir William Howe." He had had to conduct difficult negotiations that required the most undisturbed reflection, after having been under perpetual fire and spending sixteen sleepless nights, without a change of clothes. After all his misfortunes, he knew he was about to face another war "with ministers who will always lay the blame upon the employed who miscarries." He wrote to another correspondent that he expected that ministerial ingratitude would "be displayed, as in all countries and at times is usual, to remove the blame from the orders to the execution." Burgoyne was ready again to do battle and to vindicate himself in Britain.[96]

His strategy of defense was to blame Germain's orders, which he insisted gave him no alternative but to continue to Albany. He claimed to believe that his army had been deliberately sacrificed by the government as a diversionary force to assist the campaign of Howe and argued that he had merely exerted "a spirited *execution* of his orders" and that "the utmost that malevolence can say will be that I have been too bold." He took the precaution of sending a copy of his letter of explanation to the earl of Derby in case "the Ministry should curtail or mangle any part of it in their Gazette." In April 1778, Burgoyne was released on parole and returned to Britain. Upon his arrival in Plymouth in May, Nathaniel Wraxall claimed, Burgoyne met with the politician Charles James Fox, who "in a long and confidential interview" offered to support him if he blamed Lord George Germain rather than General Howe. Whether or not he made such an agreement with Fox, Burgoyne joined the opposition in attacking Germain. Together with the Howe brothers, he aimed to obtain a court martial or parliamentary inquiry to clear his name.[97]

On his return to London, Burgoyne was refused an audience with George III. He was initially granted a military tribunal, but it declined to judge his conduct of the campaign on the grounds that he was a prisoner of war. His strategy of not only holding the minister responsible for his failure, but also arguing that the war was unwinnable and courting the friendship of Fox, alienated George III who consequently supported Germain. Although the king had initially supported the idea of an inquiry, the government subsequently stonewalled such attempts. Burgoyne defied government orders to return to his captivity in America. In May 1779, a parliamentary committee was finally convened to investigate both his command and that of Sir William Howe. Although the inquiry enabled him to call and examine a succession of witnesses, it dissolved at the end of the parliamentary session and the committee never reported. On October 9, Burgoyne was given an ultimatum either to be stripped of his offices or to return to America. He chose to resign his various lucrative appointments, which left him financially ruined, in what he dramatically called a "suicide of my professional existence." Lord Jeffrey Amherst thought such treatment "severe useage" but failed to dissuade George III.[98]

Burgoyne became a much-embittered figure who was always ready with a speech to recount the details of his campaign in the House of Commons. With the encouragement of Edmund Burke, he published his defense both in a letter to his constituents on his resignation in 1779 and in a pamphlet entitled *A State of the Expedition from Canada as Laid before the House of Commons* in 1780. Burgoyne understood the value of publicity. He travelled to Beaconsfield to have Edmund Burke read and revise the manuscript of his pamphlet, which he republished in an enlarged edition in 1780 and dedicated to Major General William Phillips, whom he had left in command of his captive army in America.

The pamphlet had overtones of the Declaration of Independence, beginning: "When it becomes necessary for men who have acted critical parts in public stations to make an appeal to the world in their own justification . . ." He gave up his original intention to write his memoirs, however. In February 1782, he was finally released from his parole and was formally exchanged for Henry Laurens of South Carolina who had been taken prisoner on a diplomatic mission to Holland and kept in the Tower of London.[99]

Burgoyne was sixty years old at the end of the war in 1783. During the short coalition government of Charles James Fox and Lord North, Burgoyne was appointed commander of the army and privy councilor in Ireland where he headed an army of fifteen thousand. Following the fall of the Fox-North administration, he resigned from office in January 1784. It was the end of his military career. By throwing in his lot with his old gambling partner and club friend Charles James Fox, he precluded any chance of political favor from George III. He ceased to go to court after attending a royal levée where he "had the mortification to perceive a different countenance" from the king than he was "used to be honored with." When there was talk of war with Spain in 1788, he again offered his services as "an old soldier," saying that should death be near, "he would rather meet it in the duties of the field than amidst the sorrows and afflictions of a sick bed."[100]

Burgoyne also became less active in politics. Nathaniel Wraxall described him in the House of Commons in the late stages of the Revolutionary War, commenting that he rose above ordinary height and had clearly possessed a distinguished figure "but years had enfeebled him though he was cast in an athletic mould." Burgoyne voted for parliamentary reform. He remained in opposition, voting against the government of William Pitt the Younger. He continued to support measures to increase the public accountability of the East India Company, and he supported the impeachment trial of Warren Hastings who was charged with corruption during his tenure as governor general of India (1787). Burgoyne favored army reforms and denounced the selling of commissions, saying that officers should not rise to high rank "without ever seeing a soldier, or knowing what a firelock was." His last speech concerned army pay, when he expressed concern for the salaries of junior officers.[101]

While the revival of his military and political career eluded him after the Revolutionary War, Burgoyne had a new lease of life as a successful playwright. He wrote a musical comedy with Richard Brinsley Sheridan called *The Lord of the Manor,* which was performed at the Drury Lane Theatre in December 1780. Sheridan was the manager of the theater and at the height of his literary fame as the author of *The School for Scandal.* Burgoyne's most successful play, *The Heiress,* first performed at Drury Lane in January 1786, went through ten editions during the first year and was translated into four languages with productions in both France and Germany. Walpole quipped that "Burgoyne's battles and speeches would be forgotten, but his delightful comedy *The Heiress* still continues the delight of the stage and one of the most pleasing of domestic compositions." Written over the course of two summers spent at Knowsley, Burgoyne dedicated it to the twelfth earl of Derby, whose wedding had occasioned his first play, *The Maid of Oaks.* The earl was so enchanted with the leading actress in *The Heiress,* Elizabeth Farren, that he caused a society scandal by marrying her weeks after the death of his first wife, whom he had refused to divorce despite a long separation.

Burgoyne never remarried, but he had a long-standing affair with an actress, Susan Caulfield. They had four children, of whom the oldest, christened in August 1782, was John Fox Burgoyne who served as a colonel in the American war of 1812–15 and fought at the battle of New Orleans. Later on, he was chief engineer to Lord Raglan in the Crimea. He retired as a field marshal, and his statue in London is often mistaken for his father. His son Hugh joined the navy and won the Victoria Cross in the Crimea, and a few years after that war died when his ship, an experimental ironclad called HMS *Captain,* capsized and sank.[102]

On August 4, 1792, while working on a musical production of Shakespeare's *As You Like It,* in which he was updating the English, General John Burgoyne died suddenly at his London home. He was seventy years old. In accordance with his wishes, his funeral was a modest affair with few mourners. He was buried next to his wife and daughter in the North Cloister of Westminster Abbey. The grave remained unmarked for 160 years until it was simply identified as that of "John Burgoyne 1723–1792." His last will and testament expressed regret at his sexual transgressions and the hope that "my sensualities have never injured, nor interrupted, the peace of others." Burgoyne died virtually insolvent. He was never publicly commemorated until a plaque was recently installed on his home at 10 Hertford Street in Mayfair.[103]

X

Although he had allied himself with Howe and the opposition parties in order to place the onus of the failure of Saratoga on Germain, Burgoyne had been perceptive about the fundamental causes of British failure in America. He recognized that British strategy was predicated on the fallacy that the ordinary people were latently loyalist. Before crossing the Hudson, Burgoyne wrote to Germain that "the great bulk of the country are undoubtedly with the Congress, in principle and zeal." He described how the movements of the army were shadowed by militia who assembled three or four thousand troops within twenty-four hours, bringing their own provisions and returning to their farms when the crisis passed. Hanging on the flank of his army "like a gathering storm," there were men from the Hampshire Grants (New Hampshire and Vermont), which Burgoyne described as "a country unpeopled and almost unknown in the last war, [but] now abounds in the most active and most rebellious race of the continent." At the surrender ceremony on October 17, 1777, Burgoyne complimented Gates on having an inexhaustible fund of men who were "like the Hydra's head, when cut off, seven more spring in its stead." After his defeat at Saratoga, he had a long meeting with Germain in Pall Mall in which he represented "the truths respecting the dispositions of the people in America" which he knew to be "very different from the ideas" prevalent in the government.[104]

In his published account of the campaign of 1780, Burgoyne was scathing about the potential for loyalist support in America. He had found the loyalist units in his army to be "a tax upon time and patience." They were motivated by such diverse influences that it was impracticable to make arrangements with them. There was the man who sought to profit by mustering a corps, another who was exclusively concerned with the protection of the district in which he resided, and a third who was wholly intent upon revenge against his personal enemies. They all shared a repugnance against any idea of subordination. In sending the detachment of German troops to obtain provisions and horses in Bennington, Burgoyne had been told that "the friends of the British cause were five to one, and that they wanted only the appearance of a protecting force to show themselves." He received his information from "persons of long experience and residence . . . who had been present on the spot when the rebellion broke out; and whose information had been much respected by the administration in England."[105]

Burgoyne observed that the enemy commanders had encountered no opposition in raising troops, but "not a loyalist was found earnest enough to convey me intelligence" in the Hampshire Grants. He asked rhetorically why the loyalists had not risen around Albany to challenge the separate and distinct military corps that was gathering from remote areas to support General Gates. Why had they not risen in the populous and supposedly well-affected area along the Mohawk to support St. Leger at Fort Stanwix? He wrote ruefully that "a critical insurrection from any one point of the compass within distance to create [a] diversion, would probably have secured the success of the campaign."[106]

Burgoyne privately admitted that his conjectures about the enemy had been very different at the time of his victory at Ticonderoga. He acknowledged that his earlier views "were delusive" and regarded it as his "duty to the state to confess it." He was contemptuous of those who doubted the quality of rebel military skills, which reflected "a prejudice that it would be very absurd longer to contend with." Even during the campaign, he had conceded that the secrecy and alertness of the enemy were not to be equaled. After his surrender at Saratoga, he paid tribute to the Continental Army, which he was "sorry" to say was the equal of any British army in America. It had all the fundamentals of a well-regulated army in discipline, subordination, regularity, and courage. The militia was inferior in method and movement, "but not a jot less serviceable in woods." His awareness that he had been deluded may explain some of his rancor towards Germain, who more than ever justified the continuance of the war in terms of the potential support of loyalists.[107]

The implications of the defeat at Saratoga changed the British war for America.

Although France was already contemplating an open alliance with the United States, Saratoga demonstrated the potential of the American Revolution to succeed against Britain. By helping to ensure French entry, it transformed the war into a global struggle in which British military resources were deflected by other military priorities in the Caribbean, the Mediterranean, India, and the Channel.[108]

CHAPTER 5

"The Achilles of the American War"

LORD GEORGE GERMAIN

Betwen November 1778 and July 1779, Parliament refought the battle of Saratoga. The leading British generals and politicians were all present and played off against one another in a mutual blame game. It was parliamentary theater at its best. Sir William Howe and John Burgoyne demanded inquiries to clear their reputations. Horace Walpole salivated at the welcome prospect of the confusion likely to develop between generals, admirals, Cabinet ministers, and the returned peace commissioners. The war and the government were on trial. The issue was whether the defeat at Saratoga had been due to bad planning by the politicians or to poor implementation by the generals. The main target was the secretary of state for America, Lord George Germain, who was the chief architect of the Revolutionary War in Britain.[1]

During the course of the parliamentary debates on Saratoga, returned army officers and generals gave devastating testimonies that the war was unwinnable because the majority of Americans were determined to oppose Britain. Major General "No Flint" Charles Grey, who had commanded at the "Paoli Massacre" and at Tappan, said "that with the present force in America there can be no expectation of ending the war by force of arms." He thought that the American people "were almost unanimous in their aversion to the government of Great Britain." Throughout his time in the war, he claimed that the size of the British forces was inadequate to subdue America. Sir John Wrottesley, the member for Stafford who had served as an officer for three years in America, warned that "if 50,000 Russians were sent, they could do nothing . . . our posts are too many, and our troops too much detached . . . the chain of communication was too far extended." Wrottesley had voted with the government for nine years, and had previously supported the war, but he had come to the conclusion that we are "not able to carry on the war offensively."[2]

In March 1779, Sir William Howe made an "unexpected and direct attack" on Lord George Germain. He asserted that if his military decisions had not been based on the minister's directions, they had at least not been discouraged or contradicted by him. Howe called for an inquiry and a full examination of Germain to acquaint the nation with the true cause of the failure of the British campaign in America in 1777. Howe attributed his resignation and that of his brother to their treatment by Germain. He concluded by asserting that it would be impossible either to restore peace or to prosecute the war while the conduct of the war was continued in the hands "of the present noble secretary" for America. Germain seemed "astonished at this unexpected attack" and entered into a defense of his actions, claiming that the charge supposed "him of much more consequence than he really was, by attributing to him the sole management of the war." During the successive days of the debate, Charles James Fox accused Germain of being the author of the "miscarriage" at Saratoga, because the minister had not given sufficiently explicit orders to Howe to meet and assist Burgoyne at Albany. Fox was said to have made the case "with extraordinary temper and judgment, and without any acrimony." Languishing on the front benches of the government side of the Commons, Germain said nothing, other than to respond to specific questions. Later during the debates, he finally defended himself "in a good speech, though many thought he did not clear himself."[3]

There were well-grounded rumors that the government was so fearful of defeat that it was about to make a sacrifice and dismiss Lord George Germain. In January 1778, George III had given Lord North the choice "that either the Secretary or the General should retire." In May, Germain wrote that he had found the parliamentary session "too fatiguing and almost intolerable." He told a friend that he was ready to resign, but that he would first disprove the accusations against him in the House of Commons. Walpole thought that Germain was fearful not only of being sacrificed by the government but also of an impeachment proceeding by the opposition. In Parliament and St. James's Palace, the other Cabinet ministers physically and publicly distanced themselves from Germain. Charles James Fox publicly hinted that Germain was so dissatisfied that he was threatening to resign. By his gestures during Fox's speech, Germain implied assent, and his reply to Fox made little effort to defend his colleagues in the government. In June 1778, Germain had felt slighted by Lord North who had removed him from the Board of Trade in favor of the earl of Carlisle. Prepared to resign, Germain suggested that Carlisle assume all his duties as secretary of state for America. During these debates, Germain was painted by the artist George Romney in a manner that suggested his plight (Figure 21). The portrait shows Germain standing in front of his country house at Drayton in Northamptonshire. In the background, thunder clouds loom. His hand rests on a virtually blank piece of paper, with a finger pointing to a few words at the top, which simply read "To the King."[4]

In the period of declining government majorities in March 1780, the opposition nearly removed Germain by a margin of only seven votes with a motion to eliminate the position of secretary of state for the American Department. During the anti-Catholic Gordon Riots in London in the summer of 1780, Germain had to seek the help of friends to barricade the entrance and passages to his home along Pall Mall, and then "coolly waited for the attack of the populace." Richard Cumberland had just returned from a diplomatic mission to Spain to discover "the rebellion of America transplanted to England." At Germain's home in Pall Mall, Cumberland was ushered by night through a suite of five rooms "the door of every one of which was constantly locked" after him.[5]

I

Born Lord George Sackville, Germain was the youngest and favorite son of the duke of Dorset. At six feet tall, he had a commanding presence with clear blue eyes, a prominent nose, and a muscular physique. There was an alertness about his face combined with a look of melancholy, a trait associated with the Sackvilles. According to Nathaniel Wraxall, he had a robust and vigorous appearance, "an air of high birth and dignity," and a keen look of purpose that "pervaded every lineament of his face." Educated at Westminster School and Trinity College Dublin, Germain exuded a powerful intellect which was apparent in his eyes, "the motions of which were quick and piercing." He was, however, conscious of not being well read in literature and the classics, for which he had little inclination.[6]

Germain seemed to be reserved, reticent, proud, distant, and haughty in public. In private, he was completely relaxed, and he liked to dine at home with his family and drink a pint of claret. He judged his audience well, "always saying enough, and not too much." He spoke plainly, using the "commonest expressions." He was an entertaining conversationalist who told stories of his military exploits and indiscreet anecdotes about the royal family, raising "the curtain that concealed the vulgar eyes [from] the palaces of Whitehall, of St. James's, of Kensington, and of Hampton Court." He related gossip about famous people dating back to the beginning of the century. Wraxall maintained that no one who saw him on such social occasions would have ever suspected "that the responsibility of the American war reposed principally on his shoulders."[7]

Other than Lord North, Lord George Germain was the most prominent government spokesman in the House of Commons. The combination of a powerful voice and an impressive physique made him an imposing figure there. He spoke with vehemence and animation, and his speeches were clear and cogent. Horace Walpole thought him one of the best speakers in Parliament. According to the otherwise hostile earl of Shelburne, Germain never spoke on subjects that he had not fully mastered. Edmund Burke said of him that few members were more diligent in their attendance and that debates seemed to be his principal amusement.[8]

When he became secretary of state for America in 1775, Germain was a seasoned politician with thirty-four years of experience in Parliament. In the 1750s, he had been a principal speaker against such parliamentary luminaries as William Pitt the Elder and Henry Fox. Like Lord North, he was a master of parliamentary style, an excellent judge of "the prolongation and acceleration of debate," with a capacity to read his audience to determine the best length of his speeches. As he sat down on the government front benches, he took the pulse of the chamber by eyeing the opposition ranks to see who was present and who was absent. He used to say that it was possible to *see* everything in the Commons, while *hearing* nothing but declamations. He claimed to have acquired his skills while secretary to his father, when he was lord lieutenant of Ireland. His great weakness in debate was that he lacked the ability of North to remain placid and to turn opposition attacks into humor. He instead was irritable and easily roused. He "was less artful in debate than North," and well known for an "unguarded mode of expression." As the minister most associated with the war, he was a favorite target of the newspapers and the opposition parties.[9]

A military veteran who had commanded an army and fought in battle, Germain was in many ways unusually well qualified to provide political oversight of the war for America. He was descended from a long and distinguished military ancestry. At the battle of Fontenoy (May 11, 1745), he saw his regiment cut to pieces and only three officers escape unwounded, while he himself was shot in the breast and captured. A year later, during the Jacobite rebellion in Scotland (1745–46), he aggressively and successfully pursued the defeated clansmen through the Highlands in the aftermath of the British victory at Culloden. The duke of Cumberland described him as having shown courage and an inclination to the military trade that was not always present among the higher ranks. In 1758, he served with the Howe brothers and was wounded in a raid on the French Channel port of St. Malo. Although Horace Walpole claimed that Germain and the Howes did not get along and that this was the source of later friction in their relationship, Germain had respect for the military abilities of both and later supported their appointment as joint commanders in America. He was a protégé of one of the great strategists of the era, Field Marshal John Ligonier, and was highly regarded by one of the most revered heroes of the British army, a former lieutenant colonel in his regiment, James Wolfe, the victor of Quebec.[10]

However, Germain carried the fatal stigma of having been pronounced unfit to serve in the army by a court martial in condemnation of his role at the battle of Minden in northwestern Germany (August 1, 1759). At the time of the battle, Germain was a forty-three-year-old lieutenant general serving under Prince Ferdinand of Brunswick, who was commander of the allied forces in western Germany and the son-in-law of Frederick the Great. Minden was one of the great battles of eighteenth-century Europe, a victory of the coalition arrayed against France in the Seven Years' War that pushed the French army back toward the Rhine. Like most European battles, it dwarfed the scale of warfare in Revolutionary America. At the head of twenty-four cavalry squadrons comprising thirty-three hundred troops, Germain failed to pursue the French when they began to retreat. After waiting for a while, he moved forward slowly with only part of his cavalry and lost an opportunity to rout the enemy and gain an even more spectacular victory. It was later alleged that he had repeatedly and deliberately disobeyed orders to charge, and he was obliquely criticized in the official report of the battle by Prince Ferdinand.

Germain resigned from his command and returned to England. Although not formally charged, he insisted upon a court martial to clear his name and to explain his actions. It was a matter of personal honor and pride, even though he thereby risked the death sentence. In 1756, Admiral John Byng had been executed on his own quarterdeck when a court martial had found him guilty of not fully engaging the French fleet, inspiring Voltaire's famous line in *Candide* that the British shoot an admiral from time to time "pour encourager les autres" ("to encourage the others"). There were mitigating circumstances for Germain's inaction at Minden. His view of the battlefield was obscured by a forest, and he received contradictory orders that were imperfectly and inaudibly relayed by messengers speaking in German. Such considerations did not sway the fourteen generals at his trial who found him guilty of disobedience and "unfit to serve his Majesty in any military capacity whatever." It was the lightest punishment available to the judges. According to an unconfirmed report, he escaped the death penalty by just one vote.[11]

Walpole claimed that "the shrewdest observers thought his non-compliance with [his] orders flowed from malice to Prince Ferdinand, not from cowardice." The two commanders had quarreled throughout the campaign. Germain resented Prince Ferdinand for not allowing him to command the British infantry as well as the cavalry, while Prince Ferdinand was secretive about his plans and had not sufficiently briefed Germain. On the other hand, some Hanoverian officers had previously complained that Germain was so imperious that "none of the foreign troops can bear him." Regardless of the merits of his case, Germain had little prospect of a fair trial because he was associated with the opposition leaders who were critical of the war in Germany. George II personally called for Germain's name to be struck off the list of the Privy Council. He also ordered that the sentence be read out to every regiment of the British army, with the comment that it was "worse than death," and that it be reported in the *London Gazette*. The episode devastated Germain's father, who had doted on his younger son and who retired to solitude at the family home at Knole in Kent.[12]

The specter of Minden overshadowed Germain's career and proved a major liability in his role as secretary of state for America. Many of the generals and army officers serving in America had been present at the battle, among them Lord Cornwallis, William Phillips, and Baron Friedrich Adolf von Riedesel who commanded German troops from New Brunswick in Burgoyne's campaign. Before serving in the Revolutionary War, half of the officers of the Fusiliers or 23rd Regiment had been present at the battle of Minden. Frederick Haldimand, a Swiss-born general in the British army who became commander in chief in Canada in 1779, had been a witness in support of Germain at the court martial, as had Cornwallis's father. Some of the leading opponents of Lord North's government had been present at Minden, including the earl of Shelburne and the duke of Richmond. In 1770, after taking four days to settle his affairs for his wife and child, Germain fought a duel in Hyde Park against George Johnstone, a former governor of West Florida, who had said that it was not proper for a man to defend the honor of the House of Commons "who had forfeited his own honor." After nearly getting killed by a bullet that hit his pistol, Germain gained some public respect for his coolness and intrepidity, while the "brutality" of Johnstone made him appear a boisterous bully.[13]

Regardless of the validity of the original accusations, the decision of the court martial was a serious liability for someone overseeing a war and dealing with military men. While Germain was secretary of state for America, his opponents regularly invoked Minden. After the withdrawal of the British from Boston in 1776, Temple Luttrell said mockingly that Germain had set an example in Germany for the army. In February 1777, John Wilkes said that "Lord North, like a true *dictator,* had chose for his *Master of the Horse,* the noble lord . . . who, to his immortal honor, with great and invincible courage advanced and charged the enemies of the country at the head of the British *Horse.*" During the debates on Saratoga in May 1778, there was nearly a duel between Luttrell and Germain, after Luttrell said that Germain had been promoted for disobedience and timidity. Clasping his sword with his hand, Germain stood up in a violent rage, vowing that he would not tolerate such an insult from an assassin and a most wretched character. Luttrell left the chamber and refused to retract a word, declaring that he would prefer to be sent to prison, and left the chamber ready to fight a duel. After two hours of histrionics, he finally made an apology to Germain.[14]

Germain was a divisive figure. He was certainly able to command allegiance and respect. He was fondly regarded by the two great memoirists of the period, who were otherwise at the opposite ends of the political spectrum. Horace Walpole, whom historians accuse of having perpetuated a jaundiced view of the government in his memoirs, wrote of "the uncommon excellence of his abilities" and claimed to have "always lived on civil terms with him." Walpole particularly admired the way that Germain remained loyal to the duke of Gloucester, the younger brother of George III, who was ostracized for having married Walpole's niece without the permission of the king. Germain was the only member of the government to be portrayed in entirely laudatory terms in the contemporary memoirs of Nathaniel Wraxall, who knew him so well that in the later years of Germain's life he was "on terms of great intimacy" with him, and who regarded it as an "honor to enjoy a place in his friendship." Germain initially impressed some of the leading American loyalist exiles in Britain. Thomas Hutchinson, the American-born governor of colonial Massachusetts, wrote in his diary that Germain had "the character of a great man" and that he was a "true friend to both countries." Hutchinson found him polite, affable, and friendly. Peter Oliver, the American-born former chief justice of Massachusetts, thought that Germain had good sense and a "firmness of mind" that well qualified him to be secretary of state for America, and that was "equal to the subdual of an American Rebellion."[15]

Others detested Germain and regarded him as cunning. Charles James Fox delivered some of his most venomous personal invectives against Germain. While the British defeat at Saratoga was still only rumored in London in November 1777, Fox launched a brilliant and bitter philippic against Germain in which he accused him of being "an ill-omened and inauspicious character" who was unfit to serve the crown, and who was ignorant and incapable in his conduct of the war for America. It was an example of the opposition alienating support by being too shrill, since moderate members thought the speech too personal and severe. In another speech, in December 1777, Fox likened Germain to Dr. Sangrado, a notorious Spanish physician "who would persist in drawing blood because he had written a book on bleeding." He held Germain principally responsible for the atrocities of the war, including "the inhuman measure of employing . . . savages" not to subdue but "to exterminate a people who we still pretend to call our subjects." By the defeat at Saratoga, he declared, Germain had brought about "the final loss of our colonies." After accusing the government of stupidity and ignorance, "Fox flamed still more and charged Lord George with the whole blame of the badness of the plan" that had led to Saratoga.[16]

Oxford historian Piers Mackesy suggests that the enmity toward Germain cannot be explained simply by the events at Minden, but that the particular viciousness of these personal attacks was due to his reputed homosexuality. There had long been unsubtle mentions in the press of scandal, with references to Germain as the "buggering hero" in the scurrilous writings of John Wilkes, Charles Churchill, and the anonymous Junius. When London society was rocked with stories of the trial of the duchess of Kingston on charges of bigamy in the House of Lords in 1776, Germain was libeled in a verse publication entitled *Sodom and Onan*. The duchess had commissioned the pamphlet in revenge against Samuel Foote who had written a play in which she was unflatteringly featured. As a friend of Foote, Germain was attacked in the poem:

> Sackville, both Coward and Catamite, commands
> Department honourable, and kisses hands
> With lips that oft in blandishment obscene
> Have been employed . . .

Apart from words for explicit sexual acts, at the time there was not even a language to describe same-sex relationships. In contrast to the more ambiguous attitude of late seventeenth-century England, homosexuality was increasingly associated in literature and drama with effeminacy. There was a latent fear that the nation was becoming effeminate, which was regarded as evidence of its decline.[17]

Germain made little attempt to disguise his sexual preferences. He had been married to Diana Sambrooke, who died of measles at the age of forty-seven in the midst of the Revolutionary War in January 1778. She was fifteen years his junior, and they had two sons and three daughters. Upon their first meeting, she impressed his favorite sister as a sensible, clever, and good-tempered woman. Although the Sambrooke family was related to the earl of Salisbury, Germain was thought by some to have married beneath him. According to Horace Walpole, "she was a good woman," and "her death was a great blow to him"; it coincided with the recent arrival in London of news of the defeat at Saratoga. On her death, Germain missed a week of critical Cabinet meetings about the future of the war, while he retired to grieve at Knole. Nevertheless, the suspicion that he was homosexual or bisexual had begun long before her death. While secretary of state for America, Germain gave greater currency to such rumors by his patronage of the playwright Richard Cumberland, whom he appointed to be secretary of the Board of Trade, and of the American loyalist and scientist Benjamin Thompson, whom he made his under secretary of state. Cumberland and Thompson were both very capable and distinguished in many spheres, but they were both reputed to be lovers of Germain.[18]

Richard Cumberland had left a promising academic career at Cambridge University to be the private secretary of Lord Halifax, who was a highly regarded president of the Board of Trade. He also became one of the most successful playwrights of the period, with *The Brothers* (1769) at Covent Garden, and *The West Indian* (1771) and *The Fashionable Lover* (1772) at Drury Lane. After the Revolutionary War, he reestablished his reputation as a dramatist with *The Jew* (1794) and *The Wheel of Fortune* (1795). He eventually wrote over forty plays, as well as poetry, three novels, and several books of recollections. He was married with two daughters and four sons. In her diary in 1777, Mrs. Thrale, the friend of Samuel Johnson, wrote of Richard Cumberland, "I have a notion, *Dieu me pardonne* [God forgive me] that Cumberland is a— . . ." She continued, "Effeminacy is an odious quality in a He creature, and when joined with low jealousy, actually detestable." Long after the war for America, she was still writing that something whispered in her heart that "Cumberland did like the *Masculine* gender best." In 1780, Germain sent Cumberland on an important diplomatic mission to try to negotiate peace with Spain. After the Revolutionary War, they became neighbors, and Cumberland wrote an affectionate personal memoir in which he called Germain "one of the very best companions of the age, though he had neither the advantages of literature, the brilliance of wit, nor any superior pretensions to a fine taste in the elegant arts."[19]

Benjamin Thompson was unique among American loyalists in gaining high office in Britain and later in the Holy Roman Empire. He was even knighted, which caused the marquess of Wellesley to dub him "Sir *Sodom* Thompson, Lord Sackville's *under* Secretary." He was one of the most talented scientists of his era and an expert on gunpowder, and is credited with having been the first to suggest that heat is a mode of motion. He designed an oven called the Rumford Roaster. He became a fellow of the Royal Society, where his portrait still hangs, and a founder of the Royal Institution. He established the Rumford medals awarded by the Royal Society, together with awards in the American Academy of Arts and Sciences, and the Rumford professorship of physics at Harvard University. In later life he moved to Bavaria, where he was the founder of the English Gardens in Munich and became Count von Rumford of the Holy Roman Empire.[20]

Rumford was also twice married; he divorced his first wife and separated from the second. He was regarded as dangerously ambitious. He lived for a period with Germain during the Revolutionary War. The American loyalist Samuel Curwen described Thompson as a "shop lad" from Massachusetts who by "a strange concurrence of Evils" was serving under Germain with whom he "always breakfasts, dines, and sups . . . so great a favourite is he." Thomas Hutchinson recorded in his diary that Thompson spoke freely of living with Germain. Hutchinson commented cryptically, "some points look strange." In another of his oblique diary entries, Hutchinson wrote that he had heard "what it's shocking to think of," after someone had described Thompson as a scoundrel; he thought Germain remiss for allowing the world "to insinuate such things." When he heard Thompson repeat some private remarks made by George III to Germain, Hutchinson wrote that Germain was "extremely incautious in trusting such an amount of his conversation with the King to a young man," especially one so indiscreet.[21]

In 1782–83, Thompson served in America as a lieutenant colonel commanding his own loyalist cavalry and infantry corps, the King's American Dragoons. He fought at Charleston and saw service in Long Island. In 1785, he wrote to Germain from Munich that "rank, titles, decorations, literary distinctions . . . and some small degree of military fame I have acquired (through your availing protection)." He continued that he wished he could celebrate his happiness in "the society of my best, my only friend! Look back for a moment, my dearest friend, upon the work of your hands. *Je suis de votre ouvrage* [I am your creation]. Does it not afford you a very sensible pleasure to find your child has answered your expectations?"[22]

II

When he became secretary of state for the American Department in November 1775, Germain did not have a large parliamentary following to strengthen the government. He was chosen for his abilities and for his commitment to the cause of winning the war for America, as well as being more vigorous and less conciliatory than his predecessor, the earl of Dartmouth. Despite being a detractor of Germain, the earl of Shelburne thought he had the potential to be prime minister but for the episode at Minden. The historian Edward Gibbon believed that Germain had valuable abilities that few "country boors" were capable of understanding or valuing. Gibbon attributed his unpopularity to public knowledge of the findings of the court martial, his proud behavior, his solitary lifestyle, and his indifference to county meetings. At the time of his appointment, North thought that the government was lucky to acquire him. North felt much easier at having such a "responsible person" in the House of Commons, when so many of the Cabinet members were in the House of Lords. Nevertheless, North was not fond of him, while Germain said of North that he was "a trifling supine minister."[23]

Germain had recommended himself to the government by becoming one of the foremost champions of coercive measures in America. Despite his support of the Rockingham government, he voted against the repeal of the Stamp Act (1766). During the debates on the Townshend Duties (1767), Germain successfully pushed Charles Townshend to give an assurance that he would raise a tax in the colonies, and tried to make him guarantee that the colonial tax would cover the entire cost of keeping an army in America. He reminded the government that indulgence in the past was not rewarded by "these undutiful children." In Ireland earlier in his career, he had argued that the crown had the right to dispose of unassigned tax revenue without consulting the Irish Parliament. During the debates on the Coercive Acts in 1774, he warned against allowing America to "steal a constitution they had no right to," and he attributed the crisis to the willingness of past governments to give in to the demands of the colonies. He urged the government to adopt "a more manly method than that in which we have hitherto trifled."[24]

During the debates on the Massachusetts Governing Act (1774), Germain said that the government had not gone far enough in extending imperial oversight. He mocked the involvement of colonial merchants in politics, saying that they should follow their occupations, rather than considering "themselves as ministers of that country" and engaging in politics "which they do not understand." He suggested that the Massachusetts council be appointed by the king, the town meetings be abolished, the method of selecting juries be changed, and colonial charters be treated as revisable. He decried the tendency of past governments to make verbal assertions about sovereignty over the colonies, but not to enforce the law. He was confident that "by a manly and steady perseverance, things may be restored from a state of anarchy and confusion, to peace, quietude and due obedience to the laws of this country." In another debate during the third reading of the act, Germain said that he understood the maxim that it was better that ten guilty men should escape than that an innocent man should suffer, but he asked rhetorically, "What is the state of Boston? Anarchy and confusion. Have they at this instant a civil magistrate that dare act? Have they any redress for any one grievance but what depends upon the will of the licentious multitude?" Unless the home government took action, he warned that there would be government by the mob, acting under the guise of the banner of liberty: "they will assert every right, and they will substitute their Assembly in the place of your Parliament." In January 1775, Germain said that he would gladly approve petitions from America, "but if they resisted for what they call their rights, he would treat them with Roman severity."[25]

In a conversation with Edward Gibbon, Germain "was in high spirits and hopes to re-conquer Germany in America," in other words to redeem the stain of Minden by victory in America. The process of his rehabilitation had begun with the patronage of George III. It helped that he was able to change his name from Lord George Sackville, owing to a bequest by Lady Betty Germain in 1769 that required him to adopt her surname in order to receive the estate of Drayton House in Northamptonshire. She was an aunt by marriage who was a widow with no surviving children, and she and her husband had favored Lord George among the Sackvilles.[26]

Like George III, Germain believed that Britain would cease to be a great and powerful nation if it lost America. He became the minister responsible for the war when it had already been in progress for over six months and thereby inherited a conflict that was already going badly for Britain. Before he was appointed secretary of state for America, the British army had suffered severe casualties in its pyrrhic victory at Bunker Hill; it had lost Fort Ticonderoga and Montreal while it was besieged both in Boston, by the Continental army commanded by George Washington, and in Quebec, by forces commanded by Benedict Arnold. Britain had lost control of the colonies to radical leaders and revolutionary governments, while most of the royal governors had been forced to seek sanctuary. The decision had already been made to quit Boston, withdraw from America, and send an expedition to North Carolina, and the generals had already been appointed. Germain was left with the herculean task of masterminding the reconquest of America and the reconstruction of British government there.[27]

Germain infused a new energy into the war effort with the aim of winning in a single campaign. Like George III, he believed in the importance of the war and the need to prosecute it with vigor. They both spoke the same language of the need for bold, vigorous, and decisive measures. He "wished that the whole power of the state should be Exerted, that one Campaign might decide whether the American Provinces were to be subject to G.B. or free States." He worked feverishly to raise recruits and supplies so as to send out the largest force ever assembled by any European power for service in the Americas. It was a monumental achievement. He sent out more troops than requested by either William Howe in New York or Guy Carleton in Quebec, as well as a force to serve under Henry Clinton in the Carolinas. The Admiralty had said that it was impossible. The first lord of the Admiralty, Lord Sandwich, called it an unprecedented achievement and General Sir William Howe praised Germain. In the opening months of 1776, Germain was in great spirits, saying that the war would be won in a single campaign and that he would establish himself by it. The opposition *London Evening Post* was predicting that he would replace North as prime minister.[28]

Germain believed it necessary to negotiate from a position of strength by winning a decisive military victory, as well as being impelled by a sense of urgency about the need to forestall France from entering into the Revolutionary War. He was therefore against the conciliatory approach advocated by Lord North and the Howe brothers, writing that "the sentimental manner of making war, will, I fear, not have the desired Effect." He argued that leniency was misguided and even inhumane because it was likely to prolong the war. The opposition parties associated him with a doctrine of unconditional submission. Although he approved of the naval abilities of Admiral Howe, Germain went to great lengths to prevent the Howe brothers becoming the sole peace commissioners in America. He was against granting pardons to the revolutionaries until the elected assemblies had acknowledged the absolute authority of Parliament. He clashed with Lord North and the earl of Dartmouth, who wanted to give broad discretionary negotiating authority to the Howe brothers. Their differences were so acute that all parties threatened to resign until they were dissuaded by George III. Although he conceded to the brothers becoming the sole peace commissioners, Germain prevailed in severely restricting their authority and scope of action.[29]

All the same, Germain had a more realistic and pragmatic approach to the war than is often appreciated. He anticipated from the outset some of the difficulties posed by warfare in America. He allowed for the problem of communications with field commanders acting at great distances, arguing that they necessarily required much discretion and freedom in directing strategy. More surprisingly, he did not underestimate the potential of an enemy who used unconventional methods of warfare. He appreciated that "an enemy that avoids facing you in the open field is totally different from what young officers learn from the common discipline of the army." He was well aware of the setbacks suffered by the British army in the early stages of the French and Indian War and the defeat of General Edward Braddock at Monongahela in 1755. He recalled how Braddock's army had been sacrificed to the skill of enemies who were virtually unseen, as well as to military convention by which the troops kept together and fired as a single body but "could neither defend themselves nor annoy their opponents." He understood that the conduct of the war would require uncommon abilities in a field commander. He advocated the use of light infantry troops who had been taught to disperse and secure themselves by trees, walls, or hedges to protect the main body of the army from ambushes and surprise. He critically believed that Britain could not "support a protracted War, nor bear to have any considerable part of the National strength remain inactive or unemployed." He urged that "every Advantage must therefore be seized, every occasion profited of."[30]

Germain's strategy for winning the war in 1776 was to isolate radical New England from the rest of America. He favored the immediate conquest of New York because of its strategic location between the northern and southern colonies, and controlling the mouth of the Hudson River. The navy was to blockade and launch raids along the coast of New England. Germain expected Guy Carleton and the British army in Canada to march south and to join up with the army of William Howe. Even before he became secretary of state for America, Germain stressed that it was "absolutely necessary" for the army to win with "one decisive blow" against Washington. He thought it defied common sense to protract the war and advocated "exerting the utmost force . . . to finish this rebellion in one campaign." His strategy represented what most military historians believe to have been the best opportunity for Britain to win the American Revolution.[31]

Germain's intentions for the campaign were thwarted by his commanders, whose desire to conciliate their opponents caused them to act with less aggression and urgency in engaging the enemy than he expected. Owing partly to their negotiations and offers of amnesty, the Howe brothers lost the best opportunity of the war to defeat Washington's army and to exploit their victory at the battle of Long Island (August 27, 1776). In his descent from Canada, Guy Carleton similarly attempted to sway popular opinion by releasing prisoners of war and by refusing to make greater use of the Indians. His patron in England was the duke of Richmond, a leading opponent of the war in Parliament who had also been present at the battle of Minden. Germain and Carleton also had opposing views of the policy of conciliating the French subjects in Canada enshrined in the Quebec Act. Germain's view of Carleton was colored by negative accounts that he received from his confidant Colonel Gabriel Christie whom he had appointed quartermaster general of the army in Canada, a choice that Carleton blocked by instead appointing his own brother, Thomas Carleton. Christie's criticism of Carleton was reinforced by the accounts of the campaign from Burgoyne, serving as Carleton's second in command.[32]

Germain held Carleton rather than Howe chiefly responsible for the British failure to win the war in the campaign of 1776. He faulted him for not catching up with the rebel force before it reached Lake Champlain and for abandoning the capture of Crown Point. He believed that Carleton could have deflected Washington's army in New York and prevented the British defeat at Trenton by continuing his invasion from Canada, whereas his withdrawal from Crown Point enabled rebel troops to join the undermanned army of Washington and to fight at Trenton. Britain was never again able to equal the forces sent to America in 1776. Germain's plan had offered the best chance of a military solution, but his opponents were skeptical that a spectacular military victory would be sufficient to win back the allegiance of the American people. Even if the British had defeated Washington, it might have exceeded their resources to police North America with a large military presence comparable to the garrisons that controlled Ireland.[33]

Germain's plans for the 1777 campaign were much the same as those of 1776, with the aim of cutting off New England, though placing greater emphasis upon a naval blockade and raids along the coast of New England. He largely adopted the advice of

John Burgoyne in regard to the specifics of the invasion of America from Canada. It was Howe, not Germain, who made the decision to attack Philadelphia and to travel by sea via the Chesapeake. He changed his plans so late that he left virtually no option open to Germain other than to endorse what amounted to a fait accompli. When the campaign unraveled with the defeat at Saratoga, Burgoyne and the Howe brothers made common cause and avoided mutual blame in order to win the support of the parliamentary opposition parties, who were willing to hold an inquiry to absolve the generals and to attribute exclusive responsibility for the defeat to Germain. It was all part of a broader attack on the government and its management of the war in America. Germain was an easy and vulnerable target, given the notoriety of his court martial. He was not close to the other government ministers. He had been a political independent during most of his parliamentary career and had occasionally voted against the government of Lord North. Unlike the earl of Sandwich, he did not have a large political following whose defection might affect the stability of the government. He was dispensable.

However, his planning of the campaign revealed deficiencies that continued throughout his direction of the war for America. This was equally apparent in his direction of the war in the Caribbean and particularly his planning of a remarkably ambitious expedition to Central America.[34]

III

In 1780, Lord George Germain launched one of the most ambitious British enterprises of the American Revolutionary War. It is rarely featured in standard accounts of the war beyond biographies of the two men who first distinguished themselves in the episode: Horatio Nelson, the future victor of Trafalgar, and Lieutenant Edward Marcus Despard, who was executed in 1802 for an attempt to seize the Tower of London and assassinate George III. The expedition aimed at nothing less than the conquest of Spanish America through Central America. The chief medical officer of the expedition, Dr. Benjamin Moseley, described it as "the best concerted and most important enterprise that had been conceived during the war." It was part of a general reorientation of the British war effort from North America to the Caribbean. Germain was to write to Major General John Vaughan, commanding the British army in the Lesser Antilles, that "the West Indies will become the principal theatre of war."[35]

In June 1779, Spain had declared war on Britain with the aim of recovering former territories including the Floridas, the Bahama Islands, Jamaica, Gibraltar, and Minorca. Fearful for the consequences of revolution in its own empire in South America and the Caribbean, Spain neither became an ally of nor formally recognized the United States. It signed a treaty exclusively with France which committed France to assisting Spain in the

CHARLES EARL CORNWALLIS. 1783.

FIGURE 27. Lord Charles Cornwallis. Portrait by Thomas Gainsborough, 1783. Painted the year following his return from America to Britain, the portrait captures Cornwallis's strength of character and grim determination. It also shows his wall eye which gave him a wistful look, the result of being struck by a future bishop of Durham in a hockey game as a schoolboy at Eton. © National Portrait Gallery, London.

FIGURE 28. Banastre Tarleton. Portrait by Sir Joshua Reynolds, 1782. The life-size canvas dramatically portrays an officer whose name became synonymous with ruthlessness in the south, and whose behavior illustrated the dilemma that the British faced in pacifying the population of South Carolina. © National Gallery, London/Art Resource, NY.

FIGURE 29. John Trumbull, *Surrender of Lord Cornwallis,* 1797. Lord Cornwallis delegated the duty of surrender to a subordinate, Brigadier General Charles O'Hara. According to French sources, O'Hara first tried to give the sword to the French commander, the comte de Rochambeau. Library of Congress.

FIGURE 30. Admiral Sir George Brydges Rodney. Portrait by Sir Joshua Reynolds, 1789. After his great victory at the Saintes in 1782, Admiral Rodney was celebrated in medals, ballads, poems, and souvenir pottery, as well as by the commissioning of this portrait. "Rodney Forever" became a popular song heard daily that summer in the amusement park at Vauxhall Gardens in London. (Supplied by Royal Collection Trust/© HM Queen Elizabeth II 2012).

FIGURE 31. Nicholas Pocock, *The Battle of the Saints, 12 April 1782.* The siege of Gibraltar and the battle of the Saintes were the most popular subjects of paintings by British artists rather than battles fought in America. The anniversary of the Saintes was regularly celebrated in Britain and in the empire until it was eclipsed by Trafalgar in 1805. © National Maritime Museum, London.

S.^T GEORGE & the Dragon.

FIGURE 32. *St. George and the Dragon,* published by H. Humphrey, 1783. Following his victory at the Saintes, Sir George Rodney was depicted as Saint George, and the battle significantly became known as the "battle of the Saints" rather than by its French spelling. He emerged as one of the few British heroes of the American War. © National Maritime Museum, London.

FIGURE 33. John Montagu, fourth earl of Sandwich. Portrait by Thomas Gainsborough, 1783. Sandwich was first lord of the Admiralty between 1771 and 1782. Although blamed for the failure of the Royal Navy, he had argued vehemently for the full-scale mobilization of the fleet at the beginning of the war but was instead confronted by budgetary cuts. By 1778, he favored a withdrawal from America to give priority to the defense of Britain and its colonies in the Caribbean. His responsibilities required him to think globally and be concerned with the wider war outside America, which inevitably brought him into conflict with Germain. © National Maritime Museum, London.

restoration of Gibraltar. In New Orleans, the young Spanish governor Don Bernardo de Gálvez launched an invasion against British West Florida whose boundaries extended along the seaboard of the Gulf of Mexico, through Pensacola to Mobile, Manchac, Baton Rouge, and Natchez in the present-day states of Florida, Alabama, Mississippi, and Louisiana. By the end of September 1779, Gálvez had seized the British posts in Manchac, Baton Rouge, and Natchez, clearing British settlers from the entire region around the Mississippi. In Central America, the Spanish governor of Honduras similarly made the first strike against the principal settlement of British logwood cutters at St. George's Key.[36]

Aware that Spain was much weaker than France, Germain sought to use a combination of military and diplomatic pressure to force Spain out of the Revolutionary War. His wish to seize New Orleans was thwarted by the preparations of Gálvez, but there were more promising developments in Central America. In anticipation of a Spanish raid, Governor John Dalling of Jamaica had sent a small force of Irish volunteers commanded by Captain William Dalrymple to assist the British logwood cutters along the coast of Central America. When the relief expedition discovered that the Spanish had already attacked, Dalrymple changed his objective to the port of Omoa which was regarded as the key to the Bay of Honduras. In October 1779, his force stormed the impressive stone fortress of San Fernando whose eighteen-feet-thick walls had taken twenty years to build. The craters caused by the bombardment are still visible. The expedition also captured large amounts of gold bullion including two ships with an estimated value of three million dollars. The achievement emboldened Germain to consider more ambitious plans in Central America.[37]

Since the age of Elizabeth I, the British had had global ambitions in which possession of Central America offered the prospect of opening a path between the Atlantic and Pacific. By securing possession of the San Juan River, which flowed into the Caribbean, and its source, Lake Nicaragua, near the Pacific coast towns of Granada and León, Germain and his commanders anticipated that a single force might divide the northern and southern dominions of Spanish America. This was one of the most popular overland routes from the Atlantic to the Pacific before the building of the Panama Canal and was used during the California Gold Rush. Once in control of the San Juan River–Lake Nicaragua route, Germain and his commanders aimed to create a chain of bases to launch an invasion of "all the richest provinces of South America." As in North America, the plan anticipated the possibility of fomenting insurrections among the Indians, slaves, and creoles against Spain. The expectation of widespread support was encouraged by rebellions that had previously occurred in Santa Fé, Popayán, and many other parts of the Peru viceroyalty.[38]

The plan also aimed to take advantage of the presence of British settlers on the Mosquito Shore and of native Miskito Indians who were traditionally hostile to Spain.

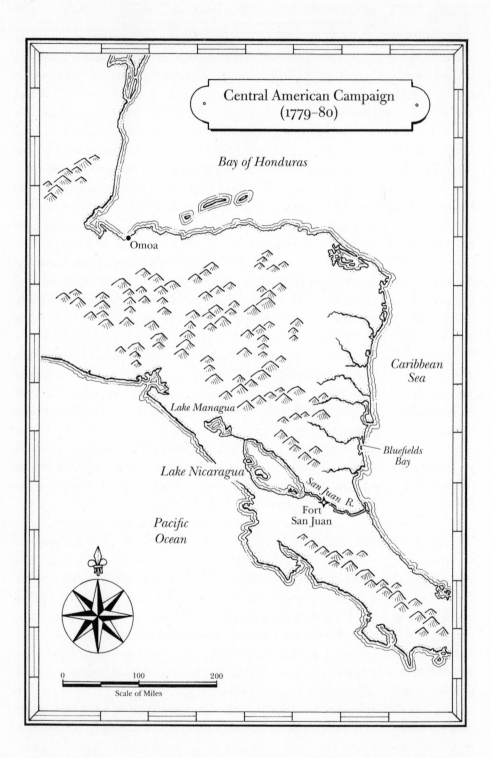

Central American Campaign
(1779–80)

Bay of Honduras

Omoa

Caribbean
Sea

Lake Managua

Bluefields
Bay

Lake Nicaragua

San Juan R.

Fort
San Juan

Pacific
Ocean

0   100   200

Scale of Miles

Since the late seventeenth century, there had been British settlements along the coast of the Bay of Honduras and later along the coast of Nicaragua. The settlers had established a logging trade that exploited the tropical rain forests in Honduras and Nicaragua for logwood and mahogany. Mahogany furniture had become fashionable in England, and the logwood yielded a dye used in the making of woolens. These informal communities of loggers were stretched along that coast at Black River, Rattan (Roatoan), St. George's Key, and Cape Gracias a Dios along the coast of Honduras, and at Sandy Bay, Pearl Key, Bluefields, and Greytown along the coast of Nicaragua. The settlements were not recognized by Spain which tried to discourage their presence by establishing garrisons like the fortress of San Fernando at Omoa. Notwithstanding the hostility of Spain, the settlements began to thrive and became informal colonies with a local superintendent general who reported to the governor of Jamaica.[39]

As with most of his plans during the Revolutionary War, Germain was acting upon proposals made by military commanders on the spot, together with the advice of leading civilians and colonial administrators. The plan of invading Central America was primarily conceived by Major General John Dalling, the governor of Jamaica. Dalling had served with William Howe under James Wolfe in the conquest of Quebec where he was wounded scaling the heights of Abraham. In 1762, he had commanded a regiment during the British occupation of Havana in Cuba. He boasted that if the home government gave him command of a force "of no great extent," he would be able to deliver "the Dominion of Spain in this part of the world." Dalling was frustrated with his civil command and admitted that he felt himself "in every respect, saving the military line unequal to the task" of civil administration. Finding the life of a governor "no satisfaction for a military man," he wanted to personally lead the expedition. He promised that he would "either present my King with Dominion on the Continent, or lay my bones in the Province of Nicaragua."[40]

Before the arrival of reinforcements from Britain, Dalling sent a small expeditionary force to capture control of the San Juan River. When it landed on the Mosquito Shore, he anticipated that it would be joined by about a thousand British settlers. After the arrival of additional troops, he expected the expedition to conquer Lake Nicaragua. It would then push ahead to take "possession of the Town of Grenada at the opposite end and, if possible, that of Leon." Indeed, Dalling was of the opinion that with fifteen hundred troops, together with volunteers and Indians, the British could take the Yucatán Peninsula.[41]

Dalling was encouraged in his plan by Major James Lawrie, the newly appointed superintendent of the British settlers on the Mosquito Shore. Lawrie was responsible for creating several of the misconceptions that proved fatal for the expedition. He gave the impression that the river was navigable and its defenses easily bypassed. He also encouraged the belief that the expedition would be supported by the settlers and Miskito

Indians. He astonishingly claimed that the health of the troops would benefit rather than suffer from tropical conditions. Lawrie had compelling reasons for wanting the expedition to be launched. He had recently been appointed superintendent general in place of his rival Robert Hodgson. The presence of troops was likely to improve the chances of logwood settlements becoming fully integrated into the British Empire. While Lawrie was encouraging Dalling with the scheme in Central America, his rival Robert Hodgson promoted a similar plan to Lord George Germain in England. He too had a vested interest. They both painted a promising picture.

Germain was initially wary of the grander design of conquering Central America, writing to Dalling that "I apprehend a greater force than your Estimate requires would be necessary, and I do not see at present how it could be spared." He subsequently changed his mind and told Dalling that "Your Ideas of the objects against which our attacks should be directed, coincide entirely with the opinions entertained here." In January 1780, Germain informed Dalling that he was sending over three thousand troops primarily for the defense of Jamaica but also to participate in the expedition to Central America. Germain now shared the optimism of the governor about the infinite possibilities of the expedition, writing that perhaps "opportunities may present themselves of enlarging your Views and extending them to Objects of still greater magnitude." Nevertheless, his primary objective was to pressure Spain to make peace. In April, he sent Richard Cumberland, his close confidant and under secretary of state, to open negotiations in Madrid, while simultaneously reinforcing Dalling in Jamaica, which would have the added advantage of strengthening Cumberland's position in Spain.[42]

The fact that Miskito Indians and slaves from the Mosquito coast had participated in the capture of Omoa in 1779 seemed to confirm British expectations of local support. In preparation for the expedition, advertisements for recruits were placed in the *Jamaica Gazette,* "inviting all free people, of whatever colour . . . to enter into the most honourable service with a bounty of Five pounds each." The light infantry and rangers were to include "two flank troops of free Mulattoes who will thereby have a favourable opportunity of displaying their courage and making their fortunes" from an equal share of the prize money. Dalling boasted to Germain that "People of colour for the free companies are now coming in fast; and it appears as if I should not want volunteers for my Expedition." Miskito Indians joined the expedition when it arrived off the coast of Nicaragua. According to Benjamin Moseley, the problems of navigating the river might have proved "insurmountable but for the skill of the Indians in managing the boats." They proved to be invaluable scouts, boatmen, and porters.[43]

Similar to the policy of deploying Native Americans and loyalists in America, Germain looked to make up the insufficient number of regular troops by finding alternative sources of manpower. He even wanted the commanders to use American prisoners of war from Jamaica and Charleston in South Carolina. There were blacks and people of mixed race in the regiments. These included the Jamaica Legion, composed chiefly of the crews of privateers, who "included some people of colour." Sir Alexander Leith's Royal Batteux Men "consisted of much the same sort of people as the legion." The light horse and dragoons also consisted "of a few people of colour" from Jamaica. Dalling expected the people of colour to "be of the first Consequence as they will be better able to bear the different fatigues in these warm Latitudes than Troops just arrived from Europe." The officers of the light dragoons were white "except one or two."[44]

The Central American campaign went dramatically wrong in ways similar to Burgoyne's campaign before Saratoga. In April 1780, without waiting for the delayed reinforcement of the three thousand regular troops from England, Dalling launched the expedition with the justification that it would confuse the enemy and deter him from counterattacks. According to one contemporary commentator, Dalling's refusal to wait for reinforcements from England was the main cause of the failure of the entire enterprise. Captain John Polson led the expedition of over a thousand men of whom only about a quarter were regulars in the British army. Like Burgoyne at Ticonderoga, Captain Polson's force initially did well and captured Fort San Juan, which Dalling "looked upon as the inland Gibraltar of Spanish America, as it commands the only water pass between the lake of Nicaragua and the Northern Ocean." Now known as El Castillo de la Inmaculada Concepción (the Fortress of the Immaculate Conception), it was located sixty-four miles up the San Juan River and thirty-two miles from Lake Nicaragua. It had a garrison of about two hundred men. Captain Polson sent Dalling a premature report of success, claiming that "now my Lord, the communicating door to the South [has] been burst open . . . Spanish America is severed in two." Anxious to resign as governor of Jamaica and assume personal command of the army on Lake Nicaragua, Dalling conjured even more grandiose plans of taking Mexico and was even musing that "at a further time . . . Peru may become as easy prey."[45]

The expedition soon began to unravel, however. The siege of Fort San Juan had been a desperate undertaking. Owing to the illness of so many of the men, Captain Horatio Nelson and Lieutenant Edward Despard personally emplaced cannon on opposite hills overlooking the fortress and thereby averted the immediate failure of the expedition. Nelson had only one field piece with which he destroyed the colors of the fortress on his first shot. On April 20, 1780, reinforcements from Jamaica consisting of 250 British troops and 270 of the locally raised Jamaica Legion arrived at Bluefields Bay. They were led by Lieutenant Colonel Stephen Kemble of the 60th Regiment, who assumed the command from Polson upon reaching Fort San Juan. Kemble was a twenty-two-year-old loyalist from a prominent New York family who had made a career in the British army. He had requested to be reassigned after General Sir Henry Clinton had overlooked him in the promotion of the more junior Major John André as adjutant general of the British army in America.

Upon arrival at Fort San Juan on May 15, Kemble found the garrison in total disorder owing to sickness, with not enough men even to change the guard. For almost two months, Kemble made a valiant attempt to revive the expedition along the San Juan River only to discover that the Spanish had been alerted and had taken additional precautions to fortify the entrance to Lake Nicaragua. It was all in vain. On July 25, Kemble withdrew to the coast and left a small garrison at Fort San Juan. His men were too weak and their numbers were insufficient to risk attack. By September, he despaired of any future prospects for the expedition, complaining that "Gen. Dalling thinks of nothing but prosecuting his Plan by this or some other River; indeed, I suppose he is so far Embarked that he cannot recede." On November 25, he finally received orders from Dalling to evacuate and blow up Fort San Juan. The destruction of the fortress was only partially completed by Lieutenant Despard before the arrival of Spanish troops in early January.[46]

As had so often proved the case in North America, the expectation of widespread support from settlers and Indians proved illusory in Central America. The expedition lost valuable time as its commander attempted to find recruits. Fearing for the future of their illicit trade with the Spanish, the English settlers showed little enthusiasm to assist and even discouraged support from the Miskito Indians by spreading rumors that the real intention of the expedition was to enslave the Indians and take them to Jamaica. Instead of recruiting a thousand settlers, Lawrie managed to gather only twelve white settlers, sixty blacks, and 230 Miskitos. The recruiting efforts in Jamaica were obstructed by the elected island assembly which opposed the removal of troops when the island faced a real threat of invasion by a joint expedition of the French and Spanish navies. The Miskitos began to desert during the siege of Fort St. Juan, taking the boats with them, and when Lawrie returned to the coast having recovered from an illness, he found that the blacks that he had recruited had abandoned the expedition.

The expedition had been conceived in ignorance of the realities of the region's geography. Dalling admitted that he had "no other charts but those of the West Indies published by Jeffries." Germain also relied on the map of Thomas Jeffreys in *The West India Atlas* (1774), which made the proposed distances of the expedition seem short, with a passage of only about a hundred miles from the coast to the lake, but of course gave no indication of the navigability of the San Juan River. Dalling had simply accepted that it was "an easy channel." In fact, the river proved a major obstacle which caused delays depriving the expedition of the vital element of surprise while exposing the troops to torrential rainfall. The expedition lacked pilots with sufficient knowledge of the river. Despite assurances to the contrary by the chief pilot, Richard Hannah, the river navigation proved dangerously shallow and impassable in some sections. The first attempt to sail up it was abandoned after some overloaded boats capsized. As a result of these difficulties, the expedition took three months rather than the anticipated four weeks, and could not carry more than fifty-three of the two hundred cannon balls intended for the siege of Fort St. Juan.[47]

The worst scourge of the expedition was disease, with men dying primarily from yellow fever and malaria, as well as from dysentery and typhoid fever. Kemble had to halt the expedition for a while when there not enough men to transport provisions from Fort San Juan. He did not have enough officers healthy enough to report the returns of troops and had to undertake most of the administrative duties himself. He vividly described how his men were half-starved and feverish, without shoes or stockings, with "fountains of water" pouring from their swollen legs, limbs, and thighs. Dr. Benjamin Moseley calculated that "Of about 1,800 people who were sent [on] this expedition, none of the Europeans retained their health above sixteen days, and not more than 380 ever returned; and those, chiefly, in a miserable condition." About 1,000 sailors who accompanied the expedition lost their lives, with combined losses amounting to around 2,500. Only 10 of the 200 crew members survived from the twenty-eight-gun frigate, HMS *Hinchinbroke,* commanded by Nelson, who was himself forced to return to Jamaica where he was nursed back to life by a slave woman, Cuba Cornwallis. It took him a further year to recover in England. They were burying between six and eight men a day, though according to Moseley, most of the men "languished in the extremist misery, and gradually mouldered away, until there was not sufficient strength alive to attend the sick, nor to bury the dead." Kemble, too, described how, upon embarking his troops back to Jamaica, there were not even enough men to bury the dead "who lay on the beach shocking to behold." Dr. John Hunter recollected the details of the high mortality rates, writing, "The mind recoils with horror from such a scene of destruction of the human species."[48]

Germain was critical when the expedition failed, complaining that it had deviated from the original plan of using Indians, settlers, volunteers, and adventurers to obtain possession of the river and "only then to send in a body of troops." The troops should not have been used under such conditions, since they could only be provisioned with the support of the natives. Germain admitted that he had had misgivings when he heard of the desertion of the Miskito Indians. He was to declare the expedition an entire failure in which "no public Benefit has been derived from the Loss of so many brave men." It not only failed but distracted from the British war effort in North America. General John Campbell, the commander in West Florida, had insufficient troops even to protect the region, let alone to attack New Orleans. On March 14, 1780, Gálvez captured Mobile, cutting off a major source of supply to the British in Pensacola. After a two-month siege on May 10, 1781, the British surrendered Pensacola and the remains of West Florida. Similarly, Spain began a counteroffensive along the coast of Honduras and captured a British post on the Rio Negro. Germain's strategy of offensive warfare had been unrealistic when there were insufficient manpower and resources even to defend existing British possessions.[49]

IV

From the siege of Boston until after the defeat at Yorktown, Germain presided over the war in America. He alone was involved in the decision making of both the operations that resulted in failure in New York at Saratoga in 1777 and in Central America in 1779–81. He was also instrumental in the decision to invade Virginia that led to the defeat of Lord Cornwallis at Yorktown. Germain was inevitably held by posterity to be more responsible than any other individual for the British loss in America. His critics have ever since argued that his strategic ideas were based on false assumptions that proved fatal to the outcome of the war. He sought an offensive strategy that required ever more troops to garrison and police new territories when military resources were already overstretched. His strategy relied heavily on naval support, which was often not forthcoming. When Britain lost the islands of Grenada and St. Vincent in the Caribbean in 1779, Germain was still planning the conquest of Puerto Rico.

In reality, Germain adopted plans urged upon him by his commanders and civil governors, whether Burgoyne in New York in 1777, Dalling in Central America in 1779–81, or Cornwallis in North Carolina in 1780–81. His plan to conquer Puerto Rico in 1779 was suggested to him by William Mathew Burt, the governor of the Leeward Islands. Although his schemes appear wildly ambitious, they were thought attainable by those who were on the spot and most familiar with local conditions. In the earliest campaign plan for 1777, Sir William Howe claimed that he only required an additional fifteen thousand troops to be able to conquer New England, unite with Burgoyne, and invade Virginia and South Carolina.

Germain prided himself upon deferring to his commanders overseas and not attempting to micromanage. In March 1778, he urged Sir Henry Clinton to feel free to "use your own discretion in planning as well as executing all operations which shall appear the most likely means of crushing the rebellion." In his instructions of January 1779, he left it to Clinton's judgment whether to make alterations to the plan of operations, because Clinton best knew the circumstances "which cannot be known here." He was indulgent towards Sir William Howe in allowing him to pursue an independent strategy to attack Philadelphia. Germain was in a dilemma because he could not easily recall a general in the middle of a campaign, and Howe was politically well connected in Britain. It was not until the campaign was too far gone that Germain became critical of the Howe brothers. Similarly with Sir Henry Clinton, Germain began to intervene when Clinton seemed to be inactive in 1779. Germain saw his role as limited to suggesting objectives in broad brush strokes and to providing the necessary logistical support from Britain. However, he invariably encouraged field commanders to undertake offensive operations, often without sufficient resources, in the belief that the risk was justified when nothing was more fatal than "a tame defensive war, which must end in the destruction of this country." He constantly proposed new objectives and lacked a clear sense of strategic priorities, which frustrated his generals who felt his expectations to be unrealistic.[50]

Germain has been accused of misplaced optimism that verged on the realm of fantasy in his belief that the deficiency of regular troops from Britain could be offset by recruiting local supporters in Central America, Canada, and North America. Indeed, Germain told the House of Commons in June 1779 that "it had never been his idea that America could be conquered." The following month, he wrote to Henry Clinton that he was convinced that "our utmost efforts will fail . . . if we cannot find means to engage the people of America in support of a cause which is equally their own and ours." He continued to believe that the revolution was the work of a minority. Again in the House of Commons in November 1780, he said that he was convinced that more than half the people in America were the friends of this country, and only the "tyranny of Congress" prevented the loyalists from taking up arms. He "denied that he ever said he should require an unconditional surrender." He had simply thought it wrong to negotiate with people in arms against Britain.[51]

Germain consistently overestimated the potential for loyalist support and under-estimated the popularity of the Revolution. He was so fixated on the idea that the loyalists were in the majority that he dismissed contrary evidence out of hand. It is often the case that wishful thinking colors outlooks and beliefs, leading to a preference for intelligence and information that corroborates an existing opinion. In 1777, Sir Henry Clinton gave a remarkable account of a meeting with the minister in London, in which he described how Germain asked questions that determined the answers and how he often answered his own questions. During a visit to London from America in January 1779, Colonel Charles Stuart wrote to Clinton of a conversation with Germain, in which he observed that, although he had already known that Germain "neglected information that did not coincide with his wishes, yet I was astonished and hurt to find that upon such shallow grounds he should be lulled into a blind security which might prove fatal to our affairs." However, Germain found plenty of people willing to confirm his views who had first-hand knowledge of America. His misconceptions were not confined to himself but were rather part of a prevalent mindset.[52]

If Germain was deceived, so were the generals and royal officials in America, all of whom shared in the expectation of popular support there. General Burgoyne had acted under the impression that he would encounter little opposition after the conquest of Ticonderoga. General Howe was convinced that he would march through friendly territory in Maryland and southern Pennsylvania. Lord Cornwallis was expectant of loyalist support in North Carolina and Virginia. Germain similarly heard support of his views from Benedict Arnold. After their return to Britain in the late fall of 1778, the Carlisle peace commissioners informed the Cabinet that there was widespread disaffection with the Continental Congress and a large reservoir of loyalist support in America. The commissioners repeated their claims in a written report to Germain. During the inquiry into the conduct of the Howe brothers in 1779, Lieutenant General James Robertson gave three days of testimony in which he claimed that large scale reinforcements were unnecessary since two-thirds of the population was loyal and that it was only necessary "to assist the good Americans to subdue the bad ones." Robertson had over twenty-three years of experience in America and was the civil governor of New York. Sir Henry Clinton was the most skeptical of the senior generals, but even he was persuaded of strong loyalist support along the eastern shore of the Chesapeake and in Pennsylvania on the very eve of the British defeat at Yorktown.[53]

Germain was also influenced by loyalist exiles in England who were especially zealous in their insistence that the revolution was the work of a minority and did not have popular support. They were members of the elite who were unrepresentative of popular feeling. Furthermore, they tended to propose strategies that concentrated military resources in their own regions and in their own estates. Germain regularly met with prominent American loyalists in London such as Thomas Hutchinson and Joseph Galloway. Richard Cumberland described in his memoirs the levees in Germain's apartment to which "great numbers of American loyalists . . . were in the habit of resorting." When Sir William Howe obtained an inquiry into his conduct in 1779, Germain found an ally in Joseph Galloway of Pennsylvania, who testified to Parliament that "more than four-fifths of Americans would prefer a union with Great Britain to independence." The loyalist perspective was shared by the under secretaries of state at the American Department. After 1778, William Knox became the senior of the two under secretaries. Although he was of Irish origin, he had lived in Georgia and acted as colonial agent for the colony, where he owned two plantations in Knoxborough on the Savannah River, with a total of 2,585 acres and 122 slaves. John Almon, who published pamphlets opposing the war, thought that the "zeal and suggestions of Knox" had unfortunate consequences in America. In 1780, Benjamin Thompson of Massachusetts became the other under secretary, at the time that he was also living with Germain.[54]

Germain was aware that it was "important to avoid being deceived in our Expectations" by the loyalists and that it was necessary to obtain accurate intelligence "thro Persons whose Knowledge of the Country & People enable them to detect & Prevent Imposition." In order to gauge the sympathies in the southern colonies, he commissioned a report in regard to the "disposition and resolution of the Back Inhabitants" from James Simpson who was the former attorney general of South Carolina. Simpson categorized the political affiliations of the population into four groups. First, there were those who were "as favorable as could be wished" and who regretted their earlier opposition to Britain. Second, there were those who feared financial ruin without the restoration of royal government. Third, there were those who were still on the revolutionary side but ready to submit, and finally there were the minority radical revolutionaries. Simpson concluded that the "number and consequence of the two first by far exceed the last." Apart from the testimonies of individual loyalists, Germain was impressed by the success of the army in obtaining oaths of allegiance from large pockets of the population in New Jersey in 1776, Philadelphia in 1778, and Charleston in 1780. In Georgia in 1778, fourteen hundred people swore an oath of allegiance and formed twenty loyalist militia companies. He mistook what was often a case of rented allegiance on the part of people who were willing to pay lip-service to whichever army was in control.[55]

The opposition parties ridiculed Germain's faith that the majority of the American population supported Britain. As early as January 1775, the earl of Chatham had accused the ministry of deluding the public into thinking that the rebel movement was confined to Boston. The opposition speakers became more merciless in their sarcasm as the evidence mounted that the army was not getting the support of the local population and that it was the Revolution that was popular. In the wake of Howe's withdrawal from New Jersey in May 1777, Edward Gibbon complained of having Charles James Fox at his elbow in the House of Commons "declaiming the impossibility of keeping America." Before the arrival of official news of Saratoga in October 1777, Lord John Cavendish referred contemptuously to the government's view of the "supposed inconsiderable party of factious men" who supported the Revolution. In the House of Lords, the marquess of Rockingham asked "where were those mighty leaders found, whom Americans obeyed so implicitly, and who governed them with so despotic a rule? They had no grandees amongst them." In November 1778, Fox spoke of the absurdity of a war waged to gain the affections of Americans. Far from the rebellion being the work of a minority or a single province, Fox asserted that Virginia was no less jealous of its rights than Massachusetts. The undisciplined rabble had transformed itself into a powerful, numerous, and well-disciplined enemy.[56]

In November 1778, Fox accused Germain of being a slave of report and "the dupe of false information of men, who were interested in deception." He ridiculed the notion that there was only a trifling mob to quell and that nine-tenths of the people were loyal, "yet strange to tell, this vast majority of people . . . suffered themselves to be fleeced and driven like sheep, by that ragged handful of their own rabble." There was suddenly a numerous and powerful army that had required the minister to ransack Europe for troops and exhaust Great Britain. Fox mocked the boasts of the early years of the war that the "Americans were all cowards" and that "a grenadier's cap was sufficient to throw" them all into panic. It was odd that "55,000 men, with an immense naval force, should be sent to reduce poltroons." With reference to Saratoga, Fox asked Germain to confirm whether he believed that a gallant army, with officers of the most distinguished merit, had been defeated by a wretched, contemptible rabble without spirit and discipline.[57]

The opposition continued to mock the contradiction between government assertions and the failures of the army in America. They asked whether there were any bounds to the credulity of the government in asserting "that many are not only most unaccounta-bly kept in bondage by the few, but they are compelled to take arms in their hands, totally contrary to their inclinations," and fight for "a vagrant congress" and a handful of factious leaders "against us whom they regard and consider their best friends." It was a recurring theme of opposition gibes that the rebellion was represented by the government as the act of a faction "who had by sort of surprize possessed themselves of the civil and military powers of that country."[58]

After the French entry into the war in 1778, Germain placed increasing emphasis upon loyalist support in a new strategy aimed at subduing the former southern colonies, in expectation of the army finding greater loyalist support than in the north. He hoped that the loyalists might make up the deficiencies in troop numbers by relieving the regular army of auxiliary and subordinate jobs, and more importantly by helping to police and retain conquered territories. With the focus of the war switching to the Caribbean and Europe, he aimed to recover the south gradually with small forces, while Sir Henry Clinton contained Washington's army in the Hudson Highlands. He hoped that success-ful military campaigns in the south and the restoration of civil government there would encourage others to side with Britain. Germain became more hopeful when the British encountered little opposition in the conquest of Georgia at the end of the year. In 1780, he was yet more optimistic, with the capture of Charleston and the defeat of the southern division of the Continental Army at Camden which gave Britain possession of South Carolina.[59]

Although the skepticism of the opposition parties proved to be justified, Ger-main had reasonable cause for his belief in the loyalists, because allegiances were fluid and continued to change throughout the war. In his essays in *The American Crisis* in 1776, Thomas Paine declaimed against the "summer soldier and the sunshine patriots," and Washington wrote of the difficulties caused by marauding "Tories." It is still much debated as to whether there was a strong sense of national identity in America during the Revolutionary War. The thirteen states did not all sign the Articles of Confederation until the year of the battle of Yorktown (1781). There was much resistance to complying with enlistments for both militia and for the army throughout the states. In early 1777, only a thousand men chose to reenlist in the Continental Army, which fell thirty-five thousand short of the target set by the Congress and eight thousand below the peak of 1776. Although there was a surge in support in 1780, the "rage militaire" and voluntary enlist-ments never again attained the level of the year of the Declaration of Independence.[60]

It is often claimed that one-third of the white colonial population was loyal to Britain, one-third was neutral, and one-third actively supported the Revolution. This assessment is almost certainly based upon a comment of John Adams written in 1775, which he repeated in a letter of 1815. However, during negotiations with the Dutch Republic, he assured his interlocutors that no more than a tenth of the population was loyalist. In the absence of opinion polls, it is impossible to calculate the actual proportion of loyalists and especially the potential latent support for Britain. The estimates of modern historians vary wildly, which is itself an indication of how difficult it was to gauge the fluctuating situation during the Revolution. William Smith, the loyalist chief justice of New York, wrote that "No Man knows his nearest Friends' real Sentiments." There was also much regional variation in the proportion and density of loyalists, with seemingly high concentrations in the Hudson Valley, southern Pennsylvania, New York, and the southern frontier between Georgia and Virginia. Nevertheless, the loyalists lost the initiative to the revolutionaries on the eve of the war when they were neither well organized nor equally motivated. They were outmaneuvered by the revolutionaries, who even succeeded in appropriating to themselves the title of Whig and dubbing the loyalists Tories, thereby associating the loyalists with the party that had espoused the divine right of kings in opposition to the Whig principles of the Glorious Revolution in England. The loyalists lacked cohesion and national leaders. Although they included many members of the elite, they were too often composed of outsiders and fringe elements of society that had scores to settle with their compatriots.[61]

The loyalists were, however, a substantial presence, so that the Revolution was a civil war as well as a rebellion. That is why the myth of loyalist strength persisted for so long among the British and deceived Lord George Germain. Although there were only 5,000 civilians in New York after the British occupation in September 1776, the arrival of loyalist refugees caused the population to grow to 25,000 by 1781 and between 33,000 and 40,000 by 1783. During the course of the Revolutionary War, some 19,000 loyalists served in provincial corps under the British. Between 1780 and 1781, 10,000 loyalists fought for Britain. An analysis of 6,000 loyalists indicates that about 15 percent of men of military age fought on the British side in the Revolutionary War. If this was indeed the average proportion of those who served in the war, the loyalists comprised about 513,000 people or the equivalent of 16 percent of the population of the United States. They included Benjamin Franklin's only son, Sir William Franklin, the former governor of New Jersey. Some 3,000 loyalists lodged claims for compensation after the war from the Royal Claims Commission. In all, a higher proportion of the American population emigrated as loyalist exiles than the proportion of refugees from France during the French Revolution. They went primarily to Canada but also to Britain and other parts of the British Empire. They dominated the population of the Bahamas, where the governor, Lord Dunmore, a former governor of Virginia now serving in a humbler position, found the loyalists just as quarrelsome as the Virginians.[62]

Despite their importance to the southern strategy, no serious consideration was given to how to attract and retain loyalist support. Sir Henry Clinton appreciated the danger of rallying the loyalists if the army was unable to give them sustained protection. He did not believe that they could act alone and maintain an independent force in the absence of the army. He opposed raids, which raised hopes only to dash them. Germain had wanted to restore civil government to replace martial law in the British-occupied territories in America, but his wish was never implemented except in Savannah. He was obstructed by his army commanders, who feared that elected assemblies and civil lawsuits might impede military operations, but who failed to appreciate the symbolic importance of constitutional government to the loyalists and the propaganda value of martial rule to the enemy. They were willing to accept nothing more than the establishment of civilian police boards in New York, Philadelphia, and Charleston. Germain was keen to create loyalist regiments but the commanders were opposed to giving the citizen soldiers of provincial corps equal status to the army. It was a delicate issue, because regular officers, who had spent their careers in the army since their teens, resented civilians being given equal rank. The officers in loyalist corps were consequently kept junior to officers of the same rank in the regular army: they did not have the same half-pay pensions, they did not receive the same gratuities if wounded, and they were not allocated funds for hospitals. Throughout the war, furthermore, there was tension between a conciliatory policy toward civilians and the use of ruthless methods deemed necessary for victory.[63]

The potential for popular loyalist support diminished the longer the war continued. From the beginning of the war, the army was notorious for plunder and indiscipline. This was not just enemy propaganda. It was admitted to be a problem at the highest levels and was condemned by Germain. The burning of towns and destruction of property alienated neutrals. Moreover, although the subject has only been studied in the context of the French and Indian War, the soldiers often appeared irreligious in a country that was being transformed by evangelical preachers who had an apocalyptic vision of the divine nature of their struggle. The regiments frequently exercised on Sundays and were rarely accompanied by their chaplains. The diaries of some officers reveal their contempt for what were known in England as "dissenting" or "nonconformist" denominations, such as Presbyterians and Congregationalists, who were the dominant religious groups in New England. The British similarly antagonized local sympathizers by their use of black slaves, Native Americans, and Hessians. The loyalists compounded the problem by seeking personal vengeance, being minorities who had their own grievances against the majority population. Furthermore, over time loyalists became less willing to be active combatants, since they resented their second-rate status in relation to the army. Despite the emphasis upon the role of loyalists in British strategy after 1778, enlistments increased but at proportionally lower rates than previously. In 1780–81, they barely replaced casualties and desertions.[64]

There was an intellectual failure among politicians and commanders in general to appreciate how the revolutionary cause broadened its appeal by embracing an increasingly radical ideology committed to liberty, consent, and equality. John Adams wrote of a second and more important American Revolution, referring to a revolution in the minds of the people and in social practices. Social historians have persuasively argued that revolutionary leaders were forced to adopt a more radical ideology in order to gain greater popular support for the cause and to win the war. There were remarkable democratic experiments like the constitution of Pennsylvania. Germain and the Cabinet took no interest in such innovations in government and did not appreciate their significance. They simply failed to comprehend this dimension of the Revolution. On the other hand, Germain ultimately believed that there was no choice but to fight the war to preserve the national importance and prosperity of Britain. He was therefore willing to clutch at every straw of hope.[65]

V

Germain contended with major constraints that are generally unappreciated in assessments of his abilities. He was particularly hampered by the disunity and weakness of the Cabinet and the lack of a dominating personality as prime minister. Like the elder Pitt in the Seven Years' War, Germain might have filled the void, since he was forceful enough, but he was handicapped by his unpopularity and the stigma of Minden.

Germain was circumscribed in his authority to decide strategy and to command the military. Although his ideas were often followed by the government, he had to defer on matters of strategy to the rest of the Cabinet and to George III. His instructions to commanders were therefore often suggestions rather than positive orders. He had to cajole and bully to get results, and he was often prevented from implementing his own ideas by his fellow ministers. In 1776, his wish to negotiate from a position of strength by a knockout victory against Washington was thwarted by the conciliatory approach of Lord North, the earl of Dartmouth, and the Howe brothers. In 1778, he complained that he was not consulted upon the creation and role of the Carlisle Peace Commission. In addition, he and his fellow ministers did not have the luxury of being able to focus on the American war alone. When Lieutenant Colonel Charles Stuart visited Britain in January 1779, he found Germain and the Cabinet "so entirely employed with the affairs of Ireland, that it was not so easy to make them attend to those of America."[66]

Germain was powerless to make up the insufficient number of troops in America. The size of the force was constrained by the budget, disappointing recruiting efforts, and anxiety even among government supporters at the prospect of an enlarged military. He had to compete for troops with the needs of the Royal Navy and the East India Company. When Germain sought to raise a new corps of Highlanders in 1776, George III resented his constant "harping" on the subject, and told Lord North to "crush the plan in the Bud." The king thought the rebellion would be crushed before a new regiment would be available for service and preferred to enlarge existing regiments. In the Recruiting Acts of 1778 and 1779, the government resorted to general impressments that extended the age of eligibility for military service. The government commuted the sentences of a small number of minor criminals to military service in disease-ridden garrisons in the Caribbean and India. It relaxed the rules against the recruitment of Catholics in Britain and Ireland. It recruited Scottish and Irish deserters both from the British and from Continental armies who made up much of Lord Rawdon's regiment, the Volunteers of Ireland. However, Germain compounded the problem of the shortage of troops by promising reinforcements that he did not deliver and annoying his commanders by disingenuously including the sick in his calculations of their military strength.[67]

After 1778, the British army actually shrank in America, overstretched by its commitments in the Mediterranean, Africa, the Caribbean, Central America, India, and Canada. In southern India in 1780, the British faced an army that was said to be of eighty thousand men under Hyder Ali of Mysore, supported by the French. Britain sent six infantry regiments, a cavalry regiment, and two Hanoverian battalions to India, which collectively far exceeded the reinforcements sent to Sir Henry Clinton in New York. Germain had to send more troops to defend the British Caribbean, whose conquest was the main strategic objective of France and Spain. In 1779, two regiments serving under Major General James Grant in St. Lucia in the Caribbean had to be redeployed into the navy, owing to the crippling shortage of men in the fleet of Admiral John Byron. In the Caribbean the mortality rates among troops were especially high. In November 1780, Brigadier General Charles O'Hara lamented that Britain had sent to the Caribbean ten old regiments from Philadelphia in November 1778 and subsequently eleven new regiments making a total of eleven thousand men of whom "above Five Thousand . . . have already perished." In the Caribbean, the army had an annual mortality rate of 15 percent, compared to 6 percent in New York and 1 percent in Canada. Without firing a single shot, the British lost 3,500 troops in three and a half years in Jamaica. Only 18 of the 1,008 men of the 79th Regiment (Royal Liverpool Volunteers), stationed in Kingston, survived to return to Liverpool. Just days after talking fondly of seeing England again, Major Thomas Stanley of the 79th Regiment, the brother of the earl of Derby, died, exclaiming "against the Ministry in the bitterest of terms, for sacrificing him to the inclemencies of an infernal Clime. He was vexed at not dying by a ball, in the field, rather than by a putrid fever, on his bed."[68]

Even though combined amphibious operations with the army were essential to success in America, Germain had no control over the Royal Navy. This meant that there was no supreme commander to ensure coordination. In April 1776, Germain was already writing that he did not understand the Admiralty and their seeming indifference to the success of expeditions in America. It was all he could do "to exhort, advise and then protest, but that will not prevent my bearing the blame if no good arises from these great armaments and immense expenses" for want of naval support. Germain wanted to permit merchants in the Caribbean to arm their vessels as privateers to attack the privateers and trade of North America. He did not have the authority to do so, and the issue became the first of his quarrels with the earl of Sandwich. While awaiting news of Cornwallis at Yorktown, Germain complained that whenever Sandwich proposed or fully approved a plan, the ships were available, but if he was not in favor, "official difficulties occur." Germain was unable to remove admirals who were incompatible with the military commanders like Sir Peter Parker with Dalling in Jamaica. From the outset of the war, Germain was unhappy with the insufficient number of naval ships to blockade the coast of North America.[69]

Germain and Sandwich openly feuded in the Cabinet. This was more than a personality conflict, and it cannot even be explained in terms of departmental rivalries; rather, it reflected different priorities in the distribution of scarce resources. The differences were reflected at lower levels among generals, governors, admirals, and other senior officers as far down as captains. After 1778, the discrepancy in his and Germain's objectives became more manifest. Sandwich favored withdrawal from America. He thereafter treated it as marginal to the defense of Britain and the West Indies. Indeed, the war in America was predicated on Britain having a superior navy to that of France, which in the course of the war ceased to be true and consistently undermined Germain's strategy for victory in America. In April 1778, Germain had to threaten resignation in order to get additional naval support in America, when he drew up "A Protest from Lord George Germain." Although his wish was granted, the reinforcement commanded by Admiral Byron was so delayed by Sandwich's caution that the French Admiral D'Estaing was able to capture Dominica in the Caribbean and nearly took Newport in Rhode Island. In 1779, Clinton's expeditions were disrupted because he did not have proper naval support so that he had to postpone his plans for the capture of Charleston. Because the French navy was superior in the Americas, Major General James Grant was unable to return the troops used in the conquest of St. Lucia to the desperate Clinton in New York. In 1781, Germain, Clinton, and Cornwallis had based their strategies on naval parity between Britain and France. In the months before Yorktown, Germain and Sandwich were at such loggerheads that Charles James Fox was claiming that Germain would be the principal witness in the event of Sandwich's impeachment.[70]

Germain had to work with a myriad of different government departments that also reported to other ministers. There were a dozen different departments that administered the army, which included the War Office led by William Viscount Barrington, who had made the logistical arrangements for the court martial of Germain in 1760. As secretary at war, Barrington had advised against sending the army to America and he eventually resigned from the government in protest against Germain. In order to transport and supply the troops in America and the Caribbean, Germain had to coordinate three different government departments, the Ordnance Board (artillery, engineers, guns, and ordnance stores), the Navy Board (infantry, cavalry, clothing, hospital stores, tents, and camp equipment), and the Treasury Board (provisions). The Treasury negotiated most of the contracts with merchants and set quality standards. After 1779, the Navy Board took over responsibility for transportation from the Treasury Board, although Germain unsuccessfully opposed the change. There were initially so many problems that he requested that the Treasury resume its oversight of shipping.[71]

Germain was also impeded by an administrative apparatus that was not well adapted to supplying and transporting troops across the Atlantic. The army required an average of thirty-three tons of food a day. There were in addition wives, common-law spouses, and women camp followers who made up the equivalent of over 12 percent of the army, while children averaged another 9 percent of the total military population. The provisions were carried in wagons pulled by two or three horses, making a total of 4,000 horses that consumed an annual average of 14,000 tons of hay and 6,000 tons of oats. There were also refugees with the army who had to be fed including growing numbers of loyalists, slave runaways, and Native Americans. In November 1779, the British were supplying provisions to 3,329 Indian refugees from twenty-two different tribes in Fort Niagara at the mouth of the Niagara River on Lake Ontario. This was just one instance among many. The Treasury consistently underestimated the amount of provisions needed because the number of refugees with the army and loyalist troops was constantly fluctuating. The lack of provisions delayed the opening of campaigns, and the army suffered some of its worst setbacks as it mounted raids to obtain forage.[72]

Germain's task of coordinating the work of departments outside his immediate scope of authority was the more difficult because he had to overcome the junior status of his position as secretary of state for America. His office had only been created as a separate department in 1768. It had been established at the expense of the two older offices of the secretaries of state for the Northern and Southern Departments, which continued in existence. His staff was smaller than the staffs of the other two secretaries in spite of the greater demands of his office. Germain's attempt to gain control of the war effort inevitably created turf battles with the other two secretaries and with Sandwich, and the other secretaries naturally resented his encroachment upon their authority and patronage in America and the Caribbean. It was a testimony to his resilience and his dominating personality that Germain was relatively successful in extending his authority in his effort to give clear direction to the war effort. It helped that he had the support of George III. Among the ministers in the Cabinet, Germain was alone in sharing the same resolution and passion for the war as George III. They spoke the same language of the need for bold strokes and the need to take major risks to achieve victory. He could do little, however, when other ministers simply failed to comply with or obstructed the implementation of policies.[73]

Like Sandwich, Germain was a dedicated and efficient administrator. He was far from the image of the languid aristocrat who preferred horseracing and gambling to managing and leading. He enjoyed committee work and administration, in which he had a genuine interest. He liked to research and master subjects under consideration. He worked rapidly, was capable of great application, and had a retentive memory. Like George III, he was punctilious to "the very point of the minute." When John Burgoyne first met him to discuss America, he was impressed that Germain "had more information upon the subject, more enlarged sentiments, and more spirit than any of the ministers with whom I had conversed." According to Richard Cumberland, Germain introduced greater standards of efficiency by his "decision and dispatch in business." He immediately put a stop to "circumlocutory reports and inefficient forms, that had only impeded business." He was precise and plain in his use of language. He disliked the contemporary vogue for florid writing aimed more at stylistic effect than at clarity. He was so religiously punctual with engagements that Cumberland recalled that "we who served under him in office" were made to sweat.[74]

As secretary of state for America, Germain had responsibility for the other British colonies in the Americas apart from the rebellious ones: Quebec, Montreal, Nova Scotia, St. John (Prince Edward Island), East and West Florida, Jamaica, Barbados, the Leeward Islands, St. Vincent, Grenada, Dominica, Tobago, the Bahamas, and Bermuda. It is still remarkable to survey the sheer volume of correspondence with which he directed not only the military commanders but also the civil administrators in Canada, America, and the Caribbean. He had a core staff of only five clerks and never more than twenty people to manage the demands of the war. Germain received dozens of letters, for example, regarding a single dispute about the military authority of the civil governor of the Leeward Islands, William Mathew Burt, in relation to the army, which culminated in a threat of resignation by the commander in chief in the eastern Caribbean, Sir John Vaughan.[75]

The government had assumed initially that the army would become relatively self-sufficient in feeding itself as Britain reacquired territory in America. In reality, the army and navy continued to be fed and supplied from Britain. During the siege of Boston in 1775–76, all the necessities such as hay, oats, vinegar, coal, beans, wood, flour, sheep, pigs, cattle, and salted provisions for the army and navy were shipped from home. There was insufficient shipping capacity. There were not even enough government packet boats to carry the official correspondence to and from the commanders and civil governors, and the boats were subject to capture and frequent delays although direction and coordination of the war required efficient communication. The transatlantic voyage took at least two months and sometimes three to four months.[76]

For much of the war, the army did not have the minimal six-month reserve of supplies thought necessary to wage a campaign, which greatly reduced its capacity to mount offensives. In 1777 and 1779, Sir William Howe and Sir Henry Clinton began their respective campaign seasons late, on the grounds that they had not received reinforcements and supplies from Britain. The delays were often due to factors beyond the control of Germain. Of a fleet of thirty-five supply ships sent to Boston, only eight arrived while the rest were mostly blown off course to Antigua. In a period when the commanders in chief were also responsible for auditing accounts, Germain had to contend with commanders who were too overwhelmed with strategy to pay sufficient attention to financial matters. Howe often failed to specify his actual requirements, and Clinton was criticized by a parliamentary audit committee after the war for the accounting practices under his command.[77]

Germain was also subject to the pressure of lobby groups like the West India merchants and planters. Unlike North America, the British Caribbean had many absentee planters who lived in Britain and sat in Parliament, whose number ranged between twenty and fifty members. They created formal associations which used petitions and the press to court public support. Before the outbreak of the war, they had attempted to obtain a parliamentary committee to present evidence to show the likely devastating effects of a war in America upon the economy of the British Caribbean. Although the leading members of the lobby like Richard Oliver were associated with the opposition parties, Germain was keen to win their support in order to argue that they were not united in opposition to the government. After 1778, Germain was subject to particularly intense lobbying to provide more troops and naval support for the British Caribbean.[78]

VI

In the early months of 1781, it was all too apparent that reliance on loyalist support had failed. Cornwallis found it difficult even to obtain guides in North Carolina, and Lord Rawdon reported the collapse of loyalist support in South Carolina. When the government was in its death throes in March 1782, Nathaniel Wraxall described a fascinating moment that he witnessed in the House of Commons, when Lord North became visibly embarrassed as he started to repeat the usual government mantra that Britain had numerous friends in America. He then excused himself, saying that the claim had not come from him but from Lord George Germain. North confessed that he had never thought such friends sufficient in numbers "either to justify our commencing or our continuing the war solely on that account." Wraxall commented that those significant expressions withdrew the curtain from around the Cabinet and admitted the audience behind the scenes to reveal the differences of opinion between the ministers.[79]

In 1781, Germain did not want to cease hostilities because he believed the outcome of the war was too close to call. He is widely regarded by historians as having been utterly deluded. This misses the point that he was equally and defensibly hopeful of the collapse of the rebel cause. He had found a general in Cornwallis who gave the war precisely the bold strokes and the momentum that Germain had urged unsuccessfully upon Howe and Clinton. He had long known of the general reluctance of Americans to enlist in the militias and the Continental Army. He was also informed of the divisions in the Continental Congress and the woeful state of the U.S. Treasury. There was runaway inflation. In Philadelphia in May 1779, the price of wheat rose to 150 shillings per bushel from 40 shillings in 1776 and increased another sevenfold before the end of the year. As early as 1779, the paper money of Congress sold at one-fortieth of its nominal value and the currency was so weak that "not worth a Continental" (a dollar) long continued a saying in the United States. The rebel economy was on the verge of collapse. There were entire regions threatened with starvation. In December 1779, civilians were rejecting Continental currency for provisions and supplies with the result that Washington and his army suffered worse conditions and deprivation in their winter camp at Morristown in New Jersey than they had experienced at Valley Forge two years earlier. According to Germain, more Americans were joining the loyalist provincial corps than the Continental army.[80]

Germain read intercepted enemy letters saying that the rebellion was close to the breaking point. The Continental Army had long been forced to resort to short-term enlistments and to drafting; it suffered high annual desertion rates of between 20 and 25 percent, and its size declined after 1777. It was perpetually short of officers. It often met with defiance when it attempted to requisition provisions and materials from civilians. Congress did not have the power to tax, but instead relied upon voluntary contributions from the states and loans from Europe. When the currency suffered its worst depreciation in 1780, the army was close to starvation and pay was in arrears. The Continental Congress attempted to shift the responsibility for the army to the states in 1780. There was a real possibility that the Revolution might destroy itself with its rhetoric and ideology of hostility toward central government, taxation, and professional armies. In May, two regiments of the Continental Army in the Connecticut Line mutinied after two and a half months on reduced rations. Between December 1780 and July 1781, the Continental Congress did not even have the funds to publish its own proceedings and journal. In January 1781, there were renewed mutinies in the Continental army beginning with the Pennsylvania Line, a thousand troops of which marched out of camp, and spreading to three regiments in New Jersey. There were rumors that Ethan Allen would declare Vermont for the British, and good reason to believe that France and Spain might end their involvement if the war continued beyond 1781.[81]

In the period leading up to Yorktown, Germain had a clear vision for victory. He was assured by the Admiralty that the navy was able to match the French fleet. He was unaware of French naval superiority and the size of the fleet of Admiral de Grasse, and he expected Admiral Rodney in the Caribbean to reach America before de Grasse and "be in Readiness to receive him when he comes upon the Coast." Confident that Clinton could continue to check Washington and the comte de Rochambeau in New York, he encouraged Cornwallis to invade Virginia and prohibited Clinton from withdrawing troops from the Chesapeake. In the event, however, what caused Cornwallis to be trapped at Yorktown was the fact that the British fleet was much inferior in size to the French.[82]

The night that the House of Commons debated the defeat at Yorktown, Germain gave a speech deploring the fate of Lord Cornwallis. He declared his readiness to quit his office, but insisted that he would neither be browbeaten nor clamored out unless asked to resign by the king. Like George III, he wanted to continue the war in America. He put forward a plan to redress "our late misfortunes in Virginia," and advocated the retention of the remaining possessions in Nova Scotia, Penobscot, New York, Charleston, Savannah, and East Florida. The main British army was still intact with 14,000 troops in New York and 13,705 in Charleston and Savannah. It would be possible to carry on an extensive trade from these posts and use them for launching attacks on the colonies of France and Spain. He warned of the consequences of losing America, which would lead to the dismemberment of the British Empire: "we must not flatter ourselves that Canada would not immediately fall, and your fisheries in Newfoundland and all your possessions in the W[est] Indies would also lie at the mercy of your enemies." He insinuated that George Washington would become a dictator under the power of France. He questioned how long the revolutionary government could last and thought that the restless spirit of the people might incline them to return to their former loyalties because of "the loss of that liberty which they thought they were fighting for, their dislike of military government," and "their natural aversion to the French nation."[83]

During a debate on December 12, 1781, Germain was even more adamant about the necessity of continuing the war in America. Although the evening was very far advanced when Germain rose from his seat in the House of Commons, the members were attentive and listened to his speech with more than ordinary interest, since it was thought likely that it would be his last as secretary of state for America. Germain said that his views about continuing the war coincided with those of the rest of the Cabinet, and vowed that he would never put his "hand to any instrument conceding the independence of the colonies." He said that Britain and its empire could not "continue after we have lost or renounced the sovereignty over America." In a debate on December 14, 1781, Lord North was attacked by both friends and opponents on the subject of continuing the war. He stood up and left the government front bench to sit in one of the seats behind Germain, who was left conspicuously alone on the government front benches. This extraordinary scene attracted all eyes and "left no doubt of the dissimilarity of opinion among Ministers on the great question respecting America." The House was then hushed in mute attention as William Pitt the Younger intervened, ironically identifying Germain with no less than two Homeric heroes: "I shall wait until . . . the sage Nestor of the Treasury bench has brought to an Agreement the Agamemnon and the Achilles of the American War."[84]

On the evening following the debate, Nathaniel Wraxall accompanied Germain to his home in Pall Mall. He recalled that Germain considered his official capacity virtually terminated. On the pretext of his daughter's wedding in January 1782, Germain told North that he would spend two or three weeks at his country home at Drayton House in Northamptonshire. It was a courtesy to enable the government to find a successor, but the government failed to reach a decision about his future before he returned to London. North valued Germain as a government spokesman in the House of Commons, and George III wanted to keep him as a symbol of continuing national commitment to the war in America. However, Henry Dundas, the lord advocate of Scotland, and Richard Rigby, the paymaster general of the forces, threatened to withdraw from the government unless North removed Germain. It was George III himself who finally decided that Germain should go, since he wanted General Sir Guy Carleton as commander in chief in America, an appointment that had long been resisted by Germain. When North notified Germain of the king's decision, he replied with great spirit, "You say I must go!—very well—but pray, why is your Lordship to stay?"[85]

George III was determined to honor Germain so as to prevent the opposition using his departure to discredit the war for America. It was an emotional moment when they came face to face for the last time as Germain delivered up his seal of office as secretary of state for the American Department. They were both aware that it was likely to mark the beginning of the end of the North government and of the war for America. The king thanked him for his services and asked whether there was anything he could do to express his gratitude. Germain asked to be given a peerage, and stated that if his first request was agreeable, he hoped that it would not be unbecoming or unreasonable if he asked a second favor, namely to be created not just a baron but a viscount. Otherwise, he said "my secretary, my lawyer, and my father's page will all take rank" over him. The king asked to know the names of the persons to whom he referred. Germain replied that the first was Lord Walsingham, who had once been under secretary of state in the American Department; the second was Lord Loughborough, who had always been his legal adviser; and the third was Lord Amherst, who was a former page to his father when he "often sat on the braces of the state-coach that conveyed him, as Lord Lieutenant of Ireland, to the Parliament House at Dublin." The king smiled and said that the request was very reasonable and asked him what title he desired. Germain requested to be called Viscount Sackville of Bolebrook in Kent, which was one of the most ancient estates belonging to the Sackvilles and was connected with the original peerage conferred by Elizabeth I upon Thomas Sackville, the first earl of Dorset. Taking a pen and ink that lay on the table where he sat, George III wrote out the new title and sent it directly to the lord chancellor. He then rose with an expression of concern and satisfaction as they parted.[86]

Germain was to suffer yet more humiliation from his opponents. In the House of Lords, the marquess of Carmarthen made a motion that it was derogatory to their honor as a body to admit a person "stamped by an incredible brand and a sentence that has never been cancelled." His motion was supported by Shelburne, Devonshire, Derby, Rutland, Portland, and Craven. George III was so angry that he immediately ordered the patent for Germain's title to be published in the newspapers, but upon taking his seat in the House of Lords, Germain underwent "one of the last and most painful trials of his life." Camarthen "like a bloodhound" renewed his earlier motion, causing the original sentence from the Minden court martial to be read aloud in the House. The debate was joined by members who had been present at the battle of Minden like the earl of Southampton, who had carried the orders from Prince Ferdinand to Germain. The earl of Abingdon dealt the harshest blow, calling Germain "the greatest criminal his country had ever known" and the author of all the calamities of the American War. In his rebuttal speech, Germain spoke of the persecution that he had suffered and the wish of some to take his life. According to Wraxall, "his enemies themselves professed that never was a more able, dignified, or manly appeal made within the walls of the House of Peers."[87]

During his brief retirement, Germain frequently visited his house in Pall Mall and spoke in the House of Lords. His last speech, in August 1785, was against the younger Pitt's proposal to relax trade regulations between Britain and Ireland, calling instead for a union of the two kingdoms. Since the time that his father had been lord lieutenant, Germain had always taken a particular interest in Irish affairs. While in the countryside at Drayton, he enjoyed shooting, coursing, and riding, after which he would casually glance through the books in his fine library. At nine thirty every morning, he appeared for breakfast, for which he allowed exactly one and a half hours. He then mounted his horse and rode about his estates with a groom who had grown gray in his service. Richard Cumberland became a neighbor and spent much time with him in his final years. He likened Germain to Sir Roger de Coverley in *The Spectator,* describing the way he would ride through his estates distributing largesse to his cottagers and tenants. Germain always carried a pocket full of sixpences to give to children. He sent medical help to his laborers whenever they were ill, purchased fruit and vegetables from their gardens, gave them the old livery clothing of his servants, and checked the state of their homes.[88]

Every Sunday, Germain "marched out his whole family in grand cavalcade" to the parish church, dressed immaculately with the formality usually reserved for the drawing room. He often stood up during the sermons to review the congregation and to overawe anyone not behaving with proper decorum. He would nod approvingly at the preacher to give encouragement, and once, in the middle of a sermon by Rev. Mr. Henry Eatoff, he cried out "Well done, Harry!" He employed "a corps of rustic psalm-singers," paying great attention to their performance with his eyes directed to the singing gallery and giving the time. On one occasion when his baker, Tom Butcher, was singing flat, Germain called out, mixing up the man's name and his trade, "Out of tune, Tom Baker."[89]

On August 26, 1785, Germain died at his second country home, Stoneland Lodge at Withyham in Sussex. He was sixty-nine years old. Although he had been suffering what Cumberland called the "dreadful malady of the stone," he never troubled his friends with any complaints despite his obvious pain. He was ill when he gave his last speech, in the course of a long sitting in a hot and crowded chamber. He spoke longer than usual, with great "agitation of mind," and at the end of his speech he was so exhausted that he nearly fainted. Upon returning to the country, he regarded his case to be without cure and believed himself to be near death. He was determined to pay his last respects to William Murray, the earl of Mansfield, who was lord chief justice and one of the major proponents of the war for America. Germain staggered into his room with "a death-like character in his countenance," visibly affecting and disturbing Mansfield, who had stood by Germain during the court martial over the battle of Minden. Germain apologized for imposing upon him by visiting in such a state, saying, "yet so great was my anxiety to return you my unfeigned thanks for all your goodness to me, all the kind protection you have shown me through the course of an un-prosperous life." He asked that he forget any differences they may have had in politics in the heat of party strife.[90]

Indeed, two hours before his death, Germain insisted upon conversing with Cumberland about Minden. He spoke of extenuating circumstances before the battle that he had not been able to reveal in the court martial. Cumberland did not elaborate upon their nature in his memoirs, but he included a reference to another account that alluded to Germain's resentment of Prince Ferdinand. Germain apologized to his physicians "for the fruitless trouble he was giving." His senses remained unimpaired, and he requested that the curtains of his bedchamber be thrown open and the sashes pulled up to allow him to take Holy Communion. Apart from Rev. Mr. Sackville Bayle, Richard Cumberland alone was present. Germain requested special prayers for a communicant on the point of death and joined in. He then clasped Cumberland by the hands to deliver his final words: "You see me now in those moments, when no disguise will serve, and when the spirit of a man must be proved; I have a mind perfectly resigned, and at peace within itself: I have not more to do with this world, and what I have done in it, I have done for the best; I hope and trust I am prepared for the next." His courage and his manliness always thrown into question, Germain wanted the world to know that he had died bravely and with a clear conscience. He ended his words to Cumberland, "these are moments in which a man must be searched, and remember I die, as you see me, with tranquil conscience and content."[91]

PART III

Victory and Defeat in the South (1778–1781)

All, all shrink from the subject, had not circumstances made me in some degree the scapegoat, I perhaps—who may also have had my share of blunders—might have found myself in the same disposition. I admit there has been blame. I admit also I may have had my share. God knows there is enough for us all.

SIR HENRY CLINTON

CHAPTER 6

"The Scapegoat"

SIR HENRY CLINTON

During the British occupation of Philadelphia in May 1778, a group of army officers arranged a most brilliant spectacle on the banks of the Delaware River to honor the departure of the popular commander in chief Sir William Howe. The guests received tickets for the event with an engraving of a shield, a view of the sea, and the setting sun, and a Latin inscription on a wreath: *Luceo descendens, aucto splendore resurgam* ("I shine as I set, I shall rise up again in increased splendor") (Figure 24). The shield was emblazoned with cannons and cannonballs, swords, pikes, and kegs of gunpowder. General Howe's crest was above the shield with the words *Viva Vale!* ("Live and be strong!").[1]

At three-thirty in the afternoon, the entertainment began with a grand regatta in the northern end of Philadelphia at Knight's Wharf. There were huge crowds of spectators aboard the ships and along the moorings. The procession was led by three flat boats, each with a regimental band and six barges, followed by three divisions of galleys, escorted by five flat boats, lined with green cloth, and filled with "ladies and gentlemen." The galleys were decorated in a variety of colors and streamers, and the flat-bottom boats displayed the flag of each galley. The *Ferret* galley led with some general officers and ladies on board; then the *Hussar* galley with General Sir William and Admiral Lord Howe, General Sir Henry Clinton, their staff officers, and ladies; and the *Cornwallis* galley in the rear with General Wilhelm, Baron von Knyphausen and his staff officers, three British generals, and a party of ladies. British warships added to the spectacle, with the *Fanny*, magnificently decorated, and Lord Howe's flagship the *Roebuck*. Transport ships lined the banks and extended the length of the city. As they arrived at the Market Wharf, the procession halted for the playing and singing of "God Save the King," which occasioned three cheers from the ships that were returned by the crowds on shore.

Owing to the high tide, the passengers disembarked onto barges at Walnut Grove, the home of the Wharton family, whose wide grounds fronted the Delaware in the location of modern-day Fifth Street below Washington Avenue. On the arrival of General

Sir William Howe, in observance of traditional navy protocol for senior commanders, a seventeen-gun salute was fired from his brother's flagship the *Roebuck,* and the same again from the *Vigilant.* Some four hundred guests promenaded through an avenue formed by two files of grenadiers, and a line of cavalry supported each file, with the colors of every regiment serving under Howe. The guests passed through two specially erected and elaborately decorated triumphal Doric arches; the first arch was in honor of Sir William Howe and the second in honor of Admiral Lord Howe.

The arch honoring Sir William was guarded by two grenadiers and was painted with military motifs: a bombshell on the right pillar and a flaming heart on the left, together with decorations inside the arch of a plume of feathers, various trophies, the figure of the ancient goddess Fame at the top, and an inscription from Horace, *I, bone, quo virtus tua te vocet; i pede fausto* ("Go, good man, whither your virtue calls you, go with an auspicious step!"). The second arch was guarded by two sailors with drawn cutlasses and had naval motifs: the figure of Neptune on top, together with depictions of three plumes of feathers on each column, and another inscription from Horace, *Laus illi debetur, et a me gratia major* ("He is due praise and greater thanks from me"). The company proceeded to a square lawn with pavilions on both sides and rows of benches rising one above the other like a stadium, while the army bands continued to play. On the front seat of each pavilion, seven daughters of the local elite sat dressed in gauze turbans and Turkish outfits to give the flavor of the Crusades. Peggy Shippen, the future wife of Benedict Arnold, was among the women invited to participate, but her father prohibited her from attending because he thought the costumes too scandalous.[2]

In accordance with the customs and ordinances of ancient chivalry, the sound of trumpets announced the beginning of a joust. The tournament was between two teams of mounted army officers: The Knights of the Blended Rose and The Knights of the Burning Mountain. Each jouster fought in honor of one of the ladies, who were chosen for their youth, beauty, and fashion. Richly attired in French Renaissance dress of pink and white silk deriving from the court of Henry IV, the seven Knights of the Blended Rose, who were all captains and lieutenants in the army, appeared first. They wore hats of white satin with red, white, and black plumes. Mounted on gray horses whose saddles and harnesses were decorated in the same colors, they were attended by their squires on foot, four trumpeters, and heralds in ceremonial robes with the symbol of the Blended Rose and their motto "We drop when separated." William Schaw, Lord Cathcart, of the 17th Light Dragoons, appeared as their chief, with his stirrups held by two young black slaves who wore sashes of blue and white silk, and silver clasps around their necks and arms. Lord Cathcart was escorted by two captains, each with two squires, one holding his lance, and the other his shield. His emblem was Cupid riding on a lion, with the motto "Surmounted by Love." The knights rode in a circuit of the square lawn and saluted the ladies as they passed before the pavilions. With a flourish of trumpets, their herald proclaimed their challenge that the ladies of the Blended Rose excelled in wit, beauty, and every accomplishment, and vowed to maintain their assertion by deeds of arms should any other knight deny it. After the third repetition of the challenge, trumpets on the other side of the square announced the arrival of the Knights of the Burning Mountain, dressed in orange and black, accented in gold. With their emblem of a volcano and the motto "I burn forever," they galloped into the arena.[3]

After a meeting between the respective heralds, the black-attired herald of the Knights of the Burning Mountain announced their defiance of the challenge of the Blended Rose. The affair was settled by a joust between the two chiefs: Lord Cathcart and Captain Watson, the chief of the Burning Mountain, who was dressed in a magnificent costume of black and orange silk, and mounted on a black horse. Lord Cathcart threw down his gauntlet and his opponent directed his squire to take it up. After receiving their lances from their squires, the two chiefs fixed their shields to their left arms and made a general salute to each other, by a very graceful movement of their lances, and then galloped toward one another until their lances clashed. In the second and third encounter, they fired their pistols at one another. In the fourth exchange, they fought with swords until the judges interceded, declaring that the honor of the ladies was satisfied and that the contest was a draw. The Knights of the Blended Rose and the Knights of the Burning Mountain then filed past one another and approached the pavilions with the ladies. The knights and their ladies retired to the mansion, ascending a flight of steps from the garden that was covered with carpets. Inside, the knights knelt to receive gifts from the ladies in return for their chivalry.

At about nine o'clock, the knights led a dance in a sumptuously decorated and brilliantly lit ballroom where the guests were showered with flowers and saw themselves reflected in eighty-five mirrors, creating an effect like the Hall of Mirrors at Versailles. After an hour of dancing, the windows were thrown open to reveal a firework display, arranged by the chief engineer of the army, which culminated in the illumination of the triumphal arch dedicated to Sir William Howe. With an irony that could only be appreciated by future generations, contemporaries described how the illuminated figure of Fame shone as if "spangled with stars." The trumpet in the mouth of the goddess blew letters of fire that contained a tribute in French to Sir William Howe, *Tes lauriers sont immortels* ("Your laurels are immortal"). At midnight, the large folding doors were thrown open to reveal an artfully concealed room where the guests were to dine. The interior was splendidly furnished with fifty-six mirrors, together with arrays of silk flowers and ribbons. The dinner was served by twenty-four black slaves in oriental dress, with silver collars and bracelets, arranged in two lines and bending to the ground at the approach of the Howe brothers. As daylight dawned, the fantasy was disrupted by a blaze in the northern part of the city and the sound of rebel gunfire, causing drums to beat an alert, the artillery to be readied, and the cavalry to be sent out in pursuit. It was a grim reminder of the reality of war in America.[4]

This event was called the Mischianza (also Meschianza), a term derived from two Italian words meaning to mix (*mescere*) or to mingle (*mischiare*). It was arranged by Major John André, who was later hanged as a spy when he was captured as the intermediary in the defection of Benedict Arnold. Described by Brigadier General Charles O'Hara as "one of the most accomplish'd Young Men in this Army," André designed the tickets, selected the costumes, and choreographed the festivities. He was one of twenty-two officers who raised a subscription to pay the costs of some three thousand guineas. The event reflected contemporary Italian influence, but the emphasis on chivalry suggests something more profound and symbolic. It reflected nostalgia for the mythical ideals of another age that valued monarchy, aristocracy, and tradition. It was a fantasy of warfare fought according to an aristocratic code, between great nations, with epic battles and armies led by aristocrats, in contrast to the reality of the fratricidal and often unconventional warfare in the hostile terrain of America. In playing the role of heroic medieval knights, the officers were enacting their ideal of warfare, which offered the opportunity for glory against a traditional enemy like France. The reality was that they were fighting a very different type of war in which they had much to lose in reputation, but little to gain, against opponents who were portrayed as amateurs and rabble. The event was more like a victory celebration than a farewell to a general who was leaving under a cloud, owing to his miscalculation in taking Philadelphia rather than relieving Burgoyne at Saratoga.[5]

At the time of the Mischianza, there seemed a greater possibility than before of Britain losing America. With the French declaration of war in March 1778, Britain would be able to devote fewer military resources to defeating the rebellion. It was now contending with a rival naval power that threatened homeland defenses, and necessitated the reinforcement of colonial posts in India, the Caribbean, the Mediterranean, and Africa. Consequently, the home government ordered the abandonment of Philadelphia. The opposition parties questioned how it would be possible to do more with less in America. In anticipation of the French declaration of war in February, Charles James Fox told the House of Commons that since it was not possible to maintain the size of the army commanded by Howe and Burgoyne, it was impossible to justify the hope or expectation of the complete conquest of the rebels. On April 7, the duke of Richmond told the House of Lords that "America was already lost." The majority of British newspapers advocated negotiating with the rebels and ending the war. Many army officers were becoming defeatists. In October, Major General James Grant wrote that he was "almost heartily tired of this cursed business" and that he had given up any hope of ever winning the war "the moment we were ordered to leave Philadelphia." In the same month, Colonel Charles Stuart wrote that "there is hardly a General Officer who does not declare his intention of going home, the same with Officers of all ranks who, could they procure the leave, wou'd be happy to leave the army." "This is an unpopular war," wrote Lieutenant Frederick Mackenzie, "and men of ability do not chuse to risk their reputation by taking an active part in it." Writing from Philadelphia, the twenty-two-year-old Lieutenant William John Hale of the 45th Regiment remarked perceptively that "Perhaps never was a Rebellion so universal and intense as this," which he regarded as a convincing refutation of the British belief that the desire for independence was limited to a small group of troublemakers.[6]

A month after the Mischianza, the British withdrew from Philadelphia. In November 1778, the parliamentary opposition at home argued that it would be folly to invest any longer in so ruinous a project as the American war when experience had proved coercion to be impractical. They condemned the government for its obstinate determination to persevere to the last in the same fatal measures that had already squandered fifteen million pounds sterling and sunk the country into humiliation, misfortune, and disgrace. They complained that the promise of reinforcements was continually held out but never achieved. The continuance of hostilities would lead to nothing but an eternity of war.[7]

Far removed from the chivalrous ideals of the Mischianza, the British were beginning to use ever more desperate methods. On October 3, 1778, as the Carlisle peace commissioners prepared to abandon their abortive mission in Philadelphia, they issued a final chilling manifesto with an implicit threat of a change in the nature and future conduct of the war. They alluded darkly to an end of former restraints in favor of a resort to the extremes of war, distressing the people and desolating the countryside. The manifesto occasioned a protest among the opposition members of the House of Lords, who warned that it implied that the army had previously shown too much leniency and that the war would be carried to extremes and desolation. With a less romantic, but arguably more accurate image of medieval warfare, the dissident lords believed that they owed it to posterity not to allow a return to the ferocity and barbarism of an earlier age, but to affirm the contemporary values of a beneficent religion, enlightened manners, and true military honor. George Johnstone, one of the Carlisle peace commissioners, acknowledged that the manifesto did threaten a war of desolation.[8]

Dressed appropriately in black, Major Banastre Tarleton was one of the Knights of the Burning Mountain at the Mischianza. His personal motto for the joust was "swift, vigilant, and bold." He was to become the commander of a loyalist cavalry regiment called the British Legion, and his reliance upon shock and terror would make his name a byword for terror in the south. He wrote that he would give "these disturbers of the peace no quarter," and that "nothing will serve these people but fire and sword, . . . and pox." Although his reputation for atrocities was exaggerated by successful Patriot propaganda, Tarleton was one of an influential group of young officers who advocated a more ruthless suppression of the rebellion. The conflict became increasingly fratricidal as the war became a civil war. Owing to the outbreak of war with France, Britain had to make greater use of American loyalists, thereby stressing the element of civil war which by its nature is always more intense, bitter, and savage.[9]

I

It was in these inauspicious circumstances that Sir Henry Clinton assumed the position of commander in chief of the British army, replacing General Sir William Howe. He was a forty-eight-year-old widower with two sons and two daughters who lived with relatives in England. He had been grief-stricken by the loss of his twenty-five-year-old wife, Harriet, who died in 1772, after giving birth to a daughter. She was the daughter of minor landowners, Thomas and Martha Carter, and they had begun their relationship when she was only sixteen and he was thirty-three; keeping the birth of their first child a secret, they had married hastily by special license when she was nineteen.[10]

In a portrait by an unknown artist of c. 1760, Clinton appears an elegantly dressed figure in full red uniform, as the aide-de-camp to Prince Ferdinand of Brunswick (Figure 22). A receding hairline and a square jaw frame a strong face with a healthy complexion, chiseled features, and a piercing glance from intense blue eyes. His tight waistcoat suggests a slight paunch, despite his regular regimen of exercise. In a miniature by John Smart in 1777, he was depicted looking out of the corner of his eyes, as if avoiding the eyes of the viewer, and contemplating the distance (Figure 23). When painted after the American War by Thomas Day in 1789, his face had become chubby, and he had lost much more of his hair. His eyes did not have the sparkle of his earlier portraits, but rather a mournful and distant quality. In the intervening time, he had become an embittered man, as a result of presiding over the defeat of the British army in America.

Clinton had tried to resign while he was still second in command, to avoid becoming the heir apparent to Howe. He told a friend that he wanted neither to serve under Sir William Howe nor to command the debris of Howe's army. He wrote in his memoirs that his promotion to commander in chief was a hopeless charge, which offered neither honor nor credit, "but on the contrary a considerable portion of blame, however unmerited seemed to be almost inevitable." He believed that every prospect of a successful outcome had been clouded by the outbreak of war with France. Clinton had fewer troops than his predecessor and a third of the naval support, while "the rebels were every day growing stronger in number, confidence and discipline." He faced a newly emboldened and more effective Continental Army which was composed of increasingly battle-hardened troops, and was transformed by the military reforms and drilling techniques introduced by "Baron" Frederick von Steuben during the winter encampment at Valley Forge (1777–78).[11]

Clinton calculated that the successful defeat of the rebellion required an army of at least 30,000 men, which at various times meant an additional 15,000 troops. He felt that a minimum of 13,000 to 15,000 troops was necessary merely for the defense of New York, and another 4,000 for the defense of Rhode Island. His estimates coincided with those of Lord Jeffrey Amherst, a successful British commander in the French and Indian War and the senior military adviser to the government during the American Revolution, who told the Cabinet that it was impossible to subdue the colonies on land without 30,000 more troops in America. The earl of Sandwich, the first lord of the Admiralty, advised his Cabinet colleagues to suspend all naval and military operations in America.[12]

Far from reinforcing Clinton, the government ordered him to abandon Philadelphia where it was feared that he might be cut off by the landing of French troops in New Jersey. His orders required him to send 5,000 choice troops for the conquest of St. Lucia in the Caribbean, which the government deemed important because of its proximity to the French naval base at Martinique; 3,000 troops to St. Augustine in Florida for an intended attack on Georgia; and 2,000 troops as reinforcements to Canada. Clinton was required to be prepared to relinquish yet more troops should they be requested by the British commander in Canada. He was reduced to a defensive posture with only 13, 661 regular troops under his command, of which 7,000 were Germans and loyalists. He had 16,000 fewer troops than the total in America under Howe and Burgoyne, and his army was insufficient by his own estimates just to hold New York. Furthermore, the Cabinet even discussed withdrawing from America to concentrate on the war in the Caribbean and the defeat of France. It had the support of George III, who thought that it would be impossible to continue the war without the wealth derived from the British island colonies in the Caribbean. Indeed, the Cabinet gave Clinton permission to leave New York and retreat to Halifax. In anticipation of having to send an additional third of his force to Canada, he informed the government that he intended to do so. Until October 1778, Lord North was braced for such an eventuality.[13]

Faced with the prospect of having fewer troops, Clinton asked to resign, insisting that the strength of his force was inadequate for the object of winning the war. He sent his aide-de-camp home to represent his request, which elicited a refusal and a rare apology from the government. Nevertheless, Clinton persisted and asked his relative the duke of Newcastle to petition the king. It was again denied. Clinton's pessimism was shared by Charles, Earl Cornwallis, who held a dormant commission to become commander in chief in the event of Clinton's death or resignation. Cornwallis also requested to return to Britain because of the reduction in the size of the army and its inability to undertake offensive operations in America. The government denied Clinton's requests to resign because it could not politically afford to let him go when the opposition was arguing that the folly of continuing the war was demonstrated by the desire of all the generals and the commander in chief to leave America. It was a remarkable moment, in the midst of the war, that the commander in chief, his second in command, and the prime minister all felt overwhelmed and wanted to quit.[14]

Like Lord North, Clinton has received little sympathy among historians, who have focused on the shortcomings of his character rather than the difficulty of his situation. He certainly had character faults. He sulked and brooded. He was jealous and tempestuous. He quarreled with colleagues. He was withdrawn and had few friends. In his journal during the voyage of the *Cerberus* to America with Burgoyne and Howe, he described himself as "a shy bitch." Unlike Howe and Burgoyne, he was not popular with his men. He failed to consult sufficiently with his senior officers. He was convinced that the enemy was attempting to assassinate him. He was hypersensitive, capricious, irascible, and unable to accept criticism. He felt it necessary to justify himself publicly for every setback and to blame everyone but himself. His emotions occasionally boiled over in his letters to the home government. His outbursts could be inconsistent, both complaining of being given too much latitude and of too much interference by Germain. In his Bancroft Prize–winning biography of 1962, William B. Willcox portrayed Clinton as a classic neurotic, an obsessive-compulsive personality. In an early experiment in psychoanalytic history, Willcox collaborated with a psychologist to postulate that the general had suffered since childhood from an unresolved conflict between craving and dreading the exercise of authority. They regarded his personality as the chief source of his difficulties.[15]

It might alternatively be suggested that Clinton's frustration and anxiety were a result of his situation. He never received significant reinforcements, including the promised return of five thousand of his best troops from the Caribbean, but he was expected to defeat Washington while assisting other commanders in Canada, the Bahamas, Bermuda, the Caribbean, Florida, Alabama, Mississippi, Georgia, and South Carolina. He was left in limbo by the government, which failed to make a decision regarding the priorities of the war, but instead overextended its resources by attempting both to continue the war in America and to defeat France. His well-conceived plans were thwarted. He complained that the expectations of him were unrealistic and that he had been set up for failure. He was in a state of constant anxiety—expected to achieve against greater odds and with fewer resources the victory that had eluded his predecessor. His daunting situation helps explain his outbursts, his indecision, and his reclusive behavior. As every suggested strategy seemed to point to failure with the resources at his disposal, he inevitably became indecisive. In a widely reprinted letter in the British newspapers, an army officer wrote that "Clinton will do all that spirit and sense can do to remedy our evils, but human exertion is a limited thing . . . remember one thing, we do not contend with an army but with a country."[16]

Sir Henry Clinton feared that he would become the chief scapegoat for the British defeat in America. His fears were justified. He is often a figure of mirth in documentaries and textbooks, where he is portrayed as doing nothing to rescue the beleaguered Lord Cornwallis in Virginia. The farcical narrative ends with his mounting a relief expedition in conjunction with the navy that arrived a week after the surrender at Yorktown. Clinton commanded the army for half the war but he remains little known beyond cameo descriptions. He was to be permanently embittered, indeed haunted, by his experience of the war. He spent his declining years writing the most comprehensive memoir written by any general on either side of the war, as well as numerous vindications of his conduct. He alone among his contemporaries continued to reflect obsessively upon the reasons why Britain lost America.

II

Clinton was a rising star in the army before the start of the American Revolution. He had grown up in America, where his father was the royal governor of New York. His family owned land in America and one of his sisters died in New England. As a result, he was familiar with the country and its people. In a military career that spanned fifty years, he had joined the army at fifteen and, when he was twenty-one years old, he was commissioned into the elite infantry regiment of the Coldstream Guards; he later transferred to the Grenadier Guards, the most senior infantry regiment in the British army. He was a veteran of many campaigns. During the War of the Austrian Succession (1740–48), he was posted to Canada. In the Seven Years' War, he served with his regiment in Germany under General John Manners, the marquess of Granby, who commanded the British contingent sent to reinforce the prince of Brunswick. He saw action at Corbach (July 10, 1760) and Closter Kampden (October 15, 1760), and was seriously wounded at the battle of Frieberg (October 29, 1762), causing him to suffer pain thereafter, especially in the summer heat in America. He was appointed aide-de-camp to Prince Ferdinand and later to the acclaimed Field Marshal Sir John Louis Ligonier. Together with Howe and Germain, he became a protégé of Ligonier, who was a veteran of campaigns of the celebrated duke of Marlborough. Clinton served as Ligonier's aide-de-camp in the Seven Years' War, in which the latter was credited with being the mastermind of the British victory.

In 1766, Clinton assumed command of his own regiment, the 12th Foot, which three years later he accompanied to Gibraltar where he became second in command of the garrison. In 1772, he was promoted to the rank of major general. His wife died the same year, however, and his grief at her death was said to have triggered his decision to travel. In 1774, Clinton crossed Europe to Vienna and the Balkans to observe the Russo-Turkish War in Bulgaria. It was a measure of his dedication to his military service and his interest in studying the art of warfare. At the time of his appointment as third in command in America in 1775, he was an experienced senior officer and a veteran of warfare who had served under some of the greatest military commanders of the era.

Clinton was the most cerebral of the generals in America. He regularly discussed tactics with fellow officers. He was fluent in French and had a preference for the works of continental authorities on warfare. He read both ancient and modern authors. From the 1760s, he began to keep the most detailed extant notes upon his military reading of any contemporary officer in the British army, which eventually filled a dozen leather-bound books with his handwritten commentaries. He was critical of "modern military history" for being too concerned with the details of skirmishes, marches, battles, and sieges while omitting "what is really useful for an officer," a broad understanding of the political, economic, and geographical context. His commentaries betray a preference for a cautious approach to warfare. He admired generals who gained victories without committing their troops in battle. He was critical of aggressive commanders who risked their armies, writing that "there is nothing I dread so much as these brave generals." This was to be characteristic of his strategy in America. As a subordinate commander, he encouraged flanking maneuvers rather than frontal assaults. As commander in chief, he mostly engaged in raids, sieges, and the gradual pacification of the population. He sought battle only when his army had the clear advantage.[17]

In contrast to the Howe brothers and Cornwallis, Clinton had not opposed the policies that led to outbreak of the American War of Independence. Nevertheless, he was not an enthusiast for the war. Like the other senior military commanders, he was less hawkish than the politicians. After becoming a member of Parliament in 1772, he was a regular supporter of the government of Lord North, but he wished for peace in America. He wrote privately that he was desirous to do everything in his power to avoid war, and that he had romantic notions of settling the affair before the effusion of blood. He was against hiring German mercenaries.[18]

Before becoming commander in chief in America in 1778, Clinton had been a brilliant critic of the strategic shortcomings of his superiors. He attempted to dissuade General Thomas Gage from the proposed plan of attack at Bunker Hill, and suggested instead a flanking attack, occupying the higher ground and blocking the enemy retreat. Although unable to persuade Gage, he led a column in the final successful attack and won praise for his bravery. Far from quarreling with his fellow generals at this stage, he was friendly with Cornwallis, Burgoyne, and Howe. In fact, he wrote that he could not wish to serve with two better people than Burgoyne and Howe. Following the removal of General Gage in September 1775, Clinton became second in command to Howe. Their relations soon became strained. Clinton wrote of his mortification at serving under Howe and his exasperation at the state of the British army in Boston. Howe avoided contact by sending him on separate missions, beginning with an expedition to the south with a fleet under the command of Commodore Sir Peter Parker.[19]

The opportunity offered by Clinton's first independent command proved disappointing. The original object of the expedition was to join and support the loyalists in North Carolina where he would be reinforced by troops from Ireland, commanded by Cornwallis. The idea was encouraged by the royal governors of the former southern colonies. Governor Samuel Martin of North Carolina had claimed that a small force would be sufficient to rouse local loyalists to subdue the rebellion in North and South Carolina, and even to threaten Virginia. Clinton was dubious at the outset about expectations of widespread loyalist support and described the optimism of the governors as a malady that had infected the Cabinet ministers in London. Sir William Howe regarded the expedition as a distraction from the more important objective of New York, and the orders from the home government required that the expedition return in time to join Howe for the opening of the campaign there. In the meantime, the governors in the south had not only failed to rally support, but were driven out to seek shelter on board warships. It was a bad omen.

After delays and a long voyage, the expedition arrived too late to reinforce the loyalists in North Carolina, who had been defeated two weeks earlier in a battle at Moore's Creek Bridge (February 27, 1776) near Wilmington. The defeated loyalists were largely composed of recently emigrated Highlanders from Scotland. One of them, Allan Mac-Donald, played a major role in the uprising and was captured in the battle at Moore's Creek. His wife was the legendary Flora MacDonald, the heroine of the Jacobite Rebellion in 1745—46 who had helped Charles Edward "the Young Pretender" (Bonnie Prince Charlie) to escape to Skye after his defeat at Culloden. She lost three sons in the Revolutionary War, and the family plantation was plundered and sequestered. The defeat at Moore's Creek was a major setback for the loyalist cause in the south. Upon finding the battle already over, Clinton and Parker had to wait another month until the arrival of the reinforcements from Ireland under Lord Cornwallis, which had been expected in January, and the failure of the original object of the expedition necessitated a total change of plan.[20]

Clinton favored establishing a base along the coast of Virginia to disrupt rebel supply lines and create a naval base. His plan was opposed by Admiral Parker, however, in favor of an attack upon the fortress at Sullivan's Island, which guarded the harbor of Charleston in South Carolina. Clinton demonstrated the diffidence that his father called a family trait and allowed himself to be persuaded by Parker. There was no expectation of taking Charleston but merely of establishing a base at Sullivan's Island, but in any case the result was a fiasco. The expedition lost all element of surprise by remaining for weeks outside the harbor because of poor weather and differences between the commanders. Finally, Clinton landed his troops on an island adjacent to the fort that flooded at high tide where his army was stuck for a fortnight and left to watch a valiant but foolhardy naval assault on the fort. Parker lost three warships in the attempt while his breeches were blown off, exposing his backside, on the deck of his own flagship. The expedition retired badly damaged. It was the last major British expedition to the south for another three years. In what became a pattern of behavior, Clinton insisted upon trying to exonerate himself from any blame and creating a public rupture with Parker.[21]

On returning to join Howe in August 1776, Clinton salvaged his reputation by distinguishing himself in the conquest of New York. At the battle of Long Island (August 27, 1776), Howe followed his suggested plan of attack which resulted in one of the great British triumphs of the war. Clinton personally led the encirclement of the left wing of Washington's army. It was the first and last time that he succeeded in having one of his plans adopted by Howe. Clinton advocated a bolder strategy than Howe to destroy Washington's army, proposing that Howe land north of Manhattan to prevent Washington from escaping across the Harlem River and the King's Bridge. In New Jersey later on, he warned Howe that his outposts and garrisons were too thinly spread, and was proved right by Washington's successes at Trenton and Princeton. When he was given the opportunity of another independent command in December 1776, Clinton fared much better than Howe in capturing Newport in Rhode Island, which was one of the best and safest harbors on the east coast of America. It did not freeze over and did not have the navigational problems of New York.

Following his success at Newport, Clinton asked and received permission to return to England. He vowed never again to serve under Howe but rather to resign or serve under the command of General Sir Guy Carleton in Canada. His primary purpose in returning to England was to defend his actions at Charleston, and besides, he was homesick and wanted to be with his children, who his sister-in-law told him were crying out to see "dear papa." In England, he met with Lord George Germain, the secretary of state for the American Department. In government circles, Clinton discovered that his success at Newport had eclipsed criticism of his role at Charleston, and that it was Howe and Carleton who were in disfavor. Clinton was told by Germain that the command of the Canadian army was his for the asking, but Clinton declined out of friendship to Carleton who would be displaced. George III then refused Clinton permission to resign and ordered him back to serve under Howe, but soothed him with a knighthood and membership in the prestigious Order of the Bath. It was a great honor, not least because there was no vacancy in the order, whose rules and traditions were jealously guarded by George III. Clinton was unhappy at his return but consoled himself with the prospect that he might replace Burgoyne when the two armies united at Albany.

Upon his arrival in America, Clinton foresaw and tried to prevent the disastrous train of events that led to Saratoga. After a painfully slow return voyage from England, he did not arrive in New York until July 1777, when he was appalled to find that the army was still in winter quarters and that Howe was planning to leave him in command of New York while leading an expedition to Philadelphia. In England, Clinton had advised

Germain against such a plan, and having recently met with Germain, he understood the expectations of the government better than Howe. He was well aware of the presumption of the government that this would be the final victorious year of the war and that Howe would march north to meet Burgoyne. For three weeks, Clinton tried to dissuade Howe from going to Philadelphia, venting his pent-up emotions and voicing his grievances of the past two years.[22]

Clinton resented being relegated to what he called "a damned starved" defensive role, and feared that Washington might seize the opportunity of Howe's absence to attack New York or crush Burgoyne. In late August 1777, Washington did indeed probe the defenses of New York, but he was foiled by Clinton who, recognizing that his opponent's three-pronged advance consisted of two feints, deployed the majority of his troops to successfully deflect the main attack of Washington's army. At the end of September, Clinton began to receive requests for help from Burgoyne. In the most daring enterprise of his career, Clinton tried to create a diversion to relieve Burgoyne by marching north into the Hudson Highlands. After routing the garrisons of the outer fortresses of Verplancks and Stony Point at the entrance to the Hudson, Clinton not only captured Fort Montgomery and Fort Clinton, but also Fort Constitution opposite West Point, and sent a small force farther north under General John Vaughan to within forty-five miles of Albany. The day of Burgoyne's surrender, Clinton received orders from Howe to withdraw from the Highlands and to send reinforcements to him in Pennsylvania. Still, the threat posed by Clinton had so alarmed General Horatio Gates that he offered Burgoyne generous terms of surrender in the Saratoga Convention.[23]

As soon as he heard of the disaster that had befallen Burgoyne at Saratoga, Clinton again tried to resign, but he was denied by Howe because of the potential for the enemy to unite his forces and attack New York. Clinton later wrote that he received the news that he was to become commander in chief of the army with great concern. After Howe, he was next in seniority and he was the only general who had won success in the last campaign. His withering critiques of his superior had been the most incisive accounts by a contemporary of the strategic shortcomings of the British war in America. He was proven right by events, but he was at a disadvantage in having few friends in government. Although he was a cousin of the duke of Newcastle, he did not have good political connections, and his cousin was a poor advocate on his behalf. In fact, he was appointed commander in chief owing to the dearth of alternative candidates and the fact that he was already in America. Lord Jeffrey Amherst had refused the offer while Cornwallis was on leave in England. The government deemed the situation too urgent to await Cornwallis's return to America, and Germain absolutely refused to countenance the appointment of the other most likely choice, Sir Guy Carleton. Lord North had advised against appointing Clinton, arguing that it was inadvisable to employ a general who wanted to resign, and who complained continually of ill treatment and slights. Clinton was aware that North was not well disposed towards him, writing that he "was never friendly to me." Clinton also suspected most of the Cabinet to be hostile to him.[24]

Having expected to receive permission to return to Britain, Clinton was not keen to assume the command and wrote to Germain that he was unprepared for the weighty charge that was now imposed upon him. Despite his criticism of Sir William Howe, he made the extraordinary suggestion that the government retain the Howe brothers on the grounds that they best knew how to remedy their mistakes and what needed to be done. He thought the two brothers individually were matched by the talents of others, but together they were an irresistible force. He further advocated dividing the army into three separate commands and pronounced himself willing to serve anywhere—even "God forbid!" in Florida.[25]

III

As commander in chief, Clinton was a gifted strategist who grasped the realities of the war and understood the precarious military situation facing the British. As the son of one admiral and the brother-in-law of another, he particularly understood the importance of British naval supremacy in supporting the army in America. He foresaw the potential for disaster in the event of the British navy being inferior to the French, and in a scenario like the one that developed at Yorktown, he constantly forewarned that an army operating outside New York was likely to be stranded should the French gain the advantage at sea. He was well aware that Britain had come close to defeat on several occasions before Yorktown. Clinton never took it for granted that he would have naval support and was consequently more hesitant about risk.

Clinton understood that force alone was not enough, but argued the need "to gain the hearts and subdue the minds of America." He doubted whether it was possible to conquer the country and "whether it was worthwhile to have it when conquered" without having the affections of the people. Although he dismissed the "idea of conquering America without the assistance of Friends," he was skeptical of government faith in the potential for loyalist support. This was apparent in a meeting with Lord George Germain in London in April 1777. During the course of their conversation, Germain asked him a rhetorical question in which he suggested that the rebels would be unable to raise an army for the next campaign and that they were growing less able every day. Clinton replied that the inability of the rebels was no "greater than ours." When Cornwallis invaded Virginia in 1781, Clinton wrote that this was a pointless endeavor if "we have not their hearts—which I fear cannot be expected in Virginia . . . we may conquer [but] we shall never keep."[26]

Clinton saw little value in taking territory only to abandon it and disappoint local loyalists who would subsequently become disillusioned. He was therefore disparaging of government plans to send expeditions to rally loyalists with a view to making them self-sustaining and then later withdrawing. Following a British withdrawal, Clinton believed, the loyalists would be left to the vengeance of the rebels, and that such examples would deter others from rallying to the royal standard. This cut-and-run policy was a betrayal of trust. It also created a refugee problem, which was an encumbrance upon the army. He spoke of the need for what he called solid campaigns that gained and retained ground. The possession of territory therefore required permanent garrisons of regular troops. He respected the fighting abilities of the Continental Army and the leadership of George Washington. After he had received news of the British defeat at Trenton (1776), he wrote that "we have held them too cheap." Clinton was also concerned with the practical difficulties of integrating loyalist regiments into the army, since it caused jealousy and desertion among the regulars.[27]

In May 1778, Clinton assumed command from Howe and began the process of withdrawal from Philadelphia. Despite orders to dispatch troops to the Caribbean and evacuate Philadelphia by sea, Clinton decided to return with all his troops overland through New Jersey to New York. He had little choice because of the shortage of shipping and the need to keep the army together when it was so vulnerable to attack during a withdrawal. At about 3:00 A.M. on May 18, he departed from Philadelphia with 1,500 wagons and artillery pieces, more than 3,000 loyalist refugees, and an army of 20,000 men, as well as sick and wounded together with women and children, crossing the Delaware in less than seven hours. Some families were later placed aboard transports to join the fleet off the coast of New Jersey where the number of loyalists swelled to 5,000. The entire train of people and wagons stretched as far as twelve miles. Along the route back to New York, Clinton found that the enemy had destroyed every bridge; the country was intersected with marshy rivulets, the roads were obstructed, and the heat was stifling. During the march, some 600 soldiers deserted of whom three-quarters were German. His army was subject to constant harassment by the enemy who even left leaflets warning him against "being Burgoyned."[28]

Despite the inherent dangers of a retreat, Clinton hoped to have "a brush" with Washington who had marched north with his army from Valley Forge. Clinton seemed to court an action by halting his army for almost two days at the town of Freehold. About four miles from the village of Monmouth on June 28, he was granted his wish when the rear of his army was suddenly attacked by an advance detachment of Washington's troops led by General Charles Lee. Sending ahead the baggage waggons, Clinton immediately rode back along two miles of his lines and ordered his soldiers "to face about and march back with all speed to attack the Rebels." It was a humid day with temperatures exceeding ninety-two degrees in what was to be the longest battle of the Revolutionary War. Clinton astonished both officers and men by his rashness in "galloping like a Newmarket jockey" into the midst of the action to the cry of "Charge, Grenadiers, never heed forming!" He was nearly shot by an enemy colonel. When the rebel attack began to falter, Lee ordered a partial withdrawal that turned into a general retreat. Cornwallis had commanded the rear and was commended for his zeal by Clinton in his official report of the engagement to Germain.[29]

The outcome of the fighting, known as the battle of Monmouth Courthouse, was indecisive but it was turned into a rebel propaganda victory in Washington's embellished report to Congress, while John Hancock claimed it had set the British back at least a year. Clinton was still fuming in his retirement against Washington's claims. Washington reported losses of 69 killed, 161 wounded, and 131 missing. It was later discovered that at least 37 of the missing had died from sunstroke. Clinton estimated his losses at 147 dead, 170 wounded and 64 missing. Nevertheless, Washington clearly regarded the battle as a great missed opportunity to defeat the British, and blamed Lee whose military career was effectively ended. Clinton had successfully defended his army in the very hazardous process of a general retreat, encumbered by a long baggage train, through very difficult country in the face of numerous enemies, and he had done so without the loss of a single wagon. The home government acknowledged that he had shown exemplary leadership.[30]

The perilous position of Clinton was highlighted during his withdrawal from Philadelphia to New York by the arrival of the French admiral, Charles Hector comte d'Estaing, with twelve ships of the line, six frigates, and 4,000 troops, outnumbering Admiral Lord Howe's squadron of nine ships in New York. They entered "the mouth of the harbor and rode at anchor in the form of an exact half-moon." Clinton had received no warning about the approach of a superior enemy fleet, owing to poor intelligence rather than government neglect. The possibility that his retreat might be intercepted made his situation very vulnerable for crossing the Hudson to New York, and he was fortunate that the French fleet had taken ten weeks to sail the Atlantic and that Admiral d'Estaing decided not to challenge Howe's inferior fleet in New York Harbor. However, when d'Estaing proceeded to sail for Rhode Island, the British garrison at Newport nearly fell to a joint attack by the French fleet and 10,000 New England troops commanded by Major General John Sullivan of the Continental Army. It was saved by the arrival of Howe's fleet which lured d'Estaing away from the siege in the hope of defeating the heavily outnumbered British. Howe's intervention merely shifted the risk from the army to the North American squadron of the Royal Navy. It succeeded but largely thanks to a sudden gale and storms that did severe damage to d'Estaing's fleet. Clinton sailed with 4,000 men to the relief of the garrison but contrary winds prevented him from cutting off the retreat of Sullivan's army.

In early October 1778, Clinton reluctantly carried out his orders to release 5,000 troops for the Caribbean, 3,000 for Florida and Georgia, 700 for Halifax, and 300 for garrisons in Bermuda and the Bahamas. The troops and transports that he sent to the Caribbean sailed unwittingly on a parallel course with Admiral d'Estaing. They might easily have been captured.[31] Clinton warned that from now on he would have to act defensively, for which he blamed the loss of troops, claiming that he would otherwise have been able to undertake a more ambitious approach. His view was supported by George Washington who thought that 5,000 additional troops would have given a dangerous advantage to Clinton.[32]

Clinton was distraught at the prospect of reducing his army and predicted that half the troops destined for the Caribbean would perish before Christmas. His fears were echoed by Sir William Howe in London, who warned that the expedition to St. Lucia would ruin the finest army in the world. Describing these troops as "the very nerves of this army," Clinton wrote an emotional letter to Germain asking to be relieved from his "mortifying command" and requested not to be forced "to remain a mournful witness of the debility" of the army. He doubted whether Britain would ever have the resources to replace them. He thought that the remaining regular troops were too few to rally the German mercenaries who in his opinion were not "equally zealous" to the British. He wrote that his request to resign did not stem from lack of ardor but from a situation in which he could no longer promote the national interest.[33]

Clinton wrote to the duke of Newcastle that he intended to tell the government "serious truths such as they are not used to" and to stop them deceiving themselves about the possibilities of success when they had denied him "the means of ensuring it." He sent his aide-de-camp to London to plead his case to Germain, who was appalled and responded, "Good God . . . is it possible that Sir Henry Clinton can think of desiring to come home at this critical time . . . when the country looks upon him as the only chance we have of saving America?" Germain wrote to Clinton denying the request, citing the lack of qualified general officers and the great military talents displayed by Clinton. He assured him that the government would do everything in its power to augment his force and enable him to act offensively.[34]

Despite the major cuts to his force, Clinton received "most secret" orders from the home government to wage a comprehensive war in the south upon the supposition that loyalist support would compensate for the lack of troops. It was a major shift in strategy to a southern war. In December 1778, Clinton complied by sending a thousand troops to attack Georgia. Although he was dubious of any "permanent advantage," the expedition offered an opportunity to test sympathies in the south, weaken the rebellion in neighboring provinces, and protect East Florida. Under the command of Lieutenant Colonel Archibald Campbell, the army captured Savannah where Campbell boasted that he had "ripped one star and one stripe from the rebel flag of America." The success caused the home government to be more optimistic about the chances of recovering the south, but Clinton was dubious, having received "no assurances of any favourable temper in the province of South Carolina." As late as April 1779, he tried to dissuade the government against its ambitious southern strategy. He thought he might at best capture Charleston but doubted whether he could retain the town for long and did "not think such a desultory advantage *in that quarter* would be beneficial to our interests." He regarded the emphasis on the south as a distraction from defeating Washington's army in New York.[35]

For the rest of the war, Clinton continued to bemoan the loss of troops to the Caribbean. The superior French naval presence prevented their return, while the high mortality rate, the lack of available convoy, and the defense needs of the islands thwarted every subsequent effort to return them northward. Between 1777 and 1779, the British had lost 15,664 troops in the western Atlantic.[36] The army was actually shrinking. In the four years after Saratoga, Clinton received only 4,700 reinforcements from Britain to make up the loss of 19,200 men. Furthermore, his naval support was reduced in favor of the Caribbean. Only 8 percent of the British navy was serving in the Caribbean in 1778, a proportion that had risen to 33 percent by the end of 1779. In contrast, North America was allocated 41 percent of the fleet in the summer of 1778, but only 9 percent in the summer of 1779, 13 percent in the summer of 1780, and 11 percent in the summer of 1781.[37]

Clinton simultaneously contended with a provision crisis. For much of the period of his command, his supplies and provisions were well below the minimum thought necessary to undertake an expedition. The Treasury estimates for food rations failed to take into account the additional amounts required for refugees and loyalist troops and did not allow for spoilage and decay. In any case, supplies were interrupted and delayed by the threat posed by the French navy. The shortage in the fall of 1778 was unparalleled since the siege of Boston in 1775. When store ships arrived on January 4, 1779, the army had only four days of food reserves. The navy had been unable to supply escorts, and Clinton had feared the capture of the entire convoy and the possibility of starvation. Although the Continental Army had suffered greater deprivations in the winters of 1778 and 1779, the implications were potentially more disastrous for Clinton because his army had to depend largely on food supplies from Britain. After some temporary relief, the food crisis continued throughout the first nine months of 1779. The army reserves were never sufficient for more than five months, well below the minimum amount deemed necessary to mount a campaign. With the opening of the campaign season in June, Clinton had less than four months' supplies and his reserves had been reduced to less than sixty days. He was only prepared to undertake major offensives when his supplies were sufficient.[38]

During the campaign season in 1779, Clinton was much criticized by contemporaries for his seeming inertia and for launching widely dispersed expeditions. As he awaited promised reinforcements and the return of his army from St. Lucia, Clinton delayed the beginning of the campaign season for five months, but the troops from Britain did not arrive until August when Chief Justice William Smith wrote in his journal that both civilians and soldiers in New York were "disgusted and dispirited" by the inactivity of Clinton. According to Smith, "The Boys in the Army hint their Contempt of the General, and common Soldiers murmur." Smith wrote deprecatingly about how Clinton was constantly on the move "and yet about Nothing." Upon visiting a post of the Queen's Rangers and light infantry, the Hessian Captain Johann von Ewald "found that all the officers of this corps were speaking badly about General Clinton." He attributed it to boredom and "continual monotony," together with the poor conditions of officers living in inadequate quarters and men sleeping in tents, with "ruined horses, worn-out clothing, and empty purses." Clinton's inactivity was even mocked in rebel satires:

> What's odd for Sir Harry, he nothing begun,
> Kept close to his works—without firing a gun.
> But, perhaps, th' poor man could not get on his legs,
> After sitting so long—like a hen o'er spoil'd eggs.

In October, William Tryon, the governor of New York, "expressed his Apprehension that the poor Man knew not what to do." Towards the end of that year in London, Thomas Hutchinson wrote in his diary of widespread belief that Clinton had "lain still all the summer, merely from indecision and a fluctuating state of mind." This was also the retrospective view of many military historians who regarded his virtual stagnation and his multiplicity of disjointed offensives as merely excuses to waver and delay.[39]

Clinton was painfully aware of the criticism and knew he would be blamed. However, he remained handicapped by lack of troops and crippled by the absence of adequate naval support. He was expected to conquer South Carolina, advance into the Hudson Valley, and attack the coast of New England all at the same time. He protested to Germain that the timely arrival of even a small reinforcement would have enabled him to attempt significant expeditions, and repeated his wish to resign. The government had other priorities, however. Between 1778 and 1783, it sent naval squadrons, eight regular regiments, and two German mercenary regiments to India. In the largest reinforcement of the Americas since 1776, the government also sent another 5,000 troops to the Caribbean and 3,000 to Central America. In 1779, Clinton had to manage with still fewer troops when the global war expanded to include Spain as a belligerent against Britain. He had to release an additional 2,000 troops for Canada. Admiral d'Estaing's fleet continued to enjoy superiority and threaten the security of the British islands in the Caribbean. During the summer, d'Estaing captured St. Vincent as well as Grenada, the second largest sugar-producing island after Jamaica in the British Caribbean. The troops sent by Clinton to St. Lucia were distributed throughout the remaining Leeward Islands to compensate for the lack of naval support. Because of the logistical difficulties of gathering enough transports to go to the different islands and the high mortality rates, their return to the mainland became even less likely.[40]

Clinton was effectively immobilized in New York because of the threat posed by the French fleet and the presence of the twenty-thousand-strong army of George Wash-

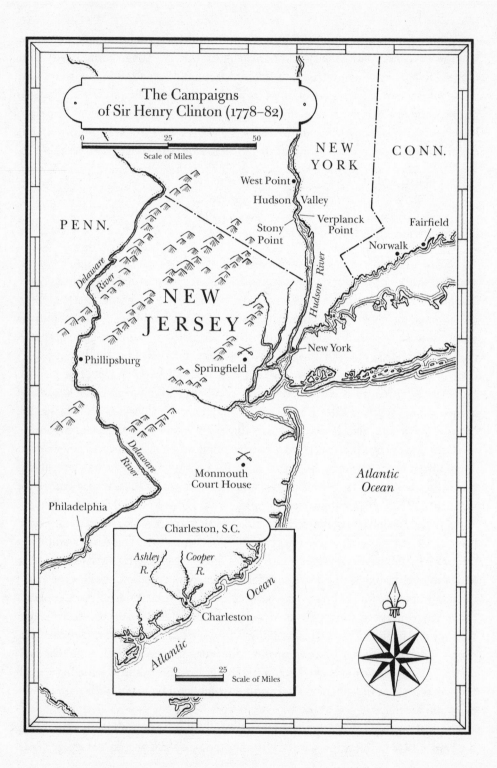

The Campaigns
of Sir Henry Clinton (1778–82)

0   25   50
Scale of Miles

NEW
YORK

CONN.

West Point

Hudson Valley

Verplanck
Point

Fairfield

PENN.

Stony
Point

Norwalk

Delaware River

Hudson River

NEW
JERSEY

New York

Phillipsburg

Springfield

Atlantic
Ocean

Delaware River

Monmouth
Court House

Philadelphia

Charleston, S.C.

Ashley
R.

Cooper
R.

Ocean

Charleston

Atlantic

0   25
Scale of Miles

ington. Like Clinton, Washington is also portrayed by biographers and military historians as inactive in 1779. He was in fact intending to launch his most daring challenge of
the war, an assault on New York in conjunction with the French fleet of Admiral d'Estaing, and made detailed plans that he was ready to carry out by October. Washington had
even recruited pilots to go aboard the French ships to navigate them through the entry
into New York Harbor. Having gathered the necessary boats and equipment for a major
siege, he was in the process of recruiting twelve thousand militiamen and concentrating
his army on the Hudson. He was only waiting for the arrival of the French fleet, whose
twenty-two ships of the line far outnumbered the five British ships of the line in New
York. Washington hoped that this would be the campaign that would end the war. It
would have been a grander and more decisive victory than Yorktown, but it was never
realized because d'Estaing returned to France instead of sailing for New York. Washington did not call a halt to the preparations until November. Clinton was therefore right
to be anxious about the security of New York, and had good reason to keep his strategic
emphasis upon the capture of the fortresses along the Hudson. He wrote that "to force
Washington to an action upon terms tolerably equal had been the object of every campaign during the war."[41]

Clinton was not inactive in 1779. Believing his force inadequate for a major
campaign and still uncertain of the number of anticipated reinforcements, Clinton resorted to launching raids aimed at causing confusion and intercepting the logistical
support of the Continental Army. In May, he began the first of a series of raids against
Virginia. With the encouragement of the home government, Clinton aimed to establish a
naval base in the Chesapeake Bay. He also hoped to cut off supplies to the rebellion and
force the state to withdraw its troops from elsewhere in America.

Nevertheless, Clinton continued to believe that the outcome of the war would be
decided in New York. In June 1779, in an effort "to stir Mr. Washington" by severing the
principal rebel supply route across the Hudson River, he successfully ordered the capture
of the fortresses at Stony Point and Verplanck Point that were situated opposite one
another along the river at a critical point of communication between the northern and
southern states, about forty miles from New York. Their capture forced enemy troops and
transports to make a detour of five to six days and forced Washington to move his army
from New Jersey. Clinton began a vigorous campaign to recruit loyalists. In Phillipsburg,
New Jersey, he ordered a proclamation to be issued offering freedom and security to
"Every NEGROE who shall desert the Rebel Standard." Although Lord Dunmore had
adopted the same expedient of recruiting slaves in Virginia in 1776, it had not been
formal policy of the British until Clinton's proclamation at Phillipsburg.[42]

Still without his anticipated reinforcements in July 1779, Clinton tried to tempt
Washington eastward by permitting William Tryon to launch coastal raids against Connecticut. As the former civil governor of New York, Tryon had long wanted to wage a war

of desolation with his loyalist troops and was an outspoken critic of the "procrastinating disposition" of Clinton. During the raids in July, Tryon's troops burned the towns of Fairfield and Norwalk, and destroyed civilian property including barns, schools, and churches. Clinton had previously made clear that he "detested" what he regarded as the buccaneering style of warfare advocated by Tryon. Although he defended Tryon to Germain, he accused him of disobeying orders and never again gave him an independent command. Such behavior only made the British more unpopular in America. Furthermore, Washington not only resisted the trap set for him by Clinton but his general "Mad" Anthony Wayne took advantage of the depleted British garrison by recapturing the fortress of Stony Point. Although it was abandoned two days later and the enemy failed in their attempt to take Verplanck Point, it was another rebel propaganda coup and forced Clinton to suspend a proposed expedition against New London. When the reinforcements arrived from Britain, they consisted of only 3,800 men rather than the 6,600 troops promised by Germain. Furthermore, these additional troops made little difference because 6,000 men were sick in hospital with fever.[43]

With reinforcements still lacking in August 1779, Clinton felt forced to abandon immediate plans for the conquest of South Carolina. He had little alternative but to act defensively owing to the urgent needs of other theater commanders and to the relative weakness of the Royal Navy in America. On August 3, he sent fourteen hundred troops to assist a recently established British garrison at Penobscot in Maine that was under siege by a rebel expedition from Boston. Uncertain of the destination of d'Estaing, Clinton felt obligated to withdraw from the recently captured fortresses along the Hudson. Before he could implement his plan on August 19, "Light Horse" Harry Lee captured the fortress of Paulus Hook which protected the Hudson. In September, Clinton received an urgent request to send reinforcements to Jamaica, the most important of the British islands in the Caribbean, where the governor was fearful of an invasion attempt by d'Estaing. He responded by embarking four thousand of his best British troops, under the command of Lord Cornwallis, together with much of the naval squadron under the command of Admiral Marriot Arbuthnot. For six days, Cornwallis and his army were at sea until they heard that d'Estaing was back in American waters, at Savannah.

Beginning on September 12, the British garrison at Savannah was surrounded by a combined force of Admiral d'Estaing and fifteen hundred American troops commanded by General Benjamin Lincoln. The siege was notable for the additional involvement of French colored troops from Saint-Domingue (Haiti), who included many of the future heroes of the Haitian Revolution. However, the Franco-American operation against Savannah was a fiasco reminiscent of the combined assault of Clinton and Parker at Charleston, for the besiegers were repulsed by the courageous actions of the defending British garrison. Nevertheless, in October, in order to concentrate his force against a combined Franco-American attack on New York, Clinton took the major decision to withdraw from Newport.[44]

Toward the end of the year, Clinton continued to be despondent and again offered his resignation. In May 1779, he had erupted in two letters to Germain. He protested at the unrealistic expectations of him when he had a smaller army than Howe and had to contend with the additional complication of a world war against France and Spain. He conceded that Germain had allowed him discretion by making recommendations rather than giving explicit orders. Nonetheless, Clinton believed that he was being set up to take the blame if he pursued his own plans and failed. He reminded the minister that he was on the spot and best able to judge the most favorable moments for action, and that he would not lose any opportunity when it offered. "For God's sake my lord," Clinton wrote to Germain, "if you wish that I should do anything leave me to myself." He later told Chief Justice William Smith that Germain "was sensible but the falsest Man alive." In his memoirs, Clinton wrote derisively of the grandiose expeditions and conquests that the minister had "chalked out" for him, when his force was smaller than that of his predecessor. He remembered how the visionary hopes raised by promises had withered and that he was the scapegoat for failure. He was too cautious and methodical to resort to the improvisation and gambles desired of him. Aware of the political need to win the war quickly, Germain was frustrated at such lack of boldness and began to settle his hopes upon the more enterprising Lord Cornwallis.[45]

In August 1779, the twenty-six-year-old Colonel Charles Stuart of the 26th Regiment described how Clinton told him with "tears in his eyes that he was quite an altered man—that business oppressed him, that he felt incapable of his station." "Believe me," said Clinton, "I envy that Grenadier who is passing the door," and would gladly exchange places with him, adding, "let me advise you never to take command of an army." He told the young colonel that "I know I am hated, nay, detested in the Army," and that he was determined to go home. In November, however, Germain wrote to Clinton denying another of his requests to resign, for it was now even less politically expedient for the government to lose its commander. Earlier in the year, the government had faced embarrassment when a court martial acquitted an opposition admiral, Augustus Keppel, in a trial widely regarded as politically motivated. The Howe brothers and Burgoyne had gone into opposition in Parliament. There was a decreasing pool of qualified and willing talent, and Germain himself threatened to resign rather than allow his personal enemy Sir Guy Carleton to succeed Clinton. In December, Germain relented and granted permission for Clinton to resign but discouraged him from doing so and assured him that he had the full support of the government for his "great military Talents."[46]

It was not until early October 1779, following the successful defense of Savannah, that Clinton felt free to begin an offensive against South Carolina. In December, for the first time since assuming his command, he had sufficient troops, provisions, and naval support to launch a major offensive. Although hesitant about the government's southern strategy, he hoped that a strike against Charleston, South Carolina, would at least enable him to secure Georgia. Ironically, he finally received permission to resign on the verge of the greatest victory of his career, and he was later to lament that he had not resigned when his reputation was at its peak. He might otherwise have been regarded as the most successful British general of the Revolutionary War.[47]

IV

In late December 1779, Clinton embarked for Charleston. His force consisted of 8,700 troops and 5,000 sailors, and 396 horses, together with ninety transports and ten warships under the command of Admiral Marriot Arbuthnot. During a stormy thirty-eight-day voyage, the horses, artillery, and much of the supplies were lost, and upon landing at daybreak on January 12, Clinton did not even have a horse to ride and his army was without baggage. For three months, he launched a classic siege of the town using cannon from the naval ships. He exhibited great personal valor during the operation. He was tirelessly energetic and showed little regard for his own safety. He made surprise inspections of the trenches at three in the morning, and stood in batteries with shells exploding around him. Captain Johann von Ewald was moved to tears by the "loud wailing of female voices" from inside the town. Washington was unable to send reinforcements to General Benjamin Lincoln, the commander of the garrison in Charleston, because of his own perilous position in New York. When Clinton summoned the town to surrender, Lincoln replied, "Duty and orders from the Congress direct me to defend myself to the utmost," but all the same the town finally capitulated. Ewald described the most "deplorable" scene of devastation that he ever witnessed throughout his military career, with "people burnt beyond recognition, half-dead and writhing like worms" who had been killed in the explosion of a gunpowder magazine. There were "mutilated bodies hanging on the farthest houses and lying in the streets" while "many of those who hurried to the scene were killed or wounded by the gunshots which came from the loaded muskets in the cellars." The "garrison consisted of handsome young men whose apparel was extremely ragged, and on the whole the people looked greatly starved." Ewald was told by one enemy officer that "the largest number had been killed by rifle bullets."[48]

It was a spectacular victory for Clinton, and all the more satisfying because he had failed in an earlier attack upon Charleston in 1776. He had not only become master of the largest and most prosperous city in the southern states, but his troops had captured seven generals of the Continental Army, three battalions of artillery, four frigates, several armed boats, numerous other vessels, four hundred pieces of ordnance, five thousand stand of arms, a vast quantity of gunpowder, and naval stores. The prisoners included 2,571 regular troops and some 800 militia. It was the largest loss sustained by the Continental Army during the Revolutionary War against only 76 British killed and 179 wounded. As the grenadiers entered the gates of the city, their band played "God Save the King." Clinton humiliated his opponents by not granting the full honors of war, which would have permitted them to surrender with their flags flying and drums beating as an acknowledgment of their honorable resistance. The British were still seething over the failure of the Continental Congress to honor the terms granted Burgoyne at the Saratoga Convention. His victory was celebrated in Hyde Park in London where 4,000 troops fired a *feu de joie*, accompanied by artillery salutes. Clinton and Arbuthnot received joint commendations voted by both Houses of Parliament.[49]

Clinton moved immediately to pacify the rest of South Carolina. In May, he issued a proclamation threatening to sequester the property of anyone who persisted in armed resistance. On June 1, he offered to pardon anyone who returned to their allegiance to the king, except those who had participated in the execution of loyal subjects. He guaranteed that those who complied would enjoy full rights of citizenship and would not be taxed, except by their own representative assemblies. His message was spread by the distribution of handbills and elicited a favorable response, with large numbers of people from the town and countryside taking the oath of allegiance, and even turning over recalcitrant rebels to the authorities. Clinton believed that he had essentially conquered South Carolina.

On June 3, 1780, suffused with victory, Clinton issued another proclamation designed to force the hand of anyone who had not taken advantage of his original offer of a pardon and withdrawing the paroles of prisoners of war. He required that they not only take a declaration of loyalty, but they be willing to take up arms in support of Britain. It effectively made neutrality impossible and gave sanction to loyalists seeking reprisals against their rebel neighbors. Like a similar proclamation in New Jersey in 1776, it backfired. It was blamed for many false declarations of support and the formation of partisan bands, under the leadership of men like Thomas Sumter and Francis Marion, who became the scourge of the British in the Carolinas. Clinton returned to New York before witnessing the impact of his policy.[50]

During the siege of Charleston, Clinton had quarreled disastrously with Admiral Arbuthnot, and with his second in command, Cornwallis, with adverse implications for British strategy in the events leading to Yorktown. Remembering, perhaps, his error in deferring to Admiral Parker during his earlier attack on Charleston in 1776, Clinton ignored the landing place suggested by Arbuthnot. Although the landing was successful, the decision embittered Arbuthnot. After the capture, they disagreed about the future government of the city. Consistent with the views of Germain, Admiral Arbuthnot advocated the restoration of full civil government with a representative assembly, but

Clinton was adamantly opposed for fear that elected assemblies and civil litigation might obstruct military operations. In the Caribbean, the army commanders were constantly vexed by the civil governors and elected assemblies. In South Carolina, the army was distrustful of the loyalties of the population. For much of the rest of the war, furthermore, Clinton and Arbuthnot wrangled about the distribution of the booty and captures from Charleston. Chief Justice William Smith suspected that this division over the plunder between the army and navy was the primary reason that "the two Chiefs have quarreled in Carolina." In his memoirs, Clinton described Arbuthnot as "false as hell." The breach became so public that it was known that the general thought the admiral "an Old Dotard." The differences essentially paralyzed any joint operations for a year until the admiral was removed.[51]

At the same time, Clinton fell out with Lord Cornwallis. Their differences had emerged gradually but became irreparable. In his first command in America, Cornwallis had been ordered to serve under Clinton during the attempted conquest of Charleston in 1776. Cornwallis had welcomed the prospect, writing that he would give his advice to Clinton "with all the sincerity of a friend," execute his orders with all the zeal and alacrity possible, and never be jealous when not consulted.[52] They remained friends despite the failure of the campaign. However, Cornwallis was closer to Sir William Howe and betrayed Clinton's trust by telling Howe that Clinton had said that he could not bear serving under him.[53] After being confronted by Howe, Clinton rebuked Cornwallis, who "made a very awkward apology." The matter was then closed. As late as October 1779, Clinton was writing of Cornwallis "that our Opinions entirely coincide." By the eve of their embarkation to Charleston in December, however, it was already apparent to Chief Justice William Smith in New York that Cornwallis had little regard for Clinton.[54]

During the seven-month interval following his request to resign, Clinton treated Cornwallis as his successor and consulted with him on all matters pertaining to the siege of Charleston. As gossip spread of his impending resignation and his fellow officers began to court the heir apparent, Clinton wrote of feeling hurt when Cornwallis told him that he intended to take command the moment word arrived from London, even if this occurred while they were besieging Charleston. In May 1780, Clinton received permission to resign from Germain who had more confidence in Cornwallis, but Clinton now declined, having just achieved a great victory, whereupon Cornwallis, having expected to succeed Clinton, withdrew from headquarters and confined himself to routine duties. Concerned by reports that a French fleet might threaten New York, Clinton departed Charleston confident of British control of Georgia and South Carolina. He left Cornwallis in command of the southern army.[55]

Clinton planned to conclude the war in a single decisive battle upon his return to New York. He therefore left comparatively few troops with Cornwallis in order to gather three-fourths of his army to surprise Washington in his encampment at Morristown in

New Jersey. His scheme was foiled when General Wilhelm von Knyphausen, a Hessian officer left in command of New York, prematurely launched raids upon the New Jersey towns of Springfield and Connecticut Farms (June 1780). Frustrated by Clinton's inactivity, loyalists and army officers like William Tryon and Lieutenant General James Robertson, who had favorable intelligence of civil unrest in New Jersey and armed protests by two Connecticut Line regiments at Basking Ridge, New Jersey, had urged Knyphausen to act. They wanted to take advantage of the absence of Clinton, whom Robertson regarded as "as inconstant as a Weather-Cock." Without awaiting Clinton's imminent return with troops from Charleston, Knyphausen ordered an assault force of five thousand men under Generals Edward Mathew and Thomas Sterling. Instead of receiving the anticipated support of loyalists, they met with determined resistance by local militiamen and were turned back by infantry and cavalry commanded by General Nathanael Greene and Henry Lee, justifying the earlier circumspection of Clinton. They further alienated the population by looting and burning Springfield. Clinton arrived too late to salvage the expedition, and the premature attack deprived him of an opportune moment to confront Washington, whose army had suffered its worst winter when encamped at Morristown where conditions were even worse than those of Valley Forge.[56]

Clinton was also forced to change objectives by the news of the sailing of a French squadron bound for Newport. He was still without significant reinforcements and short of provisions: in the words of his commissary general, "living hand to mouth." Nevertheless, he proposed to Admiral Arbuthnot a joint attack on Newport to keep the port out of the hands of the French, who would otherwise be free to menace New York or Canada. Clinton even embarked his troops, who got as far as Long Island Sound, but he was opposed by Arbuthnot, who had never favored a base at Newport. Clinton had offered two plans of attack, both of which the admiral rejected while refusing to suggest an alternative of his own. In any case. he had to postpone his plan when Washington advanced and threatened King's Bridge. In July 1780, the opportunity to seize Newport was all but lost when the garrison was reinforced with five thousand troops commanded by General Jean Baptiste Donatien de Vimeur, comte de Rochambeau, who became the senior French commander and who made Newport the main French base in America. Far from seeking a war of attrition, Clinton had wanted to go on the offensive, but was never given the chance to test either his planned surprise of Washington in New Jersey or an attack upon Newport.[57]

In August 1780, Clinton once again warned Germain that it was utterly impossible to prosecute the war without considerable reinforcements. Since it required six thousand troops just to hold South Carolina, he lacked sufficient manpower to retain the territory that he conquered. In a clear gibe at Germain, he dismissed expectations of large-scale loyalist support as fantasy and wrote sarcastically of the oppressed friends of government who pined under the usurpation of the rebels. Furthermore, he warned that if the loyalists were not supported by permanent garrisons, they would become refugees and be a drag on resources. He complained that his army was critically undermanned and that he was hampered by an admiral who simply did not share his views about the conduct of the war. In his anxiety, he believed that he had been the victim of an attempted poisoning when he and his two guests fell violently ill after each drinking a single glass of wine. By November, Clinton had still not received any of the provisions due for the year. He sent his quartermaster to give an eyewitness account of his situation and to communicate his concerns directly to Lord George Germain. Clinton insisted on the recall of Admiral Arbuthnot, the transfer of responsibility for troop transports to the army, and the addition of ten thousand troops to secure control of the Hudson. He asked again to resign, if the minister was unable to grant his request.[58]

With Washington substantially strengthened by the French troops of Rochambeau, Clinton fully expected to be attacked in New York, where he believed that the war would be decided in a decisive battle between the main forces. This was indeed the plan of the opposing allied commanders until the very eve of Yorktown. In the summer of 1780, Rochambeau and Washington had twice meditated an attack on New York, but had desisted owing to the arrival of naval reinforcements that briefly gave Britain superiority at sea. Their reluctance to proceed demonstrated the influence of the balance of the respective navies on the conduct of the land war. Far from being a timid general, Clinton had always appreciated that ultimate victory required the defeat of Washington. He was conscious of the ineffectiveness of detachments and raids, and he wanted a decisive battle between the major armies. He was thwarted by the generalship of Washington who kept his army from exposure and played for time.

V

While still despairing of success, Clinton worked on a secret plan that promised to break the deadlock. In May 1779, he had been approached by one of the most senior and most capable enemy generals, Benedict Arnold. Known to British troops as the "American Hannibal," Arnold had played a critical role in the taking of Fort Ticonderoga (1775), in delaying the advance of General Carleton at Valcour Island (1776), and in the rebel victory at Saratoga (1777). The British had hoped for a high-level defection to provide intelligence, to undermine the morale of the enemy, and to encourage others to desert the rebel cause. They regarded Arnold as potentially another George Monck, the seventeenth-century Civil War army commander who had deserted the republican cause in Britain and restored the monarchy under Charles II. Among the officers of the French army, some of whom thought the rebellion close to collapse, the chevalier de Ternay agreed with the British assessment and predicted that one highly placed traitor might decide the fate of the war.[59]

Benedict Arnold was indeed ready to betray the rebel cause. He, too, thought the rebellion close to collapse, with many of the best officers resigning in disgust at the treatment of the army by Congress. He complained about the depreciation of the currency in which the army was paid, the token size of the navy, and the virtual bankruptcy of the Treasury. His perception was skewed by his bitterness at being passed over for promotion by lesser men in decisions often based upon political considerations rather than merit. He resented a court martial that had failed to clear him fully of charges of financial impropriety. He was physically crippled by his military service and felt unappreciated by his country. His wife's family was sympathetic to the loyalist cause. His defection was not least motivated by the monetary reward, which was all the more alluring because of his extravagant lifestyle and mounting debts. He had insisted upon financial compensation and had haggled over the amount.[60]

Clinton had reservations about Arnold. He knew that Arnold was in some disgrace following charges of corruption, and that he might not be appointed to a command again. He encouraged him not to defect but to remain where he could provide intelligence and obtain another post in the army. The negotiations broke off for several months because of the price demanded by Arnold. In May 1780, they resumed their correspondence using invisible ink and code names, in which Arnold was variously known as "Gustavus" and "Monk." In July, Clinton was predicting that "the Rebellion would end suddenly in a Crash." In the meantime, Arnold's assumption of a new command at West Point put him in a position to be of real assistance to Clinton, who had long coveted control of the gateway to the Hudson. Protected by a series of rocky ridges, the fortress was the strongest post of the Continental Army. The taking of West Point offered Clinton the chance of severing the communications between Washington's army at Kingsbridge and the French army at Newport. It was a major depot of guns, ammunition, and provisions. Arnold revealed that the garrison was depleted and that the great chain in the river, blocking the passage of warships, was in such a state of decay that it could be broken by one fully loaded ship. Insisting that he meet with a senior officer, he specifically named Clinton's adjutant general, Major John André.[61]

The youthful-looking thirty-year-old André was one of the most glamorous personalities in the British army in America. An amateur thespian, a poet, and an artist, he had been the chief orchestrator of the Mischianza. He was an example of a growing number of officers who did not belong to the landed classes at home and who owed their promotion to merit rather than purchase or connections. His family income was derived from colonial trade and lands in the British Caribbean. During the siege of Charleston and the rupture with Cornwallis, André became the confidant of Clinton. Like many other young officers, he advocated a more ruthless conduct of the war, in which he suggested the hanging of merchants who supplied the rebels. He thought that fire "would be a telling weapon, applied to the homes and cornfields of rebel sympathizers."[62]

As adjutant general, André supervised the elaborate British intelligence and spy network, which had been skillfully developed from virtually nothing by Clinton. André used ciphers to communicate with his agents, including the remarkable Ann Bates, a Philadelphia schoolteacher and wife of an armorer in the British artillery, who managed to penetrate the brigades, artillery, ammunition stocks, and even the headquarters of the Continental Army. There were also many double agents working for both sides. The high drama of undercover espionage seems to have appealed to the actor in André.[63]

On September 27, 1780, André set out to meet Arnold. Clinton had instructed him not to go behind enemy lines, not to discard his uniform, and not to accept anything in writing. Largely owing to the arrangements made by Arnold, André had little alternative but to go behind enemy lines to the rendezvous, which was held in a clearing in thick woods until four o'clock in the morning, and where he received the plans of the fortress and details of the garrison which he placed in his boots. Owing to the late hour and the fact that the warship that was to carry him back via the Hudson River came under bombardment, André had to return overland to New York, which entailed his disguising his uniform. Assuming the name of John Anderson, he hoped to complete the journey in the dark with a pass and a guide, Joshua Smith, provided by Arnold. He and Smith were delayed by the numerous patrols and were finally forced to stay the night in a house near Crompound because a rebel militia captain insisted he remain because of the danger of loyalist partisans. The next morning, André became alarmed when Smith, unaware of his real identity, left him to complete the journey to within fifteen miles of the British lines. On being approached by four men near Tarrytown, he mistook them for loyalists, dismounted and, instead of showing them his pass from Arnold, introduced himself as a British officer. When they discovered the plans of West Point in his boot, they turned him over to Lieutenant Colonel John Jameson at North Castle, who forwarded the captured papers and plans to Washington. Alerted by news of André's capture, Arnold escaped, fleeing only moments before the arrival of George Washington at West Point. Arnold ordered a crew to row him downriver to the awaiting HMS *Vulture*, the British warship assigned to convey *André* back to New York.

In the meantime, André was taken back to West Point and eventually imprisoned at Marbie's Tavern in Tappan. He was tried and sentenced by a board of senior officers selected by Washington, and executed by hanging. He had asked to be shot as a soldier but his request was denied because he was wearing civilian clothing and was therefore treated as a spy. The night before his death, he drew a haunting pen-and-ink portrait of himself (Figure 26). Disclaiming ever having executed any of the rebels, Clinton tried vainly to arrange clemency but received hints that it would only be possible in exchange for Benedict Arnold. As he neared the place of execution, André asked, "Must I die in this Manner?" He pronounced himself "reconciled to my fate, but not to the mode." He added, "It will be but a momentary pang." Ascending a cart on which the scaffold was mounted, he tied his own blindfold and placed the noose over his head "with a composure which excited the admiration of the spectators." When he was told that the final moment was at hand and asked whether he had anything more to say, he replied "nothing but to request you will witness to the world *that I die like a brave man.*" Stationed in New York, Sergeant Roger Lamb recounted how "No language can describe the mingled sensations of horror, grief, sympathy, and revenge, that agitated the whole garrison; a silent gloom overspread the general countenance; the whole army, and citizens of first distinction, went into mourning." The officers wore black crepe bands around their arms. The execution of André alienated opinion in Britain and was used as a justification for hanging partisans in the south. He became a national hero, and George III gave his mother a large pension as well as making his brother a baronet. In 1824, at the request of George III's son Prince Frederick, duke of York, André's remains were returned to Britain and he was given the highest national accolade of a marble monument at Westminster Abbey designed by the architect Robert Adam.[64]

Even the captors were moved by the execution, including Alexander Hamilton, who was the personal secretary to George Washington and was one of the last people to spend time with André. Hamilton wrote to André's fiancée protesting the rigidity of Washington's refusal to grant his wish to be shot, which he thought history would condemn. Benjamin Tallmadge, a twenty-six-year-old officer who attended the execution, later wrote that he could "remember no instance of his affections being so fully absorbed by any man," and described how hundreds of onlookers at the execution "seemed to be overwhelmed by the affecting spectacle" and "many were suffused in tears." Tallmadge himself withdrew from the scene "in a flood of tears." In reality, the British had behaved in a similar manner in 1776 when General Howe had executed the Patriot spy Nathan Hale without even granting him the board of inquiry that Washington gave André.[65]

According to Major General William Phillips, the loss of André "struck poor Sir Henry to the heart.'" In his postwar memoirs, Clinton wrote that the subject affected him too deeply to continue writing. Although André wrote him a final letter absolving him of any responsibility, Clinton may well have felt guilt since the nature of the mission necessarily entailed using a disguise and going behind enemy lines. André's death was also symbolic of the demise of one of Clinton's most ambitious plans to force Washington into battle and to take West Point.[66]

Clinton made good his promises of payment to Arnold, and commissioned him a brigadier general in a loyalist regiment. Admiral Sir George Rodney thought Arnold the best general in the British army and recommended him to be commander in chief in America. However, Arnold's treason disappointed Clinton's expectations that it would persuade other Patriot generals to defect and make the loyalist cause more popular. It has been argued that it had the opposite effect of removing any lingering notion of the war as a factional struggle in favor of the understanding of it as a conflict between separate nations, in which disloyalty was treason. In the words of one historian, "Arnold as traitor helped fix a powerful new image of the United States in the minds of its people."[67]

In October 1780, Clinton was again given permission to resign but he did not take up the offer. He did not attempt to explain his motives in his memoirs. As a soldier, he clearly regarded it as his duty to obey orders, and to serve king and country, and like Lord North, he felt compelled not to indulge his private wishes. He did go out of his way in his memoirs to deny that he was influenced by patronage and the benefits of his position. The rewards were indeed considerable. His salary was larger than that of the prime minister. He had five houses in the vicinity of New York including a country house at Turtle Bay and the palatial Archibald Kennedy house at No. 1 Broadway. He regularly went fox hunting, for which he was nicknamed "the Knight." He had a mistress, his Irish housekeeper Mary Baddeley, the wife of a private soldier who had been demoted from sergeant but was promoted to captain before dying of a fever in Charleston in 1782. Clinton had five children by her and the relationship continued until his death. As with Howe, his lifestyle was a cause of derision and helped create the impression that he was not entirely serious. In November 1780, Chief Justice William Smith described how Clinton would go riding from two to five hours a day. "What a Trifler!" Smith exclaimed. "No wonder he shuns Company."[68]

Instead of resigning, Clinton wavered between self-doubt and the conviction that he was the best man for the job. In addition, he might well have stayed simply to block the promotion of Cornwallis. In a deleted section of his memoirs, he claimed that Cornwallis was motivated in his march north by the desire to usurp the post of commander in chief. His career would have been eclipsed if Cornwallis had succeeded where he had failed by winning the war for America.[69]

VI

With the collapse of his plans to capture West Point, Clinton spent much of the rest of the war playing a secondary role to Cornwallis. His main concern was the security of New York and control of the Hudson River. He regarded the retention of the city as essential, because it was the main base for the navy and an important link to Canada. He also had to consider the interests of some twenty-five thousand loyalists who lived in the city under British protection. He believed that Washington intended to attack and that the decisive battle of the war would be fought in New York.

Unable to thwart government orders, Clinton reluctantly became complicit in the fatal shift of the focus of the war to the south. Since 1776, the home government had wanted to establish a naval base in the Chesapeake Bay in Virginia. The state was the largest and most populous of the original thirteen colonies. It was an important source of food, men, and military supplies for the rebel war effort. With the conquest of South Carolina in 1780, possession of a naval base in Virginia became even more desirable as a way of cutting off communications between the southern and northern commands of the Continental Army. Clinton envisaged that a naval base in the Chesapeake could be reinforced from New York and even more speedily from South Carolina. Between May 1779 and May 1781, Clinton sent four separate detachments, amounting to nine thousand troops, to Virginia. What began as little more than what he called "desultory raids" escalated until three-fifths of his army was in the south where he had but little choice to assist Cornwallis.

Far from wishing to make the south the center of the war, Clinton had intended that Cornwallis return some of his troops for a summer offensive against Philadelphia and the eastern shore of Maryland. In August 1780, his hopes initially seemed justified when Cornwallis defeated General Horatio Gates, the victor of Saratoga and commander of the southern divisions of the Continental Army, at the battle of Camden. However, Clinton thereafter began to receive requests for more troops from Cornwallis. He had ordered Cornwallis not to proceed further north until he had fully secured South Carolina, but soon after the battle of Camden, Cornwallis wrote to him that it was necessary to invade North Carolina, in order to retain South Carolina and Georgia. He argued that reports of an advance of a large American army from the north had intimidated the loyalists, encouraged the rebels, and alienated the potential support of those who still wavered.[70]

Clinton did in fact continue to reinforce Cornwallis. In October 1780, he diverted the second of his Virginia expeditions under Major General Alexander Leslie to support Cornwallis, who urgently needed more troops in the wake of a defeat of a loyalist detachment of his army at the battle of King's Mountain (October 7, 1780). By November, however, Clinton began to despair of the southern campaign. Brigadier General Charles O'Hara, who led the Guards under Cornwallis, met with Clinton in New York, where he found him "the most perplex'd, as well as the most disappointed of all Human beings—all his Dreams of Conquests quite vanish'd, from the desperate situation of our Affairs in the Carolina's." Although reinforcements served only to encourage Cornwallis, Clinton continued to send more troops to Virginia to deflect the enemy away from the army there—fifty-seven hundred men in a six-month period. Under the mistaken impression that Cornwallis had won a great victory at Guilford Courthouse (March 15, 1781), Clinton shifted to crediting himself with having assisted in Cornwallis's success in the Carolinas.[71]

Clinton was incredulous, however, at the subsequent movements of Cornwallis and the sanction given them by the British government. The two commanders were increasingly working independently of one another with very different conceptions of future strategy. They both placed emphasis on the retention of South Carolina, but Cornwallis believed that this could only be achieved by defeating enemy forces further north and cutting off supplies. Clinton thought it an error to advance until all resistance had been quelled in Georgia and South Carolina. The two commanders were not communicating with each other. For much of the first three months of 1781, Cornwallis simply did not write to his commander. Clinton later suspected that he had become openly disobedient after Cornwallis's aide-de-camp returned from a meeting with Germain in London, where he suspected that Cornwallis was more favored by the home government than Clinton. Believing himself undermined by the home government, Clinton demurred from asserting his authority and sending positive orders to Cornwallis. He even ordered the commanders of his expeditions in Virginia to defer to orders from Cornwallis, and gave no indication of disapproving of his actions until Cornwallis marched into Virginia.

The breach between the commanders thereafter became openly hostile. Clinton was in disbelief at the diminished size of Cornwallis's army following the battle of Guilford Courthouse. In April 1781, each was accusing the other of having left him totally in the dark about future plans. Clinton had not bothered to inform Cornwallis of the orders given to Major General William Phillips and Benedict Arnold who commanded raiding expeditions that Clinton had sent to Virginia. In May, Clinton wrote scathingly to the home government that his lordship had gained honor but had lost an army, lost any sight of his objectives, and buried himself in the sea coast of North Carolina. When it was rumored that Cornwallis had marched into Virginia, Clinton told Chief Justice William Smith that he hoped "Cornwallis has not done this," correctly predicting that it would cut off General Nathanael Greene from the southern base of the Continental Army and make Greene "more desperate in the South Country." He protested that Cornwallis sought to make Virginia the main theater of the war rather than New York. Clinton conceded that it might be worth testing the loyalties of the border areas of Virginia, but not at the expense of losing New York. Clinton's letters repeatedly forewarned the home government that a superior enemy fleet could cut off troops in the Chesapeake. He alone fully appreciated the danger that Cornwallis was courting. He was in the impossible situation of having the government undermine his authority by allowing a subordinate to dictate to him.[72]

The crux of Clinton's many postwar complaints against Cornwallis was that he had disobeyed orders by advancing into Virginia before fully securing South Carolina. Indeed, Cornwallis had left the Carolinas in open rebellion and had allowed General Nathanael Greene to eliminate the chain of British army posts in North Carolina and South Carolina. Clinton regarded the invasion of Virginia as a pointless rampage. It ran totally counter to his own belief in the importance of solid operations, in which territory was conquered and secured. He had consistently argued that the continuous presence of the army would alone assure loyalists and win potential recruits to the cause of Britain.

In the weeks before Yorktown, Clinton became increasingly inconsistent, sending conflicting plans to Cornwallis. He initially ordered Cornwallis to return with his army to New York. Cornwallis began to comply and had actually embarked some troops onto their transports, when Clinton countermanded the order after receiving a letter from Germain prohibiting him from withdrawing troops from Virginia. Clinton instead ordered Cornwallis to occupy a deep-water harbor for the navy along the Chesapeake. It was his first categorical order in months. Because of Cornwallis's objections to Portsmouth, however, Clinton suggested either Old Point Comfort or Yorktown. Furthermore, the order merely required Cornwallis to maintain the port as a defensive post and gave him discretion in the choice of ports to be defended. Contrary to the claims of Cornwallis, Clinton never insisted on Yorktown, indeed he recommended that Cornwallis send the majority of his force back to New York. Cornwallis was so opposed to the plan to fortify a port that he requested to be transferred back to Charleston, in the belief that a defensive post had little military value, while it would leave the army vulnerable to attack by both land and sea. Clinton denied Cornwallis' request, and thereafter he was never able to acknowledge his own role in the disastrous events that led to Yorktown. Although he justifiably held Cornwallis responsible for the invasion of Virginia, it was he who had ordered Cornwallis to fortify and defend a port in the Chesapeake.[73]

Throughout the summer, Clinton suffered periodic spells of blindness. Shutting himself up for three to four days at a time, he refused to see anyone. He alternated between fantastical schemes to reoccupy Rhode Island and Philadelphia, and resurrected the same old shibboleths of the strength of loyalist sympathies along the east shore of Virginia and Maryland, and in Pennsylvania. The wheel had come full circle. His thinking represented the bankruptcy of ideas for the British conquest of America. Four years earlier, General Sir William Howe had tested the sympathies of the same areas only to be disappointed in his expectations of loyalist support. The army had essentially marched everywhere and tried everything.[74]

The breakdown in the relationship between Cornwallis and Clinton should not be allowed to obscure the underlying reasons for the defeat at Yorktown. Like the British commanders at Saratoga, Clinton and Cornwallis were both acting upon false assumptions and misinformation. Neither of the commanders appreciated the gravity and urgency of the situation. The operations in the south had been based on a chimera that British naval support would be sufficient to match that of the French. In March 1781, Benedict Arnold had narrowly escaped the fate of Cornwallis while commanding an expedition in Portsmouth, Virginia. Terrified of capture, Arnold became very restless and broke out into cold sweats. He carried two pistols to shoot himself rather than face the gallows as a traitor. Arnold was saved only by the timely arrival of Admiral Arbuthnot who blocked access to the French fleet of the chevalier Destouches at Lynnhaven Bay. In July, the French occupied Newport, giving them the capacity to launch naval attacks along the east coast, which further jeopardized Cornwallis's position in Virginia.[75]

For the past thirteen months, Cornwallis had been dependent on a slight British naval superiority in the Americas. Assured by the government that the British fleet would match the strength of the French, Cornwallis blithely took for granted the continued support of the navy. Clinton alone appreciated the thread by which the fate of the British army hung in the Chesapeake, but even he was beguiled by the assurances from Admiral Rodney, who commanded the British fleet in the Caribbean. The commanders were also led to expect continued naval parity between the British and French by the earl of Sandwich. Clinton and Cornwallis also acted upon faulty intelligence of the size of the likely naval reinforcement from France under Admiral de Grasse. Even when it became apparent that the Admiralty in Britain had grossly underestimated the size of the French fleet, Clinton and Cornwallis continued to be reassured by Admiral Hood that the British navy was equal to the challenge.[76]

Throughout July and August 1781, Clinton had received contradictory intelligence about enemy intentions while he privately remained convinced that Washington and Rochambeau intended to attack New York. When he discovered beyond all doubt that the combined armies of Washington and Rochambeau had marched south to Yorktown on September 1, Clinton still felt confident about Cornwallis's situation because the fleets of Admirals Hood and Thomas Graves had just sailed from New York for the Chesapeake. He did not appreciate the severity of the situation until two weeks later when Graves and Hood reappeared with their badly damaged ships after having unsuccessfully tried to dislodge the larger French fleet at the battle of the Chesapeake Capes (September 5).[77]

While Cornwallis was surrounded at Yorktown, Clinton sent word that he intended to mount a rescue expedition with four thousand troops from New York. He believed that Cornwallis could hold out for six weeks. The day that Cornwallis surrendered, Clinton finally sailed from New York. In the midst of the crisis, Clinton lavishly hosted Prince William Henry, the sixteen-year-old son of George III and the first member of the royal family to visit America. This is popularly cited as a cause of his delay, but the real reason for his failure to send timely relief was more profound. Clinton had been at the mercy of Admiral Graves, who had replaced Admiral Arbuthnot to command the navy in North America. The admiral was unwilling to sail until urgent repairs were made to the fleet; the dockyard facilities were too small to complete the task in time. There was a yet more basic reason for the delay: uncertainty about the objective once the fleet arrived off the coast of Virginia. Graves was only prepared to land the army and then return to the safety of New York, whereas Clinton wanted the navy to both land and supply the army. Graves could not afford the risk of exposing his weaker fleet in the Chesapeake. As one naval officer admitted to Major Frederick Mackenzie in New York, "the loss of two line-of-battle ships in effecting the relief of the army is of much more consequence than the loss of the army." It was unlikely that a rescue would have achieved anything, but it risked a greater disaster with the loss of a fleet as well as of the majority of the British army in America. The navy was unlikely to succeed where it had already failed in the Chesapeake. Hence the commanders dithered while Cornwallis was surrounded by enemy troops and ships at Yorktown.[78]

VII

Clinton spent the rest of his life preoccupied by the events of the American Revolution. With only a two-month leave in England between 1775 and 1782, he had spent more time in America than any of the British generals of the Revolutionary War. He believed that he had been made the scapegoat for the final defeat, and became embroiled in a public feud with Cornwallis. In November 1781, he had an initially amicable meeting with Cornwallis, who returned to New York on parole after his surrender at Yorktown, in which they pondered together about what had gone wrong. They both agreed that the battle of King's Mountain was the turning point, and they both agreed that Rodney could have won the war if he had commanded at the battle of the Chesapeake Capes. They began to argue when they discussed a letter Cornwallis had written implying that he was given no choice by Clinton but to fortify Yorktown. The rising tensions of the past five years suddenly exploded to the point that they ceased to talk to one another.[79]

Clinton became obsessed with vindicating himself and holding Cornwallis responsible for the defeat at Yorktown. While still in New York, Clinton published the first of a series of pamphlets against Cornwallis, which resulted in a half-dozen-pamphlet exchange that lasted another two years. He consulted with his friend Edward Gibbon who warned him against implicating other naval commanders and politicians in his dispute with Cornwallis. Clinton wrote repetitive tirades to himself about Cornwallis, which now fill two volumes of his papers at the William L. Clements Library at the University of Michigan in Ann Arbor. He even wrote out an imaginary dialogue from a dream in which an abject Lord Cornwallis confessed his guilt for the British defeat at Yorktown. He laboriously worked on a three-volume apologia entitled *An Historical Detail of Seven Years Campaigns in North America* which he referred to as "les campagnes de Clinton." He devoted much of the text to Cornwallis and the events leading up to Yorktown. Although it was not published until 1954, he thought it would reveal "how wantonly, how totally that Continent has been lost!"[80]

Clinton's memoirs have been characterized as an utter fabrication concerning his dealings with Cornwallis. They do indeed convey the impression that Cornwallis disobeyed positive orders, whereas Clinton had all too often deferred to him or given him latitude. It is not surprising that Clinton's memory of events became distorted, however. He must have been incensed that the war had been lost by a strategy that he had not devised, one that ran counter to his basic instincts, and that he had never really approved. He had foreseen the potential consequences, but he was in an invidious position when the government preferred the ideas of Cornwallis. He had, therefore, complied against his better judgment, only to find himself bearing the brunt of the blame for the disaster that befell the British at Yorktown. It must have been particularly galling that he was partly responsible for the defeat because he had permitted what he disapproved. He might have spared his reputation and emerged a hero if he had resigned after the conquest of Charleston in 1780.[81]

Clinton's career essentially ended with the American War. On arrival from New York in London in June 1782, he managed to obtain a two-hour private audience with George III, in which he described the frustrations of his command and the inadequate resources. He did not mention Cornwallis but the king interposed, "Come, come, you must acknowledge Lord Cornwallis rambled about, lost himself, and did not know what he was doing!" The king spoke even more scathingly of Sir William Howe. He advised Clinton to stay quiet and let the truth come out. Clinton was initially thrilled by this reception, until his return to court the next day, when he heard that the king had received Cornwallis with even greater cordiality. He was deprived of his colonelcy of a regiment without the usual courtesy of a request to resign. He even lost his parliamentary seat at Newark in the election of 1784. Seven years after the American War, he had still not been promoted nor had he received the usual honor of a pension or stipend.[82]

According to General James Grant, Clinton became "quite frantic" as he watched his rivals being promoted and receiving honors. It was particularly frustrating for him that the greatest accolades and most lucrative appointments were given to Cornwallis. As he fumed "intirely entre nous" to a confidant, he could not understand how George III could reconcile what he had said privately to Clinton about Cornwallis, only to "load, nay *overload,* his Lordship with honours & dignities, and to suffer the man whose military conduct he had so full approved & *all* whose Plans (to give you his own words) either *had* or *would* have succeeded, to be treated in the manner his ministers have been permitted to treat" him. Sir William Howe was promoted a full general and had an important role in supervising the defenses of Britain against Napoleon. Sir Guy Carleton returned to Canada as governor and became Lord Dorchester. John Burgoyne was appointed commander in chief and a privy councillor in Ireland, as well as colonel of a regiment. Lord George Germain was made a member of the House of Lords as Viscount Sackville. Clinton tried desperately to obtain some mark of honor to indicate that his services were approved by the king and the nation. He was offered and refused an Irish peerage, which was colloquially known as a potato, a vegetable that was looked down on and associated with

Ireland, because it did not confer the right to sit in the House of Lords in London. He tried to obtain a parliamentary inquiry to clear his name, but failed.[83]

The tragedy of Clinton's later life was that the public was no longer interested in the American war. Horace Walpole described the way that the Revolution was forgotten owing to the vast variety of new concerns, writing acidly that the events of the war would forever remain obscure, together with Clinton. He thought that the nation did not have the patience to sift through the multiplicity of difficult questions about the war, when the evidence had been concealed by ministers, the events had been transacted at such a great distance, many of the witnesses were absent, and the various parties affirmed or denied allegations with equal heat. Walpole reflected on the irony that the nation had originally supported the politicians and generals who had waged the war with such warmth, "and now forgot them with equal levity." Clinton was well aware of the public apathy, but he believed that Britain would one day have to contend with America. He thought that the United States would seek to expand until it had absorbed Canada, the Caribbean, and Spanish America. He believed that it was important to remember the American Revolution, because he predicted that Britain would fight another war against the United States, and he was indeed proven right in 1812. He regarded such a war as desirable because of the threat American expansionism posed to British commercial interests in the Americas and the Caribbean.[84]

Clinton continued to take an interest in the fate of the loyalists after the war and supported their claims for compensation. Like many senior officers who had served in America, he was constantly asked for help by loyalist refugees. They included the remarkable Thomas Peters, an African American who had served with the British army. When Peters arrived in London in 1790, Clinton helped introduce him to William Wilberforce and Granville Sharp. He also supported two petitions from Peters to Secretary of State William Grenville to "suffer the poor Black to tell his own melancholy Tale." The petitions were overtly critical of the failure of the government to provide sufficient land grants and provisions for blacks in Nova Scotia, and Peters became a leader in the resettlement project of black loyalists in the new colony of Sierra Leone.[85]

Despite his brooding, Clinton spent a remarkable retirement, traveling throughout Europe, including a visit to Edward Gibbon in Lausanne in Switzerland, who was in the midst of writing the final volume of *The Decline and Fall of the Roman Empire*. Clinton enjoyed reading literature and playing the violin, especially pieces by his favorite composer Haydn. He was fond of nature and liked to exercise. In addition to the children of his marriage, he kept a family by Mary Baddeley, who continued to live with him in London. It has been plausibly suggested that he tried to have parallel families, giving the children of his mistress the same names as the children of his marriage, and that he even contrived to have the children of both families born on the same day. He was to bequeath almost as much money to the children by his mistress as to those by his wife. The two sons by his marriage both became generals.

Toward the end of his life, Clinton's career began to revive. In 1790, he returned to Parliament as member for Launceston, and he was promoted a full general the following year. In 1794, he finally secured another command as governor of Gibraltar, but he became too ill to take up the appointment and he was replaced by the ruddy-faced man who had surrendered Cornwallis's sword at Yorktown, Brigadier General Charles O'Hara. Clinton died at Portland Place in London in November 1795.[86]

Quoting Macbeth, "Thou canst not say that I did it," Clinton protested to the end of his life that he had been made the scapegoat for the British loss of America. It was not the *crie de coeur* of someone who was out of his mind, but rather the lament of a rational man who had commanded with insufficient resources and whose authority had been undermined by his own government. After Yorktown, he had preserved the remainder of the British army in New York and Charleston, making it possible for George III and Germain to consider continuing the war for America. An eyewitness at the battle of Yorktown, Captain Johann von Ewald, believed that it would have been "the greatest impossibility" for Clinton to have rescued Cornwallis: "in a word, the whole thing seemed to me a delusion." Although he was critical of Clinton for not intercepting Washington's march from New York, Ewald thought that "to lay the entire blame on him is too severe, because the chief mistake lay with the admiral of the fleet, who let himself be hoaxed by the Comte de Grasse when the latter entered the Chesapeake contrary to expectations."[87]

CHAPTER 7

"Bagging the Fox"

CHARLES, EARL CORNWALLIS

On the eve of the state opening of Parliament in November 1781, George III was due to give a speech from the throne announcing expectations of a great British victory in America. Throughout the year, Lord George Germain had been enthusiastic about British prospects there. In the early months of 1781, Sir Henry Clinton had shed his usual pessimism and was beginning to think victory possible. Their optimism appears absurd in hindsight and is often cited as an example of the home government being out of touch with the realities of the war in America.[1]

Such hopes were not totally delusional, however. In 1781, the chances of success seemed very promising. In January, Admiral Sir George Rodney and General Sir John Vaughan eliminated one of the major sources of supply to the Continental Army when they conquered the Dutch island of St. Eustatius. Britain was quickly closing the gap in naval strength, and since the spring of 1780, France and Spain had begun to tire of the war. As an American diplomat in Paris, John Adams worried that France might try to arbitrate a negotiated compromise between Britain and the United States. The French foreign minister, Charles Gravier, comte de Vergennes, was simultaneously warning Louis XVI that "we have need of peace." There were well-supported rumors that France and Spain were not willing to continue the war beyond the end of 1781. Silas Deane, a former commissioner of the Continental Congress to France, had become convinced that the best option for America was reconciliation with Britain.[2]

The rebellion seemed on the verge of collapse, with a depreciated currency and a bankrupt treasury dependent on subsidies from France. By May 1781, the Continental dollar had fallen in relation to the pound from 125:1 to 700:1. There was widespread disaffection throughout the Continental Army over wage arrears and poor conditions, causing mutinies in line regiments in Pennsylvania and New Jersey. Between October and December 1780, the force commanded by Washington had dwindled from 17,586 troops

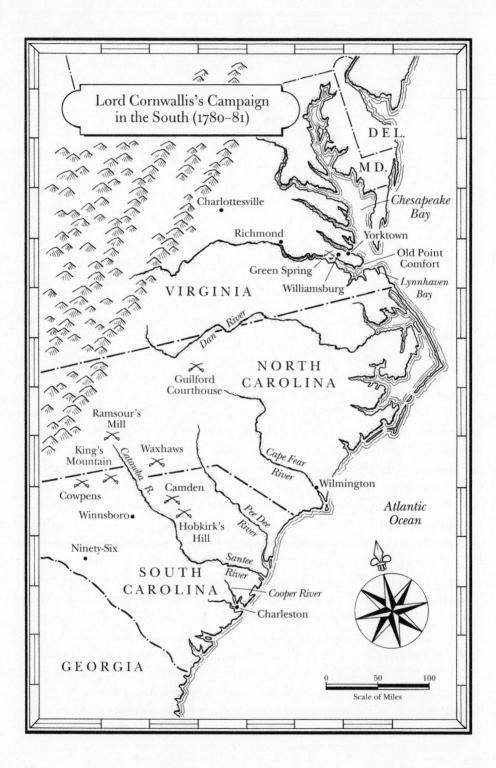

Lord Cornwallis's Campaign
in the South (1780–81)

DEL.

MD.

*Chesapeake
Bay*

Charlottesville

Richmond

Yorktown

Green Spring

Old Point
Comfort

Williamsburg

*Lynnhaven
Bay*

VIRGINIA

Dan River

NORTH
CAROLINA

Guilford
Courthouse

Ramsour's
Mill

Catawba R.

Waxhaws

*Cape Fear
River*

King's
Mountain

Wilmington

Cowpens

Camden

*Atlantic
Ocean*

Winnsboro

*Pee Dee
River*

Hobkirk's
Hill

Ninety-Six

*Santee
River*

SOUTH
CAROLINA

Cooper River

Charleston

GEORGIA

0   50   100

Scale of Miles

to 8,742, of whom only 5,982 were fit for duty. Ethan Allen gave the impression that he might declare Vermont for the British. In a letter intercepted by the British less than six months before his great victory at Yorktown, George Washington had written that if the war did not end with the next campaign, the cause would die of poverty and exhaustion: "we are at the end of our tether . . . now or never our deliverance must come."[3]

Following the success of the conquest of Georgia and South Carolina, the British government had great expectations of Charles, Earl Cornwallis. His advance through the south, they hoped, would give the war the momentum so desired by Germain and George III.

I

William Smith, the loyalist chief justice of New York, thought that Cornwallis "had an unfavorable Physiognomy," being "heavy in his Make and Gait, with a Cast in his Eye." Cornwallis referred to himself as "rather corpulent," and he undeniably had a double chin. His face was distinguished by a wall eye that gave him a quizzical and wistful look, the result of an injury in a hockey game as a schoolboy at Eton College when he was hit by the future bishop of Durham. Cornwallis was painted by Thomas Gainsborough on his final return from America to Britain in 1783 (Figure 27). The portrait captured his strength of character and grim determination. He did not have a haughty appearance, but he possessed an air of authority. After dining with Cornwallis, John Peebles, a Scottish officer in the 42nd Regiment, described how the commander exuded "ease, elegance & temperance."[4]

Cornwallis was the most aristocratic of the British commanders in America. Born in Grosvenor Square in London, he was the sixth child and oldest son of Charles, first earl Cornwallis. Since the late fourteenth century, the family had lived in Suffolk where they had established their ancestral seat at Brome Hall. In his early twenties, he succeeded to the title and became a member of the House of Lords. His later promotion and success undoubtedly owed a great deal to his status and connections. He was a lieutenant colonel by the age of twenty-three, a privy councillor at the age of thirty and, three years later, he became constable of the Tower of London. There was military tradition in his family. His uncle was a general and his brother William served with distinction in the Royal Navy during the Revolution.

Cornwallis was educated at Eton College and was a sufficiently enthusiastic alumnus that he joined the Eton Club in 1790. He briefly attended Clare College, Cambridge, but his real vocation began at the age of eighteen when he joined the Grenadier Guards. He dedicated his life to military service and later wrote that "I love the army." Like many of his fellow commanders in America, Cornwallis went to great lengths to improve his military skills and knowledge of warfare. In 1757, he obtained leave from the army to travel to Europe with a Prussian military officer. He became one of the few British officers to attend a military academy, when he studied at one of the finest in Europe at Turin. He visited many German courts where he debated battle tactics.[5]

Upon news of the outbreak of the Seven Years' War, Cornwallis immediately tried and failed to join his regiment in Germany. He was nineteen years old and determined to volunteer, writing to his father that he could never expect promotion if he did not serve in some capacity. With a determination and defiance that was characteristic of his life, he joined the army of Britain's ally Frederick the Great, though this was specifically forbidden by George II and Cornwallis's father had to extricate his son. A few weeks later, Cornwallis was appointed aide-de-camp to the marquess of Granby, a good start to an army career since the role of aide-de-camp to a prominent general was often a fast track to promotion. Cornwallis was present at the battle of Minden (1759) when Lord George Germain was disgraced and replaced by Granby. In 1761, Cornwallis became a regimental commander and served with distinction in Germany at the battle of Vellinghausen; in the following year, he saw action at Wilhelmsthal and Lutterberg. He was an experienced veteran of European warfare before his arrival in America.[6]

It was because of Cornwallis's dedication to the military life that he volunteered for service in America in 1775. He had actually disapproved of the British policies that triggered the Revolution. In 1765, he had been one of only six members of the House of Lords who voted against the Stamp Act, the first direct tax imposed by Britain upon America. The following year, he similarly supported the Rockingham Whigs in repealing the Stamp Act. His voting record demonstrated his independence in regard to colonial policy. The same year he opposed the Rockingham Whigs when they passed the Declaratory Act which asserted that Parliament had absolute authority over America.[7]

Like the Howe brothers, Cornwallis also disliked the war in America. Apart from being motivated in volunteering by a sense of duty, he was also enticed by the prospect of an expedition in the south under the command of a fellow officer in the Guards, Henry Clinton. Cornwallis's offer to serve was welcomed by Lord North as an example that would lend credit to the government and its policies in America, at a time when the "Ardor of the Nation in this cause has not hitherto arisen to the pitch one could wish." Because of his reservations about the war, Cornwallis came to be accused of being a hypocrite. In a speech in the House of Commons in November 1780, John Wilkes asked what he was to think of Cornwallis who carried "fire and sword against the Americans" but "had told him some years ago that he disapproved of the American War, and that he did not think this country had any right to exercise taxation over America." In America, however, Cornwallis became less sympathetic to the revolutionaries. He shared the view of the home government that "these unhappy people have been kept in utter darkness by the tyranny of their wicked leaders." Nevertheless, he appreciated that it was ultimately a war of opinion and persuasion, writing that there "is but one way of inducing the violent rebels to become our friends, and that is by convincing them it is in their interest to be so."[8]

As a soldier, Cornwallis was without pretension. He had no patience for pomp and fanfare. He mocked the vanity of titles and believed that reputation was more important, since no one cared whether the great generals of the past were Knights of the Garter. As a general, he personally led assaults at the front of his army. He was almost reckless in exposing himself to the enemy, and like Washington, he had horses shot from under him. He had a reputation for showing concern for the welfare of his troops. In the adversity of marches, he suffered the same deprivation as his men, eating the same food and sleeping in the same conditions. Cornwallis was committed in every way to the profession of soldiering. It was his life. According to one of his men, his army was his family: "he is the father. There are no Parties, no Competitions." Cornwallis had married in 1768. Rather than making a dynastic alliance, he had chosen Jemima Tulikens, the daughter of a modestly comfortable military family. Although she begged him not to go to America, he felt compelled to leave her and their two children whom "he loved." She even tried to get his uncle the archbishop of Canterbury to intervene to persuade him not to go to America. After eight years of a happy marriage, he would only see her once again and then only for a month. The army was and still remains a profession that demands great personal sacrifice.[9]

Before his departure to America on February 10, 1776, Cornwallis was promoted to the rank of major general. As colonel of the 33rd Regiment, he was granted the privilege of taking his unit to reinforce Sir Henry Clinton in North Carolina, and he took the regiment with him throughout his career, including in the Third Mysore War against Tipu Sultan in India (1790–92). Long before its association with Cornwallis, the regiment had fought at the battle of Dettingen in 1743, when George II was the last British monarch to personally command his troops. Established in 1702, the 33rd Regiment had the motto *Virtutis fortunae comes* ("Fortune favors the brave"). Long-lived regiments had their own distinctive traditions, uniforms, march tunes, colors, insignia, and table silver. It was gradually becoming the practice for men to serve for their entire careers in a regiment and for a regiment to recruit men from a particular region, which helped to create solidarity and to stiffen morale. As colonel of his regiment, Cornwallis was responsible for equipping the men, often at his own expense.[10]

II

On arrival in North Carolina, Cornwallis was warmly welcomed by Clinton, but he had an inauspicious introduction to the war in America. During the expedition to Charleston, Cornwallis was to observe the crippling quarrels between Clinton and Commodore

Sir Peter Parker. He witnessed the mismanagement of the campaign but did not record his thoughts for posterity. After the attempted attack was abandoned, Cornwallis and Clinton left to join Sir William Howe in the conquest of New York. If there was a window of opportunity to win the war, this was it.

After arriving at Staten Island in August 1776, Cornwallis participated in forcing Washington's army out of Long Island, Manhattan, and New Jersey. He commanded the reserve wing of the army when Howe defeated Washington at the battle of Long Island (August 27–28). In the final stages of the battle, Cornwallis led the vanguard of Clinton's successful turning movement through Jamaica Pass, and his troops foiled a counteroffensive of the enemy. Both Cornwallis and Clinton had shown courage to the point of folly by being so visible on the battlefield, which was particularly dangerous since enemy marksmen aimed at officers. Again with Clinton, Cornwallis was part of the successful rout of the enemy at Kip's Bay when the British first landed on Manhattan (September 15). He forced them to retreat along the Port Road (now Lexington Avenue). On the morning of November 20, he successfully commanded an expedition of more than four thousand troops to capture Fort Lee, one of the rebel forts guarding the Hudson. Although Washington and two thousand troops escaped shortly in advance of the attack, Cornwallis captured some fifty cannon, large quantities of flour, and the baggage of Washington's army.

During Howe's occupation of New Jersey, Cornwallis was to go in hot pursuit of Washington. He chased the retreating enemy army for more than eighty miles, but failed to fulfill his boast of "bagging the fox." His path was slowed by trees blocking the roads, destroyed bridges, and enemy sniper fire. On December 1, although he almost caught up with "the fox" on the banks of the Raritan at New Brunswick, he stopped in obedience to orders from Howe to go no further. It was to be regarded as one of the great missed opportunities of the war, but his troops were exhausted from the week-long pursuit. Insisting that his force could not have forded the river and fought a battle, he waited for four days until Howe reached him from New York. Although "the fox" had skillfully evaded capture, the revolutionary cause was at its lowest ebb and in constant retreat. With the campaign season over and the British troops about to begin their winter quarters, Cornwallis prepared to go on leave to London and was actually waiting for his ship in New York when he heard that Washington had returned across the Delaware and attacked the Hessian guard at Trenton.

On New Year's Day 1777, Cornwallis again took to the field and rode fifty miles to round up eight thousand troops in Princeton for an attack on Washington. Although the march was only a ten-mile distance, it took an entire day owing to thick mud, random enemy fire, and a group of snipers whom he mistook for the enemy army. He finally caught up with Washington at Trenton. Thinking he had "bagged his fox" and not wanting to risk a night assault, Cornwallis fatally rested his troops without placing guards to watch the enemy, satisfied that their withdrawal was blocked by the Delaware River. Sir Henry Clinton later described Cornwallis's actions at Trenton as "the most consummate ignorance ever heard of [in] any officer above a corporal." Leaving a few hundred men with camp fires burning and wrapping the wheels of his gun carriages to muffle the sound, Washington and his army escaped under cover of darkness. Cornwallis tried to dismiss this as a last defiant gasp of the enemy, but Washington turned the tables on him and advanced on Princeton, which was protected by a rearguard of Cornwallis's army. He took the precaution to destroy the bridge that would have allowed Cornwallis to follow him, and Cornwallis returned to New York. After overcoming stiff resistance from the garrison, Washington occupied Princeton. When some British troops barricaded themselves in the college hall of modern-day Princeton University, Captain Alexander Hamilton ordered a round of cannon fire and forced their surrender. Washington was to claim that, with less than a thousand extra troops, his army might have advanced further and won the war.[11]

After a brief leave in London, Cornwallis returned to America to experience yet another disastrous sequence of events, leading this time to the British defeat at Saratoga. Cornwallis again had some share of the blame. He was one of a minority of commanders who supported the intention of Sir William Howe to occupy Philadelphia. The plan was vigorously opposed by Sir Henry Clinton who urged Howe to march north to Albany in support of General John Burgoyne. With a flotilla of 228 ships and 12,500 troops, however, Cornwallis and Howe disembarked at Elkton in Maryland, about forty-five miles from Philadelphia. When Washington tried to prevent their advance on the city at Brandywine (September 11, 1777), Cornwallis was instrumental in the ensuing victory when he led eight thousand British troops in dividing the enemy, by wheeling around his opponents, crossing a creek, and reappearing at their rear, where he ensnared the forces of Major General John Sullivan. Later in the month, when Howe feigned an attack on Reading and Washington took the bait of Howe, Cornwallis marched at the head of three thousand British troops into Philadelphia. The city fell without a shot.

After news arrived of the disaster that had befallen Burgoyne at Saratoga, Cornwallis finally took advantage of his permission for a leave and returned to England aboard HMS *Brilliant*. Possibly because he was party to some of Howe's most disastrous decisions, Cornwallis always remained loyal to him and later acted as a witness for him during a parliamentary inquiry into Saratoga. He even spoke well of him in the privacy of his family, to whom he said that Howe deserved the gratitude of his country as he had served "with fidelity, assiduity, and with great ability." Cornwallis requested permission to resign, which Thomas Hutchinson thought was out of sympathy for Howe, "of whom he had been a principal favorite." Howe had consistently shown preference for Cornwallis over Clinton and had gone out of his way to praise him extravagantly in official dispatches to Germain. Cornwallis reciprocated by his continued loyalty to Howe, which affected his future relationship with Clinton.[12]

On arriving in London in January 1779, Cornwallis had a five-hour private audience with George III, in which Horace Walpole claimed that he spoke of "the hopelessness of success" in America. In March, Cornwallis and General Charles Grey advised the government that the subjugation of America was "impracticable." Despite his earlier opposition to the war, Cornwallis continued to be favored by the king, who undoubtedly appreciated his honesty, his commitment to service, his loyalty, and his professionalism. It also mattered that he was an aristocrat. George III had once chided Lord North for preferring a private gentleman over the eldest son of an earl, saying that such an attitude was diametrically opposite to what he had known all his life. In spite of his negative assessment of the war in America, Cornwallis was promoted a lieutenant general and appointed second in command to Sir Henry Clinton in America. He was additionally given a dormant commission to succeed to the command in the event of the death or resignation of Clinton. The commission was merely a precaution to prevent the elevation of Lieutenant General Baron Wilhelm von Knyphausen, who commanded the majority of the German mercenaries and was the most senior army officer after Clinton. However, the dormant commission assumed great significance, since Clinton had indicated his wish to resign in favor of Cornwallis. In his letter requesting to resign in August 1779, Clinton wrote to Germain that "I do seriously give it as my opinion that, if the endeavors of any man are likely, under the present prospects, to be attended with success, Lord Cornwallis, for many reasons, stands among the first."[13]

Traveling aboard the same ship as the Carlisle Peace Commission in April 1778, Cornwallis returned to America. Like Clinton, he was appalled when he discovered that the government at home had ordered a withdrawal from Philadelphia and the reallocation of a significant part of the army to the Caribbean. He immediately tendered his resignation on the grounds that "no offensives can be undertaken" in America. After entering the city in such glory seven months earlier, Cornwallis experienced the humiliation of the retreat to New York. He commanded the rear of Clinton's army at the battle of Monmouth against Washington (June 28, 1778) and led the elite of the troops in the final engagement of the battle. After receiving news that his wife was ill in December, Cornwallis returned to England with the failed Carlisle Peace Commission and resigned from his command in America.[14]

In England, Cornwallis rushed to the bedside of his wife, who died less than a month later. She supposedly told a servant that she was dying of a broken heart, and "she requested that a thorn-tree should be planted above the vault where she was buried, as nearly as possible over the heart—significant of the sorrow which destroyed her life." She also directed that no stone should be inscribed to her memory. She was indeed buried with a plain slab of marble over her remains in the vault at the family home in Culford. The thorn tree planted above her grave was eventually removed but was still flourishing as late as 1857. Cornwallis never remarried nor was ever rumored to have had any love affairs after her death.[15]

Disconsolate at her loss, Cornwallis changed his mind and once again resumed his role as second in command to Clinton, even though he was every bit as pessimistic as Clinton about the prospects of success in America. He wrote to his brother William that he was not motivated "with views of conquest and ambition" since "nothing can be expected" of the war in America. He explained that he was returning because he could not bear to remain at home, he wanted a change of scene, he had many friends serving in America, and he loved the army. His reasons for going back also reflected a restless quality that was a characteristic of his career. As much as Washington yearned for Mount Vernon and Jefferson for Monticello, Cornwallis claimed to desire the domestic tranquility of his Culford estate in Suffolk, but he spent most of his life abroad in Europe, in America, in Ireland and in India. He never retired.[16]

III

When he arrived at Charleston in February 1780, Cornwallis was once again warmly received by Clinton. He was treated as the heir apparent and consulted on every decision. The situation of limbo, however, became a major source of friction since Cornwallis expected at any moment to replace Clinton, and the amicability between them turned into enmity. There was already a history of tension. Clinton thought that Cornwallis had missed a golden opportunity to annihilate Washington at Trenton. He also nurtured a grudge for the rest of his life that Cornwallis had repeated a confidential conversation to Howe in which Clinton had said that he "would gladly prefer the heading of three companies at a distance" from Howe than "to serving in any capacity immediately under him." Furthermore, Clinton thought that Cornwallis had schemed for an independent command during his leave in England.[17]

While the two generals were still besieging Charleston, the breach between them became more pronounced. According to Clinton, Cornwallis suddenly began to start behaving differently toward him, ceasing to offer advice, confining himself to his routine duties, and hardly ever visiting headquarters. Clinton also suspected Cornwallis of undermining him among the other officers. He believed that Cornwallis was spreading rumors that he was about to resign to be succeeded by Cornwallis. Clinton later claimed that Cornwallis admitted that he had told the other officers that Clinton had suppressed orders from the home government clarifying the status of officers in the provincial loyalist regiments and giving them greater parity in relation to the ranks of the regular army. This was a sensitive issue because regular officers, who had spent their lives in the army, resented loyalists obtaining equal rank and pay. Clinton also attributed the withdrawal of Cornwallis from his headquarters to a desire to absolve himself of any responsibility should Clinton fail. Cornwallis did indeed ask the home government to reassign him to any theater of action where Clinton was not in command.[18]

Despite their rift, Cornwallis assisted Clinton in his crowning achievement of the war, the capture of Charleston. During the siege of the city in April 1780, Cornwallis helped cut off any possibility of escape for the garrison by blocking their retreat across the Cooper River. In conjunction with loyalist troops, he captured the few remaining enemy positions. When Clinton returned to New York and left him in command with eight thousand three hundred troops, Cornwallis set out to secure the rest of South Carolina and to destroy the remaining forces of the Continental Army, commanded by Colonel Abraham Buford, who had arrived too late to defend Charleston and had turned back to North Carolina. Unable to catch up on foot, Cornwallis ordered a pursuit of Buford by loyalist cavalry under the command of Lieutenant Colonel Banastre Tarleton.

The name of Tarleton was to become synonymous with ruthlessness in the south, and his actions were to illustrate the problems the British faced in pacifying the population of South Carolina. As the commander of a loyalist cavalry and mounted infantry regiment known as the British Legion, Banastre Tarleton became the eyes and ears of Cornwallis's army. Although his original commission was purchased, he had risen quickly in the army through merit and was only twenty-six years old at the time of the siege of Charleston. Like Major André, he was not from a traditional landed background but from a mercantile family with colonial connections. His family, like that of André, owned land in Grenada in the Caribbean. Their family backgrounds in trade may explain the social pretensions of both and their desire to excel in the army. In contrast to the majority of his fellow officers, Tarleton had not joined the army in his teens but had attended Oxford University and later volunteered for service in America.

Tarleton was described as having an "almost femininely beautiful" face and "a form that was a perfect model of manly strength and vigor." His portrait by Sir Joshua Reynolds is one of the most captivating in the National Gallery in London (Figure 28). Painted after his return from the war to England in 1782, it is a life-size canvas in which he is portrayed in a dramatic stooping posture, as if about to draw his sword, against a background of a wild-eyed horse, a plume of smoke, the open barrel of a cannon, and the flag of the British Legion. The horse is restrained by a disembodied arm that holds its bridle. Apart from the bilious white smoke, the background is painted in a bloody red hue, giving sharper focus to the arresting presence of Tarleton. He is depicted in bright colors, wearing a white neck cloth, a green tunic, pale buff breeches, and cavalry boots— the uniform of the British Legion. His eyes glance alertly to one side and avoid the gaze of the viewer. His flamboyant black headdress with swan's feathers continued to be worn by light dragoons in the British army until 1814 and became known as a "Tarleton" helmet in France as well as England.[19]

In what became known as "Buford's Massacre" at Waxhaws in South Carolina on May 29, Tarleton exhibited the bravado, courage, and energy that were to be his hallmark in pursuing reinforcements commanded by Buford and a few cavalry who had managed to escape from Charleston, representing the sole remnants of the Continental Army garrison in the South. Tarleton and about 130 loyalist cavalry rode 150 miles in fifty-four hours. He mounted his horses with two riders in order to carry some 140 infantrymen, and many of his horses died from exhaustion in the relentless pursuit. Tarleton and his British Legion caught up with Buford's troops in an area known as Waxhaws, just south of the border of North Carolina. After sending a flag of truce with an offer of surrender, Tarleton commenced an attack in which 113 enemy troops were killed and 150 wounded of a force that had consisted of between 300 and 350 soldiers of the Continental Army. Tarleton had only minor losses among his own men.[20]

Tarleton himself called the affair "a slaughter" in his memoirs. He claimed that the fatalities were so high because the enemy had been ordered not to fire until the cavalry were visible and that his approach was so fast that they were cut to pieces before they could fire. During the charge into the enemy lines, Tarleton was dismounted when his horse fell over at the sound of a volley of guns. He claimed that this "stimulated . . . [his] soldiers to a vindictive asperity not easily restrained." He was also to insist that he did everything to provide for the wounded and that it was not a total massacre. He received commendations for his action at Waxhaws from both Clinton and from Cornwallis. He became known to posterity as "Bloody Tarleton," and the killing of prisoners who had already surrendered was dubbed "Tarleton's Quarter."[21]

On August 16, Cornwallis followed up his success at Charleston with a spectacular victory at Camden, where he defeated General Horatio Gates, the victor of Saratoga. Although outnumbered, Cornwallis characteristically decided to defy the odds based on the knowledge that the majority of the enemy troops were citizen militia. Both generals had hoped to capture the respective camps of their opponents in surprise attacks, and they simultaneously ordered their armies to march at about 10:00 P.M. The advance guards of the two armies met about 2:00 A.M. nine miles north of Camden. At daybreak, there was poor visibility on the battlefield owing to hazy weather and thick smoke. The site was hemmed in by swamps on the right and left, with an open pine forest that shielded the army of Gates. With the two armies lined up in opposition to one another, Cornwallis observed movement among the Virginia and North Carolina militia who stood facing some of his finest troops, the 23rd Regiment (the Royal Welch Fusiliers) and his own 33rd Regiment. It was precisely the superior training and discipline of such troops that made the British so confident of success in America. Cornwallis ordered these regiments to advance, recounting to Germain that they did so "in good order and with the cool intrepidity of experienced British soldiers, keeping up a constant fire or making use of bayonets as opportunities offered." After encountering "an obstinate resistance for three-quarters of an hour," his troops "threw the enemy into total confusion and forced them to give way in all quarters." Breaking through the enemy forward lines, they were able to wheel behind the regular troops of the Continental Army. He then ordered his cavalry to complete the advantage gained. Tarleton described in his memoirs how "rout and slaughter ensued in every quarter."[22]

As the color bearer of the 23rd regiment, Sergeant Roger Lamb later recalled "Lord Cornwallis's judgment in planning, his promptitude in executing, and his fortitude and coolness during the action," which "justly attracted universal applause and admiration." At the battle of Camden, Gates's army lost 1,050 men who were killed or captured. Of still greater significance, the southern rebel army was dispersed and left shattered. British losses were 68 killed and 256 wounded. Among the dead on the American side was Baron Jean de Kalb, a major general in the Continental Army who introduced the marquis de Lafayette to America and had been his mentor. After his horse had been shot from under him, de Kalb continued fighting remorselessly, suffering eleven wounds before he was finally killed. Horatio Gates, the opposing commander, a former British army officer, famously fled the battlefield, galloping 180 miles in three and a half days. He had owed one of his first promotions to Cornwallis's uncle who had been a general and governor of Nova Scotia. Alexander Hamilton remarked acidly of Gates that it was an admirable pace for a man of his age, but that it was a disgrace to a general and a soldier. Gates is generally thought to have shown poor judgment in the movements of his troops before the battle and in his positioning of the militia. The mistakes of commanders were never all on one side during the American war. He was replaced in the southern command by thirty-eight-year-old General Nathanael Greene who was to be a much more equal match for Cornwallis than Gates. Greene was to compensate for the weakness of his army by coordinating with partisan resistance groups that arose throughout the south.[23]

Within two weeks of winning the battle of Camden, Cornwallis discovered that the pacification of the population was much more difficult than he and Clinton had imagined. It was difficult to distinguish between friends and foe when enemy combatants took oaths of allegiance and returned to open rebellion. He had one instance of an entire militia regiment absconding when they were accompanying some wounded and sick soldiers. Cornwallis consequently resorted to excessive methods of coercion. Although he had complained about the effect of the oath of allegiance required by Clinton, Cornwallis gave orders that anyone who had taken an oath and had subsequently joined the enemy should be imprisoned and their property confiscated. As for militiamen who had fought on his side and then joined the resistance, he ordered that they be immediately hanged, and he personally ordered several executions. The enemy newspapers published a copy of a letter he wrote to a loyalist officer, in which he ordered "the most *vigorous* measures to *extinguish the rebellion* . . . in the strictest manner." The letter as published omitted passages referring to oaths of allegiance to make it seem as if he was punishing all alike. The letter occasioned accusations of war crimes by General Washington to Sir Henry Clinton. Cornwallis retorted that "tortures and inhuman murders . . . are every day committed by the enemy." He repeatedly warned that without restraints "the war in this quarter will become truly savage."[24]

Aware of the ability of cavalry to incite terror, Cornwallis sent Tarleton to intimidate and awe the countryside, which brought momentary gains. Despite the humane image of Cornwallis, his favorite officers, such as Banastre Tarleton, Nisbet Balfour, and Lord Francis Rawdon, were advocates of brutal repression. Tarleton thought Cornwallis too lenient, and claimed that his moderation "did not reconcile enemies, but . . . discouraged friends." Cornwallis tended to indulge his officers and men for the sake of good will and unity, at the expense of disciplining them against plunder and crime. His army was notorious for its bad behavior and especially for plunder, though he had earlier disapproved of such failure to punish plunder by General Howe.[25]

The British further alienated the backcountry Scots-Irish population by their prejudice against Presbyterians, associating religious dissent and nonconformity with rebellion. Major James Wemyss burned the Presbyterian Church in Indiantown, in the belief that all such churches and meeting houses were "sedition shops." Whether it was true that pregnant women were bayoneted and graves dug up, such stories circulated in the enemy press to the disadvantage of the British. Clinton's earlier proclamations requiring oaths of allegiance, together with the use of terror, alienated people who might otherwise have remained neutral. Until the British Legion burnt his house in the High Hills of the Santee in South Carolina, Thomas Sumter, "the Carolina Gamecock," had retired from the military life, only to become one of the most inveterate and effective rebel partisan leaders in the backcountry. Rather than consent to an order to join the British army, Isaac Hayne returned to his life as a rebel militia officer, but was captured and executed, without trial, on charges of espionage and treason in Charleston. Following his hanging in August 1781, Hayne became a martyr, and the indignation at his death assisted Greene in recapturing South Carolina.[26]

The future president of the United States, Andrew Jackson, who came from a Scots-Irish family, lost all his immediate relatives and was orphaned during the war in the south. His oldest brother died of heat exhaustion during the battle of Stone Ferry (June 20, 1779). At the age of only fourteen, Andrew Jackson and his younger brother fought in the war and were taken prisoner by the British. Later dubbed "Old Hickory," he was scarred for life by the saber of a British officer, after refusing to clean the officer's boots. He and his brother contracted smallpox during their confinement and his young brother died two days after their mother had secured their release. His mother then died of cholera, which she contracted when nursing the wounded aboard one of the notorious British prisoner of war ships. He became a confirmed Anglophobe for the rest of his life and was to avenge himself when he defeated the British in 1815 at the battle of New Orleans during the War of 1812.

IV

There is symmetry between the folly of Burgoyne's march south to Saratoga and that of Cornwallis's march north to Yorktown. Military historians debate why Burgoyne risked marching south from Fort Edward in the same way that they question why Cornwallis advanced north beyond North Carolina into Virginia. Although Cornwallis had none of the outward vanity of Burgoyne, the two men were similar in that they were both junior generals and neither of them was the commander in chief of the British army in America. Both blamed their subsequent failures on rigid orders and insufficient latitude. They both expected to march through predominantly friendly territory. They both ignored the chain of command and went over the heads of their superiors to communicate independently with Lord George Germain. They both allowed their supply lines to become overextended and their forces suffered harassment by enemy militia. They presided over the two most decisive British defeats of the American Revolutionary War.

Since March 1778, the home government had intended a fundamental shift in the war from the north to the south. The strategy was predicated on the assumption that the potential for loyalist support was greater in the south, which would enable the war to be continued with more limited resources. This sea change in British strategy was never the plan of Sir Henry Clinton, who always believed that the fate of the war would be decided in the environs of New York. Until he was confident of substantial naval superiority and the arrival of reinforcements from Britain, Clinton was only interested in capturing South Carolina and establishing a post in the Chesapeake. However, Clinton gave broad discretion to Cornwallis to advance into North Carolina once he had secured South Carolina. Clinton initially left only a small part of the army for Cornwallis, but he effectively reinforced him by sending expeditions to the Chesapeake until some three-fifths of the British army in America were in the south under Cornwallis.

Since 1775, the British had toyed with the idea of detaching the southern states from the rebellion. The south seemed to offer many advantages. From the reports of the former royal governors it appeared that there was stronger loyalist sentiment in the south. With their plantation agriculture, the southern states had the richest economy in America, but they were vulnerable owing to their dependence on imports and exports. The labor on the plantations was performed by slaves, who made up over half the total population of South Carolina, a third of the population of Virginia, and the majority of the half-million slave population in America. It was a source of American weakness that the British had appreciated early in the war when Lord Dunmore had issued a proclamation inviting the slaves of rebel masters to rally to the royal standard in Virginia (November 7, 1775).[27]

The British also had the advantage in the south of an alliance with the Creek and Cherokee Indians. In South Carolina, the slaves and the Cherokees had attempted to revolt in 1776. The southern states were the most populous states, but they were vulnerable because their inhabitants were widely dispersed among plantations and throughout the backcountry. There were sectional differences between the western and eastern settlers, which had led to a virtual civil war fought by the Regulator Movement against the colonial militia in the western Carolinas in the late 1760s and early 1770s. The south offered more open territory, which allowed for the possibility of using cavalry regiments. Furthermore, after three years of relative tranquility, the southern states appeared less prepared for defense. The proximity of the south to the Caribbean allowed for more joint British naval operations with the North American fleet. There was a chance that the south might also be able to provide lumber and provisions to meet the dire need of the British Caribbean, where one-fifth of the slave population had died during a drought on the island of Antigua.

The south did indeed become the focus of the war, though this was never the objective of Clinton as commander in chief, who continued to stress the importance of New York. The change was gradual and was necessitated by the demands of Cornwallis. Clinton's ideas about strategy became increasingly irrelevant, partly because he failed to offer a good alternative other than remaining on the defensive. Cornwallis was pursuing the preferred strategy of the government of giving priority to subduing the south. Furthermore, he was better connected than Clinton with Germain and with George III. His father had been one of the very few people to appear as a favorable witness at the court martial of Germain after the battle of Minden. Germain had encouraged him to apply for his first command in America in 1776. Germain and George III had talked throughout the war about the need for bold strokes and alacrity, which was precisely the strategy that Cornwallis pursued after the capture of Charleston. They could not but contrast his movement and pace with the apparent lethargy of Clinton.

In a deleted passage of his memoirs, Clinton attributed Cornwallis's whirlwind movement through the south to naked ambition and an attempt to supplant him as commander in chief. In reality, the southern invasion was hesitant and faltering. Cornwallis revised his assessment of the military situation in the south, as he began to doubt the strength of the loyalists and their ability to pacify the areas in rebellion. He became convinced that the only way to suppress the resistance in South Carolina was to stop the supplies from the north and destroy expectations of future assistance by invading North Carolina and later Virginia. He hoped that such a strategy might create a groundswell of loyalist support for the army and cause the morale of the rebels to collapse. His ideas were consistent with those of the home government, which wanted more aggressive tactics and what the king called "bold strokes." Unlike Clinton, Cornwallis never indicated any appreciation of the importance of naval support and the perils of his situation in the event of an appearance of a larger enemy fleet. It was also against his nature to choose the safest option of remaining in a defensive posture in South Carolina. He believed essentially that the best form of defense was offense. It was a strategy that suited the restless quality of his character and his itinerant lifestyle. He believed in a war of conquest.[28]

The only opposition in the south was from irregular forces and militiamen, because Cornwallis had defeated most of the southern units of the Continental Army at the battle of Camden in 1780. The Continental Army did indeed begin to revive under the commands of Generals Nathanael Greene and Daniel Morgan, but it was outnumbered by Cornwallis. As late as February 1781, Greene told Thomas Sumter that he estimated the odds against him to be ten to one if he engaged in an open battle with Cornwallis. Like Washington, Greene aimed primarily to keep his army intact and to avoid the main British army. The vulnerability of the south was a major reason that Cornwallis was willing to gamble in invading North Carolina and Virginia.[29]

Although it offered many attractions, the south also had disadvantages. It was traversed by waterways with numerous creeks and swamps, which were perfect hideouts for rebel bands. It was crisscrossed by big rivers like the Catawba-Wataree, the Broad, the Yadkin-Pee-Dee, the Dan, the Cape Fear River, the James, and the Rivanna, which had to be forded and bridges rebuilt. The army's strength was weakened by fevers like malaria, to which locals and settlers were more resistant. Clinton did not allow for the number of sick in the southern army and therefore overestimated the number of troops available for operations. Compared to the compact region of the lower Hudson and New York, the distances in the south were great, with the consequence that supply lines were long and scattered army garrisons were isolated. The western interior was far from the coast, making it more difficult for the army to communicate with the navy, and thereby removing one of the most important advantages of the British.

The anticipated support of the Creek and Cherokee Indians proved disappointing. A Cherokee rebellion had been defeated in 1776, and at Long Island in 1777, they signed a peace treaty with the states of North Carolina and Virginia, in which they ceded all their lands east of the Blue Ridge and north of the Nolichucky River. They similarly made an agreement with Georgia and South Carolina at Dewitt's Corner, South Carolina. After uniting at Chicamauga in 1779, the Creeks and Cherokees assisted the failed attempt by the British to hold West Florida against the Spanish, which deflected them from supporting Cornwallis. In addition, their numbers were decimated by smallpox in 1779–80. Cornwallis intensified his efforts to obtain their support with promises of food, ammunition, and clothing. They were regarded as a sufficient threat in Virginia for the governor, Thomas Jefferson, to divert resources to fighting a war in the west against the Cherokees. Nevertheless, the alliance with the Creeks and Cherokees largely served to earn the British the hostility of frontiersmen and pioneers in the south.[30]

Determined to take advantage of his victory at Camden, Cornwallis marched into North Carolina, intending to gain the initiative and to rally the loyalists. For a while he seemed successful in his advance into the south but his fortune changed suddenly with the defeat of a loyalist detachment at King's Mountain (October 7, 1780) which he had sent into Tryon County to "protect our friends, who were supposed to be numerous there" and then to cross the Catawba River to protect the rear of his army in North Carolina. It was a small-scale engagement, with only one British soldier present, Major Patrick Ferguson, who commanded the loyalists. Nevertheless, Sir Henry Clinton thought in retrospect that the "unpromising turn our affairs took at the time" began with the defeat at King's Mountain; it reminded him of the old adage "that the greatest events often proceed from little causes."[31]

Major Patrick Ferguson exemplified the ambition, motivation, professional dedication and courage of young officers like Banastre Tarleton, Lord Rawdon, and John Simcoe. They all commanded loyalist units that were used to quell resistance in the backcountry and the frontier. Like Ferguson, they shared a belief in conducting the war vigorously and ruthlessly. Taking pride in their profession and regarding military operations as a science, this group of aspiring officers competed with one another for honor and glory. Although their ranks in these provincial corps were temporary, they were elevated in rank above their peers in the regular army which improved their prospects of receiving permanent promotions after the war, while causing envy and resentment among other officers. With their own independent commands, they had an opportunity to shine and eventually to become the generals of the British army. Not surprisingly, there were rivalries among them. Ferguson was not part of the coterie of officers favored by Cornwallis. He had been appointed by Clinton to be inspector general of the militia with a view to enlisting support, maintaining order, and supervising loyalist forces in western South Carolina. His responsibilities were wide-ranging, including such duties as arranging civil marriages. He was viewed with suspicion as someone who was too restless for mundane civil duties and policing. It was said that he wanted to carry on the war by himself.[32]

Ferguson had joined the army at fourteen when he became a cornet in the Scots Greys (Royal North British Dragoons). He purchased a commission in the 70th Foot in 1768 and served on the island of Tobago in the Caribbean. In response to the notoriously accurate enemy marksmen in 1776, Ferguson invented and patented the first breech-loading rifle in the British army. It was more accurate, had a faster rate of fire, and was more dependable in wet weather than the traditional Brown Bess smoothbore flintlock musket, which the British had used since the reign of Queen Anne. On arrival in Halifax in Canada in 1776, Ferguson was given permission to raise a rifle corps much like that of

Daniel Morgan. At the battle of Brandywine in 1777, his right arm was permanently shattered, and he was thereafter nicknamed by the rebels the "one-armed devil." Ferguson was far removed from the modern media image of the aristocratic dilettante officers of the British army.[33]

In October 1780, less than three months after Camden, Ferguson led 1,125 loyalists to King's Mountain, a high ridge with heavily wooded slopes in York County, South Carolina, about a mile and a half below the modern border of North Carolina. In a threat that backfired, he proclaimed his intention to march his army over the mountain, hang the rebel leaders, and "lay their country waste with fire and sword," unless they desisted from opposition. Becoming aware that large hordes of "over-the-mountain men" were assembling against him from across the Blue Ridge Mountains, he had started to retreat to join the main army of Cornwallis in Charlotte, but changed his mind and decided to face the enemy at King's Mountain. In an ill-considered appeal to the local populace, he warned them that they would be robbed and murdered, while their wives and daughters would be abused by the dregs of mankind, proclaiming that "If you choose to be pissed upon forever and ever by a set of mongrels, say so at once and let your women turn their backs upon you, and look out for real men to protect you." Ferguson began to sense that his enemies were closing in on him in large numbers and sent an urgent request to Cornwallis to send Tarleton. He never received reinforcements, however, for Tarleton was sick with malaria and Cornwallis was also ill with a fever that had affected much of his army, making it vulnerable to an attack. He had even recalled a battalion of the 71st Regiment who were on their way to King's Mountain. Ferguson was caught completely off guard by the enemy whose ranks had swelled from as far away as present Tennessee with frontiersmen and expert marksmen from South Carolina, North Carolina, and Virginia. His opponents were not well drilled, but they were skilled in Indian warfare. With about 200 men out foraging, Ferguson's remaining 900 men were outnumbered by approximately 1,790 backwoodsmen, who had appeared at about 4:00 P.M. when they tethered their horses and advanced in three parties up the sides of the mountain.[34]

Aged thirty-six, with twenty-one years of military experience behind him, Ferguson was distinctive among his men with his shattered right arm, a checkered shirt worn over his uniform, and a silver whistle with which he blew commands. His seemingly impregnable position turned out to be quite the opposite, as the surrounding trees, boulders, and ravines provided cover for the enemy, who had crept up the slopes unheard. Ferguson was trapped and ordered his men to fight back with their bayonets, which had been such a terrifying deterrent to citizen militia on so many occasions in the past. The engagement lasted only an hour. Mounted on a white horse, Ferguson made a valiant defense, galloping from one side of the summit to the other to instill morale, leading countercharges down the slopes and cutting down white flags raised by his own men. He finally made one desperate effort to break the enemy lines by charging among them. He was shot off his horse and his body fell, riddled with bullets. He did not live long enough to receive a message from Cornwallis saying that "I now consider you perfectly safe." As his men raised the white flag, the bloodshed continued: such was the spirit of revenge. Of the loyalists who had served under Ferguson, 157 were killed, 163 were too injured to move, and 700 were taken prisoner. The rebels had only 28 killed and 62 wounded.[35]

The defeat at King's Mountain "dispirited" the loyalists in North Carolina. It undermined British strategy in the south, both in enlisting support and in subduing the backcountry. It left vulnerable to attack the chain of army posts that Cornwallis had established during his advance through the Carolinas. Cornwallis had to give up his plans to launch a winter offensive in North Carolina and was forced to retreat back to South Carolina to support his posts at Camden and Ninety Six. He was unable to resume his planned attack for four months, which allowed time for General Nathanael Greene to reconstitute a southern detachment of the Continental Army in North Carolina. King's Mountain also encouraged the insurgency against the British in South Carolina. The resistance of partisan bands, especially those led by Francis Marion and Thomas Sumter, was particularly effective, with ambushes and hit-and-run raids. Marion, the "Swamp Fox," wreaked havoc on the British and loyalists in the backcountry. He had a remarkable knowledge of local geography and earned his nickname because of his ability to hide his men among the extensive marshes. The false news that Marion meditated an attack on the British arsenal at Camden caused Cornwallis to send Tarleton there. Sumter, the "Carolina Gamecock," with about a thousand men, threatened the British post at Ninety Six. His men were mounted and moved too quickly to be caught by the British. He was known for "Sumter's Law," by which he rewarded his men with plunder taken from loyalists.[36]

There were dozens of skirmishes in the interior of the lower south. As the enemy militia and partisan bands kept up the pressure on the British posts between Charleston and Winnsboro, Cornwallis found them far more troublesome than the enemy army "who always keep at a considerable distance, and retire on our approach." From North Carolina in January 1781, he wrote that the "constant incursions of refugees, North Carolinians, Back Mountain men, and the perpetual risings in different parts of the province, the invariable successes of all those parties against our militia, keep this whole country in continual alarm, and render the assistance of regular troops everywhere neces- sary." These rebel attacks weakened supply lines, retarded the progress of the army, and necessitated larger garrisons at each post. Cornwallis had some eight thousand troops just garrisoning posts stretching over two hundred miles from Savannah and Charleston in the south with strongholds at places like Augusta, Camden, Ninety Six, Orangeburg, and Georgetown. He additionally had to man fortresses like Fort Watson, Fort Motte, and Fort Granby.[37]

Cornwallis had the option of retreating to fight a defensive war in South Carolina or undoing the damage of King's Mountain by resuming his offensive in North Carolina. He chose to proceed with a second invasion of North Carolina, because he was able to redeploy a force sent by Clinton to Virginia under the command of Brigadier General Alexander Leslie. His first priority was to eliminate the threat posed by the infantry and cavalry of the newly resurgent southern detachments of the Continental Army. Generals Nathanael Greene and Daniel Morgan baited Cornwallis by dividing their army into separate detachments. Greene was playing for time because he was not yet strong enough to confront Cornwallis, and meanwhile Cornwallis ordered Tarleton to deal with Morgan. Known as "Old Wagoner," Morgan was the creator of a legendary rifle corps of marksmen who had been instrumental in the victory at Saratoga. Standing six foot tall, he still bore the scars from several hundred lashes that he had received as a punishment after brawling with a British soldier during the French and Indian War. The commanders on both sides were taking a risk and ignoring conventional military doctrine about the importance of concentrating force, but the stakes were high. Whereas Cornwallis had misgivings when he sent Ferguson to Tryon County, he was very confident that Tarleton could beat Morgan. Tarleton would be outnumbered, but he would be leading the best troops in the army, together with loyalists, against a largely militia force supported by units of the Continental Army.[38]

Like Prince Rupert when commanding the Royalist cavalry in the English Civil War, Tarleton relied on a crude formula of speed, shock, and daring. He rarely failed to appear on the horizon well ahead of the time that the enemy was warned to expect him and this occasion was no exception. Morgan was trying to make a tactical retreat and was not looking for a fight. Tarleton may have been hated but he was also feared. On discovering that Tarleton had already passed his outposts, less than five miles from his army, and having little time to prepare his ground, Morgan chose to face Tarleton in a former cattle pasture known as Cowpens, located within the borders of South Carolina about thirty miles west of King's Mountain. Tarleton and his men had marched for two days, short of food and sleep, crossing difficult creeks and rivers. They had continued to chase Morgan throughout the night before reaching Cowpens. Tarleton was satisfied that he had an advantageous position against a "vulnerable" enemy. The open field was ideal for cavalry and there was no exit for the enemy, owing to the west bend of a river behind his lines. The location had appalled Morgan's own officers. Tarleton is often criticized by military historians for not having rested his troops and waited, but such delays had led to lost opportunities for Howe at New Brunswick and Cornwallis at Trenton. It was also contrary to his temperament and tactics, which were to engage immediately and to create an aura of terror.

At the battle of Cowpens (January 17, 1781), Tarleton was lured into an elaborate and brilliantly conceived trap. Morgan arranged his troops into three lines standing about 150 yards behind one another on a slope. He ordered the first line not to fire until they could see their enemy clearly and then to fire two shots before falling back behind the next line while still firing. Morgan again had frontiersmen who were expert marksmen and veterans of partisan warfare, supported by regular troops of the Continental Army. The frontiersmen were able to run, load, and shoot with greater rapidity than the Continentals. Morgan had hidden his cavalry about half a mile behind his own front lines. He had anticipated that Tarleton would assume that the militia were withdrawing in fear and would continue forward only to be decimated by the regular soldiers on the back row. The entire battle lasted less than an hour.[39]

Cowpens was one of the few tactical defeats of the British army during the Revolutionary War. Tarleton lost at least some 800 men or the equivalent of one-sixth of Cornwallis's army. He escaped with only 250 of his dragoons, while he lost 110 killed, 200 wounded, and 527 taken prisoner. The prisoners of war included 60 former slaves who had deserted their plantations to join the British. Morgan lost 12 killed and 60 wounded. Tarleton fought to the end and narrowly managed to get away with forty of his cavalry. On hearing the news of the defeat, Cornwallis pressed down on his sword so hard that it snapped in two, and swore loudly that he would free Tarleton's captured men from Morgan "no matter what the cost." He wrote to Lord Rawdon, "the late affair has almost broke my heart." Owing to the defeat at Cowpens, Cornwallis had lost almost the whole of his light infantry troops. Daniel Morgan justifiably boasted that he had given Tarleton "a devil of a whipping."[40]

Cornwallis was undeterred. He admitted to Lord Rawdon that his situation was critical and that there was "infinite danger in proceeding," but the alternative "was certain ruin" if he retreated. He instead decided to catch up with the army of General Nathanael Greene before Greene could reunite with Morgan and slip across the Dan River into Virginia. It was the start of what became popularly known as "The Race for the Dan." Cornwallis was relentless in his efforts to press ahead in midwinter, with the army marching along red clay paths, which froze at night and turned to sticky mud during the day. When he heard that Greene had already crossed the Catawba River, Cornwallis ordered his soldiers to destroy all their baggage, leaving them without tents and almost without food. Cornwallis set an example by discarding his own belongings and wagons. According to Sergeant Roger Lamb, Cornwallis shared the army's privations and "would allow no distinction" in the treatment of the officers and men, "nor did he indulge himself even in the distinction of a tent; but in all things partook our sufferings, and seemed much more to feel for us than for himself." His officers did likewise "without a murmur." The image of him stripped down and sharing the same sleeping arrangements as his men is far removed from film portrayals of the hidebound aristocrat. He was no Burgoyne. He had turned his army into a light force to move with agility and speed. Clinton wrote mockingly that Cornwallis had been reduced to behaving like a barbaric Tartar.[41]

Cornwallis paid a price for his temerity. His troops were reduced to virtual scavengers and had to resort to plunder to live. Their health was endangered by hunger and by exposure at night. His pace was slowed by prisoners of war and the entourage of camp followers who accompanied the army. Forty-one-year-old Brigadier General Charles O'Hara lamented their "situation without Baggage, necessaries or Provisions of any sort for Officer or Soldier, in the most barren inhospitable unhealthy part of North America, opposed to the most savage, inveterate perfidious cruel Enemy with zeal and Bayonets only." Lord Cornwallis, wrote O'Hara, "was resolved to follow Greene's Army, to the end of the World." Greene ultimately retreated 250 miles through the Carolinas, comparable to the distance marched by the celebrated duke of Marlborough from the Low Countries to the Danube in the Blenheim campaign of 1704. When Greene heard that Cornwallis had burned his baggage, he supposedly said, "Then, he is ours!"[42]

As he resumed his march toward the Catawba, Cornwallis's soldiers were marching some twenty miles a day on virtually empty stomachs. They had difficulty moving through the fords, rivers, and intricate narrow roads, which were little more than clay paths. With much of his cavalry lost at Cowpens and with little knowledge of the surrounding hostile country, Cornwallis was marching blind and was uncertain about directions. His advance was contested at every stage. As his army crossed the Catawba at Cowan's Ford, the water was above waist deep and enemy militia awaited them on the other side of the bank. As they rode over the river, Cornwallis had his horse shot from under him but it did not drop until he reached the shore. Leslie's horses were carried down the river by the strong current and O'Hara's horse rolled with him for nearly forty yards. The delaying action by the enemy militia on the other side of the river exemplified the value of part-time citizen soldiers to the Continental Army. Tarleton regained some of his old magic and went in pursuit of the militia. Although heavily outnumbered at Tarrant's Tavern (February 1, 1781), Tarleton led the charge with the cry "remember the Cowpens." He later exaggerated the number of killed, but he claimed that his audacity "diffused such terror among the inhabitants" that the army passed through the rest of North Carolina without a shot fired from the militia. The pursuit of Morgan and Greene became a cat-and-mouse game, as the enemy commanders used feints and other ploys to stay ahead of the grasp of Cornwallis.[43]

Although the entire strategy of the southern campaign was based on winning local support, Cornwallis found the loyalists apathetic in North Carolina. He had difficulty obtaining reliable information about both local geography and enemy movements. In December 1780, he had written that "our friends hereabouts are so timid and so stupid that I can get no intelligence." This dearth of intelligence was to become a perennial theme of the war in the south. Tarleton described in his memoirs the impossibility of relying on the information of the inhabitants to direct the army to the best routes. Cornwallis was critically impeded by misinformation and inadequate knowledge of the local topography in the race to the Dan. When his army crossed Cowan's Ford on the

Catawba (February 1, 1781), their guide deserted them without suggesting the best of the two available routes to Virginia. Misled into believing that the lower fords were impassable, Cornwallis began to march to the upper fords of the Dan. After Cornwallis raised the royal standard and issued a proclamation for the loyalists to join him at Hillsborough (February 22), O'Hara wrote of the humiliation of having local people come "to stare at us," who then returned to their homes, with their curiosity satisfied. Tarleton similarly described the many hundreds of people who appeared at the camp "to talk over the proclamation, inquire the news of the day and take a view of the King's troops," but who showed no inclination to fight. Tarleton appreciated in retrospect that the army had never made a serious effort to assist the well-disposed inhabitants in North Carolina.[44]

This apathy reflected the popularity of the Revolution. Such spontaneous upsurge in support as took place worked, as it invariably had in the past, to the benefit of the rebellion. In North Carolina on February 27, 1776, the loyalists had risen prematurely, only to be defeated at Moore's Creek Bridge. Again in advance of the arrival of Cornwallis in North Carolina on June 20, 1780, nearly thirteen hundred poorly armed loyalists had been defeated in a battle at Ramsour's Mill. Americans fought Americans. "The violence of the Passions of these People, are beyond every curb of Religion and Humanity," wrote Brigadier General Charles O'Hara: "they are unbounded, and every Hour exhibits dreadfull, wanton, Mischiefs, Murders, and Violences of every kind, unheard of before." It was a civil war in which the opposing sides were unable to distinguish friend from foe, because neither side was wearing uniforms. Of the original force at Ramsour's Mill, only thirty loyalists survived to join Cornwallis. Although the British had made greater efforts to attract loyalist support after 1778, recruitment had actually declined. It was easier to attract officers than men. Efforts to raise two provincial corps and recruit loyalist units to replace losses in the army failed in South Carolina.[45]

In April 1781, Cornwallis wrote to Germain of the loyalists in North Carolina that "our experience has shown that their numbers are not so great as had been represented, and that their friendship was only passive." He despaired that his army endured such dangers and distresses marching hundreds of miles through hostile country, obstructed by innumerable rivers and creeks, "without one active or usefull friend, without intelligence, and without communication with any part of the country." After nearly a thousand miles of marching, O'Hara wrote in exasperation that the army never attracted more than a hundred adherents at any one time. Constantly opposed by fresh troops from every direction, the soldiers had marched barefoot, living off nothing but rotting animal flesh and small amounts of corn. With the "experiment" having been made to raise loyalist support, O'Hara found it "impossible that Government could in so important a matter, have been so grossly deceived." He dismissed such expectations of support as "total infatuation," and asked when would the "Government see these People thro the proper medium? I am persuaded never."[46]

Cornwallis was too weak to guarantee the security of those few loyalists who were willing to support his army. This was made tragically apparent in the fate that befell Dr. John Pyle, a loyalist militia colonel, and some three or four hundred followers who were on their way to answer the call of Cornwallis at Hillsboro. Upon seeing the approach of cavalry who were wearing green jackets, they assumed that this was Tarleton's British Legion, which was due to accompany them to the army camp at Hillsboro. Pyle's loyalist militia stood to attention and lined the road to greet what was actually the cavalry of the Continental Army commanded by twenty-five-year-old "Light Horse" Henry Lee. The loyalists were shot at point-blank range. Lee later claimed that they had fired first, but the casualty list suggested otherwise. He did not lose a single soldier, whereas his cavalry killed one hundred loyalists and wounded another two hundred. Lee was no backwoodsman. Educated at New Jersey College (Princeton) and at the Middle Temple at the Inns of Court in London, he was a member of one of the elite families of Virginia. He was also commanding professional soldiers. General Greene applauded the rout by Lee and the "happy effect on those disaffected Persons, of which there are too many in this Country." General Andrew Pickens told Greene that "it has knocked up Toryism altogether in this part." The incident reflected the depths to which the war in the south had fallen. There were atrocities on both sides, especially between civilians engaged in civil war. Tarleton also mistakenly killed some loyalists who were coming to join him.[47]

The potential for loyalist support receded further when Cornwallis lost the race to the Dan River. He was now outnumbered by General Greene who, emboldened by reinforcements, returned to North Carolina causing many "luke-warm friends" to abandon the British camp. Cornwallis estimated that he had just 1,950 troops against 10,000 commanded by Greene. Clinton later claimed that the disparity in numbers should not have mattered given the low quality of the southern militia. Cornwallis overestimated Greene's strength, but he was indeed outnumbered by two to one. Moreover, Greene had learned to make more effective use of his 4,400 militiamen by not attempting to place them in the traditional battle formations, but instead employing them as marksmen.[48]

Cornwallis still chose to go on the offensive. At Guilford Courthouse on March 15, 1781, the opposing armies confronted one another in battle. It was a long and particularly bloody encounter, in which there was much confusion owing to the heavy woods obscuring parts of the battlefield. Cornwallis opened the battle with his infantry advancing in quick step before charging with their bayonets against the forward lines of the enemy. A standard tactic of the British in America, it terrified the civilian militia who were generally not armed with bayonets and therefore vulnerable at close quarters. The infantry advance succeeded in breaking the lines of first the North Carolina and then the Virginia militia. It is probably a myth that Cornwallis turned the outcome of the battle by the desperate action of ordering his cannon to deliberately fire into the midst of the combat, killing many of his own men, while being begged to desist by a wounded

O'Hara. He did personally lead a dangerous assault in which he came close to death with two horses shot from under him. O'Hara was hit in the thigh, but as soon as his wounds were dressed, he returned to lead another assault when he was shot off his horse and suffered a second gunshot wound in the chest. He also lost his son in the battle. The memory of the confusion and horror of the encounter haunted many of the participants for the rest of their lives. Shortly before his death at the age of thirty-six in 1797, the Virginian Thomas Watkins wrestled with his conscience, admitting that he had killed a British officer who had asked for him to spare his life.[49]

Cornwallis won the battle of Guilford Courthouse, but at the price of losing a quarter of his men, with the worst casualties inflicted on his elite Guards. Horace Walpole quipped that "Lord Cornwallis has conquered his troops out of shoes and provisions, and himself out of troops." The army remained on the battlefield covered with the dead and wounded of both sides, leading O'Hara to write: "I never did, and hope I never shall, experience two such Nights, as these immediately after the Battle." In less than ten weeks, Cornwallis's army had been reduced by four thousand troops, leaving him with a remaining force of less than fifteen hundred. Tarleton later commented that even a major victory would have accomplished little at this stage of the war, although a defeat would have been decisive. Cornwallis had nominally established British possession of North and South Carolina. After the battle, his communications with Lord Rawdon, whom he had left to defend the remaining southern posts as far as Savannah, were cut off by Greene at the head of a meager fifteen-hundred-strong army. Despite having won a token victory, Cornwallis had to abandon seventy wounded men on the battlefield and withdraw 175 miles southeast back to Wilmington.[50]

Clinton ridiculed Cornwallis for thinking that his defeat of Greene would rally the loyalists. He wondered what Cornwallis expected when his army was so greatly reduced and so scantily supplied with provisions. In an exchange of pamphlets after the war, Clinton mocked the report that he had received from Cornwallis that "many of the inhabitants rode into the camp, shook me by the hand, said they were glad to see us, and to hear we had beat Greene, and then rode home again." Clinton commented that the inhabitants left "no doubt with aching hearts, from the melancholy scene" upon seeing the army encumbered by a long train of sick and wounded. Clinton had consistently maintained that it was both bad policy and inhumane to encourage people to defect if they could not be assured of continued protection by the army. According to one eyewitness, who thought that the majority of the population would have preferred to reunite with the mother country, local people were too afraid to join the British. They had been too often deceived in the past with promises, only to find that the army had then withdrawn. They feared that if the British left North Carolina, they would be subject to the "diabolical conduct" of the rebels who would inflict the severest punishment on their families. In his memoirs, Clinton argued that Cornwallis should have returned to South

Carolina when he did not find support in North Carolina. But despite his losses at Guilford Courthouse, Cornwallis prepared to invade Virginia.[51]

V

Just as historians have questioned why Confederate General Robert E. Lee marched into Pennsylvania, so too they ask why Cornwallis marched into Virginia. It seemed a march of folly. Like Lee, Cornwallis had inclination to fight a defensive war but preferred rather to remain on the offensive. From at least 1778, Cornwallis had appreciated that victory was unlikely, but he was determined to give it a try. Tarleton had more opportunity than anyone to examine his motives, and offered the best explanation when he wrote that Cornwallis was giving "a fair trial to the ardent wishes of government at home." It was an "experiment"—a term used by O'Hara, Clinton, Tarleton, and Germain—to test the assumptions of the home government by rousing the loyalty of the supposed majority of the population. With the invasion of Virginia, the experiment would have been tried in every state of America. The alternative was to retreat back to South Carolina.[52]

Indeed, the political situation in London demanded that he continue. Cornwallis not only carried with him the fate of America but also the future of Lord North's government in Britain. In Parliament the opposition was becoming more vociferous and their numbers were growing. In the "most personally painful and invidious" attack upon Lord North in March 1781, the opposition seized upon the size of the loans to pay for the war and the high interest rates as examples of the extravagant and improvident conduct of the war by the government. In Parliament, there was general anxiety that the fabric of the empire "seemed everywhere to be collapsing of its own weight or yielding to external attacks." In India, Hyder Ali had defeated a British force of nearly four thousand men under Colonel William Baillie and invaded the Carnatic. Ireland was demanding "political and commercial freedom sword in hand." In June, dispatches had arrived from Cornwallis describing the lack of support in North Carolina and the close action at Guilford Courthouse.[53]

In the House of Commons, Charles James Fox called upon the government to abandon the further prosecution of the war in America. He warned that the nation was weary of the contest. He cited the recent messages from Cornwallis, which he claimed proved the impracticality of conquering America. Although Cornwallis had penetrated North Carolina and defeated Greene, nothing had come of his success, neither new friends nor territory, since he had been unable to retain what he conquered. Fox observed that the only possible objection to withdrawal was the embarrassment of acknowledging American independence, but he added prophetically that "within six months of the present day," the ministers would make a similar proposition to end the war.[54]

Cornwallis was the only glimmer of hope for the future of the government. Far from seeming like a march of death, his advance inspired government supporters and helped defeat the opposition by offering a prospect of success. He was at last giving the war momentum. The normally gloomy and pessimistic newspaper accounts of the war portrayed him as an unstoppable force. The London press proclaimed him another Hannibal. Joseph Galloway, the leading American loyalist in London, compared Cornwallis to a second Caesar or Alexander. Galloway claimed that Cornwallis had proved what a handful of men could achieve, and boasted that he had always said that such a general was necessary for the conquest of America.[55]

It is remarkable not that Cornwallis was defeated in Virginia, but that he managed to create such mayhem there that the local state defenses virtually collapsed and the legislature was forced to flee as far west as Staunton in the Shenandoah Valley. Leaving political considerations aside, Cornwallis was willing to gamble, because there was already a British force in Virginia under Major General William Phillips and Benedict Arnold that had occupied Richmond in early January. Cornwallis's total force consequently numbered seven thousand men, which dissuaded Greene from following him into Virginia. Although Cornwallis had left behind thinly garrisoned posts in South Carolina and North Carolina, Greene left Virginia open to Cornwallis. Besides, Cornwallis was confident that the twenty-two-year-old Lord Rawdon could hold the British posts in South Carolina, especially after Rawdon's victory against a larger rebel force commanded by Greene at Hobkirk's Hill (April 15, 1781).

Virginia, the most populous and largest state in America, was strategically important in relation to both the north and the south. It also offered the possibility of establishing a navy base in the Chesapeake and was a major source of food and supplies. After 1778, Virginia provided between 10 and 15 percent of the men who served in the Continental Army, and it had some of the finest horses in the country. Cornwallis wanted the Chesapeake to become "the seat of the war, even (if necessary) at the expense of abandoning New York." He argued that there was more chance of success than in the north and that the successful conquest of Virginia would guarantee the security of the British hold on the other southern colonies. His aim was to occupy Virginia sufficiently to overturn the government and establish a loyalist militia to police the population. Using the plentiful supply of horses in Virginia, Cornwallis was able to mount six hundred light dragoons to travel between thirty and seventy miles a day. He mounted an additional seven or eight hundred infantrymen, which doubled his cavalry. For virtually the first time in the war, the army was able to outrun the enemy.[56]

In the absence of much of the southern detachment of the Continental Army, Virginia was poorly defended. Greene had left only a small unit of regular troops under von Steuben, who had drilled Washington's army at Valley Forge. Many of the Virginia troops in the southern Continental Army had been killed or captured in the battles of Camden and Waxhaws in South Carolina. The militia had been resistant to mobilization in the past. A third of the population was composed of slaves, who outnumbered whites in some areas. Virginia's currency was so weak that Jefferson said that it had no more value than oak leaves. There were divisions in the state government, as well as complacency because the first half of the war had been largely fought in the north. In 1779, the British army had marauded the coast and military arsenals for almost two weeks without opposition. The problem of insufficient manpower was so bad that Virginia was the only state in the south to recruit free blacks with the official sanction of the legislature before the practice was adopted by Maryland in 1780. The Assembly had to reinstate the draft in order to meet the state quota of men required for service in the Continental Army. The perilous situation of the state was slightly relieved by the arrival of three thousand troops commanded by the marquis de Lafayette who had been sent from the north by Washington to deter the British coastal raids and capture Benedict Arnold.[57]

In May 1781, Cornwallis reached the army of Benedict Arnold at Petersburg and assumed command of all the British forces in Virginia. Since Greene was in the Carolinas, Cornwallis had the benefit of superior numbers and professional troops. The governor of Virginia, the thirty-eight-year-old Thomas Jefferson, had been kept informed of the movements of Cornwallis in the south by another future president of the United States, James Monroe. The British had intercepted one of Jefferson's letters in which he urged the assembling of the militia and warned that Cornwallis's invasion had the potential to be as damaging as the French occupation of Hanover during the Seven Years' War. The state had been caught unprepared, and Cornwallis initially attempted to trap Lafayette. Upon reaching Westover along the James River, he discovered that Lafayette had abandoned the state capital at Richmond. Indeed Lafayette moved north, leaving the south and west of the state open to Cornwallis, whose army was free to roam the country "without apprehension or difficulty." Cornwallis received further intelligence that the governor and Assembly had left Richmond for Charlottesville, and that the small guard of von Steuben was overseeing the state arsenal and supplies for the Continental Army at Point of Fork. Cornwallis ordered Tarleton to capture the Assembly members in Charlottesville and Simcoe to capture the arsenal at Point of Fork.[58]

Tarleton rode towards the Shenandoah Valley with its great vista of the Blue Ridge Mountains. With 180 dragoons and 70 mounted infantry, he headed for Charlottesville, while John Simcoe and the Queen's Rangers set out for Point of Fork. The plan was to strike simultaneously. Along the route, Tarleton burned a wagon train and stores of the Continental Army; he captured some of the "principal gentlemen" of Virginia including a member of the Continental Congress. Always intent upon surprise, he covered seventy miles in twenty-four hours, overwhelmed the guard at the Rivanna River, and charged into the center of Charlottesville (a town named after the wife of George III, Queen Charlotte). Only months earlier, General John Burgoyne's Convention Army from Saratoga had been prisoners of war in Charlottesville before being hastily moved to Fort Frederick in Maryland by an order of Jefferson.

Arriving in Charlottesville on George III's birthday, June 4, 1781, Tarleton's dragoons killed several officers and men, including a Brigadier General Scott. They captured seven members of the state legislature, including the legendary Daniel Boone who represented Fayette County, together with a thousand new firelocks, four hundred barrels of gunpowder, and some clothing for the Continental Army. From a prominence near to his mountaintop home at Monticello, Jefferson had watched the approach of the dragoons through a spyglass. He had been alerted to Tarleton's approach at four-thirty in the morning by Captain John Jouett, who had ridden through the night to Monticello upon seeing Tarleton's men drinking at Cuckoo Tavern near Louisa. After arranging for his wife and children to get away, Jefferson himself escaped while Tarleton's dragoons were actually ascending the hillside of Monticello. The soldiers spent eighteen hours at the home of the author of the Declaration of Independence. According to Jefferson, they "preserved everything with sacred care." Tarleton had shown unusual sensitivity and ordered the officers to disturb nothing at Monticello, though in his memoirs, he wrote of his disappointment at the "ineffectual" attempt to capture Jefferson.[59]

The experience haunted Jefferson for the rest of his life. The expiration of his term as governor happened to coincide with the attack on Charlottesville, and because the legislature fled to Staunton, the state was without a government for a week. The Assembly considered a motion to create a dictator and later brought impeachment charges against Jefferson, who had actually demonstrated more courage than the members by remaining so close to danger at Richmond and Monticello. Jefferson had very limited power as governor. The inadequacy of the state defenses was due to many factors, not least the general expectation that the British would not invade Virginia. Nevertheless, Jefferson told friends that the wound of the accusations against him could "only be cured by the all-healing grave." On the eve of a second war with Britain in 1812, "Light Horse" Henry Lee wrote a memoir in which he accused Jefferson of culpability for the fall of Richmond and cowardice for his flight from Monticello. Jefferson never responded publicly to criticism, but he did employ others to refute Lee. Louis H. Girardin actually lived at Monticello while writing a response to Lee at Jefferson's behest.[60]

Two months before his death in 1826, Jefferson tried to persuade the younger Henry Lee not to republish his father's memoirs, or at least to expunge the passages dealing with his role in the invasion of Virginia of 1781. Jefferson even submitted an alternative version to incorporate in the new edition. In the last week of his life, Jefferson was still so obsessed with the episode that he personally met with the younger Lee at Monticello. After Jefferson's death, Lee published the original version in 1827. Like many of the "Founding Fathers," Jefferson was concerned about molding his reputation for posterity and controlling his legacy. The issue of the invasion divided the next generation. When Jefferson's nephew published a selection of his uncle's papers, he included letters that diminished Lee, as well as a letter to James Monroe that compared Lee's memoirs to a historical novel written for "the amusement of credulous and uninquisitive readers." The younger Lee replied in kind. The issue revealed that Cornwallis had still seemed a formidable enemy only weeks before his defeat at Yorktown. His army had penetrated the heart of the most important and populous state in the nation. It left a deep impression on contemporaries and not least upon Thomas Jefferson.[61]

After leaving Charlottesville, Tarleton rejoined Cornwallis at his headquarters at Jefferson's Elk Hill plantation at the mouth of Byrd Creek in western Goochland, where Cornwallis headed his letters "Jefferson's Camp." In contrast to Tarleton's dragoons at Monticello, Cornwallis's men left "an absolute waste" at Elk Hill and Jefferson accused Cornwallis of having acted in a spirit of "total extermination." The British burned his buildings and crops, ate up all the cows, sheep, and hogs, carried off his horses, and cut the throats of the mares, after which he never again bred horses. Jefferson was also to allege that the British stole thirty of his slaves and seized thirty thousand enslaved people in Virginia. His numbers were exaggerated and no coercion was involved. In fact, he lost twenty-three slaves from three of his plantations, including Robin, Barnaby, Harry, and a boy called Will, who joined the British from Monticello. Perhaps because it was easier to escape from Elk Hill, women and children like Black Sal and her three infants left with the British. Jefferson later employed an agent to recover five of his slaves who had been present at the battle of Yorktown, including Robin, Barnaby and Will. Barnaby died shortly afterwards, and Jefferson sold Robin a few months later and Will in 1790.[62]

As contemporaries understood, the existence of slavery contradicted a revolutionary ideology that celebrated liberty and equality. Some British and Hessian officers condemned American slavery, while other officers, like Banastre Tarleton, were critical of the policy of offering freedom to the runaways of rebel masters. Tarleton's family profited from the slave trade, and he later led the campaign against the abolitionists in Parliament. He correctly believed that emancipating slaves did much to antagonize white opinion in the south. The British commanders were not primarily acting from humanitarian sympathies when they emancipated enslaved people, but were rather motivated by the exigencies of war and lack of troops. They did not free the slaves of American loyalists who were relocated to the Caribbean and to the Bahamas. Britain at the time was the leading slave-trading nation in Europe and ruled over 400,000 slaves in its own colonies in the Caribbean, where the slave codes were generally harsher and mortality rates higher than in America.[63]

The British army was accompanied by some three thousand to four thousand African Americans by the time Cornwallis reached Yorktown. He had been joined by some two thousand runaways during the march through the Carolinas and at least another thousand in Virginia. They worked as laborers, foragers, artificers, servants, cooks, laundresses, and nurses. They carried the provisions and supplies, some wearing motley collections of the clothes of their masters and mistresses. The young men were generally employed to relieve regular soldiers of fatigues like digging trenches, and were not fully integrated into the regular army. In contrast to the colonial period, when runaways were mostly young males, many entire families fled to the British during the Revolutionary War. Half of the slaves who joined Cornwallis were women and children, together with the elderly and disabled. Captain Johann von Ewald estimated that there were 4,000 enslaved people accompanying the army. He described how "any place this horde approached was eaten clean, like an acre invaded by a swarm of locusts." It was a riddle to him "where these people lived." He thought it fortunate that the army "seldom stayed in one place longer than a day or a night."[64]

Although some unscrupulous individuals reneged, the British government honored the promise of freedom, which became a source of much postwar friction with the United States. Although African Americans fought on both sides of the conflict, many more joined the British—a conservative estimate suggests at least 20,000 up to as many as 100,000 people, many of whom died from smallpox and other diseases. Despite a plea from O'Hara, Cornwallis left some of the sick and "Wretched Negroes" behind, leading to accusations of attempted germ warfare. Others blended into free black society in the north. Between eight and ten thousand former slaves departed from America with the British in 1782–83. They included six runaways from George Washington at Mount Vernon and another former slave of Patrick Henry. Most were resettled in Nova Scotia and New Brunswick in Canada, while some returned with the British to London and elsewhere in the British Empire. At least eleven former slaves were among the first convicts to be shipped to the new penal colony at Botany Bay in New South Wales. They included Caesar, one of the first "bushmen," who now have an iconic status in Australia. They were to be a major force in the abolitionist experiment of founding a black colony in Sierra Leone, where they named streets in Freetown after British officers—Tarleton, Rawdon, and Howe. A former slave in Nova Scotia renamed himself "British Freedom." First raised in 1779, the Carolina Black Corps continued as a regiment in the British Caribbean and became the embryo of the largest all black force in the Americas, the famed West India Regiments.[65]

VI

The game seemed far from up in Virginia. Although Washington still believed as late as March 1781 that the outcome of the war would be decided in New York, he sent General "Mad" Anthony Wayne and a thousand Pennsylvania Continentals to Virginia, though they did not arrive to join Lafayette until June. Meanwhile, Cornwallis successively occupied Richmond and the former capital, Williamsburg. Upon receiving instructions from Clinton to secure a naval post in the Chesapeake Bay, he left Williamsburg, followed at some distance by the forces of Lafayette and Wayne. As he crossed the James River in the late afternoon of July 9, he set a trap for the enemy at Green Spring Plantation. In order to encourage them to think that his main force had crossed the river and that the rear of his army was vulnerable, he sent only his baggage and a mounted detachment ahead while he awaited them with his full force. In the ensuing battle, he was only prevented from gaining a major victory because the main body of the rebel army did not appear until almost sunset and the engagement was broken off in the darkness. Cornwallis continued to try "to trap the boy" Lafayette, who only evaded him by consummate skill. Cornwallis had won every major battle that he commanded in the south, and had created pandemonium in Virginia.

Cornwallis won victories but was unable to gain traction. The British had virtually marched the length and breadth of America. The problem was well described by O'Hara who wrote that it was impossible to conquer a country "where repeated successes cannot ensure permanent advantages," and where every trifling setback was like an "Electric fire," rousing the vast continent to persevere in resistance "upon the least and most distant dawn of Hope." Admiral Thomas Graves described the movements of the British army in America as like "the passage of a ship through the sea whose track is soon lost." Cornwallis appreciated the absurdity of his situation, writing that he was "quite tired of marching about the Country in Quest of Adventure." Clinton could not but admire the "firm intrepidity, activity, and perseverance" of Cornwallis, but he thought his maneuvers pointless and foolhardy, "an unmeaning and unprofitable ramble through Virginia," which had sacrificed the security of the Carolinas. While Cornwallis was in Virginia, Greene had attacked the posts he had left behind until the British army was reduced to the defense of Wilmington, Charleston, and Savannah.[66]

Horrified by these excursions in Virginia in July 1781, Clinton suddenly became assertive and commanded Cornwallis to send his troops back to New York. Clinton then countermanded himself with instructions for Cornwallis to establish a post at a deepwater harbor in the Chesapeake and send the remainder of his troops back for a possible assault on either Philadelphia or Newport. Cornwallis saw little purpose in maintaining a defensive naval post that would not have any influence on the rest of the south and would simply leave its garrison prey to a superior enemy fleet. He requested to return to South Carolina. In a letter to Lord Rawdon of July 23, he confided his suspicion that Clinton "is determined to throw all the blame on me, and disapprove of all I have done," and that nothing but consciousness of his duty "could possibly induce me to remain" under his command.[67]

The magnitude of the defeat at Yorktown might have been diminished if Cornwallis had returned the majority of his troops to New York. In fact, late in July 1781, he had begun to embark troops to join Clinton, and the Queen's Rangers were already aboard their transports ready to leave Virginia. He detained them, because he justifiably argued that he would otherwise not have enough troops to fortify and defend Yorktown. Cornwallis had spent weeks investigating the various deep water ports of Portsmouth and Old Point Comfort in the Hampton Roads but concluded that the only suitable location for battleships was Yorktown and Gloucester. Yorktown was a small tobacco port, only twenty-three miles from the original British settlement in America at Jamestown and also close to the former capital at Williamsburg. Cornwallis disliked the location as dangerous and easily accessible to the enemy, though both he and Clinton were unaware of the superior size of the approaching French fleet.[68]

Clinton had given Cornwallis positive orders to fortify a naval base and specifically suggested he choose Yorktown or Old Point Comfort on Hampton Road. Clinton was therefore wrong when he claimed in his memoirs that he had never expected Cornwallis to move to Yorktown. This was one of his few positive orders in months and it allowed little discretion. However, the choice of location was of marginal importance. Ewald recorded in his journal that "our fate depends on the success of the English fleet, for as long as the English remain rulers of the sea, a door stays open for us," but their exit was blocked by a superior French navy commanded by the Admiral de Grasse off the coast of the Chesapeake. Cornwallis was instead encircled and heavily outnumbered by 7,800 French and 8,850 American troops commanded by George Washington. It was checkmate.[69]

Clinton criticized Cornwallis for not having done more to save himself at Yorktown, arguing that Cornwallis had been negligent in not sufficiently fortifying the town and building redoubts. Clinton thought that he should have done more to prevent the junction of the enemy forces and cut off the army of Lafayette and the troops of the marquis de Saint-Simon from Saint-Domingue, who were landed by the fleet of Admiral de Grasse. He argued that Cornwallis had abandoned his outer works too quickly and that he should have been able to withstand the bombardment longer until he was relieved. His criticism was echoed in the memoirs of Tarleton.[70]

Cornwallis did not try to fight his way out, because he was expecting relief forces from Clinton. In August 1781, he began to fortify Yorktown at a leisurely pace owing to the heat and the sickness among his men. Until September 8, he was unaware of the approach of the combined armies of Rochambeau and Washington, who had marched some four hundred miles south from New York. Until September 23, he was similarly ignorant of the real size of the French fleet and its ability to blockade Yorktown. Nevertheless, he placed obstacles in the river and sank ships to prevent the French from sailing down the York River. On September 25, he received a message from Clinton promising him a relief expedition due to arrive on October 5. Two days after the expected arrival, Cornwallis and his army faced a classic siege, a form of warfare that had been perfected by the French, who had the best and most sophisticated artillery officers in Europe. The thirty-one-year-old General Henry Knox had turned the American artillery into a formidable corps and additionally commanded the French artillery. Ensign Ebenezer Denny of the Pennsylvania Line of the Continental Army described how after dark the shells from the opposing armies passed "high in the air, and descending in a curve, each with a long train of fire, exhibited a brilliant spectacle." Of all forms of warfare, sieges were the most formulaic, the most scientific and the most assured of success with adequate support.[71]

As the enemy closed in around him, Cornwallis withdrew from his outer defenses to within a two-thousand-yard perimeter that extended in a semicircle through and around Yorktown. His lines consisted of eight redoubts, defensive works surrounded by trenches, palisades (rows of wooden stakes), fraises (sharpened poles facing outward towards the enemy) and abatis (wooden stakes). Commencing on October 9, the enemy bombardment was so devastating that he had to move the next day from his headquarters in a private house to a grotto in the garden. He was himself nearly hit by a cannonball and took refuge on one occasion under a cliff. During the night of October 10, the horizon was lit up by the blazing forty-four-gun British frigate *Charon* which had sought shelter under the cliffs of Yorktown before being hit by French artillery fire. Four days later, Alexander Hamilton led American troops in the taking of Redoubt 9 and the French army seized Redoubt 10 which defended the southwestern flank of Yorktown. Lasting less than half-an-hour, these attacks left the British exposed to allied artillery fire at a distance of 350 yards. Cornwallis tried a desperate sortie to spike the enemy guns—an action that yielded little success. On the night of October 17, without cannon and scarcely any shells along the works facing the two captured redoubts, his army made one last bid to escape in the night to their garrison on the other side of the York River at Gloucester Point, commanded by Tarleton, but the attempt was thwarted by a freak storm. Cornwallis was outnumbered three to one and exposed to the full force of more than a hundred enemy cannon. As Sergeant Roger Lamb described it, his fortifications "were tumbling into ruin: not a gun could be fired from them, and only one eight inch [mortar], and little more than one hundred cohorn shells [as fired by mortars] remained." With his garrison "exhausted by the fatigue of constant watching and unremitting duty," Cornwallis later claimed that it would have been inhumane to make his army try to hold out any longer. It had endured nine days of incessant artillery fire and had suffered at least 156 fatalities and 326 wounded, though some contemporary accounts estimated his losses at more than twice this number.[72]

On October 17, 1781, four years to the day that Burgoyne had surrendered at Saratoga, Cornwallis sent a flag of truce to negotiate the surrender of his army of seventy-one hundred men, which represented a quarter of the total British forces in America. He failed in his wish to obtain the same generous terms granted Burgoyne, but was instead granted the same terms that Sir Henry Clinton gave to General Benjamin Lincoln at Charleston. His troops were consequently treated as prisoners of war and only his senior officers were given parole. The regiments were not allowed to unfurl their colors at the surrender ceremony, and their fifes and drums were only permitted to play their own marches. According to Knox, they were specifically prohibited from playing *Yankee Doodle*, which was originally a satirical British song mocking the low quality of citizen militia during the French and Indian War, the verses of which were often played with a prolonged note at the end to sound like a raspberry. However, there is no contemporary evidence for the popular myth that the British marched to the tune of *The World Turned Upside Down*. Cornwallis's plea of sickness was very possibly a ploy to avoid the shame of personally appearing at the surrender ceremony, but his claim may also have been genuine since he had contracted malaria and been bedridden twice with fevers during the southern campaign. The process of surrender was not without irony. Cornwallis was taken into custody by John Laurens, who had drawn up the articles of capitulation and who was the son of Henry Laurens, a former president of Congress. His father had been captured by the British on his way to negotiate a treaty with the Dutch and had become a prisoner in the Tower of London, whose absentee governor was Cornwallis, now the prisoner of John Laurens.[73]

On October 19, some fifty-six thousand soldiers, sailors, and civilians surrounded and were crowded within Yorktown and Gloucester Point. The battle site was still strewn with dead bodies, animal carcasses, and debris. Against a background of shelled buildings, there were mattresses, blankets, and sheets, saturated with blood and scattered over the beach of the York River. One eye witness described the way "the houses stood there like lanterns shot through and through with holes." The ground was full of craters caused by the bombs and mortars, making it dangerous to walk. There were corpses of dead black soldiers and black camp followers, some of whom had been forcibly evicted from the British lines. In a second formal ceremony, Tarleton surrendered to the French at Gloucester Point, having previously ordered the slaughter of over a thousand horses owing to lack of forage. Some members of Congress wanted Cornwallis executed for war crimes committed by his army in the south. Instead, he was wined and dined by the American and French commanders, and received so many invitations that he had to decline some of them. He was thereafter permitted to leave for the British headquarters in New York.[74]

Yorktown had been a disaster waiting to happen. As Tarleton pointed out, if Cornwallis had been rescued by Clinton, it would only have postponed "the evil day." The same scenario had been close to happening earlier in the war, and had only been prevented by the luck and skill of the army and mistakes by the enemy. Yorktown, however, was a superbly orchestrated campaign on the part of both the French and the Americans. Rochambeau had suggested the idea of marching south to Virginia with a force that outnumbered the Continental Army. In fact, with the addition of the sailors aboard de Grasse's fleet, the French were more numerous than the combined forces of the Continental Army and the Virginia militia. On the other hand, Washington was the commander in chief who had to approve the plan and take responsibility if it failed. The "fox" had ensnared its hunter.[75]

VII

Cornwallis enjoyed the most successful postwar career of any of the men who lost America. He was beaten but had given a good fight and created the mirage of a close finish. He had tested the assumption that there was a loyalist majority in the south. He had done the bidding of the government in fighting an offensive war, and he had remained on good terms with the king. The government reciprocated with the publication of a letter from Clinton that gave the impression that Cornwallis had been given no discretion about fortifying Yorktown.

From New York, Cornwallis was accompanied by Benedict Arnold on the voyage back to Portsmouth. He had previously tried to leave America on board a ship, the *Robuste,* in which he had spent several days at sea, but the ship had leaked so badly that it had to return to New York. After the two men finally arrived in England in early January 1782, Arnold supported Cornwallis by writing letters to the press blaming Clinton for Yorktown. Cornwallis also benefited from the reflected glory of his brother William, who became a naval hero after an action off St. Kitts in the fleet of Admiral Sir Samuel Hood. The only criticism of Cornwallis in the press was his failure to obtain provision in the articles of surrender for the safety of the loyalists, whose welfare became an issue of national conscience. Otherwise, he was treated as a hero when he returned to England. In London, crowds thronged around him and carried him on their shoulders to the Guildhall, "accompanied by an incredible Number of Spectators," according to a newspaper account, "whose Acclamations upon the occasion can be better conceived than described."[76]

The admiring feelings of the Londoners were shared by the king. George III said that he did not "lay anything at the charge of Lord Cornwallis," and in June 1782, only a day after telling Clinton that Cornwallis had rambled around and lost himself in the south, he assured Cornwallis that his conduct had proved his attachment to the crown, the country, and the army. In 1786, without conferring with members of his Cabinet, George III created Cornwallis a Knight of the Garter. Being a much smoother operator than Clinton, Cornwallis avoided becoming entangled in a bitter feud with the latter, who in 1783 published the first of his pamphlets blaming his former subordinate for Yorktown. Cornwallis thought the pamphlet "a bad performance," which was unlikely to do Clinton "much good with people of judgment." Cornwallis was much more hurt by criticisms made in the memoirs of Banastre Tarleton, which were published in 1787. Regarding the memoirs as a personal betrayal, he complained that Tarleton had known and approved of his decisions. Even after the battle of Cowpens, Cornwallis had continued to recommend his subordinate to the home government and had even helped pay off his debts after the war. Tarleton, however, incorrectly believed that Cornwallis had denied him an anticipated post in India.[77]

In his later career, Cornwallis became an imperial troubleshooter, celebrated as a successful general and administrator. In February 1786, he was appointed to succeed Warren Hastings as governor general of Bengal and commander in chief of British forces in India. He led a larger army than he had commanded in America, consisting of twenty thousand men, with whom he defeated forty thousand troops of Tipu Sultan during the Third Mysore War (1790–92). His officers included many of those who had served with him in America. Cornwallis was the first British commander to make significant use of elephants in hauling artillery. In a reversal of his position at Yorktown, Cornwallis mounted a successful siege against Tipu and nearly captured the capital city of Seringapatam (Srirangapatna). His campaign acquired half Tipu's territory in Mysore for Britain and helped pave the way for British dominance in south India. As a guarantee of the peace agreement, Cornwallis held two of Tipu's young sons as hostages. Once again extolled in England as a second Hannibal, he was given a vote of thanks by Parliament and awarded an annuity of five thousand pounds by the East India Company. The scene of him receiving the two sons of Tipu Sultan was the subject of paintings by Arthur Devis, James Northcote, Edward Bird, George Carter, Robert Homes, Robert Smirke, Mather Brown, and Henry Singleton. It was also depicted in prints, and commemorative items ranging from medallions, to tin trays. He was eulogized in popular verses with titles like "Cornwallis Triumphant" (1792). The City of London commissioned a portrait of him by the American-born artist John Singleton Copley. Upon his return from India in 1793, George III made him the first Marquess Cornwallis.[78]

During the great rebellion in Ireland in 1798, Cornwallis was appointed lord lieutenant and commander in chief. He himself led his troops into battle and defeated a French invasion force of eleven hundred men commanded by General Joseph Humbert. It was the first time in a century that a lord lieutenant had commanded troops in war in Ireland. While walking from Phoenix Park to Dublin Castle in 1799, he was the victim of an attempted assassination, when a man disguised as a sentry fired and fled.[79]

Cornwallis was known for his integrity and independence of mind. He set an example by his own personal austerity. He never had a taste for pomp and fanfare. In Ireland, he preferred to live in a lodge in Phoenix Park rather than Dublin Castle. In India, he turned down the salary of commander in chief since he thought it wrong to earn two salaries. When he returned to India for a second term of office in 1805, replacing Richard, Marquess Wellesley as governor general, he immediately did away with the ostentation and display that had distinguished the government of his predecessor. He did not accept presents from natives. He improved the salaries of officials and justices to make them less liable to accept bribes, and did much to create an efficient and uncorrupt imperial bureaucracy. However, he treated the home government as he had treated Clinton in America, reporting his decisions only when they had become virtually irreversible.[80]

There were echoes of Cornwallis's experience in America during his commands in India and Ireland. He significantly warned one of his generals about the importance of procuring sufficient intelligence, working effectively with allies, and not dividing his command. In what came nearest to an admission of his own failure in the southern campaign, he wrote of "the ill effects of hazarding small detachments and being beat in detail." He insisted upon having joint political and military authority in both India and Ireland. He was in favor of the state assuming more control over the affairs of the East India Company, writing that the appeal to chartered rights did not have "much weight with me." He was wary of allowing colonial elites to hold high office and to share power. In Ireland, he championed the civil rights of the Catholic majority as a counterweight to the disproportionate influence of the minority Anglican elite in Dublin. The Irish loyalists reminded him of American loyalists, "only much more numerous and powerful, and a thousand times more ferocious." Just as he had spoken out against British policies in America, he daringly opposed George III by supporting Catholic Emancipation, believing that only such a measure would give quiet and security to Ireland. After the great rebellion, he favored leniency and a general act of amnesty toward the rebels, though in an echo of his policy in South Carolina, he executed some of the ringleaders.[81]

In India, Cornwallis's opposition to native elites led to the racial segregation of offices, with white imperial officials gradually gaining exclusive hold of senior appointments. He debarred the children of mixed-race couples, who had previously been predominant in the administration, from holding office. In a remarkable correspondence with Arthur Lee, who had been a diplomat for the United States in France during the Revolution, Cornwallis wrote that he had never ceased to think that "rational liberty makes people virtuous" and that virtue makes them happy. He claimed to believe in universal happiness and universal liberty. He then proceeded to disagree with Lee about the potential for liberty in India. He asserted that the Hindus were incapable of enjoying civil liberty and that they were happier to be ruled by the British than by the Mughal emperor and his officials. In his letters to the home government, Cornwallis stressed the need for a large European army in India. He warned that "it cannot be expected that even the best of treatment would constantly conciliate the willing obedience of so vast a body of people" with different religions and customs. His attitudes reflected a growing invidious racial distinction in the nineteenth century between authoritarian imperial government in countries with a population composed mainly of people of color and representative government in predominantly white countries. Britain was ultimately to grant increasing autonomy to countries with white majorities, such as Canada, Australia, New Zealand, and the Cape Colony in South Africa.[82]

His zest for the military and for constant movement continued unabated to the end. After the Revolution, he briefly settled into domestic life on his estate at Culford. He enjoyed hunting and sport, and he was able to spend time with his son and daughter. He found military books agreeable reading and became "more and more convinced of the necessity of military reading." However, he was not satisfied with a life of virtual retirement, and began discussions about his Bengal appointment from the moment of his return to England. When Britain was later threatened by Napoleon, he wrote that he could not "sit down quietly by myself, without occupation or object." He found it mortifying to be inactive after the pains he had taken "to acquire knowledge and experience" in his profession. He grew restless after one or two years in any post. Within ten days of becoming lord lieutenant of Ireland, he wrote that the post was his "idea of perfect misery." Interestingly, he discouraged his own son from joining the army. He had no grandsons, but six of his great-grandchildren entered the military, of whom four were killed in the Crimean War.[83]

Soon after his return to India on October 5, 1805, the sixty-seven-year-old Cornwallis died at Ghazipur near Benares in northern India. The House of Commons voted a memorial and statue to his memory in St. Paul's Cathedral. The British inhabitants of Calcutta raised a public subscription to pay for a mausoleum in the style of a classical temple over his grave, located on a bluff overlooking the River Ganges and built of stone imported from England. The inscription reads: "This monument, raised by the British inhabitants of Calcutta, attests their sense of those virtues which will live in the remembrance of grateful millions, long after it shall have mouldered in the dust." It paid tribute to his military victories and to his "forbearance and moderation" in peace.[84]

Clinton alone had kept alive the subject of Yorktown. The quarrel between the generals over who was to blame had obscured the role of the admirals who had been equally culpable. The generals had acted throughout the southern campaign in the belief that they would receive sufficient protection from the navy. They had received assurances of adequate naval support from the home government and from the admirals serving in the Caribbean. They were unaware of the size of the French fleet until it was too late. In his obsession with Cornwallis, Clinton deflected attention away from the roles of Sir George Rodney, who commanded the fleet in the Caribbean, and the earl of Sandwich, the first lord of the Admiralty in London. Almost a year before Yorktown, General George Washington had described naval superiority as "the pivot upon which everything turned."[85]

PART IV

Victory against France and Spain (1782)

If Historiographers should be hardy enough to fill the page of
History with the advantages that have been gained with unequal numbers
(on the part of America) in the course of this contest, and attempt to
relate the distressing circumstances under which they have been obtained,
it is more than probable that Posterity will bestow on their labors the
epithet and marks of fiction; for it will not be believed that such a force as
Great Britain has employed for eight years in this Country could be
baffled in their plan of Subjugating it by numbers infinitely less,
composed of Men oftentimes half starved; always in Rags, without pay,
and experiencing, at times, every species of distress which human
nature is capable of undergoing.

GEORGE WASHINGTON

CHAPTER 8

"Saint George"

SIR GEORGE RODNEY

On November 16, 1776, Fort Orange in the Dutch island of St. Eustatius fired the first foreign salute of the flag of the United States of America. The fort was responding to a gun salute from the *Andrew Doria,* one of the first four ships of the Continental Navy, which was on a mission to purchase armaments from St. Eustatius and to present a copy of the Declaration of Independence to Governor Johannes de Graff. There had been an interval of hesitation while the fort commander checked with the governor before dipping the fortress flag and firing a nine-gun salute. The governor afterwards gave a party for the commander of the *Andrew Doria,* Captain Isaiah Robinson. In 1939, President Franklin Roosevelt presented a copper plaque to the fortress, commemorating the place where "the sovereignty of the United States of America was first formally acknowledged to a national vessel by a foreign official."[1]

Situated among the northern Leeward Islands, St. Eustatius was less than five miles long and no more than two and a half miles wide. Known also as Statia and "the Golden Rock," its wealth "as a place of vast traffick from every quarter of the globe" was derived from its status as a free port and its geographical proximity to the islands of other European powers. There were some six hundred warehouses that stretched over a mile along the shoreline of the capital, Oranjestad. The commercial district was so dense that there were warehouses on the beach, creating a lower town. Janet Schaw, a Scottish visitor to St. Eustatius on the eve of the Revolutionary War, was entranced by the diversity of the merchants who offered their goods for sale in different languages, including Dutch, French, and Spanish. The merchants were attired in the clothing of their respective countries. She described the island as a grand market where she found "rich embroideries, painted silks, flowered Muslins, with all the Manufactures of the Indies. Just by hang Sailor's Jackets, trousers, shoes, hats etc." She marveled at "the variety of merchandize in such a place, for in every store you find every thing, be their qualities ever so

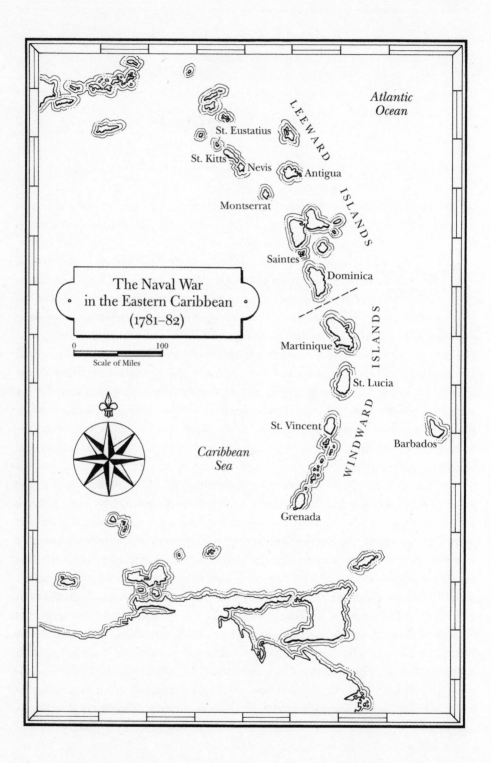

The Naval War
in the Eastern Caribbean
(1781–82)

0   100
Scale of Miles

Atlantic
Ocean

LEEWARD ISLANDS

St. Eustatius
St. Kitts
Nevis
Antigua
Montserrat

Saintes
Dominica

Martinique

St. Lucia

WINDWARD ISLANDS

St. Vincent

Barbados

Caribbean
Sea

Grenada

opposite." Schaw treated herself to some excellent French gloves and "English thread-stockings cheaper than I could buy them at home."[2]

St. Eustatius prospered during the Revolutionary War. Trade with the North Americans was "so general and done in so publick a manner, as to be no secret to any person in the West India Islands." It included the sale of guns, rifles, and ammunition that were generally imported from France and the Austrian Netherlands. Some 235 American ships visited the island in 1776 and 1777. Such was the importance of the island that it attracted agents appointed by the Continental Congress, including the resident agent, Samuel Curzon, and a frequent visitor, William Bingham, the agent for Martinique. Abraham van Bibber, representing the state of Maryland at St. Eustatius, enthused that he was "on the best terms" with the governor, who expressed "the greatest desire and intention to protect a trade with us." He described how "our flag" flew every day in the port aboard visiting merchant ships and privateers. Until 1777, Virginia had also used Bibber, whom it then replaced with John Ball. The agents of the Continental Congress in Europe found it safe to send their mail home via St. Eustatius. By September 1777, the island was so notorious for supplying the rebels that the password of General John Burgoyne's troops at the battle of Freeman's Farm was "St. Eustatius."[3]

After France entered the war in 1778, Martinique ceased to have neutral status, and St. Eustatius became the primary conduit for trade in the Caribbean with the United States. The American trade was "immense," with between seven and ten ships arriving every night and sometimes regular fleets of up to thirty ships. St. Eustatius also provided vital supplies to the French navy and colonies in the Caribbean. An armed convoy of forty to fifty French merchant ships visited the island every other week to buy provisions for Martinique and Guadeloupe. Jacques Texier was a French agent in St. Eustatius who was known to correspond with the governors of the French islands and to be "vehement in his hatred of Great Britain." In 1780, over 40 percent of ships entering the ports of Philadelphia and Baltimore arrived from St. Eustatius and another 40 percent from elsewhere in the Caribbean. Between September 1777 and June 1778, during the British occupation of Philadelphia, St. Eustatius became the mart of America, and throughout the rest of the war, it was to dominate the commerce of the mid-Atlantic and New England. British diplomatic pressure to halt the trade achieved nothing except an unenforced ban on gunpowder sales and the recall of the governor, who was back in office within a year.[4]

In December 1780, upon the pretext of the discovery of a draft treaty between the Dutch Republic and the United States, Britain finally declared war on the Netherlands in an effort to suppress its trade in both Europe and the Caribbean with France, Spain, and the United States. The British government simultaneously sent secret orders to Admiral Sir George Rodney and Major General John Vaughan, who respectively commanded the navy and the army in the eastern Caribbean, to capture St. Eustatius. It was to be a fateful decision in ways that the home government could not have anticipated. Four months later, Admiral François Joseph Paul de Grasse left the port of Brest to sail to the Caribbean and then to Virginia. Failing either to intercept de Grasse or to pursue the French fleet to America, Rodney became obsessed with St. Eustatius. In the haunting phrase of his chief subordinate Admiral Sir Samuel Hood, "The lairs of St. Eustatius were so bewitching as not to be withstood by flesh and blood."[5]

Rodney was a maverick whose actions contributed to the British defeat at York-town. He was delegated the task of intercepting de Grasse's fleet in the Caribbean and pursuing him to North America. Instead, rather than follow de Grasse to the Chesapeake Bay, Rodney returned to Britain to defend himself in Parliament against an inquiry into his conduct during the conquest of St. Eustatius in 1781. The most important sea battle of the war was consequently fought by a less illustrious admiral, Thomas Graves, whom the government had never intended to command at the Chesapeake Capes (September 5, 1781). As a result, De Grasse was able to prevent any possibility of Lord Cornwallis and his army from being rescued by the Royal Navy at Yorktown. Lord Shelburne, who was to succeed Lord North as prime minister, made the connection when he received the news of the British defeat at Yorktown with the remark that "For his part he solemnly believed that the capture of Lord Cornwallis was owing to the capture of St. Eustatius."[6]

I

Sir George Rodney was one of the few British commanders to emerge from the Revolu-tionary War with his reputation enhanced. After the British defeat at Yorktown, he won one of the most decisive naval victories against the French before the battle of Trafalgar in 1805. It is perhaps no coincidence that Rodney's victory became known at the time as the "battle of the Saints" (April 12, 1782). It is only recently that the battle has become known again by the name of its location among a group of small islands called the Saintes. Rodney's victory enabled the British to preserve much of the rest of their empire and to negotiate honorable peace terms with France in 1783.

Rodney's victory at the Saintes was the pinnacle of one of the most successful naval careers before Nelson. Despite his lack of powerful family connections and influen-tial patrons, Rodney had a meteoric rise in the navy from the time that he joined at the typically young age of fourteen, after attending Harrow School. During the War of the Austrian Succession (1740–48), he became one of the youngest captains in the navy, when he successfully captured a vessel and launched a raid on Spanish army stocks at Ventimiglia. Aboard his ship the *Eagle,* he captured six ships, and he made a fortune from prize money that enabled him to buy a country seat and to become a member of Parlia-ment for Saltash. After the war, he was appointed governor and commander in chief of Newfoundland with the rank of commodore. The appointment was an acknowledgment of his achievement in a period when naval officers were often put on leave and given half-pay during peacetime. During the Seven Years' War, he played a minor role in the taking of Louisburg and rose to the rank of rear admiral. Between 1759 and 1761, he became famous as a result of his successful blockade of the French port of Le Havre, and he was similarly celebrated for his role in the conquest of Martinique in 1762. He was promoted to vice admiral of the Blue and voted the thanks of both Houses of Parliament. In 1764, he was created a baronet and became Sir George Brydges Rodney. He again received peacetime appointments as governor of Greenwich Hospital (1765–70) and commander in chief of the naval dock at Port Royal in Jamaica (1771–74). In 1774, he was made rear admiral of Great Britain.

Despite his long list of achievements and his support of the government, he was not given an appointment in the early stages of the Revolutionary War. In February 1778, he was promoted admiral of the White, a merely honorific title because he was still without the command of a fleet. Finally in 1779, he was made commander in chief of the naval squadron in the Leeward Islands, and soon began again to dazzle the nation with his triumphs. In January 1780, Rodney distinguished himself in the relief of Gibraltar. Located along the south coast of Spain, this rocky peninsula was regarded as crucial by the British for checking the Spanish and controlling access to the Mediterranean. It was one of the many military theaters that distracted the British from the war effort in America. On January 16, during an action fought at night known as the Moonlight Battle, Rodney defeated the Spanish Admiral Juan Francisco de Lángara when he captured nine ships and destroyed another. It was Admiral Lángara who had earlier defeated and disgraced the British Admiral John Byng at the battle of Minorca in 1756, which led to Byng's court martial and execution in 1757. Lord Sandwich congratulated Rodney that he "had captured more line of battleships than had been taken in any action in either of the two last preceding wars." In May, he engaged the French fleet in the Caribbean commanded by Luc Urbain de Bouëxic, comte de Guichen. The battle averted a French attempt to capture Barbados and so shattered the enemy fleet that de Guichen abandoned his original objective of proceeding to America and instead returned to France. During the American Revolution, Rodney's fleet captured or destroyed sixteen enemy warships, and captured or killed three admirals of France, Spain, and Holland.[7]

At the time of his appointment to the command of the naval squadron in Barbados and the Leeward Islands in October 1779, Rodney was sixty-one-years-old. His portraits show a gaunt and very angular face (Figure 30). He was emaciated and tall, with a small protruding chin and prominent nose. He had high eyebrows and a look of keen concentration in his eyes. He wore a white powdered wig, and prided himself on his etiquette and courtesy toward people of all social ranks. The "sea was his element," and he talked of little else, fighting battles over dinner tables. According to the playwright Richard Cumberland, he was a singular and extraordinary man who had some striking eccentricities. "He would very commonly indulge himself in a loose and heedless style of talking," which Cumberland thought detracted from the "sound, good sense" and the "strength and dignity of mind that were natural to him."[8]

Although distantly related to the Rodneys of Delaware, he had shown no sympathy for the grievances of the colonists in North America. As a member of Parliament, in 1765 he voted with the opposition against a Rockingham administration motion to produce American papers with the intention of withdrawing the Stamp Act, and later consistently voted in support of the government of Lord North. Otherwise, he claimed to be like the majority of naval officers, having "nothing to do with parties and politics, being simply bound to carry their instructions into execution to the best of their abilities, without deliberating about men and measures, which forms no part of their duty, and for which they are in no degree responsible." Nevertheless, he was regarded by the opposition parties as a friend and supporter of the two most unpopular ministers in the government, Lord George Germain and the earl of Sandwich.[9]

Before his appointment to the Barbados and Leeward Islands squadron in 1779, Rodney had spent the previous five years ashore. His first command of a fleet for seventeen years, it was the most important naval command in the Americas because the squadron was the first line of naval defense for the British Caribbean and North America. It included surveillance of Martinique, the main base of the French operations in the Americas.

The defense of the British colonies in the Caribbean, which was a major priority of the home government, deflected precious military resources that might otherwise have served in America. The British Caribbean included Antigua, Barbados, Dominica, Jamaica, Grenada, Montserrat, Nevis, St. Kitts, Tobago, and St. Vincent. These islands produced sugar and rum, the most valuable commodities imported from any colony into Britain. Their trade was subject to constant attack from America by rebel privateers like the *Oliver Cromwell,* the *General Washington,* the *Rattle Snake,* and the *Reprisal* that hovered around popular sailing routes along the north coast of Cuba and the eastern Caribbean and found sanctuary in the neighboring islands of foreign countries. After 1778, the British possessions became more vulnerable with the escalation of the war in the Caribbean. The navy was overstretched, often having fewer ships than there were British-owned islands in the eastern Caribbean. At the beginning of 1778, the army was thinly dispersed, with a little over 1,060 men fit for duty, compared to 8,000 French troops in the Caribbean. The successes of the previous war evaporated as one island after another fell to France, beginning with Dominica in 1778, then St. Vincent and Grenada in 1779, followed by Tobago in 1781, and St. Kitts, Montserrat, and Nevis in 1782.

To the disappointment of their American allies, French objectives were primarily concentrated in the Caribbean, where France had traditionally been a dominant presence: on the eve of the American Revolution, Saint-Domingue (Haiti) produced more sugar than the entire production of the British Caribbean. This was the major reason that

France failed to provide more direct military and naval support to the United States. In September 1778, France seized the initiative with the conquest of Dominica: two thousand French troops easily overwhelmed the British garrison, which consisted of a single company of forty-one soldiers. The French invaded the island before news of the expedition reached Admiral Sir Samuel Barrington, who was in any case under strict orders to remain at Barbados in Carlisle Bay. He was to await a secret expedition of troops detached from the army of Sir Henry Clinton in New York to attack the French island St. Lucia. The capture of Dominica enabled the French to simultaneously consolidate their colonial possessions and divide the British islands in the eastern Caribbean.

After 1778, Britain temporarily subordinated military activities in North America to give priority to objectives in the Caribbean. The government even discussed withdrawing from America in favor of the Caribbean. The expedition to St. Lucia necessitated the retreat of Sir Henry Clinton from Philadelphia and effectively undermined the Carlisle Peace Commission. It was successful, however, in conquering St. Lucia, giving the British possession of the fine harbor at Gros Islet Bay, which enabled the Royal Navy to shadow the French navy in the neighboring island of Martinique. When Rodney was appointed to the command of the Leeward Island squadron, St. Lucia had become the center of the British fleet and army in the eastern Caribbean.

The Caribbean was the main route of the military supplies that sustained George Washington and the Continental Army. The rebels lacked the resources to manufacture the materials necessary to wage war. Having exhausted their gunpowder supplies within the first nine months of the conflict, they relied on imports because they could not manufacture gunpowder in sufficient quantities. The Caribbean was also a leading supplier of salt that came largely from the Turks Islands, in the southernmost chain of the Bahamas. The Continental Congress and the state governments responded to the shortage of ammunition by sending agents to Europe and to the neutral islands in the Caribbean. Through his merchant house of Willing & Morris in Philadelphia, Robert Morris owned a fleet of ships that traded with the Caribbean and supplied the Continental Army.

At the beginning of the Revolutionary War, the major conduit of supplies to the Continental Army was through the French Caribbean. In an operation parallel to the modern drug trade that often runs the same routes, the gunpowder was divided among small craft, such as Virginia pilot boats. They would steal out in the night and sail much too fast to be caught by the few and sluggish British warships. Between 1776 and 1779, the twenty-four-year-old William Bingham built a fortune representing the Continental Congress in Martinique, where he supported the activities of privateers whose commanders met in the American Coffee House. He issued blank commissions for American privateers to give them the protection of nominal French ownership. He presented Martha Washington with a Nankin china tea service for use at Mount Vernon, which had been captured on a vessel bound for England and had belonged to Lady Isabella Hamilton, known as Lady Belle, the wife of the attorney general of St. Kitts and the daughter of the tenth earl of Buchan. Bingham was assisted by Richard Harrison, who helped master-mind the rebels' activities in Martinique, which "ever since the commencement of the Rebellion [was] . . . considered by the Americans as their chief magazine and asylum in these seas." The colorful playwright, courtier, and adventurer Pierre Beaumarchais, author of *The Marriage of Figaro* and *The Barber of Seville,* under the pseudonym of Roderigue Hortalez & Co. in Paris, consigned some of his military shipments to Bingham in Martinique. Beaumarchais's ships sailed with false papers, to disguise their cargoes and destinations, usually via Saint-Domingue to North America, where they were an essential source of supply to the Continental Army.[10]

Bingham appointed other American agents throughout the Caribbean in Saint-Domingue, Guadeloupe, St. Eustatius, and Curaçao. At the beginning of the war, Samuel Curzon and Isaac Gouverneur Jr. were merchant partners who acted as the local agents of Congress in St. Eustatius, and the states also appointed agents. By 1777, Virginia had a network throughout the Caribbean including John Ball in St. Eustatius, Thomas Webb in Curaçao, Raleigh Colston in Santo Domingo, and Thomas Bretman in Surinam. Maryland shared with Virginia in the appointment of Abraham van Bibber in St. Eustatius and Richard Harrison in Martinique. In association with private merchants and sympathetic governments, the agents procured gunpowder and other military supplies. During the first two years of the war, 90 percent of the gunpowder discharged by the rebels was procured from abroad and primarily from the Caribbean. The French, Dutch, Spanish, and Danish islands in the Caribbean were all active in supplying the revolutionaries in North America. As Lord Macartney, the governor of Grenada, observed, "The Genius of all West Indians without distinction, seems turned to piracy and free-booting."[11]

As commander of the Leeward Islands squadron, Rodney imposed strict discipline on his officers and men. By discouraging desertion and by taking personal control of the exchange of prisoners of war, he improved the manning of the fleet. He reorganized the dockyard at English Harbour in Antigua, the main base of the Royal Navy in the Eastern Caribbean, and he promoted innovation, such as copper sheathing the bottoms of ships to make them seaworthy for longer periods. In 1780, Rodney appointed Dr. Gilbert Blane to accompany the fleet and study the health of the seamen, which resulted in the publication of Blane's *An Address to the Officers Serving in H.M. Ships of War in the West Indies and America.* Blane was to become a major influence on naval medicine and the modern science of epidemiology. Under his influence, Rodney rigorously insisted upon good hygiene among the sailors, ventilation, clean clothing, and fresh fruit and vegetables to prevent scurvy. By April 1782, the mortality rate of the fleet (exclusive of battle casualties) was 1.4 percent compared to 11 percent among the army in the Caribbean.[12]

II

On February 3, 1781, St. Eustatius surrendered unconditionally to the combined British naval and military forces of Rodney and John Vaughan. The inhabitants were not even aware of the outbreak of war between Britain and the Dutch Republic, and it was said that the blow was as sudden as a clap of thunder and wholly unexpected. Attacked by fifteen British warships and three thousand troops, the island was incapable of resistance with a garrison of less than sixty men. It was instantly captured together with a Dutch frigate of thirty-six guns, five warships, and 150 merchant ships in the bay. Rodney's fleet also pursued, overtook, and captured a richly laden merchant convoy of thirty ships and two naval escorts that had sailed a couple of days earlier for Holland. During a brief exchange of naval fire, the Dutch Admiral Willem Crul, aboard his sixty-gun flagship *Mars,* died after losing his leg and was buried at the Dutch Reformed Church, where his grave can still be seen on St. Eustatius. Rodney wrote to Lord Sandwich that "the capture is beyond conception." The news was celebrated with bonfires in Britain. There was a mood of triumphalism represented in a satirical engraving by James Gillray, *The DUTCH-MAN in the DUMPS,* which portrayed grieving Dutchmen contemplating ruin with one character saying, "Americans now, to Old England might bow." In Belfast and Dublin, the news was similarly greeted with bonfires, the illumination of buildings, and volunteer corps firing *feux de joie.*[13]

Following the conquest, the British commanders spent three fateful months engaged in the indiscriminate plunder of the island. They continued to fly the Dutch flag over St. Eustatius to trick unsuspecting ships from North America. They ordered a general confiscation of all private property including clothing, petty cash, and even food, and the soldiers and sailors marked the broad-arrow, a symbol of government property, "on every store particularly on iron chests." They stopped both men and women in the street to search them "in the most Shameful manner." They searched wallets and pockets, and dug up gardens and even graves for hidden treasure. They ransacked houses, seized slaves and horses, confiscated merchant inventories, accounts, and letter books, and locked the warehouses. They withheld every necessary of life "for the space of twenty days, before the retail shops were permitted to be reopened." They even broke open cabinets of the Dutch governor and his wife and took "every Thing valuable." It was alleged that the British quartermaster general told one inhabitant, who pleaded for food, "not a Mouthful; must you be told a second Time—not a Mouthful!"[14]

The commanders did not distinguish between friends and foes. In the House of Commons, Edmund Burke later evoked the scene, describing how a "Sentence of Beggary was pronounced indiscriminately against all." The troops paraded the inhabitants daily according to their nationality, in preparation for intended exile. They spared the

Dutch sugar planters, except Governor de Graff, who was "the first Man that insulted the British" by saluting the American flag; they seized his plantations and sent him a prisoner to England. Within an afternoon, they gathered all the Americans on the beach and loaded them on board boats to leave the island, including John Witherspoon, the son of the signer of the Declaration of Independence and president of the College of New Jersey (Princeton). Their tactics even forced those American loyalists who had found refuge on the island "to seek bread wherever they could find it."[15]

The commanders treated all the British inhabitants of St. Eustatius as smugglers, an erroneous assumption since not all were engaged in illicit trade. Britain had permitted a limited trade with neutral islands, in fact, in 1780, Parliament had specifically passed an act to encourage British merchants to import tobacco from such islands. British ships had sailed with valid clearances from the major ports of Britain and Ireland for St. Eustatius. The British residents there included refugees from the British islands occupied by France, and "unfortunate traders . . . driven down by losses in business" who had "preserved their faith to their creditors and their allegiance to their country."[16]

Rodney reserved the harshest treatment for the Jewish community in St. Eustatius. There were some 350 Sephardi and Ashkenazi Jewish residents, who with the support of the Jewish communities in Curaçao and Amsterdam had built a synagogue that they called *Honen Dalim,* "the one who is merciful to the poor," the ruins of which still remain on the island. On her visit there before the war, Janet Schaw encountered orthodox Jews for the first time in her life. She wrote movingly of the persecution they had suffered in Europe, describing one who had been tortured in France where "he was stretched on the wheel . . . under the hands of the executioner [until he had] . . . hardly a joint in place." Another had suffered eighteen months under the Spanish Inquisition "till he has hardly the semblance of a human creature remaining," after which he was dumped in a street at night.[17]

The conquest of St. Eustatius was "a day of desolation to the community at large & Jews in particular." The Jews not only shared in the common loss, but the men were banished and separated from their wives and children. They were not even told the destination of their exile. They "petitioned, intreated, implored, [and] remonstrated against so hard a sentence, but in vain." In contrast to the other residents, they were not allowed to keep personal possessions, and those who withheld cash were set apart for punishment. The British assembled 101 Jewish adult males, ripping open the linings of their pockets and tearing their clothes to pieces in search of money. They then hurried thirty of them "off the island, destitute of everything, to solicit the cold charity of Antigua, and St. Kitts." They locked the rest in a weighing house for three days, releasing them just in time to witness the auction of their belongings.[18]

Some of the banished Jews were exiled American loyalists. One of them had previously been persecuted by the French for his "partiality to the English," but this did not spare him from mistreatment by the British. He was taken prisoner, despite his "very infirm state of health" and died two days later. Myer Pollock was also taken prisoner, despite having been "stripped of all his worth" in Rhode Island for importing tea from the East India Company. He had lost his brother and brother-in-law in the British cause, leaving him to raise their families, as well as to care for his mother and his sister. When he tried to conceal some money from his British captors in St. Eustatius, he was separated for additional punishment. A similar fate awaited Samson Myers, the secretary to the synagogue and a loyalist refugee from Norwalk, Connecticut.[19]

General Vaughan apparently interceded on behalf of the Jews, who later sent him an address, signed by "the warden and rulers of the people," expressing gratitude for the clemency and goodness he had exhibited.[20]

III

Rodney justified these extraordinary proceedings on the grounds that the island was nothing but a nest of robbers, adventurers, traitors, and rebels who had forfeited any right to be treated as a respectable people or protected by the rules of war. The admiral was the dominant of the two commanders with his illustrious naval career and popularity in Britain. Likewise, during a daring relief expedition to supply Burgoyne in 1777, Major General John Vaughan had been responsible for the controversial burning of the towns of Kingston and Esopus in upper New York, justifying the latter action on the grounds that it was "a nursery for almost every Villain in the Country." However, Vaughan mostly deferred to Rodney throughout the conquest of St. Eustatius. Rodney insisted that the inhabitants were "Traitors to their King, and Parricides to their Country . . . mixed with Jews, and Dutch who, regardless of the Treaties subsisting between Great Britain and Holland, had traitorously conspired, and for years supported the Public Enemys of the state, and the Rebellion of our divided colonies." He felt justified that "a perfidious people, wearing the mask of friendship, traitors to their country, and rebelling against their king deserve no favour or consideration."[21]

Rodney was fully convinced that Britain would have conquered the southern states of America but for the trade of St. Eustatius. He regarded it as an "island inhabited by Rebellious Americans and their agents, disaffected British factors who from base, and lucrative motives, were the great support of the American Rebellion." He fumed that this rock had done England "more harm than all the arms of her most potent enemies, and alone supported the infamous American Rebellion." He maintained that commerce and commerce alone had sustained the rebellion, and that an end to commerce would be an end to the rebellion.[22]

Furthermore, Rodney believed that St. Eustatius had robbed him of a victory against the French fleet, that might have turned the balance of the American war dramatically in favor of Britain. On April 17, 1780, Rodney had fought an indecisive naval battle against the superior French fleet of Admiral de Guichen. Afterward, he was unable to obtain supplies from St. Eustatius where the merchants claimed insufficient stocks, but they assisted de Guichen by providing two shiploads of cordage and naval stores, together with carpenters to make repairs. The French might otherwise have lost eight ships, or have had to detach them to refit at Saint-Domingue. Instead, they retained their numerical superiority when Rodney encountered them again off Dominica and Martinique on May 15 and May 19. This lost opportunity rankled with the admiral for the rest of his life. The defeat of a French fleet would have complemented the British successes of 1780, the capture of Charleston, the defeat of General Horatio Gates at Camden, and the defection of Benedict Arnold.[23]

Rodney's defense of his actions did not justify his continuing to plunder the inhabitants after the island had surrendered. Before its capture, the British themselves had traded there, making purchases for the army in North America and in the Caribbean. British naval officers had sold prizes at St. Eustatius that were sometimes resold to the rebels in North America. Following the fall of Dominica in 1778, Governor William Mathew Burt had armed and fortified St. Kitts with supplies from St. Eustatius. Over 40 percent of the land on St. Eustatius was devoted to cultivating food crops, which were exported to the British Leeward Islands. In 1778–79, these islands had been able to reduce the "miseries of actual Famine," thanks to food imports from St. Eustatius that were "formerly received from North America." The slaves in Antigua "must have perished had they not been fed from St. Eustatius." Furthermore, by a treaty of 1678, Britain had actually acknowledged the right of the Dutch to continue trading as neutrals in wartime, without any specific prohibition of naval stores.[24]

The British commanders admitted their ignorance to Lord George Germain when they declared that "we military men . . . cannot be suppos'd to be so well vers'd, in the Laws of Nations, or the particular Law of Great Britain." Despite specific orders not to touch "the Property of British subjects, lawfully exported thither," Rodney went ahead with the sale of confiscated goods. When a delegation from the Assembly of St. Kitts protested, Rodney replied that he had a special place for their petition in his quarter gallery (the admiral's privy). He eventually conceded that "a few, a very few may have been less guilty of those atrocious practices and may have legally imported the goods . . . from Great Britain." He even began to restore their property, but again changed his mind and resumed the sale.[25]

The indiscriminate plunder by the British commanders at St. Eustatius had violated the customs and norms of warfare, which generally allowed private citizens to keep their property once they had surrendered. The concept of rules of war was well established. This was at least the convention in Europe where there was a rich literature on the ethics of warfare, by jurists like Francisco de Vitoria in Spain, Hugo Grotius in the

Netherlands, Samuel von Pufendorf in the Holy Roman Empire, and Emmerich de Vattel in Switzerland. Enlightenment thought gave emphasis to the humanitarian treatment of conquered peoples, and following the Seven Years' War (1756–63), Britain had engaged in a remarkable experiment of permitting French law and the Roman Catholic Church among the conquered French inhabitants of Canada and Grenada. The theorists of just warfare did allow latitude to commanders in cases of necessity. Nevertheless, there was a convention of paroles and exchanges, flags of truce, care of enemy wounded, and honorable terms of surrender.[26]

As a veteran of warfare in Europe, Rodney was well aware of the rules of war, but by treating the inhabitants of St. Eustatius as pirates, he was cleverly using a loophole in which outlaws had no legal status, and he was exploiting the ambiguity of law and custom in the Caribbean. There were double standards cloaked in a system of plural legal ethics, which varied according to region. Whereas slavery had been effectively abolished in England by the Somerset Case in 1772, it continued in the British Caribbean until the Emancipation Act of 1833 (which provided for gradual manumission). In the seventeenth century, it had been common for wars to continue in the Caribbean during periods of peace in Europe, giving rise to the phrase "no peace beyond the line." The majority of the slaves in America were originally captives of war in Africa, which Europeans justified not by the customs of their own countries but by practices in West Africa.

However, attitudes in Britain were changing even in relation to the Caribbean, as had been apparent in the indignation expressed against the Carib War in St. Vincent in 1772. There was awareness that local planters had deliberately provoked the war to expand their sugar plantations and remove the Caribs. The French and British were so respectful of property when they occupied one another's islands in the Caribbean that the white elites preferred to capitulate without a fight in the event of an enemy landing rather than risk their plantations in a protracted siege or face the danger of a slave insurrection. Rodney had therefore violated what were becoming recognized norms of warfare among Europeans even in the Americas. When Banastre Tarleton returned to Britain, he similarly found himself the object of disapproval for his ruthless tactics in the southern states of America. The belief in their own moral superiority and civility was an important part of self-identity among the British and more generally in western Europe.[27]

Rodney had not only transgressed moral norms but had set an unfortunate precedent that might have affected the behavior of the French. This was the concern of the powerful planters and merchants of the British Caribbean, who were so wealthy that significant numbers of them had returned as absentee landowners to Britain, where they had an influential caucus in Parliament. They feared that the French might imitate Rodney during their occupation of Dominica, St. Vincent, and Grenada, and with inadequate naval protection, the planters and merchants felt vulnerable to further French conquests. The Bristol Society of Merchant Venturers, which was closely connected with the West India Society of Merchants and Planters in London, accused Rodney and Vaughan of having waged an "uncivilized system of war," and their criticism was seconded by the opposition in Parliament. The stage was set for another inquiry and more embarrassment for the government in Britain.[28]

IV

Rodney was notorious for being unscrupulous in financial matters. Throughout his career his patriotic fervor was mixed with a large element of greed. Before the outbreak of war in America in 1775, he was so badly in debt that he fled abroad to escape creditors and imprisonment, and lived in exile in Paris. He was still unable to return when war broke out, and in 1776, his wife was reduced to trying to raise a subscription from members of White's Club in London to pay off his debts. In a petition to the earl of Sandwich as first lord of the Admiralty, she represented "the distressful situation of Sir George, herself and the four children, who must be in danger of literally starving if his Lordship is not induced to restore him that countenance and friendship with which he has formerly been honoured." French sources claimed that Rodney actually served time in prison during his exile. In May 1777, he wrote to his son, "May God grant that you may never experience the same," and asked his wife to "Think for me, for I can scarce think for myself." He was only able to return to Britain thanks to the generosity of a French nobleman, Louis Antoine de Gontaut, duc de Biron. In London, he had to seek sanctuary from his creditors by living opposite St. James's Palace, where he was able to avail himself of the ancient custom of immunity from arrest for anyone in the presence of the king or near a royal palace. While Rodney was in this "unfriended state," Richard Cumberland, the under secretary of state for America, described how he had "nothing but exclusion and despair before his eyes."[29]

For Rodney, financial difficulties were nothing new. He had been born into genteel poverty and brought up on the charity of a distant relative. His father had been reduced to penury after losing his investments in the great speculative bust of the eighteenth century, the South Sea Bubble (1720). Rodney had acquired a fortune early in his career from captures at sea and some legacies from wealthy relatives, but had frittered it away on a lavish lifestyle, the building of a country estate, and a gambling addiction. In 1768, he had been ruined in one of the most expensive elections of the eighteenth century, when he stood for Parliament in Northampton. Rodney sold his country estate but made his situation much worse when he signed a loan contract that committed him to paying almost 13½ percent interest. He was relying upon a lucrative naval command and the anticipated outbreak of war with Spain, but this did not happen. Furthermore, his loan failed to consolidate all his debts.[30]

Rodney thus had strong financial motives for his excessive greed at St. Eustatius.

His abject circumstances were suddenly transformed by the capture of the island, which offered the best chance for the sixty-three-year-old naval commander to pay off his debts and to provide for his family. His health was poor. Left a widower by the death of his first wife, he had married again to a woman twenty years his junior, and he still had young children to support. The first month's sales of the plunder at St. Eustatius netted an astounding £100,529 10s. 4d. Admiral Hood, his second in command, predicted that the commanders would "find it difficult to convince the world that they [had] not proved themselves wickedly rapacious."[31]

Rodney did not disguise his elation at the sudden transformation of his financial situation. As he wrote to his wife after the conquest, "I shall be happy as, exclusive of satisfying all debts, something will be left for my children. . . . My chief anxiety is, that neither yourself nor my girls shall ever be necessitous, nor be under obligations to others." His letters to his family were euphoric with promises of a new London home, "the best harpsichord money can purchase" for his favorite daughter, a marriage settlement for his oldest son, a commission in the Foot Guards for a younger son, a dowry for another daughter to marry an earl, and a settlement of the debts of his prospective noble son-in-law.[32]

In the month following the capture of St. Eustatius, Rodney and Vaughan held an auction in which they sold the confiscated goods to buyers of any country. It was described by critics as a grand military fair. In an allegation that Rodney denied, the sale was said to have included naval and military stores in order to promote the sale of other goods. According to a later litigant against Rodney, sales to the French were "so notoriously flagrant" that the officer on board the British flagship, "under whose stern they necessarily passed, [asked visitors] . . . not—*from where came ye;* but *have ye money on board?*" Captain Harvey "was appointed to see the Purchasers, with their Commodities, clear" of British privateers. It was claimed that the French and Americans were able to purchase stores at the sale 50 percent cheaper than they had bought from the Dutch. Meanwhile, the British commissioner of the dockyard at Antigua complained that the admiral was sending him unsuitable materials at inflated rates. Rodney countered that the commissioner and storekeepers were angry because they received a lower commission on cheaper goods. In Britain, the auction was ridiculed in contemporary cartoons and satires, which depicted Rodney with a gavel accepting the bids.[33]

Rodney even appointed as agent for the auction of the captured goods a merchant called Aretas Akers from St. Kitts, who was suspected of complicity in the contraband trade of St. Eustatius. Akers had been friendly with the agents for South Carolina and Virginia in St. Eustatius, and was said to have had loans and merchandise on the island worth between forty and fifty thousand pounds. Rodney's choice of Akers and his failure to appoint a commission to handle the capture further strained his thirty-five-year-old relationship with Hood, who wrote scathing accounts of the behavior of his superior which are sometimes dismissed as nothing more than the personal rancor of an envious subordinate, but which are all too well supported by testimonies of others at St. Eustatius.[34]

Rodney was infamous also among his contemporaries for financial impropriety. He had been forced to return a racehorse from his stables that he had improperly taken from a French merchant ship before the outbreak of war. While Rodney was commander in chief of the naval squadron in Jamaica in 1771–74, the earl of Sandwich acknowledged that the public money the admiral had expended and "the mode of procuring it" were "undoubtedly very irregular and unprecedented." Rodney responded to the accusations by pleading ignorance of the proper procedures, as he did again at St. Eustatius, but he was not eligible to receive a command on the outbreak of the American War until he reimbursed the Navy Board for expenses in Jamaica. He appointed his fifteen-year-old son a post-captain, who later had the dubious distinction of being the longest-serving captain in the Royal Navy.[35]

Eighteenth-century warfare still possessed features of the age-old practice of private profit from the plunder of war. In a period of inadequate salaries and no pensions, officers and men expected rewards in the form of what was euphemistically called prize money, which was distributed according to exact proportions between the different ranks. It was disingenuous for Rodney to plead that he was unaware of the likely benefits of his capture of St. Eustatius, when the royal grant of prize money was a standard practice, whereby commanders traditionally received one-eighth of the entire value of the captured goods. The total proceeds from St. Eustatius amounted to between four and five million pounds sterling, the largest wartime capture of the century. Because his share was split with General Vaughan, Rodney stood to gain one-sixteenth of all the possessions seized at St. Eustatius.[36]

St. Eustatius was one of many episodes in the admiral's life in which he was deflected from an official mission by the lure of prize money. During the Seven Years' War, Rodney had been given the important responsibility of taking Major General Jeffrey Amherst to his post as commander in chief of the expedition against Louisburg, but lengthened the passage by pursuing potential prizes. Rodney was similarly accused of having jeopardized a mission by sending ships to cruise for prizes when he was under orders to await the arrival at Barbados of the fleet of Admiral Sir George Pocock and troops of the earl of Albemarle to launch an attack against Cuba. Following the capture of Martinique in 1762, Rodney quarreled with the army over prize money, and during his command in Jamaica in 1771–74, the earl of Sandwich feared that he might deliberately provoke a war with Spain to obtain prize money.[37]

Only a few months before the conquest St. Eustatius, Rodney had sailed to New York, where he claimed superior authority to Admiral Marriot Arbuthnot, who commanded the fleet in North America. Since he had gone on his own initiative and did not undertake any military engagements, it was suspected that his motive was to obtain a share of prize money. This was certainly the view of Arbuthnot, who issued orders for money to be paid to his own agent and threatened legal action against Rodney. According to Arbuthnot, Rodney "displayed the most wanton unpresidented abuse of power that ever was exhibited." He "stripped the storehouses of all necessaries both for ships and men . . . carried away two frigates, impressed 400 seamen, mostly out of the victualling ships and transports, and has so debilitated me that I have not an escort to convoy them home." During his two-month sojourn in New York, Rodney made no attempt to meet with Arbuthnot. His unexpected presence merely worsened existing tensions between Arbuthnot and Sir Henry Clinton, and also contributed to the rivalry and friction between the fleets in the Caribbean and North America.[38]

Rodney's behavior at St. Eustatius not only suggested greed, but also anti-Semitism. It was said that Rodney was unaware of the treatment of the Jews until it was too late, but several witnesses contradicted this claim. He himself wrote of apprehending "a Rascal of a Jew [who] has hid a chest of 5000 joes in a cane patch." Only the humane intervention of General Vaughan allowed the remaining Jews "time to settle their affairs" and "to return, and arrange their little matters." As a naval commander in Jamaica in the early 1770s, Rodney had lashed out against the Jews, who he claimed conducted a "pernicious and Contraband Trade" at Kingston, where he insisted that "particularly the Jews" traded illegally with the Spanish. He confiscated two of their ships that were condemned for sale in the Vice-Admiralty Court. When he wanted to obtain naval intelligence from the Jews of Santo Domingo, he observed, "they will do anything for money." There were of course Jewish merchants who had traditionally engaged in illicit trade. They had the advantage of speaking several languages, together with family and religious networks throughout the islands, but a recent study argues that their dominance in such trade was exaggerated by other merchants and that they "always faced severer punishment than Christians." Rodney never attempted to demonstrate that the Jewish merchants were guiltier of illicit trade than the other merchants in St. Eustatius.[39]

Not even the friends and allies of Rodney and Vaughan felt able to exonerate them from censure for their indiscriminate plunder following the conquest of St. Eustatius. The Rev. James Ramsay, a former naval surgeon, who was close to the commanders and whose brother-in-law was agent for the sale of the goods, admitted that "the clamour raised on the proceedings at Statia is very great and it must be confessed, that the hardships imposed on individuals, in many cases, have been scandalous, in most unnecessary, and in all so notorious, that it is in vain to attempt to palliate, or conceal them." Later to become famous as a leading abolitionist in Britain, Ramsay had tried to persuade the commanders that further punishing the inhabitants of St. Eustatius was unnecessary, since they had already achieved their objective of cutting off the trade of the enemy. His words unheeded, he despaired that "the national character, and the honour of the service have received wounds, that will not easily be healed." Nevertheless, out of "regard for both Commanders," Ramsay advised Lord George Germain on how to make the best case for them before Parliament.[40]

V

There was an immediate outcry against the illegality of the proceedings at St. Eustatius. In Amsterdam, crowds rioted in protest against the plunder. The Society of West India Merchants and Planters in London drew up an address to the king complaining of the behavior of the commanders, printed the address to win public support, and sent a delegation to meet with Lord George Germain. The merchants were particularly concerned about possibilities of retaliation by the French, a legitimate concern since the merchants of St. Eustatius had requested that France indemnify their losses from the occupied British islands of Grenada, Dominica, and St. Vincent.[41]

On November 30, 1781, five days after the king had received official news of the surrender of Cornwallis at Yorktown, Edmund Burke brought the issue of St. Eustatius before Parliament, but his motion for copies of the orders sent to the commanders and for an official inquiry was defeated. Having just returned from the Caribbean, Rodney spoke in the debate and described "the attacks upon his character" and "false aspersions" as "impotent" and "wicked . . . the shafts of envy, malice, and detraction." Vaughan also participated in the debate, in which he said that the warehouses had been locked to prevent fire and theft. Lord North defended the commanders, and the motion was lost by 163 votes to 89. Undeterred, Burke began to prepare a case against Rodney that had the makings of his more famous prosecution of Warren Hastings.[42]

On February 4, 1782, Burke made his final appeal when he presented the petition of one of the Jewish merchants who appeared in person to present his case. He was the seventy-year-old Samuel Hohen, an elder of the Jewish community, a native of Amsterdam, and a twenty-five-year resident of St. Eustatius, who was personally too impoverished to bring legal proceedings against the commanders. He was a merchant who had dealt only in dry goods, not military stores. He had been reduced from a prosperous condition to poverty and absolute want. The petition was referred to a committee of the House of Commons, and Burke planned to bring criminal charges.[43]

On the subject of St. Eustatius, Nathaniel Wraxall recalled in his memoirs that Burke blazed with such eloquence in describing the sufferings of individuals that he surpassed even his usual oratorical brilliance. Burke compared the actions of Rodney and Vaughan "to the most savage outrages of the ferocious leaders of the most barbarous ages." He painted a picture of misery and oppression that inspired both the sympathies and the indignation of the House. Lord North sat silent throughout, creating the impression that he did not approve of the actions of the commanders and that the Cabinet was divided in its reaction. According to Horace Walpole, the ministers were unconvincing in their defense of the commanders and the government supporters admitted that they had voted against their consciences in order to defeat Burke. As a personal friend of both Germain and Rodney, Nathaniel Wraxall was one of the members who voted against Burke, but he acknowledged in his memoirs that he was unable, either on moral or on political grounds, to condone the events at St. Eustatius.[44]

The initiative thereafter passed to the law courts where the admiral faced suits until his death in 1792. Some of the legal cases lasted more than a decade and many were referred to the High Court of Appeals for Prizes. Ninety claims of upwards of £300,000 represented almost the entire value of the commission received by Rodney and Vaughan. The claim of one British merchant, Richard Downing Jennings, amounted to £70,000. In 1786, the claimants won a judgment for reimbursement for the full original value of the goods and not just the profits of the sales. Mr. Hoelein, one of the claimants, settled for £1,000 from the commanders, although his goods had only yielded a little over £154 in the sale. In response to diplomatic pressure, the French merchants at St. Eustatius were similarly reimbursed; Rodney had already been forced to return their household goods and slaves while he was still in St. Eustatius. The British government later paid them two million livres in compensation.[45]

Rodney blamed the success of the English lawsuits on the disappearance of crucial evidence. The merchant letterbooks and ledgers seized at St. Eustatius were shipped to England where they were kept in the offices of Lord George Germain; and William Knox, the under secretary to Germain, was thought to have taken many of them for fear that he might be prosecuted by merchants for having kept them in confinement. Rodney's supporters argued that the loss of these papers by the British government was contrived by political enemies of Lord North, whose government fell in March 1782. The fate of these papers must remain a mystery, but it is equally possible that their disappearance was to the benefit of Rodney. The surviving evidence suggests that these papers did nothing to support his case and might actually have harmed it, since merchants' records rarely contained accounts of smuggling activities and illicit trade. Rodney had ordered the sale of the captures without investigating these papers and had simply assumed the guilt of the merchants.[46]

Two months after the conquest of St. Eustatius, an army officer examined some of the merchant papers, found "nothing material or improper" in their contents, and returned some of them to their owners. The rest were shipped to England, where George Jackson, acting as counsel for the admiral, found them incomplete and confused. Before their disappearance, Rodney made no attempt to use these papers to defend himself in Parliament or in the High Court of Appeals for Prizes. Furthermore, Rodney's own letterbook contained a gap of eleven months overlapping with the period of the conquest and plunder of St. Eustatius. In 1787, Rodney wrote and published a defense of himself in a pamphlet entitled *A Plain State of Facts Relative to the Capture of St. Eustatius.* He remarkably did not even address the accusations of plunder.[47]

The fiasco of the conquest of St. Eustatius continued when the French seized a homeward-bound convoy carrying much of the remaining seized goods. The conquest never had the desired result of cutting off trade to America. As with the modern drug trade, the closing of one island merely offered opportunities to another. St. Eustatius was soon replaced as a conduit of trade with North America by Cuba, the Danish island of St. Thomas, and French-occupied Grenada. The conquest of St. Eustatius actually stimu-lated the economic revival of Pennsylvania, which was consequently able to feed the marching army of George Washington on its way to Yorktown. In November 1781, France retook St. Eustatius, together with the pay of the British forces in North America. It was a particularly enterprising and daring raid. The British officer in charge of the defending garrison was court-martialed for negligence and found guilty.[48]

VI

Beyond the momentary benefits of the original conquest, the conduct of Admiral Rodney at St. Eustatius had disastrous strategic consequences for the British war in America, for it contributed to the British defeat at Yorktown and the loss of North America.

According to Lieutenant Colonel Banastre Tarleton, Cornwallis had confidently expected the arrival of the fleet from the British Caribbean at Yorktown. Instead, Rodney remained at St. Eustatius for three crucial months during which he ceased to pursue further naval operations. His presence was hardly necessary when the island, stripped of its trade, was a mere rock "neither of real nor relative importance." Rodney was pre-occupied with the details of the sales of the captured goods and the safe return of the loot to Britain. He called off a proposed expedition against Dutch Curaçao and Surinam, the command of which he had promised to Hood. Although Rodney later justified his order on the grounds of intelligence he had received of the sailing of the French fleet to the Caribbean, Hood claimed that he had made the decision before the news arrived.[49]

These setbacks were incidental compared to the failure of Rodney to intercept de Grasse's fleet, which had left Brest to go to the Caribbean on March 22. British strategic policy was predicated on a superior British naval presence, and the government therefore expected Rodney either to prevent de Grasse from reaching Martinique or to follow him to North America. Delegating his responsibility to Admiral Hood, Rodney instead re-mained at St. Eustatius. When the homebound convoy of a hundred prizes was about to sail from St. Eustatius, Rodney ordered Hood to move from the windward to the leeward of Martinique. Hood suspected that the change was to protect the captured goods, rather than to intercept reinforcements from France. Hood complained, "doubtless there never was a squadron so unmeaningly stationed as the one under my command, and what Sir George Rodney's motive for it could be I cannot conceive, unless it was to cover him at St. Eustatius." These were not retrospective criticisms, but concerns that he had repeatedly expressed to Rodney. His fears were justified by events when de Grasse outmaneuvered him by sailing windward into Martinique.[50]

In defense of Rodney, it should be said that there were valid strategic reasons to reposition Hood. Owing to sudden changes in currents and winds, it was difficult to patrol from either the windward or the leeward side of the entrance to Fort Royal Bay in Martinique. In 1779, Vice Admiral John Byron had kept the windward position urged by Hood, but had been unable to prevent the entry of d'Estaing's fleet into the bay. Although keeping a windward position, Rodney had twice failed to intercept French fleets, those of de Blénac in 1762 and de Guichen in June 1780. Furthermore, when Rodney repositioned Hood at Martinique, he had been misinformed by intelligence reports from Britain that underestimated the strength of the French fleet. Nevertheless, the suspicion must remain that mercenary motives caused him to reposition Hood and to remain with part of the British fleet at St. Eustatius.[51]

Rodney further helped seal the fate of Cornwallis at Yorktown by failing to send timely and accurate intelligence of the French fleet to Sir Henry Clinton and Admiral Thomas Graves in New York. It was not until July 7 that Rodney warned Graves of de Grasse's sailing for America. Because Graves was out at sea, he did not receive the letter in New York until August 16. Contrary to Rodney's later claims, his message underestimated the threat, in the reasonable expectation that the French would split their fleet and send part of it to escort a homeward-bound convoy of merchant ships from the French Caribbean. Unaware that de Grasse had kept his fleet together contrary to instructions from France, Rodney gave the impression to the British generals that only part of the French fleet was bound for America. On July 31, Rodney was disabused when he received new intelligence that de Grasse had sailed with his entire fleet of twenty-eight ships of the line and was likely to be reinforced by another French squadron in North America. Because he knew that de Grasse was accompanied by Virginia pilots who had boarded the French fleet at Saint-Domingue, Rodney was the first to realize that the French intended to make their "grand effort" in Virginia.

However, Rodney did not immediately relay the report of French intentions and the revised estimate of the strength of the French fleet to Graves and Clinton. Instead, he hesitated about whether to follow the French or accompany the West India convoy back to Britain. It was not until August 13 that he finally sent a warning to the British commanders in New York. He had waited eleven days, and the message did not arrive until the fate of Cornwallis was virtually sealed. Rodney later exaggerated the extent to which he had foreseen the tragedy. When he departed with the homeward-bound convoy from the Caribbean, his information was still incomplete and he did not appreciate the full magnitude of de Grasse's force. By giving constant assurances of the surveillance of the French fleet, Rodney helped perpetuate complacency among the British commanders in both New York and Yorktown.[52]

The British government had assumed that Rodney would follow de Grasse, taking with him three British regiments from the Caribbean. After much equivocation, in which he changed his mind from day to day, Rodney instead ordered Hood to sail for America while he returned to St. Eustatius and then, only two days before the arrival of urgent dispatches from Clinton in regard to the gravity of the situation in America, sailed for Britain. It was very different from his action the previous year when he had rushed to New York. Hood believed that Rodney returned home in order to avoid defeat and protect his reputation, but such behavior was uncharacteristic of a man undaunted by the challenge of battle against a superior fleet. Rodney blamed ill health for his inaction, since he had long suffered severe gout and periods of nervous exhaustion. Only a month earlier, he had insisted that as long as he was mentally fit to give orders, he would pursue the French fleet "let them go where they will."[53]

Although ill health may have played a role, Rodney was keen to return to Britain to answer his critics about the conquest of St. Eustatius and to defend himself in Parliament. His first priority on arriving was not recuperating his health, but making an unannounced visit to George III to justify his actions at St. Eustatius. He hurried from Plymouth to Windsor where he astonished and embarrassed the king, who had just returned from hunting and who was not prepared for his unexpected guest. Dismayed by newspaper accounts of St. Eustatius, George III evaded the admiral by pleading fatigue. The *Public Advertiser* jeered that Rodney's sickness was due to "spending so much Time in the damp vaults of St. Eustatius . . . had it come about thru' action then everyman would have regretted the impaired Health of the Admiral; but no one finds himself interested in the fate of the Storekeeper." As news of the surrender of the British forces at Yorktown circulated in London, Rodney was defending himself in the House of Commons against Edmund Burke.[54]

The failure of the British fleet to dislodge de Grasse in the battle of the Chesapeake Capes (September 5–9) sealed the fate of Lord Cornwallis's army at Yorktown. The British defeat was of course due to a variety of factors, but Rodney's departure had deprived the navy of their most senior and experienced commander in North America. Despite his vociferous criticism of his commander at St. Eustatius, Hood claimed that Rodney would have won at the battle of the Chesapeake Capes. When Clinton and Cornwallis met after Yorktown in New York, they both agreed that Rodney could have won the war if he had gone to the Chesapeake. It was virtually the only subject on which they agreed after Yorktown.[55]

Furthermore, Rodney had contributed to the numerical inferiority of the British fleet at the Chesapeake Capes. He sent his flagship, the *Sandwich,* to be repaired in the naval dockyard in Jamaica, together with two other ships to provide an escort, the *Torbay,* seventy-four guns, and the *Prince William,* sixty-four guns. When he was later asked by Sir Henry Clinton about having taken these three vital ships out of action, "he made no apology" but hemmed and hawed. He later claimed that he had ordered Vice Admiral Sir Peter Parker, the commander of the Jamaican squadron, to send nine ships from Jamaica to America. In reality, however, he had simply urged Parker to send any ships that he could spare, but the latter had demurred, believing that he needed them all for the defense of the island. Rodney left for England with the *Gibraltar,* the *Triumph,* and the *Panther,* which he described as the finest ships in his fleet, while justifying their departure by claiming that they were in desperate need of repair. In any case, Hood sailed for America with only fourteen ships, a reduction of the Caribbean fleet by one-third. Even before hearing of Cornwallis's surrender at Yorktown, Sir Henry Clinton told Chief Justice William Smith that "he found great Fault with Sir George Rodney . . . and said he deserved to be ruined for his bad Conduct."[56]

In contrast to Rodney, who dispersed the British fleet, de Grasse did not split the French fleet in the Caribbean. Instead, he left the Spanish fleet of Admiral Don José Solano to protect the French West Indies, and took virtually his entire fleet to North America. He spent his own money providing transports for additional troops, under the command of the marquis de Saint-Simon in Saint-Domingue, to join the expedition to the Chesapeake and to reinforce the troops commanded by the comte de Rochambeau at Yorktown. The French fleet consequently outnumbered the British fleet at the Chesapeake Capes.[57]

Instead of Rodney, Rear Admiral Sir Thomas Graves was to command the most important naval battle of the American Revolution. Following the departure of Arbuthnot, who had quarreled with Clinton, Graves had been temporarily left in command while he awaited Arbuthnot's replacement from England. Such was the lack of government confidence in their admiral that Graves was due to be replaced by an officer of junior rank, Robert Digby. Partly because he lacked accurate information about the enemy, Graves failed to appreciate the threat, and he ignored a plea for immediate action by Hood, when he arrived from the Caribbean. Graves wasted crucial time hunting for a convoy of enemy supplies off Boston Bay. He was senior to Hood and was consequently the commander of both the North American and the Leeward Islands fleets in the Chesapeake, with Hood in command of the rear division.

It is a measure of the relative obscurity of the naval battle between the British and French off the Chesapeake Bay that it is known by multiple names, including the battle of the Virginia or Chesapeake Capes, of the Chesapeake Bay, of Lynnhaven Bay, of the Chesapeake, of Cape Henry, and of the Capes of Virginia. It was nevertheless the battle that determined the fate of Lord Cornwallis and his army at Yorktown. On September 5, 1781, Graves arrived in the morning to find that de Grasse's fleet was already in the

Chesapeake Bay. At noon, nineteen British ships of the line, with a total of fifteen hundred guns, faced twenty-four French warships with two thousand guns. The action lasted two and a half hours before nightfall, and only the vans of the two fleets were closely engaged, so much so that at one point they were almost within pistol shot. Anticipating the tactics of Rodney at the Saintes (1782) and Nelson at Trafalgar (1805), Graves attempted to concentrate his ships to isolate and overwhelm part of the French fleet. He failed, partly due to adverse winds but primarily because Admiral Hood's Leeward Islands squadron had no experience of sailing with the British North American fleet. This was a great disadvantage in the age of sail when captains needed to be able to anticipate the different speed of each ship in order to act cohesively. In addition, the simultaneous signals from Graves's flagship to form a line of battle and close with the enemy were misunderstood by Hood and his captains because the two fleets had different signal systems owing to the lack of standardization in the Royal Navy. Hood did not engage until it was too late, and Graves did not renew action the next day because his ships had suffered too much damage. Indeed, the length of time spent repairing them in New York was to be a factor in the failure of Graves and Clinton to launch a timely rescue of Cornwallis.[58]

After the action of September 5, the opposing fleets continued to sail within range of one another for two days, while drifting over a hundred miles south at some distance from Cape Hatteras. In the meantime, Admiral Jacques-Melchior Saint Laurent, comte de Barras, sailed into the Chesapeake Bay from Boston with another eight French ships of the line, together with supplies, transports, and siege artillery intended for Yorktown. In what amounted to a strategic defeat, the badly damaged and numerically inferior British fleet returned to refit in New York. De Grasse's fleet joined de Barras's ships in the Chesapeake Bay where he now had a total of thirty-five warships, which effectively precluded any chance of a British naval rescue for Cornwallis. The battle of the Chesapeake Capes was the first major French naval victory against the British since 1690.

Since the British fleet was outnumbered by the French, Rodney might well have fared no better against de Grasse than Graves. The following year, he defeated de Grasse, but the fleets were more evenly matched, with a numerically superior British fleet against larger French warships. Graves was criticized for not having dislodged de Grasse and occupying his moorings in the Chesapeake. A year later, Hood succeeded in this very maneuver against de Grasse during the French siege of St. Kitts by forcing his opponent out to sea, anchoring his ships in their place, and landing troops at Frigate Bay. It was brilliant seamanship, but it achieved nothing, for Hood was unable to assist the besieged British garrison at Brimstone Hill. Throughout his time off the coast of Virginia, furthermore, Graves was unaware of the deteriorating situation of Lord Cornwallis at Yorktown. He did not appreciate that the army needed to be rescued.[59]

Graves was commanding the only British fleet in the Americas. If he had suffered a major defeat at the Chesapeake Capes, he would have opened the way for a successful French attack on Jamaica and the remaining islands of the British Caribbean. Naval strength was the key to the balance of power among the European empires in the Americas, the Mediterranean, and the Pacific. The loss of a fleet would have had catastrophic implications for Britain. Its survival was more important than that of the army at Yorktown, which is why Graves seemingly obstructed efforts to relieve Cornwallis by what some of his own officers regarded as unnecessary delays in the time spent refitting his fleet in New York. Not even Rodney had won victories against such odds.

VII

Rodney escaped the recriminations that followed Yorktown. Having removed so many senior commanders, the government had little choice but to retain him and to defeat the attempts of Burke to make a political issue of St. Eustatius in Parliament. The government not only kept Rodney, but gambled in promoting him vice admiral of Great Britain and giving him permission to take much of the British fleet to the Caribbean to engage the French. It was a desperate last bid of the final months of the government of Lord North. The risk paid off.

The British surrender at Yorktown is traditionally regarded as the closing chapter of the Revolutionary War, but it marked an escalation of the conflict in the Caribbean. The French and Spanish prepared a grand attack on the remaining British islands, above all Jamaica. After Yorktown, de Grasse rejected the request of George Washington to assist with further operations against the British in Georgia and South Carolina. De Grasse had already overstayed his orders directing him to the Caribbean. French troops at Martinique were daily practicing embarking and disembarking, ready for another campaign. The French flagship was rumored to carry fifty thousand pairs of handcuffs and fetters intended for the slaves in Jamaica. In February 1782, de Grasse opened his campaign in the Caribbean with the capture of St. Kitts, Montserrat, and Nevis. He awaited reinforcements imminently expected from France under de Guichen, in addition to the Spanish fleet of twelve ships of the line and fifteen thousand troops commanded by Don Solano.[60]

Britain braced itself for the loss of its few remaining colonies in the Caribbean. The opposition rallied against the flagging government of Lord North. Charles James Fox warned that the ministry would "not be satisfied till they had mangled and destroyed the last miserable tenth" of the British Empire. Lord John Cavendish feared that "the great and splendid empire of Britain was nearly overturned; calamity, disgrace, and disaster were pouring on us from every quarter; and the measure of our misfortunes was likely to be soon completed by the loss of all our dominions in America and the Caribbean."

Contemporary prints lampooned the government, such as *The Royal Hunt or Prospect of the Year 1782*, which featured the devil saying, "I am sorry we have lost St. Kitts."[61]

As politicians fretted over the future of the Caribbean colonies, Rodney became the savior of the British Empire. North's government risked the defense of Britain to focus naval resources upon obtaining an overwhelming superiority in the Caribbean. The decision reflected the importance of the Caribbean to Britain, especially Jamaica. It was facilitated by an increase in the size of the navy, which had reached parity with the combined enemy fleets by 1782. In a passage through the Îles des Saintes between Dominica and Guadeloupe, Rodney's superior force intercepted de Grasse's fleet on its way from Martinique to join troops in Saint-Domingue for the invasion of Jamaica.[62]

Eighteenth-century naval warfare had a classical symmetry that was very much a characteristic of the aesthetics of the period. The opposing fleets formed parallel lines of battle with such precision that they almost mirrored one another. Each ship of the line (the largest warships) engaged an opponent of a similar size and firepower. Like land battles in the same era, naval battles were often indecisive, and victory was won through a process of attrition rather than annihilation. At the battle of the Saintes (April 12, 1782), however, Rodney departed from tradition by "breaking the line"—sailing through gaps in the opposing fleet, enabling his own ships to concentrate fire and to surround the enemy ships at close range. Assisted by the good fortune of a wind shift that divided the enemy fleet, his ships were able to fire their cannon at both sides of the enemy's ships. It was a revolutionary tactic later used by Admiral Howe at the Glorious First of June (1794), and by Nelson at Trafalgar. It became the subject of much later debate whether Rodney first conceived the tactic or merely stumbled upon it by accident. According to the playwright Richard Cumberland, Rodney had earlier elaborated the concept of "breaking the line" over dinner at Lord George Germain's country home at Stoneland. Rodney illustrated his idea by taking cherry stones from the table and arranging them into two lines to represent opposing fleets. He suddenly arrested the attention of the other guests "by declaring that he was determined to pierce the enemy's line of battle" and vowing that "he would lay the French admiral's flag at his sovereign's feet." In reality, the tactic of "breaking the line" was gaining popularity within the Royal Navy, as was demonstrated by Graves's unsuccessful attempt to use it at the Chesapeake Capes.[63]

At the battle of the Saintes on April 12, 1782, Rodney's flagship the *Formidable* was so close to the enemy ships as to be almost touching them. The battle continued "with unremitting fury till sun-set." Throughout twelve hours of action, Rodney stood on his quarterdeck, with no other refreshment than a lemon, which he held in his hand and applied frequently to his lips. As he watched several British ships concentrate their cannon fire on the French *Glorieux,* Sir Charles Douglas, who was the captain of the fleet, cried out "Behold, Sir George, the Greeks and the Trojans contending for the body of

Patroclus!" Pacing the quarterdeck, in great agitation as one of his own ships miscarried, Rodney exclaimed: "Damn the Greeks and damn the Trojans; I have other things to think of." A sudden change of wind divided the French fleet, making it possible for Rodney to break their line. As one of the ships covering the *Formidable* broke through the French line of battle and created an opening, Rodney "with a smile of joy" shouted to Douglas, "Now, my dear friend, I am at the service of your Greeks and Trojans, and the whole of Homer's *Iliad,* or as much of it as you please, for the enemy is in confusion, and our victory is secure."[64]

Captain William Cornwallis, the younger brother of Lord Charles Cornwallis, showed such gallantry aboard his seventy-four-gun ship that he was the "admiration of the whole fleet." Fighting "like Hector . . . as if emulous to revenge his brother's cause," Cornwallis engaged de Grasse's much larger 110-gun flagship, the *Ville de Paris,* which was the finest ship in the French navy, a gift to the nation from the city of Paris. He left it almost a wreck. Toward sunset, Sir Samuel Hood aboard the *Barfleur* aimed the most destructive fire for ten minutes against the *Ville de Paris,* and de Grasse finally struck his flag and surrendered. He was one of only three men aboard the upper deck who were still alive and unhurt, with four hundred crew dead and many more wounded. It made a horrific scene since the French did not follow the practice of the Royal Navy of throwing their dead overboard. The British fleet captured four other ships, together with the siege artillery intended for Jamaica. There were at least six thousand French fatalities owing to their ships being crowded with troops intended for the conquest of Jamaica. Rodney took de Grasse prisoner, making the victory all the more satisfying for public consumption.[65]

The victory caused an outburst of euphoria in Britain. Wraxall described it as "an event which electrified the whole population of Great Britain," and later recalled that "only the enthusiasm roused by Nelson at the Nile exceeded it." Written with his characteristic bravado, Rodney's account of the victory appeared in the newspapers, ending with the words "may the British flag flourish all over the globe." He became the darling of the press, and contemporary satirical prints reveled in his humiliation of de Grasse; for example, James Gillray's *The Ville De Paris Sailing for Jamaica, or Rodney Triumphant* depicted Rodney standing on the back of de Grasse heading for Jamaica, and *St. George & the Dragon* portrayed Sir George in the guise of the saint (Figure 32). The prints variously depicted de Grasse squatting to use a commode on board the British flagship and appearing on his knees on presentation at court to George III. Rodney was commemorated in medals, ballads, poems, and souvenir pottery. "Rodney Forever" became a popular song heard daily that summer in the amusement park at the Vauxhall Gardens in London. He was the subject of full-length life portraits commissioned from Thomas Gainsborough, Sir Joshua Reynolds, and Jean-Laurent Mosnier. Charles James Fox proclaimed the victory the most brilliant that the country had seen.[66]

Rodney was also celebrated in the British Caribbean, where the anniversary of his victory became a major celebration until superseded by Trafalgar. The Assembly of Jamaica commissioned John Bacon, one of the finest sculptors in England, to carve a commemorative neoclassical statue of Rodney from marble imported from Italy. It was the most impressive British monument of the Revolutionary War, depicting the admiral wearing a breastplate and with a toga thrown over his extended right arm holding a baton. The statue was housed in a splendid octagonal temple with a domed roof, surrounded by a balustrade, topped by a cupola, and flanked by two-story office buildings, which were linked to the temple by curving white colonnaded walkways. Three panels on the pedestal of the statue featured patriotic bas-reliefs of Britannia. The merchants of Kingston and the planters of Spanish Town competed for the emplacement of the monument, which survives today in the central square of the old government capital at Spanish Town. Rodney had become one of the few British heroes of the American Revolutionary War.[67]

Wraxall wrote in his memoirs that it was difficult to appreciate or imagine the effect of the news on the nation. He could not recall such emotions on any other occasion including Trafalgar, when the joy and excitement were clouded by the death of Nelson. After seven years of war and national humiliation, the intensity of the victory celebrations largely reflected public relief. Britain had stood alone against France, and the Saintes had rescued the country from the additional humiliation of the loss of its other colonies in the Caribbean. It helped to enable the British to make a separate peace agreement with the United States and to obtain much better terms with France. Wraxall described the victory as "a sort of compensation" for the years of disgrace and the loss of America: "the country, exhausted and humiliated, seemed to revive in its own estimation and to resume once more its dignity among nations."[68]

The victory at the Saintes also won Rodney immunity from public censure for his actions at St. Eustatius. He was additionally fortunate that the quarrel between Cornwallis and Clinton distracted attention from his role in the events leading up to Yorktown. Edmund Burke personally congratulated him for splendid and substantial service to the country and denied any personal animosity, telling others that he could crown the admiral with laurels as the Roman Senate had done for Julius Caesar. Fox said that if he had ever entertained any prejudices against the admiral for his conduct at St. Eustatius, the recent victory had obliterated them. He announced that he was ready to bury in oblivion all inquiry respecting the admiral's past conduct. Burke and Fox were ridiculed in one satire for dropping the case of the Jews of St. Eustatius. They were portrayed playing musical instruments including the Jew's harp with a caption, "found in the breeches pocket of the *St. Eustatius Israelite!*" According to Sir Henry Clinton, Rodney was "too high game to fly at," and no one dared hold him responsible for his role in the loss of America. Since someone had to be blamed somewhere, and no one had been held to account, Clinton said that the blame naturally fell on the absent man, in other words the one out of political favor. He meant of course himself, but he too avoided incriminating Rodney.[69]

The government of Lord North fell before the arrival of the news of Rodney's victory at the Saintes. It might very well have survived if the victory had occurred a few months earlier. In any case, unaware of the victory, the new government of Lord Rockingham had ordered the recall of Rodney to face charges relating to his actions at St. Eustatius. The government had sent out a replacement, Admiral Sir Hugh Pigot, who had not been to sea for twenty years, and who was without distinction. It was suggested that Pigot was appointed admiral because he was owed gambling debts by the new minister, Charles James Fox. Unable to rescind Rodney's recall before the arrival of Pigot in Jamaica, the new government made quick amends by giving Rodney a peerage as Baron Rodney of Rodney Stoke in Somerset and an annual pension of two thousand pounds. It closed the St. Eustatius hearings and saw to it that both houses of Parliament voted him thanks. The recall of Rodney was the mirth of the press, with graphic satires depicting Pigot as a pig. Lord North was so thrilled by the news that he appeared for some time to be "in a sort of stupor," aware that the victory reflected well on his former government and that it had embarrassed his successors who had recalled the admiral after a great victory. North called it not only the greatest victory of the present war, "but perhaps the most complete of any recorded in the naval annals of England."[70]

Rodney returned to an ecstatic welcome in Britain. In Westminster, the mob smashed the windows of houses that were not illuminated in his honor. The Guildhall presented him with the freedom of the City of London, in a box made of the heart of oak. He was also presented with the freedom of the City of Dublin and the English town of Huntingdon. He was feted with dinners, entertainments, bonfires, and balls. It was a triumphal end of his fifty-year career in the navy.[71]

VIII

Despite the accolades following his victory at the battle of the Saintes, St. Eustatius sullied the remaining ten years of Rodney's life. His homecoming was also marred by illness and family quarrels. He was taken sick in Huntingdonshire where he was staying with the earl of Sandwich to receive the Freedom of the Borough of Huntingdon, and he was ill for much of the rest of the year. His favorite daughter eloped and married at Gretna Green, the eighteenth-century equivalent of going to Las Vegas. John, his seventeen-year-old son, followed suit and married without his permission. In 1784 Rodney, who had many extra-marital affairs, separated from his wife Lady Henrietta, known as Henny, just after the couple had had another child who was younger than some of his grandchildren. Twenty years his junior, Henny was the daughter of an English merchant in Lisbon. They had married in 1764, when he was a widower, and she had accompanied him to the

Caribbean when he was in Jamaica and to France when he was a debtor in Paris. At the time of his death, she was living abroad at Fontainebleau where she had to be rescued on the outbreak of the French Revolution. She lived into her nineties and died in 1827.[72]

After the separation, Rodney left to travel in France and Italy, but in 1785, he had to return to face suits relating to St. Eustatius at Westminster Hall. The following year, the High Court of Appeals for Prizes found in favor of the litigants. It not only awarded them the amount paid for their belongings at the auction, but gave them full restitution of the original value of their property. Rodney called it a "cruel and unjust" verdict. He published a pamphlet in his defense and paid to have it widely distributed. The verdict left him ruined, and his debts plagued his oldest son George, who survived him by only ten years. He was also pursued for payments of earlier debts. His most relentless creditor was the firm of Lowther, Mackreth & Co., who even reported him for not having purchased a pass to walk across Green Park and the Horse Guards on his way to Parliament. Rodney consequently had to live modestly during his retirement. He was unable to purchase a grand country house and instead lived in a small house at Kensington Gore in London, making occasional trips to Bath. He owed the comforts he enjoyed in later life to generous relatives and to his son George.[73]

Rodney made infrequent public interventions. In 1788, he spoke against a bill to abolish the slave trade, calling it "an Act of Suicide" against the commerce of Great Britain. He appeared as a witness for the planters during a parliamentary inquiry into the trade, and was a freeman of the two major slave-trading ports of Bristol and Liverpool. His family had owned land in the Caribbean, and he had always enjoyed support from the Society of West India Merchants and Planters. Rodney argued that slaves lived better than many poor day-laborers in England and that the bill would only benefit national enemies, among whom he included "the ungrateful Americans." He spent increasing amounts of time living at the home of his oldest son in Hanover Square. He enjoyed the company of his grandchildren who he said "never plague me but contribute to my health." He was still buying lottery tickets in the final year of his life, as he never lost his appetite for gambling.[74]

Toward the end of his life, he wrote that he was very weak and his spirits so low that he was convinced that his "hour-glass is almost run out." He comforted himself that it was all he could expect from his age and infirmities. He said that he had no complaint since his days had multiplied long beyond what he had ever imagined or his physical state had warranted. He was therefore content to endure with patience and resignation "the lot of human nature." He died at the home of his son in Hanover Square on May 24, 1792, at the age of seventy-four. He had suffered the night before from such acute pain that he was delirious. He briefly regained consciousness when a doctor said to him "I hope, my dear Lord, ye feel yourself better," to which he replied "I am very ill." He died soon afterwards, at five o'clock in the morning. He was buried close to the grave of his first wife at Arlsford in Hampshire. The City of London paid for a monument of him in full naval uniform at St. Paul's Cathedral. The duke of Clarence, the third son of George III who had served in the navy during the Revolutionary War, made a speech in his honor in the House of Lords. His name was immortalized. "Rodney" became a popular Christian name for boys, and in 1809, the Royal Navy launched the first of at least four warships called the *Rodney*. Rodney's Rock was named after him in Dominica and Gros Islet Bay in St. Lucia was renamed Rodney Bay. The finest rum in St. Lucia is called "Admiral Rodney Extra Old St. Lucia Rum," featuring an engraving of Rodney on the bottle and a reproduction of a painting of the battle of the Saintes on the box.[75]

Even though Rodney's failure to follow de Grasse to North America may have contributed to the defeat of Lord Cornwallis at Yorktown, he was ironically one of the few British heroes of the Revolutionary War. Nevertheless, his blunders at St. Eustatius should not distract from the underlying reason for the British defeat at the battle of the Chesapeake Capes, namely French naval superiority. Other than Lord George Germain, the most popular target of criticism by the opposition parties was the first lord of the Admiralty, the earl of Sandwich. It was he who was held responsible for the inferior state of the Royal Navy.

CHAPTER 9

"Jemmy Twitcher"

THE EARL OF SANDWICH

John Montagu, fourth earl of Sandwich, was famously quoted as saying to John Wilkes that "you will either die on the gallows or of a pox," to which Wilkes replied, "that depends whether I embrace your Lordship's principles or your mistress." They were both notorious libertines. Both were members of the Medmenham Friars, also known as the Knights of St. Francis, who met in Medmenham Abbey, a former Cistercian monastery in Buckinghamshire. Like so much in the life of the earl of Sandwich, the salacious stories of the Friars' nocturnal gatherings in the abbey ruins were greatly embellished, beginning with the name of the society, which erroneously became known as the Hell-Fire Club. The rituals of the group deliberately mocked religious orders. The club was founded by Sir Francis Dashwood, an aggressively anti-Catholic politician who was known among the club members as "the Prior" and wore a red hat like a cardinal. The reputation of the club for satanic rites and orgies, with members dressed as monks and female prostitutes as nuns, was largely derived from a contemporary novel about an imaginary club by Charles Johnstone, *Chrysal: The Adventures of a Guinea* (1760).[1]

The Medmenham Friars virtually disbanded in the wake of libelous assertions against the members by John Wilkes in his periodical, the *North Briton*. His targets included Sir Francis Dashwood when he was chancellor of the Exchequer and the earl of Sandwich when he was first lord of the Admiralty. Immortalized in a famous Hogarth print with his squint and his lecherous grin, John Wilkes was associated with the cause of liberty in both Britain and America before the American Revolution. When Madame de Pompadour, the mistress of Louis XV, asked Wilkes how far the freedom of the press extended in England, he was said to have replied, "I do not know. I am trying to find out." In the early 1760s, Wilkes made outrageous allegations in the *North Briton,* which variously accused the king's mother of an affair with the prime minister, who was then the earl of Bute; the archbishop of Canterbury of committing buggery; and the bishop of Gloucester's wife of being a professional prostitute. George III called him "that devil Wilkes."

When issue number 45 of *The North Briton* called the Cabinet ministers "tools of despotism and corruption" and implied that the king's speech to Parliament contained falsehoods, the government tried unsuccessfully to prosecute and imprison Wilkes, and subsequent government attempts to exclude him from his seat in the House of Commons only served to raise his popularity.[2]

After the government prosecution was dismissed against Wilkes, the earl of Sandwich attempted to disgrace him in the House of Lords by reading an obscene poem and commentary called *An Essay on Woman*, which had been co-authored by Wilkes and Thomas Potter. Written for private circulation as a parody of Alexander Pope's *Essay on Man*, it ridiculed Bishop William Warburton of Gloucester, who had written a commentary on Pope's *Essay on Man*, by appending the bishop's name to a pornographic "interpretation" of the *Essay on Woman*. This was in particularly poor taste, because Potter was rumored to have seduced the wife of the bishop and to have fathered his son. The poem was also blasphemous, referring to the Holy Trinity as "cock and balls" and making a mockery of the Church of England. It became a national sensation, with the lines:

> Awake my Fanny, leave all meaner things
> This morn shall prove what rapture swiving brings!
> Let us (since life can little more supply
> Than just a few good Fucks and then we die)
> Expatiate free o'er that lov'd scene of Man
> In mighty Maze! For mighty Pricks to scan . . .

When Lord Lyttelton begged Sandwich to desist from reading the poem, the other peers cried "Go on, go on." Bishop Warburton, who was sitting on the bench of bishops with the peers, contributed to the comic relief by denying his authorship of the spoof, which he said was unfit for the ears of the "hardiest inhabitants of hell."[3]

The exposure caused Wilkes to flee to France, but Sandwich became unpopular as a result of what opponents regarded as perfidy against a fellow club member and personal friend. Horace Walpole wrote of the absurdity of Sandwich posing as a guardian of public morals "with more hypocrisy than would have been tolerable even in a professed Methodist." It did not matter that it was Wilkes who had previously turned on Sandwich, calling him "profligate," or that Sandwich was obliged to lead the government attack as secretary of state for the Northern Department. Soon after the incident in the House of Lords, there was a revival of John Gay's *The Beggar's Opera* at Covent Garden. In the last scene Macheath complains that he has been betrayed by Jemmy Twitcher, and Horace Walpole described the way the whole audience "burst into an applause of appreciation and the nickname of Jemmy Twitcher stuck by the Earl so as almost to occasion the disuse of his title."[4]

The earl of Sandwich was tall with a hooked nose, protruding jaw, and a lean, furrowed, weather-beaten face "full of expression." He had been athletic in his youth, but was stout in late middle age. He had a gangly body and an awkward careless gait, as if he were "walking down both sides of the street at once." He told a story against himself about his French dancing master requesting that he "never tell anyone of whom you learned to dance." Despite his unprepossessing appearance, he exuded social ease. Witty and convivial in private company, he was fond of the theater, the opera, and concerts. He was a capable classicist and especially proud of his rarer knowledge as an orientalist. As a young man, he commissioned a portrait of himself in exotic oriental clothing with a turban and a sumptuous silk red leotard. He was an amateur poet, musician, linguist, historian, astronomer, and numismatist. A keen sportsman, he owned his own yacht which he liked to race in the sea and along the River Thames. He also enjoyed hunting, tennis, punting, skittles, and fishing. An early patron of cricket, he captained the Old Etonians in 1751, and the first poem about cricket was dedicated to him by the author James True.[5]

Sandwich was an intellectual and a man of fashion, who belonged to prominent social and scientific societies. He was a fellow of the Royal Society and an Elder Brother of Trinity House. Owing to his interest in oriental languages, he founded the Egyptian Club. Together with Sir Joshua Reynolds, he helped establish the Royal Academy of Arts. Sandwich was a member of the Sublime Society of Beefsteaks which met in a sumptuous room at the top of the Covent Garden Theatre for festivities that included singing. The club motto was "Beef and Liberty." Sandwich was also able to share his scholarly interests in art and archaeology with fellow members of the Society of Dilettanti. Founded as a drinking society in 1732, it sponsored expeditions to classical sites. At the behest of Sandwich in 1763, the society sent an expedition to Lydia in Asia Minor, but in spite of its scholarly pretensions, the club was also reputed to be debauched. With Sir Watkin Williams Wynn in 1776, Sandwich founded the Concert of Ancient Music, which aimed to preserve music, ranging from earlier to more recent times, particularly the work of George Frederic Handel, who had died in 1759. Sandwich's secretary Joah Bates, who was known as a leading interpreter of Handel, acted as the director, conductor, and organist.[6]

Sandwich was descended from the Montagu family of Huntingdonshire. Sir Sydney Montagu had purchased the family seat at Hinchingbrooke House in 1627 from Sir Oliver Cromwell, the renowned Cromwell's uncle. The great-grandfather of Sandwich, Sir Edward Montagu commanded the principal fleet under the Commonwealth and then received an earldom for supporting the restoration of the monarchy. At the end of a distinguished career in the navy of Charles II, Montagu died at sea. Sandwich enjoyed entertaining at Hinchingbrooke House. From about 1759, he began hosting regular concerts for a week in the summer and for a week at Christmas. The solo parts were often performed by the leading professional artists of the day, and he would accompany on the kettle drums. The programs always included the oratorios of Handel, and like Burgoyne, Sandwich staged theater productions with the celebrated actor David Garrick. Sandwich liked to host guests including Omai, the Polynesian whom Captain James Cook had brought back from Otaheite (Tahiti) and who resided for several weeks at Hinchingbrooke House.[7]

Sandwich's personal life had a tragic quality. Born in London, he was only four years old when his father died, and he then became estranged from his mother after she remarried and he started boarding aged seven at Eton College. At the age of ten, he inherited the earldom on the death of his mentally ill grandfather. At the age of nineteen in 1741, he married the Hon. Dorothy Fane, whom he had met in Florence. Through her brother, Lord Fane, he became closely associated with the politically influential duke of Bedford who became his patron and later secured his appointment as first lord of the Admiralty. However, Sandwich's marriage was to prove unhappy. Although they were never formally divorced, he and his wife were living apart for over a decade before she was made a ward of court and declared insane by the Court of Chancery in 1767.[8]

Sandwich never remarried, but openly kept a mistress called Martha Ray, whom he met in 1761 when she was sixteen years old and he was forty-three. The apprentice of a milliner in the district of Clerkenwell in London and the daughter of a corset maker who lived near the Strand, she was five foot four inches tall with dark hair, rosy cheeks, smiling eyes, and a pleasant countenance. Sandwich groomed her to be a lady, to accompany him in public, and to act like a wife. He paid for her to receive language and deportment lessons in France. He also hired tutors to teach her to sing and play the harpsichord, and she performed in his private concerts at Hinchingbrooke House. They attended the theater together in London. Living in his apartment at the Admiralty House in Westminster, she presided over dinners for his male friends who included naval officers, botanists, musicians, and authors such as the composer Charles Burney and the poet Richard Owen Cambridge. She and Sandwich had nine children and were partners for nineteen years before she was sensationally murdered by a besotted admirer, when she was leaving the theater at the height of the Revolutionary War in 1779.[9]

Sandwich's lurid personal life was very different from his professional character. He was financially dependent upon his income from government service which made him eager to succeed and to dedicate his life to political office. Conscientious and intellectually gifted, he rose early and worked until dinner in the late evening; in fact, the sandwich is generally assumed to be named after him, owing to his habit of eating snacks consisting of slices of meat between two pieces of bread while working through mealtimes or when gambling. He liked memoranda and dispatches to be brief and concise. He claimed that he gave instant replies to any message of a single page but that anyone who compelled him to turn over to another sheet had to "wait my leisure." When he was first lord of the Admiralty in 1763, he met four to six days a week, including sometimes on Sundays, with the members of the Admiralty Board.[10]

When Sandwich attended Trinity College, Cambridge, with his cousin Lord Halifax, they were the first noblemen to publicly declaim classical authors. After leaving the university, he demonstrated a remarkable independence and curiosity in his choice of a grand tour. He broke with the usual convention of traveling by land in continental Europe, and instead chartered a yacht to sail the Mediterranean, visiting Corsica, Sardinia, Sicily, Cyprus, Greece, Turkey, and Egypt. On his return journey, he visited Malta, Gibraltar, Minorca, Spain, and Portugal. His journal and notes, with detailed observations, were published posthumously as *A Voyage Performed by the Late Earl of Sandwich Round the Mediterranean in the Years 1738 and 1739.* The journal anticipated his later interests in scientific inquiry and voyages of exploration. He made the first British proposal to explore the Pacific in 1749, and Captain James Cook named the Sandwich Islands in the North Pacific in his honor.[11]

I

When he became first lord of the Admiralty in January 1771, Sandwich was the most experienced member of the Cabinet of Lord North. He described himself the following year as "a very old practitioner in business and I fear a very old man, for yesterday was my 54th birthday." After thirty-seven years in Parliament, he reflected, he was one of the longest serving members, if not the oldest, of the House of Lords. A minister at the age of twenty-six, he had served in the Cabinet when Lord North was a boy at Eton and Lord George Germain a junior officer in the Horse Guards. By 1779, he was the last member of the generation in Parliament that had held political office under Sir Robert Walpole. His political experience had extended to foreign affairs when he acted as the British representative in the two-year negotiations at Breda, resulting in the peace of Aix-la-Chapelle (1748), that ended the War of the Austrian Succession. He had overseen foreign policy during the early years of the government of George Grenville in the 1760s.[12]

Sandwich had twice previously held the office of first lord of the Admiralty. He was unusual as a civilian in a position traditionally held by admirals. His own military experience was in the army where he served during the Jacobite rebellion in Scotland in 1745, but he presided over the navy by preference. It was his passion. Although it entailed a reduction in his salary, he had resigned as a secretary of state in order to become first lord of the Admiralty. It was no minor renunciation for a man who constantly complained of financial difficulties. Upon his appointment to the Admiralty, Sandwich wrote to his son that he had not accommodated the government, but rather the government had "gratified me in my request to change my department."[13]

As first lord of the Admiralty, Sandwich contended with problems common to the navy during peacetime when many of the ships were taken out of commission, and the majority of the officers were relieved of their commands. The paper strength of the fleet rarely reflected the actual force, but even so, the size of the navy grew in the second half of the century, and the dockyards, which were essential for the building, repairing, and careening (cleaning) ships, had not expanded to accommodate the increase. During the Seven Years' War, the fleet had increased by 65 percent, but the dockyards at Portsmouth and Plymouth had remained virtually unchanged since the reign of Queen Anne (1702–14). The majority of the dockyards were located on the south coast rather than the west coast facing the Atlantic. Plymouth alone was strategically placed to serve the Western squadron and North America. The timber for the ships had to be imported and too many ships were built with unseasoned "green" timber, which rapidly rotted. There was a shortage of skilled artisans to work in the dockyards, as well as a shortage of cordage and masts. The greatest problem was the cost of maintaining the fleet during a period of high national debt.[14]

Sandwich well understood the problems of the navy and devoted much of his career to remedying them. In December 1744, he had become a member of the Admiralty Board when the duke of Bedford was first lord of the Admiralty. Bedford delegated the daily running of the admiralty to Sandwich together with George Anson, who was to be regarded as one of the greatest naval administrators of the eighteenth century. In February 1748, Sandwich succeeded Bedford as first lord. During a brief stint that ended in June 1751, he introduced the first marine corps and is regarded as the founder of the Royal Marines, and began the practice of the Admiralty Board making personal tours of the dockyards, rather than relegating the task to the more junior Navy Board. The inspections helped invigorate the work of the dockyards. Sandwich also experimented with paying dockyard workers for productivity or "task-work." When he returned to the Admiralty in 1763, he gave priority to the improvement of the dockyards, but his impact was limited by his brief tenure in the office. His experience made him acutely aware of the need for a long-term shipbuilding and ship maintenance program. He appreciated the difficulty of mobilizing the navy at short notice and was therefore an exponent of keeping a larger peacetime fleet in permanent readiness for action.[15]

Sandwich continued his reforms on returning to office in 1771, implementing one of the most ambitious overhauls of naval administration undertaken by any eighteenth-century first lord. Sandwich revived the personal inspections of the dockyards by the first lord and the Admiralty Board, which had lapsed during the previous twenty years. Sandwich now visited together with members of both the Admiralty and the Navy Board, the department most responsible for the daily administration of the fleet. The innovation aimed to reduce friction between the departments and to encourage better collaboration. Sandwich worked closely with the Navy Board, and was responsible for the rise of one of the most important and gifted administrators of the navy when he appointed Captain Charles Middleton to be comptroller at the Navy Board in July 1778. Middleton always paid homage to the abilities of Sandwich and was to be highly influential in naval affairs until the battle of Trafalgar. Sandwich was especially concerned with timber supplies and the need to build stocks of seasoned wood, which his predecessor had allowed to fall perilously low. Sandwich broke a cartel of timber merchants who imported Baltic oak and arranged dry storage for the timber under cover, so that within three years, he succeeded in building up a stockpile.[16]

Sandwich carefully nurtured the interest of George III in the Royal Navy. Almost as soon as he returned to office, he took the king to watch the launch of the seventy-four-gun ship of the line HMS *Grafton* at Deptford. Under his tutelage, the king became the best-informed monarch on naval affairs since James II. Between 1771 and 1774, he began sending the king models of ships under construction, charts, and plans. They were formally presented as part of what George III called his "Naval Collection." It was an inspired move that raised the profile of the Royal Navy.[17]

Throughout the eighteenth century, Britain aimed to maintain a two-power navy that was equal to the combined navies of France and Spain. There was a constant threat of war with both countries, which had been firm allies ever since the late seventeenth century when the Bourbon dynasty inherited the Spanish throne. When war nearly broke out with Spain over the Falkland Islands in 1770, the Royal Navy seemed fully prepared, and its rapid mobilization helped deter the escalation of the conflict. The success encouraged false confidence in the readiness of the navy for war.[18]

II

After Lord George Germain, Sandwich was the favorite target of the opposition parties as the government minister most responsible for the loss of America. He was accused of negligence in failing both to equal the combined strength of the enemy navies and to maintain naval superiority off the coast of America. He was blamed for the success of enemy privateers and the inadequacy of the blockade of America. He was charged with corruption and favoritism in his appointment of senior officers that had resulted in a succession of mediocre admirals serving in North America.

Sandwich had been one of the most outspoken advocates of coercing the American colonies before the outbreak of the Revolutionary War. He had long believed that Britain's future was best assured by investment in colonial and maritime ventures rather than by military engagements in Europe. He had opposed the return of Louisburg to the French at the Treaty of Aix-la-Chapelle in 1748. He had based his political career on alliance with the parliamentary faction surrounding the duke of Bedford, who joined the government of Lord North. Known as the Bedfords, the group espoused a firm imperial policy towards the colonies and they likely strengthened the resolve of Lord North against America. Before joining the ministry of North, Sandwich had acted as a patron to James Scott, who wrote polemics attacking America under pseudonyms such as Anti-Sejanus and Old Slyboots. In what Benjamin Franklin called "a Petulant vehement Speech" on January 20, 1775, Sandwich spoke against the House of Lords receiving the earl of Chatham's plan for conciliation, "and gave his Opinion that it ought to be immediately REJECTED with the Contempt it deserv'd." He added that he could never believe the plan to be authored by a British peer but "that it appear'd to him rather the Work of some American," and, turning toward Franklin who was leaning against the bar of the House (the rail confining visitors), Sandwich said that "he fancied he had in his Eye the Person who drew it up, one of the bitterest and most mischievous Enemies this country had ever known."[19]

The most effective government speaker in the House of Lords, Sandwich was known for his clarity, his command of the issues, his gracefulness, his coolness under fire, and his ability to expose the flaws in the arguments of his opponents. On March 16, 1775, in the debate on a bill restraining the trade and fishing rights of New England, Sandwich famously dismissed the claim that America could not be conquered, citing the alleged cowardice of colonial troops at the siege of Louisburg and saying, "Suppose the colonies do abound in men, what does that signify? They are raw, undisciplined, cowardly men. I wish instead of 40 or 50,000 of these brave fellows, they would produce in the field at least 200,000, the more the better, the easier would be the conquest; if they did not run away, they would starve themselves into compliance." Although the bill was intended as a temporary punishment, Sandwich suggested that it be made permanent despite the consequences for the economy of New England.[20]

During the same debate, in which he had been so derisive and contemptuous of the fighting ability of the Americans, he was challenged by one of his own ministerial colleagues, the earl of Suffolk. Sandwich's speech occasioned sixteen peers to enter a formal protest into the journals of the Lords, to the effect that his intervention was irrelevant and derogatory to the dignity of the House. Sandwich was unperturbed and returned to the theme later in the year, when he suggested that the boasts of the colonial opposition "would only add to the facility of their defeat." In October 1775, he wrote that "the nation seems more unanimous against the Americans, than I ever remember them in any point of great national concern since I have known Parliament." In a much quoted speech in November 1776, he proclaimed that "the very sound of a cannon" would frighten the rebels off "as fast as their feet could carry them." His views were the object of satire and lampoons in America.[21]

Sandwich was frustrated in his attempts to increase the fleet by budgetary restraints imposed by Lord North. As recently as 1772, North had wanted to reduce the peacetime fleet from twenty to sixteen ships and possibly even fewer, declaring "I do not recollect to have seen a more pacific appearance of affairs than there is here." At the very time that Britain introduced legislation to punish Massachusetts in March 1774, North imposed economies on the navy that forced Sandwich to reduce the number of shipwrights from 8,114 to 7,543 by September 1775. The shipwrights were crucial in the maintenance, repair, and building of ships, but their manning levels were not restored until the outbreak of war with France in 1778. Sandwich consequently revived the expedient of trying to pay shipwrights for performance, based on their completion of tasks, rather than for the number of hours worked. Although the system won acceptance at Woolwich, it was resisted in Portsmouth and Plymouth. On the eve of the outbreak of war in America in 1775, the introduction of the task system occasioned several weeks of strikes and affected morale in the two largest naval dockyards in Britain. The government dismissed 129 shipwrights as a punishment, but was later forced to relent by hiring back most of the strikers and postponing implementation of the task system. After the passage of the Coercive Acts in December 1774, North moved to reduce the navy by 4,000 sailors, reflecting his faith in a quick victory in America. The naval estimates provided for only 18,000 sailors in 1775, 21,000 in 1776, and 45,000 in 1777, and did not allow for the likely outbreak of war in Europe. North was concerned that higher taxes to maintain a larger navy might alienate voters who supported the war.[22]

Sandwich persisted in attempts to increase the navy but was again obstructed by Lord North. The issue was not only fiscal. Lord North was fearful that a larger fleet might provoke war with France and Spain. Sandwich disagreed, believing that it was vital to make early preparations for a war against the Bourbons. In the summer of 1776, the situation became more urgent with intelligence of a French naval rearmament. In June, Sandwich sought permission to increase the pay of dockyard workers and to arm another twelve warships, and repeated his requests throughout the summer. On October 23, Sandwich presented the king with a memorandum proposing wartime mobilization, and the government finally responded by requiring that thirty-four ships be prepared for service in the Channel and ordering a general impressment, in which press gangs forcibly enlisted men into the navy. The press gangs were sent out the evening of the Cabinet decision. In December, the government thwarted an attempted sabotage of the naval dockyard at Portsmouth by James Aitken, who was on a politically motivated spree of setting fires throughout southeastern England. A rebel sympathizer known by the alias "John the Painter," Aitken was hanged, with his body suspended from a fifty-foot-high gibbet overlooking Spithead. The full-scale mobilization of the navy did not occur until the eve of war with France in January 1778, however. Sandwich was writing in the meantime that he dreaded the consequences of delaying this measure and complained that the government would have much to answer for.[23]

After 1778, the shortage of ships became more acute with the entry of France into the American War. Sandwich finally had the permission he had sought in 1776 to fully mobilize the navy, and he did so at a rate that compared favorably with the triumphant Seven Years' War. He had sufficiently built up stocks of timber and construction supplies, and the length of time to repair or build a ship was competitive with that in the previous war. His opponents still accused him of negligence and corruption. In 1779, Sandwich defended himself, saying that he had inherited a fleet "in a most deplorable state, the ships decaying and unfit for service, the storehouses empty, and a general despondency running through the whole naval department." He argued that he had increased the navy from 36 ships of the line to 90, with a total of 314 ships in commission. The navy was larger than at any time in history.[24]

Although successful in increasing productivity, Sandwich was unable to achieve even higher rates of construction because of the inadequate capacity of the dockyards, the dearth of skilled artisans, and the lack of available funding from the government. There was an additional cyclical problem of decay, for ships had a limited lifespan of about eleven to sixteen years. His predecessors in office had been assiduous in the repairing and refitting of ships, but they had done so by extending the lives of ships that were due to be broken up. The navy had often kept decayed ships on the books, because it was easier to obtain funding for a repair than for building a new ship. Sandwich appeared negligent because the fleet actually decreased in size for a while and the expansion during the war did not seem to reflect the vast amounts of money voted for the navy. Sandwich made himself the subject of suspicion by not publicly acknowledging the problem and by providing misleading information about the actual size of the fleet. He justified his deception for reasons of national security, but his lack of candor gave the impression of a cover-up.[25]

Previous ministers had also presented budgets that were merely estimates and which listed projects that were sometimes never undertaken. The method gave the navy flexibility, since it was difficult to predict the amount of work needed to restore a particular ship and the dockyards necessarily had to change their priorities during war. The vagueness of the estimates also helped to keep secret the state of the navy from foreign enemies. The real cost of the navy had often been disguised by using different budgets, which made the voting of funds more palatable. Sandwich did not stand to benefit from naval contracts and expenditure, and he presented budgets that conformed to the tradition of his predecessors. In the House of Commons in 1778, an enraged Edmund Burke threw the naval estimates at the government front benches, exclaiming that they were fictitious and that they treated the House with the utmost contempt by presenting members "with a fine gilt book of Estimates, calculated to the last farthing, for purposes to which the money granted was never to be applied." The outburst was due to the estimates listing the construction of a ship that had never been built. Sandwich was found wanting because the opposition began to demand higher levels of accountability and budgets that showed total costs with fully itemized projections. The naval budget came under greater scrutiny than before because of distrust of the government and because the mounting costs of the war seemed so overwhelming.[26]

The construction program in the naval dockyards was only sufficient to maintain a fleet of sixty ships of the line, each of which took some six and a quarter years to build. Between 1770 and 1777, the navy built twenty-two ships, but destroyed another twenty-one that were beyond repair, so that the construction program succeeded only in replacing ships rather than expanding the fleet. Between 1777 and 1782, the rate of production marginally increased to 5.6 years, but even this level of output was only made possible by contracting out the building of ships to private yards with an attendant increase in costs. Between 1771 and 1775, Sandwich commissioned half the new ships to be built in private yards; the navy would otherwise have decreased in size. He was therefore greatly handicapped when his Cabinet colleagues opposed a more ambitious construction program and an early full-scale mobilization of the navy.[27]

Sandwich contended with a related problem of manning the fleet and the dockyards. A seventy-four-gun ship required six hundred men to sail it and serve the guns, and the attrition rate was high, with an average ship discharging half its company annually. Half the recruits were raised by the unpopular expedient of press gangs, and the government also used bounties as an enticement. When the government finally consented to full mobilization in August 1777, the majority of the available manpower was already engaged on warships and transports in America. Of 70,000 men voted for the navy by Parliament in 1779, 55,906 were variously sick, discharged, killed, or missing. The Channel fleet was especially afflicted by sickness. In 1779, Vice Admiral John Byron had to take on board two army regiments, a total of one thousand men, to crew his ships at St. Lucia. These were some of the best troops in the army, whom Sir Henry Clinton had sent with the expectation of their return to America. The remaining troops were distributed among the smaller islands for want of proper naval defense. By 1781, the navy employed some 105,000 men, and between 1776 and 1782, under the direct personal supervision of Sandwich, the strength of the marines increased from 10,129 to 25,291 men. During the course of the Revolutionary War, some 230,000 to 250,000 men served in Britain and throughout the world in the Royal Navy.[28]

In Parliament, Sandwich had to defend the state of the navy against critics, despite his own reservations about strategy and his vigorous attempts to enlist his colleagues for a more ambitious plan to enlarge the fleet at the beginning of the war. Sandwich reminded opponents that he did not make decisions alone but with the consent and involvement of the Cabinet. His speeches were important because they were some of the first to expound the constitutional theory of the collective responsibility of the Cabinet in making government policy.

III

Sandwich contended with the same problem of insufficient strength that beset the army. Even before French entry into the war in 1778, the Royal Navy was too small to cope with the demands upon it. It was inadequate to the task of both blockading the east coast and supporting the army in America. The blockade was critical, given that the Continental Army depended on the import of supplies and gunpowder from Europe. The navy was additionally unable to contain rebel privateers, who preyed upon British merchant ships and were active throughout the Caribbean, the east coast of America, and the English Channel. The incapacity of the navy was due directly to the government's unwillingness to fund Sandwich's request for full mobilization of the navy at the start of the American War.[29]

Early in the war, Vice Admiral Augustus Keppel described the navy as "inadequate to a war and too large for a peace time establishment." In 1774, Admiral Samuel Graves had only twenty-six ships to support army operations and to blockade the entire eastern coastline of America. This was less than half the number thought necessary by Sir Hugh Palliser at the Admiralty, who estimated that the navy needed twenty-two ships merely to serve the army and blockade Boston. Throughout 1775, the home government failed to significantly reinforce the navy. It did not take account of the other demands on the fleet which included providing refuge for colonial officials and obtaining supplies for the army. On his return to London, Graves sought a court martial to clear him of accusations that he had been too lenient in suppressing rebel trade. Acting as a temporary replacement for Graves, Rear Admiral James Gambier summed up the dilemma of the command, which he described as a "choice of difficulties, and scarcity of means." During his brief command of the North American squadron, Admiral Molyneux Shuldham was able to assign less than seventeen ships to cruise the coast of America in July 1776. The rest of his forty-eight vessels, some of which were just armed brigs, supported the army.[30]

Between 1776 and 1778, Admiral Lord Howe gave priority to his brother and the army, but it was at the cost of preventing the importation of armaments to the rebels and suppressing the activities of privateers. Despite arriving with a larger fleet from Britain in 1776, Howe still lacked sufficient ships to both support the army and to enforce a blockade. Unlike Graves and Shuldham, he was not ordered to give the blockade "first importance," and throughout the winter of 1776–77, the ports and trade of the southern states and New England were left virtually undisturbed. When he was able to release some ships from assisting the army in December 1776, he succeeded in enforcing a relatively successful blockade between Buzzard's Bay and the Chesapeake. Upon resigning his commission in September 1778, Howe wrote a damning report about the state of the ninety-two ships of the North American squadron. He reported that only one of the thirteen ships of the line and seven of the thirty-nine frigates were "fit for sea." His fleet had been composed of the majority of the medium-range cruising ships belonging to the Royal Navy. These smaller frigates were best suited to chasing the nimble privateers, and their presence in America had prevented their use for protecting British merchant ships in European waters.[31]

Colonial British America had a seafaring tradition, and its dockyards had built a fifth of the British merchant fleet before the American Revolution. Before the alliance with France, the Continental Congress even created a small but effective Continental Navy under the command of Esek Hopkins, which carried out a successful raid against New Providence (Nassau) in the Bahamas that was notable for the first deployment of the U.S. Marines. John Paul Jones was the most famous of the naval commanders, with his ship the *Bonhomme Richard*. The Scottish-born Jones was twenty-nine years old when he enlisted in the Continental Navy in 1776, he, with considerable nautical experience, having served aboard slave ships and merchant vessels in the Caribbean. In April 1778, in one of many escapades, he launched a successful raid on the port of Whitehaven and on the home of the earl of Selkirk. It was the first foreign attack on an English town since the Dutch burning of Sheerness in 1667. In September 1779, he captured a British naval ship, the *Serapis*.

States like Virginia also had their own small navies, but it was the privateers that posed the greatest problem for the British. Like the militia on land, they fought a guerrilla war on the seas. The privateers were usually merchant ships that were armed with a view to making fortunes from captures. They proliferated in number, with the Continental Congress issuing 556 letters of marque to authorize voyages by 1781. They were also commissioned by individual states. They offered an opportunity for immense profits both for their sponsors and for the crews who divided the prizes. The Irish-born Captain Gustavus Conyngham of Philadelphia commanded the *Charming Peggy* and the *Revenge* in the North Sea, the Mediterranean, the Irish Sea, the English Channel, and the Caribbean. In less than eighteen months, he took sixty British ships, as well as making successful raids along the coasts of Ireland and Scotland. Finding safe haven in the ports of Europe, he created diplomatic tensions for Britain with Holland, France, and Spain. In late 1777, the Admiralty assigned twenty-eight warships just to chase Conyngham, and in May 1779, he was finally captured off the coast of New York. So much did they abhor the "pirate of Dunkirk," that the British sent him to be imprisoned in England. He escaped in a third attempt, to serve under John Paul Jones, but was later caught again and spent the rest of the war in prison. Between 1776 and 1777, privateers took some 350 British ships. Their activities increased insurance rates, disrupted trade, and dispersed the resources of the Royal Navy.[32]

Sandwich was forced to counter the privateers by providing naval protection and convoys for merchant ships, for which he was heavily lobbied by merchant groups like the East India Company and the Society of West India Merchants and Planters. As early as August 1775, merchant ships received permission to arm themselves for self-protection. In July 1776, the navy provided escorts for the linen trade in the Irish Sea, and in August and October, it introduced escorts respectively for the homeward-bound West India trade and the East India Company ships in the Atlantic. By January 1777, there was a comprehensive system of naval convoys for almost every branch of trade in the Atlantic

Ocean, the North Sea, the Baltic, the Mediterranean, the Indian Ocean, and the Carib-bean. The convoys protected shipping to Lisbon, Oporto, Gibraltar, Basseterre (St. Kitts), Kingston (Jamaica), New York, Newport, and beyond. The underwriters of insur-ance premiums to merchant ships often insisted that they travel with a convoy, and the premiums were cheaper for those who complied. The navy was hamstrung, however, by its inability to retaliate against neutral powers like France, Holland, and Spain, which gave sanctuary to privateers and supplied America.[33]

Sandwich disagreed with his Cabinet colleagues about the distribution of the limited forces available. He was always more preoccupied with the threat of Britain's enemies in Europe than with the war for America. Necessarily concerned with the defense of Britain, he consistently championed concentrating the navy in Europe in readiness for the outbreak of war with France and Spain. It was an approach validated by the experience of previous wars, in which French fleets had been best intercepted by guarding the Western Approaches and Bay of Biscay. It was not merely a defensive strategy, since it envisaged a loose blockade of the major French naval bases at Toulon on the Mediterranean coast and Brest on the Atlantic coast. However, North and other members of the Cabinet gambled on the hope of winning the war in America before a declaration of war by France.[34]

As early as 1777, Sandwich tried to resist requests from Lord Howe for reinforce-ments in America until an equal number of ships were available as replacements in Britain. He was overruled by the Cabinet, which supported Howe in the hope that the re-bellion might be crushed before the intervention of France and Spain. At the beginning of the year, Lord Howe commanded 80 warships of the total 250 ships, and 15,000 of a total 60,000 men of the Royal Navy. The fleet in America absorbed virtually the entire cruising ship strength of the Royal Navy, but it was still unprepared to combat the sudden surge of privateers and simultaneously support the land operations of the army in America.[35]

When news arrived in England of Burgoyne's defeat at Saratoga, Sandwich wrote a memorandum proposing a fundamental change of strategy. Dated December 8, 1777, his "Paper . . . relative to the American war" was critical of the way in which the navy had been subordinated to the army in America under Admiral Howe. He argued that the priority given to supporting the army had undermined the naval blockade and the protection of domestic trade against privateers, so that the rebels had been able to be supplied from Europe. He suggested that at least three ports be secured along the east coast as bases for the navy and that raids be made against rebel ports. In the event of war with France and Spain, British possessions were vulnerable in the Caribbean, the Medi-terranean, and the East Indies, and the fleet was not large enough to protect each colony individually. He therefore advocated having sufficient army garrisons in each colony and increasing the size of the fleet. The memorandum was consistent with his earlier appeals, that war was inevitable against Britain's "inveterate enemies," France and Spain.[36]

Adopting the strategy of previous wars, Sandwich preferred concentrating the fleet in Europe rather than America, thereby forcing the Bourbon powers to keep a considerable proportion of their fleets in Europe. He was also motivated by the uncertainty of intelligence about the direction of enemy fleets, whether to the Mediterranean, the East Indies, the Caribbean, or North America. In Europe, the Royal Navy had the advantage of being able to watch the major ports of the enemy and to pursue enemy fleets abroad, though the strategy risked the possibility that an enemy fleet might escape to inflict a major blow in North America or the East Indies before the arrival of a relief expedition from Britain. Since Sandwich had to think globally and to be concerned with the wider war outside America, his priorities inevitably collided with those of Lord George Germain who was responsible for the American war. Germain thought that Sandwich was too concerned about domestic security and too cautious. In the spring of 1780, he wrote that "I think we have little to fear at home, but Lord Sandwich will not risk the country upon any account, so that I apprehend we shall have some misfortunes abroad." Their conflicting priorities and different perspectives of reality were reflected in a series of very damaging disputes between army and navy commanders in both the Caribbean and America.[37]

IV

When the war for America escalated to involve France (1778) and Spain (1779), the Royal Navy, already overstretched by the effort to support the suppression of the revolution in America, now also had to fight the combined forces of two rival naval powers. Britain had no ally in Europe, in contrast to earlier wars, and since 1763, France and Spain had begun shipbuilding programs that proceeded at a combined rate of roughly double that of Britain. By 1775, their combined fleets exceeded that of Britain by some 25 percent, which rose to 44 percent by 1780. France and Spain continued to be able to devote the majority of their resources to their navies, because they were not entangled in a land war in Europe. Spain allied with France much earlier than she had done in the Seven Years' War, and with no ally like Prussia to divert its additional enemies in Europe, Britain was now struggling for its own survival, with the threat of attacks in the summers of 1778 through 1781.[38]

After the outbreak of war with France in 1778, Sandwich was among the most pessimistic members of the Cabinet and advocated withdrawal from America, saying that it was impossible to carry on the war there, but he was again overruled by Cabinet colleagues. Germain wanted to send a fleet to reinforce Howe in America and the Leeward Islands squadron of Admiral Samuel Barrington in the Caribbean, before the arrival of a French fleet, since the British fleet might otherwise be perilously outnumbered in both North America and the Caribbean. Sandwich, however, was adamantly opposed to sending out a fleet in advance of the French. The consequence was a paralysis in decision making, which was worsened by the irresolute state of mind of Lord North. Germain eventually triumphed, but the consequence revealed the inadequacy of the size of the navy.

In 1778, Sandwich's dilemma and the weakness of the navy became all too apparent in both America and Europe. Sandwich was ordered by the Cabinet to send a detachment of the fleet under Vice Admiral Byron to America, in advance of the French fleet of Admiral d'Estaing. Known as "Foul-Weather Jack," Byron was the grandfather of the poet Lord Byron and was known for his exploration of the South Seas. Sandwich was opposed to sending so many ships abroad, and he attempted to revoke the order, arguing unsuccessfully against the fleet wintering abroad. His hesitancy was confirmed by the massing of French troops along the Channel coast, which was actually a decoy to confuse the British about the destination of Admiral d'Estaing for America. Sandwich did not give Byron the order to sail until d'Estaing had cleared the straits of Gibraltar, and refused to spare a frigate to carry dispatches informing the commanders in America of Byron's departure from Britain. The information was instead sent by the regular packet boat system and did not arrive until three months later. During the voyage to America, Byron's fleet of thirteen ships of the line was dispersed by a storm, forcing some of them back to Europe while the rest drifted into various ports in America, where they had been long preceded by d'Estaing.[39]

In the absence of Byron, the presence of d'Estaing's superior fleet posed a major threat in both America and the Caribbean, and he might have inflicted an earlier defeat upon the British—against General Howe in New York and Rhode Island; against Clinton's army retreating from Philadelphia to New York; or against the British troop transports on their way to attack St. Lucia, which unknowingly sailed from New York to the Caribbean on a parallel course with d'Estaing. As it was, Howe barely managed to avert disaster, Clinton narrowly escaped from Philadelphia to New York, and the British troop transports were fortunate not to encounter d'Estaing. For five weeks after the French admiral's departure from Boston, Byron was unable to follow the French fleet because his ships were undergoing urgent repairs in Newport. In the Caribbean, the British captured St. Lucia only twenty-four hours ahead of the appearance of d'Estaing whose fleet outnumbered the Leeward Islands squadron of Admiral Sir Samuel Barrington. Although the British lost the island of Dominica, Byron arrived in time to save St. Lucia. It had been a lucky deliverance.[40]

Although the sailing of Admiral Byron helped save the navy in America and the Caribbean, it adversely affected the navy in Europe, where it caused a political crisis that almost brought about the downfall of Sandwich. In order to reinforce America, Sandwich had to weaken the Channel fleet, which protected Britain, by giving eleven of its ships to Byron. The commander of the Channel fleet was Sandwich's appointee Vice Admiral Augustus Keppel. A portly fifty-year-old bachelor, Keppel was the only remaining admiral, apart from Howe, who had experience of commanding a squadron, gained in the

Seven Years' War. However, Keppel was aligned with the opposition parties and had refused to serve in America. His brother, the bishop of Exeter, died thanking God that he had never voted to shed blood there; and his cousin, the duke of Richmond, was the leading opponent of the war in America in the House of Lords. Keppel was warned by Richmond not to trust Sandwich, who would make him a scapegoat in the event of any naval reversal in Europe, and on being offered the command of the Channel fleet, he demanded an audience with the king and made it a condition that he would accept only those ships he judged seaworthy. The condition foreshadowed the later acrimony between him and Sandwich. In March 1778, upon arriving in Portsmouth to assume command of the fleet, some of whose remaining ships had been stripped to fit out Byron's force, even before the detachment of ships for America, Keppel discovered only "six ships fit to meet a seaman's eye" throughout the Channel fleet.[41]

With the detachment of some of "the finest ships" in his fleet to America under Admiral Byron, Keppel feared that his fleet was inadequate to protect the country from invasion, if the French fleets at Brest and Toulon combined to take control of the Channel. His concerns were corroborated by the massing of French troops along the coast of Normandy. Because of the loss of ships to America, Keppel was unwilling to expose the fleet and cruised for only a fortnight in the Channel before returning to Portsmouth. He wrote to Sandwich that when he considered the fatal consequences of a defeat of the fleet, especially "when greatly inferior in numbers . . . I dare not put myself in the scale against so much danger to my country." Late in the afternoon on July 23, 1778, having put out to sea for a second time, Keppel engaged the French fleet in an indecisive encounter off the coast of France, known as the battle of the Ushant, which occasioned damaging recriminations that led to the court martial of Admiral Keppel and to political divisions within the Channel fleet. It was a missed opportunity to defeat France and enable Britain to focus its resources on the war for America.[42]

After a third unsuccessful cruise of the Channel fleet commanded by Keppel, an anonymous article appeared in an opposition newspaper blaming Sir Hugh Palliser for the unsuccessful outcome of the battle of the Ushant. Owing to severe damage during the battle, Palliser's ship had been unable to comply with an order for a renewed attack. A protégé of Sandwich, Palliser was representative of a rising professional class who were promoted for their merit. In contrast to the aristocratic Keppel, he had risen from humble descent to become a baronet and rear admiral; he had served as comptroller of the navy and a junior lord of the Admiralty. It was his appointment as lieutenant general of the Marines that George III thought "was the real source of the mischief that has now broke forth," since he was promoted over more senior admirals such as Howe and Keppel. His advancement caused a storm of protest, not least from Admiral Keppel, who wrote a series of letters of complaint to Sandwich and brooded darkly that "what is to follow time will discover." The anonymous newspaper article alleged that Palliser had ignored orders to join the admiral in forming the line of battle, which had prevented Admiral Keppel from attempting another attack on the French.[43]

Although he had not criticized Palliser in any of his official communications, Keppel refused to deny or repudiate the charges in the newspaper article. When confronted by Palliser in a debate in the House of Commons, Keppel demurred from either contradicting or confirming the allegation of misconduct. Instead of seeking a court martial to clear his own name, Palliser aggravated the situation by publishing his own account of the battle and asking for a court martial of Keppel. It was an impulsive decision that transformed a private dispute about personal honor into a political storm. Palliser claimed that Keppel was responsible for the failure of his ships to join the action because he had failed to form the proper line of battle and had later remained aloof from the battle without supporting Palliser. Horace Walpole reflected the opposition view that Palliser was "nothing but the tool and instrument of Lord Sandwich," who was trying to discredit Keppel.[44]

V

Beginning in January 1779, the court martial of Admiral Keppel became a *cause célèbre* of the opposition parties against the government. It occurred within living memory of the infamous court martial that had resulted in the execution of Admiral John Byng. It played well to an opposition narrative, which portrayed the government as using its commanders as scapegoats for a failed policy. On the eve of the trial, the British newspapers printed an address to the king, signed by twelve admirals, denouncing the court martial. Among the addressers, Admiral Lord Edward Hawke said that he "would sooner cut off his hand than be accessory to such a trial." The Howe brothers and General John Burgoyne were simultaneously seeking either a court martial or a parliamentary inquiry to vindicate their own conduct in the events leading up to the British defeat at Saratoga.[45]

By special act of Parliament, the trial was conducted on land rather than on board ship, on the pretext that Keppel was ill. The location was a great advantage to the opposition, whose leaders crowded the court in Portsmouth, including Charles James Fox, the duke of Richmond, the earl of Shelburne, the duke of Cumberland, the marquess of Granby, Edmund Burke, and the marquess of Rockingham. The trial lasted five weeks. It was high theater with the friends of the admiral cheering favorable evidence and hissing contrary evidence that favored Palliser. Such was the public interest that several newspapers published a diagram of the courtroom. The verdict was an acquittal for Keppel. It was a unanimous decision, which dismissed the original charges as "malicious and unfounded" and essentially condemned Palliser, who was later acquitted in another court martial in which he was the defendant. The outcome had never been in doubt, with the coffeehouse bookies refusing to take bets on the odds. It was a feast day for opponents of the war in America.[46]

With the announcement of the verdict on February 11, 1779, there was widespread rejoicing and rioting. In Portsmouth, Keppel was led in a procession with a model of his ship, followed by two thousand shipwrights and ropemakers before a crowd of ten thousand. His supporters wore blue ribbons with his name emblazoned in gold letters, and the band played "See, the Conquering Hero Comes." In Bath, the Royal Crescent was illuminated and in Dartmouth ten thousand yards of blue ribbon were purchased for cockades and decorations. In Newcastle, Germain and Sandwich were burnt in effigy as "abettors of the American war." There were three days of riots in London. The mob ordered houses to be illuminated to celebrate the victory or face ransacking. Palliser went into hiding after his London home in Pall Mall was ransacked and gutted. His furniture was set on fire in St. James's Square and he was burnt in effigy on Tower Hill. The crowds tore down the gates and broke the windows of the private apartment of the earl of Sandwich at the Admiralty House. The terrified Lord Sandwich escaped through the garden with his mistress, Martha Ray, to the Horse Guards. The mob smashed the windows of Lord George Germain, Captain (later Rear Admiral) Samuel Hood, Lord Lilburne, and Captain Constantine John Phipps, Lord Mulgrave. They threw fireworks and crackers, and the servants of opposition leaders discharged guns. The home of the prime minister was saved from destruction only by the intervention of troops and the reading of the Riot Act. As he was to do again during the Gordon Riots in August 1780, North hid on the roof of his official residence at 10 Downing Street.[47]

According to Horace Walpole, the opposition leaders encouraged the rioters. Walpole described how Charles James Fox, the earl of Derby, and his brother Major Stanley, together with a few young aristocrats, were drinking all night at Almack's club in London. At three in the morning, they joined the crowds on the street and met up with the duke of Ancaster, who had been breaking windows. Finding the mob at the home of Sir Hugh Palliser, the young aristocrats said, "Why don't you break Lord George Germaine's windows," since Germain also lived on Pall Mall. The crowds were so "little tutored" that they asked who Germain was and then proceeded to break his windows. The following evening, Sandwich excused himself from a dinner with Lord Hertford and the Spanish ambassador, saying that it was only safe for him to go out in daylight and that he "might be insulted or ill-used in the evening." In the evenings a month later, the mob was still to be found, serenading Sandwich and Martha Ray with antigovernment ballads, under the back windows of his apartment at the Admiralty. Despite the disorder in the city, Keppel was voted the thanks of both Houses of Parliament. He was presented with the honorary freedom of the cities of London, Norwich, York, Londonderry, and Dublin.[48]

Sandwich was increasingly viewed as a liability to the government. George III and Lord North were prepared to remove him in favor of Lord Howe, but the negotiations ended when Howe made unacceptable conditions that would have required the removal of Germain. On March 3, 1779, Charles James Fox made a motion of censure in the House of Commons against Sandwich. According to Walpole, Sandwich was so frightened that he begged members to attend the debate, as his life and reputation were in danger. In the Lords, the duke of Bolton complained that everything was at sea except the fleet.[49]

On the night of April 7, 1779, the political blow of the Keppel trial was followed by a personal tragedy for Sandwich with the dramatic murder of Martha Ray at the Covent Garden Theater. She had been attending a benefit concert for another actress and was about to step into her coach when an obsessed admirer rushed forward, shot her in the head, and then tried to shoot himself. His name was the Rev. James Hackman, a former soldier who had recently been ordained. He was hanged for the crime. The story of the murder was to be much embellished. There had been ruptures between Sandwich and Martha Ray. He had accused her of extravagance, and she was upset by his failure to provide financially for her and their children. She resented her exclusion from the company of married women. In 1772, when Sandwich sent Martha away in advance of a visit by his son and daughter-in-law, she threatened to leave him. She always referred to Sandwich as "lord" and signed herself as the "most affectionate M Ray." She was thirty-four at the time of her death and he was sixty. Upon hearing the news from a black servant called James, Sandwich seized a candle, ran upstairs and exclaimed in agony, "Leave me a while to myself—I could have borne anything but this." He later fled a house party when a guest inadvertently sang one of Martha's favorite airs, "Shepherds, I have lost my Love."[50]

While Sandwich was still reeling from the murder of Martha Ray, the opposition escalated their attack upon him in Parliament. On April 19, 1779, Fox made a motion in the House of Commons seeking the removal of Sandwich as first lord of the Admiralty, and later that month, the earl of Bristol made a similar motion in the House of Lords. Bristol, who had been an ally of Sandwich before becoming a peer, had been a distinguished naval officer, but had been disappointed in his wish to be promoted to flag rank and to become the second lord of the Admiralty. Lord Howe also joined the parliamentary opposition against Sandwich. The opposition argued that Sandwich had misrepresented the number of ships fit for service; that he had allowed the French Toulon squadron to escape without pursuit; that he had sent Keppel out to sea with a force inferior to the enemy, and that he had sought to make his commanders into scapegoats. The opposition tried to make the debate into a criminal prosecution, requesting that Keppel's answers to questions be taken down as evidence. Lord North objected. The debate ended in uproar with the clerk supposedly unable to finish counting the votes owing to the commotion. The motion in the Commons was defeated by 118 to 221 votes.[51]

In the summer of 1779, the inadequacy of the navy was again dramatically demonstrated by an invasion scare. In June, Spain had joined the war as an ally of France, and the combined fleets outnumbered the British. At the end of July, the combined enemy fleets sailed toward Britain from Corunna in northern Spain. At Le Havre and St. Malo along the coasts of Normandy and Brittany, the comte de Rochambeau, who later served with Washington at Yorktown, commanded a French army of thirty-one thousand men waiting to cross the Channel. On leave from the United States, the marquis de Lafayette was appointed an aide to Rochambeau and supervised the gathering of supplies at Le Havre. Sandwich asked rhetorically of his Cabinet colleagues why the enemy was superior, answering that "England till this time was never engaged in a sea war with the House of Bourbon thoroughly united, their naval force unbroken, and having no other war or object to draw off their attention and resources." Britain was additionally fighting the war in America, which was draining the national finances and deploying a considerable part of the military. It had no friends or allies; indeed, other countries were supplying the enemy. Sandwich could not resist reminding his colleagues that earlier preparations, such as he had advised, would have averted such a disaster.[52]

On August 16, 1779, news reached London of the arrival in the Channel of the combined enemy fleet. The fleet's sixty-six Spanish ships commanded by French Admiral comte Louis d'Orvilliers outnumbered the British fleet by two to one. The expedition aimed to land the French army on the Isle of Wight before seizing Gosport as a preliminary to an attack upon Portsmouth. The plan also contemplated attacks on the army depot at Cork in Ireland and the port of Liverpool. After driving the British fleet up the Channel, Admiral d'Orvilliers mounted a three-day blockade of Portsmouth. The threat caused the British government to pass a bill calling out the militia throughout the nation, and to order the removal of horses from coastal areas and of navigation aids along the Thames. There was panic among the commander and garrison at Plymouth with the enemy fleet in view, and the nationwide scare lasted until the end of the month. The planned invasion collapsed, but not because of the defense measures in Britain. It was instead due to a severe storm, together with a shortage of provisions and sickness among the crews, that persuaded d'Orvilliers to return to Brest.[53]

Meanwhile, d'Estaing seemed poised to conquer the British Caribbean. As Byron escorted the summer homeward-bound West India fleet, d'Estaing captured St. Vincent (June 19) and Grenada (July 3–4). With d'Estaing active in the eastern Caribbean, Sandwich had little option but to reinforce the Leeward Islands and risk Jamaica, writing, "I own I speak with trembling, for I see the danger with which the Island is surrounded without being able to suggest any effectual means of giving it relief." D'Estaing was reinforced by Commodore de la Motte-Picquet, giving the French naval supremacy in the Caribbean. He fought an indecisive battle with Byron with 183 British killed and 340 wounded, in which Byron's fleet sustained considerable damage to its masts and rigging, leaving the way open to d'Estaing to attack the remaining British colonies in the Caribbean. In September 1779, the threat posed by d'Estaing to Jamaica induced Lord Cornwallis to embark with four thousand troops from New York to sail to the island's defense. D'Estaing opted instead to attack the British garrison in Savannah in Georgia. The inferior British naval presence in America was a factor in the failure of Sir Henry Clinton to mount major operations in New York until December, and although d'Estaing failed in his attempt to capture Savannah, the attack influenced Clinton not to send additional troops to Georgia and to abandon Newport.[54]

The affair between Palliser and Keppel worsened existing political tensions within the Channel fleet, where naval officers were increasingly divided between "Montagues" and "Capulets." However, the impact was largely confined to the navy in home waters. True, Rodney claimed that the rancor had spread to the Leeward Islands squadron in the Caribbean, but he made the claim in the context of one of his many explanations of his failure to defeat Admiral de Guichen in 1780. It did not affect the North American squadron, where the term "Keppelite" simply meant "dilatory" or "troublesome." The real significance of the crisis was that it limited the selection of admirals to command the Channel fleet, a choice that was further reduced by the refusal of Vice Admiral Samuel Barrington to serve as commander, because he was upset that Sandwich had not applauded him more fulsomely for the conquest of St. Lucia. When Sandwich appointed Sir Samuel Hood to be second in command to Rodney in the Leeward Islands squadron, an appointment that other senior officers had refused, he commented that others had been "rendered unsuitable for their factious connections." Hood had been Commissioner of Portsmouth dockyard, an appointment that usually marked the end of an active career at sea. Of much more significance for the war in America in 1779 was Sandwich's appointment of Marriot Arbuthnot to command the North American squadron, because he was uncontroversial and not aligned with Keppel. Arbuthnot had never commanded a fleet and had not fought in a battle for twenty years. His incessant quarrels with Sir Henry Clinton were to prove debilitating in the months before Yorktown.[55]

VI

Sandwich gave such priority to other theaters of the war that he seemingly sacrificed America. He was accused of appointing mediocre admirals to command the North American squadron. At the beginning of the war in Boston, he was forced to remove Admiral Samuel Graves, whose opponents complained that he had shown too much leniency to the rebels on humanitarian grounds and had failed to enforce the Boston Port Act. Despite the best efforts of Sandwich to retain Graves, he was replaced in temporary command by Rear Admiral James Gambier, of whom Lord North said that he had seldom heard anyone describe him as a good naval officer "or as one who deserved to be trusted with any important command." Gambier was portrayed as a sixty-four-year-old fop and coxcomb who attempted to look and dress as if he were thirty. He was actually in his mid-fifties. Embarrassed by the stylistic infelicities of his letters to Lord George Germain, Gambier wrote apologetically that "the ship had been the only university he had been permitted to study . . . for upwards of forty years."[56]

Sandwich had tried to block the appointment of Admiral Howe, who proved to be the most successful of the naval commanders in North America. He opposed the Howe brothers receiving joint military and naval commands, saying that when the two brothers were partners "in deep play at whist," they were no match even for two rustics who have never played any "games beyond Putt or Loo." His main objection was that he had already promised the job to someone else, but he was overruled. Following his resignation in 1779, Howe was replaced by the sixty-eight-year-old Admiral Marriot Arbuthnot, who had been the naval commissioner at Halifax and one of the judges in the court martial of Keppel. Arbuthnot and Clinton's relationship degenerated to the point that they eventually resorted to communicating through an intermediary, to whom they uttered profanities against one another. Clinton described Arbuthnot as "false as hell," and Arbuthnot said of Clinton "The Fellow is a vain, jealous fool."[57]

Although Clinton was promised Arbuthnot's removal in 1780, Arbuthnot remained another nine months until July 1781. Despite his long-anticipated departure, the arrival of his replacement Robert Digby was delayed, and the post devolved upon Rear Admiral Thomas Graves, who was to command at the most important naval battle of the American Revolutionary War, the Chesapeake Capes in September 1781. General Sir Henry Clinton wrote disparagingly to Lord George Germain, "Is your Lord Sandwich, who to my knowledge has long considered the American war as secondary, forever to send out Gambiers and Arbuthnots?" Clinton complained that he heard "of expeditions sent out everywhere, reinforcements to every place but this. Is it because America is become no object? If so, withdraw before you are disgraced!" William Knox, the under secretary to Germain, thought that Sandwich and the Admiralty had a prejudice against the North American department and that they were hostile to requests from Germain's office for naval support in America.[58]

The accusation of neglecting America was misleading, since Sandwich appointed the best admirals and devoted the largest resources abroad to the Caribbean, which was the gateway of French fleets to North America. The majority of eighteenth-century admirals were not household names. They often pursued cautious tactics, because the fate of nations and the balance of global empires might be tipped by the loss of a fleet. Most naval battles were indecisive. The admirals serving in the Caribbean included some of the most celebrated contemporary naval commanders such as Sir Samuel Barrington, Sir Samuel Hood, and Sir George Rodney. The Leeward Islands squadron was the most important, because it was the first line of defense protecting an arc of small islands that were likened by nineteenth-century historian James Anthony Froude to the bow of Ulysses. It was also the first line of defense for Jamaica and North America, owing to the westerly direction of the trade winds. Of ninety-two British warships serving in America in early 1778, Sandwich ordered twenty home and thirteen to the Caribbean. In July, 8 percent of the British fleet was in the Caribbean; in 1779, the proportion increased to 33 percent; in July 1780, 41 percent of the fleet was in the Caribbean, and 48 percent by April 1782.[59]

The navy was too small to protect convoys, combat rebel privateers, blockade the east coast of America, and support the British army under Clinton, in addition to defending Britain, Ireland, Jersey, India, Minorca, Gibraltar, Bermuda, West Africa, Jamaica, St. Kitts, Barbados, Antigua, Tobago, Montserrat, Nevis, St. Lucia, Nova Scotia, Quebec, and Montreal. In addition to overseeing the fleet, in 1779 the Navy Board assumed responsibility from the Treasury for the transportation of the army in America and the Caribbean. It provided naval escorts to replace the previous system of armed merchant ships, and the cost of transportation became a major financial burden. As the army spread out and the number of garrisons increased, there was a need for even more supply ships and convoys. As Sandwich wrote in a memorandum to the Cabinet in September 1779, there was little purpose in forming plans "without at the same time pointing out the manner of securing their success." Given the shortage of ships, it was necessary to think in terms of "not only what ought to be done but what can be done"; what might be desirable was not necessarily feasible. Since the country had "a deep stake to play for," Sandwich reasoned that the government should husband military forces, to be employed "only on those services which are of the utmost importance and that have a probability of being attended with success."[60]

Sandwich was consistent in wanting to concentrate naval forces along the western approaches to Europe. It was a strategy based on successful experience in the two previous wars. George III wanted a less cautious policy, which risked sending out larger fleets to the Americas and leaving a smaller force in the Channel. He decried the concern with matching the size of the enemy fleets, arguing that admirals should be more aggressive. He believed that the weakness of the navy should be "made up for in activity and resolution." The alternative choices represented major risks, whether the strategic emphasis was in Europe or America.[61]

The situation was made worse by the government failing to choose between either strategy, but instead vacillating between the advice of Germain and Sandwich. The indecision reflected the absence of a dominant leader, and Sandwich was openly critical of the government's decision-making process. He faulted Lord North for not providing an agenda for Cabinet meetings and not sufficiently briefing ministers, and successfully proposed that Cabinet minutes be recorded. For seven months in the aftermath of the Keppel-Palliser affair, Lord North appeared incapable of making decisions. After Lord Suffolk had a stroke in June 1778, North failed to appoint a replacement as secretary of state for the Northern Department, and Cabinet meetings stagnated. In September 1779,

Sandwich wrote to North "to point out to you how absolutely necessary it is that you should take the lead among us, and not suffer any question to be agitated there that is not decided and carried into question." In October, he wrote to John Robinson, the secretary to the Treasury, "I think that you should not be an instant from Lord North's side till something decisive is done." When he heard that North was leaving town without having filled two vacancies in the Cabinet, he encouraged Robinson to intervene, as the only one who could "give good advice to the person upon whom the fate of this kingdom depends."[62]

Sandwich continued to be the target of opposition attacks. During the Gordon Riots in London in the summer of 1780, he was dragged out of his carriage and had his face cut before being saved by the Horse Guards. In November 1780, Nathaniel Wraxall later recalled, Sandwich was the subject of the most personal and acrimonious debate that he ever witnessed during his fourteen years in Parliament.[63]

In the wake of the Gordon Riots, the opposition parties became desperate for an issue to rally support, because the land war in America seemed to be going better and the government's popularity was improving. The poor performance of the navy, however, provided ammunition against an unpopular minister. The year began well with the successful relief of Gibraltar by Rodney and the capture of Charleston by Arbuthnot and Clinton. Off the Azores in August 1780, however, a Spanish fleet from Cadiz captured the immensely valuable East India and West India outward-bound convoy. Except for a man-of-war and some three merchant ships, the convoy of sixty-three ships was taken in its entirety. Not since 1693 had there been such a major convoy disaster, with a loss of cargoes to the value of one and a half million pounds, 1,350 seamen, and 1,255 troops of the 90th Regiment. The immediate effect was to end secret talks in Madrid aimed at luring Spain from the alliance with France.[64]

However, such setbacks did not explain the peculiar venom of the hatred against Sandwich. His unpopularity was partly because of the national importance of the navy and the huge sums expended on it. His accusers undoubtedly included many who genuinely believed that by his mismanagement he had betrayed the public trust and that he was responsible for the navy's disappointing performance. They remembered the triumphs of the navy in the previous war and made no allowance for the change in circumstances. He was the more vulnerable to attack because he was a civilian and might be presumed to know less than the naval officers in Parliament like the earl of Bristol. Sandwich was also being judged according to higher standards than his predecessors by an articulate opposition, which wanted greater accountability.

It has been suggested that the main reason for Sandwich's unpopularity was his activity as a politician in building up a base of support. Although he lacked the personal patronage and wealth of the duke of Bedford or the marquess of Rockingham, Sandwich had built the largest parliamentary following of any member of the government except Lord North. He led a personal caucus of some seventeen members of the House of

Commons, and this made him increasingly indispensable to the government as majorities declined. Earlier in his career he had relied upon the patronage of the duke of Bedford, but his growing political independence enabled him to distance himself from the Bedfords while serving in the Cabinet of Lord North. Wraxall wrote that "with consummate ability Lord Sandwich had constructed a species of political citadel within Ministerial lines which acknowledged hardly any other commander or comptroller than himself." He had influence on the election of three members of Parliament representing the town and shire of Huntingdon, and on the parliamentary seats controlled by the Admiralty. Since about 1768, furthermore, he had built up a political following in the East India Company. Wraxall described the company headquarters at India House as constituting a fortress "of which he [Sandwich] was supposed to possess the secret keys." Sandwich's involvement in the activities of the company earned him the lasting enmity of Vice Admiral Hugh Pigot and Captain George Johnstone in the House of Commons.[65]

It was Sandwich's patronage of very able administrators from obscure backgrounds that was a leading cause of jealousy and resentment against him. By surrounding himself with relatively junior officers, he aroused the suspicion and resentment of senior officers. His protégés included Sir Hugh Palliser, who Wraxall said was entirely devoid of manners, deportment, and external grace. The recipients of such patronage owed their loyalty entirely to Sandwich, and were expected to support the government. When Sandwich procured Captain Constantine Phipps the parliamentary representation of Huntingdon in 1775, it was on condition of "the thinking and acting as I do in all American points and supporting the present administration in their whole system." The opposition attack in November 1780 was occasioned by the promotion of Palliser to be governor of Greenwich Hospital. Sandwich suffered politically by his loyalty to Palliser, which was at odds with his nickname "Jemmy Twitcher," suggesting someone who snitched on his friends.[66]

VII

The overextension of the fleet was the undoing of the British war in America. It led directly to the defeat at the Chesapeake Capes and the entrapment of Cornwallis at Yorktown. Already before those disasters, with the British declaration of war against the Dutch Republic in late December 1780, the navy was confronted with the additional challenges of waging war against the Dutch colonies in the Caribbean and the East Indies, intercepting Dutch convoys in the North Sea, and blockading the Dutch coast and the mouth of the Texel. The war against the Dutch not only dissipated the resources of the British fleet but led to the distraction of Rodney's conquest of St. Eustatius.

In April 1781, the Channel fleet sailed to relieve Gibraltar, where the fortress and naval base were in the third year of a Spanish siege. While the British fleet was attempting to rescue Gibraltar, de Grasse sailed for Martinique to begin the fateful voyage that ended in the Chesapeake Capes and Yorktown. Meanwhile, Admiral Pierre André de Suffren sailed for the East Indies where he prevented another British fleet from capturing the Dutch colony of the Cape of Good Hope. Admiral de la Motte-Picquet also sailed with a French fleet and captured two-thirds of the ships in the homebound convoy of the goods confiscated by Rodney at St. Eustatius. In May, the Spanish governor Bernardo de Gálvez conquered Pensacola and West Florida, which included much of the present state of Florida. The British naval squadron in Jamaica was responsible for the protection of West Florida, and the commander in Florida blamed the navy for the colony's loss, but Admiral Sir Peter Parker made the very plausible case that his fleet was already fully occupied in the defense of Jamaica, the most valuable and most important British colony remaining in the Americas. In July, another Spanish fleet captured the British base of Minorca in the Mediterranean.[67]

In the months before Yorktown, the British fleet was rapidly gaining against the combined fleets of France and Spain. On March 16, 1781, the much-maligned Admiral Marriot Arbuthnot averted a French attempt to reinforce Lafayette in Virginia and subject Benedict Arnold's expeditionary force to the fate that awaited Cornwallis. In consequence of an action fought off Lynnhaven Bay, the French Admiral Destouches decided to return to Newport with twelve hundred troops sent by Rochambeau to double the strength of Lafayette's force in Virginia. In April, Commodore George Johnstone took six valuable Dutch East Indiamen in Saldanha Bay near Cape Town. When the enemy crews attempted to burn their ships, Johnstone personally led one of the boarding parties. In the North Sea in August, Vice Admiral Hyde Parker won a strategic victory against a Dutch fleet and convoy at Dogger Bank, and the Dutch thereafter did not attempt to escort any more convoys to the Baltic. During the summer, another combined French and Spanish armada was thwarted in attempting an attack upon Britain. On December 12, Rear Admiral Richard Kempenfelt attacked a larger French fleet and convoy commanded by de Guichen, and in a daring act of bravado, succeeded in taking twenty merchant ships. His victory also delayed an intended Franco-Spanish invasion of Jamaica.[68]

However, none of these successes could make up for the British naval failure at the battle of the Chesapeake Capes on September 5, with its disastrous implications for Cornwallis at Yorktown. There were many elements of chance and misfortune that led to this reversal. Sandwich had built a successful intelligence system with agents watching the great naval dockyards in France and Spain, but it failed him at a crucial time, with the result that the government was not informed of the size of the French fleet destined for America. He consequently did not send out a fleet in time to provide reinforcements, and did not give sufficient advance warnings to the naval and military commanders in the Caribbean and North America. However, at the time of the battle of the Chesapeake

Capes, Sandwich had provided for a larger fleet to be available for the defense of North America. He had expected Rodney to follow de Grasse, in which case Admiral Thomas Graves would have had an additional eight ships at his disposal, thereby improving the numerical odds at the Chesapeake Capes. In addition, Sandwich would not have expected de Grasse to sail with his entire fleet from Martinique to Virginia. The risk that de Grasse ran gave a numerical advantage to France.[69]

The failure of the navy, however, was due more to overwhelming demands upon it than to misfortune or incompetent commanders. The navy had been lucky to escape defeat by d'Estaing at Rhode Island and New York in 1778 and Savannah in 1779. Sir Henry Clinton reflected that the navy was outnumbered during some of each year of his command in North America, and predicted a scenario in which a detachment of the army might be cut off by land and sea. Sandwich was well aware of the deficiencies, and had urged earlier mobilization to better prepare for the war with France. When the French war broke out in 1778, he had wanted Britain to cut its losses and withdraw from America. He understood that hard choices had to be made in view of the limited resources available.

When news of Yorktown reached London in late November 1781, the opposition targeted Germain and Sandwich, in hopes of bringing down the government by undermining the two ministers most associated with the conduct of the war. In December, the opposition found further ammunition against Sandwich upon receiving news that Admiral Richard Kempenfelt had been forced to retreat against a superior French fleet off Ushant. In a debate in the House of Commons of December 20, Charles James Fox made the opening salvo, calling the incapacity of Kempenfelt "ignominious and disgraceful" and demanding an inquiry. Lord Rockingham led the attack in the House of Lords.[70]

The government was disunited. Lord Advocate Henry Dundas and Attorney General Lord Edward Thurlow wanted North to dismiss Sandwich to divert a parliamentary inquiry into the navy. Germain also blamed Sandwich. They had disagreed about the basic strategy of the American Revolutionary War, and Germain was convinced that Sandwich had kept him in the dark about naval affairs and deliberately obstructed him. Their differences had increasingly turned public, with the partisans of each writing abusive articles in the newspapers against the other. Germain wanted to recall and court-martial Graves for his conduct at the Chesapeake Capes, whereas Sandwich ordered Graves to Jamaica, thinking it was impolitic to put on trial an admiral who also happened to be the brother-in-law of Lord North. The breach between the ministers became so open that Charles James Fox said he intended to call Germain as his principal witness in the impeachment of Sandwich. George III told his brother that Sandwich had insisted to himself and Lord North that Germain should recant his implicit criticism of Sandwich in the House of Commons. Germain initially denied comments attributed to him but finally made "a sort of apology" to Sandwich.[71]

With Germain about to be removed from the Cabinet in January 1782, the opposition was able to concentrate its fire upon Sandwich. The Cabinet closed ranks in support, because its future was now tied to Sandwich's political survival. On January 24, Fox moved for an inquiry into the mismanagement of the navy in 1781, which he said "contained or exhibited an epitome of all the blunders committed during the course of the war." For the sake of dispatch, he announced that he would confine his investigation chiefly to the last year. North was unable to obstruct the motion and therefore consented on the grounds that the government had nothing to hide. Sandwich welcomed the opportunity to defend his record and to convince independent members. The debates attracted some of the largest parliamentary attendances of the decade. There had been 443 members present at the roll call in January, with independent members attending in force and the government relying on their support. On February 7, however, Fox made a motion of censure that was defeated by only 205 votes to 183, with many traditional government supporters absent and others abstaining. Lord North wrote of his own reaction, "Lord Sandwich's majority of 22 makes Lord N horrid sick." Lord Thurlow confirmed that Lord North was "worried to death and things wore a very uncertain aspect."[72]

On February 20, 1782, Fox introduced a second motion of censure against Sandwich. Such was the seriousness of the threat that both Sandwich and Treasury Secretary John Robinson wrote personally to the government supporters to request their attendance at the vote. Fox was supported by William Pitt the Younger—the first and last time that the two future political adversaries voted together. Lord Advocate Henry Dundas, a Cabinet colleague of Sandwich, had sat through the first debate with "dark and ambiguous expressions" and was silent in the second debate, which indicated that the Cabinet was divided. The second motion of censure was only defeated by 236 votes to 217. It was always remarkable if the opposition parties won more than 200 votes, and the increase in the opposition vote signaled the incipient collapse of the government. Nathaniel Wraxall was an eyewitness to the debates, and described the way that Fox "united the keenest sarcasms with the most able and laborious investigation of naval administration." Admiral Howe "flung all his weight into the scale of the Opposition," and supported by Keppel, attacked in detail the administration of Sandwich, whom "they stigmatized as deficient in judgment, energy and activity."[73]

In the House of Lords on March 6, 1782, the duke of Chandos moved "that the immediate cause of the capture of the army under Earl Cornwallis in Virginia appeared to be the want of a sufficient naval force to cover and protect the same." The motion was more easily defeated by the government in the Lords than Fox's motion in the Commons. The opposition gained additional ammunition from news of further losses abroad with the French capture of St. Kitts, Montserrat, Nevis, Demerara, and Essequibo and the Spanish capture of Minorca in February, news of which reached London in March. The attack on Sandwich was merely a preliminary for a vote of no confidence in the government. In March, North resigned before giving the opposition the satisfaction of a majority vote.

VIII

The fruition of Sandwich's work did not come to pass until after he left office in March 1782, with Rodney's victory at the Saintes, for which he had helped lay the foundation. Wraxall wrote that the victory "constituted the best reply to the charges made against Lord Sandwich." There was no more talk of impeachment or prosecution. Keppel, who replaced Sandwich as first lord of the Admiralty, was unable to claim credit for the victory, because he had recalled Rodney before receiving news of it.[74]

In late 1781, the British fleet was better-matched in relation to the combined enemy fleets than at any other time during the American war. The ship-building program was catching up. Sandwich had been successful in ensuring supplies of seasoned timber together with other essentials like masts, hemp, pitch, tar, and iron. Having inherited a low stockpile of timber and other materials necessary for the repair and building of ships, he built up at least a two-year reserve for the duration of the war. In 1779, the firepower of the ships became more effective, thanks to the introduction throughout the fleet of carronades, short-barreled cannons capable of firing heavy shot at short range that could be mounted on forecastles and poop decks where heavier guns could not be placed. About the same time, the fleet was also issued langrage for guns on upper decks, quarterdecks, and forecastles—cases filled with asymmetrical pieces of iron scrap, to be fired at sails and rigging. This had been a favored tactic of the French, used by d'Orvilliers against Keppel at the battle of the Ushant. A new signal system introduced by Kempenfelt, although not universally adopted within the Royal Navy, enlarged the tactical vocabulary of an admiral from 60 to 999 instructions. [75]

The fleet was more seaworthy, thanks to the expansion of a system of sheathing the bottoms of hulls with copper plates to prevent the dragging effect of barnacles and accumulated debris and provide protection against shipworms—actually mollusks, known as *Teredo navalis*, that bore into wood. This was a major achievement, with the entire fleet of 82 ships of the line, 14 fifty-gun ships, 115 frigates, and 102 sloops and cutters coppered by 1781. It required fourteen tons of copper plate and fastening to cover a medium-sized warship. The process had been attempted earlier, but the navy had previously been unable to solve the problem of the chemical reaction and corrosion that resulted from contact between copper and iron. Coppering reduced the frequency of careening, cleaning, and refitting ships, which helped relieve the dockyards in the longer term, though the process delayed the building and repair of ships in the short-term.

Furthermore, copper-bottomed ships were swifter, easier to maneuver, and able to undertake longer voyages at sea. It was one of the most important naval innovations of the eighteenth century.[76]

Sandwich had approved the deployment of the greatest part of the fleet to accompany Rodney to the Caribbean, which gave Rodney numerical superiority over de Grasse at the Saintes. Sandwich had also requested from William Knox that an order be issued by Germain's office to reinforce the Leeward Islands. As a result, at the time of the battle of the Saintes, the majority of the British navy was in the Caribbean—forty-two out of ninety-six ships of the line, as against thirty-four in England. Although Rodney had more ships than de Grasse, the fleets were still roughly matched at the Saintes because the French had larger ships with greater firepower. The victory was not as decisive as Trafalgar, but it shook the French navy and enabled British negotiators to recover the great majority of conquests by France in the peace treaty of 1783.[77]

During Sandwich's administration, the Royal Navy played a crucial role in preserving the rest of the British Empire while it enjoyed some success in America. It relieved Quebec in 1776 and enabled the recovery of Canada. It helped the garrison of Gibraltar withstand a three-year siege. It deflected attacks upon Barbados, Antigua, and Jamaica. It averted several attempts of the combined fleets of France and Spain to invade Britain in 1779, 1780, and 1782. It helped in the successful withdrawal of the British army from Boston in 1776 and the removal of civilians from Philadelphia in 1778. It thwarted enemy attacks on Newport in 1778 and Savannah in 1779. It deterred de Guichen from engaging in combined operations in America in 1780. Although it lacked the resources to mount a total blockade of the coast of America, it inflicted economic hardship on the rebel states and reduced their trade. The navy achieved notable success in amphibious assaults together with the army, including the capture of New York and Newport in 1776, Philadelphia (via the Chesapeake) in 1777, and Charleston in 1780. The capture and burning of the port towns hindered rebel trade and affected the economies of the surrounding regions.[78]

Even during the war, Sandwich continued to encourage the voyages of exploration by Captain James Cook, who established the British claim to Australia and New Zealand. Sandwich's passionate interest in exploration helped to bring about Cook's second Pacific voyage of 1772 to 1775, which dispelled the two-thousand-year-old myth of a southern continent in the tropics. After circumnavigating the globe for a second time, Cook returned to England. In 1773, Sandwich also sponsored an expedition of Captain Constantine Phipps to the Arctic, which disproved the possibility of a shorter route to the east via the North Pole. Sandwich similarly encouraged and planned Cook's third voyage, which took place during the American war between 1776 and 1779. In December 1777, Cook explored and named the Sandwich Isles, sailing from them to the west coast of America. It was after Cook had revisited the Sandwich Isles that he was killed by the natives of Karakakoa in Hawaii on January 17, 1779. Even in his retirement, Sandwich promoted knowledge of voyages of exploration by encouraging and editing the publication of accounts.[79]

During the period that Sandwich headed the Admiralty, there was an important effort to combat disease and reduce mortalities in the Royal Navy. When Admiral Arbuthnot arrived in New York in 1779, he had seven hundred men sick from scurvy as a result of the voyage across the Atlantic. The second voyage of Captain Cook was important in the discovery that a regular diet of limes helped prevent scurvy, which had long plagued the navy. Accompanying Admiral Rodney in 1780, Dr. Gilbert Blane also addressed scurvy and made considerable improvements to the health of the fleet. Far from being the weak link between the victories at Quiberon Bay in 1759 and Trafalgar in 1805, Sandwich and the naval administrators he promoted contributed to laying the foundations of British naval success against Napoleon.

IX

Sandwich was sixty-three years old when he left office in 1782. The following year, he was disappointed not to be named to a senior position in government when Lord North returned to power in a coalition with Charles James Fox. Instead, he was given the sinecure of Ranger of the Parks, and his son was appointed Master of the Buckhounds. When his son considered resigning from the government on the grounds that the ministers were attempting "to keep the King in perpetual subjection," Sandwich disapproved, believing that his son had a duty to uphold a government that had given him favors. Like so many of the so-called "tools" of the king who served in the government of Lord North, he was never a lackey of George III, and like Lord North, he paid a price for his independence. His political career effectively ended with the fall of the Fox-North coalition.[80]

Sandwich thrived in his retirement. He had always enjoyed country house life at Hinchingbrooke. During the war, he had had little opportunity to indulge his taste for concerts, dinners and clubs. His last holiday had been a trout-fishing trip to Newbury in June 1776, and the last concert at Hinchingbrooke had been at Christmas 1776. After the American war, however, he revived the concerts, and in 1784, he was the organizer, "moving spirit," and patron of the centenary commemoration of Handel's birth at Westminster Abbey, which the royal family attended. He arranged other Handel concerts, which proved important in the revival of Handel and the popularity of *Messiah*. It was a passion he shared with George III. With the historian Mark Noble, Sandwich also spent time collecting materials for writing a history of the House of Cromwell, the original owners of Hinchingbrooke House.[81]

Sandwich had acquired another mistress a year after the murder of Martha Ray called Nelly Gordon. He had at least one child by her, who was mentioned in his will.

Among the children of his first marriage, he was survived only by his son and heir Viscount Hinchingbrooke. His wife outlived him but remained confined for insanity at Windsor. They had had another son, who had joined the navy and died at the age of twenty-three in Lisbon, and four other children had died in childhood. Among his children by Martha Ray, the boys were educated at Charterhouse and two of them attended Cambridge University. Robert Montagu, the oldest of his children by Martha, served as a lieutenant during the American war and rose to become an admiral. Basil, the second son, became a successful lawyer and lived until 1851. Sandwich's daughter Augusta married Henry Speed, a member of Parliament and the grandson of a former Sardinian minister, who succeeded to the title of the count de Viry. Two other sons died in their youth. Sandwich took a fond interest in his grandchildren and in the families of his three nieces.[82]

On Saturday, April 30, 1792, Sandwich died at his London home in Hertford Street. It was about three o'clock on a Saturday afternoon, soon after a servant had delivered a message that "My Lord desires me to add that he is going to sleep." He died fearing imminent bankruptcy and plagued with financial worries. In 1788, he had felt obliged to apply for the repayment of a loan that he had made to his son at the time of his marriage. His will included a bequest to his black servant, James, who attended him in his last days and who had brought him the news of the murder of Martha Ray. It was the end of an era, with the French Revolution at the height of the "Year of Terror." Sandwich was followed by Admiral Lord Rodney, who died less than a month later in May, and by Lord North and General John Burgoyne who passed away in August. Sandwich's memory was to be defined by his political adversaries until the publication of his official papers in four volumes by the Navy Records Society in the 1930s. Wraxall said of Sandwich, which held true of so many of the men who lost America, that the problems "originated more in the nature of the war than from the fault of Lord Sandwich; the obloquy and the punishment, however, fell upon him."[83]

Conclusion

In one of the first published histories of the American War of Independence by a British army officer, Charles Stedman wrote that "men were obliged to conclude, either that a force of Great Britain was ill-directed, or that no invading army, in the present enlightened period, can be successful in a country where the people are tolerably united." Although critical of some of the decisions of the commanders, he argued that the experience of the southern campaign had demonstrated as "a fact beyond all contradiction" that the war was unwinnable. He recalled the process of subduing Georgia and South Carolina. He remembered when "the British commanders in those provinces had been uniformly successful in all general actions they fought, and had not in a single instance been defeated," yet their successes achieved nothing but the retention of Savannah and Charleston, which "facts naturally led to this inference, that it was madness to persist in an expensive war, in which even success failed to produce its natural consequences."[1]

The British military commanders are criticized for having been both too cautious and too bold during the American War of Independence. Like General George B. McClellan in the American Civil War, the commanders in chief in America, Sir William Howe and Sir Henry Clinton, are regarded as having failed to take sufficient initiative and pursue the war more aggressively. On the other hand, some blame the defeat upon high-risking and offensively minded deputy commanders like John Burgoyne at Saratoga and Lord Charles Cornwallis at Yorktown. The British are thought to have erred in dividing their forces, but they had little alternative if they were to give the war momentum or support loyalists in different parts of the country. Their strategies failed not as a result of incompetence and blundering, but because of insufficient resources, the unanticipated lack of loyalist support, and the popularity of the Revolution.[2]

Britain had an army of conquest, but not an army of occupation. It conquered every major city during the war, but there were insufficient troops to retain and police large areas of territory against a popular rebellion. The British were greatly outnumbered in all their major defeats: at Boston in 1776, Hubbardton in 1777, Saratoga in 1777, King's Mountain in 1780, and Yorktown in 1781. The British suffered their most serious reversals whenever they dispersed their forces, extended their supply lines, and moved away from coastal bases to penetrate the interior. They were continually impeded by insurgents like Thomas Sumter, "the Carolina Gamecock," and Francis Marion, "the Swamp Fox," who later became folk heroes in the United States. The commanders attributed their misfortunes to being defeated in detail, when detachments left the main force on separate expeditions. In other words, the British army was gradually eroded in small-scale skirmishes and expeditions, a process known in the eighteenth century as *la petite guerre,* that turned the American war into one of attrition, in which the British army was worn down in unconventional warfare against citizen soldiers. "Whenever the Rebel Army is said to have been cut to pieces," wrote Brigadier General Charles O'Hara, "it wou'd be more consonant with truth to say that they have been dispersed, determin'd to join again upon the first favourable opportunity." Although the British won the majority of the battles in America, this counted for little against an enemy in regard to whom General Nathanael Greene boasted, "we fight, get beat, rise and fight again."[3]

However, the British defeat was not solely attributable to guerrilla warfare. The citizen militias could be liabilities for the revolutionary cause, being often difficult to mobilize and not dependable in battle, and the British light infantry and German Jaegers were well suited to combating the militias. Furthermore, some British officers had experience of earlier colonial warfare and adapted their tactics to conditions in America. Above all, in spite of the prevalence of *la petite guerre,* the major victories of the war were those in which the opposing army was captured and eliminated. George Washington recognized the importance of mastering conventional European tactics and the importance of a professional army. In its code of discipline and justice in the army, Congress even adopted the British Articles of War. The Americans prided themselves on beating the British at their own game and playing by the same rules.[4]

British victories, however, merely served to reinvigorate the revolutionary cause. They stimulated recruitment in the militias and the Continental Army. They stirred pamphlet writers and propagandists to sharpen their rhetoric. They created greater unity and greater willingness of the states to cede powers to the Continental Congress. In 1780, British successes at Charleston and Camden helped stir a national movement with the granting of greater command authority to Washington, the creation of a national bank, and the appointment of Robert Morris as superintendent of finance. As Charles James Fox reflected in a speech of November 1780, "every gleam of success had been the certain forerunner of misfortune."[5]

Britain did not expect to have to occupy America. The most fundamental miscalculation of the men who lost America was the assumption that the loyalists were in a majority and that they would rally in support of the army. This was the error that led to their most disastrous decisions: the attempt to solve the imperial crisis by coercion, the slow buildup of military forces at the beginning of the war, the failure to make a more concerted effort to link the campaigns of Generals John Burgoyne and Sir William Howe in 1777, and the planning and conduct of the southern campaign after 1778. Although they were proved wrong, their overestimation of the potential for latent loyalist support was defensible because it was based on seemingly good evidence. It was a view encouraged by people with firsthand knowledge, like colonial administrators and the loyalists themselves. The government also found confirming evidence in the number of Americans who swore oaths of allegiance during the British occupation of New York and New Jersey in 1776, Philadelphia in 1777, Savannah in 1778, and Charleston in 1780. It was a view that was reinforced by evidence of apathy and dissent within the revolutionary movement. The leading loyalists persisted in the belief that the majority of Americans opposed Congress. If this assumption ultimately became a straw at which the home government clutched, it was because it believed that failure was not an option, America was too important to Britain.

Indeed, loyalties were never static and they continued to change, but to the disadvantage of the British. The very presence of the British army alienated opinion in America. Although justified by the insufficient size of the army, the use of German mercenaries against fellow subjects antagonized Americans. The granting of freedom to slave runaways from rebel masters alienated white opinion in the south. In the Declaration of Independence, George III was accused of mercilessness and cruelty in employing "savages," a reference to the British alliance with Native Americans. The use of loyalists was a double-edged sword since many loyalists were intent on vengeance, resulting in civil war and some of the most vicious episodes of the entire conflict. The depravity, plunder, and cruelty of the army were the favorite theme of revolutionary propaganda. The two sides increasingly regarded one another as foreigners rather than fellow nationals. Britain was additionally unable to compete with the promise of the republican creed of the Revolution, which held out prospects of a better future and which was peculiarly well-adapted to the relatively egalitarian social conditions among whites in America. It similarly could not replicate the apocalyptic religious zeal of the revolutionaries who believed that providence was on their side.[6]

The difficulties of the army were mirrored by the navy, which was similarly too small to meet its commitments of supporting military operations on land and mounting an effective blockade. This was apparent as early as 1775 and remained true even before the French joined the war in 1778. Owing to budgetary constraints, the navy was not fully mobilized until 1778. Just as the army contended with the citizen militia disrupting their supply lines, the navy was overwhelmed by privateers who preyed on British merchant ships. Like the army, the navy was unable to concentrate its forces sufficiently because of the multiplicity of demands ranging from providing armed convoys to giving asylum to colonial officials.

Even in the earliest stages of the war it was apparent to some in Britain that their country could not win with the resources available. After Lexington and Concord, the *Saint James's Chronicle* warned that "A Thousand English Soldiers killed in America must be supplied by a Thousand more from Great Britain; while a Thousand Americans destroyed are supplied by a Thousand more on the spot." Under such difficulties of maintaining supplies and reinforcements, "any war must be on very unequal terms." In 1777, an anonymous correspondent in the *London Chronicle* warned that it was one thing to conquer a country, and another to subdue the people. The article argued that it would require numerous armies in every province to crush the rebellion and impose order, and that the expense would be prohibitive. Another correspondent in the *Morning Chronicle* noted that it would be necessary to divide the army into small detachments in order at the same time to fight the rebel army and police the population. The process could only be carried on by coercion and force since "we have lost their affection." The article shrewdly argued that the enemy wished to protract the war because time was to their advantage and ruinous to Britain. The British would simultaneously have to fight a war and begin a process of reconstruction.[7]

In 1778, Charles James Fox brilliantly predicted the fates of the generals who served in America. He argued that whomever the government sent out to command would suffer the same criticisms as their predecessors. They would either be accused of indolence, inactivity, or want of spirit, or of behaving like knights errant, roaming around in quest of adventure, acting too independently, and disobeying their instructions. He concluded that the generals had not miscarried for want of professional skill, bravery, or devotion to duty, "but merely from being employed on a service, in which it was impossible to succeed." They were set up to fail.[8]

During the American Civil War, the Union changed its commanders more frequently than the British in the Revolutionary War and also failed to blockade the Confederacy successfully. The Union ultimately triumphed with a massive superiority in manpower, manufacturing, technology, and sea power. Grant and Sherman resorted to accepting huge losses in battle in the knowledge that the South could not make up for its corresponding losses. In the American Revolution, the British could not afford such an attrition of their forces. They lacked sufficient troops for suppressing a popular uprising and policing a continent of over two and a half million people. They were impeded by the vast distances and difficult terrain. Furthermore, owing to the fragmented and local character of authority, there was no capital or center that offered a strategic key for the British to win control over America.

In addition to the popularity of the Revolution, the eventual defeat may be ascribed to factors other than the quality of the leaders who were contending against major constraints. They were hampered by the logistics of fighting a war three thousand miles across the Atlantic. It took eight and a half months for the letter from Lord George Germain appointing John Burgoyne to the command of the army in Canada, to reach Governor Sir Guy Carleton in Quebec. Because of the particular difficulty of transporting horses by sea, the British never had a sufficient number of the animals in America. Because of the failure to conquer significant amounts of territory, the government had to supply many of the needs of the army, including coal, forage for the horses, food, and lumber. The army suffered some of its worst setbacks mounting raids to obtain forage within America. The logistical challenges led to the late arrival of provisions, troop transports, shipping, and reinforcements, which delayed military operations. During the winter of 1775, shortage of transports prevented General Howe from making an earlier withdrawal from Boston and attacking New York. In 1780–81, the "want of a proper conveyance" obstructed communication between Cornwallis and Clinton. In 1782–83, the logistical problems of shipping had become so bad that Britain was unable to deploy troops from America to the Caribbean to take advantage of the naval victory at the Saintes.[9]

Similarly, the shortage of provisions detained General Howe in Halifax before his attack on New York in 1776 and delayed Carleton in his pursuit of the Continental Army across Lake Champlain. For much the same reason, in 1777 Burgoyne's advance toward Albany became more halting after reaching Fort Edward, and it was owing to his need for forage and other supplies that he sent out the disastrous expedition to Bennington. The late arrival of provisions from Britain slowed the opening of the campaigns by General Howe in 1777 and by Clinton in 1779. It was a factor in the failure of Clinton to take advantage of the presence of Rodney to attack Rhode Island or to undertake any major operations in the late summer and early fall of 1780.[10]

The logistical problems of fighting the war overwhelmed the primitive administrative system of eighteenth-century government. It involved a myriad of different government departments which answered to different members of the Cabinet. At the outset of the war, there were a dozen different departments that administered the army, and three different government departments were responsible for the transportation and supply of the British army in America and the Caribbean. Both Generals Howe and Clinton thought that transportation should be controlled by the army. The lack of integration in the parallel activities of different departments resulted in delays. In 1778, it took seven months to arrange transport for a cargo of vinegar from Deptford to New York. The shipping problem was exacerbated by commanders abroad who detained vessels to use as warehouses, owing to inadequate storage facilities in America and the Caribbean. The supply ships were also commandeered as hospitals, prisons, and troop transports. The problem was further aggravated by the dispersion of the army throughout America and the Caribbean, with far-flung garrisons like Bermuda, Minorca, Gibraltar and Gorée in West Africa all having to be supplied. During the war, there were efforts to reform the administration, which included more stringent control of contractors and suppliers, but they could not solve the fundamental problem.[11]

Coordination between departments was impaired by the eighteenth-century British political system, which created a fractured system of command. The evolution of political parties was still very weak, which meant that governments were often coalitions of various factions, diluting unity of purpose. The prime minister did not even appoint all the members of the Cabinet, and the secretary for war was not a Cabinet member. The concept of collective Cabinet responsibility, in which ministers united behind an agreed policy, had not fully evolved. Even though combined amphibious operations were essential to success in America, the army and navy were answerable to different ministers, and there was no supreme commander. All this made it difficult to set clear strategic priorities.

The need for economy and the growing national debt were major restraints upon military operations. The government was under pressure to keep down the cost of the war in order to maintain the support of domestic taxpayers. Budgetary considerations were a factor in the decision to cut the funding of the Royal Navy at the outbreak of the war with America. They were similarly a constraint upon sending more troops to America, and were the main reason why the government denied the request of General Sir William Howe for fifteen thousand additional troops as part of his original plan for the campaign in 1777. They were also a major reason for the shortage of provisions, since the Treasury was unwilling to allow a margin for emergencies. Nor did it calculate for the demands of an increasing number of refugees among loyalists, slave runaways, and Native Americans. The rations allowed for women and children accompanying the army reflected the number officially permitted by the army but not the actual number, which greatly increased during the war. In consequence, the Treasury consistently sent insufficient food and supplies to the army in America.[12]

From 1778, the British army and navy were additionally overstretched in a global war against France, and later against Spain and Holland. From Blenheim in 1704 to Waterloo in 1815, Britain won the majority of its victories in alliance with other countries in Europe. Thus, in the Seven Years' War, Britain had Prussia to divert France to operations in Europe; likewise, Spain did not become a belligerent in that war until 1762, leaving Britain free to focus its energies against France. In the American war, on the other hand, Britain was at a great disadvantage because it had no allies and was opposed by much of the rest of Europe in the League of Armed Neutrality (1780). Spain and France were able to concentrate upon building up their navies whose combined strength outnumbered the Royal Navy and Britain faced the most serious invasion threat since the Spanish Armada in 1588. It was because the navy was overstretched that it was inadequate for the purposes of defeating the French fleet at the Chesapeake Capes or rescuing Lord Cornwallis's army at Yorktown. In consequence of the expansion of the war, the priorities of the British government were diverted from the war in America.[13]

Finally, the growing parliamentary opposition in Britain prevented the possibility of continuing the war in America. In the summer of 1774, there was virtually unanimous support in Parliament for the coercive policies that triggered the American Revolution. With the outbreak of war in 1775, opinion became more divided, with a popular antiwar petitioning movement in Britain. The government itself was split between those who favored conciliation and those who believed the situation could be resolved only by an outright military victory. Throughout the conflict, the minority opposition parties brilliantly argued the case against the war in America. The government was also subject to much greater public scrutiny, owing to the dramatic growth in newspapers and the newly won right of journalists to report the proceedings of the House of Commons. In fact, the only person to receive universal acclaim from the British press was George Washington. Yet Lord North's government remained strongly entrenched. Even after Yorktown, George III and Lord George Germain wanted to push on and continue the war. By then, however, public opinion and parliamentary majorities dictated otherwise. After Yorktown, the government majorities began to collapse until it became unable to remain in power. In March 1782, Lord North was replaced by the marquess of Rockingham, who was committed to ending the war in America.

Historians recoil from suggesting that the outcome of any event is inevitable. They are too well aware of the role of chance and other contingencies. This book has argued that conditions did not favor the British but they might yet have prevailed against less capable opponents, above all Washington, who was critical to the success of the American Revolution. He was shrewd in his choice of advisers and junior commanders like Nathanael Greene, the marquis de Lafayette, baron von Steuben, and Alexander Hamilton. Six foot four inches tall and mounted on a white charger, he became a living legend during the war. He inspired the loyalty of his men, and showed humility in allowing junior commanders to vent their frustration. He was equally dispassionate in his often trying dealings with the French. He showed the same equanimity and diplomacy in working with Congress. He understood the politics of warfare. Most importantly, he kept his army intact and mostly out of reach of the British. When the artist Benjamin West said that Washington "would retire to a private situation" after the Revolutionary War, George III responded, "if He did He would be the greatest man in the world."[14]

The British came to respect the fighting abilities of the rebels. General James Grant was to regret his much-quoted speech of 1775 when he had said that the Americans were too cowardly to fight. Less than four years later, he admitted to the House of Commons that he had been wrong and that "he never saw better troops than some of the rebel regiments." In June 1781, Cornwallis wrote that the southern militia had inflicted such high casualties as to prove "but too fatally that they are not wholly contemptible." In his memoirs, Banastre Tarleton paid his former foes some of the highest compliments of any British officer. He particularly praised General Nathanael Greene and his troops for their "judiciously" and "vigorously executed" march from the Catawba to Virginia. He admired "the wisdom and vigour of the American operations," which had foiled the designs of Cornwallis at Wilmington. Lieutenant General John Graves Simcoe similarly respected the skill of his opponents in frontier warfare, in which he thought them "excellent marksmen" who knew the country and were veterans of Indian warfare. The Hessian Captain Johann von Ewald was fulsome in his praise of the Continental Army, whose discipline and drill were not only the same manner as those of the English but as good "as the English themselves." He marveled at the achievement of soldiers who had been "nearly naked and in the greatest privation." He asked "Who would have thought a hundred years ago that out of this multitude of rabble would arise a people who could defy kings and enter into a close distance with crowned heads?" He paid tribute to what "enthusiasm—which these poor fellows call 'Liberty'—can do!" His testimony was all the more impressive given that he later became a distinguished author of military texts and commanding general of the Duchy of Holstein.[15]

The weakness of the revolutionary central government and its virtual state of bankruptcy might still have turned the war in Britain's favor. At some point in their military careers, a succession of revolutionary commanders resigned in frustration at their treatment by the Continental Congress, including Thomas Sumter, Nathanael Greene, and Daniel Morgan. It was in the months after Yorktown that the officers of the Continental Army came closest to mutiny, culminating in the famous Newburgh Conspiracy in 1783. This was a major reason that George Washington was willing to lend his reputation to chair the Continental Convention of 1787 that wrote the Constitution.

Nevertheless, the British were lucky not to be defeated earlier in the Revolutionary War. In America, their army was vulnerable whenever the Royal Navy was numerically inferior to the French navy. In a scenario similar to the defeat of Cornwallis at Yorktown, the French fleet might easily have trapped Clinton when retreating from Philadelphia in 1778, the garrison in Rhode Island in 1778, the troop transports sailing from New York to St. Lucia in 1778, and the garrison in Savannah in 1779. On these occasions, the British army was only able to persevere because of luck, skill, training, good leadership, and bravery. It was also because France was more concerned with acquisitions in the Caribbean and with supporting the ambitions of Spain. In November 1779, Washington had to abandon his plan to besiege Clinton in New York because Admiral d'Estaing returned to France. If successful, this would have been a far more decisive and spectacular victory than Yorktown. Indeed, the British survival was partially due to the failure of combined operations between the French and the Continental Army at Rhode Island in 1778 and Savannah in 1779. The mistakes were never one-sided.

The British did not entirely lose the American Revolutionary War. They were not totally defeated, even in America. After the battle of Yorktown (1781), Britain still possessed Charleston, Savannah, Penobscot, St. Augustine, and New York, and above all, it permanently retained Canada. Three-quarters of the British army remained intact in North America, with 15,240 rank-and-file effectives at New York, 7,588 in South Carolina, 1,624 in Georgia, and 541 in East Florida. During the peace negotiations of 1782–83, the British need not have conceded such favorable terms to the United States.

George Washington was unable to obtain further French naval assistance after Yorktown. The Continental Army was not strong enough to take New York, Savannah, or Charleston, and as late as April 1782, Washington was reduced to proposing to Congress the enlistment of German mercenaries. The fighting had been indecisive in the Ohio Valley and the northwest, and until the 1790s, the British held the fortresses in the upper midwest of Oswego, Niagara, Detroit, and Michilimackinac. They also continued to negotiate for the absorption of Vermont into Canada. Despite his opposition to the war, the earl of Shelburne was initially opposed to granting independence to America, and his view was shared by the commander in chief of the British army in America, Sir Guy Carleton. Shelburne was hopeful of entering separate negotiations with different states, and like Carleton, he thought it possible to create some kind of political union between Britain and America. Shelburne eventually chose to offer generous terms in order to make peace with the United States separately from France and maintain good relations with the former colonies. Far from suffering a major loss, British commerce with America not only revived, but exceeded the volume of trade before the Revolution. British influence remained so pervasive that Thomas Jefferson and the Republican Party feared that the United States might become a client state of Britain.[16]

The men who lost America were also the men who saved Canada, India, Gibraltar, and the British Caribbean. The political leadership of the North government can be credited with the victory at the Saintes in 1782; the same year, Admiral Howe raised the Spanish siege of Gibraltar which had been heroically defended by a garrison of German mercenaries and British troops. In contrast to the British navy in the Chesapeake Bay, Howe was able to shield his transports and supply vessels behind his warships to enable them to relieve the garrison. This climactic end to the three-year siege was one of the most celebrated wartime subjects of artists like John Singleton Copley. The final voyages of Captain James Cook to Australia and New Zealand took place during the era of the American Revolution, and the convicts formerly transported to America became the first settlers of Australia.

As the western empire partly disintegrated in the Americas, the British were consolidating an eastern empire in India. In the final years of the American War of Independence, General Sir Eyre Coote recovered most of the territories captured by Hyder Ali of Mysore who had earlier invaded the Carnatic in alliance with the Maratha princes and the French forces totaling 100,000 men. At the Battle of Novo Porto (July 1, 1781), Coote's army of 8,500 British soldiers and Indian sepoys defeated 47,000 Mysoris, and went on to win further victories at Pollilore and Solingar. In November 1780, Vice Admiral Sir Edward Hughes captured the Dutch fort of Negapatam whose garrison had been reinforced by 2,300 troops of Hyder Ali, who was forced to evacuate forts and posts in the Tanjore country. By mounting a successful blockade of the Malabar Coast, Hughes destroyed Ali's hopes of becoming a maritime power, destroying his shipping at Calicut and Mangalore. In 1782, Hughes fought a series of five naval battles against the French which successfully preserved the British possessions in India. At the death of George III, the British Empire comprised one-twentieth of the global population, and was already the largest empire in history, upon which "the sun never set."

Notes

The following abbreviations are used in the notes.

PRO   The National Archives (Public Record Office), Kew, UK
WLCL William L. Clements Library, University of Michigan, Ann Arbor

Introduction

1. "Military Journal of Major Ebenezer Denny 1781 to 1795," *Publications of the Historical Society of Pennsylvania* (Philadelphia: J. B. Lippincott & Co., 1860), p. 248; *The Fate of a Nation: The American Revolution Through Contemporary Eyes,* ed. William P. Cumming and Hugh Rankin (London: Phaidon, 1975), pp. 312–42; *The Spirit of Seventy-Six: The Story of the American Revolution as Told by Participants,* ed. Henry Steele Commager and Richard B. Morris, vol. 2 (Indianapolis: Bobbs-Merrill, 1958), pp. 1239, 1241–42; Robert Selig, "20 October 1781: The Day after the Surrender," *The Brigade Dispatch* 38, no. 2 (Summer 2008): 2.

2. James Thacher, *Military Journal During the American Revolutionary War, from 1776 to 1783* (1854; repr. Cranbury, N.J.: The Scholar's Bookshelf, 2005), pp. 288–90.

3. There are various different accounts of the surrender of the sword. Rochambeau and his compatriot Colonel Mathieu Dumas both mentioned in their memoirs that O'Hara offered the sword to Rochambeau. Only the French accounts mention the return of the sword via O'Hara to Cornwallis. Thacher wrote that the sword was offered to Washington who directed O'Hara to Benjamin Lincoln.

4. Thacher, *Military Journal During the American Revolutionary War,* p. 290; *Pennsylvania Packet,* November 13, 1781; Selig, "20 October 1781," p. 2; "Military Journal of Major Ebenezer Denny 1781 to 1795," p. 248; Mark Urban, *Fusiliers: The Saga of a British Redcoat Regiment in the American Revolution* (New York: Walker, 2007), p. 279; Stephen Conway, *The War for American Independence, 1775–1783* (London: Edward Arnold, 1995), p. 128.

5. Nathaniel Wraxall, *The Historical and the Posthumous Memoirs of Sir Nathaniel William Wraxall, 1772–1784,* ed. Henry B. Wheatley, 5 vols. (1836; repr. London: Bickers & Son, 1884), 2:137–138. The account of the reception of the news in London by Wraxall was totally discounted by Charles Ross in his three-volume edition of the *Correspondence of Charles, First Marquis Cornwallis* (London: John Murray, 1859), 1:129n. Ross claimed that "the story must be entirely false" because the dispatch with the official news did not arrive until midnight (according to some writing on the back of the original letter) and that it did not contain details of the capitulation. However, it is generally accepted that the king

did indeed receive the news of Yorktown on November 25 (see *The Correspondence of King George the Third from 1760 to December 1783,* ed. Sir John Fortescue, 6 vols. [London: Macmillan, 1927–28], 5:303).

6. Wheatley, *Historical and Posthumous Memoirs of Sir Nathaniel William Wraxall,* 2:138–139. Wraxall said they went to see Thurlow in his house in Great Russell Street in Bloomsbury, but Wheatley says that this was not possible and that Thurlow lived on Ormond Street.

7. Ibid., pp. 139–41.

8. Ibid.

9. Ibid., pp. 138–39.

10. In a speech in the House of Commons in June 1781, Lord Westcote said that "The American War was in his opinion better deserving of the title of any Holy War, than those of olden time," "The House Debates Whether to Continue the War," November 9, 1780, in *The American Revolution as Described by British Writers and The Morning Chronicle and London Advertiser,* ed. Elizabeth R. Miller (Bowie, Md.: Heritage Books, 1991), p. 50; William Henry Lyttelton similarly referred to it as "a holy war," *The House of Commons 1754–1790,* ed. Sir Lewis Namier and John Brooke, 3 vols. (London: HMSO, 1964), 3:77; Henry Ellis to William Knox, June 17, 1781, in *The Manuscripts of Captain Howard Vincente Knox (From Volume VI of "Reports on Manuscripts from Various Collections" Prepared by the Historical Manuscripts Commission, Great Britain)* (1909; repr. Boston: Gregg Press, 1972), p. 178; Adam Smith quoted in H. V. Bowen, "British Conceptions of Global Empire, 1756–83," *Journal of Imperial and Commonwealth History* 26, no. 3 (1998): 14.

11. Barbara Tuchman's *The March of Folly: From Troy to Vietnam* (1984; repr. London: Abacus, 1990) writes that "the American Revolution . . . succeeded by virtue of British mishandling" and that "lax management at home translated into lax generalship in the field." She attributes their defeat to a languid attitude, sluggishness, divided counsels, negligence, carelessness and misjudgment of their opponents. They demonstrated "a pervasive and peculiar folly." She explicitly links this folly with their social backgrounds, arguing that "noble circumstances did not nurture realism in government" and that their "social pleasures tended to come first." She implicitly contrasts the "lords in silk knee-breeches" with the entrepreneurial and virtuous homesteaders and pioneers in America, pp. 260, 259, 272, 278, 166, 177.

12. Ira D. Gruber, "British Strategy: The Theory and Practice of Eighteenth-Century Warfare," in *Reconsiderations of the Revolutionary War: Selected Essays,* ed. Don Higginbotham (Westport, Conn.: Greenwood Press, 1978), pp. 19–20; Ira D. Gruber, "George III Chooses a Commander in Chief," in *Arms and Independence: The Military Character of the American Revolution,* ed. Ronald Hoffman and Peter J. Albert (Charlottesville: University Press of Virginia, 1984), pp. 166–91; Ira D. Gruber, *Books and the British Army in the Age of the American Revolution* (Chapel Hill: University of North Carolina Press, 2010), pp. 25, 33.

13. Eric Robson, "Purchase and Promotion in the British Army in the Eighteenth Century," *History* 36 (February & June 1951): 57–72; Gruber, *Books and the British Army,* pp. 6–7, 26; Stephen Brumwell, *Redcoats: The British Soldier and War in the Americas, 1755–1763* (Cambridge: Cambridge University Press, 2002), pp. 84–85; Stephen Conway, "The British Army, 'Military Europe,' and the American War of Independence," *William and Mary Quarterly,* 3d ser., 67, no. 1 (January 2010): 69–101.

14. Matthew H. Spring, *With Zeal and Bayonets Only: The British Army on Campaign in North America, 1775–1783* (Norman: University of Oklahoma Press, 2008), pp. xii, 102, 172, 179, 198, 201, 202, 221.

15. Edward Thornton to James Bland Burges, April 2, 1792, in S. W. Jackman, "A Young English-

man Reports on the New Nation: Edward Thornton to James Bland Burges, 1791–1793," *William and Mary Quarterly,* 3d ser., 18, no. 1 (January 1961): 104; Sir Winston Churchill, *The Great Republic: A History of America,* ed. Winston S. Churchill (New York: Random House, 1999), p. 73. See also William Seymour, *The Price of Folly: British Blunders in the War of American Independence* (London: Brassey's, 1995), p. 10: "This complex, unique and wholly avoidable war, so full of blunders, mistakes, muddles and mismanagement, chiefly on the part of the British politicians responsible for its conduct." Paul Johnson, *A History of the American People* (New York: Harper Perennial, 1999), pp. 127, 128, 139, 161, 162; Johnson refers to the British leaders as a "dismal succession of nonentities," ibid., p. 127.

16. Michael Kammen, *A Season of Youth: The American Revolution and the Historical Imagination* (New York: Knopf, 1978), pp. 172–73; H. T. Dickinson, "Introduction," in *Britain and the American Revolution,* ed. H. T. Dickinson (London: Longman, 1998), p. 13.

17. Tim Breen, "Ideology and Nationalism on the Eve of the American Revolution: Revisions *Once More* in Need of Revising," *Journal of American History* 84, no. 1 (June 1997): 13–14; Dickinson, "Introduction," p. 2; Urban, *Fusiliers,* p. xiii. The literature published before 1978 was reviewed in David Paul Nelson, "British Conduct of the American Revolutionary War: A Review of Interpretations," *Journal of American History* 65, no. 3 (December 1978): 623–53. See also David Syrett, "Historiographical Essay: The British Armed Forces in the American Revolutionary War. Publications, 1875–1998," *Journal of Military History* 63, no. 1 (January 1999): 147–64. Since these reviews, there have been a number of notable studies by Stephen Conway, Sylvia Frey, Eliga H. Gould, P. D. G. Thomas, David Syrett, John A. Tilley, David Paul Nelson, Julie Flavell, Troy Bickham, Matthew H. Spring, and Mark Urban. There are syntheses that give emphasis to the British side by Hugh Bicheno, Don Cook, Robert Harvey, Christopher Hibbert, Michael Pearson, and Stanley Weintraub.

18. Ira D. Gruber, "The American Revolution as a Conspiracy: The British View," *William and Mary Quarterly,* 3d ser., 26, no. 3 (July 1969): 360–73; Bernard Bailyn, *The Ideological Origins of the American Revolution* (Cambridge, Mass.: Harvard University Press, 1967), pp. 150–59; P. D. G. Thomas, *Tea Party to Independence: The Third Phase of the American Revolution 1773–1776* (Oxford: Clarendon Press, 1991), pp. 51, 82; Benjamin W. Labaree, "The Idea of American Independence: The British View, 1774–1776," *Proceedings of the Massachusetts Historical Society,* 3d ser., 82 (1970): 9, 11.

19. The resurgence of revolutionary resistance by the militias and the Continental Army in 1776 and 1780 is a theme of Charles Royster, *A Revolutionary People at War: The Continental Army and American Character, 1775–1783* (Chapel Hill: University of North Carolina Press, 1979). The pamphlet writers and revolutionary propagandists also rallied in the face of British victories. See Philip Davidson, *Propaganda and the American Revolution 1763–1783* (Chapel Hill: University of North Carolina Press, 1941), p. 406; E. Wayne Carp, *To Starve the Army at Pleasure: Continental Army Administration and American Political Culture, 1775–1783* (Chapel Hill: University of North Carolina Press, 1984), p. 196.

20. Memo of conversation, February 7, 1776, Clinton Papers, WLCL, quoted in Anthony J. Scotti Jr., *Brutal Virtue: The Myth and Reality of Banastre Tarleton* (Westminster, Md.: Heritage Books, 2007), p. 132.

21. David Syrett, *Shipping and the American War 1775–83: A Study of British Transport Organization* (London: Athlone Press, 1970), pp. 9, 78, 101, 132, 222; R. Arthur Bowler, *Logistics and the Failure of the British Army in America 1775–1783* (Princeton, N.J.: Princeton University Press, 1975), pp. 12–13; Norman Baker, *Government and Contractors: The British Treasury and War Supplies 1775–1783* (London: Athlone Press, 1971), p. 21.

22. Bowler, *Logistics and the Failure of the British Army in America,* pp. 9–10, 30, 92–93; Judith L. Van Buskirk, *Generous Enemies: Patriots and Loyalists in Revolutionary New York* (Philadelphia: University of

Pennsylvania Press, 2002), p. 106; Walter Hart Blumenthal, "British Camp Women On The Ration," in *Women Camp Followers of the American Revolution* (New York: Arno Press, 1974), pp. 18–19.

23. Bowler, *Logistics and the Failure of the British Army in America*, p. 54.

24. Patrick K. O'Brien, "The Political Economy of British Taxation, 1660–1815," *Economic History Review*, 2d ser., 41, no. 1 (February 1988): 1–32; H. V. Bowen, *War and British Society, 1688–1815* (Cambridge: Cambridge University Press, 1988), pp. 17–33; John Brewer, *The Sinews of Power: War, Money and the English State, 1688–1783* (New York: Knopf, 1989), pp. 89, 91, 114, 116; Paul Langford, *A Polite and Commercial People: England 1727–1783* (Oxford: Oxford University Press, 1989), pp. 640–41.

25. Richard Middleton, *The Bells of Victory: The Pitt-Newcastle Ministry and the Conduct of the Seven Years' War 1757–1762* (Cambridge: Cambridge University Press, 1985), p. 217; Brendan Simms, *Three Victories and a Defeat: The Rise and Fall of the First British Empire, 1714–1783* (New York: Basic Books, 2007), pp. 523, 574, 584, 607, 626.

26. Simms, *Three Victories and a Defeat*, p. 598.

27. Simms explores this theme at length. See especially ibid., pp. 626–28, 653, 677–78.

Chapter 1. "The Tyrant"

1. John Adams to Timothy Pickering, August 6, 1822, in *The Works of John Adams, Second President of the United States. With a Life of the Author*, ed. Charles Francis Adams, 10 vols. (Boston: Little, Brown, 1850–56), 2:514; *Diary and Autobiography of John Adams*, ed. L. H. Butterfield, Leonard C. Faber, and Wendell D. Garrett, 4 vols. (Cambridge, Mass: Harvard University Press, 1962), 2:150.

2. Adams to Secretary John Jay, Bath Hotel, Westminster, June 2, 1785, Adams, *The Works of John Adams*, 8:256, 257, 258.

3. Ibid., p. 258; Adams to Thomas Jefferson, Bath Hotel, Westminster, June 3, 1785, *The Adams-Jefferson Letters: The Complete Correspondence Between Thomas Jefferson and Abigail and John Adams*, ed. Lester J. Cappon (Chapel Hill, N.C.: University of North Carolina Press, 1988), p. 27.

4. Abigail Adams to Jefferson, December 20, 1785, Cappon, *The Adams-Jefferson Letters*, p. 27; Marie Kimball, *Jefferson: The Scene of Europe 1774 to 1789* (New York: Coward McCann, 1950), p. 135; *Autobiography of Thomas Jefferson 1743–1790*, ed. Paul Leicester Ford (New York: Putnam's, 1914), p. 94; Adams, *The Works of John Adams*, 1:420. Charles R. Ritcheson, "The Fragile Memory: Thomas Jefferson at the Court of George III," *Eighteenth Century Life* 6, no. 2–3 (1981): 1–16, argues that there was never such an incident on the grounds that such behavior was uncharacteristic of George III; the veracity of the account is also undermined by the mention of Queen Charlotte since she did not attend levees which were an all-male affair; and John Adams said nothing about it. It is certainly true that there is no contemporary account other than Jefferson's later autobiography. Nevertheless, George III was certainly capable of vindictive behavior, as he demonstrated toward William Pitt the Elder and Charles James Fox. Furthermore, the term "levee" was used broadly during the period to describe informal royal occasions when the queen and her daughters were indeed present. Jefferson had joined Adams to obtain a trade agreement with Britain, so that they had every reason not to make the incident at court into a diplomatic row.

5. Pauline Maier, *American Scripture: Making the Declaration of Independence* (New York: Random House, 1998), p. 138; "Comments on Soulés' *Histoire*," August 3, 1786, *The Papers of Thomas Jefferson*, ed. Julian P. Boyd, Charles T. Cullen, John Catanzariti, Barbara B. Oberg, et al., 34 vols. (Princeton, N.J.: Princeton University Press, 1950–), 10:369; Jefferson to Abigail Adams, August 9, 1786, ibid., 261.

6. H. V. Bowen, "British Conceptions of Global Empire, 1756–83," *Journal of Imperial and Commonwealth History* 26, no. 3 (1998): 3.

7. Matthew Winterbottom, "Dining with George III and Queen Charlotte," in *The Wisdom of George III*, ed. Jonathan Marsden (London: Royal Collection Publications, 2004), p. 236; Horace Walpole to George Montagu, November 13, 1760, in Frank Arthur Mumby, *George III and the American Revolution: The Beginnings* (London: Constable, 1924), p. 4.

8. Jane Wess, "George III, Scientific Societies, and the Changing Nature of Scientific Collecting," in Marsden, *The Wisdom of George III*, pp. 321, 322.

9. Jane Roberts, "George III's Acquisitions on the Continent," in Marsden, *The Wisdom of George the Third*, pp. 101, 115, 116; Holger Hoock, "George III and the Royal Academy of Arts: The Politics of Culture," ibid., pp. 247, 248; David Watkin, *The Architect King: George III and the Culture of Enlightenment* (London: Royal Collections Publications, 2004), pp. 28, 74; Christopher Lloyd, "King, Queen and Family," in *George III and Queen Charlotte. Patronage, Collecting and Court Taste*, ed. Jane Roberts (London: Royal Collections Publications, 2004), pp. 8–90; Lloyd, "The King's Buildings," in Marsden, *The Wisdom of George the Third*, pp. 93–152; Jonathan Marsden, "Patronage and Collecting," ibid., pp. 169–85; Jeremy Black, *George III: America's Last King* (New Haven, Conn.: Yale University Press, 2006), pp. 167–68, 171–72; Stella Tillyard, *A Royal Affair: George III and His Scandalous Siblings* (New York: Random House, 2006), p. 45.

10. Watkin, *The Architect King*, p. 86; John Wain, *Samuel Johnson: A Biography* (New York: Viking Press, 1974), pp. 244–45.

11. *The Correspondence of King George III with Lord North 1768 to 1783*, ed. W. Bodham Donne, 2 vols. (London: John Murray, 1867; repr. New York: Da Capo Press, 1971), 1:lxxxviii; P. D. G. Thomas, "George III and the American Revolution," *History* 70, no. 228 (1985): 18–19; *The Correspondence of King George The Third from 1760 to December 1783*, ed. Sir John Fortescue, 6 vols. (London: Macmillan, 1927–28), 1:452. Thomas, "George III and the American Revolution," pp. 16–31, makes the strongest case for George III having little responsibility for the policies that led to the Revolution. Other historians have suggested that he played a role. According to John L. Bullion, "Security and Economy: The Bute Administration's Plans for the American Army and Revenue, 1762–1763," *William and Mary Quarterly*, 3 ser., 45, no. 3 (July 1988): 502, George III was a party to the momentous decision to keep ten thousand troops in America after the French and Indian War. He even suggested an ingenious method of enlarging the size of the regiments at a minimum cost. However, this was when George III was still very much the protégé of his former tutor and then prime minister, the earl of Bute. Benjamin Woods Labaree, *The Boston Tea Party* (Oxford: Oxford University Press, 1964), p. 41; Don Cook, *The Long Fuse: How England Lost the American Colonies, 1760–1785* (New York: Atlantic Monthly Press, 1995), p. 107, mentions that "the king refused to allow any political retaliation against the 167 MPs who had voted against the repeal, which left little doubt about royal unhappiness over the whole affair"; G. M. Ditchfield, *George III: An Essay in Monarchy* (Basingstoke: Palgrave-Macmillan, 2002), p. 124, argues that George III's opposition to withdrawing the tea duty influenced the decision of the Cabinet to retain it in May 1769. Hiller B. Zoebel, *The Boston Massacre* (New York: Norton, 1971), p. 235, notes that in the aftermath of the Boston Massacre of 1770 George III personally paid the legal costs of Captain Preston, an officer who was present at the incident who was later tried for murder, defended by John Adams, and acquitted.

12. Memorandum of the king, February 1769, Fortescue, *The Correspondence of King George the Third*, 2:84–85.

13. George III to Lord North, February 4, 1774, May 6, 1774, September 11, 1774, Fortescue, *The Correspondence of King George The Third*, 3:59, 104, 131; Black, *George III: America's Last King*, p. 84.

14. George III to North, September 10, 1775, Fortescue, *The Correspondence of King George The Third*, 3:256.

15. George III to North, April 15, 1774, March 21, 1774, ibid., pp. 94, 82. See also George III to North, March 14, 1774, ibid, p. 80; *The Diary and Letters of His Excellency Thomas Hutchinson, Esq.*, ed. Peter Orlando Hutchinson, 2 vols. (New York: Burt Franklin, 1971), 1:163. See also ibid., pp. 159, 174, 175; Watkin, *The Architect King*, p. 31; Hutchinson, *Diary and Letters of Thomas Hutchinson*, 1:158, 159; Bernard Bailyn, *The Ordeal of Thomas Hutchinson: Loyalism and the Destruction of the First British Empire* (London: Allen Lane, 1975), pp. 277–78.

16. George III to North, March 14, 1774, March 23, 1774, April 28, 1774, May 3, 1774, August 24, 1774, September 11, 1774, November 18, 1774, Fortescue, *The Correspondence of King George The Third*, 3:80, 84, 100, 103, 125–26, 131, 153.

17. George III to North, November 18, 1774, ibid., p. 154; P. D. G. Thomas, *Lord North* (London: Allen Lane, 1976), p. 82; George III to North, December 15, 1774, Fortescue, *The Correspondence of King George The Third*, 3:156.

18. James E. Bradley, *Popular Politics and the American Revolution in England: Petitions, the Crown and Public Opinion* (Macon, Ga.: Mercer University Press, 1986); Kathleen Wilson, *The Sense of the People: Politics, Culture and Imperialism in England, 1715–1785* (Cambridge: Cambridge University Press, 1998); John Sainsbury, *Disaffected Patriots: London Supporters of Revolutionary America 1769–1782* (Kingston, Ont.: McGill-Queen's University Press, 1987); Stephen Conway, *The British Isles and the War of American Independence* (Oxford: Oxford University Press, 2000), pp. 10, 132–41, 209; Paul Langford, "London and the American Revolution," in *London in the Age of Reform*, ed. John Stevenson (Oxford: Basil Blackwell, 1977), pp. 66–67.

19. George III to North, February 15, 1775, March 6, 1775, July 5, 1775, July 26, 1775, November 3, 1775, November 9, 1775, Fortescue, *The Correspondence of King George The Third*, 3:175, 175, 184, 233, 235, 276, 282.

20. Langford, "London and the American Revolution," p. 71; Bradley, *Popular Politics and the American Revolution in England*, p. 47; George III to North, April 7, 1775, Fortescue, *The Correspondence of King George The Third*, 3:201; North to George III, April 6, 1775, ibid., p. 199; George III to North, April 7, 1775, ibid., p. 201.

21. George III to North, August 18, 1775, ibid., p. 248.

22. Bernhard Knollenberg, *Growth of the American Revolution 1766–1775*, ed. Bernhard W. Sheehan (1975; repr. Indianapolis: Liberty Fund, 2003), p. 191; *The Parliamentary History of England from the Earliest Period to 1803*, ed. William Cobbett and Thomas Hansard, 36 vols. (London: Hansard, 1806–22), 18:cols. 695–97; Maier, *American Scripture*, p. 25.

23. Ditchfield, *George III*, p. 38; Edward Gibbon to J. B. Holroyd. October 14, 1775 in *The Letters of Edward Gibbon*, ed. J. E. Norton, 3 vols. (New York: Macmillan, 1956). 3:88; Jerrilyn Greene Marston, *King and Congress: The Transfer of Political Legitimacy, 1774–1776* (Princeton, N.J.: Princeton University Press, 1987), p. 46.

24. Bruce Ingham Granger, *Political Satire in the American Revolution 1763–1783* (Ithaca, N.Y.: Cornell University Press, 1960), pp. 73–75, 98–99; Stella F. Duff, "The Case Against George III," *William and Mary Quarterly*, 3d ser., 6, no. 3 (July 1949): 383–97; Winthrop D. Jordan, "Thomas Paine and the Killing of the King, 1776, "*Journal of American History* 60, no. 2 (September 1973): 294–308; William D. Liddle, "A Patriot King, or None: American Public Attitudes towards George III and the

British Monarchy" (Ph.D. diss., Claremont Graduate College, 1970), p. 250; Liddle, "'A Patriot King, or None': Lord Bolingbroke and the American Renunciation of George III," *Journal of American History* 65, no. 4 (March 1979): 951–70; Arthur S. Marks, "The Statue of King George III in New York and the Iconology of Regicide," *American Art Journal* 13, no. 3 (1981): 61–82; Richard Bushman, *King and People in Provincial Massachusetts* (Chapel Hill: University of North Carolina Press, 1985); Marston, *King and Congress*, chaps. 1 and 2; William. L. Hedges, "Telling Off the King: Jefferson's Summary View as American Fantasy," *Early American Literature* 22, no. 2 (1987): 166–74.

25. Liddle, "A Patriot King, or None," p. 312; Jordan, "Familial Politics," p. 301; Brendon McConville, *The King's Three Faces: The Rise and Fall of Royal America, 1688–1776* (Chapel Hill: University of North Carolina Press, 2006), pp. 286, 304, 306.

26. Thomas Jefferson, "A Summary View of the Rights of British America," in *The Writings of Thomas Jefferson*, ed. Paul Leicester Ford, 20 vols. (New York: Putnam's, 1892–99), 1:440, 446; Gordon S. Wood, "The Problem of Sovereignty," *William and Mary* Quarterly, 3d ser., 68, no. 4 (October 2011): 573–77; *London Chronicle*. no. 2758, November 12–15, 1774, p. 465.

27. *American Archives . . . A Documentary History . . . of the American Colonies,* ed. Peter Force, 4th ser., (Washington: Published by M. St. Clair and Peter Force, 1848–53), 4:399, 527; Julie Flavell, "The Plot to Kidnap King George III," *BBC History* (November, 2006): 12–16; Flavell, *When London Was Capital of America* (New Haven, Conn.: Yale University Press, 2010), pp. 159–62, 237.

28. Thomas Paine, *Common Sense* (1776; repr. London: Penguin Classics, 1986), pp. 69, 72, 78–79, 81, 92.

29. Adams to John Penn, April 28, 1776, *Papers of John Adams*, ed. Robert J. Taylor, Gregg L. Lint, and Celeste Walker, 15 vols. (Cambridge, Mass: Harvard University Press, 1979–2012), 4:149; Adams to Samuel Chase, July 9, 1776, ibid., p. 372; Butterfield, *Diary and Autobiography of John Adams*, p. 259; Maier, *American Scripture*, pp. 157, 158.

30. George III to North, June 11, 1779, Fortescue, *The Correspondence of King George The Third*, 4:351.

31. John L. Bullion, "The *Ancien Regime* and the Modernizing State: George III and the American Revolution," *Anglican and Episcopal History* 68, no. 1 (1999): 67–84; George III to North, November 14, 1778, May 31, 1777, June 11, 1779, Fortescue, *The Correspondence of King George The Third*, 4:221, 3:449, 351; George III to the earl of Sandwich, September 13, 1779, ibid., 4:433.

32. George III to North, June 11, 1779, March 7, 1780, June 13, 1781, November 3, 1781, Fortescue, *The Correspondence of King George The Third*, 4:351, 5:30, 247, 297.

33. Black, *George III: America's Last King*, pp. 118–19; Watkin, *The Architect King*, p. 87; Celina Fox, "George III and the Royal Navy," in Marsden, *The Wisdom of George III*, p. 266; N. A. M. Rodger, *The Insatiable Earl: A Life of John Montagu, Fourth Earl of Sandwich* (New York: Norton, 1993), p. 199; Stephen Conway, "The Politics of British Military and Naval Mobilization, 1775–83," *English Historical Review* 112, no. 449 (November 1997): 1185.

34. Black, *George III: America's Last King*, pp. 227, 229; *The Last Journals of Horace Walpole During the Reign of George III*, ed. A. F. Steuart, 2 vols. (London: John Lane, 1910), 1:172; Ira Gruber, "British Strategy: The Theory and Practice of Eighteenth-Century Warfare," in *Reconsiderations on the Revolutionary War: Selected Essays*, ed. Don Higginbotham (Westport, Conn.: Greenwood Press, 1978), p. 15; Alan Valentine, *Lord North*, 2 vols. (Norman, University of Oklahoma Press, 1967), 1:294; Peter D. G. Thomas, *George III: King and Politicians 1760–1770* (Manchester: Manchester University Press, 2002), p. 2; Ira Gruber, "George III Chooses a Commander in Chief," in *Arms and Independence: The Military Character of the American Revolution*, ed. Ronald Hoffman and Peter J. Albert (Charlottesville: Univer-

sity Press of Virginia, 1984), pp. 166, 174; "Remarks on '*The Conduct of the War from Canada*' from the Original Manuscript in the British Museum in the Handwriting of George III," in Edward Barrington De Fonblanque, *Political and Military Episodes in the Latter Half of the Eighteenth Century: Derived from the Life and Correspondence of the Right H. John Burgoyne, General, Statesman, Dramatist* (London: Macmillan, 1876), pp. 486–87.

35. Peter D. G. Thomas, *Tea Party to Independence: The Third Phase of the American Revolution 1773–1776* (Oxford: Clarendon Press, 1991), p. 180; Ira D. Gruber, *The Howe Brothers and the American Revolution* (Chapel Hill: University of North Carolina Press, 1972), p. 69; Piers Mackesy, *The War for America 1775–1783* (1964; repr. Lincoln: University of Nebraska Press, 1964), p. 307; George III to Sandwich, September 10, 1779, *The Private Papers of John, Earl of Sandwich, First Lord of the Admiralty 1771–1782*, ed. G. R. Barnes and J. H. Owen, 4 vols. (Navy Records Society, 1932–38), 3:144.

36. George III to North, January 31, 1778, August 12, 1778, Fortescue, *The Correspondence of King George the Third*, 4:30, 186.

37. George III to North, November 7, 1775, April 10, 1777, December 4, 1777, ibid., 3:279, 281, 440, 503; George III to North, January 31, 1778, March 22, 1778, April 21, 1779, ibid., 4:30, 72, 327.

38. George III to North, January 13, 1778, January 31, 1778, ibid., 4:15, 31. The military implications are examined in William B. Willcox, "British Strategy in America, 1778," *Journal of Modern History* 19. no. 2 (1947): 97–121; David Syrett, "Home Waters or America? The Dilemma of British Naval Strategy in 1778," *Mariner's Mirror* 77, no. 4 (November 1991): 365–77; Gerald S. Brown, "The Anglo-French Naval Crisis: A Study of Conflict in the North Cabinet," *William and Mary Quarterly*, 3d ser., 13, no. 1 (January 1956): 3–26.

39. North to George III, January 29, 1778, March 16, 1778, March 17, [1778], Fortescue, *The Correspondence of King George The Third*, 4:28, 60, 62 (emphasis in the original).

40. North to George III, March 25, 1778, March 25, 1778, ibid., pp. 73, 76, 77.

41. George III to North, March 27, 1778, ibid., pp. 84–85; North to George III, May 7, 1778, ibid., p. 133.

42. George III to North, June 2, 1778, November 2, 1778, ibid., pp. 162–63, 213; North to George III, November 14, 1778, ibid., p. 219; George III to North, November 14, 1778, ibid. p. 220.

43. Mr. Jenkinson to George III, November 30, 1779, May 15, 1779, April 14, 1780, November 12, 1779, November 28, 1779, December 9, 1779, December 1, 1779, June 17, 1780, ibid., pp. 503, 342, 5:42, 4:483, 500, 513, 505, 5:87.

44. Mr. Jenkinson to George III, June 25, 1779, ibid., 4:377; North to George III, June 30, 1779, [? September, 1779], [? November, 1779], April 7, 1780, ibid., pp. 382, 442, 494–95, 5:40; Mr. Jenkinson to George III, April 14, 1780, ibid., p. 42; North to George III, March 15, 1781, ibid., p. 207.

45. Steuart, *The Last Journals of Horace Walpole*, 2:305; *The Manuscripts of Captain Howard Vincente Knox (From Volume VI of "Reports on Manuscripts in Various Collections" Prepared by the Historical Manuscripts Commission, Great Britain)* (1909; repr. Boston: Gregg Press, 1972), p. 267; W. Baring Pemberton, *Lord North* (London: Longmans, Green, 1938), p. 253.

46. George III to North, May 31, 1777, August 9, 1775, Fortescue, *The Correspondence of King George The Third*, pp. 449, 242; North to George III, March 29 [1778], ibid., 4:79; *The Annual Register*, in *Rebellion in America: A Contemporary British Viewpoint, 1769–1783*, ed. David Murdoch (Santa Barbara, Calif.: Clio Books, 1979), p. 605; George III to North, May 12, 1778, Fortescue, *The Correspondence of King George The Third*, 4:139–40.

47. George III to North, March 16, 1778, March 17, 1778, March 18, 1778, Fortescue, *The Correspondence of King George The Third*, 4:60–61, 65, 67.

48. Charles R. Ritcheson, *British Politics and the American Revolution* (Norman: University of Oklahoma Press, 1954), pp. 247, 248; Rev. Dean of Windsor to Charles Arbuthnot, 13 January 1843, Donne, *The Correspondence of King George the Third with Lord North*, 2:127.

49. Mackesy, *The War for America*, pp. 44, 264; Herbert Butterfield, *George III, Lord North and the People, 1779–80* (New York: Russell & Russell, 1968), p. 116; George III to North, June 16, 1778, Fortescue, *The Correspondence of King George The Third*, 4:358.

50. George III to North, June 11, 1779, Fortescue, *The Correspondence of King George The Third*, 4:350–51; "The King's Speech to his Cabinet," June 21, 1779, *The Manuscripts of Captain Howard Vincente Knox*, p. 260.

51. "The King's Speech to his Cabinet," June 21, 1779, *The Manuscripts of Captain Howard Vincente Knox*, pp. 260–61; George III to North, June 21, 1779, Fortescue, *The Correspondence of King George The Third*, 4:367.

52. Butterfield, *George III, Lord North and the People*, pp. 26, 46; George III to North, March 17, 1778, June 16, 1779, June 11, 1779, June 18, 1779, Fortescue, *The Correspondence of King George The Third*, 4:65, 358, 351, 360.

53. Flora Fraser, *Princesses—The Six Daughters of George III* (London: John Murray, 2004), pp. 44–45, 66; Watkin, *The Architect King*, pp. 26, 209; Stephen Roe, "Music at the Court of George II and Queen Charlotte," in Marsden, *The Wisdom of George the Third*, p. 147; Black, *George III: America's Last King*, p. 118. George III was first portrayed in the Windsor Uniform by Thomas Gainsborough in 1781, Ditchfield, *George III: An Essay in Monarchy*, p. 145.

54. William Cowper to Unwin, February 13, 1780, Donne, *The Correspondence of George The Third with Lord North*, 2:192.

55. George III to North, April 7, 1780, April 11, 1780, Fortescue, *The Correspondence of King George The Third*, pp. 40, 42.

56. Ian R. Christie, "Economical Reform and 'The Influence of the Crown,' 1780," *Myth and Reality in Late-Eighteenth-Century British Politics and Other Papers* (London: Macmillan, 1970), p. 310; John Brooke, *King George III* (London: Constable, 1972), p. 218: "it was not the influence of the Crown that was increasing but the pretensions of the House of Commons"; Christie, "Economical Reform," p. 309; J. B. Owen, "George II Reconsidered," in *Statesmen, Scholars and Merchants: Essays in Eighteenth-Century History Presented to Dame Lucy Sutherland*, ed. Anne Whiteman, J. S. Bromley, and P. G. M. Dickson (Oxford: Oxford University Press, 1973), pp. 113–35. For a skillful refutation see Brewer, "Ministerial Responsibility and the Powers of the Crown," in *Party Ideology and Popular Politics at the Accession of George III* (Cambridge: Cambridge University Press, 1976), pp. 131–35. Jeremy Black, *George II: Party Puppet of the Politicians?* (Exeter: University of Exeter Press, 2007) argues that that king did indeed wield extensive power especially in foreign policy, and sees George III as consistent with George II in his use of power.

57. George III to North, June 22, 1779, Fortescue, *The Correspondence of King George the Third*, 4:370; Brewer, "Ministerial Responsibility and the Powers of the Crown," p. 134; George III to North, June 22, 1779, Fortescue, *The Correspondence of King George the Third*, 4:370; George III to the lord chancellor, October 16, 1779, ibid., p. 458; George III to Mr. Jenkinson, November 7, 1779, ibid., p. 477; George III to North, July 3, 1780, ibid., 5:96–97. Richard Pares, *King George III and the Politicians* (Oxford: Clarendon Press, 1953), p. 112, regarded the king's insistence as a novel addition to the Constitution: "I know of no deliberate attempts to make acceptance of office conditional upon stipulations as to policy earlier than the beginning of George III's reign."

58. *The Historical and Posthumous Memoirs of Sir Nathaniel William Wraxall 1772–1784*, ed. Henry

B. Wheatley, 5 vols. (1836; repr. London: Bickers & Son, 1884), 2:20; George III to North, March 5, B. Wheatley, 5 vols. (1836; repr. London: Bickers & Son, 1884), 2:20; George III to North, March 5, 1779, April 25, 1780, Fortescue, *The Correspondence of King George the Third*, 5:299, 5:52; George III to North, July 3 (?), 1780, Donne, *The Correspondence of King George the Third with Lord North*, 2:329; George III to North, February 22, 1780, Fortescue, *The Correspondence of King George the Third*, 5:20.

59. I. R. Christie, "The Marquis of Rockingham and Lord North's Offer of a Coalition, June–July 1780," in *Myth and Reality*, pp. 109–32.

60. Steuart, *The Last Journals of Horace Walpole*, 2:311–12; H. T. Dickinson, *The Politics of the People in Eighteenth-Century Britain* (New York: St. Martin's Press, 1994), p. 153; Wheatley, *The Historical and Posthumous Memoirs of Sir Nathaniel William Wraxall*, 1:244, 246, 247, 251; Christopher Hibbert, *King Mob: The London Riots of 1780* (New York: Dorset Press, 1958), pp. 43, 131; George III to North, November 24, 1779, Fortescue, *The Correspondence of King George the Third*, 4:497.

61. *The Annual Register*, in Murdoch, *Rebellion in America*, p. 535.

62. Wheatley, *The Historical and Posthumous Memoirs of Sir Nathaniel William Wraxall*, 2:3–4.

63. Ibid.; "The House Debates Whether to Continue the War," November 9, 1780, in *The American Revolution as Described by British Writers and The Morning Chronicle and London Advertiser*, ed. Elizabeth R. Miller (Bowie, Md.: Heritage Books, 1991), p. 29; Wheatley, *The Historical and Posthumous Memoirs of Sir Nathaniel William Wraxall*, 2:10.

64. Peter Brown, *The Chathamites: A Study in the Relationship between Personalities and Ideas in the Second Half of the Eighteenth Century* (New York: St. Martin's Press, 1967), p. 35.

65. George III to North, November 28, 1781, December 26, 1781, February 26, 1782, Fortescue, *The Correspondence of King George the Third*, 5:304, 326, 374; I. R. Christie, *The End of North's Ministry* (London: Macmillan, 1958), p. 288; *The New Annual Register, or General Repository of History, Politics, and Literature for the Year 1782* (London: G. Robinson, 1783), p. 4; Wheatley, *The Historical and Posthumous Memoirs of Sir Nathaniel William Wraxall*, 2:151–52.

66. *The New Annual Register* (London: G. Robinson, 1783), p. 4.

67. Christie, *The End of North's Ministry*, pp. 288, 273, 289; Wheatley, *The Historical and Posthumous Memoirs of Sir Nathaniel William Wraxall*, 2:178. "Removal of Lord George Germain," *The Manuscripts of Captain Howard Vincente Knox*, p. 276.

68. George III to North, February 28, 1782, Fortescue, *The Correspondence of King George the Third*, ed. Fortescue, 5:375; North to George III, March 18, 1782, ibid., p. 395; George III to North, March 19, 1782, ibid., p. 397; Steuart, *The Last Journals of Horace Walpole*, 2:211.

69. Draft message from the King, Fortescue, *The Correspondence of King George The Third*, 5:425.

70. Thomas Fleming, *The Perils of Peace: America's Struggle for Survival after Yorktown* (New York: HarperCollins, 2007), p. 241; Wheatley, *The Historical and Posthumous Memoirs of Sir Nathaniel William Wraxall*, 2:395; *The Annual Register*, in Murdoch, *Rebellion in America*, p. 987; Fraser, *Princesses*, p. 73.

71. George III to Fox, August 7, 1783, Fortescue, *The Correspondence of King George the Third*, 6:443–44; John L. Bullion, "George III and Empire, 1783," *William and Mary Quarterly*, 3d ser., 51, no. 2 (April 1994): 309 n. 7; George III to North, September 7, 1783, Fortescue, *The Correspondence of King George the Third*, 6:443–44; Eric Robson, *The American Revolution in Its Political and Military Aspects 1763–1783* (1955; repr. New York: Norton, 1966), p. 29.

72. Linda Colley, "The Apotheosis of George III: Loyalty, Royalty and the British Nation, 1760–1820," *Past and Present*, no. 102 (1984): 94–129.

73. Colley, "The Apotheosis of George III"; Black, *George III: America's Last King*, p. 287.

74. Stanley Ayling, *George The Third* (London: Collins, 1972), p. 117; Judy Rudoe, "Queen Charlotte's Jewelry: Reconstructing a Lost Collection," in Marsden, *The Wisdom of George the Third*, p. 196; Flora Fraser, "Princesses: Telling the Story," ibid., p. 221.

75. Ida Macalpine and Richard Hunter, *George III and the Mad-Business* (London: Allen Lane, 1969). The book was the outcome of earlier articles: "The 'Insanity' of George III: A Classic Case of Porphyria," *British Medical Journal*, no. 5479 (January 1966): 65–71; "A Clinical Reassessment of the 'Insanity' of George III and Some of Its Historical Implications," *Bulletin of the Institute of Historical Research* 15 (1967): 166–85; *Porphyria—A Royal Malady: Articles Published in or Commissioned by the British Medical Journal* (London: British Medical Association, 1968). See also Fraser, *Princesses*, p. 316. There are other theories about the source of his illness, but the case for porphyria is greatly strengthened by the work of J. C. G. Rohl, M. Warren, and D. Hunt, *Purple Secret: Genes, "Madness" and the Royal Houses of Europe* (London: Bantam Press, 1998).

76. Macalpine and Hunter, *George III and the Mad-Business*, pp. 160–61.

77. George III to Lord Shelburne, November 10, 1782, Fortescue, *The Correspondence of King George the Third*, 6:154; Adams, *The Works of John Adams*, 8:257.

Chapter 2. The Prime Minister

1. *The Diary and Letters of His Excellency Thomas Hutchinson, Esq.*, ed. Peter Orlando Hutchinson, 2 vols. (New York: Burt Franklin. 1971), 2:262; North to George III, June 4, 1779, *The Correspondence of King George the Third from 1760 to December 1783*, ed. Sir John Fortescue, 6 vols. (London: Macmillan, 1927–28), 4:369.

2. March 17, 1778: *The Last Journals of Horace Walpole During the Reign of George III*, ed. A. F. Steuart, 2 vols. (London: John Lane, 1910), 2:139, 210; December 9, 1779: Hutchinson, *Diary and Letters of Thomas Hutchinson*, 2:306:; Steuart, *The Last Journals of Horace Walpole*, 1:239, 2:210; William Cobbett and Thomas Hansard, eds., *The Parliamentary History of England from the Earliest Period to 1803*, 36 vols. (London: Hansard, 1806–22), 22:cols. 949, 950, quoted in Alan Valentine, *Lord North*, 2 vols. (Norman: University of Oklahoma Press, 1967), 2:112.

3. Steuart, *The Last Journals of Horace Walpole*, 1:47; *Public Advertiser*, April 21, 1778, in *Our American Brethren: A History of Letters in the British Press During the American Revolution, 1775–1781*, ed. Alfred Grant (Jefferson, N.C.: McFarland, 1995), p. 74; Steuart, *The Last Journals of Horace Walpole*, pp. 596–97.

4. Charles Daniel Smith, *The Early Career of Lord North the Prime Minister* (London: Athlone Press, 1979), pp. 47, 94. The view that Lord North's desire to resign was insincere was expressed by Charles Jenkinson; see Eric Robson, "Lord North," *History Today* 2, no. 8 (August 1952): 537. The same allegation is found in scholarly accounts, including John Brooke, *King George III* (London: Constable, 1972), p. 195. W. Baring Pemberton, *Lord North* (London: Longmans, Green, 1938), p. 4 treats North's desire to resign as genuine.

5. Pemberton, *Lord North*, p. 248; Steuart, *The Last Journals of Horace Walpole*, 1:117; George III to North, September 19, 1777, Fortescue, *The Correspondence of King George the Third*, 3:479; George III to North, May 19, 1778, ibid., 4:145–46; Brooke, *King George III*, p. 195 comments that the "promise of the tellership was not a bribe to induce North to remain but a reward for services rendered." Thomas, *Lord North*, p. 114: "These rewards had the political consequence that North felt himself unable to resign without the King's permission; and that he was never to obtain. . . . The bond had become a chain."

6. Herbert Butterfield, *George III, Lord North and the People, 1779–80* (New York: Russell & Russell, 1968), pp. 18, 19; *The Correspondence of King George the Third with Lord North,* ed. W. B. Donne, 2 vols.(London: John Murray, 1867; repr. New York: Da Capo Press, 1971), 2:154; the earl of Hillsborough commented to Thomas Hutchinson that North's father desired that he stay in power until all his extended family "were provided for, and they were numerous," Hutchinson, *Diary and Letters of Thomas Hutchinson,* 1:378.

7. Horace Walpole, *Memoirs of the Reign of King George III,* ed. Derek Jarrett, 4 vols. (New Haven, Conn.: Yale University Press, 2000), 4:143; *The Letters of Junius,* ed. John Cannon (Oxford: Clarendon Press, 1978), p. 189.

8. *The Historical and Posthumous Memoirs of Sir Nathaniel William Wraxall 1772–1784,* ed. Henry B. Wheatley, 5 vols. (1836; repr. London: Bickers & Son, 1884), 1:3, 371, 376, 361–62.

9. Hugh Bowen, "British Conceptions of Global Empire, 1756–83," *Journal of Imperial and Commonwealth History* 26, no. 3 (1998): 6, 10, 13.

10. Peter G. Dickson, *The Financial Revolution in England: A Study of the Development of Public Credit* (New York: St. Martin's Press, 1967); John Brewer, *The Sinews of Power: War, Money, and the English State, 1688–1783* (New York: Knopf, 1989); Gerald Newman, *The Rise of English Nationalism: A Cultural History* (New York: St. Martin's Press, 1987); Linda Colley, *Britons: Forging the Nation, 1707–1837* (New Haven, Conn.: Yale University Press, 1992); Eliga H. Gould, *The Persistence of Empire: British Political Culture in the Age of the American Revolution* (Chapel Hill: University of North Carolina Press, 2000).

11. Dora Mae Clark, *British Opinion and the American Revolution* (New York: Russell & Russell, 1966), pp. 133, 201; Reginald Lucas, *Lord North, 1732–1792,* 2 vols. (London: Arthur L. Humphreys, 1913) 1:70; *Proceedings and Debates of the British Parliaments Respecting North America 1754–1783,* ed. R. C. Simmons and P. D. G. Thomas, 6 vols. (Millwood, N.Y.: Kraus International, 1982–86), 3:3; P. D. G. Thomas, *The Townshend Duties Crisis: The Second Phase of the American Revolution 1767–1773* (Oxford: Oxford University Press, 1987), p. 134; Thomas, *George III: King and Politicians 1760–1770* (Manchester: Manchester University Press, 2002), p. 206; Thomas, *Lord North* (London: Allen Lane, 1976), pp. 32–33.

12. P. J. Marshall, *The Making and Unmaking of Empires: Britain, India and America c. 1750–1783* (Oxford: Oxford University Press, 2005), p. 318.

13. Simmons and Thomas, *Proceedings and Debates of the British Parliaments Respecting North America 1754–1783,* 3:210–216, 228–37; Smith, *The Early Career of Lord North the Prime Minister,* p. 226; *Rebellion in America: A Contemporary British Viewpoint 1765–1783,* ed. David H. Murdoch (Santa Barbara, Calif.: Clio Books, 1979), pp. 102–3.

14. Thomas, *The Townshend Duties Crisis,* pp. 252, 171.

15. H. T. Dickinson, "Britain's Imperial Sovereignty: The Ideological Case against the American Colonists," in *Britain and the American Revolution,* ed. H. T. Dickinson (London: Addison Wesley Longman, 1979), pp. 64–96.

16. Murdoch, *Rebellion in America: A Contemporary British Viewpoint 1765–1783,* pp. 221, 216. See also his later speech in *The Annual Register,* ibid., p. 576.

17. North's speech of March 7, 1774 in *The Annual Register,* ibid., p. 132; Steuart, *The Last Journals of Horace Walpole,* 1:317–18; P. D. G. Thomas, *Tea Party to Independence: The Third Phase of the American Revolution 1773–1776* (Oxford: Oxford University Press, 1991), p. 54; Neil Stout, *The Perfect Crisis: The Beginning of the Revolutionary War* (New York: New York University Press, 1976), p. 53; Ira Gruber, "The American Revolution as a Conspiracy: The British View," *William and Mary Quarterly,* 3d ser.,

26, no. 3 (July 1969): 360–72; Bernard Bailyn, *The Ideological Origins of the American Revolution* (Cambridge, Mass.: Harvard University Press, 1967), pp. 150–59; Benjamin Woods Labaree, "The Idea of American Independence: The British View, 1774–1776," *Proceedings of the Massachusetts Historical Society*, 3d. ser., 82 (1970): 3–20. Thomas, *Tea Party to Independence*, pp. 51, 82, 50.

18. *The Papers of Benjamin Franklin*, ed. Leonard W. Labaree, William B. Willcox, Barbara Oberg, and Ellen R. Cohn, 39 vols.(New Haven, Conn.: Yale University Press, 1959–), 21:132–133. For contemporary accounts of popular opinion see Thomas, *Tea Party to Independence*, p. 83; Benjamin Woods Labaree, *The Boston Tea Party* (Oxford: Oxford University Press, 1964), p. 206; Hutchinson, *Diary and Letters of Thomas Hutchinson*, 1:217; Charles R. Ritcheson, *British Politics and the American Revolution* (Norman: University of Oklahoma Press, 1954), p. 157; Paul Langford, "The British Business Community and the Later Nonimportation Movements, 1768–1776," in *Resistance, Politics, and the American Struggle for Independence, 1765–1775*, ed. Walther H. Conser Jr., Ronald M. McCarthy, David J. Toscano, and Gene Sharp (Boulder, Colo.: Lynne Riener, 1986), p. 281.

19. Stout, *The Perfect Crisis*, p. 52; Labaree, *The Boston Tea Party*, p. 207; Boswell, *Life of Johnson*, quoted in Smith, *The Early Career of Lord North*, p. 175.

20. Labaree, *The Boston Tea Party*, p. 238; *Peter Oliver's Origin and Progress of the American Rebellion: A Tory View*, ed. Douglass Adair and John A. Schutz, (Stanford, Calif.: Stanford University Press, 1961), p. 114.

21. Murdoch, *Rebellion in America*, p. 216; North's speech of March 7, 1774 in *The Annual Register*, ibid., p. 133. Ritcheson, *British Politics and the American Revolution*, p. 158; Stout, *The Perfect Crisis*, p. 126; Julie Flavell, "Government Interception of Letters from America and the Quest for Colonial Opinion in 1775," *William and Mary Quarterly*, 3d ser., 58, no. 2 (April 2001): 416, 418, 420, 423.

22. Thomas, *Tea Party to Independence*, p. 168, 178; Hutchinson, *The Diary and Letters of Thomas Hutchinson*, December 22, 1774, 1:330; Steuart, *The Last Journals of Horace Walpole*, 1:427; *The Annual Register*, in Murdoch, *Rebellion in America*, p. 225; Gibbon to J. B. Holroyd, February 8, 1775, in *The Letters of Edward Gibbon*, ed. J. E. Norton, 3 vols.(New York: Macmillan, 1956), 3:59.

23. Ritcheson, *British Politics and the American Revolution*, p. 178; Bernhard Knollenberg, *Growth of the American Revolution: 1766–1775* (1975; repr. Indianapolis: Liberty Fund, 2003), p. 318.

24. Benjamin Franklin to William Franklin, "Journal of Negotiations in London," March 22, 1775, Labaree et al., *The Papers of Benjamin Franklin*, 21:550, 552, 567–68, 571.

25. Weldon A. Brown, *Empire or Independence: A Study in the Failure of Reconciliation, 1774–1783* (Baton Rouge: Louisiana State University Press, 1941), pp. 36–40; Thomas, *Tea Party to Independence*, pp. 176–80; Lucas, *Lord North*, 2:36; Benjamin Franklin to William Franklin, "Journal of Negotiations in London," March 22, 1775, Labaree et al., *The Papers of Benjamin Franklin*, 21:591.

26. I. R. Christie, *Crisis of Empire: Great Britain and the American Colonies 1754–1783* (New York: Norton, 1966), p. 96; Thomas, *Lord North*, p. 84; Allan J. McCurry, "The North Government and the Outbreak of the American Revolution," *Huntington Library Quarterly* 34, no. 2 (February 1971): 153, 155; Benjamin Franklin to William Franklin, "Journal of Negotiations in London," March 22, 1775, Labaree et al., *The Papers of Benjamin Franklin*, 21:595; Virginia Resolutions on Lord North's Conciliatory Proposal [10 June 1775], Boyd et al., *The Papers of Thomas Jefferson*, 1:171. See also "Resolutions of Congress on Lord North's Conciliatory Proposal" (Jefferson's draft resolutions [25 July 1775]), ibid., 225–33. The Conciliatory Proposal initially had a favorable response from some Americans living in London, see Julie Flavell, "Lord North's Conciliatory Proposal and the Patriots in London," *English Historical Review* 107, no. 423 (April 1992): 302–22.

27. Hutchinson, *Diary and Letters of Thomas Hutchinson*, 1:400. See also Bernard Donoughue, *British Politics and the American Revolution: The Path to War, 1773–75* (London: Macmillan, 1964), p. 200.

28. *The Annual Register*, in Murdoch, *Rebellion in America*, p. 240; Steuart, *The Last Journals of Horace Walpole*, 1:437.

29. Benjamin Franklin to William Franklin, "Journal of Negotiations in London," March 22, 1775, Labaree et al., *The Papers of Benjamin Franklin*, p. 591; Gibbon to J. B. Holroyd, February 25, 1775, Norton, *The Letters of Edward Gibbon*, 3:61; *The Annual Register*, in Murdoch, *Rebellion in America*, p. 240; Steuart, *The Last Journals of Horace Walpole*, 1:437.

30. Hutchinson, *Diary and Letters of Thomas Hutchinson*, 1:454.

31. Thomas, *Tea Party to Independence*, pp. 252, 254, 260; Julie M. Flavell, "American Patriots in London and the Quest for Talks, 1774–1775," *Journal of Imperial and Commonwealth History* 20, no. 3 (1992): 357–58. Williamson and Cruger thought North and Dartmouth more anxious to avoid war than the rest of the Cabinet, but their view was not shared by Franklin and Lee: Flavell, "Lord North's Conciliatory Proposal and the Patriots in London," p. 317.

32. *The Annual Register*, in Murdoch, *Rebellion in America*, p. 562; Brown, *Empire or Independence*, p. 23; John Shy, *A People Numerous and Armed: Reflections on the Military Struggle for American Independence*, rev. ed. (Ann Arbor: University of Michigan Press, 2000), pp. 71–74.

33. Ritcheson, *British Politics and the American Revolution*, p. 192; Stanley Weintraub, *Iron Tears: America's Battle for Freedom, Britain's Quagmire, 1775–1783* (New York: Free Press, 2005), pp. 8, 53; Solomon Lutnick, *The American Revolution and the British Press 1775–1783* (Columbia: University of Missouri Press, 1967); Burke to Rockingham, February 2, 1774, *The Correspondence of Edmund Burke*, ed. Thomas W. Copeland et al., 10 vols. (Chicago: The University of Chicago Press, 1960), 2:523–524; Troy Bickham, *Making Headlines. The American Revolution as Seen through the British Press* (DeKalb: Northern Illinois University Press, 2009), argues that the press reports were mixed, that the newspapers did not split among party lines and that they were not beholden to political sponsorship (pp. 50, 75).

34. Stephen Conway, *The British Isles and the War of American Independence* (Oxford: Oxford University Press, 2000), p. 135.

35. *The Annual Register*, in Murdoch, *Rebellion in America*, p. 210.

36. Valentine, *Lord North*, 1:373; William Knox, account of first peace commission of 1776, n.d., *Knox Papers*, X, fol. 23, WLCL, cited in Ira D. Gruber, *The Howe Brothers and the American Revolution* (Chapel Hill: University of North Carolina Press, 1972), p. 74; Alexander Wedderburn to Lord George Germain, [March 7, 1776?], Historical Manuscripts Commission, *Report on the Manuscripts of Mrs. Stopford-Sackville of Drayton House, Northamptonshire*, 2 vols. (London: H.M. Stationery Office, 1910), 2:24–25.

37. "First Commissioners to the American Colonies," *The Manuscripts of Captain Howard Vincente Knox (From Volume VI of "Reports on Manuscripts in Various Collections" Prepared by the Historical Manuscripts Commission, Great Britain)* (1909; repr. Boston: Gregg Press, 1972), pp. 258–60. The peace commission is discussed in Ritcheson, *British Politics and the American Revolution*, pp. 202–8; Brown, *Empire or Independence*, pp. 75–85; Gruber, *The Howe Brothers and the American Revolution*, pp. 72–74; Steuart, *The Last Journals of Horace Walpole*, 1:551; Thomas, *Tea Party to Independence*, p. 293; *The Annual Register*, in Murdoch, *Rebellion in America*, p. 342. It was a royal rather than a parliamentary commission and therefore received little attention in Parliament.

38. Valentine, *Lord North*, 1:421; Historical Manuscript Commission, *Abergavenny Papers*, cited in Lucas, *Lord North*, 2:53; North to Eden, November 4, 1777, in Ritcheson, *British Politics and the American Revolution*, p. 233; Lucas, *Lord North*, 2:54. For newspaper comment see, for example, *Public*

Advertiser, December 12, 1777, and December 12, 1777, and British Legion in the *Morning Post,* December 30, 1777, in Grant, *Our American Brethren,* pp. 90, 115, 113; Bickham, *Making Headlines,* pp. 69–70.

39. North to Lord Chancellor Bathurst, December 9, 1777, Cirencester House Papers, cited in Lucas, *Lord North,* 2:55; North to George III, October 25, 1778, Fortescue, *The Correspondence of King George the Third,* 4:210.

40. Flavell, "American Patriots in London and the Quest for Talks," pp. 356–57; Wentworth negotiations described in Ritcheson, *British Politics and the American Revolution,* pp. 234–41; Helen Augur, *The Secret War of Independence* (New York: Little, Brown, 1955), pp. 254–61. G. H. Guttridge, *English Whiggism and the American Revolution* (Berkeley: University of California Press, 1963), pp. 282, 289.

41. *The Diaries of Sylvester Douglas (Lord Glenbervie),* ed. Francis Bickley, 2 vols. (London: Constable, 1928), 2:403; Paul David Nelson, *William Tryon and the Course of Empire: A Life in the British Imperial Service* (Chapel Hill: University of North Carolina Press, 1990), p. 160.

42. Bickley, *The Diaries of Sylvester Douglas,* 1:403; "Orders and Instructions," in *Proceedings of the British Commissioners in Philadelphia, 1778–9: Partly in Ferguson's Hand,* ed. Yasuo Amoh, Darren Lingley, and Hiroko Aoki (Kyoto: Kakenhi Supplemental Project Research Report, Kyoto University, 2007), pp. 25–41; *Sources and Documents Illustrating the American Revolution 1764–1788 and the Formation of the Federal Constitution,* ed. Samuel Eliot Morison (1923; repr. Oxford: Oxford University Press, 1965), pp. 186–204; Piers Mackesy, *The War for America 1775–1783* (1964; repr. Lincoln: University of Nebraska Press, 1993), pp. 188–89; Jerome Reich, *British Friends of the American Revolution* (Armonk, N.Y.: M. E. Sharpe, 1998), p. 121; Charles Stedman, *The History of the Origin, Progress, and Termination of the American War,* 2 vols.(London: J. Murray, J. Debrett, and J. Kerby, 1794), 2:6.

43. Cobbett and Hansard, *Parliamentary History,* 19:762–815 (February 19, 1778) quoted in Valentine, *Lord North,* 1:cols. 505; *The Annual Register,* in Murdoch, *Rebellion in America,* pp. 576, 577; Ritcheson, *British Politics and the American Revolution,* p. 261; Hutchinson, *Diary and Letters of Thomas Hutchinson,* 1:187, 189.

44. *The Annual Register,* in Murdoch, *Rebellion in America,* p. 581; Gibbon to J. B. Holroyd, February 23, 1778, Norton, *The Letters of Edward Gibbon,* 3:411; *The Annual Register,* in Murdoch, *Rebellion in America,* p. 577; Steuart, *The Last Journals of Horace Walpole,* 2:117.

45. William B. Willcox, "British Strategy in America, 1778," *Journal of Modern History,* 19 no. 2 (June 1947): 106; Addendum of George Johnstone to Germain, June 15, 1778, in Henry Clinton, William Eden, and George Johnstone to Germain, July 19, 1778 and September 5, 1778; in Amoh et al., *Proceedings of the British Commissioners at Philadelphia,* pp. 71, 81, 111.

46. Eden to North, March 30, 1778, and Eden to Wedderburn, April 12, 1778, in Valentine, *Lord North,* 1:535–36.

47. Pemberton, *Lord North,* p. 278.

48. Steuart, *The Last Journals of Horace Walpole,* 2:115; Gibbon to J. B. Holroyd, February 23, 1778, Norton, *The Letters of Edward Gibbon,* 3:411; *Morning Post,* March 10, 1778, Grant, *Our American Brethren,* p. 99; *The Annual Register,* in Murdoch, *Rebellion in America,* p. 354.

49. North to Eden, June 14, 1778, British Library, Add. MSS. 34415, cited in Lucas, *Lord North,* 2:62; "Letter of Lady Charlotte Lindsay on Lord North, Green-Street, February 18, 1839," in Henry, Lord Brougham, *Historical Sketches of Statesmen Who Flourished in the Time of George III,* 2 vols. (London: Charles Knight & Co., 1839), 1:393.

50. Wheatley, *The Historical and the Posthumous Memoirs of Sir Nathaniel William Wraxall,* 1:373; Thomas, *George III,* p. 51; Boswell, *Life of Johnson,* May 17, 1778, quoted in Valentine, *Lord North,* 2:8.

Richard Middleton, *The Bells of Victory: The Pitt-Newcastle Ministry and the Conduct of the Seven Years' War 1757–1762* (Cambridge: Cambridge University Press, 1985) questions whether Pitt had a strategy and argues that too much credit for the victory is given to him. This view is rebutted in Brendan Simms, *Three Victories and a Defeat: The Rise and Fall of the First British Empire, 1714–1783* (New York: Basic Books, 2007), pp. 423, 429–30.

51. "Letter of Lady Charlotte Lindsay on Lord North," in Brougham, *Historical Sketches of Statesmen Who Flourished in the Time of George III,* 1:392; Lucas, *Lord North, 3*:62, 88, 89, 99.

52. Boswell, *Life of Johnson,* quoted Valentine, *Lord North,* 1:363; Hutchinson, *Diary and Letters of Thomas Hutchinson,* 1:451.

53. North to George III, March 20, 1778, [May 6, 1778?], May 10, 1778, Fortescue, *The Correspondence of King George the Third,* 4:70, 132, 138.

54. Bickley, *The Diaries of Sylvester Douglas,* 1:231; Smith, *The Early Career of Lord North,* p. 238; Lucas, *Lord North, 1*:355–356.

55. William Burke to the duke of Portland, August 12, 1779, quoted in Lucas, *Lord North,* 2:93; British Library, Add. MSS. 38212, (Liverpool Papers, vol. 33), f. 56, quoted in Guttridge, *English Whiggism and the American Revolution,* p. 111; North to Dartmouth, November 34, 1779, Patshull House Papers, cited *Lord North, 2*:98; North to Guilford, April 25, 1781, quoted ibid., p. 133.

56. Lord North to the king, May 7, 1778, Fortescue, *The Correspondence of King George the Third,* 5:133; Hutchinson, *Diary and Letters of Thomas Hutchinson,* 1:404; Robinson to Jenkinson, June 13 and June [?], 1780, British Library, Add. MSS. 38213, f. 22, and 38214, f. 57, quoted in Valentine, *Lord North,* 2:218; *The Caledonian Mercury,* August 10, 1778, Grant, *Our American Brethren,* pp. 73–74.

57. Hutchinson, *Diary and Letters of Thomas Hutchinson,* 3:182; Sandwich to George III, September 14, 1779, Fortescue, *The Correspondence of King George the Third,* 4:435; Butterfield, *George III, Lord North and the People,* p. 151; John Robinson to Jenkinson, January 27, 1780; Jenkinson to Robinson, quoting Thurlow, January 27, 1780; British Library, Add. MSS. 38213, ff. 79–80, 80; cited in Valentine, *Lord North,* 2:185; North to Robinson, May 25, 1779, Historical Manuscripts Commission, *Abergavenny Papers,* no. 217, cited in Ian R. Christie, *The End of North's Ministry, 1780–1782* (London: Macmillan, 1958), p. 5.

58. Robson, "Lord North," p. 533; Butterfield, *George III, Lord North and the People,* pp. 60–81.

59. Lord North to the king, February 2, 1776, Fortescue, *The Correspondence of King George the Third,* 3:335; Hutchinson, *Diary and Letters of Thomas Hutchinson,* January 4, 1775, February 17, 1775, 1:343, 378.

60. Willcox, "British Strategy in America, 1778," pp. 97–121; Gerald S. Brown, "The Anglo-French Naval Crisis, 1778: A Study of Conflict in the North Cabinet," *William and Mary Quarterly,* 3d ser., 13, no. 1 (January 1956): 3–25; David Syrett, "Home Waters or America? The Dilemma of British Naval Strategy in 1778," *The Mariner's Mirror* 77, no. 4 (November 1991): 365–77.

61. H. M. Scott, *British Foreign Policy in the Age of the American Revolution* (Oxford: Oxford University Press, 1990), pp. 19, 256, 261; North to George III, March 21, [1778], Fortescue, *The Correspondence of King George the Third,* 4:70; *Baroness von Riedesel and the American Revolution: Journal and Correspondence of a Tour of Duty 1776–1783,* ed. Marvin L. Brown, Jr. (Chapel Hill: University of North Carolina Press, 1965), pp. 9–10.

62. Norman Baker, *Government and Contractors: The British Treasury and War Supplies 1775–1783* (London: Athlone Press, 1971), pp. 10, 23, 28, 42, 142, 247; David Syrett, *Shipping and the American War 1775–83: A Study of British Transport Organisation* (London: Athlone Press, 1970), p. 131; R. Arthur

Bowler, *Logistics and the Failure of the British Army in America 1775–1783* (Princeton, N.J.: Princeton University Press, 1975), pp. 102–3; North to George III, Fortescue, *The Correspondence of King George the Third*, 4:216–217; Eden to North, August 25, 1779, Butterfield, *George III, Lord North and the People*, p. 61.

63. Ian R. Christie, *Myth and Reality in Late-Eighteenth-Century British Politics and Other Papers* (London: Macmillan, 1970), p. 11.

64. R. B. McDowell, *Ireland in the Age of Imperialism and Revolution 1760–1801* (Oxford: Clarendon Press, 1979), pp. 254, 256, 257; Maurice R. O'Connell, *Irish Politics and Social Conflict in the Age of the American Revolution* (Philadelphia: University of Pennsylvania Press, 1965), pp. 148, 189, 194; Butterfield, *George III, Lord North and the People*, p. 103.

65. Butterfield, *George III, Lord North and the People*, pp. 120–21; *The Annual Register*, in Murdoch, *Rebellion in America*, pp. 318, 440; Valentine, *Lord North*, 2:66.

66. Christie, *Myth and Reality*, p. 296; Christie, *The End of North's Ministry*, p. 259; John Norris, *Shelburne and Reform* (London: Macmillan, 1963), pp. 102, 107, 108.

67. Conway, *The British Isles and the War of American Independence*, pp. 51–55; Butterfield, *George III, Lord North and the People*, p. 42; Daniel A. Baugh, "Why Did Britain Lose Command of the Sea During the War for America?" in *The British Navy and the Use of Naval Power in the Eighteenth Century*, ed. Jeremy Black and Philip Woodfine (Leicester: Leicester University Press, 1988), pp. 159, 161; North to George III, March 25, 1778, Fortescue, *Correspondence of King George the Third*, 4:77.

68. Bickham, *Making Headlines*, pp. 7, 14, 22, 29, 49, 51, 185–206.

69. Wheatley, *The Historical and Posthumous Memoirs of Sir Nathaniel William Wraxall*, 1:369, 364; P. D. G. Thomas, *The House of Commons in the Eighteenth Century* (Oxford: Oxford University Press, 1971), pp. 41, 234.

70. Wheatley, *The Historical and Posthumous Memoirs of Sir Nathaniel William Wraxall*, 2:35; Walpole, *Memoirs of the Reign of King George III*, 4:143; Steuart, *The Last Journals of Horace Walpole*, 1:533, 537; Wheatley, *The Historical and Posthumous Memoirs of Sir Nathaniel William Wraxall*, 1:365. See also the description of North's speeches by James Anderson, a Scottish economist who was employed by William Pitt the Younger, in Smith, *The Early Career of Lord North*, p. 127.

71. Bickley, *The Diaries of Sylvester Douglas*, 1:237–238; Steuart, *The Last Journals of Horace Walpole*, 2:94; Bickley, *The Diaries of Sylvester Douglas*, 1:403; Don Cook, *The Long Fuse: How England Lost the American Colonies, 1760–1785* (New York: Atlantic Monthly Press, 1995), p. 148; Lucas, *Lord North*, 2:99.

72. Wheatley, *The Historical and Posthumous Memoirs of Sir Nathaniel William Wraxall*, 2:33, 92.

73. Thomas, *The House of Commons in the Eighteenth Century*, pp. 1–2, 114, 125, 127, 174, 244, 262.

74. Edward Gibbon, *Memoirs of My Life*, ed. Georges Bonnard (New York: Funk & Wagnalls, 1966), p. 156; Gibbon to J. B. Holroyd, February 25, 1775, Norton, *Letters of Edward Gibbon*, 3:29; Gibbon, *Memoirs of My Life*, p. 156; Gibbon quoted in Lucas, *Lord North*, 1:44.

75. Wheatley, *The Historical and Posthumous Memoirs of Sir Nathaniel William Wraxall*, 2:101, 1:367; Gibbon to Edward Eliot, June 20, 1779, Norton, *The Letters of Edward Gibbon*, 3:219; Steuart, *The Last Journals of Horace Walpole*, p. 486; see also pp. 70, 81, 82, 427–28. Wheatley, *The Historical and Posthumous Memoirs of Sir Nathaniel William Wraxall*, 2:33, 34; see also Hutchinson, *Diary and Letters of Thomas Hutchinson*, 1:361; Steuart, *The Last Journals of Horace Walpole*, 1:81. 418; Thomas, *The House of Commons in the Eighteenth Century*, p. 221; Reich, *British Friends of the American Revolution*, p. 129; Guttridge, *English Whiggism and the American Revolution*, pp. 236–37.

76. Wheatley, *The Historical and Posthumous Memoirs of Sir Nathaniel William Wraxall*, 1:238–239; Historical Manuscripts Commission, 17th Report, Lothian MSS., p. 351, cited in Guttridge, *English Whiggism and the American Revolution*, p. 109.

77. Steuart, *The Last Journals of Horace Walpole*, 1:513; Stout, *The Perfect Crisis*, p. 173; Steuart, *The Last Journals of Horace Walpole*, 2:387.

78. Wheatley, *The Historical and Posthumous Memoirs of Sir Nathaniel William Wraxall*, 1:361, 364.

79. Patrick K. O'Brien, "The Political Economy of British Taxation, 1660–1815," *Economic History Review*, 2d ser., 41, no. 1 (February 1988): 1–32; H. V. Bowen, *War and British Society, 1688–1815* (Cambridge: Cambridge University Press, 1988), pp. 17–33; Brewer, *The Sinews of Power*, pp. 89, 91, 114, 116; Wheatley, *The Historical and Posthumous Memoirs of Sir Nathaniel William Wraxall*, 1:369–370.

80. John Cannon, *Lord North: The Noble Lord in the Blue Ribbon* (London: Historical Association, 1970), p. 14.

81. Wheatley, *The Historical and Posthumous Memoirs of Sir Nathaniel William Wraxall*, 2:138–139.

82. Ibid., pp. 51–52, 74, 77.

83. Ibid., p. 160.

84. Christie, *The End of North's Ministry*, pp. 352–63; Olive Anderson, "The Role of the Army in Parliamentary Management During the American War of Independence," *Journal of the Society for Army Historical Research* 34, no. 140 (December 1956): 147. Wheatley, *The Historical and Posthumous Memoirs of Sir Nathaniel William Wraxall*, 2:194.

85. Ibid., p. 242.

86. Ibid., p. 244; Lucas, *Lord North*, 2:144, 145. Wheatley, *The Historical and Posthumous Memoirs of Sir Nathaniel William Wraxall*, 2:247.

87. Ibid. II, p. 269.

88. Bickley, *The Diaries of Sylvester Douglas* 1:180 (February 24, 1801); Bodleian Library, North Papers, d19, f. 19, quoted in Valentine, *Lord North*, 2:347; *The Adams Papers: Adams Family Correspondence*, ed. L. H. Butterfield, Richard Ryerson, and Margaret A. Hogan, 10 vols. (Cambridge, Mass.: Harvard University Press, 1963–), 6:212–213, 242. I am grateful to Edith Gelles and Julie Flavell for these references.

89. "Letter of Lady Charlotte Lindsay on Lord North," in Brougham, *Historical Sketches of Statesmen Who Flourished in the Time of George III*, 1:391; *Memoirs of Richard Cumberland: London 1806*, ed. Henry Flanders (1856; repr. New York: Richard Bloom, 1969), p. 437; "Letter of Lady Charlotte Lindsay on Lord North," in Brougham, *Historical Sketches of Statesmen who Flourished in the Time of George III*, 1:395.

90. Lucas, *Lord North*, 2:296–297; "Letter of Lady Charlotte Lindsay on Lord North," in Brougham, *Historical Sketches of Statesmen Who Flourished in the Time of George III*, 1:392, 395.

91. Brougham, *Historical Sketches of Statesmen Who Flourished in the Time of George III*, 1:396, 397.

92. Bickley, *The Diaries of Sylvester Douglas*, 1:61; Edward Legge to a friend, August 13, 1790, Public Record Office, 30/29/6, quoted in Smith, *The Early Career of Lord North*, p. 297.

93. Wheatley, *The Historical and Posthumous Memoirs of Sir Nathaniel William Wraxall*, 2:146, 3:71; Valentine, *Lord North*, 2:373; Cobbett and Hansard, *Parliamentary History*, 24:cols. 987–97, 1073, 1143, 1167, 1202, quoted in Valentine, *Lord North*, 2:421.

Chapter 3. The Peace Commissioners?

1. The voyage is described in William B. Willcox, *Portrait of a General: Sir Henry Clinton in the War of Independence* (New York: Knopf, 1964), pp. 36–39, 43–44; Lieutenant William Fielding to Basil Fielding, earl of Denbigh, Boston, June 1775, *The Lost War: Letters from British Officers During The American Revolution*, ed. Marion Balderston and David Syrett (New York: Horizon Press, 1975), p. 29.

2. Ira D. Gruber, "George III Chooses a Commander in Chief," in *Arms and Independence: The Military Character of the American Revolution*, ed. Ronald Hoffman and Peter J. Albert (Charlottesville: University of Virginia Press, 1984), pp. 166, 170, 171, 172, 174, 181, 182, 188. The king's speech to his Cabinet, June 21, 1779, in *The Manuscripts of Captain Howard Vincente Knox (From Volume VI of "Reports on Manuscripts in Various Collections"* (1909; repr. Boston: Gregg Press, 1972), pp. 260–61.

3. *The Last Journals of Horace Walpole During the Reign of George III*, ed. A. F. Steuart, 2 vols. (London: John Lane, 1910), 1:561; *The Annual Register*, in *Rebellion in America: A Contemporary British Viewpoint, 1769–1783*, ed. David H. Murdoch (Santa Barbara, Calif.: Clio Books, 1979), p. 223; Steuart, *The Last Journals of Horace Walpole*, 1:428; *Proceedings and Debates of the British Parliaments Respecting North America 1754–1783*, ed. R. C. Simmons and P. D. G. Thomas, 6 vols. (Millwood, N.Y.: Kraus International, 1982–86), 5:347, 352; Paul David Nelson, *General James Grant: Scottish Soldier and Royal Governor of East Florida* (Gainesville: University Press of Florida, 1993), p. 85; Neil Stout, *The Perfect Crisis: The Beginning of the Revolutionary War* (New York: New York University Press, 1976), p. 177; Piers Mackesy, *The War for America 1775–1783* (1964; repr. Lincoln: University of Nebraska Press, 1993), p. 34.

4. *The Correspondence of General Thomas Gage with the Secretaries of State, and with the War Office and the Treasury 1763–1775*, ed. Clarence Edwin Carter, 2 vols. (1933; repr. Hamden, Conn.: Archon Books, 1969), 1:686–687; "Proceedings in Relation to the American Colonies," in *The Manuscripts of Captain Howard Vincente Knox*, p. 257; Gage to Barrington, November 2, 1774, in Carter, *The Correspondence of General Thomas Gage*, 2:658–59; John Richard Alden, *General Gage in America: Being Principally a History of His Role in the American Revolution* (Baton Rouge: Louisiana State University Press, 1948), pp. 219–20; 229–30; John Shy, "Thomas Gage: Weak Link of Empire," in *George Washington's Generals and Opponents: Their Exploits and Leadership*, ed. George Athan Billias, 2 vols. in 1 (1964, 1969; repr. New York: Da Capo Press, 1994), 2:24–26.

5. *The American Rebellion: The Sir Henry Clinton's Narrative of His Campaigns, 1775–1782*, ed. William B. Willcox (New Haven, Conn.: Yale University Press, 1954), p. 18; Burgoyne to Lord Rochfort, n.d. (June 1775) in Edward Barrington De Fonblanque, *Political and Military Episodes in the Latter Half of the Eighteenth Century: Derived from the Life and Correspondence of the Right H. John Burgoyne, General, Statesman, Dramatist* (London: Macmillan, 1876), pp. 137, 142–43.

6. Willcox, *The American Rebellion*, p. 19; Mark Urban, *Fusiliers: The Saga of a British Redcoat Regiment in the American Revolution* (New York: Walker, 2007), p. 39; Roger Lamb, *An Original and Authentic Journal of Occurrences During the Late American War from its Commencement to the Year 1783* (Dublin: Wilkinson & Courtney, 1809), pp. 29, 32–33; Paul Lockhart, *The Whites of Their Eyes: Bunker Hill, the First American Army, and the Emergence of George Washington* (New York: Harper, 2011), pp. 215–16.

7. Lockhart, *The Whites of Their Eyes*, pp. 211, 259, 288, 290, 307, 313–14; Willcox, *The American Rebellion*, p. 19; Bellamy Partridge, *Sir Billy Howe* (New York: Longmans, Green, 1932), p. 3; Urban, *Fusiliers*, p. 43. Michael Pearson, *Those Damned Rebels: The American Revolution as Seen Through British Eyes* (New York: Da Capo Press, 1972), pp. 100, 105; Lamb, *Original and Authentic Journal of*

Occurrences During the Late American War, p. 29; *The Diary and Letters of His Excellency Thomas Hutchinson, Esq.*, ed. Peter Orlando Hutchinson, 2 vols. (New York: Burt Franklin, 1971), 2:194.

8. Gibbon to J. B. Holroyd, September 4, 1775, *The Letters of Edward Gibbon*, ed. J. E. Norton, 3 vols. (New York: Macmillan, 1956), 2:83; memorandum of John Burgoyne in Fonblanque, *Political and Military Episodes*, p. 129.

9. Burgoyne to General Hervey, June 14, 1775, Burgoyne to Lord Rochfort, n.d (June 1775) in Fonblanque, *Political and Military Episodes in the Latter Half of the Eighteenth Century*, pp. 140, 149.

10. Maya Jasanoff, *Edge of Empire: Lives, Culture, and Conquest in the East 1750–1850* (New York: Knopf, 2005), p. 29.

11. Howard H. Peckham, *The War for Independence*, rev. ed. (Chicago: University of Chicago Press, 1979), p. 15; Urban, *Fusiliers*, p. 157.

12. Steuart, *The Last Journals of Horace Walpole*, p. 433; *The Historical and Posthumous Memoirs of Sir Nathaniel William Wraxall 1772–1784*, ed. Henry B. Wheatley, 5 vols. (1836; repr. London: Bickers & Son, 1884), 2:42; *The Earl and Countess Howe by Gainsborough: A Bicentenary Exhibition*, ed. Anne French (London: English Heritage, 1988), p. 16; Charles Stedman, *The History of the Origin, Progress, and Termination of The American War*, 2 vols. (London: J. Murray, J. Debrett, and J. Kerby, 1794), 2:192.

13. Frances Vivian, "A Defence of Sir William Howe with a New Interpretation of his action in New Jersey, June 1777," *Journal of the Society for Army Historical Research* 44, no. 178 (1966): 70; Margaret Stead, "Contemporary Responses in Print to the American Campaigns of the Howe Brothers," in *Britain and America Go to War: The Impact of War and Warfare in Anglo-America, 1754–1815*, ed. Julie Flavell and Stephen Conway (Gainesville: University Press of Florida, 2004), p. 122.

14. Lieutenant William Fielding to Basil Fielding, earl of Denbigh, November 20, 1775, in Balderston and Syrett, *The Lost War*, p. 50.

15. Matthew H. Spring, *With Zeal and Bayonets Only: The British Army on Campaign in North America, 1775–1783* (Norman: University of Oklahoma Press, 2008), pp. 246, 231–32, 233; Stephen Brumwell, *Redcoats: The British Soldier and War in the Americas, 1755–1763* (Cambridge: Cambridge University Press, 2002), pp. 231, 232, 233.

16. Edward E. Curtis, *The Organization of the British Army in the American Revolution* (New Haven, Conn.: Yale University Press, 1926), p. 4; Mackesy, *The War for America*, p. 78; Stephen Conway, *The War of American Independence 1775–1783* (London: Edward Arnold, 1995), p. 246; Germain to [Lord Suffolk], [June 16 and 17, 1775], Historical Manuscripts Commission, *Report on the Manuscripts of Mrs. Stopford-Sackville of Drayton House, Northamptonshire*, 2 vols. (London: H.M. Stationery Office, 1910), 2:2; Washington to Richard Henry Lee, December 26, 1775, *The Papers of George Washington: Revolutionary War Series*, ed. W. W. Abbot, Philander D. Chase, Theodore Crackel, and Edward G. Lengel, 20 vols. (Charlottesville: University of Virginia Press, 1985–), 2:611.

17. John Creswell, *British Admirals of the Eighteenth Century: Tactics in Battle* (Hamden, Conn.: Archon Books, 1972), p. 148; David Syrett, *Admiral Lord Howe: A Biography* (Annapolis, Md.: Naval Institute Press, 2006), pp. 15–16.

18. Syrett, *Admiral Lord Howe*, pp. 19–20.

19. Ira D. Gruber, *The Howe Brothers and the American Revolution* (Chapel Hill: University of North Carolina Press, 1972), pp. 51–52; Partridge, *Sir Billy Howe*, p. 6; Benjamin Franklin to William Franklin, Journal of Negotiations in London, March 22, 1775, *The Papers of Benjamin Franklin*, ed. Leonard W. Labaree, William B. Willcox, Barbara Oberg, and Ellen R. Cohn, 39 vols. (New Haven,

Conn.: Yale University Press, 1959–), 21:572; Simmons and Thomas, *Proceedings and Debates of the British Parliaments Respecting North America,* 5:503, 507.

20. Steuart, *The Last Journals of Horace Walpole,* 2:137; F. D. Cartwright, *Major Cartwright,* 1:75, quoted in Jerome Reich, *British Friends of the American Revolution* (Armonk, N.Y.: M. E. Sharpe, 1998), p. 18; *The Annual Register,* in Murdoch, *Rebellion in America,* p. 321; Gruber, "George III Chooses a Commander in Chief," pp. 172, 182; Mary Kinnear, "Pro-Americans in the British House of Commons in the 1770s" (Ph.D. diss., University of Oregon, 1973), p. 133; Gruber, "George III Chooses a Commander in Chief," pp. 169, 173–74; Sir Lewis Namier and John Brooke, eds., *The House of Commons 1754–1790,* 3 vols. (London: H.M. Stationery Office, 1964), 3:149; Stephen Conway, "British Army Officers and the American War for Independence," *William and Mary Quarterly,* 3d ser., 41, no. 2 (April 1984): 265–76; Ira D. Gruber, "For King and Country: The Limits of Loyalty of British Officers in the War for American Independence," in *Limits of Loyalty,* ed. Edgar Denton (Waterloo, Ont.: Wilfred Laurier University, 1980), pp. 30–31, 33.

21. *The Annual Register,* in Murdoch, *Rebellion in America,* p. 321.

22. William Howe to Samuel Kirk, February 21, 1775, Partridge, *Sir Billy Howe,* p. 7; Simmons and Thomas, *Proceedings and Debates of the British Parliaments Respecting North America,* November 20, 1775, February 20, 1776, 6:282, 396.

23. Germain to General Irwin, July 26, 1775, September 13, 1775, Historical Manuscripts Commission, *Stopford-Sackville Manuscripts,* 2:136, 137; Ira D. Gruber, "Lord Howe and Lord George Germain: British Politics and the Winning of American Independence," *William and Mary Quarterly,* 3d ser., 22, no. 2 (April 1965): 231.

24. Troyer Steele Anderson, *The Command of the Howe Brothers During the American Revolution* (1936; repr. Cranbury, N.J.: The Scholar's Bookshelf, 2005), p. 58.

25. David Hackett Fischer, *Washington's Crossing* (Oxford: Oxford University Press, 2004), p. 31; David McCullough, *1776* (New York: Simon and Schuster, 2005), p. 134; *Rebels and Redcoats,* ed. George F. Scheer and Hugh F. Rankin (New York: Da Capo Press, 1957), p. 146; North Callahan, "Henry Knox: American Artillerist," in Billias, *George Washington's Generals and Opponents,* 1:243.

26. *The Journal of Ambrose Serle,* ed. Edward H. Tatum, Jr. (San Marino, Calif.: Huntington Library, 1940), 62.

27. David Syrett, *Shipping and the American War 1775–83: A Study of British Transport Organisation* (London: Athlone Press, 1970), p. 185.

28. John A. Tilley, *The British Navy and the American Revolution* (Columbia: University of South Carolina Press, 1987), pp. xvi, 122; Urban, *Fusiliers,* p. 81.

29. Urban, *Fusiliers,* p. 107; Spring, *With Zeal and Bayonets Only,* pp. 144, 149; Stephen Conway, "The British Army, 'Military Europe,' and the American War of Independence," *William and Mary Quarterly,* 3d ser., 67, no. 1 (January 2010): 77.

30. McCullough, *1776,* p. 118; Germain to [Lord Suffolk], [June 16 or 17, 1775], Historical Manuscripts Commission, *Stopford-Sackville Manuscripts,* 2:3.

31. Anderson, *The Command of the Howe Brothers,* p. 130.

32. Gruber, *The Howe Brothers and the American Revolution,* p. 115; Hugh, Lord Percy, to the duke of Northumberland, September 1, 1776, and to Lord George Germain, September 2, 1776, *Letters of Hugh, Earl Percy, from Boston and New York, 1774–1776,* ed. Hugh Percy and Charles K. Bolton (Boston: Charles E. Goodspeed, 1902), pp. 69, 71.

33. Bruce Bliven Jr., *Battle for Manhattan* (Baltimore: Penguin, 1964), pp. 27, 29, 35–37, 40; Ruma

Chopra, *Unnatural Rebellion: Loyalists in New York City During the Revolution* (Charlottesville: University of Virginia Press, 2011), p. 46; Tatum, *The American Journal of Ambrose Serle*, p. 104.

34. Howe to Germain, September 25, 1776, Historical Manuscripts Commission, *Stopford-Sackville Manuscripts*, 2:41.

35. Washington to Samuel Washington, December 18, 1776, Abbot et al., *The Papers of George Washington: Revolutionary War Series*, 7:369–71; Nicholas Tracy, *Navies, Deterrence, and American Independence: Britain and Seapower in the 1760s and 1770s* (Vancouver: University of British Columbia Press, 1988), p. 139.

36. Stead, "Contemporary Responses in Print to the Howe Brothers," in Flavell and Conway, *Britain and America Go to War*, p. 131–32. See also Francis Hopkinson's satirical verse against Howe in Bruce Ingham Granger, *Political Satire in the American Revolution 1763–1783* (Ithaca, N.Y.: Cornell University Press, 1960), p. 172.

37. Maldwyn A. Jones, "Sir William Howe: Conventional Strategist," in Billias, *George Washington's Generals and Opponents*. 2:66; Partridge, *Sir Billy Howe*, p. 102; Anderson, *The Command of the Howe Brothers*, pp. 15, 135, 141, 145; Gruber, *The Howe Brothers and the American Revolution*, p. 126; Gruber, "Lord Howe and Lord George Germain," p. 236; Johann von Ewald, *Diary of the American War: A Hessian Journal*, trans. and ed. Joseph Tustin (New Haven, Conn.: Yale University Press, 1979), pp. 18, 19, 25.

38. Stedman, "A Reply to the Observations of Lt. Gen. Sir William Howe," pp. 146–48, in Partridge, *Sir Billy Howe*, p. 49; Howe to Germain, July 7, 1776, CO 5/93, PRO; Stedman, *The History of the Origin, Progress, and Termination of the American War*, 1:199.

39. "The Justifying Memorial of the King of Great Britain, in Answer to the Exposition, &c of the Court of France," *The Annual Register*, in Murdoch, *Rebellion in America*, p. 741; "The Humble Address of the House of Commons to the King, November 20, 1778," ibid., pp. 629, 697; *Morning Chronicle*, November 10, 1775, and *London Chronicle*, November 11, 1775, in *Our American Brethren: A History of Letters in the British Press During the American Revolution, 1775–1781*, ed. Alfred Grant (Jefferson, N.C.: McFarland, 1995), p. 170. See also ibid., pp. 86, 164, 171, 172, 174.

40. Gruber, *The Howe Brothers and the American Revolution*, pp. 90, 94–95; McCullough, *1776*, pp. 144–45, 147.

41. Anderson, *The Command of the Howe Brothers*, pp. 159–60; Gruber, *The Howe Brothers and the American Revolution*, p. 116–19; Tatum, *Journal of Ambrose Serle*, p. 101.

42. Reich, *British Friends of America*, p. 141; *The Annual Register*, in Murdoch, *Rebellion in America*, pp. 441–42; William Cobbett and Thomas Hansard, eds., *The Parliamentary History of England from the Earliest Period to 1803*, 36 vols. (London: Hansard, 1806–22), 17:cols. 1431–33, 1436–39; Gruber, *The Howe Brothers and the American Revolution*, pp. 124–26; *The Annual Register*, in Murdoch, *Rebellion in America*, p. 342.

43. Howe to Germain, April 26. 1776, Historical Manuscripts Commission, *Stopford-Sackville Manuscripts*, 2:30.

44. *The Narrative of Lieut. Gen. Sir William Howe in a Committee of the House of Commons, on the 29th of April, 1779, Relative to His Conduct During His Late Command of the King's Troops in North America: To Which Are Added, Some Observations Upon A Pamphlet, Entitled, Letters to A Nobleman* (London: Baldwin, 1780), p. 5; Christopher Duffy, *The Military Experience in the Age of Reason* (London: Routledge & Kegan Paul, 1987), p. 11; *The Narrative of Lieut. Gen. Sir William Howe*, pp. 5–7.

45. Bliven, *Battle for Manhattan*, pp. 71–109; Partridge, *Sir Billy Howe*, pp. 79–80; McCullough,

1776, pp. 218–19; Mark Mayo Boatner III, *Encyclopedia of the American Revolution* (New York: David McKay, 1966), pp. 488–91.

46. *Examination of Lieutenant General The Earl Cornwallis Before A Committee of the House of Commons, Upon Sir William Howe's Papers* (London: J. Robson, 1779), p. 14; Partridge, *Sir Billy Howe*, p. 118; McCullough, *1776*, p. 269.

47. Fischer, *Washington's Crossing*, pp. 196–97, 201, 205; Rodney Atwood, *The Hessians: Mercenaries from Hessen-Kassel in the American Revolution* (Cambridge: Cambridge University Press, 1980), pp. 87, 88; John S. Pancake, *1777: The Year of the Hangman* (Tuscaloosa: University of Alabama Press, 1977), p. 53; Stedman, *The History of the Origin, Progress, and Termination of the American War*, 1:234.

48. W. J. Wood, *Battles of the Revolutionary War 1775–1781* (New York: Da Capo Press, 1990), pp. 77, 88, 89.

49. *The Narrative of Lieut. Gen. Sir William Howe*, pp. 7–9; John Shy, *A People Numerous and Armed: Reflections on the Military Struggle for American Independence*, (Ann Arbor: University of Michigan Press, 2000), p. 225, gives the number of oaths as 3,000; Gruber, "Lord Howe and Lord George Germain," p. 237, gives it as 5,000; Tatum, *The Journal of Ambrose Serle*, p. 157; Fischer, *Washington's Crossing*, p. 360; Nelson, *General James Grant*, p. 119; *The Narrative of Lieut. Gen. Sir William Howe*, p. 6; Atwood, *The Hessians*, p. 87.

50. Partridge, *Sir Billy Howe*, p. 81; *The Narrative of Lieut. Gen. Sir William Howe*, p. 6; Sir James Murray to Elizabeth Murray, February 25, 1777, in *Letters from America 1773–1780: Being the Letters of a Scots Officer, Sir James Murray, to His Home During the War of American Independence*, ed. Eric Robson (Manchester: Manchester University Press, 1951), pp. 37–42; Fischer, *Washington's Crossing*, pp. 359, 366.

51. Mackesy, *The War for America*, p. 102; Edward E. Curtis, *The Organization of the British Army in the American Revolution* (New Haven, Conn.: Yale University Press, 1926), pp. 101–2, 143; Gruber, *The Howe Brothers*, p. 135; R. Arthur Bowler, *Logistics and the Failure of the British Army in America 1775–1783* (Princeton, N.J.: Princeton University Press, 1975), pp. 64–65, 71.

52. Syrett, *Admiral Lord Howe*, p. 63; *Reflections on a Pamphlet intitled "a Letter to the Right Honble Lord Vict. H——E" By Admiral Lord Howe*, ed. Gerald Saxon Brown (Ann Arbor: University of Michigan Press, 1959), p. 25; Gruber, *The Howe Brothers and the American Revolution*, pp. 102–3, 136, 139, 140–41, 157.

53. Anderson, *The Command of the Howe Brothers During the American Revolution*, p. 46; Vincent Morley, *Irish Opinion and the American Revolution, 1760–1783* (Cambridge: Cambridge University Press, 2002), pp. 24, 87; R. B. McDowell, *Ireland in the Age of Imperialism and Revolution 1760–1801* (Oxford: Clarendon Press, 1979), pp. 22, 59, 128, 263; Stephen Conway, "'Like the Irish'? Volunteer Corps and Volunteering in Britain during the American War," in Flavell and Conway, *Britain and America Go to War*, p. 160.

54. Richard B. Sheridan, "The Jamaican Slave Insurrection Scare of 1776 and the American Revolution," *Journal of Negro History* 61, no. 3 (1976): 290–308; Journal of the Assembly of Jamaica, December 17, 1776, CO. 140/56, PRO; Stedman, *The History of the Origin, Progress, and Termination of the American War*, 1:259.

55. Partridge, *Sir Billy Howe*, p. 6; Percy to General Harvey (?), July 28, 1775, Percy and Bolton, *Letters of Hugh, Earl Percy*, p. 58; *The Annual Register*, Murdoch, *Rebellion in America*, pp. 342, 350; Mackesy, *The War for America*, p. 38.

56. Howe to Germain, November 30, 1776, CO 5/93, PRO; *The Narrative of Lieut. Gen. Sir William Howe*, pp. 9–10.

57. *Beyond Philadelphia: The American Revolution in the Pennsylvania Hinterland*, ed. John B. Frantz

and William Pencak (University Park, Pa.: Pennsylvania State University Press, 1998), pp. xvii–xix, 197; Thomas Paine, *The American Crisis,* introd. Andrew S. Trees (New York: Barnes & Noble, 2010), p. 81; Howe to Germain, December 20, 1776, CO 5/94, PRO; *The Narrative of Lieut. Gen. Sir William Howe,* p. 19.

58. Fischer, *Washington's Crossing,* p. 366; *The Narrative of Lieut. Gen. Sir William Howe,* p. 14; Gruber, "Lord Howe and Lord George Germain," pp. 238–41; *The Narrative of Lieut. Gen. Sir William Howe,* p. 14; Stead, "Contemporary Responses in Print to the Howe Brothers," in Flavell and Conway, *Britain and America Go to War,* p. 124.

59. *The Narrative of Lieut. Gen. Sir William Howe,* pp. 12, 13–14.

60. Howe to Germain, April 2, 1777, July 7, 1777, CO 5/94, PRO.

61. Vivian, "A Defence of Sir William Howe," pp. 77–83.

62. Gerald S. Brown, *The American Secretary: The Colonial Policy of Lord George Germain, 1775–1778* (Ann Arbor: University of Michigan Press, 1963), p. 125. The number of Howe's troops is variously given, with figures ranging from 13,000 to 16,000: Stephen R. Taaffe, *The Philadelphia Campaign, 1777–1778* (Lawrence: University of Kansas Press, 2003), p. 50; Atwood, *The Hessians,* p. 117; John W. Jackson, *With the British Army in Philadelphia 1777–1778* (San Rafael, Calif.: Presidio Press, 1979), p. 280; Paul E. Kopperman, "The British High Command and Soldiers' Wives in America, 1755–1783," *Journal of the Society for Army Historical Research* 60, no. 241 (Spring 1982): 14–35.

63. Stead, "Contemporary Responses in Print to the Howe Brothers," in Flavell and Conway, *Britain and America Go to War,* p. 126; Ira Gruber, "British Strategy: The Theory and Practice of Eighteenth Century Warfare," in *Reconsiderations on the Revolutionary War: Selected Essays,* ed. Don Higginbotham (Westport, Conn.: Greenwood Press, 1978), p. 26; W. H. Moomaw, "The Denouement of General Howe's Campaign of 1777," *English Historical Review* 79, no. 312 (July 1964): 500, 502, 503–04, 506, 508, 511; Howe to Germain, August 30, 1777, CO 5/94, PRO.

64. Ewald, *Diary of the American War,* pp. 80, 87; Peckham, *The War for Independence,* p. 70; W. J. Wood, *Battles of the Revolutionary War 1775–1781,* 2d ed. (New York: Da Capo Press, 2003), pp. 92–114; Callahan, "Henry Knox: American Artillerist," in Billias, *George Washington's Generals and Opponents,* 1:250.

65. Ewald, *Diary of the American War,* pp. 91–92; Jackson, *With the British Army in Philadelphia,* pp. 16–17, 25.

66. *The Narrative of Lieut. Gen. Sir William Howe,* p. 27; Partridge, *Sir Billy Howe,* p. 186; Ewald, *Diary of the American War,* pp. 92, 96; Walter Harold Wilkin, *Some British Soldiers in America* (1914; repr. Milton Keynes: General Books, 2010), p. 12; Partridge, *Sir Billy Howe,* p. 189.

67. Jackson, *With the British Army in Philadelphia,* pp. x, 10, 53, 81, 103, 201–2, 212, 216–17; Granger, *Political Satire in the American Revolution,* p. 262; *John Peebles' American War: The Diary of a Scottish Grenadier, 1776–1782,* ed. Ira Gruber (Mechanicsburg, Pa.: Stackpole Books, 1998), pp. 161, 169, 177; Ewald, *Diary of the American War,* p. 120.

68. Jackson, *With the British Army in Philadelphia,* pp. 53, 120, 177, 188.

69. Howe to Germain, November 30, 1777, Historical Manuscripts Commission, *Stopford-Sackville Manuscripts,* 2:81; Troy Bickham, *Making Headlines: The American Revolution as Seen through the British Press* (DeKalb: Northern Illinois University Press, 2009), p. 106.

70. Germain to Carleton, March 26, 1777, Historical Manuscripts Commission, *Stopford-Sackville Manuscripts,* 2:63; Germain to Howe, May 18, 1777, CO 5/94, PRO; Historical Manuscripts Commission, *Stopford-Sackville Manuscripts,* 2:66–67; Germain to Howe, September 3, 1777, CO 5/94, PRO; *The Manuscripts of Captain Howard Vincente Knox,* pp. 276–77.

71. Brown, *The American Secretary,* p. 125; Gruber, *The Howe Brothers and the American Revolution,* pp. 207, 230.

72. Gruber, *The Howe Brothers and the American Revolution,* p. 233; Washington to Israel Putnam, July 21, 1777, Abbot et al., *The Papers of George Washington: Revolutionary War Series,* 9:346; Christopher Hibbert, *Redcoats and Rebels: The American Revolution through British Eyes* (New York: Norton, 1990), p. 142; Washington to Horatio Gates, July 30, 1777, Abbot et al., *The Papers of George Washington: Revolutionary War Series,* 10:459.

73. *The Narrative of Lieut. Gen. Sir William Howe,* p. 20.

74. Howe to Germain, July 15, 1777, July 16, 1777, CO 5/94, PRO; Brown, *The American Secretary,* p. 109; Gruber, *The Howe Brothers and the American Revolution,* p. 200; Germain to Knox, September 29, 1777, *The Manuscripts of Captain Howard Vincente Knox,* p. 139; John F. Luzader, *Saratoga: A Military History of the Decisive Campaign of the American Revolution* (New York: Savas Beatie, 2008), p. 26; George H. Guttridge, "Lord George Germain in Office, 1775–1782," *American Historical Review* 33, no. 1 (October 1927): 29.

75. Gordon S. Wood, "Rhetoric and Reality in The American Revolution," *William and Mary Quarterly,* 3d ser., 23, no. 1 (January 1966): 3–22; Jay Fliegelman, *Declaring Independence: Jefferson, Natural Language, and the Culture of Performance* (Stanford, Calif.: Stanford University Press, 1993).

76. Philip Davidson, *Propaganda and the American Revolution 1763–1783* (Chapel Hill: University of North Carolina Press, 1941), pp. 17, 292–329. Michal Jan Rozbicki, *Culture and Liberty in the Age of the American Revolution* (Charlottesville: University of Virginia Press, 2011) makes a strong case for a very restricted view of liberty as a spectrum of rights and privileges that varied according to class. He argues that the revolutionary leadership was committed to the continuance of inequality. Gordon S. Wood, *The Radicalism of the American Revolution* (New York: Knopf, 1992) discusses the social and political changes both during the Revolution and in the immediate aftermath inspired by the revolutionary creed.

77. The process is described by Shy, *A People Numerous and Armed,* pp. 175–77, 236, 237, 242.

78. Eliga H. Gould, *The Persistence of Empire: British Political Culture in the Age of the American Revolution* (Chapel Hill: University of North Carolina Press, 2000), p. 163; Stephen Conway, "From Fellow-Nationals to Foreigners: British Perceptions of the Americans, Circa 1739–1783," *William and Mary Quarterly,* 3d ser., 61, no. 1 (January 2002): 65–101; Stephen Conway, "'The Great Mischief Complain'd of': Reflections on the Misconduct of British Soldiers in the Revolutionary War," ibid., 47, no. 3 (July 1990): 370–91; Captain John Bowater to Basil Feilding, earl of Denbigh, April 4, 1777, in Balderston and Syrett, *The Lost War,* p. 121; Major John Bowater to Basil Fielding, November 17, 1777, ibid., p. 147.

79. Colonel Stuart to Lord Bute, September 16, 1778, *A Prime Minister and His Son: From the Correspondence of the Third Earl of Bute and of Lt. Gen. The Hon. Sir Charles Stuart, K.B,* ed. The Hon. Mrs. E. Stuart Wortley (London: John Murray, 1925), p. 132; Joseph E. Tiedemann, "Patriots by Default: Queens County, New York, and the British Army, 1776–1783," *William and Mary Quarterly,* 3d ser., 43, no. 1 (January 1986): 38; Mathew C. Ward, "Crossing the Line? The Application of European 'Rules of War' in North America in the Eighteenth Century" (unpublished paper, Edinburgh University), pp. 6, 7; Spring, *With Zeal and Bayonets Only,* p. 13.

80. Jackson, *With the British Army in Philadelphia,* pp. 224–25; "A Briton" in the *Public Advertiser,* January 11, 1776, in Grant, *Our American Brethren,* p. 64.

81. Rawdon to Francis, earl of Huntingdon, August 5, 1776, Historical Manuscripts Commission, *Report on the Manuscripts of the late Reginald Rawdon Hastings Esq.* ed. Francis Bickley, 4 vols. (London:

H.M. Stationery Office, 1928–47), 3:179; Gruber, *The Howe Brothers and the American Revolution,* p. 145. For examples of rapes, see also Gruber, *John Peebles' American War,* p. 74.

82. Urban, *Fusiliers,* p. 108; Charles Stuart to Lord Bute, February 4, 1777, in Wortley, *A Prime Minister and his Son,* p. 99; *Stephen Kemble's Journal,* introd. George Athan Billias (Boston: Gregg Press, 1972), pp. 96, 98; Jackson, *With the British Army in Philadelphia,* p. 97–98, 190, 268.

83. Tiedemann, "Patriots by Default," pp. 35–63; Captain John Bowater to Basil Feilding, earl of Denbigh, November 25, 1776, Balderston and Syrett, *The Lost War,* p. 108.

84. Partridge, *Sir Billy Howe,* pp. 173–74; Howe to Germain, August 30, 1777, Historical Manuscripts Commission, *Stopford-Sackville Manuscripts,* 2:75.

85. Taaffe, *The Philadelphia Campaign,* p. 89; *The Narrative of Lieut. Gen. Sir William Howe,* pp. 32–33.

86. Elizabeth A. Fenn, *Pox Americana: The Great Smallpox Epidemic of 1775–82* (New York: Hill and Wang, 2001), p. 99.

87. Howe to Germain, October 22, 1777, Historical Manuscripts Commission, *Stopford-Sackville Manuscripts,* 2:80.

88. Lady Howe to Lord North, 18 February 1778, *The Private Papers of John, Earl of Sandwich, First Lord of the Admiralty 1771–1782,* ed. G. R. Barnes and J. H. Owen, 4 vols. (London: Navy Records Society, 1932–38), 2:292; Germain to Lord Howe, August 4, 1777, Historical Manuscripts Commission, *Stopford-Sackville Manuscripts,* 2:73; Tatum, *The American Journal of Ambrose Serle,* pp. 311–12.

89. W. Hale to Admiral Hale, July 21, 1778, in Wilkin, *Some British Soldiers in America,* p. 121.

90. Gruber, *The Howe Brothers and the American Revolution,* p. 274; Stead, "Contemporary Responses in Print to the Howe Brothers," p. 131; Bickham, *Making Headlines,* p. 93; Alan Valentine, *Lord North,* 2 vols. (Norman: University of Oklahoma Press, 1967), 2:44.

91. Worthington C. Ford, "Parliament and the Howes," *Proceedings of the Massachusetts Historical Society,* 3d ser., 44 (October 1910): 120–43.

92. Syrett, *Admiral Lord Howe,* pp. 127–28.

93. *Gentleman's Magazine,* September 1799, p. 807; Ann French, "The Earl and Countess Howe: A Biography," in French, *The Earl and Countess Howe by Gainsborough,* p. 17.

Chapter 4. "The Old Gamester"

1. Alan Valentine, *Lord George Germain* (Oxford: Oxford University Press, 1962), p. 260; *The Diary and Letters of His Excellency Thomas Hutchinson, Esq.,* ed. Peter Orlando Hutchinson, 2 vols. (New York: Burt Franklin, 1971), 1:168–69; *Morning Chronicle,* December 1, 1777, *Our American Brethren: A History of Letters in the British Press During the American Revolution, 1775–1781,* ed. Alfred Grant (Jefferson, N.C.: McFarland, 1995) pp. 110–11; Richard Sampson, *Escape in America: The British Convention Prisoners 1777–1783* (Chippenham: Picton Publishing, 1995), p. 52; *The Last Journals of Horace Walpole During the Reign of George III,* ed. A. F. Steuart, 2 vols. (London: John Lane, 1910), pp. 80–81; Account in the *Edinburgh Advertiser* quoted by Troy Bickham, *Making Headlines.: The American Revolution as Seen through the British Press* (DeKalb: Northern Illinois University Press, 2009), p. 105.

2. Anthony Morris Storer to George Selwyn, December 11, 1777, quoted in Valentine, *Lord George Germain,* p. 265; Bickham, *Making Headlines,* pp. 36–37.

3. George Athan Billias, "John Burgoyne: Ambitious General," in *George Washington's Generals and Opponents: Their Exploits and Leadership,* ed. Billias, 2 vols. in 1 (1964, 1969; repr. New York: Da

Capo Press, 1994), 2:142–143; Valentine, *Lord George Germain*, p. 299; Steuart, *The Last Journals of Horace Walpole*, 2:433; *The Historical and Posthumous Memoirs of Sir Nathaniel William Wraxall 1772–1784*, ed. Henry B. Wheatley, 5 vols. (1836; repr. London: Bickers & Son, 1884), 2:45–46.

4. David Mannings, *Sir Joshua Reynolds: A Complete Catalogue of his Paintings*, 2 vols. (New Haven, Conn.: Yale University Press, 2000), 2:113; Bruce Ingham Granger, *Political Satire in the American Revolution 1763–1783* (Ithaca, N.Y.: Cornell University Press, 1960), pp. 175–79.

5. Joyce Godber, *History of Bedfordshire* (Bedford: Bedfordshire County Council, 1969), pp. 175, 200, 247–48; Richard J. Hargrove Jr., *Gentleman John Burgoyne* (Newark: University of Delaware Press, 1983), p. 17. See also ibid., p. 18 for the perpetuation of the rumor.

6. Edward Barrington De Fonblanque, *Political and Military Episodes in the Latter Half of the Eighteenth Century: Derived from The Life and Correspondence of the Right Hon. John Burgoyne, General, Statesman, Dramatist* (London: Macmillan, 1876), p. 124.

7. Gruber, "British Strategy: The Theory and Practice of Eighteen-Century Warfare," in *Reconsiderations on the Revolutionary War: Selected Essays,* ed. Don Higginbotham (Westport, Conn.: Greenwood Press, 1978), p. 15; James Lunt, *John Burgoyne of Saratoga* (London: Macdonald and Jane's, 1976), p. 17.

8. Lunt, *John Burgoyne of Saratoga*, pp. 30–31.

9. Ibid., p. 34; Fonblanque, *Political and Military Episodes in the Latter Half of the Eighteenth Century*, pp. 15–21.

10. Max M. Mintz, *The Generals of Saratoga: John Burgoyne and Horatio Gates* (New Haven, Conn.: Yale University Press, 1990), p. 19; Mannings, *Sir Joshua Reynolds*, 1:113.

11. *Observations and Reflections Upon the Present Military State of Prussia, Austria, and France,* in Fonblanque, *Political and Military Episodes in the Latter Half of the Eighteenth Century*, pp. 62–82.

12. Ibid.

13. Burgoyne to Major Warde, November 23, 1757, Burgoyne to Charles Townshend, August 10, 1762, Bute to Burgoyne, November 2, 1762, ibid., pp. 11, 46, 4, 49.

14. *The House of Commons 1754–1790,* ed. Sir Lewis Namier and John Brooke, 3 vols. (London: H.M. Stationery Office, 1964), 3:453, 1:14.

15. *The Letters of Junius,* ed. John Cannon (Oxford: Clarendon Press, 1978), pp. 154–58, 180; Steuart, *Last Journals of Horace Walpole*, 1:202.

16. Hargrove, *Gentleman John Burgoyne*, p. 43.

17. Lunt, *John Burgoyne of Saratoga*, pp. 16, 61; Hargrove, *Gentleman John Burgoyne*, pp. 44, 49.

18. Paul V. Williams, ed., *The Long and Short of General John Burgoyne's Maid of Oaks: The Story of an Eighteenth Century Play and Its Players* (Carshalton: Friends of Honeywood, 2007), pp. 23, 24, 27–31.

19. Ibid., pp. 82–84, 94, 109.

20. George III to North, February 14, 1771, March 12, 1772, *The Correspondence of King George the Third from 1760 to December 1783,* ed. Sir John Fortescue, 6 vols. (London: Macmillan, 1927–28), 2:218, 328–29.

21. H. V. Bowen, *Revenue and Reform: The Indian Problem in British Politics 1757–1773* (Cambridge: Cambridge University Press, 1991), p. 117.

22. Ibid., pp. 58–62.

23. Ibid., pp. 169, 172.

24. *Proceedings and Debates of the British Parliaments Respecting North America 1754–1783,* ed. R. C. Simmons and P. D. G. Thomas, 6 vols. (Millwood, N.Y.: Kraus International, 1982–86), 4:193, 232, 238; Steuart, *Last Journals of Horace Walpole*, 1:80, 304.

25. Memorandum by Burgoyne, in Fonblanque, *Political and Military Episodes in the Latter Half of the Eighteenth Century*, pp. 120–21.

26. Ibid., pp. 34–36.

27. Ibid., p. 122.

28. Ibid., pp. 122–33.

29. Ibid., pp. 129, 128, 132.

30. John Burgoyne, *The Speech of a General Officer in the House of Commons, February 20th, 1775* (n.p., n.d.), pp. 3, 4; February 27, 1775, Simmons and Thomas, *Proceedings and Debates of the British Parliaments Respecting North America 1754–1783*, 5:475, 476.

31. Burgoyne, *The Speech of a General Officer in the House of Commons*, pp. 4, 5, 6, 7, 8; February 27, 1775, Simmons and Thomas, *Proceedings and Debates of the British Parliaments Respecting North America 1754–1783*, 5:476, 477; Steuart, *The Last Journals of Horace Walpole*, 1:439; Benjamin Woods Labaree, "The Idea of American Independence: The British View, 1774–1776," *Proceedings of the Massachusetts Historical Society*, 3d. ser., 82 (1970): 6.

32. Hutchinson, *Diary and Letters of Thomas Hutchinson*, March 30, 1775, I, p. 420; Burgoyne to George III, April 18, 1775, Fonblanque, *Political and Military Episodes in the Latter Half of the Eighteenth Century*, pp. 133–34.

33. Hargrove, *Gentleman John Burgoyne*, p. 73; Burgoyne to North, June 14, 1775, Burgoyne to Rochford [1775], Fonblanque, *Political and Military Episodes in the Latter Half of the Eighteenth Century*, pp. 136–37, pp. 145, 146.

34. Burgoyne to Palmerston, [1775], Burgoyne to North, June 14, 1775, ibid., pp. 154, 137.

35. Billias, "John Burgoyne," p. 160; Fonblanque, *Political and Military Episodes in the Latter Half of the Eighteenth Century*, pp. 146, 152; Billias, "John Burgoyne," pp. 157–58.

36. John W. Shy, "Charles Lee: The Soldier as Radical," in Billias, *George Washington's Generals and Opponents*, 1:22–54; Lee to Burgoyne, June 7, 1775, Burgoyne to Lee, July 8, 1775, Fonblanque, *Political and Military Episodes in the Latter Half of the Eighteenth Century*, pp. 161–67, 168–72.

37. Lieutenant William Feilding to Basil Feilding, earl of Denbigh, January 19, 1776, in *The Lost War: Letters of British Officers During The American Revolution*, ed. Marion Balderston and David Syrett (New York: Horizon Press, 1975), pp. 58–59; Mark Urban, *Fusiliers; The Saga of a British Redcoat Regiment in the American Revolution* (New York: Walker, 2007), p. 60; Fonblanque, *Political and Military Episodes in the Latter Half of the Eighteenth Century*, p. 188; Mintz, *The Generals of Saratoga*, p. 67; Sylvia Frey, *The British Soldier in America* (Austin: University of Texas Press, 1981), p. 67; Hargrove, *Gentleman John Burgoyne*, p. 82.

38. Burgoyne to North, June 14, 1775, in Fonblanque, *Political and Military Episodes in the Latter Half of the Eighteenth Century*, pp. 138–39.

39. Burgoyne to Rochford [1775], Burgoyne to North [1775], Burgoyne to Germain, August 20, 1775, Burgoyne to Thurlow [1775], ibid., pp. 147, 148, 149; pp. 180, 182; pp. 194, 197; p. 200.

40. Burgoyne to Rochford [1775], ibid., pp. 151, 152–53.

41. Burgoyne to Rochford [1775], Burgoyne to North [1775], ibid., pp. 153, 178; Hoffman Nickerson, *The Turning Point of the Revolution, or Burgoyne in America* (1928; repr. Cranbury, N.J.: The Scholar's Bookshelf, 2005), pp. 39–40; Valentine, *Lord George Germain*, p. 274; Paul David Nelson, *General Sir Guy Carleton, Lord Dorchester. Soldier-Statesman of Early British Canada* (Teaneck, New Jersey: Fairleigh Dickinson University Press, 2000), pp. 64–65.

42. "Reflections upon the War in America," in Fonblanque, *Political and Military Episodes in the Latter Half of the Eighteenth Century*, pp. 208–9.

43. Ibid.

44. Jefferson to Virginia delegates in Congress, May 10, 1781, *The Papers of Thomas Jefferson,* ed. Julian P. Boyd, Charles T. Cullen, John Catanzariti, Barbara B. Oberg, et al., 34 vols. (Princeton, N.J.: Princeton University Press, 1950–), 5:632–33; Michael Kranish, *Flight from Monticello: Thomas Jefferson at War* (Oxford: Oxford University Press, 2010), p. 249; Robert P. Davis, *Where a Man Can Go: Major General William Phillips, British Royal Artillery, 1731–1781* (Westport, Conn.: Greenwood Press, 1999), p. 48.

45. Elizabeth A. Fenn, *Pox Americana: The Great Smallpox Epidemic of 1775–82* (New York: Hill and Wang, 2001), pp. 64–67.

46. Roger Lamb, *An Original and Authentic Journal of Occurrences During the Late American War from Its Commencement to the Year 1783* (Dublin: Wilkinson & Courtney, 1809), p. 82; Paul H. Smith, "Sir Guy Carleton," in Billias, *George Washington's Generals and Opponents,* 2:108; Gustave Lanctot, *Canada and the American Revolution 1774–1783* (Cambridge, Mass.: Harvard University Press, 1967), p. 26; Reginald Coupland, *The Quebec Act* (Oxford: Clarendon Press, 1925).

47. Burgoyne to Germain, June 22, 1776, Historical Manuscripts Commission, *Report on the Manuscripts of Mrs. Stopford-Sackville of Drayton House, Northamptonshire,* 2 vols. (London: H.M. Stationery Office, 1910), 2:37.

48. Nelson, *General Sir Guy Carleton,* pp. 64, 86–87, 95.

49. John H. G. Pell, "Philip Schuyler: The General as Aristocrat," in Billias, *George Washington's Generals and Opponents,* 1:64.

50. Burgoyne to Clinton, July 7, 1776, and November 7, 1776, in Douglas R. Cubbison, *Burgoyne and the Saratoga Campaign: His Papers* (Norman: University of Oklahoma Press, 2012), pp. 150–53, 160.

51. George III to North, March 3, 1778, Fortescue, *The Correspondence of King George the Third,* 4:45; Smith, "Sir Guy Carleton," pp. 127–28; Alfred L. Burt, "The Quarrel Between Germain and Carleton: An Inverted Story," *Canadian Historical Review* 11 (September 1930): 202–22.

52. John Burgoyne, *A State of the Expedition from Canada as Laid Before the House of Commons by Lieutenant-General John Burgoyne,* 2d ed. (London: J. Almon, 1780), p. 2.

53. George III to North, December 13, 1776, Fortescue, *The Correspondence of King George the Third,* 3:406–7; Nickerson, *The Turning Point of the Revolution,* p. 81.

54. Nickerson, *The Turning Point of the Revolution,* pp. 83–89 reproduces the "Thoughts." Piers Mackesy, *The War for America 1775–1783* (1964; repr. Lincoln: University of Nebraska Press, 1993), pp. 58–59; John F. Luzader, *Saratoga: A Military History of the Decisive Campaign of the American Revolution* (New York: Savas Beatie, 2008), p. 18; Jane Clark, "Responsibility for the Failure of the Burgoyne Campaign," *American Historical Review* 35, no. 3 (April 1930): 544; Hargrove, *Gentleman John Burgoyne,* p. 95.

55. "Extracts from General Burgoyne's Plan of the Campaign from the Side of Canada with the Remarks Thereon of George the Third," in Fonblanque, *Political and Military Episodes in the Latter Half of the Eighteenth Century,* pp. 483–86; Burgoyne, "Thoughts for Conducting the War, from the Side of Canada," in Cubbison, *Burgoyne and the Saratoga Campaign,* pp. 178–87, 36, 75.

56. Mackesy, *The War for America,* pp. 115–16, 142; Fonblanque, *Political and Military Episodes in the Latter Half of the Eighteenth Century,* pp. 486–87; Nickerson, *The Turning Point of the Revolution,* p. 90; Burgoyne to Fraser, May 6, 1777, quoted in Eric Robson, *The American Revolution in Its Political and Military Aspects 1763–1783* (1955; repr. New York, Norton, 1966), p. 139; Clark, "Responsibility for the Failure of the Burgoyne Campaign," pp. 542–43,

57. Burgoyne, *A State of the Expedition,* pp. 9, 22; Hargrove, *General John Burgoyne,* p. 113; Howe to Carleton, April 5, 1777, Historical Manuscripts Commission, *Stopford-Sackville Manuscripts,* 2:65–66.

58. Burgoyne to General Harvey, May 19, 1777, in Fonblanque, *Political and Military Episodes in the Latter Half of the Eighteenth Century,* p. 242; Valentine, *Lord George Germain,* p. 195.

59. Burgoyne, *A State of the Expedition,* p. 10; Colin G. Calloway, *The American Revolution in Indian Country: Crisis and Diversity in Native American Communities* (Cambridge: Cambridge University Press, 1995), pp. 85, 72.

60. Nelson, *General Sir Guy Carleton,* p. 119; Burgoyne, *A State of the Expedition,* p. 14 gives the original number as 250; Carleton to Burgoyne, May 29, 1777, in Fonblanque, *Political and Military Episodes in the Latter Half of the Eighteenth Century,* p. 240.

61. *Baroness von Riedesel and the American Revolution: Journal and Correspondence of a Tour of Duty 1776–1783,* ed. Marvin L. Brown Jr. (Chapel Hill: University of North Carolina Press, 1965).

62. Burgoyne, *A State of the Expedition,* p. 15; Hargrove, *Gentleman John Burgoyne,* p. 122; Christopher Hibbert, *Redcoats and Rebels: The American Revolution through British Eyes* (New York: Norton, 1990), p. 178.

63. "Manifesto issued by Lieut. Genl Burgoyne, Camp at the River Bouquet, June 24," in Cubbison, *Burgoyne and the Saratoga Campaign,* pp. 201–3.

64. Burgoyne, *A State of the Expedition,* p. 10; "To the Indians in Congress at the Camp upon the River Bouquet June the 21st, 1777, and their Answer," in Cubbison, *Burgoyne and the Saratoga Campaign,* pp. 198–201.

65. Fonblanque, *Political and Military Episodes in the Latter Half of the Eighteenth Century,* p. 243; Steuart, *The Last Journals of Horace Walpole,* 2:41. For a parody by William Livingston under the name of "A New Jerseyman" see Philip Davidson, *Propaganda and the American Revolution 1763–1783* (Chapel Hill: University of North Carolina Press, 1941), pp. 379–80.

66. This theme is discussed in Robert Glenn Parkinson, "Enemies of the People: The Revolutionary War and Race in the New American Nation" (Ph.D. diss., University of Virginia, 2005), pp. 5–6.

67. *With Burgoyne from Quebec: An account of the life at Quebec and of the famous battle of Saratoga. First published in 1789 as Volume One of Travels Through the Interior Parts of North America, by Thomas Anburey,* ed. Sydney Jackman (Toronto: Macmillan, 1963), pp. 131–32.

68. Hargrove, *Gentleman John Burgoyne,* p. 127; Davis, *Where a Man Can Go,* p. 65.

69. Steuart, *The Last Journals of Walpole,* 2:42; Charles R. Ritcheson, *British Politics and the American Revolution* (Norman: University of Oklahoma Press, 1954), p. 214.

70. The earl of Derby to Germain, [August 1777], in Fonblanque, *Political and Military Episodes in the Latter Half of the Eighteenth Century,* pp. 249–50; Washington to Schuyler, July 22, 1777, quoted in Valentine, *Lord George Germain,* p. 222.

71. Mintz, *The Generals of Saratoga,* p. 136; Carleton to Germain, June 26, 1777, CO 42/36, PRO, ff. 343–48, cited in Hargrove, *General John Burgoyne,* p. 124.

72. Davis, *Where a Man Can Go,* p. 68; Burgoyne, *A State of the Expedition,* p. 60; Mintz, *The Generals of Saratoga,* pp. 156, 163.

73. Burgoyne, *A State of the Expedition,* pp. 17, 18; Luzader, *Saratoga,* pp. 74–82 makes a good case that the lake route would not have made much difference in time.

74. Burgoyne, *A State of the Expedition,* pp. 21, 269; Jackman, *With Burgoyne from Quebec,* pp. 152, 154; Burgoyne, *A State of the Expedition,* pp. 77, 128.

75. Parkinson, "Enemies of the People," pp. 2–5; Lunt, *John Burgoyne of Saratoga,* pp. 175–77; Hargrove, *General John Burgoyne,* p. 151; Calloway, *The American Revolution in Indian Country,* p. 295.

76. *The American Rebellion: Sir Henry Clinton's Narrative of His Campaigns, 1775–1782*, ed. William B. Willcox (New Haven, Conn.: Yale University Press, 1954), p. 70.

77. Burgoyne, *A State of the Expedition*, pp. 18, 19, 135.

78. Ibid., pp. 19–20; Nickerson, *The Turning Point of The Revolution*, pp. 229, 247, 260, 265; Luzader, *Saratoga*, pp. 103, 111.

79. Nickerson, *The Turning Point of The Revolution*, pp. 189, 190; Hargrove, *Gentleman John Burgoyne*, pp. 155, 156; Fonblanque, *Political and Military Episodes in the Latter Half of the Eighteenth Century*, pp. 274–75.

80. Ibid., pp. 275–76.

81. "Observations, memoranda and evidence upon General Burgoyne's expedition in 1777," Historical Manuscripts Commission, *Stopford-Sackville Manuscripts*, 2:89; Burgoyne, *A State of the Expedition*, pp. 15–16.

82. *The Annual Register*, in *Rebellion in America: A Contemporary British Viewpoint, 1769–1783*, ed. David H. Murdoch (Santa Barbara, Calif.: Clio Books, 1979), p. 705; Burgoyne, *A State of the Expedition*, pp. 62, 68, 23.

83. Fonblanque, *Political and Military Episodes in the Latter Half of the Eighteenth Century*, p. 275; "Notes of General Burgoyne's Speech to the House of Commons," May 26, 1778, Historical Manuscripts Commission, *Stopford-Sackville Manuscripts*, 2:113; Brown, *Baroness von Riedesel and the American Revolution*, p. 47.

84. W. J. Wood, *Battles of the Revolutionary War 1775–1781*, 2d ed. (New York: Da Capo Press, 2003), pp. 132–72.

85. Lamb, *An Original and Authentic Journal of Occurrences During the Late American War*, pp. 160–61.

86. Burgoyne, *A State of the Expedition*, pp. 23, 57, 69, 70, 103, 162, 163; Jackman, *With Burgoyne from Quebec*, pp. 176–77.

87. Burgoyne, *A State of the Expedition*, p. 166; Lamb, *An Original and Authentic Journal of Occurrences During the Late American War*, p. 166.

88. Willcox, *The American Rebellion*, pp. 72, 83; Fonblanque, *Political and Military Episodes in the Latter Half of the Eighteenth Century*, pp. 286–87.

89. Nickerson, *The Turning Point of The Revolution*, p. 353; Lamb, *An Original and Authentic Journal of Occurrences During the Late American War*, p. 163; Luzader, *Saratoga*, pp. 323–24; ibid., pp. 287–89, Luzader makes an interesting case against the importance or reality of the role of Arnold. Burgoyne and his officers certainly credited Arnold in *A State of the Expedition*, pp. 26, 60.

90. Burgoyne, *A State of the Expedition*, pp. 169, 170–71, 172, 173, 174.

91. *Baroness von Riedesel and the American Revolution*, ed. Brown, pp. 55–56, 59.

92. Luzader, *Saratoga*, pp. 323–24.

93. Lamb, *An Original and Authentic Journal of Occurrences During the Late American War*, p. 174; Nickerson, *The Turning Point of the Revolution*, p. 400; Luzader, *Saratoga*, p. 335.

94. Jane Clark, "The Convention Troops and the Perfidy of Sir William Howe," *American Historical Review* 37, no. 4 (July 1932): 721–22; Sampson, *Escape in America*, p. 55.

95. Ibid., p. 184; Kranish, *Flight from Monticello*, pp. 105–7, 109–13; Philander D. Chase, "Years of Hardship and Revelations: The Convention Army at Albemarle Barracks 1779–1781," *Magazine of Albemarle County History*, no. 41 (1983): 9–53; Peter Nicolaisen, "Thomas Jefferson and Friedrich Wilhelm von Giesmar: A Transatlantic Friendship," ibid., no. 64 (2006): 1–27; Davis, *Where a Man Can Go*, pp. 101–2.

96. Burgoyne to his nieces, October 20, 1777, Burgoyne to Colonel Phillipson, October 20, 1777 in Fonblanque, *Political and Military Episodes in the Latter Half of the Eighteenth Century,* pp. 316–17, 313.

97. Ibid., pp. 313–15; Wheatley, *The Historical and Posthumous Memoirs of Sir Nathaniel William Wraxall,* p. 47.

98. Burgoyne, *A State of the Expedition,* p. 187; Hargrove, *Gentleman John Burgoyne,* p. 231.

99. Hargrove, *Gentleman John Burgoyne,* p. 230; Burgoyne, *A State of the Expedition,* pp. vii, 122.

100. Burgoyne to Lord Sydney, October 29, 1784, in Fonblanque, *Political and Military Episodes in the Latter Half of the Eighteenth Century,* p. 439; Hargrove, *Gentleman John Burgoyne,* p. 259.

101. Wheatley, *The Historical and Posthumous Memoirs of Sir Nathaniel William Wraxall,* 2:45–46; Hargrove, *Gentleman John Burgoyne,* p. 250.

102. William Seymour, *The Price of Folly: British Blunders in the War of American Independence* (London: Brassey's, 1995), pp. 247–48. The author is the great great grandson of John Fox Burgoyne.

103. Hargrove, *Gentleman John Burgoyne,* p. 263; Lunt, *John Burgoyne of Saratoga,* p. 329; Fonblanque, *Political and Military Episodes in the Latter Half of the Eighteenth Century,* pp. 463–64, 466.

104. Burgoyne to Germain, August 20, 1777, in Fonblanque, *Political and Military Episodes in the Latter Half of the Eighteenth Century,* pp. 274–75; John Burgoyne, *A Letter from Lieut. Gen. Burgoyne to his Constituents upon his Late Resignation with Correspondence between the Secretaries of War and him relative to his Return to America* (London: J. Almon, 1779), p. 8.

105. Burgoyne, *A State of the Expedition,* pp. 133–34, 135.

106. Ibid., pp. 140, 152.

107. Lunt, *John Burgoyne of Saratoga,* p. 273; Burgoyne, *A State of the Expedition,* p. 167; Burgoyne to Germain, August 20, 1777, Burgoyne to Phillipson, October 20, 1777 in Fonblanque, *Political and Military Episodes in the Latter Half of the Eighteenth Century,* pp. 274, 315–16; Lunt, *John Burgoyne of Saratoga,* p. 273.

108. Richard W. Van Alstyne, "Great Britain, the War of Independence, and the 'Gathering Storm' in Europe, 1775–1778," *Huntington Library Quarterly* 27, no. 4 (August 1964): 339–40, argues that France was already committed to war before receiving news of Saratoga, and that the turning point was in September 1777 with France, Spain, and Britain deciding to concentrate more naval power in the West Indies.

Chapter 5. "The Achilles of the American War"

1. A. F. Steuart, ed., *The Last Journals of Horace Walpole During the Reign of George III,* 2 vols. (London: John Lane, 1910), 2:208–9.

2. His testimony was part of a parliamentary inquiry; see John Almon and John Debrett, eds., *Parliamentary Register; or History of the Proceedings and Debates of the House of Commons,* 62 vols. (London: J. Debrett, 1775–96), 13:1–1539. To follow the full development of the investigation, from Howe's initial motion to make public his correspondence with Germain until the inquiry lapsed on June 30, it is necessary to consult ibid., vols. 10–12; William Cobbett and Thomas Hansard, eds., *The Parliamentary History of England from the Earliest Period to 1803,* 36 vols. (London: Hansard, 1806–22), col. X; Alan Valentine, *Lord North,* 2 vols. (Norman: University of Oklahoma Press, 1967), 2:84; *The History of Parliament: The House of Commons 1754–1790,* ed. Sir Lewis Namier and John Brooke, 3 vols. (London: H.M. Stationery Office, 1964), 3:666; Steuart, *The Last Journals of Horace Walpole,* 2:208.; C. F. Adams, "Contemporary Opinion on the Howes," *Proceedings of the Massachusetts Historical Society* 3d ser., 44 (November 1910), p. 115.

3. *The Annual Register,* in *Rebellion in America: A Contemporary British Viewpoint 1765–1783,* ed.

David H. Murdoch (Santa Barbara, Calif.: Clio Books, 1979), p. 694; Steuart, *The Last Journals of Horace Walpole*, 2:142, 144.

4. George III to North [January 1778], *The Correspondence of King George the Third from 1760 to December 1783*, ed. Sir John Fortescue, 6 vols. (London: Macmillan, 1927–28), 4:13; Germain to North, May 12, 1778, Historical Manuscripts Commission, *Report on the Manuscripts of Mrs. Stopford-Sackville of Drayton House, Northamptonshire*, 2 vols. (London: H.M. Stationery Office, 1910), 1:73; Steuart, *The Last Journals of Horace Walpole*, 2:143, 67, 172; Germain to North, September 13, 1779, Historical Manuscripts Commission, *Stopford-Sackville Manuscripts*, 2:141; George H. Guttridge, "Lord George Germain in Office, 1775–1782," *American Historical Review*, 33, no. 1 (October 1927): 38.

5. *The Annual Register*, in Murdoch, *Rebellion in America*, p. 766; *The Historical and Posthumous Memoirs of Sir Nathaniel William Wraxall 1772–1784*, ed. Henry B. Wheatley, 5 vols. (1836; repr. London: Bickers & Son, 1884), 1:240; *Memoirs of Richard Cumberland: London 1806*, ed. Henry Flanders, (1856; repr. New York: Richard Bloom, 1969), pp. 232, 233.

6. Edmond G. P. Fitzmaurice, *Life of William Earl of Shelburne afterwards First Marquis of Lansdowne with Extracts of his Papers and Correspondence*, 3 vols. (London: Macmillan, 1875–76), 1:362, 363; Richard Cumberland, *Character of the Late Lord Viscount Sackville* (London: C. Dilly, 1785), p. 4; Wheatley, *The Historical and Posthumous Memoirs of Sir Nathaniel William Wraxall*, 1:385.

7. Cumberland, *Character of the Late Lord Viscount Sackville*, pp. 3–4, 7, 9, 11; Wheatley, *The Historical and Posthumous Memoirs of Sir Nathaniel William Wraxall*, 1:208, 385.

8. Namier and Brooke, *The History of Parliament*, 3:390, 394.

9. Wheatley, *The Historical and Posthumous Memoirs of Sir Nathaniel William Wraxall*, 1:388–89, 366; Troy Bickham, *Making Headlines: The American Revolution as Seen through the British Press* (DeKalb: Northern Illinois University Press, 2009), p. 95.

10. Cumberland, *Character of the Late Lord Viscount Sackville*, p. 18; Piers Mackesy, *The Coward of Minden; The Affair of Lord George Sackville* (London: Alan Lane, 1979), p. 29; Alan Valentine, *Lord George Germain* (Oxford: Oxford University Press, 1962), pp. 13, 39, 42.

11. Gerald S. Brown, "The Court Martial of Lord George Sackville, Whipping Boy of the Revolutionary War," *William and Mary Quarterly*, 3d ser., 9, no. 3 (July 1952): 325; Richard Middleton, *The Bells of Victory: The Pitt-Newcastle Ministry and the Conduct of the Seven Years' War 1757–1762* (Cambridge: Cambridge University Press, 1985), p. 130.

12. Steuart, *The Last Journals of Horace Walpole*, 2:223; Brown, "The Court Martial of Lord George Sackville," pp. 326, 333; Brendan Simms, *Three Victories and a Defeat: The Rise and Fall of the First British Empire, 1714–1783* (New York: Basic Books, 2007), p. 452.

13. Mark Urban, *Fusiliers: The Saga of a British Redcoat Regiment in the American Revolution* (New York: Walter, 2007), p. 8; Valentine, *Lord George Germain*, p. 46; Steuart, *The Last Journals of Horace Walpole*, 2:47; Horace Walpole, *Memoirs of the Reign of King George III*, ed. Derek Jarrett, 4 vols. (New Haven, Conn.: Yale University Press, 2000), 4:211–12.

14. Steuart, *The Last Journals of Horace Walpole*, 2:541, 8, 180.

15. Ibid., 1:47, 326, 328, 2:48, 61; Wheatley, *The Historical and Posthumous Memoirs of Sir Nathaniel William Wraxall*, 1:326, 383; *The Diary and Letters of His Excellency Thomas Hutchinson, Esq.*, ed. Peter Orlando Hutchinson, 2 vols. (New York: Burt Franklin, 1971), January 25, 1775, 2:11; entry in diary of Judge Oliver, December 1, 1776, ibid., 2:12, 120.

16. Cumberland, *Character of the Late Lord Viscount Sackville*, p. 3; Steuart, *The Last Journals of Horace Walpole*, 2:75, 80; *The Annual Register*, in Murdoch, *Rebellion in America*, p. 53; Steuart, *The Last Journals of Horace Walpole*, 2:81.

17. Mackesy, *The Coward of Minden*, pp. 254, 258; Kathleen Wilson, *The Sense of the People: Politics, Culture and Imperialism in England, 1715–1785* (Cambridge: Cambridge University Press, 1998), p. 220.

18. Steuart, *The Last Journals of Horace Walpole*, 2:91; Valentine, *Lord George Germain*, pp. 19–20, 286.

19. Mackesy, *The Coward of Minden*, pp. 254–55; Cumberland, *Character of the Late Lord Viscount Sackville*, p. 5; Flanders, *Memoirs of Richard Cumberland*, p. 203.

20. Mackesy, *The Coward of Minden*, p. 256.

21. *The Journal of Samuel Curwen, Loyalist*, ed. Andrew Oliver, 2 vols. (Boston: Harvard University Press, 1972), 2:758; Hutchinson, *Diary and Letters of Thomas Hutchinson*, 2:184, 289, 339.

22. Thompson to Sackville, August 16, 1785, Historical Manuscripts Commission, *Stopford-Sackville Manuscripts*, 1:255–56;

23. Mackesy, *The Coward of Minden*, p. 33; Gibbon to J. B. Holroyd, August 20, 1774, in *The Letters of Edward Gibbon*, ed. J. E. Norton, 3 vols. (New York: Macmillan, 1956), 2:26; Lady North to North's father, London, November 10, 1775, in Edward Hughes, "Lord North's Correspondence, 1766–83," *English Historical Review* 64, no. 243 (April 1947): 228.

24. Guttridge, "Lord George Germain in Office," p. 24; P. D. G. Thomas; *The Townshend Duties Crisis: The Second Phase of the American Revolution 1767–1773* (Oxford: Oxford University Press, 1987), p. 21; Germain to Irwin, February 18, 1767, Historical Manuscripts Commission, *Stopford-Sackville Manuscripts*, 1:119; R. C. Simmons and P. D. G Thomas, eds., *Proceedings and Debates of the British Parliaments Respecting North America 1754–1783*, March 9, 1774, 6 vols. (Millwood, N.Y.: Kraus International, 1982–86), 6:50; Valentine, *Lord George Germain*, pp. 23–24.

25. Simmons and Thomas, *Proceedings and Debates of British Parliaments Respecting North America 1754–1788*, March 28, 1774, 6:148–49, 151–52; May 2, 1774, ibid., p. 360; Namier & Brooke, *The History of Parliament*, 3:395; Simmons and Thomas, *Proceedings and Debates of British Parliaments Respecting North America 1754–1788*, January 26, 1775, 5:309–10.

26. Gibbon to J. B. Holroyd. November 4, 1776, in Norton, *The Letters of Edward Gibbon*, 2:120.

27. Steuart, *The Last Journals of Horace Walpole*, 2:389.

28. Ibid., 1:510; Germain to General Irwin, June 13, 1775, Historical Manuscripts Commission, *Stopford-Sackville Manuscripts*, 1:135; Ira Gruber, "Lord Howe and Lord George Germain, British Politics and the Winning of American Independence," *William and Mary Quarterly*, 3d ser., 22, no. 2 (April 1965): 229; Steuart, *The Last Journals of Horace Walpole*, 2:49; Ira D. Gruber, *The Howe Brothers and the American Revolution* (Chapel Hill: University of North Carolina Press, 1972), p. 83; Piers Mackesy, "British Strategy in the War of American Independence," in *Essays on the American Revolution*, ed. David L. Jacobson (New York: Holt, Rinehart and Winston, 1970), p. 172; P. D. G. Thomas, *Tea Party to Independence: The Third Phase of the American Revolution 1773–1776* (Oxford: Clarendon Press, 1991), p. 286.

29. Gruber, "Lord Howe and Lord George Germain, British Politics and the Winning of the American Independence," p. 229; *The Annual Register*, in Murdoch, *Rebellion in America*, pp. 353, 368.

30. Germain to Lord Suffolk, June 16 or 17, 1775, Historical Manuscripts Commission, *Stopford-Sackville Manuscripts*, 2:2; Germain to Clinton, January 3, 1781, CO 5/101 no. 76, PRO.

31. Germain to General Irwin, July 26, 1775, September 13, 1775, Historical Manuscripts Commission, *Stopford-Sackville Manuscripts*, 2:136, 137.

32. Paul David Nelson, *General Sir Guy Carleton, Lord Dorchester: Soldier-Statesman of Early British Canada* (Teaneck, N.J.: Fairleigh Dickinson University Press, 2000), pp. 63–64, 86–87, 90, 95.

33. Germain to Carleton, March 26, 1777, Historical Manuscripts Commission, *Stopford-Sackville*

Manuscripts, 2:60; Nelson, *General Sir Guy Carleton, Lord Dorchester*, pp. 88, 91–92, 107; Hoffman Nickerson, *The Turning Point of The Revolution, or Burgoyne in America* (1928; repr. Cranbury, N.J.: The Scholar's Bookshelf, 2005), p. 94; Thomas, *Tea Party to Independence*, p. 289; Alfred L. Burt, "The Quarrel Between Germain and Carleton: An Inverted Story," *Canadian Historical Review* 11 (September 1930): 202–22.

34. Guttridge, "Lord George Germain in Office," pp. 35, 36.

35. Dr. Benjamin Moseley, M.D., *A Treatise on Tropical Diseases; on Military Operations; and on the Climate of the West-Indies* (London: T. Cadell, 1789), p. 130; Germain to Vaughan, February 8, 1780, CO. 318/6, PRO.

36. H. M. Scott, *British Foreign Policy in the Age of the American Revolution* (Oxford: Oxford University Press, 1990), pp. 312–13; Clifford D. Conner, *Colonel Despard: The Life and Times of an Anglo-Irish Rebel* (Conshohocken, Pa.: Combined Publishing, 2000); Sir Charles Oman, *The Unfortunate Colonel Despard and Other Studies* (New York: Burt Franklin, 1922); Peter Linebaugh and Marcus Rediker, *The Many-Headed Hydra: Sailors, Slaves, Commoners, and the Hidden History of the Revolutionary Atlantic* (Boston: Beacon Press, 2000), pp. 249–86; Tom Pocock, *The Young Nelson in the Americas* (London: Collins, 1980); Joseph J. Gallo, *Nelson in the Caribbean: The Hero Emerges, 1784–1787* (Annapolis, Md.: Naval Institute Press, 2003).

37. Charles Stedman, *The History of the Origin, Progress, and Termination of the American War*, 2 vols. (London: J. Murray, J. Debrett and J. Kerby, 1794), 2:169–75.

38. Moseley, *A Treatise on Tropical Diseases*, 122.

39. For the diplomatic background see Scott, *British Foreign Policy in the Age of the American Revolution*, pp. 71–72.

40. Dalling to Germain, February 4, 1780, September 12, 1779, April 26, 1780, CO 137/76, f. 194, CO 137/75, f. 176, CO 137/77, f. 141, PRO.

41. Dalling to Germain, February 7, 1780, CO 137/77, f. 20, PRO.

42. Germain to Dalling, June 17, 1779, February 2, 1780, January 4, 1780, March 1, 1780, Germain Papers, WLCL, vols. 18, f. 68, 11 (unfoliated), 18, f. 116, vol. 12 (unfoliated).

43. *St. James's Chronicle*, December 18–21, 1779; *Royal Gazette* (New York), June 24, 1780; *New York Gazette and Weekly Mercury*, June 26, 1780; Moseley, *A Treatise on Tropical Diseases*, p. 129; Dalling to Germain, February 4, 1780, CO 137/76, f. 196, PRO.

44. Minutes of the Assembly of Jamaica, December 15, 1780, CO 140/59, PRO; Piers Mackesy, *The War for America 1775–1783* (1964; repr. Lincoln: University of Nebraska Press, 1993), pp. 334–37; Dalling to Germain, July 2, 1780, CO 137/78, f. 168, PRO.

45. Dalling to Germain, February 4, 1780, CO 137/77 PRO; Moseley, *A Treatise on Tropical Diseases*, p. 123; Dalling to Germain, February 4, 1780, CO 137/76, f. 194, PRO; Captain John Polson to Dalling, April 30, 1780, CO, 137/77, ff. 158–60; Dalling to Germain, June 23, 1780, CO 137/78, PRO.

46. "Kemble's Journal 1780," in *The Kemble Papers*, 2 vols. (New York: New-York Historical Society, 1885), 2:4; John Polson to Dalling, April 30, 1780, CO 137/77, f. 160, PRO; Kemble to Capt. Dixon, September 18, 1780, November 26, 1780, *Kemble Papers*, 2:306, 352.

47. Dalling to Germain, February 7, 1780, CO 137/77, PRO.

48. "Kemble's Journal 1780," *Kemble Papers*, 2:24, 31; Moseley, *A Treatise on Tropical Diseases*, p. 133; Sir John Fortescue, *The War of Independence: The British Army in North America, 1775–1783*, introd. John Shy (abridged ed., 1911; London: Greenhill Books, 2001), pp. 196–97; "Kemble's Journal 1780," *Kemble Papers*, 2:36; John Hunter, *Observations on the Diseases of the Army in Jamaica*, 3d ed. (London: T. Payne, 1808), pp. 20, 48.

49. Germain to Dalling, December 7, 1780, CO 137/78, f. 335, PRO; J. Barton Starr, *Tories, Dons, and Rebels: The American Revolution in British West Florida* (Gainesville: University Press of Florida, 1976), pp. 1, 141, 143, 144–45, 160, 173–74, 190–92, 211.

50. Germain to Clinton, March 8, 1778, Historical Manuscripts Commission, *Stopford-Sackville Manuscripts,* 2:99; Germain to Clinton, January 23, 1779, CO 5/97, PRO; Germain to North, September 13, 1779, Historical Manuscripts Commission, *Stopford-Sackville Manuscripts,* 2:142; Gruber, *The Howe Brothers and the American Revolution,* pp. 215, 220–21; John Shy, *A People Numerous and Armed: Reflections on the Military Struggle for American Independence,* rev. ed. (Ann Arbor: University of Michigan Press, 2000), p. 203.

51. 11 June 1779 in Namier and Brooke, *The History of Parliament,* 3:395; Germain to Clinton, August 3, 1779, CO 5/98, PRO; ibid., Historical Manuscripts Commission, *Stopford-Sackville Manuscripts,* 2:135; Namier and Brooke, *The History of Parliament,* 3:390.

52. Stuart to Clinton, January 1779, *A Prime Minister and His Son: From the Correspondence of the Third Earl of Bute and of Lt. Gen. The Hon. Sir Charles Stuart, K.B.,* ed. The Hon. Mrs. E. Stuart Wortley (London: John Murray, 1925), p. 146.

53. *Twilight of British Rule in Revolutionary America: The New York Letter Book of General James Robertson 1780–1783,* ed. Milton M. Klein and Ronald W. Howard (Cooperstown, N.Y.: New York State Historical Association, 1983), pp. 7, 40.

54. Flanders, *Memoirs of Richard Cumberland,* p. 291; Mary Beth Norton, *The British-Americans: The Loyalist Exiles in England 1774–1789* (Boston: Little, Brown, 1972), pp. 153–54; Leland J. Bellot, *William Knox: The Life and Thought of an Eighteenth-Century Imperialist* (Austin: University of Texas Press, 1977), pp. 113, 146; 163–64; Margaret Specter, *The American Department of the British Government 1768–1782* (New York: Columbia University Press, 1940), pp. 38, 136.

55. Germain to Clinton, March 31, 1779, CO 5/97, PRO; James Simpson to Clinton, May 15, 1780, in "James Simpson's Reports on the Carolina Loyalists, 1779–1780," ed. Alan S. Brown, *Journal of Southern History* 21, no. 4 (November 1955): 518–19; Shy, *A People Numerous and Armed,* pp. 207, 230, 235.

56. *The Annual Register,* January 20, 1775, in Murdoch, *Rebellion in America,* p. 212; Gibbon to J. B. Holroyd, May 3, 1777, in Norton, *The Letters of Edward Gibbon,* 3:140; *The Annual Register,* February 2, 1778, February 11, 1778, November 28, 1778, in Murdoch, *Rebellion in America,* pp. 436, 535, 562, 567, 540.

57. *The Annual Register,* November 28, 1778, in Murdoch, *Rebellion in America,* p. 540.

58. Ibid., May 1779, May 3, 1779, pp. 698, 704.

59. Germain to Clinton, March 8, 1778, CO 5/95, PRO; Same to Same, September 27, Historical Manuscripts Commission, *Stopford-Sackville Manuscripts,* 2:144.

60. Thomas Paine, "The Crisis Number 1," in *The American Crisis,* introd. Andrew S. Trees (New York: Barnes & Noble, 2010), p. 1; James Kirby Martin and Mark Edward Lender, *A Respectable Army: The Military Origins of the Republic, 1763–1789* (Wheeling, Ill.: Harlan Davidson, 2006), pp. 68, 89, 206; Shy, *A People Numerous and Armed,* pp. 127, 128–29.

61. John Adams originally made the observation in relation to the Continental Congress in 1775. He repeated the estimate after the war in Adams to Jedediah Morse, December 22, 1815, *The Works of John Adams, Second President of the United States: With a Life of the Author,* ed. Charles Francis Adams, 10 vols. (Boston: Little, Brown and Company, 1850–56), 10:194; Don Cook, *The Long Fuse: How England Lost the American Colonies, 1760–1785* (New York: Atlantic Monthly Press, 1995), p. 325; Paul H. Smith, "The American Loyalists: Notes on Their Organization and Numerical Strength," *William*

and Mary Quarterly, 3d ser., 25, no. 2 (April 1968): 260. William Smith seems to have been unaware of Adams's letter of 1815 which was brought to my attention by Richard Bernstein. *Historical Memoirs of William Smith 1778–1783,* ed. W. H. W. Sabine, 2 vols. (New York: New York Times, 1971), 1:380.

62. Ruma Chopra, *Unnatural Rebellion: Loyalists in New York City During the Revolution* (Charlottesville: University of Virginia Press, 2011), pp. 136–37, 199; Paul H. Smith, *Loyalists and Redcoats: A Study in British Revolutionary Policy* (Chapel Hill: University of North Carolina Press, 1964), p. 60; Smith, "The American Loyalists," pp. 266, 267, 268, 269; William H. Nelson, *The American Tory,* 2d ed. (Boston: Northeastern University Press, 1992), pp. 87, 92, 115.

63. Germain to Clinton, December 3, 1778, CO 5/96, PRO; Clinton to Germain, May 5, 1779, CO 5/97, PRO; Don Higginbotham, *The War of American Independence: Military Attitudes, Policies, and Practices 1763–1789* (1971; repr. Boston: Northeastern University Press, 1983), p. 138; Shy, *A People Numerous and Armed,* p. 201.

64. Stephen Brumwell, *Redcoats: The British Soldier and the War in the Americas, 1755–1763* (Cambridge: Cambridge University Press, 2002), p. 117; Fred Anderson, *A People's Army: Massachusetts Soldiers and Society in the Seven Years' War* (London: Norton, 1984), pp. 111–42; Smith, *Loyalists and Redcoats,* pp. 74, 78; Nelson, *The American Tory,* pp. 143, 144; Shy, *A People Numerous and Armed,* pp. 130, 193.

65. Smith, *Loyalists and Redcoats,* p. 60. For historians who have argued that the Founders were forced to adopt radical policies "from below," see Michael McDonnell, *The Politics of War: Race, Class, and Conflict in Revolutionary Virginia* (Chapel Hill: University of North Carolina Press, 2007); Woody Holton, *Forced Founders: Indians, Debtors, and the Making of the American Revolution in Virginia* (Chapel Hill: University of North Carolina Press, 1999); Terry Boulton, *Taming Democracy* (Oxford: Oxford University Press, 2007); and Gary B. Nash, *The Unknown American Revolution: The Unruly Birth of Democracy and the Struggle to Create America* (New York: Viking, 2005). This is also an important theme in the writings of Edward B. Countryman and Alfred F. Young.

66. Germain to Carleton, July 10, 1777, in *The Manuscripts of Captain Howard Vincente Knox (From Volume VI of "Reports on Manuscripts from Various Collections" Prepared by the Historical Manuscripts Commission Great Britain)* (1909; repr. Boston: Gregg Press, 1972), p. 132; Ritcheson, *British Politics and the American Revolution,* p. 242; Germain to Irwin, February 3, 1778, Historical Manuscripts Commission, *Stopford-Sackville Manuscripts,* 1:139; Colonel Charles Stuart to Sir Henry Clinton, January 1779, in Wortley, *A Prime Minister and His Son,* p. 146.

67. Higginbotham, *The War of American Independence,* pp. 123, 124; Stephen Conway, "British Governments and the Conduct of the American War," in *Britain and the American Revolution,* ed. H. T. Dickinson (London: Addison Wesley Longman, 1998), p. 175; Ritcheson, *British Politics and the American Revolution,* p. 209; Stephen Conway, "The Recruitment of Criminals into the British Army, 1775–81," *Bulletin of the Institute of Historical Research* 57 (1985): 46–58.

68. Stephen Conway, "The Politics of British Military and Naval Mobilization, 1775–83," *English Historical Review* 112, no. 449 (November 1997): 1181, 1182–83, 1192, 1195, 1201; P. J. Marshall, *The Making and Unmaking of Empires: Britain, India and America c. 1750–1783* (Oxford: Oxford University Press, 2005), p. 237; Mackesy, *The War for America,* p. 368; Valentine, *Lord George Germain,* pp. 146, 337, 339; Paul David Nelson, *General James Grant: Scottish Soldier and Royal Governor of East Florida* (Gainesville: University Press of Florida, 1993), p. 136; Sylvia Frey, *The British Soldier in America* (Austin: University of Texas Press, 1981), p. 37; David Patrick Geggus, *Slavery, War, and Revolution: The British Occupation of Saint Domingue, 1793–1798* (Oxford: Oxford University Press, 1982), p. 363; Hunter, *Observations on the Diseases of the Army in Jamaica,* pp. 11, 37, 47, 58, 60; Mackesey, *The War for*

America, pp. 368, 526; Roger Norman Buckley, *The British Army in the West Indies: Society and the Military in the Revolutionary Age* (Gainesville: University Press of Florida, 1998), pp. 60, 104, 210, 218, 219, 229, 237; *The Diary of the Revd. William Jones 1777–1821*, ed. O. F. Christie (London: Brentano's, 1929), pp. 64–65.

69. Thomas, *Tea Party to Independence*, p. 320; Germain to William Knox, November 1, 1778, *The Manuscripts of Captain Howard Vincente Knox*, p. 180.

70. Gerald S. Brown, "The Anglo-French Naval Crisis: A Study of Conflict in the North Cabinet," *William and Mary Quarterly*, 3d ser., 13, no. 1 (January 1956): 16–17; Mackesy, *The War for America*, p. 451.

71. Edward E. Curtis, *The Organization of the British Army in the American Revolution* (New Haven, Conn.: Yale University Press, 1926), p. 120; R. Arthur Bowler, *Logistics and the Failure of the British Army in America 1775–1783* (Princeton, N.J.: Princeton University Press, 1975), p. 20.

72. Curtis, *The Organization of the British Army in the American Revolution*, p. 132; Paul E. Kopperman, "The British High Command and Soldiers' Wives in America, 1755–1783," *Journal of the Society for Army Historical Research* 60, no. 241 (Spring 1982): 20, 22; Bowler, *Logistics and the Failure of the British Army in America*, p. 9; Colin G. Calloway, *The American Revolution in Indian Country: Crisis and Diversity in Native American Communities* (Cambridge: Cambridge University Press, 1995), pp. 135, 137, 147–48.

73. Bellot, *William Knox*, pp. 107, 150, 162; Specter, *The American Department of the British Government*, pp. 30, 34, 48; R. Arthur Bowler, "Logistics and Operations in the American Revolution," in *Reconsiderations on the Revolutionary War: Selected Essays*, ed. Don Higginbotham (Westport, Conn.: Greenwood Press, 1978), p. 66.

74. Cumberland, *Character of the Late Lord Viscount Sackville*, pp. 5, 14; Wheatley, *The Historical and Posthumous Memoirs of Sir Nathaniel William Wraxall*, 1:386–87; memorandum by Burgoyne, in *Political and Military Episodes in the Latter Half of the Eighteenth Century: Derived from the Life and Correspondence of the Right H. John Burgoyne, General, Statesman, Dramatist*, ed. Edward Barrington De Fonblanque (London: Macmillan, 1876), p. 126; Flanders, *Memoirs of Richard Cumberland*, p. 201.

75. Specter, *The American Department of the British Government*, p. 34; Fortescue, *The War of Independence*, pp. 191–92.

76. *The Annual Register*, in Murdoch, *Rebellion in America*, p. 326; Bowler, "Logistics and Operations in the American Revolution," pp. 66, 67.

77. Bowler, "Logistics and Operations in the American Revolution," pp. 66, 70; R. A. Bowler, "Sir Henry Clinton and Army Profiteering: A Neglected Aspect of the Clinton-Cornwallis Controversy," *William and Mary Quarterly*, 3d ser., 31, no. 1 (January 1974): 111–23; Bowler, *Logistics and the Failure of the British Army in America*, p. 148.

78. David S. Reid, "An Analysis of British Parliamentary Opinion on American Affairs at the Close of the War of Independence," *Journal of Modern History* 18, no. 3 (September 1946): 214–15; Andrew O'Shaughnessy, "The Formation of a Commercial Lobby: The West India Interest, British Colonial Policy and the American Revolution," *Historical Journal* 40, no. 1 (1997) 71–95; O'Shaughnessy, "The West India Interest and the Crisis of American Independence," in *West Indies Accounts: Essays on the British Caribbean and the Atlantic Economy in Honour of Richard Sheridan*, ed. Roderick A. McDonald (Kingston: University of the West Indies Press, 1996), pp. 126–49.

79. Wheatley, *The Historical and Posthumous Memoirs of Sir Nathaniel William Wraxall*, 2:231.

80. E. Wayne Carp, *To Starve the Army at Pleasure: Continental Army Administration and American Political Culture, 1775–1783* (Chapel Hill: University of North Carolina Press, 1984), pp. 68, 72, 106; Germain to Clinton, March 1781, CO 5/101, no. 81, PRO.

81. Richard Buel Jr. "Samson Shore: The Impact of the Revolutionary War on Estimates of the Republic's Strength," in *Arms and Independence: The Military Character of the American Revolution*, ed. Ronald Hoffman and Peter J. Albert (Charlottesville: University of Virginia Press, 1984), pp. 149–50; Higginbotham, *The War of American Independence*, pp. 403–5; Charles Royster, *A Revolutionary People at War: The Continental Army and American Character, 1775–1783* (Chapel Hill: University of North Carolina Press, 1979), pp. 48, 71, 86, 131, 300; Carp, *To Starve the Army at Pleasure*, pp. 78, 97, 173, 180–81, 184, 220.

82. Germain to Clinton, April 4, 1781, CO 5/101, PRO; Germain to Major General John Vaughan, 4 April, 1781, July 4, 1781, CO 318/8, ff. 103, 127, PRO; Germain to Clinton, August 2, 1781, CO 5/102, PRO.

83. Wheatley, *The Historical and Posthumous Memoirs of Sir Nathaniel William Wraxall*, p. 146; memorandum, in Lord George Germain's handwriting, on American Affairs in Historical Manuscripts Commission, *Stopford-Sackville Manuscripts*, 2:216, 218–19.

84. Ian R. Christie, *The End of North's Ministry, 1780–1782* (London:, 1958), pp. 275, 276; Wheatley, *The Historical and Posthumous Memoirs of Sir Nathaniel William Wraxall*, pp. 157–58, 159–60, 161.

85. Christie, *The End of North's Ministry*, pp. 290, 292; Steuart, *The Last Journals of Horace Walpole*, 2:396.

86. Wheatley, *The Historical and Posthumous Memoirs of Sir Nathaniel William Wraxall*, pp. 176–78; Walpole, *The Last Journals of Horace Walpole*, ed. Steuart, 2:400.

87. "The Removal of Lord George Germain," *The Manuscripts of Captain Howard Vincente Knox*, pp. 272–76; Steuart, *The Last Journals of Horace Walpole*, p. 400; Fitzmaurice, *Life of William, Earl of Shelburne*, 3:125–29; Cumberland, *Character of the Late Lord Viscount Sackville*, p. 20; Steuart, *The Last Journals of Horace Walpole*, p. 400; Valentine, *Lord George Germain*, p. 457; Wheatley, *The Historical and Posthumous Memoirs of Sir Nathaniel William Wraxall*, pp. 178–79.

88. Wheatley, *The Historical and Posthumous Memoirs of Sir Nathaniel William Wraxall*, 1:385–386; Flanders, *Memoirs of Richard Cumberland*, pp. 322–23.

89. Flanders, *Memoirs of Richard Cumberland*, p. 323.

90. Ibid., pp. 326–27.

91. Ibid., pp. 329; Cumberland, *Character of the Late Lord Viscount Sackville*, pp. 22–23.

Chapter 6. "The Scapegoat"

1. The description that follows was printed in *The Annual Register* in 1779 in "Particulars of the Mischianza, exhibited in America at the Departure of General Howe in a copy of a letter from an officer in Philadelphia to his correspondent in London," and is reproduced in *Rebellion in America: A Contemporary British Viewpoint 1765–1783*, ed. David H. Murdoch (Santa Barbara, Calif.: Clio Press, 1979), pp. 621–25. See also *John Peebles' American War: The Diary of a Scottish Grenadier, 1776–1782*, ed. Ira Gruber (Mechanicsburg, Pa.: Stackpole Books, 1998), pp. 180–83.

2. Nicholas Cole of St. Peter's College, Oxford University, identified the two quotes as from Horace, *Epistles* 2 and *Satires* 1.6.

3. The dress was chosen by Major John André, whose description is found in Robert McConnell Hatch, *Major John André: A Gallant in Spy's Clothing* (Boston: Houghton Mifflin, 1986), p. 99. For other details of the Mischianza see ibid., pp. 99–105.

4. Ibid., p. 103. The term "star-spangled" was also used in the description in *The Annual Register*.

5. O'Hara to Grafton, November 1, 1780, in "Letters of Charles O'Hara to the Duke of Grafton,"

ed. George C. Rogers Jr., *South Carolina Historical Magazine* 65, no. 3 (July 1964): 162; Armstrong Starkey, "War and Culture, a Case Study: The Enlightenment and the Conduct of the British Army in America, 1755–1781," *War and Society* 8 (May 1990): 17–18; Linda Colley, *Britons: Forging the Nation 1707–1837* (New Haven, Conn.: Yale University Press, 1992), p. 147; Piers Mackesy, *The War for America 1775–1783* (1964; repr. Lincoln: University of Nebraska, 1992), p. 4, regarded the war as "the last great war of the *ancien régime.*" Stephen Conway, *The War of American Independence 1775–1783* (London: Edward Arnold, 1995), p. xi, treats the conflict as a novel form of warfare especially on the side of the Americans.

6. *The Annual Register,* in Murdoch, *Rebellion in America,* p. 563; Troy Bickham, *Making Headlines: The American Revolution as Seen through the British Press* (DeKalb: Northern Illinois University Press, 2009), p. 108. Paul David Nelson, *General James Grant: Scottish Soldier and Royal Governor of East Florida* (Gainesville: University Press of Florida, 1993), p. 131; Charles Stuart to Lord Bute, October 7, 1778 in *A Prime Minister and His Son: From the Correspondence of the Third Earl of Bute and of Lt.-Gen. The Hon. Charles Stuart, K.B.,* ed. The Hon. Mrs. E. Stuart Wortley (London: John Murray, 1925), p. 139; Don Higginbotham, *The War of American Independence: Military Attitudes, Policies, and Practices 1763–1789* (1971; repr. Boston: Northeastern University Press, 1983), p. 125; William John Hale to Admiral Hale, April 2, 1778, in Walter Harold Wilkin, *Some British Soldiers in America* (1914; repr. Milton Keynes: General Books, 2010), p. 114.

7. The House of Commons, November 20, 1778, *The Annual Register,* in Murdoch, *Rebellion in America,* pp. 525–26.

8. Manifesto and Proclamation of the Commissioners, October 8, 1778, *Proceedings of the British Commissioners at Philadelphia, 1778–9: Partly in Ferguson's Hand,* ed. Yasuo Amoh, Darren Lingley, and Hiro Aoki (Kyoto: Kakenhi Supplemental Project Research Report, Kyoto University, 2007), pp. 146–47; Protest of the Lords, December 7, 1778, *The Annual Register,* in Murdoch, *Rebellion in America,* pp. 631–32, 735.

9. Anthony J. Scotti, Jr. *Brutal Virtue: The Myth and Reality of Banastre Tarleton* (Westminster, Md.: Heritage, 2007), p. 92; Stephen Conway, "To Subdue America: British Army Officers and the Conduct of the Revolutionary War," *William and Mary Quarterly,* 3d ser., 48, no. 3 (July 1986) 382–83, 393, 398, 399, 404–5; Scotti, *Brutal Virtue,* pp. 47, 132; Paul H. Smith, *Loyalists and Redcoats: A Study in British Revolutionary Policy* (Chapel Hill: University of North Carolina Press, 1964), p. 115.

10. Marvin Stern, *Thorns and Briars: Bonding, Love and Death 1764–1870* (New York: Foundation of Thanatology, 1986), pp. viii, 3, 5, 6, 7.

11. *The American Rebellion: Sir Henry Clinton's Narrative of His Campaigns, 1775–1782, with an Appendix of Original Documents,* ed. William B. Willcox (New Haven, Conn.: Yale University Press, 1954), p. 84; *The Diary and Letters of His Excellency Thomas Hutchinson, Esq.,* ed. Peter Orlando Hutchinson, 2 vols. (New York: Burt Franklin, 1971), February 30, 1777, 2:181; Willcox, *The American Rebellion,* pp. 85, 107; Robert K. Wright Jr., "'Nor Is Their Standing Army to Be Despised': The Emergence of the Continental Army as a Military Institution," in *Arms and Independence: The Military Character of the American Revolution,* ed. Ronald Hoffman and Peter J. Albert (Charlottesville: University of Virginia Press, 1968), pp. 69–71; Charles Royster, *A Revolutionary People at War: The Continental Army and American Character, 1775–1783* (Chapel Hill: University of North Carolina Press, 1979), pp. 211, 216, 218, 219.

12. Willcox, *The American Rebellion,* p. 119; Clinton to Germain, July 27, 1778, September 15, 1778, CO 5/96, PRO; Willcox, *The American Rebellion,* p. 209; Charles R. Ritcheson, *British Politics and the American Revolution* (Norman: University of Oklahoma Press, 1954), pp. 257, 156.

13. William B. Willcox, "British Strategy in America, 1778," *Journal of Modern History* 19, no. 2 (June 1947): 109; Willcox, *The American Rebellion*, pp. 106–7; Stephen Conway, *The War of American Independence 1775–1783* (London: Edward Arnold, 1995), pp. 103, 108, 157; Piers Mackesy, *The War for America 1775–1783* (1964; repr.: University of Nebraska Press, 1992), pp. 221, 232; David Syrett, *The Royal Navy in American Waters 1775–1783* (Aldershot: Scolar Press, 1989), pp. 115, 118; Eric Robson, *The American Revolution in Its Political and Military Aspects 1763–1783* (1955; repr. New York: Norton, 1966), pp. 192, 193–94, 105, 206, 209–10, 212.

14. Cornwallis to Germain, June 17, 1779, CO/5/96, PRO; Willcox, *The American Rebellion*, p. 107; Mackesy, *The War for America*, pp. 244–45.

15. William B. Willcox, *Portrait of a General: Sir Henry Clinton in the War of Independence* (New York: Knopf, 1964), pp. xiv–xv, 44; *Historical Memoirs of William Smith 1778–1783*, ed. W. H. W. Sabine, 2 vols. (New York: New York Times, 1971), 2:92; Willcox, *The American Rebellion*, p. 203; Mackesy, *The War for America*, p. 268; Frederick Wyatt and William B. Willcox, "Sir Henry Clinton: A Psychological Exploration in History," *William and Mary Quarterly*, 3d ser., 16 (January 1959): 3–26.

16. Bickham, *Making Headlines*, p. 197.

17. Ira D. Gruber, *Books and the British Army in the Age of the American Revolution* (Chapel Hill: University of North Carolina Press, 2010), pp. 3–4, 10, 44, 73–78; Gruber, "The Education of Sir Henry Clinton," *Bulletin of the John Rylands University Library of Manchester* 72 (1990): 133, 135, 139, 140–41, 145. The notebooks are not located with the rest of the Clinton Papers in the Clements Library in Ann Arbor, Michigan. In 1958, they were deposited at the John Rylands Library, and Gruber was the first to consult these papers in the summer of 1986.

18. Willcox, *Portrait of a General*, pp. 36, 64.

19. Ibid., p. 46.

20. Eric Robson, "The Expedition to the Southern Colonies, 1775–1776," *English Historical Review* 66 (October 1951): 539; Willcox, *Portrait of a General*, p. 68; Elizabeth Gray Vining, *Flora MacDonald: Her Life in the Highlands and in America* (London: Geoffrey Bles, 1967); Vining, "Flora Macdonald (1722–1790): A Loyalist from the Scottish Highlands," in *Loyalist Mosaic: A Multi-ethnic Heritage*, ed. Joan Magee (Toronto: Dundurn Press, 1984), pp. 137–55.

21. Smith, *Loyalists and Redcoats*, p. 24.

22. Willcox, "British Strategy in America, 1778," pp. 157–59.

23. Willcox, *The American Rebellion*, p. 92; Paul David Nelson, *William Tryon and the Course of Empire: A Life in the British Imperial Service* (Chapel Hill: University of North Carolina Press, 1990), pp. 154–55.

24. Willcox, *The American Rebellion*, p. 85; Willcox, "British Strategy in America," p. 168; Willcox, *Portrait of a General*, p. 20.

25. Clinton to Germain, May 2, 1778, CO/5/96, PRO; Willcox, "British Strategy in America, pp. 201, 109.

26. Memo of conversation, February 7, 1776, Clinton Papers, WLCL, quoted in Scotti, *Brutal Virtue*, p. 132; Sir Henry Clinton, "Account of his conversation with Germain," April 7, 1777, Clinton Papers, WLCL, vol. 20, f. 47; Smith, *Loyalists and Redcoats*, p. 91; Clinton to Germain, June 9, 1781, CO 5/102, no. 130, PRO; Willcox, *The American Rebellion*, pp. 528–29.

27. Clinton to Germain, August 25, 1780, CO 5/100, PRO; Willcox, *Portrait of a General*, pp. 126, 127, 831.

28. Clinton to Germain, June 5, 1778, CO/5/96, PRO; John W. Jackson, *With the British Army in Philadelphia 1777–1778* (San Rafael, Calif.: Presidio Press, 1979), pp. 259–60; Clinton to Germain, July

5, 1778, CO/5/96, PRO; Johann von Ewald, *Diary of the American War: A Hessian Journal,* trans. and ed. Joseph Tustin (New Haven, Conn.: Yale University Press, 1979), p. 132; Brendan Morrissey, *Monmouth Courthouse 1778: The Last Great Battle in the North* (Botley: Osprey Publishing, 2004), pp. 11, 32–33, 35; Willard M. Wallace, *Appeal to Arms: A Military History of the American Revolution* (New York: Harper, 1951), p. 190.

29. Willcox, *The American Rebellion,* p. 91; Gruber, *John Peebles' American War,* p. 193; Clinton to Germain, July 5, 1778, CO/5/96, PRO; John William Hale to Admiral Hale, July 1778, in Wilkin, *Some British Soldiers in America,* p. 118.

30. Morrissey, *Monmouth Courthouse 1778,* p. 69. Willcox, *The American Rebellion,* p. 97; Germain to Clinton, September 2, 1778, CO/5/96, PRO; Howard H. Peckham, *The War for Independence,* rev. ed. (Chicago: University of Chicago Press, 1979), p. 97; Morrissey, *Monmouth Courthouse 1778,* p. 76.

31. Clinton to Germain, July 27, 1778, CO/5/96, PRO; Ewald, *Diary of the American War,* p. 140; Charles Stedman, *The History of the Origin, Progress, and Termination of The American War,* 2 vols. (London: J. Murray, J. Debrett and J. Kerby, 1794), 2:34–37.

32. Clinton to Germain, October 8, 1778, CO/5/96, PRO; Willcox, *Portrait of a General,* p. 270.

33. Willcox, *Portrait of a General,* p. 242; Clinton to Germain, New York, October 8, 1778, CO/5/96, PRO, also printed in the appendix to Willcox, *The American Rebellion,* p. 97.

34. Willcox, *Portrait of a General,* pp. 242, 252; Germain to Clinton, 1778, December 3, 1778, CO/5/96, PRO.

35. Germain to Clinton, March 8, 1778, in Historical Manuscripts Commission, *Report on the Manuscripts of Mrs. Stopford-Sackville of Drayton House, Northamptonshire,* 2 vols. (London: H.M. Stationery Office, 1910), 2:97–100; Ira Gruber, "Britain's Southern Strategy," in *The Revolutionary War in the South: Power, Conflict, and Leadership,* ed. W. Robert Higgins (Durham, N.C.: Duke University Press, 1979), pp. 220–21; Willcox, *The American Rebellion,* p. 127; Clinton to Germain, April 4, 1779, Historical Manuscripts Commission, *Stopford-Sackville Manuscripts,* 2:124–25.

36. Mackesy, *The War for America,* p. 368.

37. William B. Willcox, "Sir Henry Clinton: Paralysis of Command," in *George Washington's Generals and Opponents,* ed. George Athan Billias, 2 vols. in 1 (1964, 1969; repr. New York: Da Capo Press, 1994), 2:100 n. 8; Conway, *The War of American Independence,* p. 158; Jonathan R. Dull, *The French Navy and American Independence: A Study of Arms and Diplomacy, 1774–1787* (Princeton, N.J.: Princeton University Press, 1975), pp. 359–76; R. Arthur Bowler, "Logistics and Operations in the American Revolution," in *Reconsiderations on the Revolutionary War: Selected Essays,* ed. Don Higginbotham (Westport, Conn.: Greenwood Press, 1978), p. 67.

38. R. Arthur Bowler, *Logistics and the Failure of the British Army in America 1775–1783* (Princeton, N.J.: Princeton University Press, 1975), pp. 98, 109–32, 245; David Syrett, *Shipping and the American War 1775–83: A Study of British Transport Organisation* (London: Athlone Press, 1970), p. 157.

39. Clinton to Germain, August 20, 1779, CO 5/98, PRO; Sabine, *Historical Memoirs of William Smith 1778–1783,* 2:173, 157, 177; Ewald, *Diary of the American War,* pp. 159–60, 178; Bruce Ingham Granger, *Political Satire in the American Revolution 1763–1783* (Ithaca, N.Y.: Cornell University Press, 1960), pp. 185–88; Hutchinson, *Diary and Letters of Thomas Hutchinson,* November 24, 1779, 2:298.

40. Conway, *The War of American Independence,* p. 150; Mackesy, *The War for America,* p. 314.

41. Matthew H. Spring, *With Zeal and Bayonets Only: The British Army on Campaign in North America 1775–1783* (Norman: University of Oklahoma Press, 2008), p. 14. The real threat posed by Washington to Clinton in New York in 1779 is the subject of recent research by the editors of the George Washington Papers. See Benjamin Lee Huggins, "'A Speedy and Decisive Effort': George

Washington's Prospective 1779 Campaign Against New York," paper presented to the 78th Annual Meeting of the Society for Military History, Lisle, Ill., June 11, 2010; William M. Ferraro, "Active, Aggressive and Aware: George Washington's Response to the Raids on Connecticut, July 1779," ibid.

42. Clinton to Germain, May 5, 1779, CO5/97, PRO; Same to Same June 18, 1779, CO/5/98, PRO; Ewald, *Diary of the American War,* p. 168; Philip Morgan and Andrew Jackson O'Shaughnessy, "Arming Slaves in the American Revolution," in *Arming Slaves from Classical Times to the Modern Age,* ed. Christopher Leslie Brown and Philip Morgan (New Haven, Conn.: Yale University Press, 2006), p. 190.

43. Clinton to Germain, November 4, 1779, CO/5/98, PRO; Nelson, *William Tryon and the Course of Empire,* pp. 169–73; Clinton to Germain, June 18, 1779, CO 5/98, no. 58, PRO; Willcox, *The American Rebellion,* p. 140.

44. Clinton to Germain, August 21, 1779, CO/5/98, no. 69; Arbuthnot to Sandwich, September 29, 1779, *The Private Papers of John, Earl of Sandwich, First Lord of the Admiralty 1771–1782,* ed. G. R. Barnes and J. H. Owen, 4 vols. (London: Navy Records Society, 1932–38), 3:134.

45. Clinton to Germain, May 22, 1779, CO/5/97, PRO; Sabine, *Historical Memoirs of William Smith 1778–1783,* 2:452; Willcox, *The American Rebellion,* pp. 127, 155.

46. Colonel Stuart to Lord Bute, August 1779, in Wortley, *A Prime Minister and his Son,* p. 49; Germain to Clinton, December 3, 1778, Clinton Papers, vol. 47, f. 32, WLCL.

47. Willcox, *The American Rebellion,* pp. 189, 363.

49. Ewald, *Diary of the American War,* pp. 196, 225, 227, 238–39; Willcox, *Portrait of a General,* p. 306.

49. Royster, *A Revolutionary People at War,* p. 282; Willcox, *The American Rebellion,* p. 171; George Smith McCowen Jr., *The British Occupation of Charleston, 1780–82* (Columbia: University of South Carolina Press, 1972), p. 10.

50. McCowen, *The British Occupation of Charleston,* pp. 52–55; Willcox, *The American Rebellion,* pp. 174–75, 181.

51. Mary Beth Norton, *The British-Americans: The Loyalist Exiles in England 1774–1789* (Boston: Little, Brown, 1972), p. 33; Sabine, *Historical Memoirs of William Smith,* 2:295; Willcox, *The American Rebellion,* p. 166; Sabine, *Historical Memoirs of William Smith,* 2:390; Robson, *The American Revolution in Its Political and Military Aspects,* p. 145.

52. Willcox, *Portrait of a General,* p. 86.

53. Willcox, *The American Rebellion,* p. 163.

54. Sabine, *Historical Memoirs of William Smith,* p. 201; Willcox, *Portrait of a General,* p. 160; Clinton to Germain, October 29, 1779, CO 5/98, PRO.

55. Willcox, *The American Rebellion,* pp. 183, 184; Sabine, *Historical Memoirs of William Smith,* 2:498.

56. Thomas Fleming, *The Forgotten Victory: The Battle for New Jersey—1780* (New York: Reader's Digest Press, 1973); *Twilight of British Rule in Revolutionary America: The New York Letter Book of General James Robertson 1780–1783,* ed. Milton M. Klein and Ronald W. Howard (Cooperstown, N.Y.: New York State Historical Association, 1983), pp. 55, 59.

57. Bowler, *Logistics and the Failure of the British Army in America,* p. 13.

58. Clinton to Germain, August 25, 1780, CO/5/100, PRO; Willcox, *The American Rebellion,* p. 203; Mackesy, *The War for America,* p. 439; Syrett, *Shipping and the American War,* pp. 157, 228.

59. Mackesy, *The War for America,* p. 350; Roger Lamb, *An Original and Authentic Journal of Occurrences During the Late American War from Its Commencement to the Year 1783* (Dublin: Wilkinson & Courtney, 1809), p. 81.

60. Carl Van Doren, *Secret History of the American Revolution* (1941; repr. Clinton, N.J.: Augustus M. Kelley, 1973), p. 375.

61. Clinton to Germain, October 11, 1780, CO/5/100, PRO; Hatch, *Major John André*, p. 203; Sabine, *Historical Memoirs of William Smith*, 2:300, 334. Clinton's account of the episode is contained in a "Narrative" enclosed in his letter to Germain.

62. Hatch, *Major John André*, p. 82.

63. Roger Kaplan, "British Intelligence Operations During the American Revolution," *William and Mary Quarterly*, 3d ser., 47, no. 1 (January 1990): 121, 123, 124; Hatch, *Major John André*, pp. 156–58.

64. Willcox, *The American Rebellion*, p. 217; Lamb, *An Original and Authentic Journal of Occurrences During the Late American War*, pp. 329, 332–33; Ewald, *Diary of the American War*, p. 250; Sarah Knott, *Sensibility and the American Revolution* (Chapel Hill: University of North Carolina Press, 2009), pp. 159, 161.

65. Hatch, *Major John André*, pp. 269, 273–74; Knott, *Sensibility and the American Revolution*, p. 156.

66. Hatch, *Major John André*, p. 276; Willcox, *The American Rebellion*, p. 218.

67. Van Doren, *Secret History of the American Revolution*, p. 394.

68. Germain to Clinton, October 13, 1780, CO/5/100, PRO; Stanley Weintraub, *Iron Tears: America's Battle for Freedom, Britain's Quagmire, 1775–1783* (New York: Simon and Shuster, 2005), p. 202; Sabine, *Historical Memoirs of William Smith*, 2:347; Judith L. Van Buskirk, *Generous Enemies: Patriots and Loyalists in Revolutionary New York* (Philadelphia: University of Pennsylvania Press, 2002), p. 30; Christopher Hibbert, *Redcoats and Rebels: The American Revolution through British Eyes* (New York: Norton, 1990), pp. 59–60,

69. Willcox, *The American Rebellion*, p. 294.

70. Ibid., p. 209; Cornwallis to Clinton, August 6, 1780, *The Cornwallis Papers: The Campaigns of 1780 and 1781 in the Southern Theatre of the American Revolutionary War*, ed. Ian Saberton, 6 vols. (Uckfield: Naval & Military Press, 2010), 1:175–79.

71. O'Hara to Grafton, November 15, 1780, in Rogers, "Letters of Charles O'Hara to the Duke of Grafton," p. 169.

72. Clinton to Germain, April 23, 1781, CO/5/101, PRO; Cornwallis to Clinton, April 10, 1781, CO/5/101, PRO; William B. Willcox, "The British Road to Yorktown: A Study in Divided Command," *American Historical Review* 52, no. 1 (October 1946): 15; Sabine, *Historical Memoirs of William Smith*, 2:417; Willcox, "The British Road to Yorktown," pp. 12, 15; Clinton to Germain, April 23, 1781, CO/5/101, PRO; Clinton to Germain, May 18, 1781, CO/5/101, PRO; Willcox, "Sir Henry Clinton: Paralysis of Command," p. 86. From the fall of Charleston, Clinton's letters repeatedly emphasized the importance of adequate naval support.

73. Willcox, "Sir Henry Clinton: Paralysis of Command," pp. 91–92; Clinton to Cornwallis, July 15, 1781, Cornwallis to Clinton, July 27, 1781, Clinton to Cornwallis, August 2, 1781, CO 5/103, PRO.

74. Randolph G. Adams, "A View of Cornwallis's Surrender at Yorktown," *American Historical Review* 37, no. 1 (October 1931): 30, 31, 36.

75. William B. Willcox, "Rhode Island in British Strategy, 1780–81," *Journal of Modern History* 17, no. 4 (December 1945): 320; Ewald, *Diary of the American War*, p. 295.

76. Germain to Clinton, April 4, 1781, CO 5/101, no. 83, PRO; Adams, "A View of Cornwallis's Surrender at Yorktown," p. 34.

77. Ibid., pp. 25–26, 37, 39.

78. Don Cook, *The Long Fuse: How England Lost the American Colonies, 1760–1785* (New York: Atlantic Monthly Press, 1995), p. 347.

79. Willcox, *Portrait of a General*, p. 447. Rumors circulating in London that Clinton intended to challenge Cornwallis to a duel are mentioned in *The Last Journals of Horace Walpole During the Reign of George III*, ed. A. F. Steuart, 2 vols. (London: John Lane, 1910), 2:377, 402.

80. Edward Gibbon to Sir Henry Clinton [December 1782], *The Letters of Edward Gibbon*, ed. J. E. Norton, 3 vols. (New York: Macmillan, 1956), 3:31; Willcox, *Portrait of a General*, pp. 480, 481; Howard H. Peckham, "Sir Henry Clinton's Review of Simcoe's Journal," *William and Mary Quarterly*, 2d ser., 21, no. 4 (October 1941): 367.

81. Willcox, *Portrait of a General*, p. 406.

82. Sir Henry Clinton to William Henry, duke of Gloucester, April 24, 1780, Clinton Papers, vol. 254, f. 40, WLCL; Willcox, *Portrait of a General*, pp. 471–72.

83. Nelson, *General James Grant*, p. 156; Peckham, "Sir Henry Clinton's Review of Simcoe's Journal," p. 367.

84. Steuart, *The Last Journals of Horace Walpole*, 2:402; Willcox, *Portrait of a General*, p. 485n.

85. Maya Jasanoff, *Liberty's Exiles: American Loyalists in the Revolutionary World* (New York: Knopf, 2011), pp. 287–88.

86. Stern, *Thorns and Briars*, pp. ix, 31.

87. Willcox, *Portrait of a General*, p. 490; Ewald, *Diary of the American War*, pp. 337, 338.

Chapter 7. "Bagging the Fox"

1. Paul H. Smith, *Loyalists and Redcoats: A Study in British Revolutionary Policy* (Chapel Hill: University of North Carolina Press, 1964), p. 98: "government relied less and less on military might, it fell victim to every unfounded report that American resistance was crumbling"; ibid., p. 163.

2. John Ferling, "John Adams, Diplomat," *William and Mary Quarterly*, 3d ser., 51, no. 2 (April 1994): 239, 240; Ferling, *Setting the World Ablaze: Washington, Adams, Jefferson, and the American Revolution* (New York: Oxford University Press, 2000), pp. 216–17; Thomas Fleming, *The Perils of Peace: America's Struggle for Survival after Yorktown* (New York: HarperCollins, 2007), p. 79.

3. James Kirby Martin, "A 'Most Undisciplined, Profligate Crew': Protest and Defiance in the Continental Ranks, 1776–1783," in *Arms and Independence: The Military Character of the American Revolution*, ed. Ronald Hoffman and Peter J. Albert (Charlottesville: University of Virginia Press, 1984), pp. 134–36; James Kirby Martin and Mark Edward Lender, *A Respectable Army: The Military Origins of the Republic, 1763–1789* (Wheeling, Ill.: Harlan Davidson, 2006), pp. 161–63; E. Wayne Carp, *To Starve the Army at Pleasure: Continental Army Administration and American Political Culture, 1775–1783* (Chapel Hill: University of North Carolina Press, 1984), p. 68; Fleming, *The Perils of Peace*, p. 107; William B. Willcox, *Portrait of a General: Sir Henry Clinton in the War of Independence* (New York: Knopf), p. 393; Marcus Cunliffe, *George Washington: Man and Monument* (London: Collins, 1959), p. 97.

4. *Historical Memoirs of William Smith 1778–1783*, ed. W. H. W. Sabine, 2 vols. (New York: New York Times, 1971), 2:144, 200–201; Frank and Mary Wickwire, *Cornwallis and the War of Independence* (London: Faber and Faber, 1971), pp. 7–8; *John Peebles' American War: The Diary of a Scottish Grenadier, 1776–1782*, ed. Ira Gruber (Mechanicsburg, Pa.: Stackpole Books, 1998), p. 287.

5. Quoted in Wickwire and Wickwire, *Cornwallis and the War of Independence*, 1:115; Ira Gruber, "British Strategy: The Theory and Practice of Eighteenth-Century Warfare," in *Reconsiderations on the*

Revolutionary War: Selected Essays, ed. Don Higginbotham (Westport, Conn.: Greenwood, 1978), p. 15; Cornwallis to Thomas Townshend, September 2, 1758, in *Correspondence of Charles, First Marquis Cornwallis,* ed. Charles Ross, 3 vols. (London: John Murray, 1859), 1:7; Wickwire and Wickwire, *Cornwallis and the War of Independence,* pp. 38–39.

6. Wickwire and Wickwire, *Cornwallis and the War of Independence,* pp. 27–28.

7. Ibid. p. 46.

8. Lord North to George III [November 26, 1775], *The Correspondence of King George the Third from 1760 to November 1783,* ed. Sir John Fortescue, 6 vols. (London: Macmillan, 1927–28), 3:294–95; "The House Debates Whether to Continue the War," November 9, 1780, in *The American Revolution as Described by British Writers and The Morning Chronicle and London Advertiser,* ed. Elizabeth R. Miller (Bowie, Md.: Heritage Books, 1991), p. 31; *The Historical and Posthumous Memoirs of Sir Nathaniel William Wraxall 1772–1784,* ed. Henry B. Wheatley, 5 vols. (1836; repr. London: Bickers & Son, 1884), 1:265; *The Last Journals of Horace Walpole During the Reign of George III,* ed. A. F. Steuart, 2 vols. (London: John Lane, 1910), 2:338; Benton Rain Patterson, *Washington and Cornwallis: The Battle for America, 1775–1783* (New York: Taylor Trade Publishing, 2004), p. 50; Cornwallis to Vice Admiral Arbuthnot, June 29, 1780, in *The Cornwallis Papers: The Campaigns of 1780 and 1781 in the Southern Theatre of the American Revolutionary War,* ed. Ian Saberton, 6 vols. (Uckfield: Naval & Military Press, 2010), 1:159.

9. Quoted in Hugh F. Rankin, "Charles Lord Cornwallis: Study in Frustration," *George Washington's Generals and Opponents: Their Exploits and Leadership,* ed. George Athan Billias, 2 vols. in 1 (1964, 1969; repr. New York: Da Capo Press, 1994), 2:204; Steuart, *The Last Journals of Horace Walpole,* 1:498; Rankin, "Charles Lord Cornwallis: Study in Frustration," in Billias, *George Washington's Generals and Opponents.,* 2:194. The name of Cornwallis's wife is variously spelled in different reference works. The spelling here is that used in the *Oxford Dictionary of National Biography.*

10. Matthew H. Spring, *With Zeal and Bayonets Only: The British Army on Campaign in North America, 1775–1783* (Norman: University of Oklahoma Press, 2008), pp. 105, 116; Stephen Brumwell, *Redcoats: The British Soldier and War in the Americas, 1755–1763* (Cambridge: Cambridge University Press, 2002), pp. 113, 119, 127; Ian S. Hallows, *Regiments and Corps of the British Army* (London: New Orchard Edition, 1994), pp. 194–95.

11. Rankin, "Charles Lord Cornwallis: Study in Frustration," p. 197; *The American Rebellion: Sir Henry Clinton's Narrative of His Campaigns, 1775–1782,* ed. William B. Willcox (New Haven, Conn.: Yale University Press, 1954), p. 60.

12. Quoted in Wickwire and Wickwire, *Cornwallis and the War of Independence,* p. 116; *The Diary and Letters of His Excellency Thomas Hutchinson, Esq.,* ed. Peter Orlando Hutchinson, 2 vols. (New York: Burt Franklin, 1971), 2:231.

13. Steuart, *The Last Journals of Horace Walpole,* 2:91; March 9, 1779; Hutchinson, *Diary and Letters of Thomas Hutchinson,* 2:257; Richard Pares, *King George III and the Politicians* (Oxford: Clarendon Press, 1953), p. 57; Hutchinson, *Diary and Letters of Thomas Hutchinson,* 2:201–2; Clinton to Germain, August 20, 1779, in Ross, *Correspondence of Charles, First Marquis Cornwallis* 1:40.

14. Quoted in Wickwire and Wickwire, *Cornwallis and the War of Independence,* p. 109.

15. Ross, *Correspondence of Charles, First Marquis of Cornwallis,* 1:14.

16. Quoted in Wickwire and Wickwire, *Cornwallis and the War of Independence,* p. 115.

17. Willcox, *The American Rebellion,* p. 65; Wickwire and Wickwire, *Cornwallis and the War of Independence,* p. 122.

18. Willcox, *The American Rebellion,* p. 184.

19. Michael Pearson, *Those Damned Rebels: The American Revolution as Seen Through British Eyes* (New York: Da Capo Press, 1972), p. 334; John Mollo and Malcolm McGregor, *Uniforms of the American Revolution* (Poole: Blandford Press, 1985), p. 211; David Mannings, *Sir Joshua Reynolds: A Complete Catalogue of His Paintings*, 2 vols. (New Haven, Conn.: Yale University Press, 2000), 1: 439–40.

20. Lieutenant-Colonel Banastre Tarleton, *A History of the Campaigns of 1780 and 1781 in the Southern Provinces of North America* (1787; repr. Cranbury, N.J.: The Scholar's Bookshelf, 2005), p. 32.

21. Ibid., p. 31; Anthony J. Scotti Jr., *Brutal Virtue: The Myth and Reality of Banastre Tarleton* (Westminster, Md.: Heritage Books, 2007), pp. 102, 103–4. For the battle of Waxhaws see ibid., pp. 173–80.

22. Gruber, "British Strategy," p. 29; Cornwallis to Germain, August 21, 1780, Historical Manuscripts Commission, *Report on the Manuscripts of Mrs. Stopford-Sackville of Drayton House, Northamptonshire*, 2 vols. (London: H.M. Stationery Office, 1910), 2:180. The description here is based on the memoirs of Banastre Tarleton, in conjunction with modern reference sources which generally support his account; see Tarleton, *A History of the Campaigns of 1780 and 1781 in the Southern Provinces of North America*, pp. 104–10.

23. Roger Lamb, *An Original and Authentic Journal of Occurrences During the Late American War*, p. 305; Howard H. Peckham, *The War for Independence*, rev. ed. (Chicago: University of Chicago Press, 1979), p. 147; Don Higginbotham, "Reflections on the War of Independence, Modern Guerrilla Warfare, and the War in Vietnam," in Hoffman and Albert, *Arms and Independence*, p. 23.

24. Cornwallis to Lieut. Colonel Cruger, August 18, 1780, in Saberton, *The Cornwallis Papers*, 2:19; Cornwallis to Clinton, August 29, 1780, ibid., pp. 41–42; Washington to Clinton, October 16, 1780, ibid., 3:17–18; Clinton to Washington, October 23, 1780, ibid., pp. 19–20; Cornwallis to Clinton, December 4, 1780, ibid., pp. 27–28; Cornwallis to Clinton, January 18, 1781, CO 5/101, PRO; Smith, *Loyalists and Redcoats*, p. 146.

25. John Shy, *A People Numerous and Armed: Reflections on the Military Struggle for American Independence*, rev. ed. (Ann Arbor: University of Michigan Press, 2000), pp. 187, 208; Scotti, *Brutal Virtue*, p. 209, refers to Cornwallis's "ambiguous stance on terror"; Tarleton, *A History of the Campaigns of 1780 and 1781 in the Southern Provinces of North America*, p. 90.

26. Russell F. Weigley, *The Partisan War: The South Carolina Campaign of 1780–1782* (Columbia: University of South Carolina Press, 1970), p. 13.

27. The advantages of a southern campaign were outlined in a memorial of the former royal governors: Memorial of governors of the southern colonies regarding the practicality of military operations, attachment of Howe to Germain, July 16, 1777, CO 5/94, PRO.

28. Willcox, *The American Rebellion*, p. 294; Smith, *Loyalists and Redcoats*, pp. 156–57.

29. Lawrence E. Babits and Joshua B. Howard, *Long, Obstinate, and Bloody: The Battle of Guilford Courthouse* (Chapel Hill: University of North Carolina Press, 2009), p. 29.

30. John E. Selby, *The Revolution in Virginia 1775–1783* (1988; repr. Charlottesville: University of Virginia Press, 2007), pp. 187–88; Colin G. Calloway, *The American Revolution in Indian Country: Crisis and Diversity in Native American Communities* (Cambridge: Cambridge University Press, 1995), pp. 197–98, 203, 204; Hugh Bicheno, *Rebels and Redcoats: The American Revolutionary War* (New York: HarperCollins, 2003), p. 200.

31. Willcox, *The American Rebellion*, pp. 230, 228; Lord Rawdon to the Hon. Major General Leslie, October 24, 1780, Historical Manuscripts Commission, *Stopford-Sackville Manuscripts*, 2:185. For the government's southern strategy see Germain to Clinton, March 8, 1778, ibid., pp. 97–100.

32. Rankin, "Charles Lord Cornwallis: Study in Frustration," p. 205.

33. W. J. Wood, *Battles of the Revolutionary War 1775–1781*, 2d. ed. (New York: Da Capo Press, 2003), p. 190.

34. Ibid.; Rankin, "Charles Lord Cornwallis: Study in Frustration," p. 208; Wood, *Battles of the Revolutionary War*, pp. 194–95.

35. Quoted in Rankin, "Charles Lord Cornwallis: Study in Frustration," p. 208; Peckham, *The War for Independence*, p. 149.

36. Rawdon to Clinton, October 29, 1780, CO 5/101, PRO; Tarleton, *A History of the Campaigns of 1780 and 1781 in the Southern Provinces of North America*, p. 171; Weigley, *The Partisan War*, pp. 15, 23, 55.

37. Don Higginbotham, *The War of American Independence: Military Attitudes, Policies, and Practices 1763–1789* (1971; repr. Boston: Northeastern University Press, 1983), p. 362; Cornwallis to Clinton, January 6, 1781, in Saberton, *The Cornwallis Papers*, pp. 33–34.

38. For the relative numbers at the Battle of Cowpens, see Spring, *With Zeal and Bayonets Only*, p. 285 n. 27; Don Higginbotham, "Daniel Morgan: Guerrilla Fighter," in Billias, *George Washington's Generals and Opponents*, 1:292–93.

39. Willard M. Wallace, *Appeal to Arms: A Military History of the American Revolution* (New York: Harper, 1951), p. 234.

40. Rankin, "Charles Lord Cornwallis: Study in Frustration," p. 210; Peckham, *The War for Independence*, p. 152; Cornwallis to Rawdon, January 21, 1781, in Saberton, *The Cornwallis Papers*, 3:251; Selby, *The Revolution in Virginia*, p. 226.

41. Lamb, *An Original and Authentic Journal of Occurrences During the Late American War*, p. 381; John Buchanan, *The Road to Guilford Courthouse: The American Revolution in the Carolinas* (New York: Wiley, 1997), p. 367; O'Hara to Grafton, April 20, 1781, "Letters of Charles O'Hara to the Duke of Grafton," ed. George C. Rogers Jr., *South Carolina Historical Magazine* 65, no. 3 (July 1964): 174; Lieutenant-General Sir Henry Clinton, *Observations on Some Parts of the Answer of Earl Cornwallis to Sir Henry Clinton's Narrative* (1783; repr. Cranbury, N.J.: The Scholar's Bookshelf, 2005), p. 6.

42. Babits and Howard, *Long, Obstinate, and Bloody*, p. 36; Spring, *With Zeal and Bayonets Only*, pp. 47–48; O'Hara to Grafton, April 20, 1781, in Rogers, "Letters of Charles O'Hara to the Duke of Grafton," p. 174.

43. Lamb, *An Original and Authentic Journal of Occurrences During the Late American War*, p. 345; Tarleton, *A History of the Campaigns of 1780 and 1781 in the Southern Provinces of North America*, p. 226.

44. Cornwallis to Tarleton, December 18, 1780, Saberton, *The Cornwallis Papers*, 3:352; Tarleton, *A History of the Campaigns of 1780 and 1781 in the Southern Provinces of North America*, p. 169; Roger Kaplan, "British Intelligence Operations During the American Revolution," *William and Mary Quarterly*, 3d ser., 47, no. 1 (January 1990): 130; O'Hara to Grafton, April 20, 1781, Rogers, "Letters of Charles O'Hara to the Duke of Grafton," p. 176; Tarleton, *A History of the Campaigns of 1780 and 1781 in the Southern Provinces of North America*, p. 231.

45. O'Hara to Grafton, January 6, 1781, Rogers, "Letters of Charles O'Hara to the Duke of Grafton," p. 171; Smith, *Loyalists and Redcoats*, pp. 74–75, 139, 142.

46. Cornwallis to Germain, April 18, 1781, in Saberton, *The Cornwallis Papers*, 4:106; Cornwallis to Clinton, April 23, 1781, ibid., pp. 112–13; O'Hara to Grafton, April 20, 1781, Rogers, "Letters of Charles O'Hara to the Duke of Grafton," p. 177; Shy, *A People Numerous and Armed*, p. 211.

47. Buchanan, *The Road to Guilford Courthouse*, p. 364.

48. Tarleton, *A History of the Campaigns of 1780 and 1781 in the Southern Provinces of North America*, p. 233; Willcox, *The American Rebellion*, p. 206.

49. Piers Mackesy, *The War for America 1775–1783* (1964; repr. Lincoln: University of Nebraska Press, 1993), p. 406; Stephen Conway, *The War of American Independence 1775–1783* (London: Edward Arnold, 1995), pp. 123–24; Buchanan, *The Road to Guilford Courthouse*, p. 374; Babits and Howard, *Long, Obstinate, and Bloody*, pp. xiv, 122, 126, 159, 161–62, 207.

50. Walpole to William Mason, June 14, 1781, quoted in Stanley Weintraub, *Iron Tears: America's Battle for Freedom, Britain's Quagmire, 1775–1783* (New York: Free Press, 2005), p. 275; O'Hara to Grafton, April 20, 1781, Rogers, "Letters of Charles O'Hara to the Duke of Grafton," pp. 177–78; Tarleton, *A History of the Campaigns of 1780 and 1781 in the Southern Provinces of North America*, pp. 277, 217–18; Babits and Howard, *Long, Obstinate, and Bloody*, p. 175.

51. Clinton, *Observations on Some Parts of the Answer of Earl Cornwallis to Sir Henry Clinton's Narrative*, pp. 9–10; Smith, *Loyalists and Redcoats*, p. 153: Cornwallis issued a Proclamation on March 18 in what Smith calls a "final halfhearted attempt to rally support"; Wickwire and Wickwire, *Cornwallis and the War of Independence*, p. 315.

52. Tarleton, *A History of the Campaigns of 1780 and 1781 in the Southern Provinces of North America*, pp. 209, 210; Wickwire and Wickwire, *Cornwallis and the War of Independence*, p. 285; O'Hara to Grafton, November 6, 1780, Rogers, "Letters of Charles O'Hara to the Duke of Grafton," p. 168.

53. Mackesy, *The War for America*, p. 391; Wheatley, *The Historical and Posthumous Memoirs of Sir Nathaniel William Wraxall*, 2:89–90, 105.

54. Wheatley, *The Historical and Posthumous Memoirs of Sir Nathaniel William Wraxall*, 2:125; Ian R. Christie, *The End of North's Ministry, 1780–1782* (London: Macmillan, 1958), pp. 263–64.

55. Troy Bickham, *Making Headlines: The American Revolution as Seen through the British Press* (DeKalb: Northern Illinois University Press, 2009), pp. 154–55, 156; Mary Beth Norton, *The British-Americans: The Loyalist Exiles in England 1774–1789* (Boston: Little, Brown, 1972), p. 170.

56. Cornwallis to Clinton, April 10, 1781, Saberton, *The Cornwallis Papers*, 4:111; Cornwallis to Germain, April 18, 1781, ibid., p. 106; Cornwallis to Major General Phillips, April 10, 1781, ibid., pp. 114–15; Selby, *The Revolution in Virginia*, p. 131; Gregory J. W. Urwin, "Cornwallis in Virginia: A Reappraisal," *Military Collector & Historian* 37, no. 3 (Fall 1985): 118.

57. Selby, *The Revolution in Virginia*, pp. 131, 211, 213; Michael A. McDonnell, *Race and Conflict in Revolutionary Virginia* (Chapel Hill: University of North Carolina Press, 2007), pp. 318, 340, 434, 460–61, 3. McDonnell explains the divisions in terms of incipient class war and describes Virginia as "a society at war almost as much with itself as with Britain," ibid., pp. 342–44; Dumas Malone, *Jefferson the Virginian*, vol. 1 of *Jefferson and His Time* (Boston: Little Brown, 1948), p. 260.

58. Tarleton, *A History of the Campaigns of 1780 and 1781 in the Southern Provinces of North America*, pp. 294, 295.

59. Ibid., p. 297. Monticello was of a different design from the house that now appears on the nickel, but some of the original rooms remain including the cabinet and library. Michael Kranish, *Flight from Monticello: Thomas Jefferson at War* (New York: Oxford University Press, 2010), pp. 275–82; Scotti, *Brutal Virtue*, pp. 172, 97; Tarleton, *A History of the Campaigns of 1780 and 1781 in the Southern Provinces of North America*, p. 297.

60. Selby, *The Revolution in Virginia*, pp. 282–83, 315; Francis D. Cogliano, *Thomas Jefferson: Reputation and Legacy* (Charlottesville: University of Virginia Press, 2006), pp. 62–64.

61. Cogliano, *Thomas Jefferson*, pp. 64–65.

62. Malone, *Jefferson the Virginian*, pp. 390, 445; Kranish, *Flight from Monticello*, pp. 287–88; Cassandra Pybus, *Epic Journeys of Freedom: Runaway Slaves of the American Revolution and Their Global Quest for Liberty* (Boston: Beacon Press, 2006), pp. 48, 54, 105; Pybus, "Jefferson's Faulty Math: The

Question of Slave Defections in the American Revolution," *William and Mary Quarterly,* 3d ser., 62, no. 2 (April 2005): 243, 245–46; John R. Maas, "'The Greatest Terror': Cornwallis Brings His Campaign to Goochland, June 1781," *Goochland County Historical Society Magazine* 41 (2009): 55–56.

63. Buchanan, *The Road to Guilford Courthouse,* p. 20; Rodney Atwood, *The Hessians: Mercenaries from Hessen-Kassel in the American Revolution* (Cambridge: Cambridge University Press, 1980), p. 165; John A. Tilley, *The British Navy and the American Revolution* (Columbia: University of South Carolina Press, 1987), p. 111; Tarleton, *A History of the Campaigns of 1780 and 1781 in the Southern Provinces of North America,* pp. 89–90.

64. Pybus, "Jefferson's Faulty Math," pp. 254, 256, 258; Johann von Ewald, *Diary of the American War: A Hessian Journal,* trans. and ed. Joseph Tustin (New Haven, Conn.: Yale University Press, 1979), p. 305.

65. Pybus, *Epic Journeys of Freedom,* pp. 148, 150; Pybus, "Jefferson's Faulty Math," pp. 249, 261, 263–64; Elizabeth A. Fenn, *Pox Americana: The Great Smallpox Epidemic of 1775–82* (New York: Hill and Wang, 2001), pp. 130–31; George F. Tyson Jr., "The Carolina Black Corps: Legacy of Revolution," *Revista/Review Interamericana* 5 (Winter 1975–76): 648–63; Roger Norman Buckley, *Slaves in Red Coats: The British West India Regiments, 1795–1815* (New Haven, Conn.: Yale University Press, 1979). Cassandra Pybus disputes the higher numbers for runaways given by Sylvia Frey, *Water From the Rock: Black Resistance in a Revolutionary Age* (Princeton, N.J.: Princeton University Press, 1993), p. 211 n. 22.

66. O'Hara to Grafton, November 1, 1780, Rogers, "Letters of Charles O'Hara to the Duke of Grafton," p. 160; Buchanan, *The Road to Guilford Courthouse,* p. 359; Cornwallis to Phillips, April 10, 1781, Saberton, *The Cornwallis Papers,* 4:114–15; Willcox, *The American Rebellion,* pp. 270–71, 308.

67. Cornwallis to Rawdon, July 23, 1781, Saberton, *The Cornwallis Papers,* 6:62–63.

68. Clinton to Cornwallis, July 8, 1781, Saberton, *The Cornwallis Papers,* 5:140–42; Clinton to Rawdon, July 23, 1781, ibid., 6:62–63; Rawdon to Clinton, July 26, 1781, ibid., 1:22–23.

69. Willcox, *The American Rebellion,* p. 323 n. 17; Ewald, *Diary of the American War,* p. 319.

70. Tarleton, *A History of the Campaigns of 1780 and 1781 in the Southern Provinces of North America,* p. 393.

71. "Military Journal of Major Ebenezer Denny 1781 to 1795," *Publications of the Historical Society of Pennsylvania* (Philadelphia: Lippincott, 1860), p. 245.

72. Jerome A. Greene, *The Guns of Independence: The Siege of Yorktown, 1781* (New York: Savas Beatie, 2009), pp. 42, 59, 205, 210, 252, 276, 307; Cornwallis to Clinton, September 16, 1781, October 20, 1781, CO 5/103, PRO; Selby, *The Revolution in Virginia,* p. 302; Rankin, "Charles Lord Cornwallis: Study in Frustration," p. 217; Lamb, *An Original and Authentic Journal of Occurrences During the Late American War,* pp. 378–79.

73. Greene, *The Guns of Independence,* p. 296; *The Annual Register,* in *Rebellion in America: A Contemporary British Viewpoint 1765–1783,* ed. David H. Murdoch (Santa Barbara, Calif.: ABC-Clio, 1979), p. 920; North Callahan, "Henry Knox: American Artillerist," in Billias, *George Washington's Generals and Opponents,* 1:255.

74. Robert Selig, "20 October 1781: The Day After the Surrender," *The Brigade Dispatch,* 34, no. 2 (Summer 2008): 2, 5–6; Greene, *The Guns of Independence,* p. 315.

75. Tarleton, *A History of the Campaigns of 1780 and 1781 in the Southern Provinces of North America,* p. 393; Edward C. Lengel, *General George Washington: A Military Life* (New York: Random House, 2005), p. 149.

76. Steuart, *The Last Journals of Horace Walpole,* 2:379; *Our American Brethren: A History of Letters in*

the British Press During the American Revolution, 1775–1781, ed. Alfred Grant (Jefferson, N.C.: McFarland, 1995), p. 121; Bickham, *Making Headlines,* p. 161.

77. Franklin and Mary Wickwire, *Cornwallis: The Imperial Years* (Chapel Hill: University of North Carolina Press, 1980), p. 5; Willcox, *Portrait of a General,* pp. 472, 459; Jeremy Black, *George III: America's Last King* (New Haven, Conn.: Yale University Press, 2006), p. 28; Cornwallis to Lieut. Colonel Ross, January 15, 1783 in Ross, *Correspondence of Charles, First Marquis Cornwallis,* 1:144; Cornwallis to the Bishop of Lichfield, December 12, 1787, ibid., 1:59.

78. Wickwire and Wickwire, *Cornwallis: The Imperial Years,* pp. 165, 131, 138; Maya Jasanoff, *Edge of Empire: Lives, Culture and Conquest in the East 1750–1850* (New York: Alfred A. Knopf, 2005), p. 161; P. J. Marshall, "'Cornwallis Triumphant': War in India and the British Public in the Late Eighteenth Century," in *War, Strategy, and International Politics: Essays in Honour of Sir Michael Howard,* ed. Lawrence Freedman, Paul Hayes, and Robert O'Neill (Oxford: Clarendon Press, 1992), pp. 61, 62, 63, 64, 71.

79. G. M. Ditchfield, *George III: An Essay in Monarchy* (Basingstoke: Palgrave Macmillan, 2002), p. 135; Wickwire and Wickwire, *Cornwallis: The Imperial Years,* p. 224.

80. William Dalrymple, *White Mughals: Love and Betrayal in Eighteenth-Century India* (New York: Penguin, 2002), p. 308; Wickwire and Wickwire, *Cornwallis: The Imperial Years,* pp. 540–54, 83; P. J. Marshall, *The Making and Unmaking of Empires: Britain, India, and America c. 1750–1783* (Oxford: Oxford University Press, 2005), p. 225.

81. Wickwire and Wickwire, *Cornwallis: The Imperial Years,* pp. 135, 228; Piers Mackesy, "What the British Army Learned," in Hoffman and Albert, *Arms and Independence,* p. 197; Cornwallis to Lieut.-Col. Ross, November 21, 1783, Ross, *Correspondence of Charles, First Marquis Cornwallis,* 1:150, 2:418; Wickwire and Wickwire, *Cornwallis: The Imperial Years,* p. 250.

82. Wickwire and Wickwire, *Cornwallis: The Imperial Years,* pp. 68, 8; Dalrymple, *Love and Betrayal in Eighteenth-Century India,* p. 3; Wickwire and Wickwire, *Cornwallis: The Imperial Years,* pp. 92, 98, 175.

83. Cornwallis to Lieut.-Col. Ross, November 13, 1783, Ross, *Correspondence of Charles, First Marquis Cornwallis,* 1:149; Wickwire and Wickwire, *Cornwallis: The Imperial Years,* p. 262; Ross, *Correspondence of Charles, First Marquis Cornwallis,* 2:355, 1:16.

84. Wickwire and Wickwire, *Cornwallis: The Imperial Years,* p. 267.

85. Washington, December 20, 1780, in Harold A. Larrabee, *Decision at the Chesapeake* (New York: Clarkson N. Potter, 1964), p. 91.

Chapter 8. "Saint George"

1. John Colpoys to Admiral Young, November 27, 1776, Adm 1/309 (Pt. III), f. 589, PRO; Barbara W. Tuchman, *The First Salute: A View of the American Revolution* (New York: Knopf, 1988), pp. 5–6, 16, 43, 54–55, 57. For salute of the flag in St. Croix see H. Kelly to Vice Admiral Young, Antigua, October 27, 1776, enclosed in Germain to Suffolk, March 14, 1777, Adm 1/309 (Pt. III and IV), PRO; *The Danish American Gazette,* April 16, 1777; Franklin L. Jameson, "St. Eustatius and the American Revolution," *American Historical Review* 8 (1902–3): 691.

2. Helen Augur, *The Secret War of Independence* (New York: Little, Brown, 1955), p. 52; *Journal of a Lady of Quality; Being the Narrative of a Journey from Scotland to the Caribbean, North Carolina and Portugal, in the Years 1774 to 1776,* ed. Evangeline W. Andrews and Charles M. Andrews (New Haven, Conn.: Yale University Press, 1921), pp. 136–37.

3. Young to Heylinger, May 20, 1776, Adm 1/309 f. 488, PRO; John Colpoys to Young, November 27, 1776, Adm 1/309, f. 589, PRO; F. C. van Oosten, "Some Notes Concerning the Dutch Caribbean During the American Revolutionary War," *American Neptune* 36 (1976): 165; letters of Van Bibber (November 1776), *Maryland Archives*, 12:423, 436, quoted by Jameson, "St Eustatius in the American Revolution," pp. 690–91; Florence Lewisohn, "St. Eustatius: Depot for Revolution," *Revista/Review Interamericana* 5 (1975–76): 625; John E. Selby, *The Revolution in Virginia, 1775–1783* (1988; repr. Charlottesville: University of Virginia Press, 2007), pp. 171–72; Richard Sampson, *Escape in America: The British Convention Prisoners 1777–1783* (Chippenham: Picton Publishing, 1995), p. 19.

4. Lewisohn, "St. Eustatius: Depot for Revolution," 625; "Extract of a private letter from a gentleman in St. Kitt's, to his friend in Stirling, dated June 14," *Morning Post*, August 17, 1779; Lewisohn, "St. Eustatius: Depot for Revolution," p. 626; [James Ramsay], "Observations on the Caribbean Station," January 1780, Germain Papers, WCLC, vol. 11; [James Ramsay] "Thoughts on the Charibbean Station," December 5, 1778, Germain Papers, WCLC, vol. 8; Richard Buel Jr., *In Irons: Britain's Naval Supremacy and the American Revolutionary Economy* (New Haven, Conn.: Yale University Press, 1998), pp. 229, 120, 178, 180; Christie to Germain, 8 February, 1781, James Ramsay to Germain, March 1, 1781, [James Ramsay]. "Of St. Eustatius," March 1781, Germain Papers, WLCL, vol. 14 (unfoliated); speech of Lord George Germain in the House of Commons, May 14, 1781, *St. James's Chronicle,* May 12–14, 1781.

5. Hood to Jackson, June 24, 1781, *Letters Written by Sir Samuel Hood, Viscount Hood in 1781–83,* ed. David Hannay (London: Navy Records Society, 1895), p. 18.

6. Shelburne quoted in Kenneth Breen, "Sir George Rodney and St. Eustatius in the American War: A Commercial and Naval Distraction, 1775–81," *Mariner's Mirror* 84 (May 1998): 100.

7. Sandwich to Rodney, March 8, 1780, *The Private Papers of John, Earl of Sandwich, First Lord of the Admiralty 1771–1782,* ed. G. R. Barnes and J. H. Owen, 4 vols. (London: Navy Records Society, 1932–38), 3:206; N. A. M. Rodger, *The Insatiable Earl: A Life of John Montagu, Fourth Earl of Sandwich* (New York: Norton, 1994), pp. 327, 305; John Creswell, *British Admirals of the Eighteenth Century: Tactics in Battle* (Hamden, Conn.: Archon Books, 1972), p. 151; Piers Mackesy, *The War for America 1775–1783* (1964; repr. Lincoln: University of Nebraska Press, 1993), p. 473.

8. *Memoirs of Richard Cumberland: London 1806,* ed. Henry Flanders (1856; repr. New York: Benjamin Blom, 1969), p. 208.

9. *The House of Commons 1754–1790,* ed. Sir Lewis Namier and John Brooke, 3 vols. (London: H.M. Stationery Office, 1964), 3:368–69; Flanders, *Memoirs of Richard Cumberland,* p. 209.

10. Young to Stephens, April 7, 1776, March 9, 1777, Adm 1/309, ff. 458, 657; Macartney to Germain, October 22, 1777, CO 101/21, PRO; Robert C. Alberts, *The Golden Voyage: The Life and Times of William Bingham 1752–1804* (Boston: Houghton Mifflin, 1969), 44; Augur, *The Secret War of Independence,* pp. 54, 105–10, 114–28, 203–4, 206–7; Andrews, *Journal of a Lady of Quality,* pp. 120, 124, 275–77.

11. Orlando W. Stephenson, "The Supply of Gunpowder in 1776," *American Historical Review* 30, no. 2 (1925): 271, 274, 277, 279, 281; Macartney to Germain, October 22, 1777, CO 101/21, PRO; Selby, *The Revolution in Virginia,* p. 172; Augur, *The Secret War of Independence,* pp. 54, 85–86.

12. Alan G. Jamieson, "War in the Leeward Islands 1775–1783" (D.Phil. thesis, Oxford University, 1981), p. ix; David Spinney, *Rodney* (London: Allen & Unwin, 1969), pp. 298, 354; N. A. M. Rodger, *The Command of the Ocean: A Naval History of Britain, 1649–1815* (New York: Norton, 2004), pp. 399, 487.

13. Rodney to Sandwich, February 7, 1781, Barnes and Owen, *Sandwich Papers,* 4:148; Brendan

Simms, *Three Victories and a Defeat: The Rise and Fall of the First British Empire, 1714–1783* (New York: Basic Books, 2007), p. 646; James Gillray, *The DUTCHMAN in the DUMPS* (London: William Humphrey, April 9, 1781), JCB Political Cartoons, BM 5837, John Carter Brown Library, Brown University; Vincent Morley, *Irish Opinion and the American Revolution, 1760–1783* (Cambridge: Cambridge University Press, 2002), p. 343.

14. "Extract of a Letter from St. Eustatia," March 6, *London Chronicle*, April 12–14, 1781; Richard Downing Jennings, "Case of an English Subject at the Capture of St. Eustatius by Lord Rodney and General Vaughan in the year 1781" (1784), Sydney Papers, vol. 12, f. 14, WLCL; speech of Edmund Burke, December 4, 1782, *St. James's Chronicle*, February 2–February 5, 1782; ibid., May 14, 1781, May 12–14, 1781; Ronald Hurst, *The Golden Rock: An Episode of the American War of Independence, 1775–1783* (London: Leo Cooper, 1996), p. 139.

15. Rodney to Stephens, February 12, 1781, Adm 1/314, f. 50, PRO; *Royal Gazette*, April 14, 1781; Sheldon Cohen, *British Supporters of the American Revolution, 1775–1783: The Role Of The "Middling-level" Activists* (Woodbridge: Boydell Press, 2004), p. 37; James Ramsay to Germain, March 31, 1781, Germain Papers, vol. 14 (unfoliated), WLCL.

16. Revd. James Ramsay to Germain, March 31, 1781, Germain Papers, vol. 14 (unfoliated), WLCL.

17. Hurst, *The Golden Rock*, p. 7; Norman F. Barka, "Citizens of St. Eustatius, 1781: A Historical and Archaeological Study," in *The Lesser Antilles in the Age of European Expansion*, ed. Robert L. Paquette and Stanley L. Engerman (Gainesville; University Press of Florida, 1996), p. 228; Andrews, *Journal of a Lady of Quality*, pp. 136–37.

18. Jennings, "The Case of an English Subject at the Capture of Saint Eustatius," Sydney Papers, vol. 12, f. 14, WLCL; speech of Edmund Burke, 14 May, 1781, *St. James's Chronicle*, May 12–14, 1781; James Ramsay to Germain, March 31, 1781, Germain Papers, vol. 14 (unfoliated), WLCL.

19. Jennings, "Case of an English Subject at the Capture of Saint Eustatius," Sydney Papers, vol. 11, f. 14, WLCL; speech of Edmund Burke, May 14, 1781, *St. James's Chronicle*, May 12–14, 1781.

20. *The New Annual Register, a General Repository of History, Politics and Literature, for the Year 1782* (London: G. Robinson, 1783), p. 29.

21. Spinney, *Rodney*, p. 369; Hurst, *The Golden Rock*, p. 26; Rodney to Stephens, February 12, 1781, Adm 1/314, ff. 48–49, PRO; Vaughan to Howe, October 17, 1777, CO/5/94, PRO; "Copy of a Letter from Admiral Rodney to the Marquis de Bouillé," *Maryland Gazette*, May 31, 1781.

22. Rodney to Stephens, March 9, 1781 quoted in *General Advertiser*, July 4, 1786; Rodney and Vaughan to Germain, June 25, 1781, CO 28/58, PRO; Rodney to Lady Rodney, April 23, 1781, in G. B. Mundy, *Life and Correspondence of the Late Admiral Lord Rodney*, 2 vols. (London: J. Murray, 1830), 2:97; Rodney to Stephens, June 29, 1781, Adm 1/314, f. 214, PRO.

23. Rodney to Stephens, March 6, 1781, Adm 1/314, PRO; Rodney to Stephens, March 17, 1781, Adm 1/314, f. 61, PRO.

24. General Howe to Admiral James Young, 30 January, 1776, Adm 1/309, f. 415, PRO; Sir Henry Calder to Germain, St. Lucia, September 19, 1779, CO 318/7, PRO; "Petition of the West India Merchants and Planters to the King," April 6, 1781, Shelburne Papers, vol. 79, f. 173, WLCL; Anon., *A Speech which was Spoken in the House of Assembly of St. Christopher Upon a motion made on Tuesday the 6th of November, 1781, For Presenting An Address to His Majesty, Relative to The Proceedings of Admiral Rodney and General Vaughan at St. Eustatius And the Present Dangerous Situation of The West India Islands* (London: J. Debrett, 1782), p. 28; Jennings, "Case of an English Subject at the Capture of Saint Eustatius," Sydney Papers, vol. 12, f. 5, WLCL; H. M. Scott, *British Foreign Policy in the Age of the American Revolution* (Oxford: Clarendon Press, 1990), p. 287.

25. Vaughan and Rodney to Germain, July 3, 1781, CO 318/7, PRO; Spinney, *Rodney,* pp. 375, 377; Hurst, *The Golden Rock,* p. 137; "Orders given by Sir George Bridges Rodney to his Agents," July 31, 1781, Sydney Papers, vol. 9 (unfoliated), WLCL; Anon., *A Speech which was Spoken in the House of the Assembly of St. Christopher,* p. 25.

26. Armstrong Starkey, "War and Culture, a Case Study: The Enlightenment and the Conduct of the British Army in America, 1755–1781," *War and Society* 8 (May 1990): 8–9.

27. Eliga H. Gould, "Zones of Laws, Zones of Violence: The Legal Geography of the British Atlantic, circa 1772," *William and Mary Quarterly,* 3d ser., 60, no. 3 (July 2003): 474–75, 476, 479, 483, 486, 489–90, 496, 497, 507.

28. Speech of Edmund Burke, 14 May, 1781, *St. James's Chronicle,* May 12–14, 1781; Anon., *A Speech which was Spoken in the House of Assembly of St. Christopher,* p. 16; Richard Neave to Germain, April 26, 1781, Germain Papers, vol. 14 (unfoliated), WLCL; Germain to Vaughan, March 30, 1781, CO 318/8, PRO.

29. Spinney, *Rodney,* pp. 268, 274, 278, 284–85, 286, 287, 290; Christopher Lloyd, "Sir George Rodney: Lucky Admiral," in *George Washington's Generals and Opponents: Their Exploits and Leadership,* ed. George Athan Billias, 2 vols. in 1 (1964, 1969; repr. New York: Da Capo Press, 1994), 2:332; Flanders, *Memoirs of Richard Cumberland,* p. 207.

30. See Spinney, *Rodney,* pp. 20–21 for childhood and father; for gambling, ibid., pp. 111, 225, 239, 273, for lavish lifestyle, ibid., p. 219; for Northampton election, ibid., p. 236; for loans and financial decline, ibid., pp. 217, 238, 240, 241, 246, 249, 264, 266.

31. Hood to Jackson, May 21, 1781, quoted in W. M. James, *The British Navy in Adversity: A Study of the War of American Independence* (London; Longmans, Green, 1926), p. 257; Hood to Jackson, June 24, 1781, Hannay, *Letters Written by Sir Samuel Hood,* p. 18; N. A. M. Rodger, *The Wooden World: Anatomy of the Georgian Navy* (London: Fontana Press, 1990), p. 323; David Syrett, *The Royal Navy in American Waters 1775–1783* (Aldershot: Scolar Press, 1989), p. 154; John A. Tilley, *The British Navy and the American Revolution* (Columbia: University of South Carolina Press, 1987), p. 201; Spinney, *Rodney,* pp. 129, 215, 216, 367.

32. Rodney to Lady Rodney, 23 April, 1781, in Mundy, *Life and Correspondence of the Late Admiral Lord Rodney,* 2:100; Rodney to Lady Rodney, March 18, 1781, Greenwich 35 MS 0292, quoted in Spinney, *Rodney,* p. 367; Rodney to George Rodney, February 6, 1781, Rodney Papers (Belsize Park) quoted in Spinney, *Rodney,* 380; Donald G. F. W. MacIntyre, *Admiral Rodney* (London: Peter Davies, 1962), p. 16; Hood to Jackson, June 24, 1781, Hannay, *Letters Written by Sir Samuel Hood,* p. 18.

33. Jennings, "Case of an English Subject at the Capture of Saint Eustatius," Sydney Papers, vol. 12, f. 20, WLCL; ibid., ff. 15, 20, 17; speech of Edmund Burke, December 4, 1781, *St. James's Chronicle,* December 4–6, 1781; *The Annual Register* (1783), p. 26; Spinney, *Rodney,* p. 368.

34. Byron to Stephens, August 3, 1779, Adm 1/312, f. 111, PRO; Aretas Akers to Charles Lyell, July 27, 1779, Adm 1/312, f. 115, PRO; Richard Downing Jennings, "Account of the proceedings of Lord Rodney and General Vaughan at St. Eustatius," April 9, 1789, Sydney Papers, vol. 15 (unfoliated), WLCL; James Ramsay to Vaughan, June 26, 1780, CO 318/6, f. 169, PRO, acknowledges help of Akers in procuring information; Akers to Rodney, December 28, 1780, January 19, 1781, January 31, 1781, 30/20/261, ff. 9, 14–15, 17, PRO; Capt. W. Young to Sir Charles Middleton, December 26, 1780, *Letters and Papers of Charles, Lord Barham, Admiral of the Red Squadron, 1758–1813,* ed. Sir J. K. Laughton, 3 vols. (London; Navy Records Society, 1906–10), 1:86.

35. Spinney, *Rodney,* pp. 121, 266–67, 275; Rodger, *The Insatiable Earl,* p. 196.

36. *The Annual Register* (1783), p. 27; Tilley, *The British Navy and the American Revolution*, p. 201; Syrett, *The Royal Navy in American Waters*, pp. 154–55; Tuchman, *The First Salute*, p. 172.

37. Spinney, *Rodney*, pp. 141, 201–2, 206, 255. Ibid., p. 201, David Spinney defends Rodney against what he calls myths and legends that treat the admiral as "a self-centered and rapacious careerist."

38. Spinney, *Rodney*, pp. 346, 347, 349; Rodger, *The Insatiable Earl*, pp. 284–88; Syrett, *The Royal Navy in American Waters*, pp. 152–59; Tilley, *The British Navy and the American Revolution*, p. 198; Arbuthnot to Germain, December 19, 1780, Historical Manuscripts Commission, *Report on the Manuscripts of Mrs. Stopford-Sackville of Drayton House, Northamptonshire*, 2 vols. (London: H.M. Stationery Office, 1910), 2:190.

39. Hurst, *The Golden Rock*, p. 143; Revd. James Ramsay to Germain, March 1, 1781, Germain Papers, vol. 14 (unfoliated), WLCL; Jennings, "Case of an English Subject at the Capture of Saint Eustatius," Sydney Papers, vol. 12, f. 14, WLCL; Rodney to Vaughan, February 6, 1781, Vaughan Papers, vol. 3, f. 21, WLCL; James Ramsay to Germain, March 11781, Germain Papers, vol. 14 (unfoliated), WLCL; "The Most Humble Address of the Wardens and Elders of the Hebrew Congregation to His Excellency the Hon. John Vaughan, Major General and Commander in Chief of His Majesty's Army in the Leeward Islands," CO 28/58, PRO; Rodney to Stephens, February 8, 1772, Adm 1/238, PRO; Rodney to Stephens, March 12, 1774, Adm 1/239, PRO; *Westminster Journal* April 18, 1772; Hurst, *The Golden Rock*, p. 143; Stephen Alexander Fortune, *Merchants and Jews: The Struggle for British West Indian Commerce, 1650–1750* (Gainesville: University Press of Florida, 1984), pp. 104, 126, 139, 145.

40. Revd. James Ramsay to Germain, March 1, 1781, Germain Papers, vol. 14 (unfoliated), WLCL. Rodney has never received from historians such uncritical veneration as Nelson: Lloyd, "Sir George Rodney: Lucky Admiral," p. 327, referred to his "rapacity for prize money" which "robbed his victories of their full military impact." Rodger, *The Insatiable Earl*, p. 176, has argued that the navy was relatively free of the insidious effects of corruption and patronage with the major exception of Rodney, who "never displayed that reliability and trustworthiness" so necessary to "a senior officer's position," often attributing "to others those qualities of avarice and malice which independent observers thought characteristic of him." Syrett, *The Royal Navy in American Waters*, p. 154, writes, "Rodney had a long history, known throughout the service, for usurping authority and grasping every penny that came near him." David Spinney, although intent upon clearing the name of the admiral "whose case has gone by default," admits in regard to St. Eustatius that "Sir George's action, emotional and vindictive, cannot be defended." See also Rodger, *Wooden World*, pp. 124, 323, 324, 325, 338, 339; on Rodney's nepotism, Spinney, *Rodney*, pp. 250, 251, 274, 354, 380, 407; on his financial malfeasance, ibid., pp. 266, 267, 275.

41. Ramsay to Germain, March 15, 1781, Germain Papers, vol. 14 (unfoliated), WLCL; *Pennsylvania Journal*, August 4, 1781; petition of the West India Planters and Merchants to the king, April 6, 1781, Shelburne Papers, vol. 79, f. 173, WLCL; Richard Neave, chairman of the society, to Germain, April 26, 1781, Germain Papers, vol. 14 (unfoliated), WLCL; *Pennsylvania Journal*, December 22, 1781. The petition does not appear in the minutes of the West India Merchants, but it was printed in the *London Chronicle*, April 12–14, 1781, and *Lloyd's Evening Post*, April 13–15, 1781.

42. Ian R. Christie, *The End of North's Ministry, 1780–1782* (London: Macmillan, 1958), p. 261; *The Last Journals of Horace Walpole During the Reign of George III*, ed. A. Francis Steuart, 2 vols. (London: John Lane, 1910), 1:362; *The Annual Register* (1783), pp. 24–30.

43. *The Annual Register* (1783), pp. 68–69.

44. *The Historical and Posthumous Memoirs of Sir Nathaniel William Wraxall 1772–1784*, ed. Henry B. Wheatley, 5 vols. (1836; repr. London: Bickers & Son, 1884), 2:115, 116, 166; Steuart, *The Last Journals of Horace Walpole*, 2:385.

45. Spinney, *Rodney,* pp. 420–21, 423, 426; Hurst, *The Golden Rock,* p. 139; Jennings, "Case of an English Subject at the Capture of Saint Eustatius," Sydney Papers, vol. 12, f. 22, WLCL; Breen, "Sir George Rodney and St. Eustatius in the American War," pp. 200–202.

46. Spinney, *Rodney,* p. 420; Jennings, "Case of an English Subject at the Capture of Saint Eustatius," Sydney Papers, vol. 12, ff. 15, 19, WLCL; Margaret Marion Spector, *The American Department of the British Government, 1768–1782* (New York: Columbia University Press, 1940), p. 129; Augur, *The Secret War of Independence,* pp. 324–25.

47. Affidavit of Major Nichols, March 24, 1786, quoted in the *General Advertiser,* 4 July, 1786; Spinney, *Rodney,* 383; "Account of the controversy over Rodney's actions in the St. Eustatius Affair," *General Advertiser,* 4 July, 1786, copy in the Sydney Papers, vol. 13 (unfoliated), WLCL. There was testimony accusing Arthur Savage, an American loyalist employed in the American Department, of selling the papers to one of the British merchants in St. Eustatius, Richard Downing Jennings. However, Rodney made no use of the documents in his possession. Indeed, Savage admitted returning the papers of Jennings because they contained nothing that incriminated their owner. See Hurst, *The Golden Rock,* p 229; declaration of Arthur Savage concerning St. Eustatius, July 1786, Sydney Papers, vol. 13 (unfoliated), WLCL.

48. *General Advertiser,* 4 July, 1786, copy in the Sydney Papers, vol. 13 (unfoliated), WLCL; Buel, *In Irons,* pp. 44, 190. The fall of St. Eustatius was in reality due to a classic coup de main that became a popular example in military manuals: Robert Selig, "The French Capture of St. Eustatius, 26 November, 1781," *Journal of Caribbean History* 27, no. 2 (1993): 129–43.

49. Banastre Tarleton, *A History of the Campaigns of 1780 and 1781 in the Southern Provinces of North America*(1787; repr. Cranbury, N.J.: The Scholar's Bookshelf, 2005), pp. 363–64; Anon., *A Speech which was Spoken in the House of Assembly of St. Christopher,* p. 11; Spinney, *Rodney,* pp. 362–63.

50. Hood to George Jackson, May 21, 1781, Hannay, *Letters Written by Sir Samuel Hood,* pp. 13–15.

51. Spinney, *Rodney,* pp. 339, 368.

52. Harold A. Larrabee, *Decision at the Chesapeake* (New York: Clarkson N. Potter, 1964), pp. 255–56, 272–73.

53. Germain to Vaughan, 4 April, 1781, July 4, 1781, CO 318/8, PRO; Germain to Clinton, August 2, 1781, CO 5/102; Tilley, *The British Navy and the American Revolution,* p. 243; Rodney to Philip Stephens, June 29, 1781, *Letters from Sir George Brydges now Lord Rodney, To His Majesty's Ministers, &c. &c. Relative to the Capture of St. Eustatius, And Its Dependencies; And Shewing the State of the War in the West-Indies, at that Period* (London: A. Grant, 1789), pp. 81–82.

54. Spinney, *Rodney,* pp. 381–82; *Public Advertiser,* 24 September 1781, quoted in Breen, "Sir George Rodney and St. Eustatius in the American War," p. 201.

55. William B. Willcox, *Portrait of a General: Sir Henry Clinton in the War of Independence* (New York: Knopf, 1964), p. 447.

56. Ibid., pp. 410–11, 412; *Historical Memoirs of William Smith 1778–1783,* ed. W. H. W. Sabine, 2 vols. (New York: New York Times, 1971), 2:452.

57. Jonathan R. Dull, *The French Navy and American Independence: A Study of Arms and Diplomacy, 1774–1787* (Princeton, N.J.: Princeton University Press, 1975), p. 243.

58. Sam Willis, *Fighting at Sea in the Eighteenth Century: The Art of Sailing Warfare* (Woodbridge: Boydell Press, 2008), pp. 59, 71, 101.

59. Syrett, *The Royal Navy in American Waters,* p. 269.

60. *Correspondence of General Washington and Comte De Grasse,* ed. Institut français de Washington (Washington, D.C.: U.S. Government Printing Office, 1931), pp. 37, 46, 47, 58, 76, 121, 130–31, 138; *St. James's Chronicle,* January 3–5, 1782; "Extract of a letter from a clergyman in the Island of Jamaica," May 13, 1782, *London Chronicle,* August 6–8, 1782; *Morning Herald,* August 7, 1782.

61. Debate on the resolution moved by General Conway against the further prosecution of offensive warfare on the continent of North America, February 27, 1782, *Parliamentary History of England from the Earliest Period to 1803,* ed. William Cobbett and Thomas Hansard, 36 vols. (London: Hansard, 1806–20), 22:cols. 1096, 1110; *Catalogue of Political and Personal Satires Preserved in the Department of Prints and Drawings in the British Museum 1771–1783,* ed. Dorothy M. George, vol. 5 (London: British Museum, 1935), nos. 5961 and 5986.

62. Daniel Baugh, "Why Did Britain Lose Command of the Sea?" in *The British Navy and the Use of Naval Power in the Eighteenth Century,* ed. Jeremy Black and Philip Woodfine (Leicester: Leicester University Press, 1988), p. 152; Wheatley, *The Historical and Posthumous Memoirs of Sir Nathaniel William Wraxall,* 2:326.

63. Flanders, *Memoirs of Richard Cumberland,* p. 207; Willis, *Fighting at Sea in the Eighteenth Century,* pp. 130–31.

64. Willis, *Fighting at Sea in the Eighteenth Century,* pp. 208–9.

65. Flanders, *Memoirs of Richard Cumberland,* p. 208.

66. Stephen Conway, "'A Joy Unknown for Years Past': The American War, Britishness and the Celebration of Rodney's Victory at the Saints," *History* 86, no. 282 (April 2001): 187, 189, 190, 197, 198; Troy Bickham, *Making Headlines: The American Revolution as Seen through the British Press* (DeKalb: Northern Illinois University Press, 2009), pp. 164–67.

67. *Journals of the Assembly of Jamaica,* vol. 8 (1805), pp. 565, 567; Maya Jasanoff, *Liberty's Exiles: American Loyalists in the Revolutionary World* (New York: Knopf, 2011), p. 252.

68. Wheatley, *The Historical and Posthumous Memoirs of Sir Nathaniel William Wraxall,* 2:319, 320, 321.

69. Ibid., pp. 328, 337; Edmund Burke to Lord Rodney, July 1782, PRO 30/21/6, f. 73, PRO; *The Parliamentary Register* (London, 1782), v., 92 quoted in Lloyd, "Sir George Rodney: Lucky Admiral," p. 343; *Morning Herald and Daily Advertiser,* November 6, 1783; Willcox, *Portrait of a General,* p. 461.

70. Reginald Lucas, *Lord North, 1732–1792,* 2 vols. (London: Arthur L. Humphreys, 1913) 1:381; Wheatley, *The Historical and Posthumous Memoirs of Sir Nathaniel William Wraxall,* 2:335, 332.

71. Conway, "'A Joy Unknown for Years Past,'" p. 183; Spinney, *Rodney,* pp. 414–15.

72. Spinney, *Rodney,* pp. 416, 418–19, 425, 427.

73. Ibid., pp. 416–17, 420–21.

74. Ibid., pp. 422–23, 424.

75. Ibid., pp. 424, 425.

Chapter 9. "Jemmy Twitcher"

1. George Martelli, *Jemmy Twitcher* (London: Jonathan Cape, 1962), pp. 58, 44–49; Evelyn Lord, *The Hell-Fire Clubs: Sex, Satanism, and Secret Societies* (New Haven, Conn.: Yale University Press, 2008), pp. 93, 97–103.

2. Martelli, *Jemmy Twitcher,* pp. 48, 55; N. A. M. Rodger, *The Insatiable Earl: A Life of John Montagu, Fourth Earl of Sandwich* (New York: Norton, 1993), pp. 83, 98.

3. Lord, *The Hell-Fire Clubs,* pp. 117–21; Martelli, *Jemmy Twitcher,* p. 63.

4. Rodger, *The Insatiable Earl,* pp. 103, 104; Martelli, *Jemmy Twitcher,* pp. 56, 63–64, 66.

5. Martelli, *Jemmy Twitcher,* pp. 23, 25, 39, 85–86; *The Historical and Posthumous Memoirs of Sir Nathaniel William Wraxall 1772–1784,* ed. Henry B. Wheatley, 5 vols. (1836; repr. London: Bickers & Son, 1884), 1:398–99; Rodger, *The Insatiable Earl,* pp. 71, 85, 86, 117.

6. Martin Levy, *Love and Madness: The Murder of Martha Ray, Mistress of the Fourth Earl of Sandwich* (New York: HarperCollins. 2004), p. 18; Martelli, *Jemmy Twitcher,* pp. 23, 43–44, 86.

7. Rodger, *The Insatiable Earl,* p. 2; Martelli, *Jemmy Twitcher,* p. 84; Levy, *Love and Madness,* p. 27.

8. James M. Haas, "The Pursuit of Political Success in Eighteenth-Century England: Sandwich, 1740–71," *Bulletin of the Institute of Historical Research* 43 (May 1970): 58; Rodger, *The Insatiable Earl,* pp. 1, 71.

9. Levy, *Love and Madness,* p. 2; John Brewer, *A Sentimental Murder: Love and Madness in the Eighteenth Century* (New York: Farrar, Straus and Giroux, 2004), p. 119.

10. Haas, "The Pursuit of Political Success in Eighteenth-Century England: Sandwich," pp. 56–57; Wheatley, *The Historical and Posthumous Memoirs of Sir Nathaniel William Wraxall,* 1:398–99; Clive Wilkinson, *The British Navy and the State in the Eighteenth Century* (Woodbridge: Boydell Press, 2004), p. 15.

11. Martelli, *Jemmy Twitcher,* p. 22; Rodger, *The Insatiable Earl,* pp. 4–6.

12. Rodger, *The Insatiable Earl,* pp. 19, 20, 216; H. M. Scott, *British Foreign Policy in the Age of the American Revolution* (Oxford: Oxford University Press, 1990), p. 54.

13. Rodger, *The Insatiable Earl,* pp. 75, 131, 173, 174.

14. N. A. M. Rodger, *The Wooden World: Anatomy of the Georgian Navy* (London: Fontana Press, 1990), p. 331; Rodger, *The Insatiable Earl,* p. 132.

15. Rodger, *The Insatiable Earl,* pp. 17, 18; Martelli, *Jemmy Twitcher,* pp. 33, 278.

16. Wilkinson, *The British Navy and the State in the Eighteenth Century,* p. 168; Nicholas Tracy, *Navies, Deterrence, and American Independence: Britain and Seapower in the 1760s and 1770s* (Vancouver: University of British Columbia Press, 1988), p. 34.

17. Celina Fox, "George III and the Royal Navy," in *The Wisdom of George the Third,* ed. Jonathan Marsden (London: Royal Collection Publications, 2004), pp. 293, 303, 305.

18. Tracy, *Navies, Deterrence, and American Independence,* p. 31.

19. Brendan Simms, *Three Victories and a Defeat: The Rise and Fall of the First British Empire, 1714–1783* (New York: Basic Books, 2007), pp. 349, 351, 373; "To William Franklin: Journal of Negotiations in London," March 22, 1775, in *The Papers of Benjamin Franklin,* ed. Leonard W. Labaree, William B. Willcox, Barbara Oberg, and Ellen R. Cohn, 39 vols. (New Haven, Conn.: Yale University Press, 1959–), 21:581.

20. P. D. G. Thomas, *Tea Party to Independence: The Third Phase of the American Revolution 1773–1776* (Oxford: Clarendon Press, 1991), pp. 16, 210; Rodger, *The Insatiable Earl,* p. 217; David Syrett, *Shipping and the American War 1775–83: A Study of British Transport Organisation* (London: Athlone Press, 1970), p. 123.

21. *The Annual Register,* in *Rebellion in America: A Contemporary British Viewpoint, 1769–1783,* ed. David H. Murdoch (Santa Barbara, Calif.: Clio Books, 1979), pp. 175, 211; Frank Arthur Mumby, *George III and the American Revolution: The Beginnings* (London: Constable, 1924), p. 384; N. A. M. Rodger, *The Command of the Ocean: A Naval History of Britain, 1649–1815* (New York: Norton, 2004), p. 330; Neil Stout, *The Perfect Crisis: The Beginning of the Revolutionary War* (New York: New York

University Press, 1976), p. 177; *The Parliamentary History of England from the Earliest Period to 1803*, ed. William Cobbett and Thomas Hansard, 36 vols. (London: Hansard, 1806–22), 18:cols. 436–46; Philip Davidson, *Propaganda and the American Revolution 1763–1783* (Chapel Hill: University of North Carolina Press, 1941), p. 192.

22. P. D. G. Thomas, *Lord North* (London: Allen Lane, 1976), pp. 94, 96; Charles R. Ritcheson, *British Politics and the American Revolution* (Norman: University of Oklahoma Press, 1954), p. 174; Rodger, *The Insatiable Earl*, pp. 150–52, 232–33; John A. Tilley, *The British Navy and the American Revolution* (Columbia: University of South Carolina Press, 1987), p. 31; Tracy, *Navies, Deterrence, and American Independence*, p. 119; Daniel A. Baugh, "Why Did Britain Lose Command of the Sea During the War for America?" in *The British Navy and the Use of Naval Power in the Eighteenth Century*, ed. Jeremy Black and Philip Woodfine (Leicester: Leicester University Press, 1988), pp. 155–56.

23. Rodger, *The Insatiable Earl*, p. 232, 233; Scott, *British Foreign Policy in the Age of the American Revolution*, p. 235; Tracy, *Navies, Deterrence, and American Independence*, p. 137; Ritcheson, *British Politics and the American Revolution*, p. 175; David Syrett, "The Failure of the British Effort in America, 1777," in Black and Woodfine, *The British Navy and the Use of Naval Power in the Eighteenth Century*, p. 173; David Syrett, *The Royal Navy in European Waters During the American Revolutionary War* (Columbia: University of South Carolina Press, 1998), pp. 14–15, 64; Tilley, *The British Navy and the American Revolution*, p. 79; Martelli, *Jemmy Twitcher*, p. 110; Jessica Warner, *John the Painter: The First Modern Terrorist* (London: Profile Books, 2005).

24. Martelli, *Jemmy Twitcher*, p. 183.

25. Wilkinson, *The British Navy and the State in the Eighteenth Century*, pp. 70, 75, 181, 193; Rodger, *The Command of the Sea*, p. 371.

26. Wilkinson, *The British Navy and the State in the Eighteenth Century*, pp. 95, 192, 193; Rodger, *The Command of the Sea*, p. 369, 370.

27. Rodger, *The Insatiable Earl*, pp. 148–49.

28. Rodger, *The Command of the Ocean*, pp. 334, 394, 396, 398, 399, 400; Syrett, *The Royal Navy in European Waters*, p. 66; Paul David Nelson, *General James Grant: Scottish Soldier and Royal Governor of East Florida* (Gainesville: University Press of Florida, 1993), p. 143; *The Lost War: Letters from British Officers During the American Revolution*, ed. Marion Balderston and David Syrett (New York: Horizon Press, 1975), p. 14.

29. Daniel A. Baugh questions the view that Britain had naval supremacy in America before 1778 in "The Politics of British Naval Failure, 1775–1777," *American Neptune* 52 (1992): 221–46.

30. *The Annual Register*, in Murdoch, *Rebellion in America*, p. 340; Neil Stout, *The Perfect Crisis*, p. 89 says that Graves had only nineteen ships in 1774; Tilley, *The British Navy and the American Revolution*, p. 12; David Syrett, "The Failure of the British Effort in America," p. 174; William B. Willcox, "Arbuthnot, Gambier and Graves: 'Old Women' of the Navy," in *George Washington's Generals and Opponents: Their Exploits and Leadership*, ed. George Athan Billias, 2 vols. in 1 (1964, 1969; repr. New York: Da Capo Press, 1994), 2:263; Baugh, "The Politics of British Naval Failure," pp. 225–26, 227, 229.

31. Baugh, "The Politics of British Naval Failure," pp. 233, 234, 236, 240; Robert Greenhalgh Albion, *Forests and Sea Power: The Timber Problem and the Royal Navy, 1652–1862* (1926; repr. Annapolis, Md.: Naval Institute Press, 2000), pp. 300–301.

32. David L. Preston, "The Royal Navy Lost the Revolution," *Naval History* 10, no. 1 (January/February 1996): 13.

33. David Syrett, "The Organization of British Trade Convoys During the American War 1775–1783," *Mariner's Mirror* 62 (1976): 170, 171, 178; *The Annual Register,* in Murdoch, *Rebellion in America,* p. 522.

34. Rodger, *The Insatiable Earl,* pp. 232, 271, 273; Piers Mackesy, *The War for America 1775–1783* (1964; repr. Lincoln: University of Nebraska Press, 1993), pp. 192, 193, 194; Tilley, *The British Navy and the American Revolution,* p. 199.

35. Syrett, *The Royal Navy in European Waters,* p. 3.

36. Sandwich sent two slightly different versions to North dated December 7 and 8, 1777. "A Paper sent to Lord North on 8 December relative to the American war and urging more efforts to be made at home," *The Private Papers of John, Earl of Sandwich, First Lord of the Admiralty 1771–1782,* ed. G. R. Barnes and J. H. Owen, 4 vols. (London: Navy Records Society, 1932–38), 1:327–35.

37. Willcox, "Arbuthnot, Gambier and Graves," in Billias, *George Washington's Generals and Opponents,* p. 285.

38. Simms, *Three Victories and a Defeat,* pp. 574, 629.

39. Mackesy, *The War for America,* pp. 155, 182, 251; Ritcheson, *British Politics and the American Revolution.* p. 256; Gerald S. Brown, "The Anglo-French Naval Crisis: A Study of Conflict in the North Cabinet," *William and Mary Quarterly,* 3d ser., 13, no. 1 (January 1956): 19.

40. Stephen Conway, *The War of American Independence 1775–1783* (London: Edward Arnold, 1995), pp. 223–24; Tilley, *The British Navy and the American Revolution,* p. 128.

41. Martelli, *Jemmy Twitcher,* p. 126; Syrett, *The Royal Navy in European Waters,* p. 24; Ritcheson, *British Politics and the American Revolution,* p. 246; J. H. Broomfield, "The Keppel-Palliser Affair 1778–1779," *Mariner's Mirror* 47, no. 3 (August 1961): 197.

42. Keppel to Sandwich, June 21, 1778, Barnes and Owen, *Sandwich Papers,* 2:98; Albion, *Forests and Sea Power,* pp. 295, 296.

43. Broomfield, "The Keppel-Palliser Affair," pp. 196–97; George III to North, February 13, 1779, *The Correspondence of King George the Third from 1760 to December 1783,* ed. Sir John Fortescue, 6 vols. (London: Macmillan, 1927–28), 4:277–78.

44. Broomfield, "The Keppel-Palliser Affair," pp. 200–202: *The Last Journals of Horace Walpole During the Reign of George III,* ed. A. F. Steuart, 2 vols. (London: John Lane, 1910), 2:222.

45. Troy Bickham, *Making Headlines: The American Revolution as Seen through the British Press* (DeKalb: Northern Illinois University Press, 2009), p. 131.

46. Broomfield, "The Keppel-Palliser Affair," p. 203; Bickham, *Making Headlines,* p. 131.

47. Bickham, *Making Headlines,* p. 131; Steuart, *The Last Journals of Horace Walpole,* pp. 247–48; Broomfield, "The Keppel-Palliser Affair," p. 204–05.

48. Steuart, *The Last Journals of Horace Walpole,* pp. 247–48; Martelli, *Jemmy Twitcher,* pp. 158–59; Syrett, *The Royal Navy in European Waters,* pp. 55–57; Levy, *Love and Madness,* pp. 1–2.

49. Steuart, *The Last Journals of Horace Walpole,* p. 256; Mary Kinnear, "Pro-Americans in the British House of Commons in the 1770s" (Ph.D. diss., University of Oregon, 1973), p. 262.

50. Levy, *Love and Madness,* pp. 29, 30; Brewer, *A Sentimental Murder,* pp. 23, 215; Martelli, *Jemmy Twitcher,* pp. 87–88.

51. Wheatley, *The Historical and Posthumous Memoirs of Sir Nathaniel William Wraxall,* 1:226; J. H. Broomfield, "Lord Sandwich at the Admiralty Board; Politics and the British Navy, 1771–1778," *Mariner's Mirror* 51, no. 1 (February 1965): 14; Syrett, *The Royal Navy in European Waters,* p. 57; Wilkinson, *The British Navy and the State in the Eighteenth Century,* p. 203; Martelli, *Jemmy Twitcher,* pp. 181, 182–83.

52. "Memorandum. Paper Read in the Cabinet by Lord Sandwich, Delivered to the King and Communicated to Lord North—Sept 14, 1779," Barnes and Owen, *Sandwich Papers,* 3:170–71; How-

ard H. Peckham, "Marquis de Lafayette: Eager Warrior," in Billias, *George Washington's Generals and Opponents,* 1:224.

53. Syrett, *The Royal Navy in European Waters,* pp. 68–71.

54. "Memorandum. Paper Read in the Cabinet by Lord Sandwich, Delivered to the King and Communicated to Lord North—Sept 14, 1779," Barnes and Owen, *Sandwich Papers,* 3:167; Arbuthnot to Sandwich, September 19, 1779, ibid., 3:134; Mackesy, *The War for America,* p. 278; Jonathan R. Dull, *The French Navy and American Independence: A Study of Arms and Diplomacy, 1774–1787* (Princeton, N.J.: Princeton University Press, 1975), pp. 160, 162.

55. Rodger, *The Insatiable Earl,* p. 253; K. R. Perry, *British Politics and the American Revolution* (London: Palgrave Macmillan, 1990), p. 89; Mackesy, *The War for America,* p. 341; Tilley, *The British Navy and the American Revolution,* p. 231; Kenneth Breen, "Graves and Hood at the Chesapeake," *The Mariner's Mirror,* 56 (1980), p. 55.

56. North to Sandwich, April 30, 1778, Barnes and Owen, *Sandwich Papers,* 2:39; Willcox, "Arbuthnot, Gambier and Graves," in Billias, *George Washington's Generals and Opponents,* pp. 265–66.

57. Ira D. Gruber, *The Howe Brothers and the American Revolution* (Chapel Hill: University of North Carolina Press, 1972), p. 86; Willcox, "Arbuthnot, Gambier and Graves," pp. 268, 269, 270.

58. William B. Willcox, *Portrait of a General: Sir Henry Clinton in the War of Independence* (New York: Knopf, 1964), p. 355; Leland J. Bellot, *William Knox: The Life and Thought of an Eighteenth-Century Imperialist* (Austin: University of Texas Press, 1977), pp. 150, 162.

59. Conway, *The War of American Independence,* p. 157; Stephen Conway, "British Governments and the Conduct of the American War," in *Britain and the American Revolution,* ed. H. T. Dickinson (London: Addison Wesley Longman, 1979), p. 167.

60. David Syrett, *Shipping and the American War 1775–83: A Study of British Transport Organisation* (London: Athlone Press, 1970), pp. 89, 161; Norman Baker, *Government and Contractors: The British Treasury and War Supplies 1775–1783* (London: Athlone Press, 1971), p. 91; "Memorandum. Paper Read in the Cabinet by Lord Sandwich, Delivered to the King and Communicated to Lord North—Sept 14, 1779," Barnes and Owen, *Sandwich Papers,* 3:165, 171.

61. George III to Sandwich, September 13, 1779, Fortescue, *The Correspondence of King George the Third,* 4:432–34.

62. I. R. Christie, *Myth and Reality in Late-Eighteenth-Century British Politics and Other Papers* (London: Macmillan, 1970), p. 83; British Library, Add. MSS 70990, ff. 32, 14, September 1779, in Rodger, *The Command of the Ocean,* p. 340; Rodger, *The Insatiable Earl,* p. 219; Martelli, *Jemmy Twitcher,* p. 210.

63. Steuart, *The Last Journals of Horace Walpole,* 2:309; Wheatley, *The Historical and Posthumous Memoirs of Sir Nathaniel William Wraxall,* 1:261.

64. Martelli, *Jemmy Twitcher,* p. 231; Syrett, *The Royal Navy in European Waters,* p. 136.

65. Broomfield, "Lord Sandwich at the Admiralty Board," pp. 7–17; Syrett, *The Royal Navy in European Waters,* p. 51; Martelli, *Jemmy Twitcher,* p. 235; Mackesy, *The War for America,* pp. 10, 19; Wheatley, *The Historical and Posthumous Memoirs of Sir Nathaniel William Wraxall,* 1:403, 404; Haas, "The Pursuit of Political Success in Eighteenth-Century England: Sandwich," pp. 76–77.

66. Broomfield, "Lord Sandwich at the Admiralty Board," pp. 8, 9; Wheatley, *The Historical and Posthumous Memoirs of Sir Nathaniel William Wraxall,* 1:268; Ian R. Christie, *The End of North's Ministry, 1780–1782* (London: Macmillan, 1958), p. 62.

67. Jeremy Black, *War for America: The Fight for Independence 1775–1783* (New York: St. Martin's Press, 1994), p. 204.

68. Rodger, *The Insatiable Earl*, p. 292.

69. Tracy, *Navies, Deterrence, and American Independence*, p. 14; Martelli, *Jemmy Twitcher*, p. 258.

70. Christie, *The End of North's Ministry*, pp. 285–86.

71. Ibid., p. 2; Mackesy, *The War for America*, pp. 451, 452; Steuart, *The Last Journals of Horace Walpole*, 2:381, 382.

72. Christie, *The End of North's Ministry*, pp. 304–13.

73. Ibid., pp. 313–19; *The Annual Register* in Murdoch, *Rebellion in America*, p. 919; Steuart, *The Last Journals of Horace Walpole*, 2:391; Wheatley, *The Historical and Posthumous Memoirs of Sir Nathaniel William Wraxall*, 1:271, 281, 2:171, 182, 184, 186, 187.

74. Wheatley, *The Historical and Posthumous Memoirs of Sir Nathaniel William Wraxall*, pp. 304, 328.

75. Baugh, "Why Did Britain Lose Command of the Sea?" p. 153; Tracy, *Navies, Deterrence, and American Independence*, pp. 34, 36; Conway, *The War of American Independence*, pp. 230–31; Syrett, *The Royal Navy in European Waters*, pp. 64–65; Tilley, *The British Navy and the American Revolution*, p. 135.

76. Rodger, *The Command of the Ocean*, pp. 374–75; Syrett, *The Royal Navy in European Waters*, pp. 62–63; Rodger, *The Insatiable Earl*, pp. 296, 298.

77. Syrett, *The Royal Navy in European Waters*, p. 153.

78. Richard Buel Jr., *In Irons: Britain's Naval Supremacy and the American Revolutionary Economy* (New Haven, Conn.: Yale University Press, 1998), pp. 33, 41, 45, 107, 113.

79. Rodger, *The Command of the Ocean*, p. 328; Martelli, *Jemmy Twitcher*, pp. 86–87, 92–93; Rodger, *The Insatiable Earl*, pp. 204, 205, 206, 208, 209.

80. Martelli, *Jemmy Twitcher*, pp. 282–83.

81. Rodger, *The Insatiable Earl*, pp. 310, 313, 314; Levy, *Love and Madness*, p. 142.

82. Brewer, *A Sentimental Murder*, p. 32; Martelli, *Jemmy Twitcher*, pp. 25, 136, 177, 285.

83. Martelli, *Jemmy Twitcher*, p. 286; Wheatley, *The Historical and Posthumous Memoirs of Sir Nathaniel William Wraxall*, 2:184.

Conclusion

1. Charles Stedman, *The History of the Origin, Progress, and Termination of The American War*, 2 vols. (London: J. Murray, J. Debrett and J. Kerby, 1794), 2:421, 449.

2. The argument advanced in this book to explain why the British lost the Revolutionary War is consistent with the views of John Shy at the University of Michigan, who was much influenced by his experience of living through the era of the Vietnam War. Shy shared the general admiration for the most comprehensive work on the British side of the American Revolution by Piers Mackesy, *The War for America* (1964), but disagreed with the conclusions reached by Mackesy. Although his approach was nuanced and his book impressively demonstrated the global demands of the war on the British, Mackesy continued the tradition of explaining the outcome of the war in terms of personal mistakes while shifting the main onus of the blame from the politicians to the commanders in America. He believed that the war was winnable (Mackesy, *Could the British Have Won the War of Independence?* Chester Bland—Dwight E. Lee Lectures in History [Worcester, Mass.: Clark University Press, 1976], p. 13). Shy acknowledged that "perhaps the majority of military historians of the American Revolution . . . explain British defeat in terms of British mistakes" (*A People Numerous and Armed: Reflections on the Military Struggle for American Independence*, rev. ed. [Ann Arbor: University of Michigan Press, 2000], p. 215). He, on the contrary, thought "the British commanders as a group, were not usually bad, and I think it is a mistake to tie the can of British defeat to their tails" (ibid., p. 18).

3. Russell F. Weigley, "American Strategy: A Call for a Critical Strategic History," in *Reconsiderations on the Revolutionary War: Selected Essays,* ed. Don Higginbotham (Westport, Conn.: Greenwood Press, 1978), p. 39; O'Hara to Grafton, November 1, 1780, in "Letters of Charles O'Hara to the Duke of Grafton," ed. George C. Rogers Jr., *South Carolina Historical Magazine* 65, no. 3 (July 1964): 159; Mathew H. Spring, *With Zeal and Bayonets Only: The British Army on Campaign in North America, 1775–1783* (Norman: University of Oklahoma Press, 2008), p. 268.

4. Jeremy Black, "Could the British Have Won the American War of Independence?" *Journal of the Society for Army Historical Research* 74 (1996): 145–47.

5. Charles Royster, *A Revolutionary People at War: The Continental Army and American Character, 1775–1783* (Chapel Hill: University of North Carolina Press, 1979); Philip Davidson, *Propaganda and the American Revolution 1763–1783* (Chapel Hill: University of North Carolina Press, 1941), p. 406; E. Wayne Carp, *To Starve the Army at Pleasure: Continental Army Administration and American Political Culture, 1775–1783* (Chapel Hill: University of North Carolina Press, 1984), pp. 196, 203, 208; "The House Debates Whether to Continue the War," November 9, 1780, *The American Revolution as Described by British Writers and The Morning Chronicle and London Advertiser,* ed. Elizabeth R. Miller (Bowie, Md.: Heritage Books, 1991), pp. 28–29.

6. Davidson, *Propaganda and the American Revolution,* pp. 365–75; Rodney Atwood, *The Hessians: Mercenaries from Hessen-Kassel in the American Revolution* (Cambridge: Cambridge University Press, 1980), p. 157; Stephen Conway, "The British Army, 'Military Europe,' and the American War of Independence," *William and Mary Quarterly,* 3d ser., 67, no. 1 (January 2010): 78; Eliga H. Gould, *The Persistence of Empire: British Political Culture in the Age of the American Revolution* (Chapel Hill: University of North Carolina Press, 2000), p. 163; Stephen Conway, "From Fellow-Nationals to Foreigners: British Perceptions of the Americans, Circa 1739–1783," *William and Mary Quarterly,* 3d ser., 61, no. 1 (January 2002): 65–101.

7. Troy Bickham, *Making Headlines: The American Revolution as Seen through the British Press* (DeKalb: Northern Illinois University Press, 2009), p. 80; *London Chronicle,* September 6, 1777, in *Our American Brethren: A History of Letters in the British Press During the American Revolution, 1775–1781,* ed. Alfred Grant (Jefferson, N.C.: McFarland, 1995); "Cato," in the *Morning Chronicle,* September 4, 1977, ibid, p. 147.

8. *The Annual Register,* in *Rebellion in America: A Contemporary British Viewpoint, 1765–1783,* ed. David H. Murdoch (Santa Barbara, Calif.: Clio Books, 1979), p. 570.

9. Clinton to Germain, February 28, 1781, CO 5/101, PRO; Paul David Nelson, *General Sir Guy Carleton, Lord Dorchester: Soldier-Statesman of Early British Canada* (Teaneck, N.J.: Fairleigh Dickinson University Press, 2000), p. 98.

10. R. Arthur Bowler, *Logistics and the Failure of the British Army in America 1775–1783* (Princeton, N.J.: Princeton University Press, 1975), pp. 135, 137, 222–23, 225; David Syrett, *Shipping and the American War 1775–83: A Study of British Transport Organisation* (London: Athlone Press, 1970), pp. 191, 207, 129, 235, 242; Norman Baker, *Government and Contractors: The British Treasury and War Supplies 1775–1783* (London: Athlone Press, 1971), p. 205.

11. Syrett, *Shipping and the American War,* pp. 13, 51, 162, 167, 168, 173, 177; Baker, *Government and Contractors,* p. 142.

12. Bowler, *Logistics and the Failure of the British Army in America,* pp. 144–45; Baker, *Government and Contractors,* p. 43.

13. Richard Middleton, *The Bells of Victory: The Pitt-Newcastle Ministry and the Conduct of the Seven Years' War 1757–1762* (Cambridge: Cambridge University Press, 1985), p. 217.

14. *The Farington Diary By Joseph Farington, R.A.,* ed. James Greig, 8 vols., 3d ed. (New York: George H. Doran, 1922–28), 1:278. The source of the quote is rarely cited. I am indebted for the reference to Ted Crackel, the former editor of the *Washington Papers.*

15. Cornwallis to Clinton, June 30, 1781 in *Correspondence of Charles, First Marquis Cornwallis,* ed. Charles Ross, 3 vols. (London: John Murray, 1859), 1:102; Paul David Nelson, *General James Grant: Scottish Soldier and Royal Governor of East Florida* (Gainesville: University Press of Florida, 1993), pp. 86–87, 91, 143; Banastre Tarleton, *A History of the Campaigns of 1780 and 1781 in the Southern Provinces of North America* (1787; repr. Cranbury, N.J.: The Scholar's Bookshelf, 2005), pp. 229, 283; Lieutenant Colonel J. G. Simcoe, *Simcoe's Military Journal: A History of the Operations of a Partisan Corps, Called the Queen's Rangers, Commanded by Lieut. Col. J. G. Simcoe, During the War of the American Revolution,* (1844; repr. Cranbury N.J.: The Scholar's Bookshelf, 2005), p. 75.

16. Syrett, *Shipping and the American War 1775–83,* p. 233; Thomas Fleming, *The Perils of Peace: America's Struggle for Survival after Yorktown* (New York: HarperCollins, 2007), p. 187; Nelson, *General Sir Guy Carleton, Lord Dorchester,* pp. 150, 196; Johann von Ewald, *Diary of the American War: A Hessian Journal,* trans. and ed. Joseph Tustin (New Haven, Conn.: Yale University Press, 1979), pp. 340–41, 108.

Bibliography

Manuscripts

THE NATIONAL ARCHIVES (Kew, UK)

CO 5/93–106   Original Correspondence of the Secretary of State (America and the West Indies) 1775–1782.

CO 5/167   Original Correspondence of the Secretary of State (America and the West Indies) and the Secretary at War 1772–1775.

CO 5/174   Original Correspondence of the Secretary of State (America and the West Indies) and Commander-in-Chief 1779–1782.

CO 5/253–56.   Original Correspondence of the Secretary of State (America and the West Indies) Entry Books of Letters, Instructions, Commissions, Warrants, etc.

CO 28/58   Barbados: Original Correspondence with the Secretary of State.

CO 137/75–78   Jamaica: Original Correspondence of the Board of Trade.

CO 140/56   Jamaica: Council and Assembly Minutes.

CO 318   Military Despatches.

PRO 30/20   Admiral Rodney Papers, West Indies.

WO 1/49–57   Military Papers.

Adm1/239   Despatches from Admirals on the Jamaica Station.

Adm 1/309–14   Despatches from Admirals on the Leeward Island Station.

WILLIAM L. CLEMENTS LIBRARY, University of Michigan, Ann Arbor

Sir Henry Clinton Papers.

Lord George Germain Papers.

William Knox Papers.

Lord Shelburne Papers.

DRAYTON HOUSE, Northamptonshire, UK

Letter Book of Lord George Germain, January 1777.

Military Despatches (Lord George Germain), Vol. 1: North America, November 18, 1775 to March 7, 1781.

Military Despatches (Lord George Germain), Vol. 2: the Caribbean, March 1781 to February 1782.

Printed Primary Sources

Abbot, W. W, Philander D. Chase, Theodore Crackel, and Edward G. Lengel, eds., *The Papers of George Washington: Revolutionary War Series,* 20 vols. (Charlottesville: University of Virginia Press, 1985–).

Adair, Douglass, and John A. Schutz, eds., *Peter Oliver's Origin and Progress of the American Rebellion; A Tory View* (Stanford, Calif.: Stanford University Press, 1961),

Adams, Charles Francis, ed., *The Works of John Adams, Second President of the United States. With a Life of the Author,* 10 vols. (Boston: Little, Brown, 1850–56).

Almon, John, and John Debrett, eds., *Parliamentary Register; or History of the Proceedings and Debates of the House of Commons,* 62 vols. (London: J. Debrett, 1775–96).

Amoh, Yasuo, Darren Lingley, and Hiroko Aoki, eds., *Proceedings of the British Commissioners in Philadelphia, 1778–9: Partly in Ferguson's Hand* (Kyoto: Kakenhi Supplemental Project Research Report, Kyoto University, 2007).

Andrews, Evangeline W., and Charles M. Andrews, eds., *Journal of a Lady of Quality; Being the Narrative of a Journey from Scotland to the Caribbean, North Carolina and Portugal, in the Years 1774 to 1776* (New Haven, Conn.: Yale University Press, 1921).

Balderston, Marion, and David Syrett, ed., *The Lost War. Letters from British Officers during The American Revolution* (New York: Horizon Press, 1975).

Barnes, G. R., and J. H. Owen, eds., *The Private Papers of John, Earl of Sandwich, First Lord of the Admiralty 1771–1782,* 4 vols. (London: Navy Records Society, 1932–38).

Bickley, Francis, ed., *The Diaries of Sylvester Douglas (Lord Glenbervie).* 2 vols. (London: Constable, 1928).

Boyd, Julian P., Charles T. Cullen, John Catanzariti, Barbara B. Oberg, et al., eds., *The Papers of Thomas Jefferson,* 34 vols. (Princeton, N.J.: Princeton University Press, 1950–).

Brougham, Henry, Lord, *Historical Sketches of Statesmen Who Flourished in the Time of George III,* 3 vols. (London: Charles Knight & Co., 1839).

Brown, Alan S., ed., "James Simpson's Reports on the Carolina Loyalists, 1779–1780," *Journal of Southern History* 21, no. 4 (November 1955): 513–519.

Brown, Gerald Saxon, ed., *Reflections on a Pamphlet Intitled "A Letter to the Right Honble Lord Vict. H—E" By Admiral Lord Howe* (Ann Arbor: University of Michigan Press, 1959).

Brown Marvin L., Jr., ed., *Baroness von Riedesel and the American Revolution: Journal and Correspondence of a Tour of Duty 1776–1783* (Chapel Hill: University of North Carolina Press, 1965).

Burgoyne, John, *The Speech of a General Officer in the House of Commons, February 20th, 1775* (n.p., n.d.).

——, *A Letter from Lieut. Gen. Burgoyne to his Constituents upon his Late Resignation with Correspondence between the Secretaries of War and him relative to his Return to America* (London: J. Almon, 1779).

——, *A State of the Expedition from Canada as Laid Before the House of Commons by Lieutenant-General John Burgoyne,* 2d ed. (London: J. Almon, 1780).

Butterfield, L. H., Leonard C. Faber, and Wendell D. Garrett, eds., *Diary and Autobiography of John Adams,* 4 vols. (Cambridge, Mass.: Harvard University Press, 1962).

Butterfield, L. H., Richard Ryerson, and Margaret A. Hogan, eds. *The Adams Papers: Adams Family Correspondence,* 10 vols. (Cambridge, Mass.: Harvard University Press, 1963–).

Cannon, John, ed., *The Letters of Junius* (Oxford: Clarendon Press, 1978).

Cappon, Lester J., ed., *The Adams-Jefferson Letters: The Complete Correspondence between Thomas Jefferson and Abigail and John Adams* (Chapel Hill: University of North Carolina Press, 1988).

Carter, Clarence Edwin, ed., *The Correspondence of General Thomas Gage with the Secretaries of State, and with the War Office and the Treasury 1763–1775,* 2 vols. (1933; repr. Hamden, Connecticut: Archon Books, 1969).

Christie, O. F., ed., *The Diary of the Revd. William Jones 1777–1821* (London: Brentano's, 1929).

Clinton, Sir Henry, *The American Rebellion: Sir Henry Clinton's Narrative of his Campaigns, 1775–1782,* ed. William B. Willcox (New Haven, Conn.: Yale University Press, 1954).

Cobbett, William, and Thomas Hansard, ed., *The Parliamentary History of England from the Earliest Period to 1803,* 36 vols. (London: Hansard, 1806–22).

Commager, Henry Steele, and Richard B. Morris, eds., *The Spirit of Seventy-Six: The Story of the American Revolution as Told by Participants* (Indianapolis: Bobbs-Merrill, 1958).

Copeland, Thomas W., Lucy S. Sutherland, George H. Guttridge, John A. Woods, Holden Furber, P. J. Marshall, Alfred Cobban, Robert A. Smith, R. B. McDowell, and Barbara Lowe, eds., *The Correspondence of Edmund Burke,* 10 vols. (Chicago: University of Chicago Press, 1958–78).

Cornwallis, Charles, *Correspondence of Charles, First Marquis Cornwallis,* ed. Charles Ross, 3 vols. (London: John Murray, 1859).

Cumberland, Richard, *Character of the Late Lord Viscount Sackville* (London: C. Dilly, 1785).

Cumming, William P., and Hugh Rankin, eds., *The Fate of a Nation: The American Revolution Through Contemporary Eyes* (London: Phaidon, 1975).

Davies, K. G., ed., *Documents of the American Revolution, 1770–1783,* 20 vols. (Shannon: Irish University Press, 1972–81).

Donne, W. Bodham, ed., *The Correspondence of King George III with Lord North 1768 to 1783,* 2 vols. (1867; repr. New York: Da Capo Press, 1971).

Ewald, Johann von, *Diary of the American War: A Hessian Journal,* trans. and ed. Joseph Tustin (New Haven, Conn.: Yale University Press, 1979).

Examination of Lieutenant General The Earl Cornwallis Before A Committee of the House of Commons, Upon Sir William Howe's Papers (London: J. Robson, 1779).

Fitzpatrick, John C., ed., *The Writings of George Washington from the Original Manuscript Sources, 1745–1799,* 39 vols. (Washington, D.C.: U.S. Government Printing Office, 1931–44).

Flanders, Henry, ed., *Memoirs of Richard Cumberland: London 1806* (1856; repr. New York: Richard Bloom, 1969).

Force, Peter, ed., *American Archives: . . . A Documentary History . . . of the American Colonies,* 4th ser., 4 vols. (Washington: Published by M. St. Clair and Peter Force, 1848–53).

Ford, Paul Leicester, ed., *The Writings of Thomas Jefferson,* 20 vols. (New York: Putnam's, 1892–99).

——, ed., *Autobiography of Thomas Jefferson 1743–1790* (New York: Putnam's, 1914).

Fortescue, Sir John, ed., *The Correspondence of King George The Third from 1760 to December 1783,* 6 vols. (London: Macmillan, 1927–28).

Gibbon, Edward, *Memoirs of My Life,* ed. Georges Bonnard (New York: Funk & Wagnalls, 1966).

Grant, Alfred, ed., *Our American Brethren: A History of Letters in the British Press During the American Revolution, 1775–1781* (Jefferson, N.C.: McFarland, 1995).

Gruber, Ira, ed., *John Peebles' American War: The Diary of a Scottish Grenadier, 1776–1782* (Mechanicsburg, Pa.: Stackpole Books, 1998).

Hannay, David. ed., *Letters written by Sir Samuel Hood, Viscount Hood in 1781–83* (London: Navy Records Society, 1895).

Historical Manuscripts Commission, *Charlemont Manuscripts,* 2 vols. (London: H.M. Stationery Office, 1891).

——, *Carlisle Manuscripts* (London: H.M. Stationery Office, 1891–94).

——, *Report on the Manuscripts of Mrs. Stopford-Sackville of Drayton House, Northamptonshire,* 2 vols. (London: H.M. Stationery Office, 1910).

——, *Report on the Manuscripts of the late Reginald Rawdon Hastings Esq.,* ed. Francis Bickley, 4 vols. (London: H.M. Stationery Office, 1928–47).

Howe, Sir William, *The Narrative of Lieut. Gen. Sir William Howe in a Committee of the House of Commons, on the 29th of April, 1779, Relative to His Conduct During His Late Command of the King's Troops in North America: To Which Are Added, Some Observations Upon A Pamphlet, Entitled, Letters to A Nobleman* (London: Baldwin, 1780).

Hunter, John, *Observations on the Diseases of the Army in Jamaica,* 3d ed. (London: T. Payne, 1808).

Hutchinson, Peter Orlando, ed., *The Diary and Letters of His Excellency Thomas Hutchinson, Esq.,* 2 vols. (New York: Burt Franklin, 1971).

Institut français de Washington, ed., *Correspondence of General Washington and Comte De Grasse* (Washington, D.C.: U.S. Government Printing Office, 1931).

Jackman, Sydney, ed., *With Burgoyne from Quebec: An Account of the Life at Quebec and of the Famous Battle of Saratoga. First Published in 1789 as Volume One of Travels Through the Interior Parts of North America, by Thomas Anburey* (Toronto: Macmillan, 1963).

Kemble Papers, The: Journals of Lieut-Col. Stephen Kemble, 1773–1789, 2 vols. (New York: New-York Historical Society, 1885).

Klein, Milton M., and Ronald W. Howard, eds., *Twilight of British Rule in Revolutionary America; The New York Letter Book of General James Robertson 1780–1783* (Cooperstown, N.Y.: New York State Historical Association, 1983).

Labaree, Leonard W., William B. Willcox, Barbara Oberg, and Ellen R. Cohn, eds., *The Papers of Benjamin Franklin,* 39 vols. (New Haven, Conn.: Yale University Press, 1959–).

Lamb, Roger, *An Original and Authentic Journal of Occurrences During the Late American War from Its Commencement to the Year 1783* (Dublin: Wilkinson & Courtney, 1809).

Laughton, Sir J. K, ed., *Letters and Papers of Charles, Lord Barham, Admiral of the Red Squadron, 1758–1813,* 3 vols. (London: Navy Records Society, 1906–10).

Manuscripts of Captain Howard Vincente Knox, The, (From Volume VI of "Reports on Manuscripts in Various Collections" Prepared by the Historical Manuscripts Commission, Great Britain) (1909; repr. Boston: Gregg Press, 1972).

"Military Journal of Major Ebenezer Denny 1781 to 1795," *Publications of the Historical Society of Pennsylvania* (Philadelphia: J. B. Lippincott & Co., 1860), pp. 205–409.

Miller, Elizabeth R., ed., *The American Revolution as Described by British Writers and The Morning Chronicle and London Advertiser* (Bowie, Md.: Heritage Books, 1991).

Morison, Samuel Eliot, ed., *Sources and Documents Illustrating the American Revolution 1764–1788 and the Formation of the Federal Constitution* (1923; repr. Oxford: Oxford University Press, 1965).

Moseley, Dr. Benjamin, *A Treatise on Tropical Diseases; on Military Operations; and on the Climate of the West-Indies* (London: T. Cadell, 1789).

Murdoch, David H., ed., *Rebellion in America: A Contemporary British Viewpoint, 1769–1783* (Santa Barbara, Calif.: Clio Books, 1979).

Norton, J. E., ed., *The Letters of Edward Gibbon*, 3 vols. (New York: Macmillan, 1956).

Oliver, Andrew, ed., *The Journal of Samuel Curwen, Loyalist*, 2 vols. (Cambridge, Mass.: Harvard University Press, 1972).

Paine, Thomas, *The American Crisis*, introd. Andrew S. Trees (New York: Barnes & Noble, 2010).

Percy, Hugh, and Charles K. Bolton, eds., *Letters of Hugh, Earl Percy, from Boston and New York, 1774–1776* (Boston: Charles E. Goodspeed, 1902).

Robson, Eric, ed., *Letters from America 1773–1780: Being the letters of a Scots Officer, Sir James Murray, to His Home During the War of American Independence* (Manchester: Manchester University Press, 1951).

Rodney, Sir George, *Letters from Sir George Brydges now Lord Rodney, To His Majesty's Ministers, &c. &c. Relative to the Capture of St. Eustatius, And Its Dependencies; And Shewing the State of the War in the West-Indies, at that Period* (London: A. Grant, 1789).

Rogers, George C., Jr., ed., "Letters of Charles O'Hara to the Duke of Grafton," *South Carolina Historical Magazine* 65, no. 3 (July 1964): 158–80.

Ross, Charles, ed., *Correspondence of Charles, First Marquis Cornwallis*, 3 vols. (London: John Murray, Albemarle Street, 1859).

Saberton, Ian, ed., *The Cornwallis Papers: The Campaigns of 1780 and 1781 in the Southern Theatre of the American Revolutionary War*, 6 vols. (Uckfield: Naval & Military Press, 2010).

Sabine, W. H. W., ed., *Historical Memoirs of William Smith 1778–1783*, 2 vols. (New York: New York Times, 1971).

Scheer, George F, and Hugh F. Rankin, eds., *Rebels and Redcoats* (New York: Da Capo Press, 1957).

Simcoe, Lieutenant Colonel J. G., *Simcoe's Military Journal: A History of the Operations of a Partisan Corps, Called the Queen's Rangers, commanded by Lieut. Col. J. G. Simcoe, During the War of the American Revolution* (1844; repr. Cranbury, N.J.: The Scholar's Bookshelf, 2005).

Simmons, R. C., and P. D. G Thomas, eds., *Proceedings and Debates of the British Parliaments Respecting North America 1754–1783*, 6 vols. (Millwood, N.Y.: Kraus International, 1982–86).

A Speech which was Spoken in the House of Assembly of St. Christopher Upon a motion made on Tuesday the 6th of November, 1781, For Presenting An Address to His Majesty, Relative to The Proceedings of Admiral Rodney and General Vaughan at St. Eustatius And the Present Dangerous Situation of The West India Islands (London: J. Debrett, 1782).

Stedman, Charles, *The History of the Origin, Progress, and Termination of The American War,* 2 vols. (London: J. Murray, J. Debrett and J. Kerby, 1794).

Steuart, A. F., ed., *The Last Journals of Horace Walpole During the Reign of George III,* 2 vols. (London: John Lane, 1910).

Tarleton, Lieutenant-Colonel Banastre, *A History of the Campaigns of 1780 and 1781 in the Southern Provinces of North America* (1787; repr. Cranbury, N.J.: The Scholar's Bookshelf, 2005).

Tatum, Edward H., Jr., ed., *The Journal of Ambrose Serle* (San Marino, Calif.: Huntington Library, 1940).

Taylor, Robert J., Gregg L. Lint, and Celeste Walker, eds., *Papers of John Adams,* 14 vols. (Cambridge, Mass.: Harvard University Press, 1979–2012).

Thacher, James, *Military Journal During the American Revolutionary War, from 1776 to 1783* (1854; repr. Cranbury, N.J.: The Scholar's Bookshelf, 2005).

Walpole, Horace, *Memoirs of the Reign of King George III,* ed. Derek Jarrett, 4 vols. (New Haven, Conn.: Yale University Press, 2000).

Wheatley, Henry B., ed., *The Historical and Posthumous Memoirs of Sir Nathaniel William Wraxall 1772–1784,* 5 vols. (1836; repr. London: Bickers & Son, 1884).

Wortley, The Hon. Mrs. E. Stuart, ed., *A Prime Minister and His Son: From the Correspondence of the Third Earl of Bute and of Lt. Gen. The Hon. Sir Charles Stuart, K.B.* (London: John Murray, 1925).

SECONDARY SOURCES

Adams, C. F. "Contemporary Opinion on the Howes," *Proceedings of the Massachusetts Historical Society,* 3d ser., 44 (November 1910): 94–120.

Adams, Randolph G., "A View of Cornwallis's Surrender at Yorktown," *American Historical Review* 37, no. 1 (October 1931): 25–49.

Alberts, Robert C., *The Golden Voyage: The Life and Times of William Bingham 1752–1804* (Boston: Houghton Mifflin, 1969).

Albion, Robert Greenhalgh, *Forests and Sea Power: The Timber Problem and the Royal Navy, 1652–1862* (1926; repr. Annapolis, Md.: Naval Institute Press, 2000).

Alden, Richard, *General Gage in America: Being Principally a History of His Role in the American Revolution* (Baton Rouge: Louisiana State University Press, 1948).

Anderson, Fred, *A People's Army: Massachusetts Soldiers and Society in the Seven Years' War* (London: Norton, 1984).

Anderson, Olive, "The Role of the Army in Parliamentary Management During the American War of Independence," *Journal of the Society for Army Historical Research* 34, no. 140 (December 1956): 146–49.

Anderson, Troyer Steele, *The Command of the Howe Brothers During the American Revolution* (1936; repr. Cranbury, N.J.: The Scholar's Bookshelf, 2005).

Atwood, Rodney, *The Hessians: Mercenaries from Hessen-Kassel in the American Revolution* (Cambridge: Cambridge University Press, 1980).

Augur, Helen, *The Secret War of Independence* (New York: Little, Brown, 1955).

Ayling, Stanley, *George The Third* (London: Collins, 1972).

Babits, Lawrence E., and Joshua B. Howard, *Long, Obstinate, and Bloody: The Battle of Guilford Courthouse* (Chapel Hill: University of North Carolina Press, 2009).

Bailyn, Bernard, *The Ideological Origins of the American Revolution* (Cambridge, Mass.: Harvard University Press, 1967).

——, *The Ordeal of Thomas Hutchinson: Loyalism and the Destruction of the First British Empire* (London: Allen Lane, 1975).

Baker, Norman, *Government and Contractors: The British Treasury and War Supplies 1775–1783* (London: Athlone Press, 1971).

Baugh, Daniel A., "The Politics of British Naval Failure, 1775–1777," *American Neptune* 52 (1992): 221–46.

Bayly, C. A., *Imperial Meridian: The British Empire and the World 1780–1830* (London: Longman, 1989).

Bellot, Leland J., *William Knox: The Life and Thought of an Eighteenth-Century Imperialist* (Austin: University of Texas Press, 1977).

Bicheno, Hugh, *Rebels and Redcoats: The American Revolutionary War* (New York: HarperCollins, 2003).

Bickham, Troy, *Making Headlines: The American Revolution as Seen through the British Press* (DeKalb: Northern Illinois University Press, 2009).

Billias, George Athan, ed., *George Washington's Generals and Opponents: Their Exploits and Leadership.* 2 vols. (1964, 1969; repr. New York: Da Capo Press, 1994).

Black, Jeremy, *War for America: The Fight for Independence 1775–1783* (New York: St. Martin's Press, 1994).

——, "Could the British Have Won the American War of Independence?" *Journal of Army Historical Research,* 74 (1996): 145–47.

——, *George III: America's Last King* (New Haven, Conn.: Yale University Press, 2006).

——, *George II: Party Puppet of the Politicians?* (Exeter: University of Exeter Press, 2007).

Black, Jeremy, and Philip Woodfine, eds., *The British Navy and the Use of Naval Power in the Eighteenth Century* (Leicester: Leicester University Press, 1988).

Bliven Bruce, Jr. *Battle for Manhattan* (Baltimore: Penguin Books, 1964).

Blumenthal, Walter Hart, "British Camp Women On The Ration," in *Women Camp Followers of the American Revolution* (New York: Arno Press, 1974), pp. 15–57.

Bonwick, Colin, *English Radicals and the American Revolution* (Chapel Hill: University of North Carolina Press, 1977).

Boulton, Terry, *Taming Democracy* (Oxford: Oxford University Press, 2007).

Bowen, H. V., *War and British Society, 1688–1815* (Cambridge: Cambridge University Press, 1988).

——, *Revenue and Reform: The Indian Problem in British Politics 1757–1773* (Cambridge: Cambridge University Press, 1991).

——, "British Conceptions of Global Empire, 1756–83," *Journal of Imperial and Commonwealth History* 26, no. 3 (1998): 1–27.

Bowler, R. Arthur, "Sir Henry Clinton and Army Profiteering: A Neglected Aspect of the Clinton-Cornwallis Controversy," *William and Mary Quarterly,* 3d ser., 31, no. 1 (January 1974): 111–23.

——, *Logistics and the Failure of the British Army in America 1775–1783* (Princeton, N.J.: Princeton University Press, 1975).

Bradley, James E., *Popular Politics and the American Revolution in England: Petitions, the Crown, and Public Opinion* (Macon, Ga.: Mercer University Press, 1986).

Breen, Kenneth, "Graves and Hood at the Chesapeake," *Mariner's Mirror* 56 (1980): 53–65.

——, "Sir George Rodney and St. Eustatius in the American War: A Commercial and Naval Distraction, 1775–81," *Mariner's Mirror* 84 (May 1998): 193–203.

Breen, Tim, "Ideology and Nationalism on the Eve of the American Revolution: Revisions *Once More* in Need of Revising," *Journal of American History* 84, no. 1 (June 1997): 13–39.

Brewer, John, *Party Ideology and Popular Politics at the Accession of George III* (Cambridge: Cambridge University Press, 1976).

——, *The Sinews of Power: War, Money, and the English State, 1688–1783* (New York: Knopf, 1989).

——, *A Sentimental Murder: Love and Madness in the Eighteenth Century* (New York: Farrar, Straus and Giroux, 2004).

Brooke, John, *King George III* (London: Constable, 1972).

Broomfield, J. H., "The Keppel-Palliser Affair 1778–1779," *Mariner's Mirror* 47, no. 3 (August 1961): 195–207.

——, "Lord Sandwich at the Admiralty Board; Politics and the British Navy, 1771–1778," *Mariner's Mirror* 51, no. 1 (1965): 7–17.

Brougham, Henry, Lord, *Historical Sketches of Statesmen Who Flourished in the Time of George III*, 2 vols. (London: Charles Knight & Co., 1839).

Brown, Christopher Leslie, and Philip Morgan, eds., *Arming Slaves from Classical Times to the Modern Age* (New Haven, Conn.: Yale University Press, 2006).

Brown, Gerald S., "The Court Martial of Lord George Sackville, Whipping Boy of the Revolutionary War," *William and Mary Quarterly*, 3d ser., 9, no. 3 (July 1952): 317–37.

——, "The Anglo-French Naval Crisis: A Study of Conflict in the North Cabinet," *William and Mary Quarterly*, 3d ser., 13, no. 1 (January 1956): 3–26.

——, *The American Secretary: The Colonial Policy of Lord George Germain, 1775–1778* (Ann Arbor: University of Michigan Press, 1963).

Brown, Peter, *The Chathamites: A Study in the Relationship between Personalities and Ideas in the Second Half of the Eighteenth Century* (New York: St. Martin's Press, 1967).

Brown, Weldon A., *Empire or Independence: A Study in the Failure of Reconciliation, 1774–1783* (Baton Rouge: Louisiana State University Press, 1941).

Brumwell, Stephen, *Redcoats: The British Soldier and War in the Americas, 1755–1763* (Cambridge: Cambridge University Press, 2002).

Buchanan, John, *The Road to Guilford Courthouse: The American Revolution in the Carolinas* (New York: Wiley, 1997).

Buckley, Roger Norman, *Slaves in Red Coats: The British West India Regiments, 1795–1815* (New Haven, Conn.: Yale University Press, 1979).

——, *The British Army in the West Indies: Society and the Military in the Revolutionary Age* (Gainesville: University Press of Florida, 1998).

Buel, Richard, Jr. *In Irons: Britain's Naval Supremacy and the American Revolutionary Economy* (New Haven, Conn.: Yale University Press, 1998).

Bullion, John L., "George III and Empire, 1783," *William and Mary Quarterly,* 3d ser., 51, no. 2 (April 1994): 304–10.

——, "The *Ancien Regime* and the Modernizing State: George III and the American Revolution," *Anglican and Episcopal History* 68, no. 1 (1999): 67–84.

Burt, Alfred L. "The Quarrel between Germain and Carleton: An Inverted Story," *Canadian Historical Review* 11 (September 1930): 202–22.

Bushman, Richard, *King and People in Provincial Massachusetts* (Chapel Hill: University of North Carolina Press, 1985).

Butterfield, Herbert, *George III, Lord North and the People, 1779–80* (New York: Russell & Russell, 1968).

Calhoon, Robert McCluer, *Revolutionary America: An Interpretive Overview* (New York: Harcourt Brace Jovanovich, 1976).

Calloway, Colin G. *The American Revolution in Indian Country: Crisis and Diversity in Native American Communities* (Cambridge: Cambridge University Press, 1995).

Cannon, John, *Lord North: The Noble Lord in the Blue Ribbon* (London: Historical Association, 1970).

Carp, E. Wayne, *To Starve the Army at Pleasure: Continental Army Administration and American Political Culture, 1775–1783* (Chapel Hill: University of North Carolina Press, 1984).

Chase, Philander D., "Years of Hardship and Revelations: The Convention Army at Albemarle Barracks 1779–1781," *Magazine of Albemarle County History,* no. 41 (1983): 11–53.

Chopra, Ruma, *Unnatural Rebellion: Loyalists in New York City During the Revolution* (Charlottesville: University of Virginia Press, 2011).

Christie, Ian R., *The End of North's Ministry, 1780–1782* (London: Macmillan, 1958).

——, *Crisis of Empire: Great Britain and the American Colonies 1754–1783* (New York: Norton, 1966).

——, *Myth and Reality in Late-Eighteenth-Century British Politics and Other Papers* (London: Macmillan, 1970).

Clark, Dora Mae, *British Opinion and the American Revolution* (New York: Russell & Russell, 1966).

Clark, Jane, "The Command of the Canadian Army for the Campaign of 1777, *Canadian Historical Review* 10 (June 1929): 129–35.

——, "Responsibility for the Failure of the Burgoyne Campaign," *American Historical Review* 35, no. 3 (April 1930): 542–59.

——, "The Convention Troops and the Perfidy of Sir William Howe," *American Historical Review* 37, no. 4 (July 1932): 721–22.

Cohen, Sheldon, *British Supporters of the American Revolution, 1775–1783: The Role of the "Middling-level" Activists* (Woodbridge: Boydell Press, 2004).

Colley, Linda, "The Apotheosis of George III: Loyalty, Royalty and the British Nation, 1760–1820," *Past and Present,* no. 102 (1984): 94–129.

——, *Britons: Forging the Nation, 1707–1837* (New Haven, Conn.: Yale University Press, 1992).

Conner, Clifford D. *Colonel Despard: The Life and Times of an Anglo-Irish Rebel* (Conshohocken, Pa.: Combined Publishing, 2000).

Conser, Walter H., Jr., Ronald M. McCarthy, David J. Toscano, and Gene Sharp, *Resistance, Politics, and the American Struggle for Independence, 1765–1775* (Boulder. Colo.: Lynne Riener, 1986).

Conway, Stephen, "British Army Officers and the American War of Independence," *William and Mary Quarterly,* 3d ser., 41, no. 2 (April 1984): 265–77.

——, "The Recruitment of Criminals into the British Army, 1775–81," *Bulletin of the Institute of Historical Research* 57 (1985): 46–58.

——, "To Subdue America: British Army Officers and the Conduct of the Revolutionary War," *William and Mary Quarterly,* 3d ser., 48, no. 3 (July 1986): 381–408.

——, "'The Great Mischief Complain'd of': Reflections on the Misconduct of British Soldiers in the Revolutionary War," *William and Mary Quarterly* 47, no. 3 (July 1990): 370–91.

——, *The War of American Independence 1775–1783* (London: Edward Arnold, 1995).

——, "The Politics of British Military and Naval Mobilization, 1775–83," *English Historical Review* 112, no. 449 (November 1997): 1179–1201.

——, *The British Isles and the War of American Independence* (Oxford: Oxford University Press, 2000).

——, "'A Joy Unknown for Years Past': The American War, Britishness and the Celebration of Rodney's Victory at the Saints," *History* 86, no. 282 (April 2001): 180–99.

——, "From Fellow-Nationals to Foreigners: British Perceptions of the Americans, Circa 1739–1783," *William and Mary Quarterly,* 3d ser., 61, no. 1 (January 2002): 65–101.

——, "The British Army, 'Military Europe,' and the American War of Independence," *William and Mary Quarterly,* 3d ser., 67, no. 1 (January 2010): 69–100.

Cook, Don, *The Long Fuse: How England Lost the American Colonies, 1760–1785* (New York: Atlantic Monthly Press, 1995).

Coupland, Reginald, *The Quebec Act* (Oxford: Clarendon Press, 1925).

Creswell, John, *British Admirals of the Eighteenth Century: Tactics in Battle* (Hamden, Conn.: Archon Books, 1972).

Cubbison, Douglas R., *Burgoyne and the Saratoga Campaign: His Papers* (Norman: University of Oklahoma Press, 2012).

Cunliffe, Marcus, *George Washington: Man and Monument* (London: Collins, 1959).

Curtis, Edward E. *The Organization of the British Army in the American Revolution* (New Haven, Conn.: Yale University Press, 1926).

Dalrymple, William, *White Mughals: Love and Betrayal in Eighteenth-Century India* (New York: Penguin, 2002).

Davidson, Philip, *Propaganda and the American Revolution 1763–1783* (Chapel Hill: University of North Carolina Press, 1941).

Davis, Robert P., *Where a Man Can Go: Major General William Phillips, British Royal Artillery, 1731–1781* (Westport, Conn.: Greenwood Press, 1999).

De Fonblanque, Edward Barrington, ed., *Political and Military Episodes in the Latter Half of the Eighteenth Century: Derived from the Life and Correspondence of the Right H. John Burgoyne, General, Statesman, Dramatist* (London: Macmillan, 1876).

Dickinson, H. T., *The Politics of the People in Eighteenth-Century Britain* (New York: St. Martin's Press, 1994).

——, "The Representation of the People in Eighteenth-Century Britain," in *Realities of Representation: State Building in Early Modern Europe and European America,* ed. Maija Jansson (London: Palgrave Macmillan, 2007), pp. 19–44.

——, "George III and Parliament," *Parliamentary History* 30, pt. 3 (2011): 395–413.

——, ed., *Britain and the American Revolution* (London: Addison Wesley Longman, 1979).

Dickson, Peter G., *The Financial Revolution in England: A Study of the Development of Public Credit* (New York: St. Martin's Press, 1967).

Ditchfield, G. M., *George III: An Essay in Monarchy* (Basingstoke: Palgrave Macmillan, 2002).

Donoughue, Bernard, *British Politics and the American Revolution: The Path to War, 1773–75* (London: Macmillan, 1964).

Duff, Stella F., "The Case Against George III," *William and Mary Quarterly,* 3d ser., 6, no. 3 (July 1949): 383–97.

Duffy, Christopher, *The Military Experience in the Age of Reason* (London: Routledge & Kegan Paul, 1987).

Dull, Jonathan R., *The French Navy and American Independence: A Study of Arms and Diplomacy, 1774–1787* (Princeton, N.J.: Princeton University Press, 1975).

Fenn, Elizabeth A., *Pox Americana: The Great Smallpox Epidemic of 1775–82* (New York: Hill and Wang, 2001).

Ferling, John, "John Adams, Diplomat," *William and Mary Quarterly* 3d ser., 51, no. 2 (April 1994): 227–52.

——, *Setting the World Ablaze: Washington, Adams, Jefferson, and the American Revolution* (New York: Oxford University Press, 2000).

Fischer, David Hackett, *Washington's Crossing* (Oxford: Oxford University Press, 2004).

Fitzmaurice, Edmond G. P., *Life of William Earl of Shelburne afterwards First Marquis of Lansdowne with Extracts of his Papers and Correspondence,* 3 vols. (London: Macmillan, 1875–76).

Flavell, Julie, "Lord North's Conciliatory Proposal and the Patriots in London," *English Historical Review* 107, no. 423 (April 1992): 302–22.

——, "American Patriots in London and the Quest for Talks, 1774–1775." *Journal of Imperial and Commonwealth History* 20, no. 3 (1992): 335–69.

——, "Government Interception of Letters from America and the Quest for Colonial Opinion in 1775," *William and Mary Quarterly,* 3d ser., 58, no. 2 (April 2001): 403–30.

——, "The Plot to Kidnap King George III," *BBC History* 7, no. 11 (November 2006): 12–16.

——, *When London Was Capital of America* (New Haven, Conn.: Yale University Press, 2010).

Flavell, Julie, and Stephen Conway, eds., *Britain and America Go to War: The Impact of War and Warfare in Anglo-America, 1754–1815* (Gainesville: University Press of Florida, 2004).

Fleming, Thomas, *The Forgotten Victory: The Battle for New Jersey—1780* (New York: Reader's Digest Press, 1973).

——, *The Perils of Peace: America's Struggle for Survival after Yorktown* (New York: HarperCollins, 2007).

Fliegelman, Jay, *Declaring Independence: Jefferson, Natural Language, and the Culture of Performance* (Stanford, Calif.: Stanford University Press, 1993).

Ford, Worthington C., "Parliament and the Howes," *Proceedings of the Massachusetts Historical Society,* 3d ser., 44 (October 1910): 120–43.

Fortescue, Sir John, *The War of Independence: The British Army in North America, 1775–1783,* introd. John Shy (abridged ed., 1911; London: Greenhill Books, 2001).

Fortune, Alexander, *Merchants and Jews: The Struggle for British West Indian Commerce, 1650–1750* (Gainesville: University Press of Florida, 1984).

Frantz, John B., and William Pencak, eds., *Beyond Philadelphia: The American Revolution in the Pennsylvania Hinterland* (University Park: Pennsylvania State University Press, 1998).

Fraser, Flora, *Princesses—The Six Daughters of George III* (London: John Murray, 2004).

Fremont-Barnes, Gregory, and Richard A. Ryerson, *The Encyclopedia of The American Revolutionary War: A Political, Social, and Military History,* 5 vols. (Santa Barbara, Calif.: ABC-Clio, 2006)

French, Anne, ed., *The Earl and Countess Howe by Gainsborough: A Bicentenary Exhibition* (London: English Heritage, 1988).

Frey, Sylvia, *The British Soldier in America* (Austin: University of Texas Press, 1981).

——, *Water from the Rock: Black Resistance in a Revolutionary Age* (Princeton, N.J.: Princeton University Press, 1993).

Gallo, Joseph J., *Nelson in the Caribbean: The Hero Emerges, 1784–1787* (Annapolis, Md.: Naval Institute Press, 2003).

Geggus, David Patrick, *Slavery, War, and Revolution: The British Occupation of Saint Domingue, 1793–1798* (Oxford: Oxford University Press, 1982).

George, Dorothy M., ed., *Catalogue of Political and Personal Satires Preserved in the Department of Prints and Drawings in the British Museum 1771–1783* (London: British Museum, 1935).

Godber, Joyce, *History of Bedfordshire* (Bedford: Bedfordshire County Council, 1969).

Gould, Eliga H., "A Virtual Nation: Greater Britain and the Imperial Legacy of the American Revolution," *American Historical Review* 104, no. 2 (April 1999): 476–89.

——, *The Persistence of Empire: British Political Culture in the Age of the American Revolution* (Chapel Hill: University of North Carolina Press, 2000).

——, "Zones of Laws, Zones of Violence: The Legal Geography of the British Atlantic, circa 1772," *William and Mary Quarterly,* 3d ser., 60, no. 3 (July 2003): 471–510.

Granger, Bruce Ingham, *Political Satire in the American Revolution 1763–1783* (Ithaca, N.Y.: Cornell University Press, 1960).

Greene, Jack P., "The Seven Years' War and the American Revolution: The Causal Relationship Reconsidered," *Journal of Imperial and Commonwealth History* 8 (1980): 85–105.

Greene, Jerome A., *The Guns of Independence: The Siege of Yorktown, 1781* (New York: Savas Beatie, 2009).

Gruber, Ira D., "Lord Howe and Lord George Germain: British Politics and the Winning of American Independence," *William and Mary Quarterly,* 3d ser., 22, no. 2 (April 1965): 225–43.

——, "The American Revolution as a Conspiracy: The British View," *William and Mary Quarterly,* 3d ser., 26, no. 3 (July 1969): 360–72.

——, *The Howe Brothers and the American Revolution* (Chapel Hill: University of North Carolina Press, 1972).

——, "For King and Country: The Limits of Loyalty of British Officers in the War for American Independence," in Edgar Denton III, ed. *Limits of Loyalty* (Waterloo, Ont.: Wilfred Laurier University Press, 1980), pp. 23–40.

——, "The Education of Sir Henry Clinton," *Bulletin of the John Rylands University Library of Manchester* 72 (1990): 131–53.

——, *Books and the British Army in the Age of the American Revolution* (Chapel Hill: University of North Carolina Press, 2010).

Guttridge, George H., "Lord George Germain in Office, 1775–1782," *American Historical Review* 33, no. 1 (October 1927): 23–43.

——, *English Whiggism and the American Revolution* (Berkeley: University of California Press, 1963).

Haarmann, Albert W., "The Spanish Conquest of British West Florida, 1779–1781," *Florida Historical Quarterly* 39, no. 2 (October 1960): 107–34.

Haas, James M., "The Pursuit of Political Success in Eighteenth-Century England: Sandwich, 1740–71," *Bulletin of the Institute of Historical Research* 43 (May 1970): 56–77.

Hallows, Ian S., *Regiments and Corps of the British Army* (London: New Orchard Edition, 1994).

Hargrove Richard J., Jr., *Gentleman John Burgoyne* (Newark: University of Delaware Press, 1983).

Harvey, Robert, *"A Few Bloody Noses": The Realities and Mythologies of the American Revolution* (Woodstock, N.Y.: Overlook Press, 2001).

Hatch, Robert McConnell, *Major John André: A Gallant in Spy's Clothing* (Boston: Houghton Mifflin, 1986).

Hedges, William. L., "Telling Off the King: Jefferson's Summary View as American Fantasy," *Early American Literature* 22, no. 2 (1987): 166–74.

Hibbert, Christopher, *King Mob: The London Riots of 1780* (New York: Dorset Press, 1958).

——, *Redcoats and Rebels: The American Revolution through British Eyes* (New York: Norton, 1990).

Higginbotham, Don, *The War of American Independence: Military Attitudes, Policies, and Practices 1763–1789* (1971; repr. Boston: Northeastern University Press, 1983).

——, ed., *Reconsiderations on the Revolutionary War: Selected Essays* (Westport, Conn.: Greenwood Press, 1978).

Higgins, W. Robert, ed., *The Revolutionary War in the South: Power, Conflict, and Leadership* (Durham, N.C.: Duke University Press, 1979).

Hoffman, Ronald, and Peter J. Albert, eds., *Arms and Independence: The Military Character of the American Revolution* (Charlottesville: University of Virginia Press, 1984).

Holton, Woody, *Forced Founders . . . Indians, Debtors, and the Making of the American Revolution in Virginia* (Chapel Hill: University of North Carolina Press, 1999).

Hughes, Edward, "Lord North's Correspondence, 1766–83," *English Historical Review* 64, no. 243 (April 1947): 218–38.

Hurst, Ronald, *The Golden Rock: An Episode of the American War of Independence, 1775–1783* (London: Leo Cooper, 1996).

Jacobson, David L., ed., *Essays on the American Revolution* (New York: Holt, Rinehart and Winston, 1970).

Jackson, John W., *With the British Army in Philadelphia 1777–1778* (San Rafael, Calif.: Presidio Press, 1979).

James, W. M., *The British Navy in Adversity: A Study of the War of American Independence* (London; Longmans, Green, 1926).

Jameson, Franklin L., "St. Eustatius and the American Revolution," *American Historical Review* 8 (1902–3): 683–708.

Jasanoff, Maya, *Edge of Empire: Lives, Culture and Conquest in the East 1750–1850* (New York: Knopf, 2005).

——, *Liberty's Exiles: American Loyalists in the Revolutionary World* (New York: Knopf, 2011).

Jordan, Winthrop D., "Thomas Paine and the Killing of the King, 1776," *Journal of American History* 60, no. 2 (September 1973): 294–308.

Kammen, Michael, *A Season of Youth: The American Revolution and the Historical Imagination* (New York: Knopf, 1978).

Kaplan, Roger, "British Intelligence Operations During the American Revolution," *William and Mary Quarterly*, 3d ser., 47, no. 1 (January 1990): 115–38.

Kimball, Marie, *Jefferson: The Scene of Europe 1774 to 1789* (New York: Coward-McCann, 1950).

Knollenberg, Bernhard, *Growth of the American Revolution 1766–1775* (1975; repr. Indianapolis: Liberty Fund, 2003).

Knott, Sarah, *Sensibility and the American Revolution* (Chapel Hill: University of North Carolina Press, 2009).

Kopperman, Paul E., "The British High Command and Soldiers's Wives in America, 1755–1783," *Journal of the Society for Army Historical Research* 60, no. 241 (Spring 1982): 14–34.

Kranish, Michael, *Flight from Monticello: Thomas Jefferson at War* (New York: Oxford University Press, 2010).

Labaree, Benjamin Woods, *The Boston Tea Party* (Oxford: Oxford University Press, 1964).

——, "The Idea of American Independence: The British View, 1774–1776," *Proceedings of the Massachusetts Historical Society*, 3d ser., 82 (1970): 3–20.

Lanctot, Gustave, *Canada and the American Revolution 1774–1783* (Cambridge, Mass.: Harvard University Press, 1967).

Langford, Paul, "London and the American Revolution," in *London in the Age of Reform*, ed. John Stevenson (Oxford: Basil Blackwell, 1977).

——, *A Polite and Commercial People: England 1727–1783* (Oxford: Oxford University Press, 1989).

Larrabee, Harold A., *Decision at the Chesapeake* (New York: Clarkson N. Potter, 1964).

Lengel, Edward C., *General George Washington: A Military Life* (New York: Random House, 2005).

Levy, Martin, *Love and Madness: The Murder of Martha Ray, Mistress of the Fourth Earl of Sandwich* (New York: HarperCollins. 2004).

Lewisohn, Florence, "St. Eustatius: Depot for Revolution," *Revista/Review Interamericana* 5 (1975–76): 623–37.

Liddle, William D., "'A Patriot King, or None': Lord Bolingbroke and the American Renunciation of George III," *Journal of American History* 65, no. 4 (March 1979): 951–70.

Linebaugh, Peter, and Rediker, Marcus, *The Many-Headed Hydra: Sailors, Slaves, Commoners, and the Hidden History of the Revolutionary Atlantic* (Boston: Beacon Press, 2000).

Lockhart, Paul, *The Whites of Their Eyes: Bunker Hill, the First American Army, and the Emergence of George Washington* (New York: Harper, 2011).

Lord, Evelyn, *The Hell-Fire Clubs: Sex, Satanism, and Secret Societies* (New Haven, Conn.: Yale University Press, 2008).

Lucas, Reginald, *Lord North, 1732–1792*, 2 vols. (London: Arthur L. Humphreys, 1913).

Lunt, James, *John Burgoyne of Saratoga* (London: Macdonald and Jane's, 1976).

Lutnick, Solomon, *The American Revolution and the British Press 1775–1783* (Columbia: University of Missouri Press, 1967).

Luzader, John F., *Saratoga: A Military History of the Decisive Campaign of the American Revolution* (New York: Savas Beatie, 2008).

Maas, John R., "'The Greatest Terror': Cornwallis Brings His Campaign to Goochland, June 1781," *Goochland County Historical Society Magazine* 41 (2009): 12–102.

Macalpine, Ida, and Richard Hunter, *George III and the Mad-Business* (London: Allen Lane, 1969).

McConville, Brendon, *The King's Three Faces: The Rise and Fall of Royal America, 1688–1776* (Chapel Hill: University of North Carolina Press, 2006).

McCowen, George Smith, Jr., *The British Occupation of Charleston, 1780–82* (Columbia: University of South Carolina Press, 1972).

McCullough, David, *1776* (New York: Simon and Schuster, 2005).

McCurry, Allan J., "The North Government and the Outbreak of the American Revolution," *Huntington Library Quarterly* 34, no. 2 (February 1971): 141–57.

McDonnell, Michael, *The Politics of War: Race, Class, and Conflict in Revolutionary Virginia* (Chapel Hill: University of North Carolina Press, 2007).

McDowell, R. B., *Ireland in the Age of Imperialism and Revolution 1760–1801* (Oxford: Clarendon Press, 1979).

MacIntyre, Donald G. F. W., *Admiral Rodney* (London: Peter Davies, 1962).

Mackesy, Piers, *The War for America 1775–1783* (1964; repr. Lincoln: University of Nebraska Press, 1993).

——, *Could the British Have Won the War of Independence?* Chester Bland—Dwight E. Lee Lectures in History (Worcester, Mass.: Clark University Press, 1976)

——, *The Coward of Minden: The Affair of Lord George Sackville* (London: Alan Lane, 1979).

Magee, Joan, ed., *Loyalist Mosaic; A Multi-ethnic Heritage* (Toronto: Dundurn Press, 1984).

Maier, Pauline, *American Scripture: Making the Declaration of Independence* (New York: Random House, 1998).

Malone, Dumas, *Jefferson the Virginian*, vol. 1 of *Jefferson and His Time* (Boston: Little, Brown, 1948).

——, *Jefferson and the Rights of Man*, vol. 2 of *Jefferson and His Time* (Boston: Little, Brown, 1951).

Mannings, David, *Sir Joshua Reynolds: A Complete Catalogue of His Paintings*. 2 vols. (New Haven, Conn.: Yale University Press, 2000).

Marks, Arthur S., "The Statue of King George III in New York and the Iconology of Regicide," *American Art Journal* 13, no. 3 (1981): 61–82.

Marsden, Jonathan, ed., *The Wisdom of George III* (London: Royal Collection Publications, 2004).

Marshall, P. J., "'Cornwallis Triumphant': War in India and the British Public in the Late Eighteenth Century," in *War, Strategy, and International Politics: Essays in Honour of Sir*

Michael Howard," ed. Lawrence Freedman, Paul Hayes, and Robert O'Neill (Oxford: Clarendon Press, 1992), pp. 57–75.

——, *"A Free and Conquering People": Eighteenth-Century Britain and Its Empire* (London: Ashgate Publishing, 2003).

——, *The Making and Unmaking of Empires: Britain, India, and America c. 1750–1783* (Oxford: Oxford University Press, 2005).

Marston, Jerrilyn Greene, *King and Congress: The Transfer of Political Legitimacy, 1774–1776* (Princeton, N.J.: Princeton University Press, 1987).

Martelli, George, *Jemmy Twitcher* (London: Jonathan Cape, 1962).

Martin, James Kirby, and Mark Edward Lender, *A Respectable Army: The Military Origins of the Republic, 1763–1789* (Wheeling, Ill.: Harlan Davidson, 2006).

Middleton, Richard, *The Bells of Victory: The Pitt-Newcastle Ministry and the Conduct of the Seven Years' War 1757–1762* (Cambridge: Cambridge University Press, 1985).

Mintz, Max M., *The Generals of Saratoga: John Burgoyne and Horatio Gates* (New Haven, Conn.: Yale University Press, 1990).

Mollo, John, and Malcolm McGregor, *Uniforms of the American Revolution* (Poole: Blandford Press, 1985).

Moomaw, W. H., "The Denouement of General Howe's Campaign of 1777," *English Historical Review* 79, no. 312 (July 1964): 498–512.

Morley, Vincent, *Irish Opinion and the American Revolution, 1760–1783* (Cambridge: Cambridge University Press, 2002).

Morrissey, Brendan, *Monmouth Courthouse 1778: The Last Great Battle in the North* (Botley: Osprey Publishing, 2004).

Mumby, Frank Arthur, *George III and the American Revolution: The Beginnings* (London: Constable, 1924).

Mundy, G. B., *Life and Correspondence of the Late Admiral Lord Rodney,* 2 vols. (London: J. Murray, 1830).

Namier, Sir Lewis, and John Brooke, eds., *The House of Commons 1754–1790,* 3 vols. (London: H.M. Stationery Office, 1964).

Nash, Gary B. *The Unknown American Revolution: The Unruly Birth of Democracy and the Struggle to Create America* (New York: Viking, 2005).

Nelson, Paul David, "British Conduct of the American Revolutionary War: A Review of Interpretations," *Journal of American History* 65, no. 3 (December 1978): 623–53.

——, *William Tryon and the Course of Empire: A Life in the British Imperial Service* (Chapel Hill: University of North Carolina Press, 1990).

——, *General James Grant: Scottish Soldier and Royal Governor of East Florida* (Gainesville: University Press of Florida, 1993).

——, *General Sir Guy Carleton, Lord Dorchester: Soldier-Statesman of Early British Canada* (Teaneck, N.J.: Fairleigh Dickinson University Press, 2000).

Nelson, William H., *The American Tory,* 2d ed. (Boston: Northeastern University Press, 1992).

Newman, Gerald, *The Rise of English Nationalism: A Cultural History, 1740–1830* (New York: St. Martin's Press, 1987).

Nickerson, Hoffman, *The Turning Point of The Revolution, or Burgoyne in America* (1928; repr. Cranbury, N.J.: The Scholar's Bookshelf, 2005).

Nicolaisen, Peter, "Thomas Jefferson and Friedrich Wilhelm von Giesmar: A Transatlantic Friendship," *Magazine of Albemarle County History*, no. 64 (2006): 1–27.

Norton, Mary Beth, *The British-Americans: The Loyalist Exiles in England 1774–1789* (Boston: Little, Brown, 1972).

O'Brien, Patrick K., "The Political Economy of British Taxation, 1660–1815," *Economic History Review*, 2d ser., 41, no. 1 (February 1988): 1–32.

O'Connell, Maurice R., *Irish Politics and Social Conflict in the Age of the American Revolution* (Philadelphia: University of Pennsylvania Press, 1965).

Oman, Sir Charles, *The Unfortunate Colonel Despard and Other Studies* (New York: Burt Franklin, 1922).

Oosten, F. C. van, "Some Notes Concerning the Dutch Caribbean During the American Revolutionary War," *American Neptune* 36 (1976): 155–69.

O'Shaughnessy, Andrew, "The West India Interest and the Crisis of American Independence," in *West Indies Accounts: Essays on the British Caribbean and the Atlantic Economy in Honour of Richard Sheridan*, ed. Roderick A. McDonald (Kingston: University of the West Indies Press, 1996), pp. 126–49.

——, "The Formation of a Commercial Lobby: The West India Interest, British Colonial Policy and the American Revolution," *Historical Journal* 40, no.1 (1997): 71–95.

Owen, J. B., "George II Reconsidered," in *Statesmen, Scholars and Merchants. Essays in Eighteenth-Century History presented to Dame Lucy Sutherland*, ed. Anne Whiteman, J. S. Bromley, and P. G. M. Dickson (Oxford: Oxford University Press, 1973), pp. 113–35.

Pancake, John S., *1777: The Year of the Hangman* (Tuscaloosa: University of Alabama Press, 1977).

Paquette, Robert L., and Engerman, Stanley L., eds., *The Lesser Antilles in the Age of European Expansion* (Gainesville: University Press of Florida, 1996)

Pares, Richard, *King George III and the Politicians* (Oxford: Clarendon Press, 1953).

Partridge, Bellamy, *Sir Billy Howe* (New York: Longmans, Green, 1932).

Patterson, Rain, *Washington and Cornwallis: The Battle for America, 1775–1783* (New York: Taylor Trade Publishing, 2004).

Pearson, Michael, *Those Damned Rebels: The American Revolution as Seen Through British Eyes* (New York: Da Capo Press, 1972).

Peckham, Howard H. "Sir Henry Clinton's Review of Simcoe's Journal," *William and Mary Quarterly*, 2d ser., 21, no. 4 (October 1941): 361–70.

——, *The War for Independence*, rev. ed. (Chicago: University of Chicago Press, 1979).

Pemberton, W. Baring, *Lord North* (London: Longmans, Green, 1938).

Perry, K. R., *British Politics and the American Revolution* (London: Palgrave Macmillan, 1990).

Pocock, Tom, *The Young Nelson in the Americas* (London: Collins, 1980).

Preston, David L., "The Royal Navy Lost the Revolution," *Naval History* 10, no. 1 (January/February 1996): 10–14.

Pybus, Cassandra, "Jefferson's Faulty Math: The Question of Slave Defections in the American Revolution," *William and Mary Quarterly*, 3d ser., 62, no. 2 (April 2005): 243–64.

——, *Epic Journeys of Freedom: Runaway Slaves of the American Revolution and Their Global Quest for Liberty* (Boston: Beacon Press, 2006).

Reich, Jerome, *British Friends of the American Revolution* (Armonk, N.Y.: M. E. Sharpe, 1998).

Reid, David S. "An Analysis of British Parliamentary Opinion on American Affairs at the Close of the War of Independence," *Journal of Modern History* 18, no. 3 (September 1946): 202–21.

Reitan, Earl A., *Politics, War, and Empire: The Rise of Britain to a World Power 1688–1792* (Arlington Heights, Ill.: Harlan Davidson, 1994).

Ritcheson, Charles R, *British Politics and the American Revolution* (Norman: University of Oklahoma Press, 1954).

——, "The Fragile Memory: Thomas Jefferson at the Court of George III," *Eighteenth Century Life* 6, no. 2–3 (1981): 1–16.

Roberts, Jane, ed., *George III and Queen Charlotte: Patronage, Collecting and Court Taste* (London: Royal Collections Publications, 2004).

Robson, Eric, "Purchase and Promotion in the British Army in the Eighteenth Century," *History* 36 (February & June 1951): 57–72.

——, "The Expedition to the Southern Colonies, 1775–1776," *English Historical Review* 66 (October 1951): 535–60.

——, *The American Revolution in Its Political and Military Aspects 1763–1783* (1955; repr. New York, Norton, 1966).

Rodger, N. A. M., *The Wooden World: Anatomy of the Georgian Navy* (London: Fontana Press, 1990).

——, *The Insatiable Earl: A Life of John Montagu, Fourth Earl of Sandwich* (New York: Norton, 1993).

——, *The Command of the Ocean: A Naval History of Britain, 1649–1815* (New York: Norton, 2004).

Rogers, George C., Jr., ed., "Letters of Charles O'Hara to the Duke of Grafton," *South Carolina Historical Magazine* 65, no. 3 (July 1964): 158–80.

Rohl, J. C. G., Warren, M., and Hunt, D., *Purple Secret: Genes, "Madness" and the Royal Houses of Europe* (London: Bantam Press, 1998).

Royster, Charles, *A Revolutionary People at War: The Continental Army and American Character, 1775–1783* (Chapel Hill: University of North Carolina Press, 1979).

Rozbicki, Michal Jan, *Culture and Liberty in the Age of the American Revolution* (Charlottesville: University of Virginia Press, 2011).

Sainsbury, John, *Disaffected Patriots: London Supporters of Revolutionary America 1769–1782* (Kingston, Ont.: McGill-Queen's University Press, 1987).

Sampson, Richard, *Escape in America: The British Convention Prisoners 1777–1783* (Chippenham: Picton Publishing, 1995).

Scott, H. M., *British Foreign Policy in the Age of the American Revolution* (Oxford: Oxford University Press, 1990).

Scotti, Anthony J. Jr., *Brutal Virtue: The Myth and Reality of Banastre Tarleton* (Westminster, Md.: Heritage Books, 2007).

Selby, John E., *The Revolution in Virginia 1775–1783* (1988; repr. Charlottesville: University of Virginia Press, 2007).

Selig, Robert, "20 October 1781: The Day after the Surrender," *Brigade Dispatch* 38, no. 2 (Summer 2008): 2–14.

Seymour, William, *The Price of Folly: British Blunders in the War of American Independence* (London: Brassey's, 1995).

Sheridan, Richard B., "The Jamaican Slave Insurrection Scare of 1776 and the American Revolution," *Journal of Negro History* 61, no. 3 (1976): 290–308.

Shy, John, *A People Numerous and Armed: Reflections on the Military Struggle for American Independence,* rev. ed. (Ann Arbor: University of Michigan Press, 2000).

Simms, Brendan, *Three Victories and a Defeat: The Rise and Fall of the First British Empire, 1714–1783* (New York: Basic Books, 2007).

Smith, Charles Daniel, *The Early Career of Lord North the Prime Minister* (London: Athlone Press, 1979).

Smith, Paul H., *Loyalists and Redcoats: A Study in British Revolutionary Policy* (Chapel Hill: University of North Carolina Press, 1964).

——, "The American Loyalists: Notes on Their Organization and Numerical Strength," *William and Mary Quarterly,* 3d ser., 25, no. 2 (April 1968): 259–78.

Spector, Margaret Marion, *The American Department of the British Government 1768–1782* (New York: Columbia University Press, 1940).

Spinney, David, *Rodney* (London: Allen & Unwin, 1969).

Spring, Matthew H., *With Zeal and Bayonets Only: The British Army on Campaign in North America, 1775–1783* (Norman: University of Oklahoma Press, 2008).

Starkey, Armstrong, "War and Culture, a Case Study: The Enlightenment and the Conduct of the British Army in America, 1755–1781," *War and Society* 8 (May 1990): 1–28.

Starr, J. Barton, *Tories, Dons, and Rebels. The American Revolution in British West Florida* (Gainesville: University Press of Florida, 1976).

Stephenson, Orlando W., "The Supply of Gunpowder in 1776," *American Historical Review* 30, no. 2 (1925): 271–81.

Stern, Marvin, *Thorns and Briars: Bonding, Love and Death 1764–1870* (New York: The Foundation of Thanatology, 1986).

Stout, Neil, *The Perfect Crisis: The Beginning of the Revolutionary War* (New York: New York University Press, 1976).

Syrett, David, *Shipping and the American War 1775–83: A Study of British Transport Organisation* (London: Athlone Press, 1970).

——, "Lord George Germain and the Protection of Military Storeships, 1775–1778," *Mariner's Mirror* 60 (November 1974): 395–405.

——, "The Organization of British Trade Convoys During the American War 1775–1783," *Mariner's Mirror* 62 (1976): 169–81.

——, *The Royal Navy in American Waters 1775–1783* (Aldershot: Scolar Press, 1989).

——, "Home Waters or America? The Dilemma of British Naval Strategy in 1778," *Mariner's Mirror* 77, no. 4 (November 1991): 365–77.

——, *The Royal Navy in European Waters During the American Revolutionary War* (Columbia: University of South Carolina Press, 1998).

——, "Historiographical Essay: The British Armed Forces in the American Revolutionary War. Publications, 1875–1998," *Journal of Military History* 63, no. 1 (January 1999): 147–64.

——, *Admiral Lord Howe: A Biography* (Annapolis, Md.: Naval Institute Press, 2006).

Taaffe, Stephen R., *The Philadelphia Campaign, 1777–1778* (Lawrence: University of Kansas Press, 2003).

Thomas, P. D. G., *The House of Commons in the Eighteenth Century* (Oxford: Oxford University Press, 1971).

——, *British Politics and the Stamp Act Crisis; The First Phase of the American Revolution 1763–1767* (Oxford: Clarendon Press, 1975).

——, *Lord North* (London: Allen Lane, 1976).

——, "George III and the American Revolution," *History* 70, no. 228 (1985): 16–31.

——, *The Townshend Duties Crisis: The Second Phase of the American Revolution 1767–1773* (Oxford: Oxford University Press, 1987).

——, *Tea Party to Independence: The Third Phase of the American Revolution 1773–1776* (Oxford: Clarendon Press, 1991).

——, *George III: King and Politicians 1760–1770* (Manchester: Manchester University Press, 2002).

Tiedemann, Joseph F., "Patriots by Default: Queens County, New York, and the British Army, 1776–1783," *William and Mary Quarterly*, 3d ser., 43, no. 1 (January 1986): 35–63.

Tilley, John A., *The British Navy and the American Revolution* (Columbia: University of South Carolina Press, 1987).

Tillyard, Stella, *A Royal Affair: George III and His Scandalous Siblings* (New York: Random House, 2006).

Tracy, Nicholas, *Navies, Deterrence, and American Independence: Britain and Seapower in the 1760s and 1770s* (Vancouver: University of British Columbia Press, 1988).

Tuchman, Barbara W., *The First Salute: A View of the American Revolution* (New York: Knopf, 1988).

——, *The March of Folly: From Troy to Vietnam* (1984; repr. London: Abacus, 1990).

Tyson George F. Jr., "The Carolina Black Corps: Legacy of Revolution," *Revista/Review Interamericana* 5, no. 4 (Winter 1975–76): 648–63.

Urban, Mark, *Fusiliers: The Saga of a British Redcoat Regiment in the American Revolution* (New York: Walker, 2007).

Urwin, Gregory J. W., "Cornwallis in Virginia: A Reappraisal," *Military Collector & Historian* 37, no. 3 (Fall 1985): 111–126.

Valentine, Alan, *Lord George Germain* (Oxford: Oxford University Press, 1962).

——, *Lord North*, 2 vols. (Norman: University of Oklahoma Press, 1967).

Van Alstyne, Richard W., "Great Britain, the War of Independence, and the 'Gathering Storm' in Europe, 1775–1778," *Huntington Library Quarterly* 27, no. 4 (August 1964): 311–46.

Van Buskirk, Judith L., *Generous Enemies: Patriots and Loyalists in Revolutionary New York* (Philadelphia: University of Pennsylvania Press, 2002).

Van Doren, Carl, *Secret History of the American Revolution* (1941; repr. Clinton, N.J.: Augustus M. Kelley, 1973).

Vining, Elizabeth Gray, *Flora MacDonald: Her Life in the Highlands and in America* (London: Geoffrey Bles, 1967).

Vivian, Frances, "A Defence of Sir William Howe with a New Interpretation of His Action in New Jersey, June 1777," *Journal of the Society for Army Historical Research* 44, no. 178 (1966): 77–83.

Wain, John, *Samuel Johnson: A Biography* (New York: Viking Press, 1974).

Wallace, Willard M., *Appeal to Arms: A Military History of the American Revolution* (New York: Harper, 1951).

Warner, Jessica, *John the Painter: The First Modern Terrorist* (London: Profile Books, 2005).

Watkin, David, *The Architect King: George III and the Culture of Enlightenment* (London: Royal Collections Publications, 2004).

Weigley, Russell F., *The Partisan War: The South Carolina Campaign of 1780–1782* (Columbia: University of South Carolina Press, 1970).

Weintraub, Stanley, *Iron Tears: America's Battle for Freedom, Britain's Quagmire, 1775–1783* (New York: Free Press, 2005).

Wickwire, Franklin B., *British Subministers and Colonial America 1763–1783* (Princeton, N.J.: Princeton University Press, 1966).

——. and Wickwire, Mary, *Cornwallis and the War of Independence* (London: Faber and Faber, 1971).

——, *Cornwallis: The Imperial Years* (Chapel Hill: University of North Carolina Press, 1980).

Wilkin, Walter Harold, *Some British Soldiers in America* (1914; repr. Milton Keynes: General Books, 2010).

Wilkinson, Clive, *The British Navy and the State in the Eighteenth Century* (Woodbridge: Boydell Press, 2004).

Willcox, William B., "Rhode Island in British Strategy, 1780–81," *Journal of Modern History* 17, no. 4 (December 1945): 303–31.

——, "The British Road to Yorktown: A Study in Divided Command," *American Historical Review* 52, no. 1 (October 1946): 1–35.

——, "Why Did the British Lose the American Revolution?" *Michigan Alumnus Quarterly Review* 62 (1956): 317–24.

——, "British Strategy in America, 1778," *Journal of Modern History* 19, no. 2 (June 1947): 97–121.

——, "Too Many Cooks: British Planning Before Saratoga," *Journal of British Studies* 2, no. 1 (November 1962): 56–90.

——, *Portrait of a General: Sir Henry Clinton in the War of Independence* (New York: Knopf, 1964).

Williams, Paul V., ed., *The Long and Short of General John Burgoyne's Maid of Oaks: The Story of an Eighteenth Century Play and Its Players* (Carshalton: Friends of Honeywood, 2007).

Willis, Sam, *Fighting at Sea in the Eighteenth Century: The Art of Sailing Warfare* (Woodbridge: Boydell Press, 2008).

Wilson, Kathleen, *The Sense of the People: Politics, Culture and Imperialism in England, 1715–1785* (Cambridge: Cambridge University Press, 1998).

Wood, Gordon S., "Rhetoric and Reality in The American Revolution," *William and Mary Quarterly*, 3d ser., 23, no. 1 (January 1966): 3–22.

——, *The Radicalism of the American Revolution* (New York: Knopf, 1992).

——, "The Problem of Sovereignty," *William and Mary Quarterly,* 3d ser., 68, no. 4 (October 2011): 573–77.

Wood, W. J., *Battles of the Revolutionary War 1775–1781* (New York: Da Capo Press, 1990; 2d ed., 2003).

Wyatt, Frederick, and William B. Willcox, "Sir Henry Clinton: A Psychological Exploration in History," *William and Mary Quarterly,* 3d ser., 16 (January 1959): 3–26.

York, Neil L., "Ending the War and Winning the Peace: The British in America and The Americans in Vietnam," *Soundings* 70 (1987): 445–74.

Zoebel, Hiller B., *The Boston Massacre* (New York: Norton, 1971).

THESES

Jamieson, Alan G., "War in the Leeward Islands 1775–1783" (D.Phil. thesis, Oxford University, 1981).

Kinnear, Mary, "Pro-Americans in the British House of Commons in the 1770s" (Ph.D. diss., University of Oregon, 1973).

Liddle, William D., "A Patriot King, or None: American Public Attitudes Towards George III and the British Monarchy" (Ph.D. diss., Claremont Graduate University, 1970).

Parkinson, Robert Glenn, "Enemies of the People: The Revolutionary War and Race in the New American Nation" (Ph.D. diss., University of Virginia, 2005).

Struan, Andrew, "'Judgement and Experience'? British Politics, Atlantic Connexions and the American Revolution" (Ph.D. thesis, University of Glasgow, 2010).

Index

Note: Page numbers in *italics* refer to illustrations.

and blockade, 104, 106, 119, 133, 138, 177, 331, 333, 345, 350, 355

in the Caribbean, 295, 296, 310–11, 335; *see also* Rodney, Sir George

and classic lines of battle, 314

and coppering, 349–50

and French navy, 195, 199–200, 220, 222, 224, 241–42, 279, 285, 295, 309, 311–13, 326, 346, 360

and French Revolutionary Wars, 121

and George III, 36, 326, 343

lack of standardization in, 312

limited resources of, 5, 14, 103–4, 106, 193, 228, 319, 330–35, 336, 339–41, 343, 345–49, 355, 358

and Navy Board, 12, 195–96, 343

New York invaded by, 92

and privateers, 331, 332–33, 355

roles of, 14, 343, 347, 358

Spithead mutiny, 122

throwing their dead overboard, 315

and Yorktown, 241–43, 279, 285, 292, 308–12

Rutledge, John, 99

"Sagittarius," 75

Saintes, battle of, *Fig.31*, *Fig.32*, 6, 292, 312, 314–17, 349, 350, 357, 361

St. Eustatius, 289, 291–92, 297–305, 306, 307–10, 313, 316–18, 319, 345, 346

St. John, Jack, 74

St. Leger, Barry, 144, 145, 149, 152, 163

St. Lucia, 63, 194, 195, 213, 223, 224–25, 295, 335, 341

Saint-Simon, marquis de, 279, 311

Salem, Peter, 135

Sambrooke, Diana, 172

Sandwich, John Montagu, 4th Earl of [1718–92], *Fig.33*, 320–52

cultural interests of, 10, 322–23, 352

death of, 352

as first lord of the Admiralty, 5, 7, 29, 30, 35, 68, 78, 120, 175, 213, 242, 285, 297, 319, 320, 323, 324–26, 327–34, 339–44, 345–51

and George III, 326, 338–39, 343, 351

and Germain, 195–96, 334, 342, 347

and Hell-Fire Club, 320–21

and House of Lords, 324, 327, 330

and Howe brothers, 119, 333–34, 342

and Keppel, 335–37, 338, 339

and North, 60, 67, 120, 339, 343, 345, 348

and opposition parties, 70, 326, 330, 338–39, 344, 345, 347–49

personal life of, 323, 324, 339, 351–52

personal traits of, 321–22

political career of, 178, 324–26, 344–45, 348, 349, 351

retirement of, 351–52

and Rodney, 293, 294, 304, 317

unpopularity of, 294, 321, 338–39, 344–45

and war in America, 326–34, 341–43, 345–49

and war with France, 334–37

and Wilkes, 320–21

Saratoga:

Bemis Heights (second battle), 154–56, 157

British defeat at, 31, 39, 61, 70, 75, 86, 105, 111, 113–14, 118, 120, 123–24, 157–59, 163–64, 165, 171, 172, 178, 186, 189, 218, 219, 231, 241, 253, 266, 280, 333, 337, 353

Burgoyne in environs of, 155–59, 183, 260, 353

Freeman's Farm (first battle), 155, 291

Sauders, M. L., portrait attributed to, *Fig.22*

Savannah, *see* Georgia

Sawbridge, John, 59

Sayers, James, *Fox Vox Populi*, *Fig.4*

Sayre, Stephen, 27

Schaw, Janet, 289, 291, 298

Schuyler, Philip, 142, 149, 150

Scott, James, 326

Scott, Sir Walter, 44

Serle, Ambrose, 99

Seven Years' War, 13, 19, 65, 250, 358

in America, *see* French and Indian War

British officers in, 89–90, 119, 125, 139, 215, 293, 304

effects of, 49, 50, 168–69, 301

and peace commission, 119

Royal Navy in, 325, 328, 336

Shakespeare, William, 45, 79, 110, 125, 126

Sharp, Granville, 64, 245

Shaw, George Bernard, *The Devil's Disciple*, 124

Shebbeare, John, 75

Shelburne, earl of, 34–35, 39, 40–41, 112, 167, 170, 174, 337, 360–61

Sheridan, Richard Brinsley, 76–77, 161

Shippen, Peggy, 208

Shuldham, Molyneux, 331

Sierra Leone, settlement of, 245, 277

Simcoe, John Graves, 274, 359